A Wildlife Guide to Chile

Continental Chile
Chilean Antarctica
Easter Island
Juan Fernández Archipelago

Sharon Chester

A&C Black
LONDON

First published in the United Kingdom by A&C Black Publishers in 2008
Reprinted by Bloomsbury Publishing in 2014

Copyright © 2008 by Princeton University Press

The moral right of this author has been asserted.

No part of this publication may be reproduced or used in any manner whatsoever without written permission from the Publisher except in the case of brief quotations embodied in critical articles or reviews.

Every reasonable effort has been made to trace copyright holders of material reproduced in this book, but if any have been inadvertently overlooked the publishers would be glad to hear from them.

Bloomsbury Publishing Plc
50 Bedford Square
London
WC1B 3DP

www.bloomsbury.com

BLOOMSBURY and the Diana logo are trademarks of Bloomsbury Publishing Plc

Bloomsbury Publishing, London, New Delhi, New York and Sydney

A CIP catalogue record for this book is available from the British Library

ISBN 978-1-4081-0536-8

The publisher would like to acknowledge the author of this volume for providing the camera-ready copy from which this book was printed

This book has been composed by Myriad Pro and Garamond Premier Pro

Printed on acid free paper

Printed in China by Everbest

10 9 8 7 6 5 4 3

CONTENTS

ACKNOWLEDGMENTS	iv
PREFACE	v
INTRODUCTION	vi
CONVERSION FACTORS	vii
MAP OF THE REPUBLIC OF CHILE	viii
CHILE AND HER SOVEREIGNTIES	1
MARINE RESOURCES	21
FLORISTIC ZONES AND FLORA	32
BOTANICAL DESCRIPTIONS	73
BUTTERFLIES AND MOTHS	90
REPTILES AND AMPHIBIANS	106
BIRDS	126
MAMMALS	291
WHERE TO SEE WILDLIFE	350
GLOSSARY	376
SPANISH–ENGLISH DICTIONARY	378
BIBLIOGRAPHY	379
INDEXES	380

Los Cuernos del Paine and Lago Pehoé, Torres del Paine National Park

ACKNOWLEDGMENTS

First, I would like to thank all of the staff at Princeton University Press, especially Robert Kirk, Ellen Foos, Dimitri Karetnikov, Neil Litt, and Leslie Flis for taking on this project and seeing it to its conclusion.

Thanks also to Alvaro Jaramillo, Claudio Vidal and Enrico Couve of Fantástico Sur, Ned Brinkley, and Judith Hoffman who read the manuscript for Princeton University Press. They pointed out areas that needed improvement and suggested the inclusion of topics that I had overlooked. Judith Hoffman deserves additional recognition for taking on the Herculean task of checking the text for consistency and accuracy.

The following scientists, researchers and academics generously provided advice, time, and corrections in the subjects listed below.

Flora: Claudio Donoso, Professor Emeritus, Universidad Austral de Chile, Valdivia. Martin Gardner, Coordinator of the International Conifer Conservation Programme, Royal Botanic Garden of Edinburgh, Scotland.

Lepidoptera: John B. Heppner, Curator of Lepidoptera, Florida State Collection of Arthropods. Pedro Vidal, Pontificia Universidad Católica de Chile, Santiago. Carlos Rojas, Insectos de Chile web site.

Reptiles and Amphibians: Daniel Pincheira-Donoso, University of Exeter, United Kingdom. Rafael Marquez, Museo Nacional de Ciencias Naturales, Madrid, Spain. James A. Schulte II, Clarkson University, Potsdam, New York. José Alejandro Scolaro, Universidad Nacional de la Patagonia, Argentina. Alberto Veloso, Universidad de Chile, Santiago.

Birds: Juan Tessara, Aves de Chile web site. Braulio Araya, former professor at the Universidad de Valparaíso, and Miguel Gallegos of Latour, Santiago, both of whom fostered my entry into the field of ornithological literature.

Mammals: Jaime E. Jiménez, Laboratorio de Ecología, Universidad de Los Lagos, Osorno, Chile. Charles Wheatley, Science on the Sea. Jim Sanderson, Center for Applied Biodiversity Science, Small Cat Conservation Alliance, Washington, D.C.

Taxonomy: Sheila Brands, Universal Taxonomic Services, compiler of The Taxonomicon and Systema Naturae 2000, Amsterdam, The Netherlands.

I would also like to thank Deborah Robbins and Justine Frederiksen, who dusted off their editing skills and corrected innumerable errors in this manuscript. Their comments and those of my colleagues Sue Kelly and Sue Butler at the Peninsula Humane Society in northern California were invaluable.

Lastly, my thanks go to my family, especially to James Oetzel who took on my labor of love as his own, quietly supplying endless cups of coffee and keen observations on the flow of text and quality of illustration. His unflagging warmth and good spirits kept me going and his sharp editorial eye kept me honest.

I am deeply indebted to all of you. This book would never have been realized without your guidance and support.

PREFACE

This book is the product of thirteen very enjoyable intervals of work and travel in Chile and the Antarctic from 1983 to 1996. For much of this time I acted as one of the natural history lecturers aboard the expedition cruise ships *M/S Explorer* and *M/V World Discoverer*.

Passengers were always quick to pose questions about Chile and the natural wonders that met us at every turn. There is no doubt that their seemingly unending quest for answers prompted me to create this book.

When I started writing the guide I intended to include only the birds and mammals of Chile—a project I estimated would take about two years to complete. But soon into the writing, it became apparent that this approach was too limited and that brief accounts of the general geography and common flora of Chile should be included. Much later, it was pointed out that butterflies and lizards were also an important part of the Chilean landscape, and it was at that point that I realized months or even years of drawing, writing and research loomed ahead.

In the end, the text and illustrations took over five years to complete. The work was intense and continual, but there were many satisfying moments when a picture or phrase would evoke a happy memory from my days in Chile. Most gratifying was the response of Chilean and international experts who unfailingly and graciously answered any questions I had about topics well beyond my expertise. Through them, I learned more about Chilean flora and fauna than I ever thought possible.

Some of you may be interested in the mechanics of producing a guide such as this one. Descriptions of the plants and animals were garnered from my old field notes and logs, reference books, internet sources, and specialists in the various fields of science. The illustrations are based on my field sketches and slides as well as images loaned to me by colleagues. I based each drawing on a number of scanned pictures and then drew a final, composite figure in Adobe Photoshop on a Cintiq touch-screen monitor. The latter proved an essential tool for creating the numerous illustrations and maps.

Chile is an extraordinary destination that is bound to delight and inspire. As the famed laureate Pablo Neruda put it, "Whoever created Chile must have been a poet." It is my sincere hope that this guide will enhance your travels through Chile and allow you to revel in the lyricism and beauty of the special plants and animals that live in her great deserts, rainforests, mountains, seas and far-flung sovereignties.

Sharon Chester
San Mateo, California

INTRODUCTION

This guide covers the common plants and animals of continental Chile, the Juan Fernández Archipelago, Easter Island, and the Chilean Antarctic Territory. It also contains maps of mainland Chile and the outlying territories.

Annotated and illustrated checklists of the common flora and fauna of Chile comprise the bulk of the guide. The floral and faunal families are arranged in phylogenetic sequence, beginning with the most primitive and ending with the most advanced. The latest taxonomic order based on DNA analysis was employed, but note that taxonomy is a system in flux and what was current at the time of writing may be outdated by the time of printing.

While efforts were made to include all the animals and plants that a visitor might encounter, in order to keep the guide portable enough to fit in a backpack, many rare or vagrant species of plants and animals were excluded from illustration. In some cases they are described under RELATED SPECIES.

Each species account starts with the common English and Chilean names followed by the scientific name in italics. Each scientific name consists of two words, or binomial, usually derived from Latin or Greek. The first word is the name of the genus; the second indicates the species within the genus. Local Chilean names for species as well as European language equivalents, where known, are listed under OTHER NAMES.

The identification section (ID) presents information about an organism's approximate size, shape, color and distinguishing marks. Brief descriptions of behavior, habitat and food preference, and vocalizations of birds and mammals are given where known. The status of species that are endangered or threatened with extinction are also noted.

Local and world distribution and altitudinal limits are detailed under RANGE, followed by information regarding SUBSPECIES.

A GUIDE TO THE CHAPTERS

CHILE AND HER SOVEREIGNTIES: The basics of Chilean geography are presented in this chapter. Here you will find information on political regions, climate, landforms, rivers, lakes, straits, plate tectonics and submarine topography. This chapter also includes relief and outline maps of Chile and descriptions of her territorial possessions.

MARINE RESOURCES: This chapter contains information on the marine environment. The color plates illustrate some of the marine resources of Chile, including common commercial fishes, shellfish, marine algae, and mollusks. Mollusk measurements represent the maximum length or diameter of an adult specimen's shell in inches and centimeters.

FLORISTIC ZONES: This section contains maps and descriptions of the vegetation zones of Chile. Each zonal description is accompanied by illustrations of common plants found within the zone. BOTANICAL DESCRIPTIONS of common trees, shrubs and other flowering plants appear at the end of the chapter. Abbreviations that are given in the plant descriptions include the height (H) of a mature specimen; the length of a simple leaf (L); the length of compound leaf (CL); deciduous foliage (D); perennial foliage (P); shrub (S); and tree (T).

BUTTERFLIES AND MOTHS: Chile's common butterflies and moths are described and illustrated in this chapter. The measurements in the captions refer to the wingspan (WS) of the insect measured across outspread wings. It should be noted that most of these insects have no common Chilean or English name and that many of the names given in the captions were created by Peña and Ugarte in their 1992 publication *Las Mariposas de Chile*.

REPTILES AND AMPHIBIANS: This chapter has descriptions and illustrations of the common reptiles and amphibians of Chile. The captions give the average total length of a turtle, snake, toad or frog measured from the snout to the end of the tail. The measurement of lizards and geckos represents the length from snout to vent (SV). Some lizards and frogs have no common English or Chilean names and are listed by their scientific name only.

BIRDS: The common birds of Chile are described and illustrated in this chapter. The measurements represent the average length from bill tip to tail tip, with the bird held on its back in a relaxed position. Wingspan (WS), height (HT) and weight (WT) are given in the main body of the text where pertinent. Plumage differences of species that exhibit sexual dimorphism are described and in most cases illustrated. Vagrant species are not illustrated and most are listed only by name, followed by places where they have been seen in Chile. Taxonomic order and names are generally in accord with Jaramillo's *Birds of Chile* and the South American Checklist Committee of the American Ornithologists' Union.

MAMMALS: Terrestrial mammals are described and illustrated in the first part of this chapter. Marine mammals (with the exception of the marine otter) occupy the last pages. The caption measurements represent the average total length from nose to tail tip of an adult animal. These measurements are sometimes separated into head and body length (HB) plus the tail length (T). Where males and females of a species vary greatly in total length (TL) and weight (WT), that information appears in the body of the text. In some cases, the height at the shoulder or withers (SH) is given. The names of mammalian families and species are in accord with the Third Edition of Wilson and Reeder's *Mammal Species of the World*.

WHERE TO SEE WILDLIFE: This chapter provides regional maps, park maps, and descriptions of some of the best places for wildlife observation in Chile. Brief accounts of each site's location, total area, climate, terrain, and typical flora and fauna are presented. The scientific name is given for flora and fauna that have no known common name.

APPENDIX: The Appendix contains a glossary of geographic and biological terms used in this guide and a small Spanish–English dictionary. This is followed by a short list of books and web sites consulted for the text. The last pages contain an Index of Scientific Names, an Index of Common Names, and a Quick Index to the Color Plates and Maps.

CONVERSION FACTORS USED IN THIS BOOK

1 inch (in)	= 2.5 centimeters (cm)
1 centimeter (cm)	= 0.4 inches (in)
1 centimeter (cm)	= 10 millimeters (mm)
1 foot (ft)	= 0.3 meters (m)
1 meter (m)	= 3.3 feet (ft)
1 mile (mi)	= 1.6 kilometers (km)
1 kilometer (km)	= 0.6 miles (mi)
1 square mile (sq mi)	= 2.6 square kilometers (sq km)
1 square mile (sq mi)	= 260 hectares (ha)
1 square mile (sq mi)	= 640 acres (acre)
1 pound (lb)	= 0.45 kilograms (kg)
1 kilogram (kg)	= 2.2 pounds (lb)

Chilean Blue, Licena morena
Pseudolucia chilensis
WS 0.8 in (2 cm)

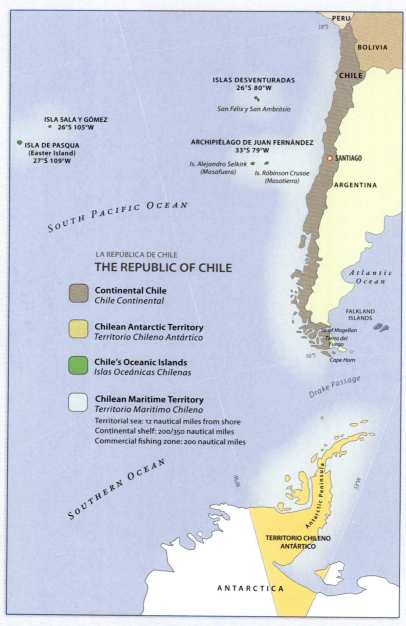

Chile is a long, narrow country lying on the southwestern flank of the South American continent. It is bounded by the Pacific Ocean to the west, Argentina to the east, Bolivia to the northeast and Peru to the northwest. Its territories include the Islas Desventuradas, Isla Sala y Gómez, Isla de Pasqua (Easter Island), Archipiélago de Juan Fernández and Territorio Chileno Antártico.

CHILE AND HER SOVEREIGNTIES

Chile is sometimes called the "stringbean" of South America due to its long, narrow shape. It is the longest country in the world. The mainland extends through 38 degrees of latitude, a distance of 2700 miles (4345 km) from north to south. This span is equal to one-tenth of the earth's perimeter, or the distance between Ketchikan, Alaska, and the southern tip of the Baja California Peninsula. In contrast, the average width is only 110 miles (177 km), with a maximum of 217 miles (350 km) near Antofagasta.

Chile's topographical profile is unique. The land slopes steeply from the High Andean summits into the central longitudinal valleys, then rises briefly in the coastal mountains before plunging into the depths of the Pacific Ocean. If one examines the narrowest sector of the Atacama Region, one finds that there is a vertical differential of some 40,000 ft (12,200 m) between the peaks of the High Andes and the bottom of the submarine trench that parallels the Pacific coast.

As one would suspect in a country of such latitudinal and altitudinal ranges, the climate is extremely varied. A hyper-arid desert extends across the northern regions. Central Chile has a mild, Mediterranean-type climate, while the south is cool and rainy, and the High Andes are cold and snowy. The land to the east of the Patagonian Andes in Aisén and Magallanes has a cool, semi-arid climate.

The great variety of climates and natural environments has produced a widely diverse flora and fauna. Chile has more than 4600 flowering plant species, 1187 mollusk species, 606 crustacean species, 10,133 insect species, 617 arachnid species, 1179 species of fish, 43 amphibian species, 94 reptile species, 456 bird species, and 148 species of mammals.

EARLY HISTORY: At the time of European discovery, indigenous tribes were living in what is now Chile. The Aymara, who are descended from the Incas, inhabited the High Andes in the north. Araucanian tribes such as the Mapuche and Pehuenche occupied the central regions. The Chonos, Yahgans, Onas, and Alacalufs were some of the tribes who lived in the south.

Ferdinand Magellan, a Portuguese navigator in the service of Spain, was the first European to reach Chile. In 1520 he arrived at Tierra del Fuego ("Land of Fire"), which he named for the Indian campfires burning on the island's shore. He also transited the strait that would later bear his name. The Spanish explorer Pedro de Valdivia founded the city of Santiago in 1541, but settlement of regions to the south was delayed for almost 300 years due to conflicts with the hostile Araucanian tribes. Chile remained under Spanish rule until 1818 when José de San Martin and Bernardo O'Higgins, who would later become Chile's first president, achieved independence from Spain.

TODAY: In 2007 Chile's total population was estimated at 16,284,741. Ninety-five percent of the population are of European descent or mestizo; five percent are indigenous. The majority of the population lives in central Chile. The country's largest city is the capital, Santiago, which has about 6.3 million people in the metropolitan area.

Chile is a multiparty Republic with an elected president and congress. The white stripe on Chile's flag represents the snow of the Andes. It is set next to a dark blue canton, which stands for blue sky. The large white star is said to guide Chile on the path to progress and honor, and the red stripe stands for the blood of those who sacrificed themselves for the homeland.

	REGIÓN	CAPITAL	PROVINCE	PROVINCIAL CAPITAL
NORTE GRANDE	XV ARICA–PARINACOTA	ARICA	ARICA PARINACOTA	ARICA PUTRE
NORTE GRANDE	I TARAPACÁ	IQUIQUE	IQUIQUE TAMARUGAL	IQUIQUE POZO ALMONTE
NORTE GRANDE	II ANTOFAGASTA	ANTOFAGASTA	TOCOPILLA EL LOA ANTOFAGASTA	TOCOPILLA CALAMA ANTOFAGASTA
NORTE CHICO	III ATACAMA	COPIAPÓ	CHAÑARAL COPIAPÓ HUASCO	CHAÑARAL COPIAPÓ VALLENAR
NORTE CHICO	IV COQUIMBO	LA SERENA	ELQUI LIMARI CHOAPA	COQUIMBO OVALLE ILLAPEL
CENTRO	V VALPARAÍSO	VALPARAÍSO	PETORCA LOS ANDES SAN FELIPE QUILLOTA VALPARAÍSO SAN ANTONIO ISLA DE PASCUA	LA LIGUA LOS ANDES SAN FELIPE QUILLOTA VALPARAÍSO SAN ANTONIO HANGA-ROA
CENTRO	METROPOLITANA DE SANTIAGO (RM XIII)	SANTIAGO	SANTIAGO CHACABUCO CORDILLERA MAIPO MELIPILLA TALAGANTE	SANTIAGO COLINA PUENTE ALTO SAN BERNARDO MELIPILLA TALAGANTE
CENTRO	VI LIBERTADOR GENERAL BERNARDO O'HIGGINS	RANCAGUA	CACHAPOAL COLCHAGUA CARDENAL CARO	RANCAGUA SAN FERNANDO PICHILEMU
CENTRO	VII MAULE	TALCA	CURICÓ TALCA LINARES CAUQUENES	CURICÓ TALCA LINARES CAUQUENES
SUR	VIII BIOBÍO	CONCEPCIÓN	ÑUBLE BIOBÍO CONCEPCIÓN ARAUCO	CHILLÁN LOS ANGELES CONCEPCIÓN LEBU
SUR	IX ARAUCANÍA	TEMUCO	MALLECO CAUTÍN	ANGOL TEMUCO
SUR	XIV LOS RIOS	VALDIVIA	VALDIVIA RANCO	VALDIVIA LA UNIÓN
SUR	X LOS LAGOS	PUERTO MONTT	OSORNO LLANQUIHUE CHILOÉ PALENA	OSORNO PUERTO MONTT CASTRO CHAITÉN
PATAGONIA	XI AISÉN DEL GENERAL CARLOS IBAÑEZ DEL CAMPO	COIHAIQUE	COIHAIQUE AISÉN GENERAL CARRRERA CAPITÁN PRATT	COIHAIQUE PUERTO AISÉN CHILE CHICO COCHRANE
PATAGONIA	XII MAGALLANES Y ANTÁRTICA CHILENA	PUNTA ARENAS	ÚLTIMA ESPERANZA MAGALLANES TIERRA DEL FUEGO ANTÁRTICA CHILENA	PUERTO NATALES PUNTA ARENAS PORVENIR PUERTO WILLIAMS

ADMINISTRATIVE REGIONS AND GEOGRAPHIC ZONES

ADMINISTRATIVE REGIONS

Chile has 15 administrative units called REGIONS. They are presently identified by Roman numerals. Recently however, the Chilean Congress declared two new regions—Región XIV Los Rios (Valdivia) and Región XV Arica-Parinacota. These newly assigned numbers break the former geographical numerical order from north to south and the numeric system may soon be dropped in favor of formal names.

The names of the regions are often abbreviated. For example, Aisén (also spelled Aysén) is the short form of Región XI Aisén del General Carlos Ibañez del Campo.

CAPITAL

SANTIAGO is the nation's capital and seat of political administration. It is located at 33° 27′ S, 70° 40′ W in the Región Metropolitana de Santiago (RM XIII). The city of VALPARAÍSO is the legislative capital.

GEOGRAPHIC ZONES

NORTE GRANDE (The Big North) includes the Arica-Parinacota, Tarapacá, and Antofagasta Regions. This zone contains the vast Atacama Desert and the High Andean steppes of the Altiplano.

NORTE CHICO (The Little North) includes the semi-arid, fertile plains of Atacama and Coquimbo.

NÚCLEO CENTRAL (Central Chile), includes the Valparaíso, Metropolitan Santiago, O'Higgins, and Maule Regions. The majority of the population lives in this zone and most administrative and agricultural activity occurs here.

SUR (South-Central Chile) includes the Regions of Biobío, Araucanía, Los Lagos, and Los Rios. Cautín Province in Araucanía is sometimes referred to in its historical function as LA FRONTERA (The Frontier). This zone has many volcanoes, lakes, and forests.

PATAGÓNICO NORTE Y SUR (North and South Patagonia), also known as LOS CANALES (The Channels), includes the Aisén and Magallanes Regions. Most of this zone is cold and wet, and has great icefields, fjords, and forests. The southeastern portion is semi-arid and covered in grassy plains called PAMPAS.

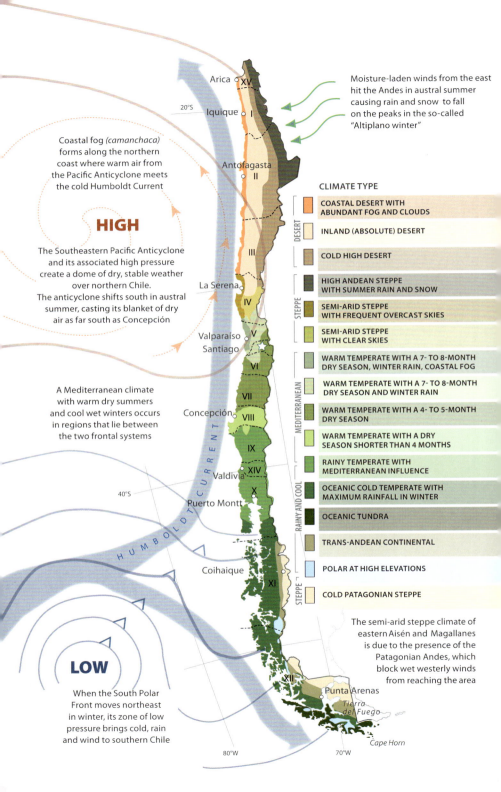

CLIMATE

The Meteorological Department of Chile lists sixteen climate types for continental Chile. These range from desert in the north to Mediterranean in the Central Valley to cold temperate in the south. The diversity is due to the extreme length of the mainland, the presence of high mountains, proximity of the Humboldt Current, El Niño events, and atmospheric effects of the Southeastern Pacific Anticyclone and South Polar Front. As a general rule, temperature decreases as elevation and latitude increase, and the south has more precipitation than the north.

AVERAGE ANNUAL PRECIPITATION	AVERAGE TEMPERATURE
Rain 0.08 in (2.1 mm) Some years with no rain	January 77°F (25°C); July 64°F (18°C) Daytime and night temperatures similar
Rain 0.5 in (15 mm) Some places with no rain ever recorded	Daytime 77°F (25°C); Night 32°F (0°C) No seasonal variation
Rain 0.08 in (2.1 mm) Some places with no rain ever recorded	Daytime 73°F (23°C); Night 32°F (0°C) No seasonal variation
Up to 16 in (400 mm) of rain and snow Most precipitation falls in January and February	Daytime January 50°F (10°C); July 37°F (3°C) Night 32°F (0°C)
Rain 3–11 in (78–270 mm) Most rain falls from June to August	January 73°F (23°C); July 61°F (16°C) Daytime and night temperatures similar
Rain/snow 8 in (200 mm) Most precipitation falls from June to August	January 81°F (27°C) July 63°F (17°C)
Rain 13–16 in (340–400 mm) Rainy season is May to August	January 73°F (23°C) July 61°F (16°C)
Rain 13–16 in (340–400 mm) Rainy season is May to August	January 73°F (23°C) July 61°F (16°C)
Rain 28–39 in (700–1000 mm) in lowlands Rain/snow 39–98 in (1000–2500 mm) in Andes	Lowlands January 88°F (31°C); July 57°F (14°C) Andes July 32°C (0°C)
Rain 39–51 in (1000–1300 mm) in lowlands Rain/snow 118 in (3000 mm) in Andes	Lowlands January 62°F (16°C); July 50°F (10°C) Andes July 32°C (0°C)
Rain/snow 39–79 in (1000–2000 mm) No dry season	Lowlands January 77°F (23°C); July 52°F (11°C) Andes July 32°C (0°C)
Rain/snow 66–157 in (1700–4000 mm) Maximum precipitation in winter; no dry season	January 63°F (18°C) July 45°F–50°F (7°C–10°C)
Rain/snow 96–180 in (2450–4700 mm) No dry season	January 45°F (7°C) July 32°F (0°C)
Rain 10–47 in (250–1200 mm) No dry season	January 50°F (10°C) July 34°F (1°C)
Snow 145–265 in (3700–6700 mm) No dry season	Below 32°F (0°C) No seasonal variation
Rain 10–24 in (250–612 mm) Variable dry season	January 54°F (12°C) July 40°F (4°C)

CLIMATE is the condition of the atmosphere at a particular location over a long period of time, normally 30 years or more. It is the sum of atmospheric elements including temperature, humidity, clouds, precipitation, atmospheric pressure, solar radiation and wind.

WEATHER is sometimes used as a synonym for climate, but weather is a short-term event—the climatic conditions over a brief period of time, at a certain place and time of year. As the great science fiction writer Robert A. Heinlein put it, "Climate is what we expect. Weather is what we get."

SEASONS in the Southern Hemisphere are the opposite of the Northern Hemisphere's. Austral summer extends from December to February and austral winter from May through July.

LANDFORMS AND PLATE TECTONICS

Landforms are naturally produced surface features of our planet's crust. They are the result of forces working deep within the Earth over eons of time.

Scientists have only begun to understand the many intricate processes that mold the land. They have discovered that surface and submarine physical features are the result of a building process called PLATE TECTONICS that continually reshapes the face of Earth. Plate tectonics revolves around the idea that the Earth's thin crust is split into numerous PLATES, which are about 50 miles (80 km) thick and which float in slow motion on top of the Earth's hot, pliable interior. Each plate moves as a unit and interacts with adjacent plates at its boundaries.

In the case of Chile, two tectonic plates are of great interest—the dense, basaltic NAZCA PLATE, which forms the seabed of the Southeastern Pacific Ocean, and the SOUTH AMERICAN CONTINENTAL PLATE, which is made of relatively lighter granitic materials. How these plates move and react when they collide explains many of the features of Chile's topography.

Movement of the Nazca Plate and other oceanic plates adjacent to Chilean territory is generated at the submarine MID-OCEAN RIDGES. Magma, which is molten rock from beneath the Earth's crust, erupts through rifts in the ridges and quickly solidifies in the cold bottom water. The buildup of new land causes the oceanic plate to shift away from a ridge in a process called SEA FLOOR SPREADING. This theory was formulated independently in the 1960s by Princeton geology professor Harry H. Hess and another geologist, Robert Dietz.

The Nazca Plate originates at an elevated ridge called the EAST PACIFIC RISE. The rise extends as a jagged ridge from Acapulco, Mexico, to the Ross Sea in Antarctica. Molten basalt erupts through the rift that runs along the ridge's crest, and provides new crust for the Pacific Plate to the west and the Nazca Plate to the east. The crust in this area is expanding at an average rate of 7 in (18 cm) per year.

The Challenger Fracture Zone, Chile Rise, Nazca Ridge, Sala y Gómez Ridge and Juan Fernández Ridge are submarine SECONDARY PLATE SPURS situated above localized melting regions in the Earth's mantle. These areas called HOTSPOTS are characterized by intense volcanic activity. Most of the volcanic peaks generated at hotspots never reach the ocean surface, but in exceptional cases, islands such as Easter Island, Sala y Gómez and the Islas Desventuradas emerge from the sea and become a visible part of the oceanic landscape.

An abyssal, V-shaped, submarine canyon called the PERU–CHILE TRENCH extends for 1100 miles (1770 km) along the continental shelf of Chile and Peru. The trench reaches depths of some 26,250 feet (8000 m) below sea level at Bartholomew Basin off Antofagasta and Richard's Depths off Valparaíso.

The trench marks the convergence of the Nazca Plate and the South American Continental Plate, which are moving in opposite directions. The South American Plate moves westward away from the Mid-Atlantic Ridge and the Nazca Plate moves eastward away from the East Pacific Rise. The convergence area is part of the RING OF FIRE, a great band of volcanic and seismic activity that encircles the Pacific seabed. At the trench, the dense Nazca Plate sinks

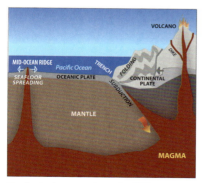

Geological events along the Chilean coast.

under the lighter continental crust in a process known as SUBDUCTION. The plate descends at an angle into the Earth's mantle where it returns to a molten state.

Molten crust erupting through fissures in the overriding continental plate caused the formation of the Andean volcanoes. In contrast, the Coastal Range was formed from accreted material scraped off the sea floor at the trench margin. Over time, the accreted material was uplifted, compressed and folded into mountains.

Earthquakes occur when the plates lurch past each other or when rock surfaces slip along a fracture—a process called FAULTING. Chile is very susceptible to this type of seismic activity. The strongest earthquake ever recorded to date occurred off the coast of southern Chile in 1960, measuring 9.5 on the Richter Scale.

In 1836 Charles Darwin witnessed a series of earthquakes at Valdivia and Concepción. In his *Beagle* diary, Darwin described the effects of the earthquake and tidal wave at Concepción as follows:

"Shortly after the shock, a great wave was seen from the distance of three or four miles, approaching in the middle of the bay with a smooth outline; but along the shore it tore up cottages and trees, as it swept onwards with irresistible force. At the head of the bay it broke in a fearful line of white breakers, which rushed up to a height of 23 vertical feet above the highest spring-tides. Their force must have been prodigious, for at the Fort a cannon with its carriage, estimated at four tons in weight, was moved 15 feet inwards. A schooner was left in the midst of the ruins, 200 yards from the beach."

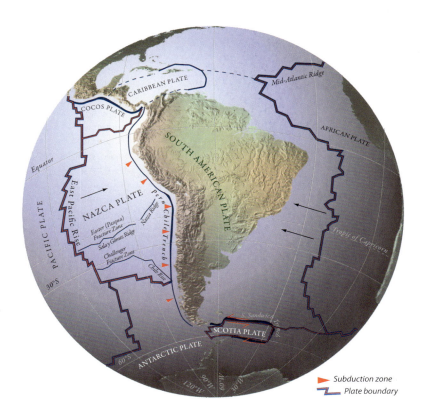

MAINLAND TOPOGRAPHY

Chile's landscape is dominated by three longitudinal relief features: the Andes Mountains, the Coastal Mountains and the Longitudinal Depression.

CORDILLERA DE LOS ANDES
Andes Mountains

The Andes Mountain Range is the world's longest mountain system, measuring some 5500 mi (8900 km) from north to south. It comprises a complex series of parallel and transverse mountain ranges, or CORDILLERAS, with intervening plateaus and depressions. There are numerous peaks over 22,000 ft (6700 m) high, making the Andes loftier than any other mountain range except the Himalayas. Cerro Aconcagua, the highest peak in the Western Hemisphere, rises to 22,826 ft (6959 m) above sea level just east of the Argentine-Chilean border.

The western arm of the Andes Range is called the CORDILLERA OCCIDENTAL. The range extends about 2500 mi (4000 km) along Chile's borders with Bolivia and Argentina. The cold, arid mountain slopes that extend to the treeline—the upper limit of arboreal growth—are called the ALTO ANDINO, or High Andes. The cordillera has 46 active volcanoes, or about 10 percent of our planet's active ones. NEVADO OJOS DEL SALADO is the world's highest active volcano at 22,566 ft (6880 m) and is also the highest point in Chile.

The ALTIPLANO ("high plain") and the PUNA (Quechua for "windswept tableland") are intermontane plateaus that lie above 12,000 ft (3650 m) in extreme northeastern Chile. They are separated by a fault at 22° S latitude, with the Altiplano to the north and the Puna to the south. It should be noted that Altiplano and Puna are terms used in a very different sense for habitats and floral communities of the High Andes.

To the east of Santiago lie the ANDES MEDITERRÁNEOS, or Mediterranean Andes. The highest peaks are Tupungato at 21,555 ft (6570 m), Marmelejo at 20,039 ft (6108 m) and Maipo at 17,270 ft (5264 m).

Summits of the CORDILLERA DE LA ARAUCANÍA, or Araucanian Range, average under 11,500 ft (3500 m) in height. What they lack in elevation, they make up for in beauty. The perfect, snow-covered, volcanic cones of Osorno, Llaima, Tronador and others provide a dramatic backdrop for the many lakes of the Los Lagos Region.

The CORDILLERA PATAGÓNICA runs from Puerto Montt to the Strait of Magellan. Except for peaks such as San Clemente and Torres del Paine, the summits of the Patagonian Andes average about 6550 ft (2000 m) in elevation. About 7000 sq mi (18,000 sq km) of the range is buried under ice. The PATAGONIAN ICEFIELDS *(Campos de Hielo Norte y Sur)* contain the largest ice mass in the Southern Hemisphere with the exception of Antarctica. Recent studies indicate that the icefields are melting at an accelerating pace and account for nearly 10 percent of global sea level change from mountain glaciers.

The Andes are reduced to low hills near the Strait of Magellan, then resurface to the south as the Fuegian Andes. This sector contains the CORDILLERA DARWIN, which runs on an east-west axis along the Beagle Channel. Mount Darwin is the highest peak at 7970 ft (2430 m).

Although the Andes appear to reach their terminus on Tierra del Fuego, in reality they continue as an arc of undersea mountains. The tallest peaks emerge from the sea as islands of the Scotia Arc—South Georgia, the South Orkneys and South Sandwich Islands—and finally rise as the mountains of the Antarctic Peninsula.

CORDILLERA DE LA COSTA
Coastal Mountains

The Coastal Range comprises very old folded mountains formed from accreted material that was scraped off the seabed between 100 to 70 million years ago. The peaks have eroded over time and now exist as rounded hills or flattened summits, with most elevations under 6550 ft (2000 m). The range parallels the Pacific seacoast from Arica to Puerto Montt—a distance of about 1865 miles (3000 km).

The Coastal Cordillera rises at MORRO DE ARICA, a massive headland to the south of Arica. It continues south to La Serena as a wide chain of arid mountains. Wave erosion has sculpted its western slopes into steep cliffs and marine terraces, which are bordered by a narrow coastal plain that is nearly devoid of natural harbors. Deep, transverse ravines called QUEBRADAS mark the places where rivers flowing from the Andes have cut a course to the Pacific Ocean across the coastal mountains.

The Coastal Range declines in elevation as it nears central Chile, forming a wide, low boundary along the Central Valley. Its seaward slopes open to broad littoral plains, oceanside resorts and major port cities.

South of Concepción, the Coastal Range is called the NAHUELBUTA CORDILLERA. Its highest peak is Alto de la Cueva at 4500 ft (1400 m). This massive cordillera stretches without break from the Río Biobío to the Río Imperial, a distance of some 120 miles (190 km). The range forms a major barrier to westward flowing rivers, whose courses are deflected to the north or south.

The rolling, forested hills of ISLA DE CHILOÉ represent the final major rise of the Coastal Cordillera before the range sinks into the Golfo de Corcovado. Summits of the drowned range reappear to the south as an archipelago of 3000 islands that extend along a fjord-lined coast to CAPE HORN at the southern tip of South America.

DEPRESIÓN INTERMEDIA (VALLE LONGITUDINAL)
Longitudinal Depression

The Longitudinal Depression lies between the western foothills of the Andes and the Coastal Range. It is a narrow valley with a maximum width of about 50 miles (80 km). A few river gorges *(quebradas)* and transverse valleys *(cajones)* cut across the area to the north of Valparaíso. These excepted, the depression extends in a nearly continuous line from Arica to Puerto Montt, where it falls into the sea at Reloncaví Sound.

The northern sector of the longitudinal valley extends from Arica to Antofagasta and runs straight through the heart of the Atacama Desert. The basin was created by a localized sinking of the Earth's crust. It subsequently filled with materials eroded from the Andes. The basin floor, which slopes gently from east to west, now lies at elevations of 2000–4000 ft (600–1200 m).

A plain called the PAMPA DEL TAMARUGAL covers a large part of the northern valley, extending 185 miles (300 km) from the Azapa Valley near Arica to the Quebrada de Tiliviche northeast of Iquique. Water flowing down from the Andes seeps into the pampa's porous alluvial soil and fills the subterranean aquifers *(napas)* lying just below the desert surface. Water from the aquifers sustains the growth of TAMARUGO *(Prosopis tamarugo)*. The wood and pods from these leguminous trees were exploited for fuel and fodder for mule trains in the early nitrate mining period. Plantations were established in the 1960s to restore this tree to its former abundance, thus stabilizing the fragile desert soils and indirectly preserving other plants and animals associated with this habitat.

SODIUM NITRATE (Chile saltpeter) deposits occur near the Pampa del Tamarugal. They originated as sediments eroded from the Andes and washed down into the Pampa over the last 65 million years. Nitrate was mined by 19th century Chilean and British entrepreneurs for use in the manufacture of gunpowder, explosives and fertilizers. A dispute over the mineral rights led to the War of the Pacific, fought from 1879 to 1884 between Chile and the joint forces of Peru and Bolivia, all of whom laid claim to the territory. Chilean victory led to the annexation of the former Peruvian province of Tarapacá and the former Bolivian province of Litoral, along with the major nitrate ports and railways that had been developed from Iquique to Pisagua and across the Atacama to Taltal.

Chile's CENTRAL VALLEY extends from the Aconcagua River Valley to Puerto Montt. It is probably the most important physical feature of Chile insofar as human settlement and agriculture are concerned. This is the most densely populated area of Chile, and the capital city of Santiago lies at its apex. The mild Mediterranean climate, moderate spring rainfall, and mineral-rich alluvial soils deposited by Andean rivers, provide near perfect conditions for orchards and vineyards. Chile exports about US$4 billion worth of agricultural products annually. A large amount of fruit is exported to the Northern Hemisphere countries, especially in boreal winter, and vintage wines are sold to connoisseurs around the world.

The southern part of the Central Valley contains fluvial and alluvial deposits, which have created soils suitable for growing wheat and for pasturing dairy cows. The country's growing dairy industry is being targeted by the government as another potential key export industry. Dairy exports presently include cheese, condensed milk and milk powder. The majority is exported to Mexico.

The Central Valley ends south of Puerto Montt. It descends into the Golfo de Ancud and Golfo de Corcovado and becomes a drowned valley that winds beneath the intercoastal channels of southern Chile.

RIVERS

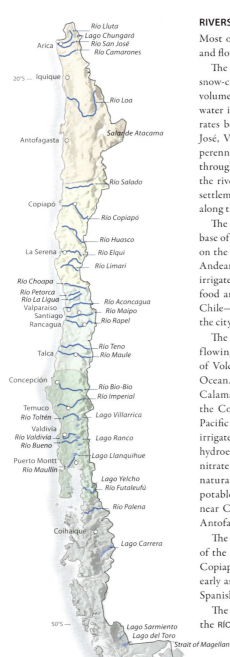

Most of Chile's rivers originate in the Andes and flow westward toward the Pacific Ocean.

The rivers of northern Chile flow from the snow-capped volcanoes of the Altiplano. Their volume is so slight in most cases that their water is either absorbed by the soil or evaporates before reaching the sea. The Lluta, San José, Vitor, Camarones and Loa are the only perennial rivers of the north. Their courses flow through QUEBRADAS—deep, wide ravines that the rivers have carved out over time. Human settlement in the north has historically been along these perennial watercourses.

The headwaters of the RÍO LLUTA lie near the base of the Volcán Parinacota, which is located on the Altiplano. The Lluta flows through the Andean foothills and across the Atacama. It irrigates the fertile Azapa Valley—the main food and citrus producing valley of northern Chile—before discharging into the Pacific near the city of Arica.

The RÍO LOA is the longest river in Chile, flowing 275 miles (443 km) from the base of Volcán Miño in the Andes to the Pacific Ocean. It runs southwest to the oasis city of Calama, then across the Atacama Desert and the Coastal Range before emptying into the Pacific north of Tocopilla. Waters of the Loa irrigate oases in the Atacama and generate hydroelectric power for Chile's copper and nitrate mines. The Loa's waters have a high natural arsenic concentration and are not potable unless treated. A purification plant near Calama provides drinking water for the Antofagasta Region.

The RÍO COPIAPÓ marks the southern limit of the Atacama Desert. It irrigates the fertile Copiapó Valley, which has been farmed as early as the Inca Period and certainly prior to Spanish settlement in 1540.

The basin of the RÍO LIMARI extends from the RÍO ELQUI in the north to the RÍO CHOAPA to the south. The basin has become the bread basket of Norte Chico thanks to the largest irrigation system in South America. Three large dams feed water into hundreds of miles of irrigation canals, watering the area's inland valleys and foothill meadows. A well-known product of the area is Pisco, a brandy *(aguardiente)* made from grapes grown in the Elqui Valley.

Heavy winter rains and spring snowmelt from the Andes feed the rivers of central Chile. Their wide, stony courses are exposed at the height of the summer drought. A complex system of irrigation canals divert water from rivers such as the ACONCAGUA, MAIPO and MAULE to the area's vineyards, orchards, croplands and dairy farms.

The RÍO BIOBÍO marks the dividing line between central and southern Chile. It is an historical boundary where the native Mapuches held back Spanish settlement for almost three hundred years (1599–1882). Today the Biobío provides fresh drinking water for over one million people, as well as hydroelectric power, irrigation and water sport recreation.

Valdivia is located at the junction of the RÍOS CALLE CALLE and CRUCES, which unite to form the RÍO VALDIVIA. These are among the few navigable rivers of the south.

Heavy rainfall keeps the rivers such as the RÍO BAKER at full volume throughout the year. Although their extremely steep drainage renders many unsuitable for navigation, these same conditions make rivers like the RÍO FUTALEUFÚ, RÍO AZUL and RÍO ESPOLON ideal for whitewater rafting and kayaking. The Class Five rapids of the "Fu" storm through gorges with nearly vertical, black, basalt walls. Farther downstream, the Fu offers calmer pools, which are legendary fly fishing locations for brook, brown and rainbow trout.

LAKES

The Altiplano of n Chile is the site of LAGO CHUNGARÁ, one of the world's highest lakes with an elevation of 14,820 ft (4517 m) and a surface area of 8 sq mi (20.5 sq km). It is a scenically glorious lake, backed by the twin volcanoes Parinacota and Pomerape and inhabited by countless Andean waterbirds.

Northern Chile is known for its large saline lakes and salt flats called *salares*. The largest is the SALAR DE ATACAMA, situated at 7550 ft (2300 m) in the desert of Antofagasta. The Salar de Atacama is 6 mi (10 km) long and 37 mi (60 km) wide. Its saline lagoons are recharged by groundwater and springs flowing from surrounding volcanic peaks.

Deep, scenic lakes fed by snow-capped volcanoes typify the LOS LAGOS REGION. From north to south the lakes are named Villarrica, Calafquén, Panguipulli, Riñihue, Ranco, Puyehue, Rupanco, Todos los Santos and Llanquihue. LAGO LLANQUIHUE is Chile's largest lake, measuring 22 mi (35 km) long by 25 mi (40 km) wide, with depths to 5000 ft (1500 m). Llanquihue is Mapuche for "Place of Peace."

LAGO GENERAL CARRERA is South America's second-largest lake. It extends from eastern Aisén into Argentina and has a surface area of 377 sq mi (978 sq km).

Lago Chungará and Volcán Parinacota

SOUTHERN STRAITS AND PASSAGES

The STRAIT OF MAGELLAN separates the South American mainland from Tierra del Fuego and other islands to the south. The strait passes through Chile for most of its length. It is about 330 mi (530 km) long and averages 15 mi (24 km) wide. Its narrowest width of 2.5 mi (4 km) lies near the Atlantic entry at ANGOSTURA PRIMERA (First Narrows).

In 1520 Ferdinand Magellan discovered the strait that would later bear his name. Three of his four small ships transited the passage in 38 days, sailing from Cabo Virgenes at the Atlantic entry to Isla Desolation and the Pacific Ocean. The Strait of Magellan gained importance in the days of the sailing ships, especially before the Panama Canal was built in 1914. Despite the frequent fog, wind, storms and narrow passages, sailing ships could pass through the strait removed from the greater danger of rounding Cape Horn.

The largest town on the Strait is PUNTA ARENAS. The economy of the port centers on shipping, oil and coal. The first oil strike occurred in 1945 at Mantianales on Tierra del Fuego. Onshore and offshore platforms operated by ENAP–Magallanes in the Strait of Magellan supply about half of Chile's oil and almost all of its liquid gas. In 1987 the Pecket Mine opened coal fields at Otway Sound near Punta Arenas.

The BEAGLE CHANNEL separates Tierra del Fuego from smaller islands to the south and forms a navigable passage between the Pacific and Atlantic Oceans. The channel is named after the British vessel *HMS Beagle* that conducted two hydrographic surveys of coastal South America. The ship's second voyage (1831–1836) was led by Captain Robert FitzRoy. Charles Darwin, who acted as ship's naturalist, recounted the journey in his famed journal, *The Voyage of the Beagle*.

The Beagle Channel is about 150 mi (241 km) long and 3 mi (5 km) wide at its narrowest point. The main settlements on the channel are PUERTO WILLIAMS, Chile, and USHUAIA, Argentina. Darwin Sound links the Beagle Channel to the Pacific at Londonderry and Stewart Islands. The channel's eastern sector forms the border between Chile and Argentina. The small islands of Picton, Lennox and Nueva lie in the channel between the two countries. They were ceded to Chile in the 1984 Peace and Friendship Treaty.

DRAKE PASSAGE is an open water sector of the Southern Ocean. It lies off the southern tip of South America between 56°S and 60°S latitudes—a distance equal to 400 miles (645 km). The Drake Passage separates the continent of South America from the South Shetland Islands and the Antarctic Peninsula.

Seas in Drake Passage are notoriously rough, often having waves over 33 ft (10 m) high. The waves are fueled by strong westerly winds that drive the waters of the Antarctic Circumpolar Current through the narrow passage that lies between the continents. On days when the fierce winds abate, the Drake Passage is pleasantly calm. On stormy days, it recalls the sailor's axiom, "Below 40 degrees, there is no law. Below 50 degrees, there is no God."

Drake Passage is named after the 16th-century English privateer Sir Francis Drake whose ships were storm-driven into the open Pacific south of the Strait of Magellan. The first recorded ship to transit the Drake Passage was the *Eendracht*, commanded by the Dutch Captain Willem Schouten and Jacob LeMaire in 1616. They also discovered CAPE HORN (Kap Hoorn), which they named for their home port in Holland.

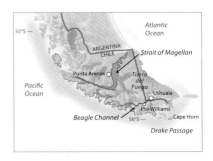

TERRITORIOS CHILENOS
CHILEAN TERRITORIES

Chile's far-flung sovereignties stretch from the tropics to the South Pole. Chile claims the Islas Desventuradas, Isla de Pascua (Easter Island, or Rapa Nui), Isla Sala y Gómez, the islands of the Juan Fernández Archipelago, and a sizeable wedge of the Antarctic continent.

Desventuradas Islands
Islas Desventuradas

The rugged Islas Desventuradas (meaning "Misfortunate Islands") lie about 528 miles (850 km) west of Chañaral on the Chilean mainland. Their discovery is credited to the Spanish navigator Juan Fernández who sighted the islands around 1574.

The Desventuradas include Islas San Félix y San Ambrosio, Islote González, and several rocks and stacks. The total area of the islands is 4 sq mi (10 sq km).

The islands lack permanent watersources and have no permanent residents. There is a single-runway military airfield on San Félix that is manned by a detachment of Chilean Navy personnel. Artisanal fisheries harvest lobster around San Ambrosio.

The islands are of volcanic origin and are primarily basaltic. Island formation dates to about 2.86 million years ago. There is evidence of volcanic eruptions occurring as recently as 100,000 years ago on San Félix.

San Félix is triangular in shape and has a total area of about one sq mi (2.5 sq km). Its surface is relatively flat in the eastern sector, but rises to 633 ft (193 m) in the west at Cerro San Félix. The coast shows evidence of intense erosion by the sea.

San Ambrosio lies 12.5 mi (20 km) east of San Félix. It rises abruptly from the sea, with sea cliffs on almost all sides. The massif is topped by a ravine-ridden plain about 833 ft (254 m) high, with the high point being over 1560 ft (478 m) in elevation.

The climate is humid, warm and oceanic. The temperature averages 64°F (18°C). The rainy season is about 7 months long, with maximum rainfall occurring from May through August. Fog is common.

There are 19 species of flowering plants, 14 of which are endemic. The flora includes perennial herbs and ferns, low bushes, and a single tree species, *Thamnoseris lacerata* (Asteraceae) that grows to about 16 ft (5 m) high. Several alien species were introduced in the past and now threaten native plants.

The fauna includes 10 bird species. The Cernícalo, or American Kestrel subspecies (*Falco sparverius fernandensis*), is resident on San Ambrosio. Seabirds include Kermadec Petrel, Masatierra Petrel, Masked Booby, Sooty Tern, Brown Noddy, Grey Noddy and White-bellied Storm-Petrel. There are no native land mammals. Dogs, cats, goats and the house mouse are introduced.

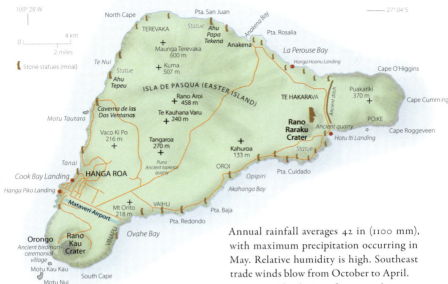

Easter Island
Isla de Pascua, Rapa Nui

Polynesians are thought to have arrived at Easter Island around AD 800. They called the island *Rapa Nui,* or more familiarly *Te Pito o Te Henua,* the Navel of the World.

The name Easter Island was bestowed by the Dutch Captain Jakob Roggeveen who sighted it on Easter Sunday in 1722. Chile claimed the island in 1888. It presently has the status of a National Park, established to protect the ancient stone statues *(moai)* and other archaelogical treasures dating from the 10th to the 16th centuries.

The island lies in southeastern Polynesia, 2355 mi (3790 km) west of Chañaral on the Chilean mainland. It has an area of 64 sq mi (164 sq km). About 3800 people, including native Polynesians, Chilean residents and Chilean temporary workers *(los continentales)* live on the island. Pascuense, a Polynesian dialect also called Rapanui, is the common language. Spanish is the official language. English is widely spoken.

The climate is subtropical. Temperatures range between 63°F and 86°F (17°C–30°C), with the warmest month being February. Annual rainfall averages 42 in (1100 mm), with maximum precipitation occurring in May. Relative humidity is high. Southeast trade winds blow from October to April.

Easter Island rises from a submarine volcanic chain known as the Easter Island or Pascua Ridge. The triangular-shaped island is built around a number of volcanic cones and two large volcanic craters, or calderas. Maunga Terevaca is the island's highest point at 1969 ft (600 m). The Rano Kao and Rano Raraku craters are filled with boggy ponds of accumulated rainwater. Most of the coastline is bounded by cliffs ranging from 65–985 ft (20–300 m) high. The cliffs are riddled with lava tubes and caves. There are sandy beaches with small coral formations on the northeast coast.

The thin and stony soils are suitable for livestock grazing and growing crops such as taro, yams and bananas. Native vegetation includes 30 flowering plant species and 16 species of ferns. Introduced grasses, eucalyptus and palms comprise the rest of the vegetation. More information is given in the chapter on flora on pages 68 and 69.

There are no extensive coral reefs, but the subtropical waters of the island support a variety of marine life including Easter Island Butterflyfish *(Chaetodon litus),* Easter Island Flyingfish *(Cheilopogon rapanouiensis),* Easter Island Mitten Lobster *(Parribacus perlatus),* Easter Island Slipper Lobster *(Scyl-*

larides roggeveeni) and the Easter Island Spiny Lobster *(Panulirus pascuensis).*

Mollusks include Planaxis *(Planaxis akuana)*, Black Nerite *(Nerita morio)*, Pyramid Pricklywinkle *(Nodilittorina pyramidalis)*, Dragon's Head Cowrie *(Cypraea caputdraconis)*, and the rare Father Englert's Cowrie *(Cypraea englerti).*

Reptiles include the Mourning Gecko *(Lepidodactylus lugubris)* and the Snake-eyed Skink *(Cryptoblepharus poecilopleurus).*

Fifteen species of tropical seabirds have been recorded on Easter Island, including Kermadec Petrel, Phoenix Petrel, Christmas Shearwater, White-tailed Tropicbird, Red-tailed Tropicbird, Masked Booby, Great Frigatebird, Wandering Tattler, Sanderling, Grey-backed Tern, Sooty Tern, White Tern, Brown Noddy, and Grey Noddy. Introduced birds include the Chilean Tinamou, Chimango Caracara, Rock Pigeon, Common Diuca-Finch and House Sparrow.

There are no native mammals. Dogs, cats, horses, cattle and rodents have been introduced.

Isla Sala y Gómez

This tiny, remote, uninhabited island is situated 258 mi (415 km) ne of Easter Island and 2110 mi (3400 km) w of Chile. It comprises two low hills of bare volcanic rock joined by a narrow arm that is covered by water at high tide. The island measures 0.25 mi long by 0.5 mi wide (402 m x 805 m)—an area of only one sq mi (2.5 sq km). Sala y Gómez is a sanctuary for marine life and seabirds.

Juan Fernández Archipelago
Archipielago Juan Fernández

The Juan Fernández Archipelago comprises three volcanic islands that rose from the undersea Juan Fernández Ridge within the last 5.8 million years.

ISLA RÓBINSON CRUSOE, formerly named MASATIERRA, and Isla Santa Clara lie about 416 mi (670 km) west of Valparaíso, the archipelago's administrative seat.

ISLA ALEJANDRO SELKIRK, formerly called MASAFUERA, lies about 520 mi (835 km) west of the Chilean mainland and 104 mi (167 km) west of Róbinson Crusoe.

The islands have a combined total area of 71 sq mi (183 sq km). All the islands are mountainous, and have steep sea cliffs and deep ravines called *quebradas*. Maximum elevations are 3000 ft (915 m) on Róbinson Crusoe, 1230 ft (375 m) on Santa Clara, and 5413 ft (1650 m) on Alejandro Selkirk.

The climate is Mediterranean with some oceanic influences. Average annual rainfall is 37 in (950 mm) and the average annual temperature is 59°F (15°C).

Islas Masatierra and Santa Clara were discovered in 1563 by the Spanish navigator Juan Fernández. It is said that he stocked the islands with goats and pigs and lived there for several years. The islands were virtually forgotten until 1704, when the Scottish sailor Alexander Selkirk was put ashore on Masatierra after a quarrel with his captain. He remained there alone, living in a cave until 1709 when he was picked up by British privateers. Selkirk's adventures inspired Daniel Defoe's novel, *Robinson Crusoe*, published in 1719.

The archipelago passed into Chilean possession in the early 1800s. The main island was used for a short time as a penal settlement for political prisoners. Today the archipelago has about 600 residents, most of whom live in the town of San Juan Bautista on Isla Róbinson Crusoe (Masatierra). The principal occupations are tourism and lobster fishing.

The islands have a rich, diverse flora with 423 species of vascular plants—132 of which are endemic to the archipelago. Sixty-five species are classed as Endangered and thirty-five as Vulnerable. Sandalwood *(Santalum fernandezianum)*, which was harvested for the China trade in the 1800s, was once common but is now extinct.

Some 58 bird species have been recorded in the archipelago. Endemic species include the Masafuera Rayadito, Juan Fernández Tit-Tyrant, Juan Fernández Firecrown, Juan Fernández Petrel and Stejneger's Petrel. Endemic at subspecies level are the Juan Fernández Variable Hawk *(Buteo polyosoma exsul)* and the Juan Fernández Kestrel *(Falco sparverius fernandensis)*.

There are no native land mammals. Dogs, cats, goats, rabbits, cattle, coati and rats are introduced. The only indigenous mammal is the Juan Fernández Fur Seal *(Arctocephalus philippii)*, a marine pinniped that was thought to be extinct until the species was rediscovered in 1967.

Marine life includes 146 species of fish, including Juan Fernández Jackfish *(Caranx georgianus)*, Jerguilla *(Girella albostriata)* and Vidriola *(Seriola lalandii)*. The Juan Fernández Lobster *(Jasus frontalis)* is endemic to the islands. Mollusks include the Juan Fernández Coral-shell *(Coraliophila scala)* and Juan Fernández Limpet *(Cellana ardosidea)*.

Chilean Antarctic Territory
Territorio Chileno Antártico

Chile claims the wedge of Antarctica lying between meridians 53°W and 90°W, and between the South Pole and 60°S latitude, as a natural extension of her landmass. The total area of the territory is 482,625 sq mi (1,250,000 sq km).

Some waggishly note that the first men to reach Antarctica were not South Americans but Europeans. The British Captain James Cook was the first known explorer to enter Antarctic waters. Between 1772 and 1776, he crossed the Antarctic Circle three times, but never sighted land. Among the first to land in Antarctica was American sealer Nathaniel Palmer who reached Deception Island in 1820. In the same year, British Captain Edward Bransfield discovered the Trinity Peninsula and Russian Admiral von Bellingshausen landed on the isolated islands of Alexander I and Peter I.

Chile's Antarctic claim overlaps that of Great Britain's and Argentina's. However, under the Antarctic Treaty System territorial claims are not recognized, nor are the claims seriously pursued. The main purpose of claimant nations is to establish scientific research stations for biological and atmospheric studies—a protocol of cooperative study established by universal accord in the International Geophysical Year of 1957–1958.

Chilean Antarctic Territory is part of the Chilean Antarctic Province, which is divided into two municipalities called *comunas*. The *Comuna de Cabo de Hornos* is administered from Puerto Williams, a naval base and civilian settlement on Isla Navarino in the Magallanes Region. The *Comuna de la Antártica* is administered from Puerto Covadonga, the civilian name for Chile's main Antarctic base, General Bernardo O'Higgins Riquelme (O'HIGGINS).

Another major Chilean base is Eduardo Frei Montalva Station (FREI), located on the shores of Admiralty Bay on King George Island. This large complex includes Teniente Rodolfo Marsh Martin airfield

Chile claims the wedge of Antarctica between meridians 53°W and 90°W and between the South Pole and 60°S latitude

and a civilian settlement, Villa Las Estrellas, which comes complete with a bank and Rotary Club. The research bases of thirteen other nations, including Russia, Korea and Brazil, share the Admiralty Bay location with Frei Base.

Chile maintains several other scientific research stations on the Antarctic Peninsula and in the South Shetland Islands. Some of the older stations are temporarily closed or have been abandoned. The Chilean station on Deception Island was destroyed in 1967 by volcanic activity.

The territory claimed by Chile is only a small part of a vast continent that lies asymmetrically centered on the South Pole. Antarctica is the fifth largest continent with an area of 5.4 million sq mi (14 million sq km). In austral winter, 8 million sq mi (20 million sq km) of sea ice forms over the surrounding ocean, almost doubling the continent's surface area.

Antarctica divides into two subcontinents. EAST ANTARCTICA, which comprises the bulk of the continental landmass, is an elevated, ice-covered plateau with underlying ancient bedrock. WEST ANTARCTICA consists largely of an archipelago of mountainous islands that are covered with ice.

The ANTARCTIC PENINSULA is part of West Antarctica. An arc of mountains topped by a narrow ice-capped plateau runs for about 1000 mi (1610 km) along the length of the Peninsula. Glaciers flow in both directions from the plateau, feeding the Larsen Ice Shelf to the east and calving icebergs into ocean waters to the west.

Because the Antarctic Peninsula extends farther north than the rest of Antarctica, the climate is warmer, and it is common for noontime temperatures to be above freezing in austral summer.

The Antarctic ecosystem is characterized by an impoverished terrestrial biota and an extraordinarily rich marine system. The dispersal of terrestrial fauna and flora is limited by the hostile polar climate and the great distance from other landmasses. Ice-free areas along the Antarctic coast serve as breeding grounds for marine birds and mammals, and support the growth of grasses, mosses, bryophytes and lichens.

Antarctica has only two seed-producing plants—Antarctic Hairgrass *(Deschampsia antarctica)* and Antarctic Pearlwort *(Colobanthus quitensis)*—and about 500 species of non-flowering plants.

Fossil remains of marsupials, crocodiles, ferns and tropical tree species suggest that Antarctica was once positioned near the equator and supported a great variety of life forms. But today there are no ferns, trees or terrestrial mammals, and now that sled dogs have been banished from Antarctica, there are no introduced mammals. The little Wingless Fly, *Belgica antarctica,* is the largest native land animal. Small invertebrates such as mites, springtails, flies, ticks, lice and fleas comprise the main body of terrestrial fauna.

Seals, whales and seabirds form the main bulk of the marine fauna. Six species of seals are present. Eared seals, the Otariidae, are represented by a single species, the Antarctic Fur Seal. True seals, the Phocidae, include the Southern Elephant Seal, Weddell Seal, Crabeater Seal and Leopard Seal. The Ross Seal is also present in Chilean Antarctica, but is very rarely seen due to its habit of remaining within the virtually impassable, consolidated pack ice.

At least 14 species of whales occur in antarctic waters. The Humpback Whale, Antarctic Minke and Orca are the species most commonly seen around the Antarctic Peninsula.

In the austral summer, the Antarctic coast is home to millions of birds, including 6 species of penguins and 43 species of flying seabirds. Common birds of the Antarctic Peninsula include Gentoo, Chinstrap and Adelie Penguins, Southern Giant-Petrel, Cape Petrel, Snow Petrel, Southern Fulmar, Blue-eyed Shag, Snowy Sheathbill, Brown Skua, Kelp Gull and Antarctic Tern.

Most seabirds move north beyond the ice edge at the onset of winter. Some birds such as the Wilson's Storm-Petrel *(Oceanites oceanicus)* undertake an arduous transequatorial migration to the Northern Hemisphere where they spend the boreal summer before returning to the Antarctic. A few species such as the Adelie Penguin, Antarctic Petrel and Snow Petrel winter on the sea ice. They feed on krill and other small marine organisms that live in open leads in the ice.

The food resources of Antarctic birds and mammals reside in the highly productive Southern Ocean—the polar waters of the South Pacific, South Atlantic and South Indian Oceans. As you will see in the next chapter, this extraordinary abundance of marine life is not restricted to Antarctic waters, but extends up the entire Pacific coast of continental Chile.

Antarctica is the highest continent. The average elevation is 6500 ft (1980 m). Mount Vinson in the Ellsworth Mountains is the highest point at 16,850 ft (5140 m).

About 95 percent of Antarctica is covered by an icecap that contains 6 million cubic miles (25 million cubic km) of ice—the largest reservoir of freshwater on Earth.

Despite being covered by so much ice, Antarctica is the driest continent—a huge polar desert that receives less than 10 in (254 mm) of precipitation per year.

Antarctica is also the coldest continent. Vostok Station in the continental interior recorded the world's coldest temperature of −129°F (−89°C) on July 21, 1983.

Antarctica is the windiest continent. Cold, gravitational winds called katabatic winds sweep down from interior elevations, at times reaching speeds of 100 miles per hour (160 km/hr) at the coast.

Most of Antarctica lies within the Antarctic Circle—a line of latitude at 66°33'S where sun does not set below the horizon on December 22, nor does the sun rise above the horizon on June 21.

Antarctica's seas lie within the Antarctic Convergence, a marine barrier zone that oscillates between 50°S and 60°S latitudes and marks the place where polar water meets and sinks beneath warmer, subantarctic water.

MARINE RESOURCES

The Pacific seacoast of continental Chile is about 4000 miles (6436 km) long. The coastal waters are rich and productive due to the cold currents and upwellings that exist along the mainland coast.

The HUMBOLDT (PERU) CURRENT is a fairly slow, coldwater flow that carries abundant nutrients from the Antarctic to the Chilean coast. The current is named after the 19th-century German scientist Alexander von Humboldt who measured its temperature and rate of flow, and described its effects on the surrounding atmosphere.

As the Humboldt Current reaches 40°S latitude, the stream bisects. One portion flows around the southern tip of South America into the South Atlantic Ocean. The other stream, which is about 550 mi (900 km) wide, flows north to parallel the Pacific coast of Chile and Peru. At about 4°S latitude, it turns west and joins the warmer South Pacific Equatorial Current.

The richness of the Humboldt Current is augmented by upwelling of cold bottom water, which is caused by the pull of the southeast trade winds at the ocean surface and by the Earth's rotation. The upwellings bring nutrients to the sea surface where they sustain a diverse food web of plankton, mollusks, fish, seabirds and mammals.

Marine productivity is interrupted in El Niño years, which are historically linked to the warming of Peruvian coastal waters and the coming of the Christ Child, El Niño. The event—also known as the EL NIÑO SOUTHERN OSCILLATION (ENSO)—is a warming of the tropical Pacific Ocean that occurs every three to six years. It is a response to a weakening of the trade winds that blow from South America toward Asia.

Normally, the trade winds induce cool surface water in the eastern Pacific Ocean through evaporation and upwelling of cold subsurface water. But when the trade winds weaken, cold bottom water is no longer drawn to the surface and sea temperatures rise. This results in diminished marine nutrient production and destructive algal blooms called "red tides," which in turn cause a decline in the number of fish and squid and a die-off of the marine birds and mammals that feed on them.

South American sea lions

THE MARINE FOOD WEB

Plankton—the little marine plants and animals that drift on ocean currents—form the basis of the marine food web.

PHYTOPLANKTON are free-floating unicellular plants such as dinoflagellates and silicoflagellates. These microscopic plants use solar energy to convert carbon dioxide into sugars and other organic compounds. They are fed upon by small herbivorous zooplankton, and thus are the first tier in the food web.

ZOOPLANKTON are the tiny, free-floating marine animals that are carried in the ocean flows. They include organisms such as jellyfish, polychaete worms, copepods and a crustacean known as krill.

KRILL are shrimp-like filter feeders. They range in size from 0.25–5.5 in (0.7–14 cm) long. The most common species found in Chilean waters are *Euphausia mucronata* and *Euphausia superba*. These euphausids swarm in large, dense shoals that tend to rise to the sea surface at night and retreat to the depths by day. They emit a bluish-green bioluminescence at night that may help them congregate and swarm in the dark.

Krill is the main food of baleen whales, seals, penguins, seabirds, fish and squid. The marine fauna's dependence on krill and the effects of a commercial krill harvest are matters of concern. The krill fishery is now the largest of any in the Southern Ocean. Nations such as the Ukraine, Poland and Japan, who operate major krill fisheries, have signed agreements to limit their catch. Hopefully this will ensure that a viable population of krill remains intact for marine fauna in the future decades.

FISHERIES

Chile is the chief fishery of South America. Chilean fish products represent about 12 percent of total national exports, with a value of some two billion US dollars. Fish products are exported primarily to Japan, China and the USA.

The Chilean Under-Secretary of Fisheries, in conjunction with the National Fishery Service (SERNAPESCA) and the non-profit Fisheries Development Institute (IFOP), regulate both the commercial fleet (*flota industrial*) and the smaller artisan fishery (*flota artesanal*). Their attempts to prevent the over-exploitation of stocks have been for the most part successful.

Commercial fishing takes place mainly off the north and central coasts of Chile. The commercial fleet harvests a total of 36 pelagic fish species. Five species represent 90 percent of the total Chilean fish catch: Jack Mackerel (*Jurel*), Hake (*Merluza*), Anchovy (*Anchoveta*), Chub Mackerel (*Caballa*) and Sardines (*Sardinas*). These pelagic species are deemed undesirable for human food because they are very bony. Most are used as raw material for fish meal and fish oil. The fish are processed at privately-owned plants in the north, and then exported for the production of animal feed and industrial oil. China, Japan and Taiwan are the chief importing nations of fishmeal from Chile.

Chilean and multinational factory and freezer trawlers operate demersal fisheries south of 41°S latitude, harvesting bottom-feeding fish such as the Congrío dorado (*Genypterus blacodes*), Patagonian Hake (*Merluccius australis*), and the Patagonian Toothfish (*Dissostichus eleginoides*), also known as Chilean Seabass, for export and local consumption.

Chile captures Mackerel Ice Fish (*Champsocephalus gunnari*) in international waters using its trawler-freezing vessels. Because of their very slow reproductive rate the ice fish catch is subject to a quota and is taken only in periods of high abundance. Ice fish are able to rest almost motionless

Mackerel Ice Fish
Champsocephalus gunnari

COMMERCIAL FISH 23

**South American Pilchard
Sardina del Pacífico**
Sardinops sagax
Arica–Magallanes
16 in (40 cm)

**Anchovy
Anchoveta**
Engraulis ringens
Arica–Los Lagos
8 in (20 cm)

Chilean Herring, Sardina común
Strangomera bentincki
Coquimbo–Biobío
11 in (28 cm)

Jack Mackerel, Jurel
Trachurus symmetricus
Arica–Los Lagos
31 in (80 cm)

**Chub Mackerel
Caballa**
Scomber japonicus
Arica–Biobío
23.5 in (60 cm)

Drum, Corvina
Cilus gilberti
Arica–Los Lagos
23.5 in (60 cm)

**Pacific Hake
Merluza común**
Merluccius gayi
Arica–Los Lagos
31 in (80 cm)

Tailed Hake, Merluza de cola
Macrouronus magellanicus
Magallanes
45 in (115 cm)

**Bigeye Flounder
Lenguado de ojos grandes**
Hippoglossina macrops
Arica–Magallanes
14.5 in (37 cm)

Pacific Pomfret, Reineta
Brama australis
Coquimbo–Magallanes
18.5 in (47 cm)

**Golden Conger, Pink Cusk-Eel
Congrío dorado**
Genypterus blacodes
Arica–Magallanes
79 in (200 cm)

Black Cusk-Eel, Congrío negro
Genypterus maculatus
Arica–Los Lagos
23.5 in (60 cm)

Patagonian Toothfish, Chilean Seabass, Bacalao
Dissostichus eleginoides
Arica–Magallanes
80 in (200 cm)

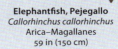

Elephantfish, Pejegallo
Callorhinchus callorhinchus
Arica–Magallanes
59 in (150 cm)

on the underwater ledges of icebergs and ice shelves because of a unique adaptation to extreme cold. Ice fish are the only vertebrates that lack the oxygen-carrying red pigment hemoglobin in the blood. This may reduce blood viscosity in near-freezing temperatures and reduce the energy needed to pump blood through the system. In addition, a glycoprotein in the blood acts as antifreeze, enabling ice fish to survive temperatures below the normal freezing point of body fluids.

The artisan fishery involves over 50,000 fishermen, divers and coastal subsistence food gatherers. Their catch includes fish such as Drum *(Corvina)*, Pomfret *(Reineta)*, Sole *(Lenguado)*, Elephantfish *(Pejegallo)* and Smelt *(Puye)*. The artisan fleet harvests about 500,000 tons of fish and other marine products annually, selling them to local and export markets.

Atlantic Salmon *(Salmo salar)* and Coho Salmon *(Oncorhychus kisutch)* are farmed for export. The salmon spend eight to ten months in cages in freshwater lakes in the southern regions. When salmon reach the stage that necessitates a salt water environment, they are moved to coastal bays and inlets. Salmon farming is growing at more than 30 percent a year in Chile. In 1990, Chile's 60 salmon farming companies exported 23,000 tons of salmon valued at 112 million US dollars. In contrast, more than 200,000 tons valued at one billion US dollars were exported in 2004. Chile is expected to surpass Norway as the leader in world salmon export in the near future.

MARISCOS

"Mariscos" means shellfish—the delectable items you are likely to see on restaurant menus throughout Chile or encounter at local seaside markets. Chile harvests about 60 kinds of shellfish, including crustaceans *(crustáceos)*, echinoderms *(equinodermos)*, mollusks *(moluscos)* and tunicates *(piures)*. At the present time, shellfish account for an annual commercial catch of about 150,000 tons, with an export value of more than 100 million US dollars. Many of the most valuable species are endangered due to historical exploitation. Today the shellfish harvest is closely regulated. Current laws allow only a few months of legal harvest and completely prohibit the catch of females of certain crustacean species.

Crustaceans

Crustaceans belong to a highly diverse phylum of joint-limbed animals known as arthropods. They include crabs *(centolla, jaiba)*, lobsters *(langostas)*, prawns *(langostinas)*, shrimp *(camarónes)* and barnacles *(picorocos)*. All except barnacles are commercially valuable. Barnacles are eaten locally after the outer protective structure that contains the living animal is pried from the rocks and coarse materials are washed away. The flesh is scooped out and eaten after cooking it in salt water. The calcified shells are usually discarded, but in some coastal communities they are used to hold items such as toothbrushes or pencils.

Tunicates

Piures, or sea squirts, are tidal pool tunicates that live attached to rocks in the tidal zone. The outer, grey-green layer is a filmy, cellulose coating called the "tunic." The salmon-red body has two siphons for drawing in seawater. Piure filter out nutrients from the water, including iodine, which imparts a strong metallic flavor. Piures are a popular delicacy in the north, especially around Antofagasta, where one sees them packed in plastic bags at local markets. At least two species, *Pyura chilensis* and *P. praeputialis* occur in Chile. The latter species is native to Australia and South Africa, and was probably transported to northern Chile on ships' hulls.

Mollusks

Most mollusks secrete calcium carbonate shells. The mollusk phylum is diverse and includes animals such as cephalopods, echinoderms, chitons, bivalves and gastropods.

MARISCOS 25

Scallop, Ostión del norte
Argopecten purpuratus
Arica–Coquimbo
5 in (13 cm)

Littleneck Clam, Almeja
Ameghinomya antiqua
Coquimbo–Valdivia
3 in (8 cm)

Chilean Wedge Clam, Macha
Mesodesma donacium
Arica–Magallanes
3.5 in (9 cm)

**Chilean Oyster
Ostra chilena**
Tiostrea chilensis
Arica–Los Lagos
3 in (8 cm)

Chilean Blue Mussel, Chorito
Mytilus chilensis
Biobío–Los Lagos
2 in (5 cm)

Red Abalone, Abalone
Haliotis rufescens
12 in (30 cm)
Farmed in Chile
Native to California

False Abalone, Loco
Concholepas concholepas
Arica–Magallanes
4.5 in (11.5 cm)

**Giant Mussel
Choro zapato**
Choromytilus chorus
Arica–Magallanes
8 in (20 cm)

Barnacles, Picorocos
Megabalanus psittacus
Arica–Magallanes
2–4 in (5–10 cm)

**Magnificent Chiton
Quitón**
Chiton magnificus
Arica–Magallanes
4 in (10 cm)

**Centolla
Chilean King Crab**
Lithodes antarctica
Valdivia–Magallanes
Cephalothorax 8 in (20 cm)

**Green Sea Urchin
Erizo colorado**
Loxechinus albus
Los Lagos–Magallanes
4 in (10 cm)

**Centollón
Chilean Snow Crab**
Paralomis granulosa
Aisén–Magallanes
Cephalothorax 3 in (8 cm)

**Jaiba
Chilean Stone Crab**
Cancer edwardsii
Arica–Magallanes
Cephalothorax 4 in (10 cm)

CEPHALOPODS: Cephalopod derives from the Greek words *kephale*, meaning head, and *pod*, meaning foot. This class of marine mollusks includes the octopuses *(pulpo)*, squid *(calamare)*, flying squid *(jibia)* and nautiloids *(nautilo)*. These organisms are bilaterally symmetrical and have a circle of prehensile tentacles. Cephalopods propel themselves by exhaling a current of water through a muscular funnel.

Squid and octopuses are very important components of the marine ecosystem. These cephalopods consume up to 100 million tons of krill per year in the Antarctic. In turn, they provide food for sperm whales, seals, penguins, albatrosses and fish.

OCTOPUSES have eight arms, usually with sucker cups on them. They have entirely soft bodies, having neither an outer nor internal shell. Ink sacs, camouflage and the ability to detach a limb are their main defense mechanisms. They have specialized color-changing skin cells called chromatophores, which they use to blend into the environment and hide. The Changos Octopus *(Octopus mimus)* is caught for human consumption by small-scale scuba fisheries in Peru and Chile.

SQUID have a distinct head, eight arms and two tentacles with suckers. They have chromatophores in the skin for camouflage and the ability to expel ink if threatened. The skeleton is internal; it consists of a single flat bone plate within the soft tissues. Squid have a specialized foot called a siphon that enables them to move by expelling water under pressure. The mouth of the squid is beak-like and made of chitin. Squid feed on fish, krill and other invertebrates. Common to Chile is the Patagonian Squid *(Loligo gahi)*, which is caught by trawlers. Natural predators include Commerson's dolphins, pilot whales and spiny dogfish. The species ranges in deep water from s Peru to s Chile, and also occurs in the South Atlantic from s Argentina to Tierra del Fuego.

FLYING SQUID can grow to enormous size. The Humboldt Flying Squid, or Jibía *(Dosidicus gigas)*, can weigh up to 110 lb (50 kg) and grow to 56 in (140 cm) long. This aggressive predator is equipped with powerful arms, long tentacles, excellent underwater vision and a razor-sharp beak that can easily tear through the flesh of prey. Its natural predators include the Sperm Whale and Juan Fernández Fur Seal. Flying squid are harvested by commercial and artisan fleets in nc Chile. The animal's normal range is the e Pacific from Mexico to Chile, at depths to 1650 ft (500 m). But since 1997 flying squid have been washing up on California beaches, possibly a result of El Niño currents. In October 2004, a 5-ft (1.5-m) specimen was caught offshore Sitka, Alaska—the first Humboldt squid recovered from waters of the Far North.

The **NODOSE PAPER NAUTILUS** *(Argonauta nodosa)* is a small, surface-dwelling octopus of the open ocean around the Islas Juan Fernández. It once was thought that these cephalopods used their large dorsal tentacles as sails—thus, the name Argonaut. We now know that only the female has these structures and uses them to secrete a parchment-like shell in which she broods her eggs. She takes shelter in the egg casing with her head and tentacles protruding from the opening. The male nautilus is a dwarf, less than an inch (2 cm) long. He mates only once, depositing his spermatophore in a female's mantle cavity where he will often live out his life.

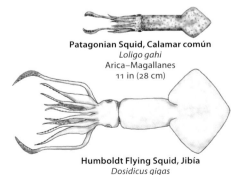

Patagonian Squid, Calamar común
Loligo gahi
Arica–Magallanes
11 in (28 cm)

Humboldt Flying Squid, Jibía
Dosidicus gigas
Arica–Magallanes
56 in (140 cm)

ECHINODERMS: These animals have skeletons made of limy, sometimes spiny, plates. This group includes sea urchins *(erizos)*, starfish *(estrellas)*, sea cucumbers *(pepinos de mar)*, sea lilies or crinoids *(lirios de mar)* and brittle stars *(estrellas frágiles)*. Of these, only the Black Sea Urchin *(Erizo negro)* and Green Sea Urchin *(Erizo colorado)* are commercially harvested for food. Fresh roe from sea urchins is sometimes referred to as "Poor Man's Caviar."

CHITONS: Chitons *(quitones)* are primitive, flattened mollusks that are covered with eight, shingle-like, overlapping, calcareous plates attached to a muscular ring called a girdle. There are 6 families and 62 species of chitons in Chile. They live on or under rocks in shallow water. They become active at twilight and move very slowly in search of food. Most are grazers, using their rasp-like teeth (radula) to feed on algae and other tiny organisms. Some prey on small crustaceans by smothering them with the girdle. None are marketed commercially, but some are harvested and eaten by people of the Chilean seacoast.

BIVALVES: Bivalves are marine mollusks that have two oval or elongated hinged shells, or valves. The group includes clams *(almejas, machas)*, scallops *(ostiones)*, mussels *(cholgas, choritos, choros)* and oysters *(ostras)*. These bivalves have been harvested for food since humans inhabited the Chilean coast. The indigenous tribes also devised clever ways to utilize the parts of certain bivalves. They used the large shells of the *choro zapato* ("shoe mussel") as soles for sandals.

GASTROPODS: Gastropods—also known as univalves—have a single, spirally-coiled shell. Most are collectively called *caracoles* in Chile. CARACOLE is a term applied both to the living organism that people harvest for food and to the empty seashell that is greatly admired by malacologists and amateur collectors alike.

Only the CHILEAN FALSE ABALONE, or LOCO, is considered commercially valuable. Locos are taken for domestic consumption and for export to Japan. Seasonal limits or complete bans on harvesting locos are enforced in order to foster their recovery in the wild. Locos are not true abalones, but the meat has a texture and taste similar to the California Red Abalone *(Haliotis rufescens)* and Asian Disk Abalone *(Haliotis discus)*, which are farmed in Chile for the commercial export market.

Some common gastropods you may see in tidepools or find cast up on beaches are illustrated on the plates. Many exhibit complex behaviors and most have a shape adapted to their marine environment.

LIMPETS have a flattened, conical shape that keeps them from being crushed by strong surf; their large flat foot acts like a powerful suction cup. Limpets move about the rocks at night while grazing on vegetation and detritus. At dawn, they return to their original location, orienting their body to the exact scar they had previously excavated into the rock surface.

KEYHOLE LIMPETS *(lapas)* have a conical shell with a natural keyhole at the apex of their volcano-shaped shell. It serves as an exit port for waste products.

TOP SHELLS, TEGULAS and NERITES are in the family Trochidae. Their pyramidical shape also helps them adhere to rocks. Their dull or dark exterior conceals a nacreous layer prized for making buttons.

PERIWINKLES and PRICKLY-WINKLES live on intertidal rocks and in mangroves. Their small size and drab color protect them from most predators.

SLIPPER SHELLS and CUP-AND-SAUCER SHELLS like the Chocha *(Calyptrea trochiformes)* have a shelf or cup located inside the shell to protect the soft parts. These mollusks often grow on top of each another. Males are smaller than females, but males can change their sex and grow to be larger.

OLIVE SHELLS and COWRIE SHELLS have a glossy sheen and oval shape. They live on sandy bottoms and prey on small mollusks and other marine organisms at night.

Juan Fernandez Limpet
Cellana ardosidea
Juan Fernández
2 in (5 cm)
Interior surface shown

South Polar Limpet
Nacella concinna
Antarctic
2 in (5 cm)

Chinese Hat Limpet
Colle, Sombrerito chino
Scurria scurra
Arica–Cape Horn
1.4 in (3.5 cm)
Seaweed in shallow water

Dark Keyhole Limpet, Lapa
Fissurella latimarginata
Arica–Cape Horn
3.4 in (8.5 cm)
On intertidal rocks

Grand Keyhole Limpet, Lapa
Fissurella maxima
Arica–Cape Horn
4 in (10 cm)
Subtidal rocky reefs

Sombrerito
Lottia ceciliana
Arica–Cape Horn
0.8 in (2 cm)
Flat intertidal rocks

Black Tegula, Caracól negro
Tegula atra
Arica–Cape Horn
2.2 in (5.5 cm)
Intertidal rocks

Chilean Top Shell
Calliostoma chilena
Valparaíso
1.4 in (3.5 cm)
Rare in deep water

Macdonald's Margarite
Bathybembix macdonaldi
Arica– Valparaíso
2.2 in (5.5 cm)
Rare in deep water

Black Monodont, Caracól
Diloma nigerrima
Arica–Cape Horn
1 in (2.5 cm)
Black rocks in shallow water

Black Turban, Lilihuen
Prisogaster niger
Arica–Cape Horn
1.2 in (3 cm)
Coastal rocks in shallow water

Black Nerite
Nerita morio
Easter Island
0.8 in (2 cm)
Under intertidal rocks

Pyramid Prickly-Winkle
Nodilittorina pyramidalis
Easter Island
0.6 in (1.5 cm)
On coastal rocks

Peru Periwinkle, Caracól de Pijama
Littorina peruviana
Arica–Cape Horn
0.6 in (1.5 cm)
On coastal rocks

Banded Turitella, Tirabuzón
Turitella cingulata
Arica–Los Lagos
2.1 in (5.5 cm)
Sand or mud bottom

Planaxis Akuana, Hanga omiti
Planaxis akuana
Easter Island
0.4 in (1 cm)
Under rocks

MARINE MOLLUSKS 29

Boat Ear Moon
Sinum cymba
Arica–Atacama
2 in (5 cm)
Sand in shallow water

Maculated Conch
Strombus maculatus
Easter Island
1 in (2.5 cm)
Reefs, tide pools

Father Englert's Cowrie
Cypraea englerti
Easter Island
1 in (2.5 cm)
Rare in intertidal zone

Dragon's Head Cowrie
Cypraea caputdraconis
Easter Island
1.4 in (3.5 cm)
Tide pools

Magellanic Wentletrap
Epitonium magellanicum
Arica–Cape Horn
1.2 in (3 cm)
Deep water

Dogwinkle, Caracól panal
Crassilabrum crassilabrum
Arica–Maule
1.4 in (3.5 cm)
Tidal zone

Juan Fernández Coral-shell
Coralliophila scala
Juan Fernández
1.2 in (3 cm)
Shallow water

Chocolata Rock-shell Locate
Thais chocolata
Arica–Maule
2 in (5 cm)
Rocks in shallow water

Chilean Triton Palo palo
Argobuccinum ranellieformi
Valparaíso–Cape Horn
2.75 in (7 cm)
Rocky sea bottom

Helmet Trophon Caracól rubio
Xanthochorus cassidiformis
Arica–Valparaíso
2.4 in (6 cm)
Shallow water

Gever's Trophon Caracol de mar
Trophon geversianus
Magallanes
3 in (8 cm)

Choca, Trochita
Calyptrea trochiformes
Arica–Maule
2.75 in (7 cm)
Shallow water

Giant Rock-shell Caracól trumulco
Chorus giganteus
Atacama–Los Lagos
4 in (10 cm)
Sand in shallow water

Maidservant Volute Piquilhue
Adelomelon ancilla
Los Lagos–Cape Horn
6.4 in (16 cm)
Offshore in deep water

Magellanic Volute Picuyo
Odontocybiola magellanica
Los Lagos–Cape Horn
7.2 in (18 cm)
Offshore

Female nautilus with her tentacles over the egg case

Nodose Paper Nautilus Nautilo del papel
Argonauta nodosa
Pelagic around Juan Fernández
5 in (13 cm)

Peruvian Olive (Two color forms)
Oliva peruviana
Arica–Aisén
1.75 in (4 cm)
Shallow water

MARINE ALGAE

Chile's coastal waters contain about 350 species of marine algae. Seaweeds are plants even though they lack true leaves, stems and roots. Instead, they have a leaf-like blade, a stem-like stipe, and a holdfast that resembles an aerial root. They are classed according to their color—green, brown or red. Green algae tend to grow in the shallow intertidal zone; brown algae in the mid- and subtidal zones; and red algae in the lower intertidal and deep water zones.

Red and brown algae are commercially valuable. They yield colloids such as agar, carrageenan and alginate, which are used in several food, pharmaceutical, cosmetic and industrial applications. The export of phycocolloids and dried algae is very profitable for Chile.

AGAR is employed as a culture medium for microbiological work; it is also used to clarify wines, juices and vinegars, to solidify canned meats, bind pharmaceutical capsules, stabilize jellies, and make agarose, a moistening additive for bread. In Chile, agar is extracted mainly from the red algae PELILLO (*Gracilaria chilensis*) and to a lesser degree from CHASCA (*Gelidium lingulatum*). Pelillo is usually harvested by traditional divers from the Puerto Montt area. They use dive suits with breathing tubes that allow them to work underwater for long periods of time without the need for oxygen tanks.

CARRAGEENAN (also called galactose) is a natural gel-forming substance that is used as a thickener, stabilizer and emulsifier in dairy products, baby formula and chocolates. In Chile, the colloid is derived from the red algae CHICORIA DE MAR (*Gigartina* spp.), LUGA (*Sarcothalia crispata*) and LUGA-LUGA (*Mazzaella laminarioides*) that grow in the marine meadows of southern Chile. *Gigartina* and *Sarcothalia* are harvested by divers who use hooks to drag the seaweed off the rocks. In a productive bed, a good diver can harvest up to 150 lb (70 kg) per hour. *Mazzaella* is normally pulled by hand from rocks exposed at low tide.

Chascón (*Lessonia nigrescens*) and Huiro (*Macrocystis pyrifera, M. integrifolia*) are known as brown kelp. They are sources of ALGINATE, a colloid that has water-holding, gelling, emulsifying and stabilizing properties. Most alginate is used for making ice cream and other dairy products, the rest in shaving creams, hair conditioners, medical dressings and dental impression material.

CHASCÓN is found in the intertidal and subtidal zones, in wave-exposed sites along most of Chile's coast. Its leathery, dark olive blades with delicately toothed margins can grow to 18 ft (5.5 m) long.

HUIRO forms enormous kelp forests on Chile's coast and offshore islands. Some specimens of Huiro have a conical holdfast up to 3 ft (1 m) in diameter, fifty or more stipes measuring up to 130 ft (40 m) long, and hundreds of blades measuring 6 ft (2 m) or longer. The blades are held to the surface at the end of a hollow stem. At the base of each blade is a gas-filled bladder called a pneumatocyst, which acts as a float.

COCHAYUYO (*Durvillaea antarctica*) grows in exposed, turbulent waters found in intertidal zones along the mainland and Antarctic coasts. The thick, leathery, strap-like blades are fixed to rocks by a large holdfast measuring to 1.5 ft (0.5 m) across. Plants can grow to more than 32 ft (10 m) long, and the largest specimens weigh many pounds. Cochayuyo is scraped from the rocks using iron knives and then sun-dried on the beach. The algae is shaped into rectangular bundles for sale at local markets. The stipe base (*ulte*) is eaten fresh in salads. The blades (*cochayuyo*) are used in stews or cooked in pastries.

LUCHE is a name applied to Sea Lettuce (*Ulva rigida*) and to Red Laver (*Porphyra columbina*). The paper-thin fronds of Sea Lettuce are rinsed in sea water and eaten like spinach; dried *Ulva* is reconstituted in water and added to fillings or soup. Dried *Porphyra* is exported to Asian nations such as Japan where it is known as *nori*, the seaweed sheets that are used to wrap sushi.

FLORISTIC ZONES AND FLORA

Copihue, Chilean Bellflower
Lapageria rosea
Chile's national flower is named in honor of Napoleon's Empress, Josephine Lapagerie, in recognition of her many services to botany and the propagation of exotic plants in her Malmaison garden near Paris.

This section of the guide contains a sampler of the common plants one can see while travelling throughout Chile. Many plants will be familiar to the weekend botanist as Chilean trees and shrubs are widely grown in temperate climate parks and gardens.

Those who have a deep interest in identifying the native flora are advised to secure a knowledgeable guide who is intimate with the regional flora. A few of the botanical field guides currently available in Chile are listed in the bibliography on page 379. This page also lists some of the excellent web sites covering Chilean flora.

Most of the plant species mentioned in the text are illustrated on the color plates and many are accorded detailed botanical descriptions on pages 73 to 89. The plate captions contain the scientific and common names, and information on the height (H) of a mature tree (T) or shrub (S), the length of a simple (L) or compound leaf (CL), and if the plant is deciduous (D) or perennial (P).

Maps of the floristic zones and forest types appear throughout the chapter. Note that the maps illustrate the general range of the plant communities, not their precise occurrence in nature. The boundaries of vegetation zones are indistinct and amorphous, with one type melding into the other so subtly that it is often impossible to tell where one begins and another ends.

The information in this section is based on the work of two contemporary Chilean botanists, Claudio Donoso and Rudolfo Gajardo. In 1981 Donoso defined the twelve forest types of Chile, based on the dominant tree species found in a general area. In 1994 Gajardo described eight zones of vegetation based on plant communities.

Donoso's and Gajardo's works represent the apex of centuries of botanical exploration. In 1767 Philibert Commerson and Louis Bougainville undertook the first collection of Chilean plants while on an expedition sponsored by the Paris Museum of Natural History. In 1773 German botanists Johann and Georg Forster catalogued the flora of southern Chile during an expedition led by British Captain James Cook.

In 1782 the Jesuit priest and naturalist Juan Molina produced his monumental work on Chilean flora and fauna, *Saggio sulla storia naturale del Chili*. This natural history classic was published in Italy after Molina and the Jesuit clergy were expelled from the Spanish territories in 1768. The Bohemian Tadeo Haenke collected floral specimens while on the Malaspina Expedition of 1789. He mused, "In a country like Chile, it is difficult to resist the temptation to become a botanist."

In the early 1800s, the Spanish botanists Hipólito Ruíz and José Pavon catalogued the plants of central Chile, and the French botanist Claudio Gay was engaged to conduct a botanical survey for the Chilean government. Gay's collection earned him the French Legion of Honor and honorary membership in the University of Chile. He was followed by the Chilean naturalist Rudolfo Philippi who described over 3800 new plant species for the Santiago Natural History Museum.

These initial works were amplified by a host of contemporary botanists. A few of the many naturalists and botanists who contributed time and resources to this end include Carlos Reiche, Iván Johnston, Otto Urban, Carlos Muñoz, Adriana Hoffmann, Melica Muñoz Schick, Roberto Rodriguez, Oscar Matthei, and Max Quezada.

Appreciation of Chilean flora extends far beyond the scientific community. The famed Chilean poet Pablo Neruda is often quoted as saying, "Who doesn't know the Chilean forest, doesn't know this planet."

FLORISTIC ZONES AND FLORA 33

Desert Zone. Desierto
Regions XV and I–IV, 18°S–30°S latitude, on the coast and inland
Arid, with coastal fog; less than 2 in (50 mm) annual precipitation
Vegetation: Cacti, grasses, xerophytic scrub

High Andean Steppe. Estepa Alto-Andina
Regions XV and I–VII, 18°S–36°S latitude, in the High Andes
Cold, semi-arid; up to 16 in (400 mm) precipitation in summer
Vegetation: Grasses, shrubs, low trees, cacti, cushion-plants

Matorral and Sclerophyll Woodland. Matorral y Bosque Esclerófilo
Regions IV–VIII, 30°S–37°S latitude, on the coast and inland
Warm dry summers; cool winters; 15–50 in (384–1270 mm) precipitation
Vegetation: Thorn trees, low scrub, cacti; vineyards, orchards, pastures
Forest types: Sclerophyll and Chilean Palm Forest
Typical trees: Espino, Chilean Palm, Quillay, Maiten, Litre, Peumo,
 Boldo, Lingue, Belloto, Patagua, Arrayán, Canelo

Deciduous Woodland. Bosque Caducifolio
Regions V–X and XIV, 34°S–41°S latitude, on coast and mountain slopes
Warm dry summers; cool winters; 20–80 in (500–3000 mm) precipitation
Vegetation: Deciduous broadleaf trees, some Cordilleran Cypress
Forest types: Roble-Hualo, Roble-Raulí-Coigüe, Coigüe-Raulí-Tepa
Typical trees: Roble, Raulí, Coigüe, Tepa (in the south), Peumo, Quillay,
 Litre, Hualo, Lingue, Radal, Avellano, Boldo, Canelo, Mañío, Queule,
 Pitao, Arrayán, Tineo, Trevo, Luma, Lenga, Ulmo (second growth)

Valdivian Laurel-leaved Forest. Bosque Laurifolio
Regions X–XI, 38°S–47°S latitude, on the coast and in foothills
Cool temperate; 80–200 in (2000–5000 mm) precipitation
Vegetation: Evergreen broadleaf trees, conifers, ferns, lianas
Forest types: Siempreverde (Evergreen) and Alerce
Typical trees: Tepa, Luma, Canelo, Tineo, Tiaca, Coigüe, Ulmo, Mañío,
 Trevo, Lingue, Alerce, Arrayán, Fuinque, Ñirre

Forests of the Patagonian Andes. Bosque Andino Patagónico
Regions VII–XII and XIV, 37°S–56°S latitude, in the Patagonian Andes
Trans-Andean continental; 40–200 in (1000–5500 mm) precipitation
Vegetation: Broadleaf trees, conifers; dwarf shrubs at treeline
Forest types: Araucaria and Lenga
Typical trees: Araucaria, Lenga, Coigüe, Roble, Ñirre, Canelo, Alerce,
 Tineo, Arrayán, Fuinque, Mañío

Magellanic Rainforest, Bogs and Moorland
Bosque Siempreverde y Turberas
Regions XI–XII, 48°S–56°S latitude, on the coast
Oceanic cold temperate; precipitation to 300 in (7500 mm)
Vegetation: Evergreen broadleaf trees, conifers, scrub, bog plants
Forest types: Guaitecas Cypress and Magellanic Coigüe
Typical trees: Guaitecas Cypress, Coigüe de Chiloé, Magellanic Coigüe,
 Canelo, Tineo, Ñirre, Lenga, Notro

Patagonian Steppe. Estepa Patagónica
Eastern sectors of Regions XI and XII
Cold Patagonian steppe; 10–24 in (250–612 mm) precipitation
Vegetation: Grasses and low shrubs

REGIÓN DEL DESIERTO
DESERT ZONE

The Desert Zone extends through the Atacama Desert between 18°S and 30°S latitude, from Arica-Parinacota to the Río Elqui in the Coquimbo Region (IV). It can be divided into four subzones: the Coastal Desert, Absolute Desert, Andean Desert and the Flowering Desert.

The Atacama is extremely arid and largely barren, with cacti and grasses being the dominant plants. Drought-tolerant trees and shrubs can grow only where adequate water is available. This includes river courses, ponds and marshes fed by runoff from the Andes, places where aquifers lie close to the soil surface, and areas where the mountain slopes catch and hold the coastal fog.

Coastal Desert, Desierto Costero

The coastal desert subzone extends from Arica to La Serena along the western slopes of the Coastal Cordillera at elevations below 5000 ft (1500 m).

The coastal desert has a rich diversity of plant species, with many endemics. This plenitude can be attributed to moderate temperatures and the presence of moisture carried on the coastal fog known as CAMANCHACA. The fog provides enough moisture for plants and animals to survive without rain. Water for irrigation is obtained from fog catchment systems. Large nets strung across mountain slopes catch the fog, which condenses on the mesh, drips into a trough, and flows through pipes to reservoirs on the Pacific coast.

Over 200 species of native desert plants such as *Copiapoa* and *Eulychnia* cacti and *Puya* and *Tillandsia* bromeliads grow in the LOMAS FORMATIONS—the "fog meadows" that occur in about fifty isolated localities in the coastal desert between 18°S and 30°S. The coastal fog also sustains the Bosque Fray Jorge, an extraordinary woodland located some 95 miles (150 km) south of La Serena. Relict trees, shrubs and vines reminiscent of the Valdivian rainforest grow here, all nourished by the *camanchaca*.

Candelabra cactus in the desert near Arica

Absolute Desert, Desierto Absoluto

The Absolute Desert lies between 18°S and 27°S at elevations of 3250–6500 ft (1000–2000 m). It corresponds to the part of the Atacama that receives little or no rain, and to where any water for plant growth comes from rivers or underground aquifers.

The QUEBRADAS—the wide, deep river gorges that cut across Norte Grande—contain riparian scrubland composed of ligneous thorny shrubs and trees such as Algarrobo blanco (*Prosopis alba*), Pimiento (*Schinus molle*), Tara (*Caesalpinia spinosa*) and Carbonillo (*Cordia decandra*). Irrigation sustains agricultural crops, plantations of exotic fruits such as guava, citrus and olives, and palms and tropical flowers. However, the desert has mostly gravel and sandy soils with great surface salt accumulations and thus salinity is a limiting factor for agriculture even in the quebradas.

The PAMPA DEL TAMARUGAL sits above a subterranean aquifer (*napa*) that provides enough water for the growth of tamarugo (*Prosopis tamarugo*). TAMARUGO is a native mesquite cultivated for its pods, which are used as livestock fodder. The trees have very long tap roots that extend more than 25 ft (8 m) down to the groundwater table. Tamarugo was nearly extirpated in the nitrate mining heyday. Mule train drivers used the tree's leaves and leguminous pods to feed their mules, and then cut the branches for firewood. Plantations established in the 1960s restored the tamarugo to the pampa and inadvertently rescued the wildlife associated with this ecosystem.

Tamarugo is central to a wide variety of animals. Its flowers are pollinated by bees such as the honeybee, *Apis mellifera*. The endemic Tamarugo Conebill (p. 277), nests in the tamarugal in spring. During this time, the birds feed on larvae of tamarugo blue butterflies, which feed in turn on tamarugo leaves. Small mammals such as Darwin's Mouse (page 316) feed on fallen tamarugo seeds, and the Tuco-tuco del Tamarugal (page 321) digs its burrows amid the tree roots. These rodents attract predators such as grisons (page 297) and foxes (page 299). Two *Microlophus* lizards—the Desert Lizard and Corredor de Pica (page 113)—also occur in tamarugo groves.

Andean Desert, Desierto Andino

This sub-region contains vegetation of the High Desert, which lies on the western slopes of the Andes from Arica–Parinacota to Atacama at elevations of 5900–11,500 ft (1800–3500 m). The area is extremely arid, and some places have never recorded any rainfall. Most plant life occurs near oasis towns and around ponds and marshes fed by rivers and snowmelt. These include areas in the Upper Río Loa basin, the Domeyko Cordillera and the Salar de Atacama.

Cacti are very well suited to the habitat. Most have shallow roots that quickly soak up infrequent desert rainfalls and runoff from the mountain slopes. They do not have leaves, which are easily desiccated, and photosynthesis takes place in their thick, succulent stems. Columnar cactus scrub is widespread east of Calama and San Pedro de Atacama. Of special interest is CARDÓN (*Echinopsis atacamensis*), a tall, saguaro-like cactus that grows in the arid hills near the Chiu Chiu in the Antofagasta Region (II).

The Atacama Desert near Chiu Chiu

The old adobe church at Chiu Chiu has doors made from flattened Cardón skeletons, which are tied together with leather strips. CANDELABRA CACTUS *(Browningia candelaris)* can be found in the foothills east of Arica on the road to Putre. It often grows in association with other cacti such as Chastudo and Acachaño *(Oreocereus* sp.*)* and "Jumping Cholla" *(Opuntia* sp.*)* whose sole purpose of existence seems to be to attach its hair-like barbs deep into the flesh of passersby.

The plazas of oasis towns are planted with shade trees such as Algarrobo blanco *(Prosopis alba)*, Pimiento *(Schinus molle)* and Chañar *(Geoffroea decorticans)*. Their timber is used in construction. An example of this can be seen in Iglesia de San Pedro de Atacama where the massive church rafters are made of Algarrobo.

Flowering Desert, Desierto Florido

The Flowering Desert extends between 27°S and 28°S latitudes in the area between the Copiapó River and the city of Vallenar.

Normally, the sandy desert plains in this area receive about 2 in (50 mm) of rainfall per annum. But in El Niño years, atypical storms bring greatly increased precipitation to the Flowering Desert. Ephemerid flower seeds, some of which have been lying dormant in the soil for years, begin to germinate. The arid wasteland bursts into bloom, reaching the peak of its flowering in September and October. For a few weeks the desert is like a beautiful garden, then everything dies and awaits the next opportunity to flower after one, five or ten years.

North of Copiapó, the interval between rains is so long that seeds cannot survive. Flowers appear in only a few isolated places with special microclimates. This is the case in the mountains around Vicuña in northern Coquimbo. The area experiences a flowering in years of adquate rainfall, but the effect is diminished because many of the wildflower seeds are destroyed by cultivation and goat pasturing.

Pata de guanaco
Cistanthe grandiflora

Suspiro del mar
Nolana paradoxa

Pajarito
Schizanthus sp.

Don Diego de la noche
Oenothera acaulis

Flor del minero
Centauria chilensis

Añañuca roja
Rhodophilia phycelliodes

Alstroemeria arrepollada
Alstroemeria spathulata

Huilli, Spring Onion
Leucocoryne ixioides

Lirio del campo
Alstroemeria magnifica

Cuerno de cabra
Haplopappus foliosus

Lion's Claw
Garra de león
Leonthochir ovallei

ESTEPA ALTO-ANDINA
HIGH ANDEAN STEPPE

The High Andean steppe extends from Arica–Parinacota (XV) to the Maule Region (VII) at the upper limit of plant growth. Cushion-plants, resilient grasses and reeds, and low shrubs with reduced foliage are plant forms that have adapted to the severe climate.

The Altiplano and Puna

The Altiplano and Puna are large intermontane plateaus with a mean elevation of 13,000 ft (4000 m). The Altiplano receives about 16 in (400 mm) of precipitation in summer; the Puna, which lies to the south of the summer rains, is more arid.

The floral landscape—confusingly also called *puna*—can be described as a plains grassland with steppe plants and spots of meadow-like vegetation, surrounded by volcanic peaks. The entire area is rich in wildlife and supports 160 plant species. There are many variations in plant cover and the indigenous people have local names for the plant communities.

TOLARES are areas containing a resinous, sagebrush-like scrub. Tola is a term collectively applied to shrubs such as *Baccharis*, *Parastrephia* and *Senecio*, which are used for fuel and medicine.

LLARETALES are dominated by Llareta *(Azorella compacta)*, a bright green, hard cushion-plant that forms large mounds on arid slopes. Umbels of tiny yellow flowers appear in summer.

QUEÑOALES refers to the presence of queñoa trees *(Polylepis tarapacana* and *P. rugulosa)*. They grow to 12 ft (3.5 m) high and have twisted branches and reddish scaling bark. Queñoa is one of the world's highest altitude trees, growing at elevations of 15,500 ft (4800 m) under conditions of extreme aridity, strong winds and intense solar radiation.

PAJONALES contain *Festuca*, *Stipa* and *Oxychloe* grasslands. The *pajonales* are used for pasturing llamas and alpacas, and many wild mammals and birds also feed there.

BOFEDALES are permanent wetlands with a dense green cover of small herbs, rushes and grasses. The *bofedales* are used for pasturing livestock and growing crops such as Quinoa *(Chenopodium quinoa)*—the Mother Grain of the Incas, which has been under cultivation for at least 3000 years.

Mediterranean Andes, Andes Mediterráneos

This sub-region extends through the Andes of central Chile from Atacama (III) to Maule (VII). The area has cold temperatures, strong winds and mountainous relief. Most precipitation occurs in winter and increases as one moves south. The flora includes Espinillo *(Adesmia spinosissima)*, Pingo-pingo *(Ephedra andina)*, Yerba blanca *(Chuquiraga oppositifolia)*, Quiaca *(Calandrinia compacta)* and Clavel del campo *(Mutisia sinuata)*.

Left: The Andean steppe outside Santiago
Opposite: Alpacas on the Puna at Lauca National Park

FLORA OF THE HIGH ANDEAN STEPPE 39

Llareta
Azorella compacta
Andes of n Chile
H 1 ft (0.3 m)
To 10 ft (3 m) across

Polylepis tarapacana

Queñoa
Polylepis sp.
Arica–Tarapacá
T, H 12 ft (3.5 m)
P, CL 0.25 in (0.9 cm)

Polylepis rugulosa

Quiaca
Calandrinia compacta
Coquimbo–Maule
H 2–5 in (6–12 cm)

**Bunchgrass
Paja**
Festuca orthophylla
Stipa pungens

Yerba blanca
Chuquiraga oppositifolia
Coquimbo–Linares
S, H 1.5 ft (0.5 m)

Tola
Baccharis sp.
High Andes of n Chile
S, H 2 ft (0.6 m)

Tola
Parastrephia sp.
High Andes of n Chile
S, H 1.5 ft (0.5 m)

Pingo-pingo
Ephedra andina
Arica–Aisén
S, H 5 ft (1.5 m)

Espinillo, Añahuilla
Adesmia spinosissima
Andes of n Chile
S, H 5 ft (1.5 m)

Mutisia, Clavel del campo
Mutisia sp.
Atacama–Biobío
S, H 20 in (50 cm)

Quinoa
Chenopodium quinoa
Andes of n Chile
S, H 3 ft (1 m)

MATORRAL is a scrubland that resembles the California chaparral or Mediterranean maquis, although the plant species of those habitats are different. The word matorral derives from the Spanish *mata*, meaning "bush" or "shrub."

SCLEROPHYLL FOREST contains trees and shrubs with hard (sclerophyllous) leaves. Sclerophyll derives from the Greek *sclero* (hard) and *phyllon* (leaf).

The **SPINY FOREST** or **ESPINAL** is a grassy savanna sparsely dotted with drought tolerant trees and shrubs, many of which are armed with thorns or spines.

MATORRAL MEDITERRÁNEO Y BOSQUE ESCLERÓFILO
MATORRAL AND SCLEROPHYLL FOREST

The Mediterranean matorral and sclerophyll forest extend the length of central Chile, from the Coquimbo Region (IV) to Biobío (VIII). The vegetation is well-suited to the Mediterranean climate with its cold, wet winters and warm, dry summers. Many of the plants that are native to this zone have made their way to gardens in distant places including California and the Cape region of South Africa.

Because this zone is Chile's most heavily populated region, the land has been greatly modified and for the most part it is difficult to find unaltered vegetation. Most of the native vegetation was cut or burned long ago in the name of urban development and agriculture. What is left is a melange of pastures, lush vineyards, orchards, pine plantations, wheat fields, towns and cities. They have largely displaced the thornbrush and scrub that once covered the Central Valley and adjacent foothills.

Introduced poplar species, which are collectively called Alamo or Black Poplar, are commonly planted as windbreaks along property lines and highways. Roadsides are edged with "weeds" such as chicory, fennel and thistle. A common spring flower along railroad embankments is the Dedal de oro, or California Poppy *(Eschscholzia californica)* that was introduced to Chile in the mid-1800s.

The Espinal in late summer

The remaining native vegetation occupies habitats known as matorral steppe, sclerophyll forest and spiny forest. To the untrained eye, these habitats are almost indistinguishable. However, their characteristics are described below for those who have a deep interest in botany.

Matorral
Matorral Estepario

The matorral occupies semi-arid sectors of the Mediterranean zone, extending along the coast and coastal mountain slopes of Coquimbo (IV) and n Valparaíso (V).

The land has been profoundly altered by intense gathering of firewood, logging, livestock pasturing and agriculture to the point where most of the original vegetation has been completely destroyed or occurs in small patches. This has left a scrubland with a cover of annual grasses and hard-leaved, often resinous, shrubs and trees that seldom grow to over 10 ft (3 m) in height.

The semi-arid, sunny slopes of the Coastal Range will often contain a scrub composed of Quisco (*Echinopsis chiloensis*), Chagual (*Puya berteroana* and *Puya chilensis*), Tebo (*Trevoa trinervis*), Crucero (*Colletia hystrix*) and Espino (*Acacia caven*), under which grow an herbal tapestry of spring-flowering perennials. Undeveloped land near river mouths and rocky beaches is often edged with a dense cover of small shrubs and trees. The mix may include Coliguay (*Colliguaja odorifera*), Boldo (*Peumus boldus*), Huingán (*Schinus polygamus*) and Molle (*Schinus latifolius*) with an understory of wildflowers typical of the Flowering Desert.

Spiny Forest
Bosque Espinoso, Espinal

This sub-region occurs in the Central Valley and on inland slopes of the Coastal Cordillera from Coquimbo (IV) to Biobío (VIII). The entire area has been so intensely degraded by agriculture that it is difficult to find remnants of the original vegetation.

Known locally as the *espinal*, the vegetation of the spiny forest is dominated by the small, deciduous Acacia tree called Espino (*Acacia caven*), which is common in overgrazed pastures and abandoned fields. The tree seldom reaches its full height as it is repeatedly cut for firewood or cleared to make room for grazing and cultivation. Round clusters of fragrant, yellow flowers bloom from September to December. New leaves form during this period, followed by hard leguminous pods (*quirincas*), which turn from bright green to dark brown as they mature. The majority of pods fall to the ground in autumn, but some remain on the trees for several months.

It is interesting to note that Espino is a relative newcomer to Chile. Its seeds are thought to have been disseminated by pack animals travelling from the Incan mines to the coast hundreds of years ago. Even when the first Spaniards arrived, Espino still had only a small role in the landscape. But with the advent of livestock farming, Espino sprang up everywhere, spread by cattle who fed on the plant's pods.

Sclerophyll Forest
Bosque Esclerófilo

Patches of this woodland type can be found from Valparaíso (V) to the Biobío Region (VIII), mainly on the western slopes of the Andes and the eastern slopes of the Coastal Cordillera between 2000–4250 ft (600–1300 m). Sclerophyll forest normally occurs as a mixed woodland with Peumo (*Cryptocarya alba*), Boldo (*Peumus boldus*), Quillay (*Quillaja saponaria*) and Litre (*Lithrea caustica*) as the dominant trees.

Gallery forests with trees such as Belloto del Norte (*Beilschmiedia miersii*), Arrayán (*Luma apiculata*), Patagua (*Crinodendron patagua*), Peumo (*Cryptocarya alba*), Lingue (*Persea lingue*), Maitén (*Maytenus boaria*), Chilean Willow (*Salix chilensis*) and Canelo (*Drimys winteri*) grow in watered ravines and along rivers and streams.

Chilean Palm Forest
Bosque Palma Chilena

Chilean Palm *(Jubaea chilensis)* is native to central Chile, growing on the sides of ravines and ridges in sclerophyll woodland, from sea level to 2000 ft (610 m). It is one of the southernmost palms of the world, second only to the Nikau Palm *(Rhopalostylis sapida)* of New Zealand.

At maturity it is a massive palm, jokingly referred to as the "Incredible Hulk" of the palm world. It can grow to 80 ft (25 m) tall. The trunk, which is thicker in the middle than at the base, can be up to 5 ft (1.5 m) in diameter. The large head of stiff, pinnate-leaved fronds, each to 10ft (3 m) long, can form a crown up to 30 ft (9 m) across.

The Chilean Palm has many names. The indigenous people call it Kan-Kán. It is also called the Coquito or Pygmy Coconut Palm because of its small edible nuts, and the Chilean Wine Palm for the wine made from fermented sap. It is known as the Syrup Palm for its sugary sap, which is used to make palm honey *(miel de palma)*. The honey is made from an old recipe consisting of palm sap, coconut milk, and cane or corn sugar, which are boiled down to the consistency of treacle. The quality and amount of each ingredient gives each maker's product a special flavor. It was the passion for palm wine and honey that brought the Chilean Palm to its present scarcity, for many palms have to be felled in order to harvest the sap.

In 1834, Charles Darwin attended a palm harvest and wrote: "Every year in the early spring, in August, very many are cut down, and when the trunk is lying on the ground, the crown of leaves is lopped off. The sap then immediately begins to flow from the upper end, and continues so doing for some months: it is, however, necessary that a thin slice should be shaved off from that end every morning, so as to expose a fresh surface. A good tree will give ninety gallons, and all this must have been contained in the vessels of the apparently dry trunk."

Chilean palms appear as ornamentals in gardens around the world. Some have been introduced to Easter Island where there is fossil evidence that a very similar species once grew. Large stands of Chilean palms can be viewed in protected areas in mainland Chile. The largest forests occur at Ocoa in La Campana National Park near Valparaíso and at Cocalán in the O'Higgins Region. In these environments, the palms grow amid bromeliads, cacti, and sclerophyllous trees and shrubs typical of central Chile's matorral.

Chilean Palms at Cocalán

BOSQUE CADUCIFOLIO
DECIDUOUS FOREST

Deciduous forest dominated by southern beech trees occurs between 33°S and 41°S latitudes—roughly from Santiago to the Los Lagos Region (X). Throughout much of this area, deciduous forest occupies the mountains and foothill ravines. Typical tree species found in these environments include Roble, Hualo, Huala, Raulí and the rare Ruil. South of 40°S, the latitude of Valdivia, the perennial *Nothofagus* species Coigüe and Coigüe de Chiloé make their appearance in the montane forests, but are generally absent from lower elevations in the Valdivian Rainforest.

The Deciduous Forest Zone is divided into three sub-regions: Montane, Llanos (Plains) and Andean Deciduous Forests. The extent of these sub-regions is outlined on the adjacent map. However, it should be noted that the deciduous forests of central Chile are mostly discontinuous in distibution. This is due to clearcutting for timber or agriculture prior to 1900. Thus the forests that exist today, especially in the lower elevations, represent a regeneration of growth and often lack species that were present in the original floral association.

Deciduous Forest Types

The deciduous forest zone has four forest types, each named for the dominant tree species. The maps on the following pages indicate their approximate locations.

ROBLE–HUALO FOREST TYPE: This forest type, which is dominated by Roble and Hualo, occurs mainly in the montane forests from Santiago to the Maule Region (VII). Many of these forests have not recovered their former profusion and vigor after they were clearcut in the 19th century.

Nonetheless, some pure stands of Roble can still be found in the Andean foothills between Colchagua and the Río Ñuble (34°30′S–35°S) at elevations above 3300 ft (1000 m). In addition, the Roble–Hualo forest type occurs as a continuous strip of

---

GENUS NOTHOFAGUS
THE SOUTHERN BEECHES

Forests to the south of Santiago are characterized by the continual presence of southern beech trees. In Chile, these trees are collectively called ROBLE—the Spanish word for oak—which suggests that early Spanish explorers and seamen noted similarites to the timber of European Oak.

The ten Chilean species are in the genus *Nothofagus*, a word that is derived from the Greek *nothos* meaning "false" and *fagus* meaning "beech."

Nothofagus includes both deciduous and evergreen species. Leaves of the deciduous species turn brilliant colors of red and gold in autumn just before they fall from the trees. The deciduous species comprise:

Roble *(Nothofagus obliqua)*
Hualo *(Nothofagus glauca)*
Huala *(Nothofagus x leonii)*
Raulí *(Nothofagus nervosa)*
Ruil *(Nothofagus alessandrii)*
Lenga *(Nothofagus pumilio)*
Ñirre *(Nothofagus antarctica)*

The perennial species, which are known as Coigüe or Coihue, keep their leaves year round. These comprise:

Coigüe *(Nothofagus dombeyi)*
Coigüe de Chiloé *(Nothofagus nitida)*
Coigüe de Magallanes *(Nothofagus betuloides)*

ROBLE–HUALO

ROBLE–RAULÍ–COIGÜE

woodland south of 35°S in the Andes of Maule, with Roble growing mainly on the south-facing slopes and Hualo on the warmer northern slopes.

In the Coastal Cordillera, patches of Roble-Hualo forest occupy the higher elevations. (Forests of the lower elevations have been displaced by exotic pine plantations). Between 33°S and 35°S, the highland Roble-Hualo forest occurs as an open woodland, which often contains a sparse growth of Peumo *(Cryptocarya alba)*, Maitén *(Maytenus boaria)*, Quillay *(Quillaja saponaria)* and Litre *(Lithrea caustica)*. South of 35°S, Hualo dominates the forest belt that runs along the summits of the Coastal Range.

Some watered ravines in the Coastal Cordillera contain Roble and Hualo growing with Canelo *(Drimys winteri)*, Olivillo *(Aextoxicon punctatum)*, Lingue *(Persea lingue)*, Huala *(Nothofagus leonii)*, Coigüe *(Nothofagus dombeyi)* and Long-leaved Mañió *(Podocarpus saligna)*. On slopes with a southwest exposure, one can sometimes find isolated groves of the rare and endangered Ruil *(Nothofagus alessandrii)*.

ROBLE–RAULÍ–COIGÜE FOREST TYPE: This forest type occurs roughly from the Maule Region (VII) to Los Lagos (X) between 36°30′S and 40°30′S latitudes. It occupies mountain valleys and slopes facing the Central Valley at elevations of 330–3300 ft (100–1000 m). The dominant trees are Roble *(Nothofagus obliqua)*, Raulí *(Nothofagus nervosa)* and Coigüe *(Nothofagus dombeyi)*. In the southern part of the range, elements of the laurel-leaved forest appear, including evergreen trees such as Laurel *(Laurelia sempervirens)*, Lingue *(Persea lingue)*, Olivillo *(Aextoxicon punctatum)*, Avellano *(Gevuina avellana)*, Ulmo *(Eucryphia cordifolia)* and Short-leaved Mañió *(Saxegothaea conspicua)*.

Deciduous forest at the Saltos de Petrohué, Los Lagos

DECIDUOUS FOREST TYPES 47

Historical clearing of the land and forest fires have caused many of the original plant associations to disappear. In their place are the *renovales* (restored lands). These areas of second growth woodland are composed of Roble in lower elevations, Roble–Raulí at mid-elevations, and Raulí–Coigüe or pure Coigüe in the upper level of growth.

COIGÜE–RAULÍ–TEPA FOREST TYPE: This forest type occupies the southern sectors of the Deciduous Forest Zone between 37°S–40°30′S. It occurs from the Biobío Region (VIII) to Los Lagos (X), mainly in the Andes, at elevations of 2000–2300 ft (600–700 m) in the north and around 1650 ft (500 m) in the extreme south. It is common around Valdivia.

COIGÜE–RAULÍ–TEPA

The Coigüe–Raulí–Tepa forests have been profoundly altered by logging, forest fires and other natural disasters. As a result, in many areas the forests take the form of second growth woodland. This produces an interesting mix of deciduous and evergreen species, especially in the southern part of the range where there is abundant rainfall. Coigüe *(Nothofagus dombeyi)*, Raulí *(Nothofagus nervosa)* and Tepa *(Laureliopsis philippiana)* are dominant throughout the natural range. Trevo *(Dasyphyllum diacanthoides)*, Tineo *(Weinmannia trichosperma)* and Olivillo *(Aextoxicon punctatum)* are also common. Short-leaved Mañió *(Saxegothaea conspicua)* forms a secondary canopy to Coigüe in the Andes, rising above a dense understory of Canelo *(Drimys winteri)* and Quila bamboo *(Chusquea quila)*. In the higher Andean elevations, this forest type merges with Lenga *(Nothofagus pumilio)* and Araucaria *(Araucaria araucana)*.

CORDILLERAN CYPRESS FOREST: Isolated stands of Cordilleran Cypress *(Austrocedrus chilensis)* can be found in the mountains of south-central Chile between 34°S–38°S and 42°S–44°S. The species is more common in the Andes, but also occurs in a few places in the Coastal Cordillera south of Concepción. It generally occupies north-facing slopes at elevations of 3000–6000 ft (900–1800 m) in the north and 1300–2300 ft (400–700 m) in the southern part of its range.

Cordilleran Cypress is normally found in pure, old-growth stands. Andean groves appear to prefer warm, dry, exposed sites in the same general location as the Roble-Hualo forest. Although the timber is strong, resistant to decay and ideal for exterior construction, Cordilleran Cypress has escaped clear-cutting because it occupies difficult sites with poor soil—places where other timber trees cannot grow. Where it has been logged, it occurs in mixed forest with Radal *(Lomatia hirsuta)*, Maitén *(Maytenus boaria)*, Maqui *(Aristotelia chilensis)*, Repu *(Rhaphithamnus spinosus)* and occasionally Coigüe *(Nothofagus dombeyi)*.

CORDILLERAN CYPRESS

DECIDUOUS FOREST FLORA 49

Coigüe, Coihue
Nothofagus dombeyi
Santiago–Aisén
T, H 165 ft (50 m)
P, L 1.25 in (3 cm)

Coigüe can live over 1000 years

Roble
Nothofagus obliqua
Valparaíso–Los Lagos
T, H 130 ft (40 m)
D, L 1–2 in (2–5 cm)

Ruil
Nothofagus alessandrii
Maule
T, H 100 ft (30 m)
D, L 3–5 in (7–13 cm)

Cordilleran Cypress
Ciprés de la Cordillera
Austrocedrus chilensis
Santiago–Biobío
T, H 65 ft (20 m)

Some Cordilleran Cypress trees are almost 1500 years old

Hualo
Nothofagus glauca
Santiago–Biobío
T, H 100 ft (30 m)
D, L 2–3.5 in (5–9 cm)

Tepa
Laureliopsis philippiana
Araucanía–Chiloé
T, H 100 ft (30 m)
P, L 2–3.5 in (5–9 cm)

Raulí
Nothofagus nervosa
Santiago–Biobío
T, H 100 ft (30 m)
D, L 2–3.5 in (5–9 cm)

Autumn leaves

BOSQUE DE ARAUCARIA
ARAUCARIA FOREST

Araucarias can be found in Biobío (VIII) and Araucanía (IX) between 37°S and 40°S at elevations above 2000 ft (600 m). They grow in areas of high precipitation and low temperatures, and can tolerate poor soils, frequently growing on lava fields or in crevices between rocks and boulders.

Araucarias are among the earliest types of seed-bearing plants. Fossils have been carbon-dated to the Jurassic Period, 180 million years ago. The tree grows to 165 ft (50 m), lives over 1500 years and takes more than 20 years to bear seeds. At maturity it has a parasol-like shape—a tall, knobby trunk topped with a whorled crown of tangled branches bearing prickly, scale-like leaves. The term "Monkey Puzzle Tree" was coined by a 19th-century English gardener who remarked that the tree would be a puzzle for a monkey to climb.

The indigenous Pehuenche, whose name means "People of the Araucaria Forests," consider the trees to be sacred. They have been harvesting Araucaria nuts *(piñones)* for thousand of years. In ancient times, the people waited for the seed cones to fall spontaneously when ripe, since they believed this would please the spirits of the Araucaria. Today the cones are often gathered by climbers who wear leather foot wraps or by men who strike the trees with a long cane. The ivory-colored nuts are eaten raw, toasted or boiled. Bread flour is ground with a flat friction mill. A drink called *chavid* is made by fermenting the nuts. Some Araucaria seeds are roasted in stone-heated pits, and some are strung into necklaces called *menken*.

In the Andes, Araucaria grow in pure stands. In the Nahuelbuta they grow in a mixed forest with Lenga *(Nothofagus pumilio)*, Coigüe *(Nothofagus dombeyi)*, Ñirre *(Nothofagus antarctica)*, Canelo enano *(Drimys winteri* var. *andina)* and Notro *(Embothrium coccineum)*. The mixed forest normally has a dense substory of Colihue bamboo *(Chusquea culeou)* whose canes are used to make reproductions of early Araucanian spears, flutes and panpipes. Wild Strawberry *(Fragaria chiloensis),* Zarzaparilla *(Ribes cucullatum)* and Alstroemeria *(Alstroemeria ligtu)* grow in the understory. Calafate *(Berberis trigona)* and Zarcilla *(Berberis empetrifolia)* are common in the surrounding *Festuca* grasslands.

The Araucaria has been protected to some degree since the 18th century, originally in order to ensure a supply of timber for the Spanish navy. The trees were declared a Natural Monument in 1976, but large-scale clearing in the past and present-day illegal logging have brought this species close to extinction. Natural disaster has also played a part in the species' decline. A forest fire in August 2003 destroyed 71 percent of the Araucaria forest in Malleco National Reserve, where some trees were estimated to be 2000 years old.

Araucaria forest is protected at Laguna del Laja National Park in Araucanía, at Conguillio National Park in Biobío, and at the Cañi Forest Sanctuary, a Lahuén Foundation preserve in Pucón, Los Lagos.

Old-growth Araucaria forest

ARAUCARIA FOREST FLORA 51

Male pollen-bearing cone

Female seed-bearing cone

Araucarias begin to bear fruit at about 25 years of age. The male cones appear in August, the female cones in November. Piñon nuts are gathered between March and May for sale or for home use.

Piñones in the husk
2 in (4–5 cm)

Female cone showing the spiral arrangement of seeds

Araucaria, Pehuén
Monkey Puzzle Tree
Araucaria araucana
Araucanía–Biobío
T, H 165 ft (50 m)

Michay
Berberis darwinii
Biobío–Aisén
S, H 3–10 ft (1–3 m)
L 1 in (2.5 cm)

Calafate
Berberis trigona
Araucanía–Magallanes
S, H 7 ft (2 m)
L 0.75 in (2 cm)

Alstroemeria
Alstroemeria ligtu
Nahuelbuta
H 20 in (50 cm)

Wild Currant
Zarzaparilla
Ribes cucullatum
Valparaíso–Magallanes
S, H 32 in (80 cm)

Canelo Enano
Drimys winteri var. *andina*
Andes of Araucanía–Los Lagos
S, H 7 ft (2 m)
L 2–3.5 in (5–9 cm)

Chilean Bamboo
Colihue, Culeú
Chusquea culeou
Maule–Aisén
H 30 ft (8 m)

Wild Strawberry
Frutilla silvestre, Lahueñe
Frageria chiloensis
Ñuble–Aisén
Creeping

THE FORESTS OF SOUTHERN CHILE

The great temperate rainforests of Southern Chile stretch from Valdivia south to Tierra del Fuego. Rather than being a homogenous mass, they vary in composition in relation to latitude, altitude, temperature and precipitation.

The VALDIVIAN FOREST occupies the areas of Valdivia (XIV) and Los Lagos (X) that have not been cleared for agriculture. The zone contains dense forests of evergreen broadleaf trees and shrubs with waxy, dark green, laurel-like *(laurifolio)* leaves.

Scattered throughout the Valdivian cordilleras and the boggy slopes of Los Lagos is the SIEMPREVERDE (EVERGREEN) FOREST. The forest contains isolated stands of Alerce and Guiatecas Cypress, and a few of the coastal areas contain Olivillo. Siempreverde forest is fairly continuous along the marine coasts and archipelagos of the Aisén Region (XI).

The MAGELLANIC RAINFOREST extends in a vast swath along the Pacific coast from the Taito Peninsula of Aisén to s Magallanes (XII). This area is exposed to strong gales and heavy rain. The wet, often boggy forest is dominated by Magellanic Coigüe *(Nothofagus betuloides)*.

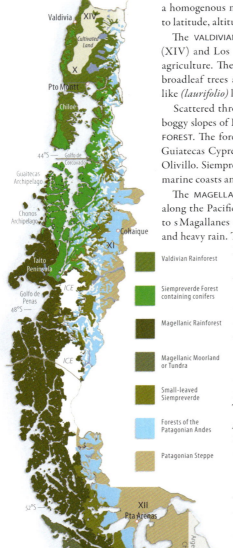

The outermost islands of extreme south-western Magallanes contain a habitat called MAGELLANIC MOORLAND. This area experiences extremely harsh climatic conditions and has impoverished soils that support only low growing shrubs, dwarfed trees and tundra vegetation.

The FORESTS OF THE PATAGONIAN ANDES extend along the ridgeline of the Andes from Los Lagos (X) to Magallanes (XII). The deciduous beech, Lenga *(Nothofagus pumilio)*, is a major component of this forest, and is especially abundant in the southern sector of the Patagonian Andes.

Sandwiched between the Magellanic and Andean forests is a transitional forest known as SMALL-LEAVED SIEMPREVERDE. It is a mixed forest composed of evergreen and deciduous trees and shrubs that are tolerant of poor, acidic, peaty soils.

BOSQUE LAURIFOLIO DE VALDIVIA
VALDIVIAN LAUREL-LEAVED FOREST

This zone, also known as the Valdivian Rainforest (*Pluviselva Valdiviana*), occurs in geographically-fragmented sites along the slopes of the Coastal and Andean Cordilleras, from Temuco to south of the Taito Peninsula (38° S–47° S). The zone has abundant precipitation year round, ranging from 60 in (1500 mm) in the Central Valley to 157 in (4000 mm) in the foothills and mountain areas.

The dense rainforests are composed of evergreen broadleaf trees and shrubs that have waxy, dark green, laurel-like leaves (*laurifólio*). These include trees such as Ulmo (*Eucryphia cordifolia*), Tineo (*Weinmannia trichosperma*), Tepa (*Laureliopsis philippiana*), Luma (*Amomyrtus luma*), Canelo (*Drimys winteri*) and Tiaca (*Caldcluvia paniculata*). The Valdivian cordilleras contain pocket forests of Patagonian Cypress, or Alerce (*Fitzroya cupressoides*) and isolated stands of Guiatecas Cypress (*Pilgerodendron uviferum*).

Ferns, bamboos, epiphytes and vines are thick in the understory, giving it a tropical appearance while making passage through the forest difficult. The dense understory contains plants such as Picha (*Myrceugenia planipes*), Murta blanca (*Ugni candollei*), Tepú (*Tepualia stipularis*) and *Chusquea* bamboo, which is often so thick it prevents other forest plants from regenerating.

Climbing plants include Coicopihue (*Philesia magellanica*), Copihue (*Lapageria rosea*), and red-flowered gesneriads such as Botellita, Medallita and Estrellita. At maturity, many of these species have long adventitious roots called *voqui*, which is also a native term for any climbing plant. Canelilla (*Hydrangea integerrima*), a giant rainforest hydrangea, can engulf even the tallest forest tree, smothering it with its dense foliage and sheer weight.

Most of the Valdivian Pacific coast was once covered by dense forests of Olivillo (*Aextoxicon punctatum*), an endemic tree species. Olivillo trees grew in profusion from the shoreline to 9800 ft (3000 m) in the Valdivian Coastal Range. Over the last 100 years, Olivillo forests have been reduced by 50 percent in size from deforestation, forest conversion and other human impact.

In 2003 the Nature Conservancy and the World Wildlife Fund acquired 147,500 acres (6000 ha) of this biologically rich coastal forest at public auction, following the bankruptcy of a timber company. The Valdivian Coastal Reserve was established in March 2005. Ownership will eventually be transferred to Chilean hands to ensure that the land and its flora and fauna are protected for future generations. The Valdivian Coastal Reserve is an invaluable reservoir of wildlife. It not only contains important trees such as the Olivillo and Alerce, but also shelters rarely-seen animals such as the world's smallest deer, the Pudu (p. 307), the tiny tree-dwelling marsupial Monito del Monte (p. 293), and wonderful curiosities such as the giant Forest Snail.

Forest Snail
Caracol de bosque
Macrocyclis peruvianus
Araucanía–Aisén
2.5 in (6.5 cm) shell

BOSQUE DE SIEMPREVERDE
SIEMPREVERDE (EVERGREEN) FOREST

The floristically rich Siempreverde forest extends between 38°30′ S and 47° S. In the Coastal Range, it is found from Temuco south to Chiloé, the Chonos Archipelago and the Taito Peninsula. In the Andes, it occurs between 40° S–47° S at elevations below 3300 ft (1000 m). The Siempreverde forest also appears in the Central Valley in seasonal bogs (*ñadis*) and other areas of poor soil drainage.

The composition of Siempreverde forest varies greatly with latitude and altitude. It often merges with other forest types such as deciduous Roble in the north and perennial Magellanic Coigüe in the south.

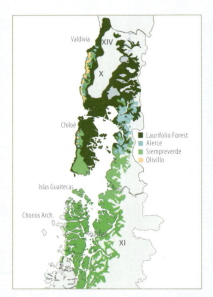

In its purest form, Siempreverde grows as a multi-canopied forest with evergreen vegetation similar to that of the Valdivian Rainforest. The uppermost tier comprises old growth coigües *(Nothofagus betuloides, N. dombeyi, N. nitida)*, Ulmo *(Eucriphya cordifolia)* and Tineo *(Weinmannia trichosperma)*. The lower story contains trees such as Tepa *(Laureliopsis philippiana)*, Luma *(Amomyrtus luma)*, Canelo *(Drimys winteri)* and Tiaca *(Caldcluvia paniculata)*.

A forest type known as BOSQUE SIEMPREVERDE CON CONÍFERAS occupies boggy areas from Valdivia to Aisén (40°S–54°S). It is a forest with low species diversity, an open canopy and dense understory. This forest type typically contains small groves of Guaitecas Cypress *(Pilgerodendron uviferum)* and Alerce *(Fitzroya cupressoides)* growing in association with a variety of southern beech and laurel-leaved trees and shrubs. Some important trees of this zone include Coigüe de Chiloé *(Nothofagus nitida)*, Magellanic Coigüe *(Nothofagus betuloides)*, Ñirre *(Nothofagus antarctica)*, Canelo *(Drimys winteri)*, Prickly-leaved Mañió *(Podocarpus nubigena)* and Tineo *(Weinmannia trichosperma)*.

Guaitecas Cypress
Ciprés de las Guaitecas

The Guaitecas Cypress, or *Ciprés de las Guaitecas (Pilgerodendron uviferum)*, is a narrowly pyramidal conifer measuring anywhere from 5 to 65 ft (1.5–20 m) high. Its gold-colored, aromatic timber is highly prized for making furniture and cabinets.

The species can be found from Valdivia to Tierra del Fuego in *Drimys–Nothofagus betuloides* coastal forest. It is fairly common in the Guaitecas and Chonos Archipelagos where it forms pure stands of dwarfed trees. This species prefers water-logged soil, and throughout its range it grows amid a dense understory of Tepú *(Tepualia stipularis)*. The common practice of setting fire to the Tepú undergrowth in order to harvest the valuable cypress timber has destroyed most of the stands. So although the estimated life span of the Guaitecas Cypress is 3000 years, trees of that age no longer exist.

In 1938 a reserve was established on the Huichas Islands in the Chonos Archipelago to protect the Guaitecas Cypress. No other protection was afforded the species until 1994, when the Conservation Land Trust in partnership with the North American philanthropist Peter Buckley acquired 200,000 acres (81,000 ha) on the southern Chilean coast near Palena. The tracts contain one of the most extensive stands of Guaitecas Cypress left in Chile. The land will eventually be donated to the Chilean Park Service with the intent of being declared a national park.

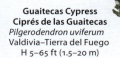

Guaitecas Cypress
Ciprés de las Guaitecas
Pilgerodendron uviferum
Valdivia–Tierra del Fuego
H 5–65 ft (1.5–20 m)

ALERCE FOREST

Alerce, Patagonian Cypress

Alerce *(Fitzroya cupressoides)* is the second oldest living tree species after the Bristlecone Pine *(Pinus longaeva)* of the western USA. One living Alerce tree in Chile is estimated to be over 3600 old.

Alerce grows in Chile and Argentina between 39°50′S and 43°30′S latitudes at elevations of 2300–4000 ft (700–1200 m). The majority of trees in Chile are located in remote Andean valleys, on slopes and terraces in the Los Lagos Region; the remainder occur in the Coastal Cordillera south of Valdivia and in the San Pedro Range of Isla Chiloé.

In the Andes, Alerce grows in association with the three perennial species of Coigüe *(Nothofagus dombeyi, N. betuloides,* and *N. nitida).* The understory is composed of *Chusquea* bamboo, Canelo enano *(Drimys winteri* var. *andina)*, heaths, barberry, ferns and epiphytes. In the Coastal Range, Alerce grows with Magellanic Coigüe, Coigüe de Chiloé, Prickly-leaved Mañío *(Podocarpus nubigena),* Canelo *(Drimys winteri)* and Tineo *(Weinmannia trichosperma).*

Alerce contains resins that resist decomposition, making it especially valuable in exterior construction and thus vulnerable to overcutting. Only about 15 percent of the original Alerce forest is in existence today due to historic large-scale logging. However, Alerce is now protected by a law that prohibits the cutting of live trees, but allows people to use dead, fallen trees for any purpose. The Alerce has been declared a Natural Monument in Chile. Large stands are fully protected at the Alerce Andino, Vicente Pérez Rosales and Chiloé National Parks, at Hornopirén and Alerce Costero Natural Monuments, and in the privately endowed Parque Pumalín in Los Lagos.

**Alerce, Lahuán
Patagonian Cypress**
Fitzroya cupressoides
Valdivia–Los Lagos
H 130 ft (40 m)
Alerce can live over 3000 years

Central market in Castro, Isla Chiloé

The shingles that clad the outer walls and roofs of many buildings in southern Chile are made from Alerce bark. In the past, the bark was stripped from live Alerce, a process that killed the trees. Today bark is taken only from dead trees. It is then flattened and carved into traditional shapes. The shingles are either painted a bright color or left to weather naturally to a soft tan.

VALDIVIAN AND SIEMPREVERDE FOREST FLORA 57

BOSQUE SIEMPREVERDE
MAGELLANIC RAINFOREST

The Magellanic Rainforest occupies a zone of complex physical relief. It includes the foothills of the Patagonian Andes, vast ice fields and innumerable islands and fjords of southern Chile. It exists in a region of high precipitation, continual low temperatures and thin organic soils that overlay a rocky subsoil—all of which limit the type of vegetation that can grow there.

The stark beauty of this remote wilderness goes largely unappreciated. Some people are fortunate enough to sail or steam through the southern channels and fjords, catching glimpses of dark greenery rising up misty mountain slopes and edging cobalt glaciers. However, it is the truly blessed who have a chance to step ashore and explore the verdure of this wondrous, wild terrain.

The Magellanic rainforests often appear battered and torn, with broken branches haphazardly strewn throughout the understory. The trees are festooned with lichens, filmy ferns and parasitic mistletoe *(Misodendrum* sp*.)* that forms large, yellowish, stick-like clusters on the tree branches.

Another growth seen on trees is DARWIN'S BREAD or Pan de Indio *(Cyttaria darwinii)*, a knobby sac fungus in the same family as truffles and morels. Charles Darwin noted in 1835: "In Tierra del Fuego the fungus in its tough and mature state is collected in large quantities by the women and children, and is eaten uncooked. It has a mucilaginous, slightly sweet taste, with a faint smell like that of a mushroom. With the exception of a few berries, chiefly of a dwarf *Arbutus*, the natives [Yaghans] eat no vegetable food besides this fungus."

Magellanic Coigüe Forest

Magellanic Coigüe *(Nothofagus betuloides)* is the dominant tree species found between Valdivia and Magallanes.

In the north, Magellanic Coigüe intermingles with deciduous Lenga *(Nothofagus pumilio)* in what is called a mixed evergreen-deciduous forest. It becomes the dominant species in southern Chile where there is more precipitation. There it associates with small-leaved evergreen trees and shrubs, which grow in the poor acidic soils that overlay a thick substratum of peat.

Romanche Glacier, Beagle Channel

MAGELLANIC RAINFOREST FLORA 59

Darwin's Bread
Cyttaria darwinii

Mistletoe
Misodendrum sp.

Coigüe is host to epiphytes and parasites such as Darwin's Bread, Mistletoe, and the lichen known as Old Man's Beard

Old Man's Beard
Usnea sp.

Magellanic Coihue
Coigüe de Magallanes
Nothofagus betuloides
Valdivia–Magallanes
T, H 80 ft (25 m)
P, L 0.5–1 in (1–2.5) cm

Tepú
Tepualia stipularis
Maule–Magallanes
S, H 25 ft (8 m)
P, L 0.75 in (2 cm)

Magellanic Maitén
Maytenus magellanica
Biobío–Magallanes
T, H 17 ft (5 m)
P, L 1–3 in (2.5–7 cm)

Sauco del Diablo
Pseudopanax laetevirens
Maule–Magallanes
S, H 25 ft (8 m)
CL 2–6 in (5–15 cm)

Fuchsia, Chilco
Fuchsia magellanica
Maule–Magallanes
S, H 13 ft (4 m)
P, L 2 in (5 cm)

Taique, Chapico
Desfontainea spinosa
Maule–Magallanes
S, H 10 ft (3 m)
L 2–2.5 in (5–6 cm)

Guaitecas Cypress
Ciprés de Guaitecas, Lahuán
Pilgerodendron uviferum
Valdivia–Magallanes
T, H 5–65 ft (1.5–20 m)

Fuinque, Romerillo
Lomatia ferruginea
Maule–Magallanes
T, H 25 ft (8 m)
P, CL 4–8 in (10–20 cm)

Canelo, Winter's Bark
Drimys winteri
Coquimbo–Magallanes
T, H 23 ft (7 m)
P, L 2.5–5 in (6–13 cm)

Notro, Firebush
Embothrium coccineum
Maule–Magallanes
T, H 35 ft (10 m)
P, L 1.5–4 in (4–10 cm)

Pure stands of Magellanic Coigüe develop away from the coast on shallow, peaty soils that do not accumulate excessive moisture. These stands normally occupy glacial valleys and sheltered streamside areas at elevations below 1150 ft (350 m). Near the snowy timberline, Magellanic Coigüe can be seen in its dwarf form where it often grows in association with *Blechnum* ferns, Barberry *(Berberis* spp.*)* and Red Crowberry *(Empetrum rubrum)*.

Along the coast, Magellanic Coigüe is found in association with Canelo *(Drimys winteri)*. In sites with good soil drainage, it grows with Magellanic Maitén *(Maytenus magellanica)*, Fuinque *(Lomatia ferruginea)* and Notro *(Embothrium coccineum)*. Sites in the coastal forest having poor drainage are often occupied by sphagnum bogs, the hummocks of which provide ideal places for the growth of Guaitecas Cypress *(Pilgerodendron uviferum)*.

Distinctive shrub communities are also present in the coastal *Nothofagus–Drimys* forest. A low scrub of Magellanic Fuchsia *(Fuchsia magellanica)* often extends to the tidal mark. Exposed coastal areas such as the seacliffs of Cape Horn contain a dense scrub often dominated by white-flowered Native Box *(Hebe elliptica)*.

Magellanic Moorland

The outermost archipelagos of Fuegia, from the Golfo de Penas to Cape Horn (48°S–56°S), are exposed to fierce westerly gales, heavy rainfall and continually low temperatures. This is the realm of the Magellanic moorland *(tundra magallánica)*. Although fragments of Magellanic Coigüe forest appear in sheltered areas, this habitat is dominated by dwarfed or prostrate trees, cushion plants, bog flora, heaths, reeds and bryophytes, all of which grow from a thick blanket of peat. A close inspection of the plants, best made while on one's hands and knees, reveals a magical miniature mosaic of *Gunnera, Gaultheria, Ugni, Empetrum* and dwarf *Nothofagus*.

Especially wet areas of moorland contain rich, raised bog communities. Cushion bogs, as their name suggests, contain cushion-forming plants such as *Bolax, Donacia, Naussavia* and *Oreobolus*. The graminoid bogs hold mosses, liverworts, rushes, reeds, ferns and sundews—the tiny, glistening *atrapamoscas* ("trappers of flies").

Maritime tussock grassland is one of the most conspicuous vegetation types of the coastal moorland. Closely spaced mounds of tussock grass *(Poa flabellata)* grow to 10 ft (3 m) high along the outer coasts. Tussock is an important terrestrial ecological niche; it provides nesting habitat for penguins, albatrosses and petrels, and shelter for seals and various forms of invertebrate fauna.

Magellanic penguins in the tussock

FLORA OF THE MAGELLANIC MOORLAND AND BOGS

Siete Camisas
Escallonia serrata
Aisén–Magallanes
S, H 12–20 in (30–50 cm)
P, L 0.5 in (1.7 cm)

Sundew, Atrapamosca
Drosera uniflora
Valdivia–Magallanes
Prostrate in bogs, wet places

**Swamp Berry
Mutilla, Chaura**
Gaultheria pumila
Aisén–Magallanes
Prostrate in heath, bogs,
wet forest

**Mountain Berry
Chaurita**
Gaultheria antarctica
Vadivia–Magallanes
Prostrate in heath, bogs

**Pig Vine
Palacoazir**
Gunnera magellanica
Southern Magallanes
H 6 in (15 cm)
L 3 in (8 cm)

**Red Crowberry
Diddle-dee
Murtilla**
Empetrum rubrum
Biobío–Magallanes
Prostrate in bogs, wet forest

**Acaena
Cadillo**
Acaena sp.
Biobío–Magallanes
H 8 in (20 cm)
Coast, forest, bog margins

**Small Fern
Pinque**
Blechnum penna-marina
Biobío–Magallanes
H 6 in (15 cm)

Native Box
Hebe elliptica
Magallanes
S, H 10 ft (3 m)
Coastal cliffs and rocks

Juncus Rush
Juncus scheuchzerioides
Maule–Magallanes
H 7–10 in (18–25 cm)

**Holly-leaved Barberry
Michay, Cheila**
Berberis ilicifolia
Los Lagos–Magallanes
S, H 16 ft (5 m)
Coast, forests

Sea Cabbage
Senecio candicans
Magallanes
H 3 ft (1 m)
Sandy beaches

Tussock Grass
Poa flabellata
Magallanes
H 3.25–10 ft (1–3 m)

Thrift, Guaicurú
Armeria maritima
Maule–Cape Horn
H 6 in (15 cm)
Coastal cliffs and rocks

BOSQUE PATAGÓNICO-ANDINO
FORESTS OF THE PATAGONIAN ANDES

This deciduous forest type extends along the Andes Range from Biobío to Tierra del Fuego. The forests are known for their intense autumn color that turns the hillsides into masses of red and gold.

A major component of these montane forests is the deciduous southern beech, LENGA *(Nothofagus pumilio)*. The species is especially abundant in the Andes of Aisén and Magallanes where it forms the upper level of arboreal growth. Trees that grow in snowpack areas at the treeline occur in a dwarf form known as "krummholz."

Lenga forest also occupies lower elevations. From sea level to 2300 ft (700 m), it occurs as transitional forest lying between the evergreen Magellanic rainforests to the west and the semi-arid Patagonian grasslands to the east. In sheltered lower elevations, Lenga trees can reach a height of 120 ft (40 m) or more. They also attain considerable height along the marine coast, where they grow close together, crowns entwined, thus offering resistance to the gale force winds that accompany frequent storms. When mature lenga trees finally fall, their rotting hulks shelter the nearby flora and return vital nutrients to the soil.

Ñirre *(Nothofagus antarctica)* is common in wet, windy sites throughout Fuegia and also thrives in cold, very wet places in the high mountains. This species seldom grows to more than 30 ft (9 m) high and often has a contorted trunk.

One can also encounter bogs *(turberas)* in areas with poor soil drainage. Sphagnum moss *(Sphagnum magellanicum)*, a main component of the bogs, grows in association with plants such as *Carex* sedge, *Festuca* grasses and Maillico *(Caltha sagittata)*. In contrast, a dwarf shrub heath occupies sites that have shallow soils with good drainage. Typical flora includes Murtilla, or Red Crowberry *(Empetrum rubrum)*, and the cushion-plant Llareta *(Bolax gummifera)*.

The Patagonian forest-edge community is dominated by the daisy-flowered shrub, Fachine *(Chiliotrichum diffusum)*. It forms a brush or scrubland that is particularly attractive in the warmer seasons when embellished with the colorful flowers of Notro *(Embothrium coccineum)*, Calafate *(Berberis buxifolia)*, Ranúnculo *(Ranunculus penduncularis)*, Anémona *(Anemone multifida)*, Yellow Orchid *(Gavilea lutea)* and Dog Orchid *(Codonorchis lessonii)*.

Fachine scrub in Tierra del Fuego

FLORA OF THE PATAGONIAN ANDES 63

Lenga
Nothofagus pumilio
Maule–Magallanes
T, H 50–100 ft (15–30 m)
D, L 1–1.5 in (2.5–4 cm)

Ñirre
Antarctic Beech
Nothofagus antarctica
Maule–Magallanes
T, H 20–50 ft (6–15 m)
D, L 0.5–1.5 in (1–4 cm)

Box-leaf Barberry
Calafate, Michay
Berberis buxifolia
Biobío–Magallanes
H 14 ft (4 m)
L 0.5 in (1.25 cm)

Fachine, Mata verde
Chiliotrichum diffusum
Valdivia–Magallanes
S, H 3–5 ft (1–1.5 m)
L 0.5–1.25 in (1–3 cm)

Sand Calafate
Zarcilla, Brecillo
Berberis empetrifolia
Valparaíso–Araucanía
S, H 20 in (50 cm)
L 0.75 in (2 cm)

Arrow-leaved Marigold
Maillico
Caltha sagittata
Santiago–Magallanes
L 1 in (2.5 cm)
Prostrate

Chilco de Magallanes
Baccharis magellanica
Maule–Magallanes
S, H 4–16 in (10–40 cm)

Yellow Orchid
Orchídea amarilla
Gavilea lutea
Biobío–Magallanes
H 8–24 in (20–60 cm)

Smith's Senecio
Senecio smithii
Los Lagos–Magallanes
P, H 1–4 ft (25–120 cm)

Dog Orchid
Palomita
Codonorchis lessonii
Valdivia–Magallanes
H 5–14 in (20–35 cm)

Marsh Lady's Slipper
Capachito de las vegas
Calceolaria biflora
Coquimbo–Magallanes
H 4–14 in (10–35 cm)

Pilludén
Violeta amarilla
Viola maculata
Biobío–Magallanes
H 8 in (20 cm)

Anémona, Centella
Anemone decapetala
Maule–Magallanes
H 18 in (45 cm)
White, yellow or
red flowers

ESTEPA PATAGÓNICO
PATAGONIAN STEPPE

The vast Patagonian Steppe of Aisén and Magallanes occupies the eastern slopes of the Patagonian Andes and stretches across southern Argentina to the Atlantic Ocean. Due to the rainshadow effect of the mountains, the steppe receives less than 24 in (612 mm) of annual rainfall. The area experiences continually cool temperatures and fierce, unrelenting winds. The soils are sandy, stony and poor in organic matter. The vegetative cover is quite uneven, with hummocks of plants separated by stretches of barren land.

Surprisingly, what results from this dismal forecast is a rolling, windswept landscape of great majesty and beauty. This is the realm of the graminae—fescue grasses (*Festuca gracillima* and *F. magellanica*), low tussock (*Poa alopecurus*) and Antarctic Hairgrass (*Deschampsia antarctica*)—which wave in synchrony as they are buffeted by the wind.

Here and there woody bushes spring up, a few growing to 10 ft (3 m) tall, but most assuming a prostrate or creeping form. In the sandy, saline soils along the Strait of Magellan, one finds Greenbush, or Mata verde (*Lepidophyllum cupressiforme*). This low-growing shrub with its scale-like leaves is covered in small yellow florets from November through January.

In the austral spring and summer, wildflowers add patches of color to the steppe mosaic. Flowering herbs such as Zapatilla de la Virgen (*Calceolaria uniflora*), Primula (*Primula magellanica*), Flor de la cuncuna (*Phacelia secunda*), Sisi Iris (*Sisyrinchium patagonicum*), Draba (*Draba magellanica*), Senecios (*Senecio magellanicus, S. patagonicus*), Violeta amarilla (*Viola maculata*) and Dandelion (*Taraxacum gilliesii*) bloom in the dry grasslands and coastal sands.

In the valleys and depressions with poor soil drainage, one finds wet meadows of *Carex* sedge and *Juncus* rush. Growing in the damp margins of the marshes (*vegas*) are water-loving plants such as Pico de Loro orchids (*Chloraea magellanica*) and Magellanic Gentian (*Gentianella magellanica*).

The grasslands give way to moors in areas where sheep and cattle have long been permitted to graze. These areas are dominated by the red-berried shrub Murtilla or Diddle-dee (*Empetrum rubrum*), which grows with Arjona (*Arjona patagonica*), Falkland Lavender (*Perezia recurvata*) and other plants typical of the Fuegian heath communities.

Unsound land use and the introduction of rabbits, cattle, horses and sheep have greatly altered the Patagonian steppe flora. It is fortunate that the Chilean grasslands have escaped some of this damage. It is still possible to travel great distances across Chile's pampas and meet only wilderness. Even around the estáncias of Magallanes, one can often see guanacos (*Lama guanicoe*) grazing with the sheep or a stately Ñandú (*Pterocnemia pennata*) striding across the grasslands, a line of little striped chicks running behind.

A Ñandú on the Patagonian steppe

FLORA OF THE PATAGONIAN STEPPE 65

Greenbush, Mata Verde
Lepidophyllum cupressiforme
Strait of Magellan
P, S, H 8–24 in (20–60 cm)
Scale-like leaves

Fescue
Festuca magellanica
Valdivia–Magallanes
H 12 in (30 cm)

Lupine
Lupinus sp.
H 3 ft (1 m)
Widespread garden plant

Sedge, Cárex
Carex magellanica
Aisén–Magallanes
H 12 in (30 cm)

Perezia Falkland Lavender
Perezia recurvata
O'Higgins–Magallanes
H 5–18 in (12–45 cm)

Sisi Iris
Sisyrinchium patagonicum
Aisén–Magallanes
H 11 in (27.5 cm)

Flor de la Cuncuna
Phacelia secunda
Coquimbo–Magallanes
H 5–14 in (12–35 cm)

Arjona
Arjona patagonica
Biobío–Magallanes
H 6 in (15 cm)

Magellanic Primula
Primula magellanica
Aisén–Magallanes
H 11 in (27.5 cm)

Adesmia
Adesmia pumila
Aisén–Magallanes
H 6 in (15 cm)
Coastal sand

Native Dandelion Diente de león
Taraxacum gilliesii
Biobío–Magallanes
H 7 in (17.5 cm)

Magellanic Gentian Genciana de Magallanes
Gentianella magellanica
Biobío–Magallanes
H 10 in (25 cm)

Pico de Loro Orchid
Chloraea magellanica
Aisén–Magallanes
H 16 in (40 cm)

Patagonian Senecio
Senecio patagonicus
Magallanes
H 15 in (37.5 cm)

Magellanic Senecio
Senecio magellanicus
Magallanes
H 8 in (20 cm)

Draba, Wiengu
Draba magellanica
Aisén–Magallanes
P, H 8 in (20 cm)

Maiden's Slipper Zapatilla de la Virgen
Calceolaria uniflora
Biobío–Magallanes
H 2–4 in (5–10 cm)

Hahn's Leucheria
Leucheria hahnii
Aisén–Magallanes
H 12 in (30 cm)

BOSQUE LAURIFOLIO DEL JUAN FERNÁNDEZ
FORESTS OF JUAN FERNÁNDEZ

The oceanic archipelago of Juan Fernández has some 50 fern and 150 flowering plant species, of which 130 are endemic. Many of the genera present in the islands also occur in the Valdivian rainforest. Isla Róbinson Crusoe (Masatierra) and Alejandro Selkirk (Masafuera) have similar forests, but there are fewer plant species on Masafuera.

Sandalwood (*Santalum fernandezianum*), which once covered the hills, was exploited for the lucrative China trade and was exterminated by the late 1800s. Invasive plants such as Maqui (*Aristotelia chilensis*) and Zarzamora blackberries (*Rubus ulmifolius*) were introduced to the islands in the past and now threaten to overrun the endemic plant species. It is estimated that 75 percent of the endemic plants are endangered. The problem is augmented by introduced goats and rabbits that browse on seedlings and foliage, preventing the regeneration of the native forest.

As a result, many of the lower elevation forests have been displaced by introduced shrubbery and grasses. The Chilean Forestry Department (CONAF) has planted fast-growing exotic conifers and eucalyptus to provide erosion control and timber sources for the islanders. Eucalyptus has value in that it produces nectar for the endemic hummingbird, the Juan Fernández Firecrown (*Sephanoides fernandensis*).

The waterfront of San Juan Bautista, the only permanent settlement of the islands, has been planted with flowering shrubs such as Tupa (*Lobelia tupa*) and the endemic Col de Juan Fernández (*Dendroceris litoralis*) with its bright orange blossoms.

There are small patches of native *Myrceugenia* and *Fagara* dry forest at elevations below 1650 ft (500 m). But for the most part, one must hike to considerable heights to see pristine native forest on Masatierra.

Forests above 1650 ft (500 m) contain perennial trees such as Luma de Masatierra (*Myrceugenia fernandeziana*), Canelo (*Drimys confertifolia*), Manzano (*Boehmeria excelsa*), Peralillo (*Coprosma pyrifolia*), Juan Bueno (*Rhaphithamnus venustus*) and the Chonta Palm (*Juania australis*) as well as Michay de Juan Fernández (*Berberis corymbosa*), the island's only deciduous endemic plant.

The slopes that lie above 2000 ft (600 m) receive substantial rainfall. There one finds lush rainforests with ferns such as *Dicksonia berteroana, Thyrsopteris elegans, Lophosoria quadripinnata* and *Blechnum cycadifolium*. Two species of *Gunnera* grow in the deep ravines. At the highest elevations, one can find endemic *Dendroseris* and *Robinsonia* shrubs growing with *Escallonia callcottiae* on the cliffs. Open, exposed ridges contain *Gaultheria rigida, Haloragis masatierrana, Plantago fernandezia* and *Lactoris fernandeziana*, a weedy endemic shrub that is the sole member of the Family Lactoraceae.

TREE FERN FORESTS
Above 2000 ft (> 600 m)

MONTANE FORESTS
1650–2000 ft (500–600 m)

TALL LOWLAND FORESTS
1000–1650 ft (300–500 m)

INTRODUCED SHRUBS & GRASSLANDS
Sea level–1000 ft (0–300 m)

San Juan Bautista, Isla Róbinson Crusoe

FLORA DE ISLA DE PASQUA
FLORA OF EASTER ISLAND (RAPA NUI)

Easter Island lies 2355 mi (3790 km) off the coast of northern Chile. Thirty vascular plants and sixteen ferns are native to this high volcanic island.

The fossil record suggests that prior to human settlement around AD 800 Rapa Nui was covered low scrub, woodland and large thickets of the extinct palm *Paschalococos dispersa*, which was very similar to the Chilean Palm *(Jubaea chilensis)*.

By the time Roggeveen's ships arrived in 1722, the island was largely treeless. Deforestation was probably the result of land clearance for cultivation, intense gathering of firewood and the gnawing of palm nuts and seedlings by Polynesian rats *(Rattus exulans)* introduced by the first colonists. The final blow to the indigenous flora was delivered in the mid-1800s when rabbits, sheep, pigs, horses and cattle were introduced to Rapa Nui and began to browse and graze their way across the island.

Today the main features of the floral landscape are grasses, introduced eucalyptus, Polynesian crop plants, and a few coconut and Chilean palms. With the exception of grasses, the native flora is restricted to a few sites. The majority of indigenous ferns grow within the craters of Rano Kau and Rano Aroi. At the bottom of the craters are ponds and peat bogs lined with TOTORA REED *(Scirpus californicus)*, a pan-American species known to the islanders as *Nga'atu* and to Californians as Tule Bulrush. In his book *Aku-Aku*, Norwegian explorer Thor Heyerdahl hypothesized that prehistoric voyagers from South America brought the reeds to Rapa Nui. However, botanists now believe that Totora colonized the island by natural means thousands of years ago.

One lost piece of Easter Island's flora is TOROMIRO *(Sophora toromiro)*, a species that survives in only a few botanical gardens. One of the last trees in Rano Kao crater was photographed in 1934 by the Frenchman Alfred Métraux. In 1953 Swedish botanist Carl Skottsberg found one remaining tree, which later died. In 1956 Thor Heyerdahl found four seedpods, which he gave to the Göteborg Botanical Garden in Sweden for possible propagation.

The Toromiro Management Group and the Chilean Forestry Department (CONAF) are working to repatriate Toromiro to Rapa Nui. They have located all available trees in cultivation, including those at the Chilean Jardín Botánico Nacional, England's Kew Gardens, the Bonn Botanischer Garten and the Göteborg Botanical Garden. In 1995 an experimental reintroduction of the trees was undertaken. If proven successful, Toromiro will again bloom on Rapa Nui.

Peat bogs and Totora Reed in Rano Kau crater

Snow algae at Cuverville Island

Antarctic Pearlwort

Lichens, mosses and liverworts flourish in rock crevices watered by melting snow

FLORA DE ANTÁRTICA CHILENA
FLORA OF CHILEAN ANTARCTICA

The harsh climate, lack of ice-free soil suitable for plant growth, and the long distance from other large landmasses has limited the number of plants that can grow in the Antarctic. Most plants occur along the coast of the Antarctic Peninsula and on offshore islands, in areas that are relatively free of ice and snow. They do particularly well around nesting colonies of penguins and other seabirds. Decomposing guano (the accumulated droppings of birds), and nitrogenous gases rising from the guano, nourish the surrounding flora.

Antarctic flora includes only two species of FLOWERING PLANTS—Antarctic Hairgrass *(Deschampsia antarctica)* and the cushion-forming Antarctic Pearlwort *(Colobanthus quitensis)*—both of which also grow in southern Chile. Most of the vegetation is composed of the so-called lower plants such as lichens, bryophytes, algae and fungi.

The abundance of beautiful LICHENS is one of the delights and wonders of the Antarctic Peninsula landscape. Over 200 species are known from the region. Lichens are composed of a fungus and algae living together in what is called a symbiotic relationship. The fungus provides a "house" for the algae, and the algae provide the fungus with food in the form of organic sugars manufactured in photosynthesis.

Lichens are slow-growing, long-lived, and able to survive incredible extremes of climate. They grow on almost any surface, at any altitude and in any environment. They are even found growing on exposed rock surfaces close to the South Pole.

Lichens grow in a great variety of forms. There are three main kinds that are distinguished by their general habit of growth and the manner of attachment to the object on which they grow. The FOLIOSE LICHENS have a prostrate, leaf-like thallus (body) that attaches itself to a substratum by root-like threads called phizinae. The entire plant often forms a rosette, with the young, growing lobes at the margins. Conspicuous foliose forms include the vivid yellow-orange xanthoriads.

FRUTICOSE LICHENS resemble miniature shrubs. They have an erect or pendant thallus with a bushy or tasseled top.

CRUSTOSE LICHENS have a crusty thallus that usually lacks distinct lobes. The entire thallus is normally so closely attached to the substratum that it is impossible to disengage it without breakage. The surface is often divided into tiny hexagonal areas called areolae, which allow expansion and contraction upon wetting and drying.

Two algal forms can be readily seen and identified. Most obvious is the terrestrial alga, PRASIOLA CRISPA, which forms a leafy green mat that can be mistaken for moss. *Prasiola* meadows are very fragile and are often trampled into muck by penguins walking to and from their nests. They can similarly be damaged by people crossing from one place to another.

Colonies of microscopic SNOW ALGAE are a colorful feature of snow and ice fields that experience annual thawing. The algae reproduce rapidly in the snow when the nutrient and temperature conditions are optimal. They "bloom" on melting snow, turning it red, green or yellow depending on the pigmentation contained in the vegetative or spore cells. The pigments protect the algal cells from damaging sunlight and ultraviolet radiation during the summer months. Snow algae in bloom is often seen where penguins regularly toboggan down slopes standing between their nests and the sea. The continual use of the slides results in glossy runs of color in the snow.

Mosses and liverworts form a group of primitive plants called BRYOPHYTES. There are over 100 species of these plants in the Antarctic. They possess some unique characteristics that enable them to withstand drying and freezing, and they thrive in rock crevices and other places that receive water from melting snow.

Certainly the most intriguing species are cryptoendolithic plants—those plants that lie hidden within the rocks of Antarctica. These communities of algae, fungi, bacteria and lichens live in the interstices of mineral grains in certain rocks. Just enough light passes through the rock's surface layers to allow plant photosynthesis and survival.

*Antarctic Hairgrass and Xanthoria lichens
King George Island, Antarctica*

ILLUSTRATIONS OF TERMS USED IN DESCRIPTIONS OF LEAVES, FLOWERS AND FRUIT
Adapted from L. H. Bailey, 1938. *Manual of Cultivated Plants*

BOTANICAL DESCRIPTIONS

There are about 2400 species of native plants in Chile. Almost half of them are endemic (found only in Chile). This section contains brief botanical descriptions of the more familiar, distinctive and widespread native trees and shrubs. The descriptions do not include lower plants such as mosses, fungi and ferns, but concentrate on the larger seed-plants, which are known as SPERMATOPHYTES or PHANEROGAMS.

Spermatophytes produce seeds containing an embryo or dormant plant, which germinates (becomes active) under favorable conditions. Spermatophytes are usually divided into GYMNOSPERMS (plants that bear naked seeds, e.g., seeds not enclosed in an ovary) and ANGIOSPERMS (plants that bear seeds enclosed in an ovary).

GYMNOSPERMAE: Gymnosperms

FAMILY ARAUCARIACEAE

ARAUCARIAS
Araucaria, Pehuén
Araucaria araucana
OTHER NAMES: Piñonero, Chilean Pine, Monkey Puzzle Tree.
ID: National tree of Chile. Tall, evergreen, cone-bearing tree, 100–165 ft (30–50 m) high. Pyramidal, whorled crown of branches at the top of mature specimens resembles a parasol. Scale-like leaves, to 2 in (5 cm) long, radially arranged, triangular-ovate, leathery, dark green, pointed, may persist for 10 years. Ovoid female cones, to 6 in (15 cm) long, ripen over 2 to 3 years. Each mature cone may contain 200 or more, 1.5 in (3.75 cm) long, creamy-white, edible pine nuts *(piñones)*, which are a staple food of the native Pehuenche people. Historically, the tall straight trunks were used as masts for sailing ships. PROTECTED species. ILLUS. P. 51.
RANGE: Maule to Araucanía; sw Argentina. Found on volcanic slopes in the Cordillera de Nahuelbuta (37°S–38°S) at 2000–4600 ft (600–1400 m); Cordillera de los Andes (37°S–40°S) at 3000–5600 ft (900–700 m).

FAMILY CUPRESSACEAE

CYPRESSES, JUNIPERS AND CEDARS
Cordilleran Cypress, Ciprés de la cordillera
Austrocedrus chilensis
OTHER NAMES: Cedro, Len, Mountain Cypress, Chilean Incense Cedar. Formerly in the genus *Libocedrus*.
ID: Narrowly columnar, densely branched conifer, to 65 ft (20 m) high, with coppery bark, peeling in threads. Scale-like, flattened leaves are arranged in sets of two unequal pairs, often with silvery bands on the reverse side. Ovoid-oblong, green to brown cones (Jan–Feb), to 0.5 in (1.25 cm) long. The cream-colored, aromatic, wood is used for making furniture and stakes for grapevines. Widely planted ornamental. Long-lived; some living trees more than 1500 years old. In decline from unknown causes. VULNERABLE. ILLUS. P. 49.
RANGE: Valparaíso to Los Lagos; San Felipe de Aconcagua to Río Palena in the Andes, and in parts of the Coastal Cordillera; also Argentina. In temperate forests on steep, dry mountain slopes that have winter precipitation and a pronounced dry season; 3000–5900 ft (900–1800 m).

Guaitecas Cypress, Ciprés de la Guaitecas
Pilgerodendron uviferum
ID: Narrowly pyramidal conifer, 5–33 ft (1.5–10 m) high. Bark dark brown, flaking in long strips. Leaves scale-like, imbricate, in four rows, ovate, obtuse, sometimes bent. Male and female cones on different branches. Female cones, 0.35 in (8 mm) long, borne on short shoots; 4 to 6 oblanceolate scales, the outer pair with a rigid dorsal spine, sometimes bowed. Seeds have one wide, oblique wing and a shorter, narrower wing. Yellow-orange, aromatic wood used in construction and woodworking. ILLUS. P. 54.
RANGE: Valdivia to Tierra del Fuego; also w Argentina. In *Drimys winteri–Nothofagus betuloides* coastal forest or inland in lowland bogs; sea level to 500 ft (0–150 m).

Alerce, Patagonian Cypress
Fitzroya cupressoides
OTHER NAMES: Lahuén, Lahual. *Fitzroya* honors the British Captain Robert Fitzroy, commander of the *HMS Beagle* (1831–36).
ID: Conical conifer to 130 ft (40 m) high; reddish-brown bark peels in strips. Oblong, dark green needles, to 0.25 in (0.6 cm) long, arranged in whorls of three. World's second oldest living tree species—3622 years in a Chilean specimen. Wood used to make carved shingles for building exteriors, especially around Puerto Montt and Chiloé. Protected as a Natural Monument in Chile. VULNERABLE. ILLUS. P. 55.
RANGE: Between 41°S–43°S in the Coastal Range and Andes; also Argentina.

FAMILY PODOCARPACEAE
PODOCARPS
Southern Hemisphere conifers with simple, persistent, needlelike or scalelike leaves.

Prickly-leafed Mañío
Mañío de hojas punzantes
Podocarpus nubigena
OTHER NAMES: Pino amarillo, Mañío hembra (in Chiloé), Mañío macho.
ID: Pyramidal tree to 80 ft (25 m) high. Grey, scaly, fissured bark and a convoluted trunk. Leaves pointed, linear-lanceolate, dark green, yew-like, to 1.25 in (3.25 cm) long. Greenish-yellow racemes of flowers at tips of branches. Ovoid, dark purple drupe, 0.3 in (0.9 cm) long, set in a reddish, funnel-shaped aril (outer covering). Yellow wood, streaked with rose, is used for furniture, flooring, decks, masts, oars and plywood. Grows with *Nothofagus dombeyi–Drimys winteri*. One of the few conifers of the lowland rainforests. ILLUS. P. 56.
RANGE: Araucanía to Magallanes (39°S–48°S); especially in Chiloé and the Coastal Range. Rainforests, in wet or swampy soil.

Long-leaved Mañío
Mañío de hojas largas
Podocarpus saligna
OTHER NAME: Willowleaf Podocarp.
ID: Columnar or broadly conical tree to 65 ft (20 m) high. Spreading, later pendant branches. Green shoots become grey-brown with age. Fibrous, peeling, red-brown bark. Linear, often sickle-shaped leaves, 2–4.5 in (5–11.5 cm) long, bluish-green above, yellow-green beneath. Male flowers borne in yellow, catkin-like cones; female flowers in green cone-like structures. Egg-shaped, dark violet fruit, to 0.35 in (0.9 cm) long. Lightweight, fibrous, malleable, yellow wood used to make furniture and carvings. ILLUS. P. 56.
RANGE: Maule to Los Lagos. In foothills, along rivers from Río Maule to Osorno, and in mixed forests with *Nothofagus obliqua*.

Short-leaved Mañío
Mañío de hojas cortas
Saxegothaea conspicua
OTHER NAMES: Mañío macho, Mañío hembra, Prince Albert's Yew. The latter name refers to Belgian Prince Albert von Sachsen-Coburg, a botanical aficionado.
ID: Shaped like a Christmas tree, to 65 ft (20 m) high, with whorled branches bearing green shoots. Leaves yew-like, linear to lanceolate, dark green, to 1.25 in (3.25 cm) long, each with two pale crossbands on the reverse. Fleshy, spherical, prickly, greyish-green, female cones, 0.5 in (1.25 cm) across, borne at terminal cluster of scales. Cylindrical, dark purple male cones borne at base of shoots. Yellowish-rose wood is used in making fine furniture, veneer and posts. Associates with *Drimys winteri*, *Nothofagus dombeyi* and *Luma apiculata*. ILLUS. P. 48.
RANGE: Maule to Aisén. Coastal rainforests; 2600–3250 ft (800–1000 m).

Lleuque
Mountain Grape
Prunopitys andina
OTHER NAMES: Uva de cordillera, Plum Yew.
ID: Conical when young; ovoid-shaped at maturity, 30–65 ft (10–20 m) high. Smooth, bluish-grey bark. Leaves yew-like, linear, soft, dull bluish-green, to 1.25 in (3.25 cm) long, with two pale bands on reverse. Ovoid, yellow cones in racemes of 5 to 20. Plum-shaped, pale yellow fruit, 0.75 in (2 cm) long, has a thin, edible aril. Yellow veined wood used for furniture. ILLUS. P. 48.
RANGE: Maule to Valdivia. Isolated groves in the Andes; 1600–3250 ft (500–1000 m).

GNETOPSIDA; EPHEDRALES; FAMILY EPHEDRACEAE
EPHEDRAS
New World shrubs known as Jointfirs because they have long slender branches that bear tiny, scale-like leaves at their nodes. The alkaloids ephedrine and pseudoephedrine are active plant constituents.

Pingo-pingo
Ephedra andina
ID: Branching shrub to 5 ft (1.5 m) high. Greyish-green stems. Very small leaves; appears almost leafless. Tiny, salmon-colored flowers (Aug–Feb). ILLUS. P. 39.
RANGE: Widespread in Chile in arid, steep, mountainous terrain.

ANGIOSPERMAE: Angiosperms
The Class Magnoliopsida comprises seed-bearing plants of two types, DICOTYLEDONS and MONOCOTYLEDONS. The seedlings of dicots have two seed-leaves, or cotyledons. Mature dicot leaves are usually net-veined and flowers 5-merous, in which the parts of each kind or series are five or in fives. Monocotyledons have a single seed-leaf, or cotyledon; monocots are often placed in their own class, Liliopsida.

DICOTYLEDONS: CLASS MAGNOLIOPSIDA

MAGNOLIALES: FAMILY WINTERACEAE
WINTERAS

Canelo, Winter's Bark
Drimys winteri
OTHER NAMES: Boighe, Pepper Bark. The English name "Winter's Bark" is attributed to Captain Winter who commanded one of Sir Francis Drake's vessels in 1578. Natives gave him a Canelo bark tea, which cured his stomach ailment. Winter took the plant to Europe where it was used to combat scurvy.
ID: Vigorous, pyramidical, hardwood tree or shrub to 23 ft (7 m) high. Aromatic bark. Oblong-elliptical to inversely lanceolate, leathery leaves, 8 in (20 cm) long, dark green above, bluish-white to buff below. Large umbels of 5 to 20 fragrant, ivory-colored flowers, to 1 in (2.5 cm) across, are followed by edible, aromatic, glossy black berries. Canelo is a sacred tree to the Araucanian people; its branches symbolize peace, ritual sacrifice and soothsaying. Timber is used for shingles and general construction. VULNERABLE in Magallanes. ILLUS. P. 59.
RANGE: Valparaíso to Magallanes. In wet or swampy ground in mixed forests; sea level to 5600 ft (0–1700 m).
RELATED SPECIES: CANELO ENANO *(Drimys winteri* var.*andina)* occurs in montane areas in sc Chile. CANELO DE JUAN FERNÁNDEZ, *Drimys confertifolia*, occurs on Islas Masatierra and Masafuera on exposed slopes and in ravines above 1650 ft (500 m).

LAURALES: FAMILY MONIMIACEAE
SOUTHERN HEMISPHERE LAURELS
Southern Hemisphere subtropical trees, shrubs or vines with aromatic leaves and oily drupes.

Laurel, Tihue, Trihue
Laurelia sempervirens
ID: Tree to 130 ft (40 m) high. Straight, cylindrical trunk, to 6.5 ft (2 m) in diameter. Upright branches. Leaves perennial, simple, opposite, aromatic, bright green, oblong to lanceolate, to 4 in (10 cm) long, with a toothed margin. Leaves, pale yellow flowers (Oct–Nov) and bark contain cineol, which is used medicinally. Yellowish-olive wood with irregular rosy veins is used for cabinets and furniture. ILLUS. P. 56.
RANGE: O'Higgins to Los Lagos. In Andean foothill forests to 3100 ft (950 m).

Tepa, Huahuán
Laureliopsis (Laurelia) philippiana
OTHER NAMES: Laurela.
ID: Large evergreen tree, to 100 ft (30 m) high. Straight, cylindrical trunk, with warty, ash-brown bark. Leaves perennial, simple, opposite, lanceolate, to 3.5 in (8.75 cm) long, with dentate margin. Hard, fine-textured wood is used for furniture and woodworking. ILLUS. P. 49.
RANGE: Biobío to Aisén. Common in rainforests and deep shade.

Boldo
Peumus boldus
ID: Tree to 65 ft (20 m) high. Short trunk to 3 ft (1 m) in diameter. Rough, greyish bark.

Leaves perennial, simple, opposite, oblong, to 2 in (5 cm) long; dark green, shiny, glandular, bumpy, strongly veined above; paler green and hairy below. Medicinal alkaloid is extracted from the leaves. ILLUS. P. 43.

RANGE: Coquimbo to Los Lagos, on slopes from sea level to 3250 ft (5–1000 m).

LAURALES: FAMILY GOMORTEGACEAE

QUEULE

A monotypic species native to central Chile, with oil cells in the aromatic leaves and stem, and small needles of calcium oxalate in the parenchyma cells.

Queule, Keule
Gomortega keule

ID: Sturdy tree to 50 ft (15 m) high, with pyramidical crown and lush green foliage. Straight, cylindrical trunk to 24 in (60 cm) in diameter. Rough, longitudinally striated, ashy-brown bark. Long branches held perpendicular to trunk. Leaves perennial, simple, opposite, oblanceolate, aromatic, to 4 in (10 cm) long; shiny bright green above, pale green and hirsute below. Yellow-green, round drupe, 2–3 in (5–7 cm) in diameter, is used to make marmalade. ENDANGERED; natural range has been largely converted to pine plantations. PROTECTED as a Natural Monument in Chile. ILLUS. P. 48.

RANGE: ENDEMIC. Río Maule to Biobío, in humid ravines.

LAURALES: FAMILY LAURACEAE

LAURELS

Tropical and subtropical evergreen trees and shrubs with aromatic or flavorful parts.

Belloto del Norte
Beilschmiedia miersii

ID: Sclerophyllous forest tree, to 80 ft (25 m). Leaves simple, opposite, oblong, aromatic, 1.5–4 in (4–10 cm) long, with undulating margin. Elliptical yellow drupe. ILLUS. P. 43.

RANGE: Coquimbo to O'Higgins. Coastal Range valleys and foothills to 3900 ft (1200 m).

Belloto del Sur
Beilschmiedia berteroana

OTHER NAME: Belloto del Centro.

ID: Tree to 50 ft (15 m) high, with scaly grey bark. Leaves perennial, simple, opposite, smooth, aromatic, with prominent veins. Fruit looks like a small, green avocado pit. PROTECTED as a Natural Monument in Chile. ENDANGERED.

RANGE: ENDEMIC. O'Higgins to Maule. On wet soils in forests to 5900 ft (1800 m).

Peumo
Cryptocarya alba

ID: Tree to 50 ft (15 m) high. Dense foliage. Leaves perennial, simple, leathery, ovate, aromatic, 0.5–2 in (1–5 cm) long, with entire, undulating margin. Reddish, edible drupe, 0.75 in (2 cm) long, forms in clusters at branch tips (Jan–Apr). Beautifully veined, water-resistant wood is used for firewood and tanning hides. ILLUS. P. 43.

RANGE: ENDEMIC. Coquimbo to Biobío. On foothill slopes to 5000 ft (1500 m).

Lingue
Persea lingue

ID: Large forest tree to 100 ft (30 m) high, with rounded crown. Straight, cylindrical trunk to 30 in (80 cm) in diameter. Dark grey bark. Leaves perennial, alternate, elliptical, lustrous, to 5 in (12 cm) long; shiny green above, pubescent and prominently veined below; smooth margins tend to turn under. Fruit is a small, smooth, blackish-purple drupe. Brownish-red wood is used for furniture and skis. ILLUS. P. 56.

RANGE: Valparaíso to Chiloé, in forests to 3000 ft (900 m).

RELATED SPECIES: *Persea meyeniana*, grows to 23 ft (7 m) high. Valparaíso to Colchagua.

FAMILY BERBERIDACEAE

BARBERRIES

Herbs and shrubs, many armed with thorns, native to the temperate Northern Hemisphere and the Andes south to the Strait of Magellan.

Calafate, Michay, Zarcilla
Berberis spp.

The names above are commonly applied to various barberry species that have yellow or orange, cup-shaped flowers and dark blue or purple, round berries.

CALAFATE, BOX-LEAVED BARBERRY, *Berberis*

buxifolia. Erect shrub to 13 ft (4 m) high. Greyish-brown bark. Branches armed with triads of short, brown spines. Leaves small, lustrous green, ovate, with a sharp, rigid, pointed spine and entire margin. Yellow flowers. Edible, dark blue, round berry. Linares to Magallanes; Argentina. Coastal scrub, forest edge, riverbanks. ILLUS. P. 63.

CALAFATE, *Berberis trigona*. Shrub to 6 ft (2.2 m) high. Grey bark. Stems have triads of short, pale spines. Sparse clusters of 3 to 9 oblong leaves, to 2 in (5 cm) long, shiny above, glaucous below. Clusters of 5 to 6 yellow-orange to red, cup-shaped flowers, to 0.5 in (1 cm), borne on long drooping stems (Sep–Jan). Edible, dark blue, egg-shaped berry. Local legend says, "If you eat the calafate berry, you will return to Tierra del Fuego." Araucanía to Magallanes. In Alerce and Araucaria understory. ILLUS. P. 51.

ZARCILLA, SAND CALAFATE, *Berberis empetrifolia*. Perennial shrub to 20 in (50 cm) high, with slender branches and trios of spines on stems. Small, linear, fleshy leaves, with a sharp rigid apical spine and entire margin. Yellow flowers (Oct–Jan), borne singly or in clusters of 2 to 3. Dark blue berry. Santiago to Araucanía. In Araucaria, Lenga, Ñirre understory; near rivers and lakes; in sandy, volcanic, rocky soils. ILLUS. P. 63.

MICHAY, *Berberis darwinii*. Spiny shrub to 6.5 ft (2 m) high. Branches covered in reddish hairs. Leaves small, hard, obovate, palmately-spined, to 1 in (2.5 cm) long, bright green above, dull reddish below. Long racemes of 12 to 16 bright orange flowers (Oct–Feb). Edible, bluish-black, round berry. Biobío to Aisén; Argentina. ILLUS. P. 51.

HOLLY-LEAVED BARBERRY, MICHAY, CHELIA, *Berberis ilicifolia*. Shrub with lined grey bark, dark red when young. Many short spines on stems. Tips of stems bear 2 to 8 obovate, holly-like leaves, to 2 in (5 cm) long, with sharply dentate margins. Clusters of small, 6-petalled, yellow flowers, borne in long corymbs (Nov–Mar). Dark blue berry. Araucanía to Magallanes. In swampy areas, along coasts and rivers, in montane *Nothofagus* forests. ILLUS. P. 61.

FAGALES: FAMILY FAGACEAE
SOUTHERN BEECHES
A large family of chiefly monoecious trees and shrubs. In Chile, the family is represented by NOTHOFAGUS, *a genus of about 40 species found throughout the Southern Hemisphere.*

Roble
Nothofagus obliqua
OTHER NAMES: Coyan, Hualle, Roble-Pellín, Oak.
ID: Woodland tree to 130 ft (40 m) high. Straight, cylindrical trunk to 6.5 ft (2 m) in diameter. Dark brown bark cracks into plates with age. Grows in a dwarf or twisted form at high elevations. at the timberline. Leaves deciduous, simple, alternate, ovate, 1–2 in (2–5 cm) long; smooth and dark green above, bluish-green below, turning yellow in autumn. Fruit is a small, scaly husk enclosing three nuts. Esteemed for its beautiful wood veined in rose and chestnut. The wood contains tannin, which confers a slight sheen and makes the wood very solid and durable. The timber is used for many purposes, including bridge framework and cabinetry. ILLUS. P. 49.
RANGE: Central Valley and foothills from Santiago to Los Lagos.
VARIETAL: ROBLE DE SANTIAGO, *Nothofogus obliqua* var. *macrocarpa*, has leaves to 3.5 in (9 cm) long. Valparaíso to O'Higgins. In foothill forests; 2625–7300 ft (800–2220 m).

Raulí, Ruilí, Roblí
Nothofagus nervosa (alpina)
ID: Tree to 100 ft (30 m) high. Straight trunk to 6.5 ft (2 m) in diameter. Dark grey bark cracks into plates with age. Branches somewhat hairy. Leaves deciduous, simple, alternate, oval to lanceolate, to 0.5 in (1.1 cm) long, with pleated, slightly serrate margin; 15 to 18 prominent veins on hirsute underside of leaf. Young leaves are bronze becoming dark green with age and turning yellow in fall. Fruit is a resinous, hairy capsule containing three nuts. Commercial hardwood is used in cabinets, furniture and fine woodworking. VULNERABLE. ILLUS. P. 49.
RANGE: Maule to Valdivia. In deciduous forests; 325–1650 ft (100–500 m).

Ruil
Nothofagus alessandrii
ID: Tree to 100 ft (30 m) high. Straight trunk to 3 ft (1 m) in diameter. Greyish bark that forms plates with maturity. Leaves deciduous, simple, opposite, obovate, to 5 in (12.5 cm) long, with fine-toothed margins. Small, multi-winged husk encloses 3 to 7 nuts. No known specimens of mature age. Protected as a Natural Monument in Chile. ENDANGERED. ILLUS. P. 49.
RANGE: Maule. RARE in the Coastal Range between 35°S–36°S; on south-facing slopes; 525–1450 ft (160–440 m).

Ñirre
Antarctic Beech
Nothofagus antarctica
OTHER NAME: Low Antarctic Beech.
ID: Tree 20–30 ft (5–9 m) high. Also grows as a tall shrub alongside Lenga. Contorted trunk, with rough, dark grey bark. Twisted branches with soft, finely-haired branchlets. Deciduous, simple, alternate, ovate leaves, to 1.25 in (3.25 cm) long, with fine toothed margin and 4 pairs of parallel veins. Leaves turn yellow and red in autumn. Fruit is a small husk enclosing 3 nuts. Thrives in cold, rainy conditions of s Chile. Forms forests called *ñirantales*. ILLUS. P. 63.
RANGE: Maule to Tierra del Fuego.

Lenga
Nothofagus pumilio
OTHER NAMES: Monte alto, Tall Deciduous Beech, Magallanes Oak. *Lenga* is a Mapuche word; *pumilio* means "dwarf."
ID: Tree 50–100 ft (15–30 m) high, with a pyramidal crown. Straight, cylindrical trunk to 5 ft (1.5 m) in diameter. Purplish-brown bark is fissured at base, with horizontal raised pores (lenticels) and wrinkles. Leaves deciduous, simple, alternate, elliptical to ovate, to 1.25 in (3.25 cm) long; dark green above, slightly hairy on both sides; turning yellow to red in autumn. Fruit is a small, scaly husk enclosing three nuts. Dominant tree in the Patagonian Andes, where it may assume a dwarf form. Grows in soils less than 4 in (10 cm) deep. Wood used for floors, doors, beams and furniture. ILLUS. P. 63.
RANGE: Maule to Magallanes. Forests in the Andes and at Nahuelbuta and Valdivia.

Hualo
Nothofagus glauca
OTHER NAMES: Roble maulino, Roble colorado.
ID: Tree to 100 ft (30 m) high. Cylindrical trunk to 6.5 ft (2 m) in diameter. Rough, reddish-grey bark flakes and cracks with age. Leaves deciduous, simple, alternate, oval, to 3.5 in (8.75 cm) long, with lobed, irregularly serrated margins; bright green above, greyish below. Fruit is a triangular husk enclosing 3 nuts. Historically exploited for timber. VULNERABLE. ILLUS. P. 49.
RANGE: Santiago to Biobío.

Huala
Nothofagus x leonii
ID: Natural hybrid of *N. glauca* x *N. obliqua*. Tree to 100 ft (30 m) high, with a straight, cylindrical trunk. Sooty-grey bark flakes and cracks with age. Leaves deciduous, simple, alternate, elliptical, 1–4 in (3–10 cm) long, with pleated margin. VULNERABLE.
RANGE: Maule, in *Nothofagus* forest in the Andes and on the coast. NOT ILLUSTRATED.

Coigüe, Coihue
Nothofagus dombeyi
ID: Densely-foliaged, broadly columnar tree to 165 ft (50 m) high. Trunk to 8 ft (2.5 m) in diameter. Dark grey bark cracks and flakes with age. Stratified branches. Perennial, alternate, simple, narrowly ovate leaves, to 2 in (5 cm) long, with finely- and sharply-toothed margins; glossy dark green above, paler green and finely veined below. Fruit is a bristly husk, to 0.25 in (0.6 cm) across, enclosing 3 nuts. Smooth-grained reddish wood is used in heavy construction, boats, piers and for plywood and railroad ties. Dominant *Nothofagus* species of the Valdivian Rainforest, where it is heavily exploited for timber. The species is often a host for the edible sac fungus, Darwin's Bread *(Cyttaria darwinii)*. Largest Chilean broadleaf tree. ILLUS. P. 49.
RANGE: Santiago to Aisén; s Argentina. On wet soils from sea level to the timberline.

Magellanic Coigüe
Coigüe de Magallanes
Nothofagus betuloides
OTHER NAMES: Evergreen Beech, Coihue, Guindo, Ouchpaya, Roble colorado.
ID: Broadly columnar tree to 80 ft (25 m) high. Straight trunk to 6.5 ft (2 m) diameter. Dark-grey bark flakes and cracks with age. Twisted, upright branches. Leaves perennial, simple, alternate, ovate to elliptical, to 1 in (2.5 cm) long; bluntly toothed; glossy dark green above, paler and finely veined below. Fruit is a tiny, bristly husk enclosing three nuts. Strong, pale yellow wood is used in construction and furniture. ILLUS. P. 59.
RANGE: Valdivia to Cape Horn, in Magellanic rainforest.

Coigüe de Chiloé
Nothofagus nitida
ID: Tree to 115 ft (35 m) high, with smooth, dark grey bark. Dense foliage borne on strong, straight branches; branchlets very hirsute. Leaves perennial, simple, alternate, trapezoidal-shaped, to 1.5 in (4 cm) long and 1 in (2.5 cm) wide at the base. Rot-resistant wood used in construction. Grows in association with Canelo *(Drimys winteri)* and Mañío *(Podocarpus* sp.*)*. ILLUS. P. 57.
RANGE: Valdivia to Capitán Prat, Aisén. Mainly in the Coastal Cordillera.

FAMILY ELAEOCARPACEAE
ELAEOCARPS
Maqui, Clon
Aristotelia chilensis
ID: Small tree or ornamental shrub with many branches, to 13 ft (4 m) high. Simple, opposite, serrate, elliptical, perennial or deciduous leaves, to 3 in (8 cm) long. Small, white flowers (Sep–Dec). Fruit is an edible blue berry favored by birds; also made into jam and medicinal wines. ILLUS. P. 48.
RANGE: Coquimbo to Aisén. Cut areas and forest edge in the Central Valley; foothill ravines to 8200 ft (2500 m). Introduced to Juan Fernández.

Patagua, Patahua
Crinodendron patagua
ID: Ornamental tree, 20–25 ft (6–8 m) with an uneven, rounded crown and arching branches. Grey, cracked bark. Leaves are perennial, simple, oval-oblong, leathery, smooth, to 3.5 in (8 cm) long, with serrate margin. Flowers (Oct–Dec) 5-petalled, white, pendulous, bell-shaped. Green, ripening to red, papery seed capsule (Mar). ILLUS. P. 43.
RANGE: Valparaíso to Biobío. In wet soils and along streams, to 4000 ft (1200 m). Introduced to Juan Fernández.
RELATED SPECIES: POLIZÓNTE, *Crinodendron hookeranum*. ILLUS. P. 47.

VIOLALES: FAMILY FLACOURTIACEAE
FLAUCORTIAS
Lilén, Corcolén, Aromo de castilla
Azara spp.
ID: These perennial shrubs all have a single large leaf with one to two small stipules located at the leaf base.

LILÉN, MAQUICILLO, *Azara petiolaris*. Arching, evergreen shrub or tree to 20 ft (6 m) high. Ovate, leathery, alternate, dark green leaves, to 2 in (5 cm) long, with dentate margin. Fragrant, creamy-yellow flowers (Oct–Nov), to 1 in (2.5 cm) across, in catkin-like racemes. Small, round, black berry. Coquimbo to Biobío. Wet slopes of Sclerophyll or Roble-Hualo forest; 1800–5900 ft (540–1800 m). ENDEMIC. ILLUS. P. 43.

LILÉN, *Azara celastrina*. Shrub or small tree to 10 ft (3 m) high. Dark, cracked bark. Perennial, simple, alternate, oval, serrate leaves, to 1.5 in (4 cm) long. Yellow flowers in an axillary corymb. Coquimbo to Biobío. In semi-arid sites, to 3250 ft (0–1000 m).

CORCOLÉN, *Azara integrifolia*. An upright, evergreen shrub or small tree to 26 ft (8 m) high. Diamond-shaped, glossy, alternate, dark green leaves, to 2 in (5 cm), with a rounded stipule at base. Fragrant, yellow, petal-less flowers with showy stamens in mimosa-like clusters (Oct–Nov). Fruit is a rounded blackish berry, with 4 to 5 orange-colored seeds. Valparaíso to Los Lagos. In damp, lowland ravines. ENDEMIC.

AROMO DE CASTILLA, *Azara serrata*. Evergreen shrub to 12 ft (4 m) high, with downy branches. Leaves oval, toothed, glossy, dark green, to 2.5 in (6.25 cm) long. Bears fragrant, dark yellow flowers in dense, spherical, umbel-like corymbs, to 0.75 in (2 cm) across (Sep–Dec). Fruit is a small bluish-white berry. Valparaíso to Chiloé. On lower slopes of the coastal range and to 6500 ft (2000 m) in the Andes. ENDEMIC.

SALICALES: FAMILY SALICACEAE
WILLOWS
Chilean Willow, Sauce chileno
Salix chilensis

ID: Tree to 60 ft (18 m) high, with slightly pendulous branchlets, a straight trunk, and rough, dark grey bark. Leaves simple, alternate, linear-lanceolate, to 3.25 in (8.25 cm), with serrate margin and prominent central vein. Pale yellow flowers held in catkins (Sep–Oct). Fruit is ovoid capsule enclosing many seeds. Bark yields medicinal astringents. NOT ILLUSTRATED.
RANGE: Atacama to Biobío. Riverbanks, lakes, marshes; sometimes in sandy soils.

ERICALES: FAMILY ERICACEAE
HEATHS
Red Crowberry, Diddle-dee, Murtilla
Empetrum rubrum
OTHER NAMES: Brecillo, Uvilla.

ID: Prostrate, evergreen shrub, to 3.25 ft (1 m) high. Small, whitish flowers enclosed by a calyx. Small, round, edible but tasteless, red berries are eaten by sheldgeese and shorebirds. Forms dense mats on dry, well-drained areas, such as hard peat on rocky ridges. Widespread in dwarf shrub heath, feldmark communities, bogs and swamps, in open *Nothofagus* forest and occasionally in the forest understory. ILLUS. P. 61.
RANGE: s Chile, s Argentina, Falklands.

Mountain Berry, Chaurita
Gaultheria antarctica

ID: Prostrate evergreen shrub of *Empetrum* heath and sphagnum bog. Simple, alternate, leather-like leaves, stipules absent. Stems to 7 in (21 cm), rooted at intervals. Small whitish flowers enclosed by pink calyx. Globose, pink or white, berry-like capsule.
RANGE: s Chile, Argentina; Falklands; sea level to 1650 ft (0–500 m). ILLUS. P. 61.

RELATED SPECIES: MUTILLA, CHAURA, SWAMP BERRY, *Gaultheria pumila*. Small pink to white flowers (Dec–Apr). Round, purple to white berry. Biobío to Magallanes. In open, wet, *Nothofagus–Drimys* forest. ILLUS. P. 61. PRICKLY HEATH, MURTA, *Gaultheria (Pernettya) mucronata*. Similar to above. Occurs in s Chile in heath, bogs, sand, *Nothofagus* forest, rock crevices; sea level to 2950 ft (0–900 m). NOT ILLUSTRATED.

FAMILY CUNONIACEAE
CUNONIAS
Southern Hemisphere shrubs, trees or woody climbers that are strongly tanniferous.

Tiaca, Triaca, Quiaca
Caldcluvia paniculata

ID: Ornamental tree to 50 ft (15 m) high, with a rounded crown. Leaves perennial, simple, alternate, elliptical, prominently veined, 2–5 in (5–12.5 cm) long, with serrate margin and acute tip. Small, rounded tufts of sessile, ivory flowers. ILLUS. P. 56.
RANGE: Concepción to Aisén. In wet, shady ravines along rivers, lakes and estuaries, and in temperate rainforests to 3280 ft (1000 m).

Tineo, Palo santo
Weinmannia trichosperma

ID: Tree to 100 ft (30 m) high. Straight trunk. Grey, lightly fissured bark. Leaves perennial, compound, opposite, unequally pinnate, 2–4 in (5–10 cm) long; 5 to 8 pairs of opposite, oblanceolate, serrated leaflets, with a diamond-shaped midrib extension (rachis) between each pair of leaflets. Panicles of creamy white flowers. Numerous colorful reddish-brown capsules, each enclosing four seeds, borne on a one-inch (2.5-cm) raceme. Durable timber. Bark is used in tanning hides. ILLUS. P. 56.
RANGE: Santiago to Magallanes. Rainforests, near rivers and lakes; 0–3000 ft (0–940 m).

ROSALES: FAMILY EUCRYPHIACEAE
EUCRYPHIAS
Single genus of trees or shrubs with unicellular hairs and producing mucilage and tannin.

Ulmo, Muermo
Eucryphia cordifolia

ID: Narrowly columnar, evergreen tree, to

80 ft (25 m) high. Trunk to 6.5 ft (2 m) in diameter. Smooth, thick, grey-brown bark. Leaves oblong, to 3 in (7.5 cm) long, with a heart-shaped base and toothed margin; dark green above, grey and hairy below. White, 4-petalled, fragrant flowers, 2 in (5 cm) across, with numerous pink-tipped stamens (Jan–Mar). Seeds are borne in a small, woody capsule. Durable timber used in buildings, bridges, railways, mine shaft supports, and for panelling, parquet and charcoal. Bark is used for tanning. Bees feeding on the flowers produce a flavorful honey *(miel de ulmo)*. ILLUS. P. 56.
RANGE: Concepción to Chiloé. Temperate rainforests in the Andean and coastal foothills, to 2300 ft (700 m).

Guindo Santo
Eucryphia glutinosa
ID: Small, columnar, deciduous tree to 17 ft (5 m), with smooth, reddish-brown bark. Shiny, dark green, compound leaves, to 2.5 in (6.25 cm) long; 3 to 5 leaflets with toothed margins. Fall color is orange to red. White, 4-petalled, fragrant flowers (Jan–Feb), to 2 in (5 cm) across, with yellow stamens and crimson anthers. Small, woody capsule with 12 valves, each with 2 to 3 seeds. ILLUS. P. 48.
RANGE: O'Higgins to Biobío. Uncommon in wet ravines and along rivers in Andean foothills; 800–2950 ft (250–900 m).

FAMILY ROSACEAE
ROSES AND ALLIES
Bollén, Huayu
Kageneckia oblonga
ID: Tree to 50 ft (15 m) high. Dark grey trunk. Twisted branches. Leaves perennial, simple, alternate, obovate, to 4 in (10 cm) long, greyish-green above, paler below, with glandular-serrate margin. ILLUS. P. 43.
RANGE: Coquimbo to Biobío, in mixed sclerophyll forest in Andean and coastal foothills.

Queñoa, Queñoa de altura
Polylepis tarapacana
ID: Tree or shrub to 12 ft (3.5 m) high, with open crown, reddish scaling bark, and twisted branches. Perennial leaves, trifolate compound, with leaflets less than 1 in (2 cm) long; dark green above, dull white below. Tiny, solitary flowers. Fruit is a winged seed. Wood is used for firewood and light construction. VULNERABLE. ILLUS. P. 39.
RANGE: Arica to Tarapacá; Peru, Bolivia; 13,000–15,500 ft (4000–4800 m).
RELATED SPECIES: *Polylepis rugulosa* has trifoliate leaflets with a dentate margin. Andes of ne Chile, Peru, Bolivia, nw Argentina; 9850–13,800 ft (3000–4200 m). ILLUS. P. 39.

Quillay
Quillaja saponaria
ID: Tree to 50 ft (15 m). Trunk to 3.25 ft (1 m) in diameter. Peeling brown bark. Perennial, simple, alternate, elliptical, shiny, light green leaves, to 1.5 (4 cm) long, with a slightly dentate margin. Small white flowers with five spatulate petals and ten long stamens; blooms at the end of spring. Woody, star-shaped fruit with five chambers enclosing many winged seeds. The bark, called *Palo de Panamá*, contains saponin that is used in shampoos and laundry soap. ILLUS. P. 42.
RANGE: Coquimbo to Biobío. In the mountains and Central Valley; sea level to 5000 ft (0–1600 m). VULNERABLE in Region IV.

PROTEALES: FAMILY PROTEACEAE
PROTEAS
Notro, Firebush
Embothrium coccineum
OTHER NAMES: Ciruelillo, Fosforito, Magu, Trumún.
ID: Forest tree or shrub to 35 ft (10 m), with a shaggy crown, reddish flexible branchlets, straight trunk and thin grey bark. Leaves perennial, simple to whorled, obovate to elliptical, to 4 in (10 cm) long, bright green above and pale green below. Corymbs of bright red, fuchsia-like flowers, to 1.5 in (3.75 cm) long, form at tips of branches. Dehiscent pod, to 1.5 in (3.75 cm) long, encloses many brown, winged seeds. Yellow to chestnut wood is used in woodcarving. Planted as a garden ornamental. ILLUS. P. 59.
RANGE: Biobío to Magallanes. Common.

Avellano, Gevuín
Gevuina avellana
ID: Tree to 60 ft (18 m) high, with a rounded crown and dense branches. Straight cylindrical trunk. Thin, grey bark marked with

white spots. Leaves perennial, alternate, compound, unequally pinnate, 3–14 in (7.5–35 cm) long, with 9 to 11 smooth, ovate leaflets, to 2 in (5 cm) long, with serrate margins, and often unequally divided at the base; bright green above, pale green below. Creamy-white flowers, with protruding red stamens, borne in axillary racemes, 4–6 in (10–15 cm) long. Rounded, edible nut with a pointed tip, 0.75 in (2 cm) long, green ripening to red or purple-black at maturity; appears at same time as flowers. Planted as an ornamental. Finely veined wood used for carvings and musical instruments. Nuts are eaten raw, toasted or ground. ILLUS. P. 56.
RANGE: Maule to the Islas Guaitecas, Aisén. In foothill forests.

Fuinque, Romerillo
Lomatia ferruginea
ID: Tree to 25 ft (8 m) high, with long branches, narrow trunk and thin, dark bark. Leaves perennial, compound, bipinnate, fern-like, to 8 in (20 cm) long; 8 to 12 pairs of opposite leaflets to 3.5 in (8.75 cm) long. Asymetric, 4-petalled flowers are greenish yellow with rosy centers. Blackish pod, to 2 in (5 cm) long, encloses numerous, rough, obovate, brown, winged seeds. Planted as an ornamental for its fern-like foliage and attractive flowers. Finely grained wood used in woodworking. ILLUS. P. 59.
RANGE: Biobío to Magallanes. In woodland; sea level to 3700 ft (0–1125 m).

Radal
Lomatia hirsuta
ID: Tree to 50 ft (15 m) high, with a rounded crown, long flexible branches. Fairly narrow trunk. Dark grey, fairly rough bark. Leaves perennial, simple, alternate, ovate-elliptical, to 5 in (12 cm) long, with a serrate margin; lustrous dark green above, paler below, with prominent veining. Axillary racemes of small greenish-yellow, asymetric flowers with orange-red stamens. Persistent, dark brown pod, to 1.5 in (3.75 cm) long, enclosing many dark brown seeds. Finely grained wood used in fine furniture. Bark contains tannin that yields a coffee color in hides. ENDANGERED in Coquimbo. ILLUS. P. 48.

RANGE: Coquimbo to Chiloé. Especially in Valdivian rainforest, on foothill slopes to 4000 ft (1200 m).

HALORAGIDALES: GUNNERACEAE FAMILY
GUNNERAS
Southern Hemisphere perennial herbs, often gigantic, with creeping rhizomes.

Nalca, Pangue, Gunnera
Gunnera tinctoria
ID: Perennial shrub, to 6.5 ft (2 m) high, with thick, semi-subterranean, blood-red stems covered with brown stipules. Palmately-lobed, alternate, dark green leaves, 2–5 ft (0.6–1.5 m) across, covered in fine hairs. Blood red leaf pedicels, to 5 ft (1.5 m) long, bear small stipules. Reddish spike, to 3 ft (1 m) high, with many small spikes bearing inconspicuous, apetalous flowers (Oct–Jan). Fruit is a small, oval, reddish-orange drupe. Planted as an ornamental. ILLUS. P. 57.
RANGE: Coquimbo to Magallanes; Argentina, Peru, Ecuador, Colombia, Venezuela. Shady, wet places, including bogs, swamps, marshes.

Pig Vine, Palacoazir, Gunnera
Gunnera magellanica
OTHER NAME: Devil's Strawberry.
ID: Creeping perennial herb to 6 in (15 cm) high. Dark green leaves, to 2.5 in (6.25 cm) across, with crenulated margins and prominent veins. Reddish stems, to 4 in (10 cm) long, covered in fine, pale red hairs. Inconspicuous flowers followed by erect clusters of bright red drupes. ILLUS. P. 61.
RANGE: Río Ñuble, Maule, to Magallanes; also Argentina, Peru, Ecuador, Colombia. Bogs, marshes and oceanic tundra.

FAMILY LEGUMINOSAE (FABACEAE)
LEGUMES
This family of trees, shrubs, vines and herbs that bear bean pods is divided into Mimosaceae, Caesalpinaceae and Papilinaceae.

MIMOSACEAE: Spiny, woody plants, usually shrubs or small trees, that are widespread in the dry tropics and subtropics. Small flowers are borne in racemes. The genera *Acacia*, *Mimosa* and *Prosopis* contain the mesquites of the New World deserts.

Espino, Cavén, Churque
Acacia caven

ID: Small thorn tree, 6–20 ft (2–6 m) high, with twisted trunk; deciduous, bipinnately compound leaves, to 2 in (5 cm) long, with 12 to 20 pairs of tiny leaflets. Small yellow flowers (Aug–Oct) with 4 to 5 tiny petals with long stamens form spherical heads, to 0.25 in (0.6 cm) across. Fruit is a dark, hard bean pod. Dominant in dry, poor soils of the *espinal*. Hardwood is used for carvings, firewood and charcoal. ILLUS. P. 42.

RANGE: Atacama to Araucanía. Semi-arid slopes of Coastal Range, Central Valley and Andes, to 4000 ft (1200 m).

Algarrobo, Algarrobo chileno
Prosopis chilensis

ID: Grows as an isolated tree to 33 ft (10 m) high; spreading crown and flexible branches. Trunk to 24 in (60 cm) in diameter, with wrinkled reddish-brown bark. Each stem node has two spines, to 2.5 in (6.25 cm) long. Leaves deciduous, compound, bipinnate, feathery, with 10 to 20 leaflets. Catkins of small, pale yellow to pale green flowers (Oct–Dec). Fruit is a brown, slightly curved pod, 2.5–6 in (6.25–15 cm) long, with sweet tasting, brownish-yellow, oval beans. Pods are used for animal fodder. ILLUS. P. 42.

RANGE: Atacama to Maule. Common in the Central Valley; s Peru, Bolivia, n Argentina.

Tamarugo
Prosopis tamarugo

ID: Tree to 50 ft (15 m), with an irregular rounded crown. Buttressed trunk to 3 ft (1 m) in diameter. Rough, fissured, dark bark. Flexible, twisted, reddish-brown branches bear pairs of thorns, to 2 in (6 cm) long. Leaves deciduous, compound, bipinnate, alternate, to 2 in (5 cm) long, with 6 to 12 pairs of leaflets. Catkins of pale flowers (Sep–Dec). Stubby, shiny, yellowish, curved pod, to 2 in (5 cm) long, enclosing 8 to 10 beans. Nearly exterminated in the nitrate mining period, when it was harvested for firewood and fodder for mule trains transporting ore across the Atacama. ILLUS. P. 35.

RANGE: Arica to Tarapacá, especially on the Pampa del Tamarugal.

Argentine Mesquite, Algarrobo blanco
Prosopis alba

ID: Tree to 50 ft (15 m) high, with a full rounded crown. Narrow trunk, with grey, striated bark. Sinuous branches have a few small thorns. Leaves deciduous, compound, bipinnate, alternate, to 4 in (10 cm) long, with 20 to 25 tiny leaflets. Racemes of small yellowish flowers (Nov–Dec). Fruit is a brown pod, 5–10 in (12–25 cm) long, enclosing 15 to 30 beans. ILLUS. P. 35.

RANGE: Antofagasta, near desert aquifers; also Peru, Bolivia, Argentina.

CAESALPINIACEAE: Tropical and subtropical species planted for their showy flowers.

Tara
Caesalpinia spinosa

ID: Small ornamental tree to 15 ft (5 m) high, with rounded crown, spindly trunk, and rough grey bark. Short, stiff, striated branches, with strong, short, conical spines. Perennial, compound, bipinnate leaves, with 5 to 8 pair of shiny, sessile, elliptical leaflets, to 1 in (2 cm) long. Racemes of golden yellow, sweetpea-like flowers. Flattened, wine-red pod, to 3.5 in (8.75 cm) long, enclosing 7 round peas. Pods and beans harvested for fodder and to obtain *goma*, a starch used to thicken ice cream. ILLUS. P. 35.

RANGE: Arica to Coquimbo, in arid to semi-arid habitats.

PAPILIONACEAE: Leguminous herbs, shrubs and trees whose flower corollas are shaped like butterflies.

Espinillo, Jarrilla, Varilla brava
Adesmia sp.

ID: Small, spiny shrub to 5 ft (1.5 m) high. Leaves alternate, compound, with small oval leaflets arranged in pairs. Yellow, papilionate flowers (Aug–Nov). Flattened pod is covered with long hairs. ILLUS. P. 39.

RANGE: North-central and central Chile, on warm, dry slopes.

Chañar
Geoffroea decorticans

ID: Tree to 23 ft (7 m) high. Twisted and branched trunk with grey, peeling bark. Sinuous branches, with branchlets having a sharp terminal spine. Leaves deciduous, compound, unequally pinnate, alternate or clustered, with 5 to 11 oblong leaflets, to 1 in (2.5 cm) long. Small, yellowish-orange flowers with reddish streaks. Smooth, reddish, ovoid drupe, to 1.25 in (3 cm) long, enclosing a single edible seed. Yellowish wood is used for furniture. Bark and leaves are used in local medicines. ILLUS. P. 35.

RANGE: Arica to Coquimbo; Peru, Bolivia, Argentina. Arid places to 7500 ft (2300 m).

Mayu
Sophora macrocarpa
ID: Shrub to 10 ft (3 m) high, with branched, dark brown trunk. Perennial, compound leaves, with 15 to 21 unequally pinnate, oval leaflets. Clusters of yellow flowers (Aug–Dec). Fruit is a string-of-beads pod, 4–6 in (10–15 cm) long. ILLUS. P. 43.

RANGE: Coquimbo to Malleco. On open foothill slopes and matorral, and in understory of Hualo forest in the Andes.

RELATED SPECIES: TOROMIRO, *Sophora toromiro*. Small tree to 7 ft (2 m), with a twisted trunk that is branched at the base. Perennial, compound leaves, to 2 in (5 cm) long, with 7 to 21 oval leaflets. Yellow flowers. ENDEMIC to Easter Island where it became extinct; reintroduced recently. ILLUS. P. 69.

MAYU-MONTE, *Sophora fernandeziana*. Tree to 15 ft (5 m). Branched trunk. Dark brown, striated bark. Leaves perennial, unequally pinnate, compound, with 15 to 23 elliptical leaflets. Racemes of yellow flowers. ENDEMIC to Isla Masatierra, Juan Fernández.

MAYU-MONTE, *Sophora masafuerana*. ENDEMIC to Isla Masafuera, Juan Fernández.

PELÚ, *Sophora microphylla*. Tree to 30 ft (10 m). Maule to Aisén, sea level to 1650 ft (500 m).

MYRTALES: FAMILY MYRTACEAE
MYRTLES
Aromatic trees and shrubs that grow worldwide in the tropics and subtropics.

Arrayán, Palo colorado, Temu
Luma apiculata
ID: Broadly spreading tree to 65 ft (20 m) high with rounded crown, sinuous branches and dense foliage. Bright cinnamon-orange bark, that flakes off to show white ovals when freshly exposed. Leaves perennial, simple, opposite, almost sessile, broadly elliptical, short-pointed, to 1 in (2.5 cm) long; bronze-purple when young, glossy dark green at maturity. Small, fragrant, white, urn-shaped, 4-petalled flowers with many white stamens (Dec–May). Rounded, fleshy red to purple-black berry, to 0.35 in (1 cm) in diameter. ILLUS. P. 56.

RANGE: Valparaíso to Aisén; also Argentina. In humid forests, especially along streams; sea level to 3250 ft (0–1000 m).

Luma, Palo Madroño, Reloncaví
Amomyrtus luma
ID: Broadly spreading tree to 65 ft (20 m) high, with shaggy, reddish-brown bark. Leaves are perennial, simple, opposite, elliptical, pointed, aromatic, to 2 in (5 cm) long. Small, white, fragrant flowers (Sep–Feb), with 5 fused sepals, 5 petals and many stamens. Fruit *(cauchao)* is a red to purple, round berry, to 0.4 in (1 cm) in diameter, enclosed in a 5-lobed calyx. Fruit is used to make jam. Wood is used for tool handles.

RANGE: Maule to Aisén; also Argentina. In rainforests and along wooded riverbanks.

RELATED SPECIES: MELI, *Amomyrtus meli*. Pyramidal-shaped tree to 65 ft (20 m) high, with bark mottled in red and cream. Leaves are perennial, opposite, elliptical, aromatic, 0.75–2 in (2–5 cm) long. White, fragrant, 5-petalled flowers (Oct–Dec), with prominent stamens and 5-lobed calyx. Small, dark violet berry with 3 seeds. Biobío to Chiloé. Along rivers and streams in the Valdivian and Siempreverde forest.

LUMA DEL NORTE, *Legrandia concinna*. Tree to 30 ft (10 m), with narrow trunk. Reddish to cream exfoliating bark. New branches are reddish and squared. Leaves perennial, simple, opposite, oblong, aromatic, to 3 in (7.5 cm) long; lustrous dark green above, light green with prominent veins below. Small, white, 4-petalled flowers with many stamens (Dec–Feb). Fruit is a small, round, red to purple berry. Maule to Biobío. In Andean foothills to 3250 ft (1000 m).

Carza, Pacama, Huacán
Myrica pavonis

ID: Tree to 30 ft (10 m) high with twisted, pendant branches. Rounded crown. Sinuous trunk with fissured grey bark. Leaves perennial, aromatic, alternate, simple, linear-lanceolate, to 3.5 in (8.75 cm) long; dark green above, yellowish green and resinous below. Small, round, dark red drupe.
RANGE: Arica to Tarapacá; Ecuador, Peru; 3250–7200 ft (1000–2200 m).

GENUS MYRCEUGENIA: A combination of the *Myrcia* and *Eugenia* genera found in Chile, Juan Fernández, Argentina, Brazil. Leaves are bright green, opposite and aromatic.

Pitra, Picha-picha
Myrceugenia planipes
ID: Small tree to 25 ft (8 m) high. Smooth grey bark. Leaves lustrous green, perennial, opposite, elliptical, to 1 in (2.5 cm) long, with entire margin, pointed tip and prominent veins. Small white flowers (Jan–Feb). Round, purple berry. NOT ILLUSTRATED.
RANGE: Biobío to Aisén; Argentina. Siempreverde forest; 1300–2300 ft (400–700 m).
RELATED SPECIES: LUMA BLANCA, *Myrceugenia chrysocarpa*; Malleco to Chiloé; rainforests. LUMA DE MASAFUERA, *Myrceugenia schulzei*; Isla Masafuera, Juan Fernández. LUMA DE MASATIERRA, *Myrceugenia fernandeziana*; Isla Masatierra, Juan Fernández; coastal and hillside forests. ILLUS. P. 67.

Tepú
Tepualia stipularis
ID: Small shrub or tree, 10–25 ft (3–8 m) high. Dense foliage; twisted trunk, with a peeling, red to grey bark. Leaves opposite, ovate to lanceolate, to 0.5 in (1.25 cm), dotted with aromatic glands. Tiny, white, 5-petalled flowers (Jan–Mar). Fruit is a tiny, woody capsule. Cut for firewood. ILLUS. P. 59.
RANGE: ENDEMIC. Maule to Magallanes. In very wet areas, rainforest, sphagnum bogs. Forms dense forest understory.

Murta, Murtilla, Uñi, Mortillo
Ugni molinae
ID: Shrub to 6.5 ft (2 m) high. Leaves bright green, shiny, aromatic, opposite, ovate, to 1 in (2.5 cm) long. Small, pendulous, bell-shaped, white to pink flowers have 5 inward-curved petals and 5 outward-turned sepals (Dec–Feb). White berry ripens to rosy-red.
RANGE: Maule to Los Lagos. In wet soils in cleared and disturbed habitats, pine plantations and forest edge.
RELATED SPECIES: MURTA BLANCA, *Ugni candollei*; Maule to Valdivia. ILLUS. P. 57.

MYRTALES: FAMILY ONAGRACEAE
FUCHSIAS AND ALLIES
Herbs and shrubs having epidermal oil cells.

Magellanic Fuchsia, Chilco
Fuchsia magellanica
ID: Shrub to 7 ft (2 m) high. Elliptical-ovate, pointed leaves, to 2 in (5 cm) long. Flowers (Sep–Apr) are red to violet, bell-shaped, pendulous, to 1.5 in (3.8 cm) long; pollinated by hummingbirds. ILLUS. P. 59.
RANGE: Maule to Magallanes. In *Nothofagus* and *Drimys* coastal forest.

CELASTRALES: FAMILY CELASTRACEAE
BITTERSWEETS AND ALLIES
Trees and shrubs whose leaves contain alkaloids, including caffeine.

Maitén, Mayten
Maytenus boaria
ID: Graceful tree to 50 ft (15 m) high, with a rounded feathery crown. Thin, pendulous branchlets. Thick trunk. Cracked dark bark. Leaves perennial, simple, alternate, lanceolate, to 2.4 in (6 cm) long, with a lightly serrate margin. Small, green axillary flowers (Aug–Dec). Small, smooth, 2-valved, 2-lobed capsule, enclosing 1 to 2 oval seeds covered with a blood red aril. White wood with red heartwood used in woodworking. Foliage used for fodder. ILLUS. P. 48.
RANGE: Atacama to Chiloé. On dry sites.
RELATED SPECIES: LEÑA DURA, MAITÉN DE MAGALLANES, *Maytenus magellanica*. Small tree to 17 ft (5 m) high. Many upright, reddish-brown branches. Grey bark. Leaves perennial, simple, alternate, lanceolate or elliptical, pointed, to 1.5 in (3.75 cm) long, with serrate margin. Clusters of 5-petalled red flowers (Oct–Dec). Fruit is an oval,

2-valved capsule that opens to reveal two dark red seeds covered with a yellow aril. Cut for firewood *(leña)*. Biobío to Cape Horn. Forests of both cordilleras; sea level to 4250 ft (0–1300 m). ILLUS. P. 59.

CELASTRALES: FAMILY AEXTOXICACEAE
OLIVILLO
This family consists of a single tree species, native to Chile, which has peltate scales on the twigs, flowers and lower side of the leaf.

Olivillo
Aextoxicon punctatum
ID: Tree to 65 ft (20 m) high, with rounded crown. Sinuous, unbranched trunk. Pale grey bark. Leaves perennial, opposite, simple, oblong-elliptical, 1.25–3.75 in (3.2–9 cm) long; dark green and smooth on top, pale brown and pitted beneath; cinnamon-colored leafstalk. Racemes of 5-petalled yellow flowers (Apr–Dec). Small, elliptical, purple drupes. Beautiful light chestnut, veined wood is used for panelling, floors and furniture. VULNERABLE. ILLUS. P. 56.
RANGE: Coquimbo to Chiloé. In protected areas; sea level to 3250 ft (0–1000 m).

SAPINDALES: FAMILY ANACARDIACEAE
SUMACS
Trees, shrubs or woody vines with resins, often with poisonous or allergenic bark and foliage.

Litre
Lithrea caustica
ID: Small tree or shrub to 15 ft (5 m) high, with dense, rounded crown. Branched, twisted trunk; grey, shaggy bark. Leaves perennial, simple, alternate, ovate-elliptical, to 2.25 in (6.25 cm) long, with an undulating, entire margin, and pale yellow veins that exude a caustic sap. Slightly pendant panicles of very small, pale flowers (Feb–Mar). Clusters of small, flattened, white drupes with a thin brown husk. Veined wood used for carvings. ILLUS. P. 42.
RANGE: Coquimbo to Biobío. In matorral and dry coastal forest.

Peppertree, Pimiento
Schinus molle
OTHER NAMES: Pimentero, Molle, Pimiento bolviano, Peruvian Mastic-tree.
ID: Tree to 80 ft (25 m) high, with a dense, rounded crown. Pendulous branches. Stout trunk with dark grey resinous bark, lightly scaled with pale grey and rust. Perennial, compound, pinnate, alternate, aromatic, feathery leaves, with 10 to 39 sessile, lanceolate leaflets, to 1.5 in (3.75 cm) long. Small, greenish-white flowers in panicles, to 8 in (20 cm) long. Clusters of small, reddish, round, spicy and aromatic drupes. Ornamental tree of town plazas. ILLUS. P. 35.
RANGE: Arica to Atacama. In oases and quebradas in the interior desert.

Molle
Schinus latifolius
ID: Tree 13–30 ft (4–10 m) high; dense, round crown. Twisted trunk with flaking dark grey or brown bark. Leaves perennial, simple, alternate, elliptical-oblong, pointed, to 2 in (5 cm) long; sinous-dentate margin; prominent veins. Racemes of small, round, cream to red drupes (Jan). ILLUS. P. 42.
RANGE: Coquimbo to Biobío, mainly in the Coastal Range on seaward slopes, in low coastal scrub and dry hills.
RELATED SPECIES: HUINGÁN, *Schinus polygamus*. Tree to 13 ft (4 m) high. Twisted trunk has spiny branches emerging at the base; peeling grey bark. Perennial, simple, spatulate leaves, to 1.5 in (3.5 cm) long, with entire to lightly serrate margin. Fruit is a small, round drupe, violet to black in maturity. Sometimes planted as a living fence. Atacama to Valdivia, in poor soils of the matorral and Central Valley. ILLUS. P. 43.

APIALES: FAMILY ARALIACEAE
ARALIAS

Sauco del diablo, Sauco cimarrón
Pseudopanax laetevirens
ID: Densely branched tree to 25 ft (8 m) high, with rounded crown. Spindly trunk with smooth, ash-grey bark. Perennial, palmately compound leaves on a long stem; 3 to 5 lanceolate leaflets, 1.5–3.5 in (3.75–8.75 cm) long, with serrate margin. Red, 5-petalled flowers held in umbels to 3 in (7.5 cm) long. Small, greenish-blue ripening to intense blue berry, encloses 4 to 5 chestnut-colored seeds. Planted as an ornamental. ILLUS. P. 59.

UMBELLIFERAS AND CACTI

RANGE: Maule to Magallanes. In *Drimys–Nothofagus betuloides* forest in the Coastal Range, to 4250 ft (1300 m).

APIALES: FAMILY UMBELLIFERAE
UMBELLIFERAS
Llareta, Yareta
Azorella sp.
ID: Bright green, resinous cushion-plant. Forms broad, irregular, hard mounds about 12 in (30 cm) high and 10 ft (3 m) across. Very slow-growing on rocky slopes; large specimens composed of hundreds of small individual plants may be more than a century old. Umbels of tiny yellow flowers borne on top of the cushion. Used for tinder and folk remedies. ILLUS. P. 39.
RANGE: Arica to Atacama; rocky slopes and barren ground on the Altiplano of n Chile, Peru and Bolivia above 10,000 ft (3200 m).
RELATED SPECIES: BALSAM BOG, LLARETA, *Bolax gummifera*. Resinous cushion plant with stellate hairs and closely-imbricated, aromatic leaves. Umbels of 3 to 20 greenish-white flowers borne on the cushion's surface (Oct–Feb). Aisén to Magallanes. On cliffs, rocks, open scrub, heath, and well-drained soils at forest edge to 2950 ft (900 m).

FAMILY CACTACEAE
CACTI
Spiny stemmed succulents whose spines are highly modified leaves.

Candelabra Cactus
Cacto candelabro, Quisco candelabro
Browningia (Azureocereus) candelaris
ID: Erect, tree-like cactus to 16.5 ft (5 m), with arms that branch from near the crown like a candelabra. Tubercled ribs produce round areoles with long spines on lower part of trunk. Funnel-shaped flowers (rarely seen); spherical green fruits. ILLUS. P. 35.
RANGE: Andes east of Arica; 6900–8500 ft (2100–2600 m).

Cardón
Echinopsis (Helianthocereus) atacamensis
ID: Tree-like columnar cactus, to 23 ft (7 m) high. Single or branched, cylindrical stems have many deep ribs with brown areoles, each bearing 30 to 40 spines, to 4 in (10 cm) long. Dried skeleton is used in construction and crafts. ILLUS. P. 35.
RANGE: Arica to Antofagasta; in the Andes, 4250–8500 ft (1300–2600 m). Widespread east of Calama and San Pedro de Atacama; also Argentina and Bolivia.

Quisco
Echinopsis (Trichocereus) chiloensis
ID: Numerous, upright, cylindrical stems to 23 ft (7 m) high. Spines to 2 in (5 cm) long cover the stems. Solitary, white, hermaphroditic flowers (Oct–Nov), to 4 in (20 cm) across. Edible fruit called *guillaves*. Dried skeleton is made into a musical instrument (a rainstick, *palo de agua*) by filling the interior with rice, beans, gravel and nails. ILLUS. P. 42.
RANGE: ENDEMIC. Coquimbo to Maule; on dry hillsides. Coastal in the north; inland south of La Serena.

Eulychnia
Eulychnia (Cereus) iquiquensis
ID: Tall, columnar, tree-like cactus to 23 ft (7 m) high, with a stem to 10 in (25 cm) in diameter. Grey-green with rounded, warty ribs, narrowly furrowed between. White, wooly, closely set aureoles, each with 12 to 15 spines, to 0.5 in (1.25 cm) long. White to pink flowers, to 3 in (7.5 cm). ILLUS. P. 35.
RANGE: Atacama and Coquimbo. Common in n Chile; sea level to 3150 ft (0–960 m).

Opuntia
Opuntia (Tephrocactus) sp.
ID: Genus with diverse species with stems and branches consisting of chains of ribless joints that may be globular, cylindrical or flattened. The SPINELESS PRICKLY PEAR is raised for goat fodder. The small, ground-hugging CHOLLA has areoles armed with tiny barbed bristles that are easily detached and readily penetrate the skin. ILLUS. P. 35.
RANGE: Arica to Santiago, on arid sites.

Copiapoa
Copiapoa sp.
ID: Genus of 10 to 20 species of slow-growing, mound-forming cacti. Stems have warty ribs and spiny aureoles. Funnel-shaped, diurnal flowers, usually yellow, emerge from dense,

wooly crowns. Turban-shaped green fruit; glossy dark brown seeds. ILLUS. PP. 35, 110.
RANGE: Arica to Coquimbo, mainly in the lomas formations along the desert coast.

FAMILY VERBENACEAE
VERBENAS
Juan Bueno
Rhaphithamnus venustus
ID: Tree to 30 ft (10 m) high. Rounded crown. Dense branches with spines to 1 in (2.5 cm). Cylindrical trunk with grey bark. Perennial, simple, opposite, oblong, dark green, waxy leaves, 0.5–2 in (1.25–5 cm) long, with entire margin. Bluish-red tubular flowers (Oct–Feb) are pollinated by hummingbirds. Tiny, round, blue-violet drupe. ILLUS. P. 67.
RANGE: Juan Fernández Archipelago; on wet slopes to 1800 ft (550 m).
RELATED SPECIES: ARRAYÁN MACHO, REPU. *Rhaphithamnus spinosus*. Tree to 20 ft (6 m). Coquimbo to Aisén. In Andean and coastal foothills to 3100 ft (950 m). ILLUS. P. 48.

SCROPHULARIALES: FAMILY SCROPHULARIACEAE
FIGWORTS
Native Box, Wiengu
Hebe elliptica
ID: Evergreen shrub to 10 ft (3 m) high. Elliptical, opposite, shiny, dark green leaves, 0.5–1 in (1.2–2.5 cm) long; opposite, alternating pairs give a squared look to each branch. White flowers crowded together at tips of new growth (Nov–Feb). ILLUS. P. 61.
RANGE: Valdivia to Cape Horn; s Argentina, Falklands, New Zealand. On coastal cliffs.

ASTERALES: FAMILY COMPOSITAE (ASTERACEAE)
SUNFLOWERS AND ALLIES
Fachine, Mata verde
Chiliotrichum diffusum
ID: Bushy evergreen shrub, 3–5 ft (1–1.5 m) high. Dark green, elliptical-lanceolate leaves are hairy on underside. White, daisy-like flowers, to 1 in (2.5 cm) across. Dominant shrub at edge of evergreen and deciduous *Nothofagus* forest. ILLUS. P. 63.
RANGE: Valdivia to Magallanes; s Argentina; sea level to 1300 ft (400 m).

Tola, Tolita
Baccharis sp., *Parastrephia* sp., *Senecio* sp.
ID: Several genera of plants are called *tola*. They are typically low shrubs with small, resinous leaves. ILLUS. P. 39.
RANGE: Andes from Arica-Parinacota to Atacama. On the Puna and Altiplano.

MONOCOTYLEDONS: CLASS LILIOPSIDA

ARECALES: FAMILY ARECACEAE
PALMS
Tropical to warm temperate species of slender trees or stout shrubs with an unbranched trunk and terminal crown of large leaves.

Chilean Palm, Palma chilena, Kan-Kán
Jubaea chilensis
OTHER NAMES: Chilean Wine Palm, Honey Palm, Palmera de coquitos.
ID: Slow-growing to 50 ft (15 m) high, with a robust, erect, scarred, cracked grey trunk, usually swollen in the midsection. Pinnate, oblong-ovate fronds, to 15 ft (5 m) long, consist of many linear, rigid, folded, yellow-green to deep green leaflets. Small, bowl-shaped, dull maroon and yellow flowers borne in panicles, to 5 ft (1.5 m) long. Woody, ovoid fruit *(coquitos)*, to 2 in (5 cm) diameter. Sap is used to make palm honey *(miel de palma)*; nuts are used in pastries and confections. VULNERABLE. ILLUS. P. 43.
RANGE: Formerly widespread in the Central Valley; now found mainly in small groves in Valparaíso and the O'Higgins Region. World's southernmost palm.

Juania Palm, Chonta
Juania australis
ID: Palm to 50 ft (15 m) high. Straight, cylindrical trunk with prominent, brown, oblique leaf scars. About 12 to 20 pinnately compound fronds, to 5 ft (1.5 m) long, with 80 to 85 leaflets per side. Pendant flower racemes, to 3 ft (1 m) long, develop from leaf axils that are guarded by persistant green bracts (spathes). Fruit is a small, round drupe, green when immature and reddish-orange when mature. ILLUS. P. 67.
RANGE: ENDEMIC to Isla Masatierra, Juan Fernández; 625–3000 ft (190–900 m).

CYPERALES: FAMILY POACEAE
BAMBOOS AND ALLIES

Chilean Bamboo, Colihue, Culeú
Chusquea culeou
ID: Green to yellowish-brown canes to 18 ft (5.5 m) long and 1.5 in (4 cm) in diameter. Prominent nodes, 4–6 in (10–15 cm) apart. Creamy white sheaths contrast with bright olive-green new culms (stems). Pale green, lanceolate leaves, to 8 in (20 cm) long. Flowers at 10 to 15 years (Oct–Mar), after which the plant dies. Grows in thickets, forming dense, almost impassable undergrowth. Small, edible stalk base. ILLUS. P. 51.
RANGE: Maule to Aisén; forests and around lakes to 47°S; also Argentina.

Chilean Weeping Bamboo, Quila
Chusquea quila
ID: Semi-climbing bamboo. Green to brown flexible canes to 18 ft (5.5 m) long and 1.5 in (4 cm) in diameter. Pale green, lanceolate leaves with serrate margin, to 8 in (20 cm) long, arranged in a "bottle-brush" fashion around the culm (stem) nodes. Flowers at 10 to 30 years, after which the plant dies. Aggressive growth; forms dense secondary undergrowth called *quilantales*. Canes are used for handicrafted furniture. Fruit was eaten by indigenous tribes. ILLUS. P. 48.
RANGE: Valparaíso to Chiloé. In humid soils in the rainforest understory.
RELATED SPECIES: QUILA ENANA, *Chusquea nigricans*. 20 in (50 cm). Hard, stiff, sharp-edged, lanceolate leaves. Valdivia to Magallanes. Peat bogs and forest understory. Most southern bamboo.

BROMELIALES: FAMILY BROMELIACEAE
BROMELIADS
Tropical epiphytes with stiff, succulent leaves that are edged with hooked thorns.

Chagual
Puya chilensis
ID: Bromeliad to 10 ft (3 m) high. Leaves very narrow, glaucous, recurved, to 3 ft (1 m) long, with sharply hooked margins. Showy greenish-yellow flowers, 2 in (5 cm) across, sessile or nearly so, in a tall, branching, bracted inflorence (Sep–Nov). Leaf fiber used for making fish nets. Plants can trap mammals in the recurved spines. ILLUS. P. 42.
RANGE: Hillsides in central Chile.
RELATED SPECIES: CHAGUAL, *Puya berteroana*, has deep metallic blue-green flowers and orange, pollen-tipped stamens. Ranges in central Chile. ILLUS. P. 42.

Tillandsia
Tillandsia landbeckii
ID: Terrestrial bromeliad with pale greenish-grey, lanceolate, basal leaves. Bears orange to red tubular flowers at the tip of a thin stalk, to 24 in (60 cm) high. ILLUS. P. 35.
RANGE: Lomas formations and sand dunes on coastal slopes, mainly outside of Iquique; 2800–4000 ft (850–1200 m).

LILIALES: FAMILY SMILACACEAE (PHILESIACEAE)
COPIHUE AND ALLIES

Chilean Bellflower, Copihue
Lapageria rosea
OTHER NAMES: Voqui-copihue, Copihuero, Nupo, Copiu, Pepino.
ID: Chile's national flower. Woody, twining climber or creeper to 10 ft (3 m), spreading slowly by suckers. Ovate, dark green leaves, to 5 in (13 cm) long. Flowers bell-shaped, pink to red, 4-petalled, to 3.5 in (8.75 cm) long, borne singly or in twos or threes in the upper leaf axils. Branches of flowers and fern leaves are sold locally in autumn markets. Fruit is edible. ILLUS. P. 57.
RANGE: Valparaíso to Los Lagos. Damp sites in the Coastal Range and Central Valley.

Coicopihue
Philesia magellanica
ID: Perennial, leafy shrub, growing 16–36 in (40–90 cm) high without support; to 10 ft (3 m) or higher as a climbing vine. Oblong, alternate, shiny dark green leaves, to 1 in (2.5 cm) long. Flowers (Nov–Apr) are bell-shaped, pink, rarely white, to 2 in (5 cm) long, and isolated at the branch tips. Separated from Copihue by 3-petalled flowers. Small, greenish-brown berry. ILLUS. P. 57.
RANGE: Valdivia to Magallanes. Especially common in Chiloé and in rainforests in the Coastal Range and Andean foothills; sea level to 350 ft (0–100 m).

BUTTERFLIES AND MOTHS

Butterflies *(mariposas)* and moths *(polillas)* are in the order Lepidoptera—a word that derives from the Greek *lepidos* for "scales" and *ptera* for "wings." It refers to the feature that separates the Lepidoptera as a group from all other insects—the powder-like wing scales that contain a pigment that gives lepidopterids some of their color.

Adult butterflies and moths have three body regions: head, thorax, and abdomen. The head has a pair of segmented antennae and a pair of large, rounded eyes. Butterflies and many moths have a coiled proboscis that unrolls into a long sucking tube used for feeding on nectar and other fluids. Most have a pair of five-jointed legs on each of the three thorax segments, and two pairs of membranous wings attached to the second and third thorax segments. Both male and female sex organs lie at the end of the ten-segmented abdomen.

Butterflies and moths physically develop in a biological process called metamorphosis. This involves a conspicuous, relatively abrupt change in the insect's structure or form through cell growth and differentiation. In lepidopterids, metamorphosis proceeds in distinct stages, beginning with the eggs, passing through larval and pupal states, and ending with adults.

The first larval stage, the instar, eats its egg casing.

The larva, or caterpillar, feeds on a specific host plant as it grows.

Female adult butterflies and moths lay dozens of pinhead-sized, sticky eggs in a specific pattern on a plant that will provide food for the larvae. When the eggs hatch, they enter the first larval state—the instar. Their own egg casings provide the first nourishment for the caterpillars, or *cuncunas*.

Soon after, the larvae begin to feed on their host plant's leaves and flowers. Larvae that feed on plants containing alkaloids store the toxins in their systems and pass them on to later stages. Adults of these species are distasteful and often advertise their toxicity with boldly colored markings. This is such an effective protection that some non-toxic species have grown to mimic noxious ones.

"Who are YOU?" said the Caterpillar.

Alice replied, rather shyly, "I hardly know, sir, just at present—at least I know who I WAS when I got up this morning, but I think I must have been changed several times since then…and being so many different sizes in a day is very confusing."

"It isn't," said the Caterpillar.

"Well, perhaps you haven't found it so yet," said Alice, "but when you have to turn into a chrysalis—you will some day, you know—and then after that into a butterfly, I should think you'll feel it a little queer, won't you?"

"Not a bit," said the Caterpillar.

—Rev. Charles "Lewis Carroll" Dodgson
Alice's Adventures in Wonderland
Original 1865 illustration by John Tenneil

Just before a butterfly larva enters the pupal state, it spins a silk button and attaches it to a twig using hooks on its hind legs. It pulls itself into a "J" shape as the pupal shell, or chrysalis, forms. Triggered by hormones, the pupa secretes digestive enzymes that cause its cellular structure to disintegrate. A few cells remain intact. Over time, these reorganize to form an adult butterfly.

Most larvae are brightly colored and some are covered in bumps or knobs. Some larvae have toxin-bearing spines or stinging hairs, which act as deterrents against predators. Larvae also have a pair of short antennae and a pair of simple, or more rarely, compound eyes. Mouth parts include two segmented, sensory structures called palpi, and a pair of strong jaws. The lower lip, or labium, often has a spinneret used for spinning silk filaments. On each of the three segments of the thorax is a pair of short, jointed legs ending in claws. On each side of the first thoracic segment is a spiracle, or breathing pore.

After a caterpillar grows and molts several times, it enters the pupal stage where the larva transforms into an adult. The process is slightly different in moths and butterflies. Before its final molt, a butterfly larva spins a button of silk by which it attaches itself to a firm support such as a branch. As its skin molts and drops away, a tough, flexible casing forms around the naked pupa, or chrysalis. Moths have different strategies. A few types, most famously the Asian silk moths, spin a silken cocoon. But most moths of the Americas pupate in dead leaves or debris, or burrow into the ground and winter inside a hard casing.

The pupal state is one of regeneration and rebirth. Hormones trigger the pupa to excrete digestive juices that break down its own organs and tissues. A few cells are left intact and, in one of Nature's little miracles, the remaining tissue cells and nutrients reorganize and grow into an adult butterfly or moth.

The winged adult emerges with soft, limp, damp wings. It rests immobile until its body fluids pulse into the wing veins, which expand and harden to provide a rigid support for the delicate wing membrane. Within minutes, the wings flutter into flight. The next two to six weeks—the average life span of an adult lepidopterid—will be occupied with finding a mate and reproduction. Aided by chemical messengers called pheromones, the sexes find each other, mate and produce eggs.

By the end of summer, the life of most adults is over. But hidden somewhere in the shrubbery or damp earth of winter are the chrysalises of nascent winged creatures that will flitter about the countryside and drink from the flowers of summer.

The adult butterfly emerges from the chrysalis with damp, limp wings. It pumps body fluids into the wing veins and after a few minutes is able to fly.

Within the next few weeks the adult butterflies will mate. A female will seek out and lay her eggs on a host plant that can provide food for her offspring, thus renewing the cycle of life.

IS IT A BUTTERFLY... OR IS IT A MOTH?

Danaus erippus

It's a butterfly if it—
- Feeds and flies by day
- Has clubbed antennae
- Rests with its wings held upright over the back

Adetomeris erythrops ♀

It's a moth if it—
- Feeds and flies by night
- Has feathered or thread-like antennae (no clubbed tip)
- Rests with its wings outspread

Butterflies can be found in a wide variety of habitats in spring and summer. They are most common in open sunny areas, which contain native plants that provide a good food supply for their larvae.

Moths are more difficult to observe due to their nocturnal habits. But again, they are more likely to be seen in places that contain preferred host plants for adults and larvae.

It can be difficult to identify butterflies and moths at the species level. However, one can usually place them within a family group by comparing the color, habitat and range of a species to the descriptions and illustrations in this guide.

LEPIDOPTERA: Butterflies and Moths

Lepidoptera, or "scale-wings," are grouped in two suborders—Heterocera (Moths) and Rhopalocera (Butterflies). Rhopalocera is further divided into Hesperioidea (Skippers) and Papilionidea (True Butterflies).

Over 160 species of Lepidoptera are present in Chile. Many do not have common Chilean or English names, so names created by Peña and Ugarte for their 1992 guide LAS MARIPOSAS DE CHILE are used here. Measurements indicate approximate wingspan (WS).

SUPERFAMILY HEPERIOIDEA
FAMILY HESPIRIIDAE: SKIPPERS

SKIPPERS

Skippers are named for their fast, erratic, skipping flight. They have a stout, hairy body, a large head, fully developed and functioning forelegs in both sexes, small pointed wings, a unique pattern of forewing venation, and curved or hooked tips to the antennae. They bask in the sun with the forewings halfway open and the hindwings fully open. Skipper larvae are green with tapered bodies; they hide in shelters made of leaves and silk. There are 35 species of skippers in Chile.

SUBFAMILY PYRGINAE: SPREAD-WING SKIPPERS

Long-tailed Skipper, Hesperia de proteo
Urbanus proteus

ID: WS 2 in (5 cm). Long tail. Upperside of wings is dark blackish-brown with whitish spots; body and wing bases are iridescent blue-green. Wing undersides brown, with blackish bands and a creamy margin on the underside of the hindwing. Adults roost upside down under leaves and limbs, and feed on flower nectar. Displaying males perch in sunlit shrubs about 4 ft (1.2 m) above the ground. Females lay clusters of about 20 eggs under leaves. Larvae feed on vine legumes and rest during the day in rolled leaves held together by silken threads.

RANGE: Azapa and Lluta Valleys, Arica, and similar habitats in n Chile. Widespread from s USA to Argentina; fields, woodland edge, gardens, disturbed open habitats.

SKIPPERS AND TRUE BUTTERFLIES 93

Long-tailed Skipper, Hesperia de proteo
Urbanus proteus
Arica–Tarapacá
2 in (5 cm)

Basking posture

♀

♂

**Little Yellow Terias
Mariposa amarilla**
Terias deva chilensis
Atacama–Santiago
1.75 in (4.5 cm)

**Gold-winged Skipper
Lluvia de oro**
Argopteron aureipennis
Biobío–Valdivia
1.5 in (3.75 cm)

**Spot-winged Skipperling
Hesperia de alas manchadas**
Butleria flavomaculata
Coquimbo–Aisén
1 in (2.5 cm)

**Alfalfa Sulphur
Colias de la alfalfa**
Colias vauthierii
Atacama–Chiloé
1.5 in (3.75 cm)

**Eufala Skipper
Hesperia eufala**
Lerodea eufala
Atacama–Valdivia
1.25 in (3.25 cm)

**Grizzled Skipper
Hesperia de tres manchas**
Pyrgus bocchoris
Arica–Valdivia
1.25 in (3.25 cm)

**Funereal Duskywing
Hesperia negra**
Erynnis funeralis
Atacama–Araucanía
1.5 in (3.75 cm)

**Branded Skipper
Hesperia del pasto**
Hylephila fasciolata
Atacama–Magallanes
1 in (2.5 cm)

**Southern Dogface
Mariposa amarilla boliviana**
Zerene caesonia
Arica–Tarapacá
2 in (5 cm)

**Aristolochia Swallowtail
Papillo negro**
Battus polydamus
Atacama–Biobío
3–4.5 in (7.5–11.5 cm)

Pipevine, Oreja de Oso
Aristolochia chilensis

**Cloudless Sulphur
Mariposa limonera**
Phoebis sennae
Atacama–Valdivia
3 in (7.5 cm)

RELATED SPECIES: DORANTES LONGTAIL, HESPERIA DORANTES, *Urbanus dorantes,* is olive with small yellow spots on the forewings. Long greenish tail. Azapa Valley, Arica.

Grizzled (Checkered) Skipper
Pyrgus spp.
ID: WS 1.25 in (3.25 cm). Chilean species are dusky brown with pale squared spots. Larvae feed on mallows.
HESPERIA DE OCTAVIO, *Pyrgus barrosi,* is dark brown with white and yellow spots; hindwings have a black margin. Occurs in Antofagasta, in sandy sites with leguminous vegetation, around 13,000 ft (4000 m).
HESPERIA DE TRES MANCHAS, *P. bocchoris,* is dark brown. Dorsal hindwings have a large quadrate white spot; ventral face of hindwings white with narrow black markings. Common from Arica to Bíobío.
HESPERIA PARDA, *P. fides,* is olive with cream-colored spots. Fairly common from Arica to central Chile.
HESPERIA PARDA COMÚN, *P. notatus,* is olive-brown with white spots. Fairly common from Santiago to Valdivia.
HESPERIA GRIS COMÚN, *Heliopyrgus americanus,* is greyish-brown with white spots that appear to unite as a whitish band in the distal area. Flight is September to May. Atacama to Bíobío.

Funereal Duskywing, Hesperia negra
Erynnis funeralis
ID: WS 1.5 in (3.75 cm). Blackish with a white margin on the hindwings. Larvae feed on alfalfa and other grasses.
RANGE: Atacama to Araucanía; s USA to South America. Towns and farms.

SUBFAMILY HESPERIINAE: GRASS SKIPPERS

Skipperlings
Butleria spp.
ID: WS 1 in (2.5 cm). Dark brown with yellow, orange or white spots.
HESPERIA DE ALAS MANCHADAS, *Butleria flavomaculata,* is brown with yellow spots. **ENDEMIC.** Common from Coquimbo to Aisén.
HESPERIA MANCHADA, *Butleria fruticolens patagonica,* is similar. Common in s Chile.
CHILEAN SKIPPERLING, HESPERIA CHILENA, *B. paniscoides,* is olive-brown with white spots. Common from Coquimbo to Aisén.
HESPERIA DE ELWES, *B. elwesi,* is olive brown with varying amounts of yellow dots; occurs in bamboo thickets. Aconcagua to Chiloé.
HESPERIA DE PHILIPPI, *B. philippi,* is dark brown with varying numbers of yellow-orange spots on the wings. Uncommon from Ñuble to Osorno in bamboo thickets.

Gold-winged Skipper
Lluvia de oro
Argopteron spp.
ID: WS 1.5 in (3.75 cm). Golden-brown with yellow wingspots. Ventral side of wings is bright gold.
LLUVIA DE ORO, *Argopteron aureipennis,* is brown with 3 yellow spots on the dorsal side of the forewings. Underside of wings is bright gold in males and dark gold in females. Common from Bíobío to Valdivia in bamboo thickets.
HESPERIA DE PUELMA, *A. puelmae,* has brown forewings with 2 yellow spots and a broad, dark brown margin. Common from Maule to Aisén in *Nothofagus* forest where red, pink or white flowers are present.
HESPERIA DORADA, *A. aureum,* has brown forewings with 2 yellow spots, Hindwings are gold with a brown margin. A rare species found in bamboo thickets in the Cordillera de Parral, Linares.

Branded Skipper, Hesperia del pasto
Hylephila spp.
ID: WS 1 in (2.25 cm). Golden with dark brown "scorch" marks. These skippers rest with their forewings held upright and hindwings spread flat.
HESPERIA DEL PASTO, *Hylephila fasciolata,* has typical coloration. Atacama to Magallanes. In gardens, pastures, and woodland.
HESPERIA AMARILLA COMÚN, *H. signata,* has yellow base color. Atacama to Magallanes.

HESPERIA ELEGANTE, *Hylephila venusta*, has black wing margins. Ñuble to Aisén.

Eufala Skipper, Hesperia eufala
Lerodea eufala
ID: WS 1.25 in (3.25 cm). Upperside of wings is grey-brown. Forewing has 3 to 5, small, transparent spots. Underside of hindwings are brown with dense gray overscaling. Displaying males perch in flat grassy areas on low vegetation. Caterpillars eat grasses, and rest in rolled leaves tied with silken filaments. Adults feed on nectar from flowering alfalfa and daisies.
RANGE: Atacama to Valdivia, and north to s USA. Open, sunny areas in vacant lots, agricultural fields, road edges and lawns.

SUPERFAMILY PAPILIONOIDEA
FAMILY PAPILIONIDAE: SWALLOWTAILS

SWALLOWTAILS
Swallowtails are the largest and best known group of butterflies. Adults bear bold color patterns, and most have tail-like projections on the hindwings.

Aristolochia Swallowtail, Papillo negro
Battus polydamas archidamas
ID: WS 3–4.5 in (7.5–11.5 cm). Black, with pale yellow spots. Hindwings have a green or blue iridescence; no tails on hindwings. All stages feed on *Aristolochia chilensis*, a foul-smelling birthwort called *Oreja de Oso* (Bear's Ear) or Pipevine. They ingest toxic chemicals from the plant, which gives both larvae and adults a noxious taste and makes birds avoid them as a food source. This is the only known Papilionidae from Chile and is also one of Chile's largest butterflies.
RANGE: Common around *Aristolochia* from the Atacama Desert to Biobío.

FAMILY PIERIDAE: SULPHURS, WHITES

WHITES, YELLOWS AND SULPHURS
These medium-sized butterflies are colored white, yellow or orange. Males often differ in color from females. Green, striped larvae feed on crop plants and are considered an agricultural pest. Just before changing into pupae, larvae spin a silken girdle around the waist and a silk button at their anal end, then attach themselves to twigs or leaves. There are 36 Pieridae species in Chile.

SUBFAMILY COLIADINAE: SULPHURS

Alfalfa Sulphur, Colias de la alfalfa
Colias vauthierii
ID: WS 1.5 in (3.75 cm). Sexually dimorphic. MALE's wings are orange with black margins. FEMALE's wings are grey with black or dark grey patches. Found in alfalfa fields.
RANGE: Atacama to Chiloé.
RELATED SPECIES: COLIAS DE BLANCHARD, *Colias flaveola*, is pale greyish-green. Males have an orange spot on the hindwing. This is a common species, living in high Andean valleys in Argentina and Chile.
COLIAS DE MENDOZA, *C. mendozina*, is pale grey. Rare on hillsides and quebradas of the Aconcagua Valley near Portillo.
LUCEN'S BUTTERFLY, COLIAS ARGENTINA, *C. lesbia*, is sexually dimorphic. MALE's wings are orange with black margins. FEMALES are grey with darker grey spots. Ranges in Ñuble, Malleco, and Magallanes.

Southern Dogface
Mariposa amarilla boliviana
Zerene caesonia
ID: WS 2 in (5 cm). Lemon-colored. Broad, irregular, black margins on the forewings suggest a dog's head in silhouette. Lays its eggs on leguminous plants, especially those used for livestock fodder.
RANGE: Valleys of Arica and Tarapacá; also s USA to Mexico and Argentina.

Cloudless Sulphur
Mariposa limonera
Phoebis sennae amphitrite
ID: WS 3 in (7.5 cm). MALE's upperwings are lemon yellow with no markings. FEMALE is yellow-ochre; outer edges of both wings have dark borders; upper forewing has dark spot in distal cell. Ventral surface of hindwing has 2 pink-edged, silvery spots. Males cluster on moist sand. Eggs are laid singly on host plants. Caterpillars eat leaves

of legumes and rest on the underside of leaf stems. Adults feed on nectar of tubular flowers and wild senna.

RANGE: Atacama to Valdivia, and Argentina north to s USA. Parks, gardens, beaches, roadsides, open fields, scrub.

Little Yellow Terias, Mariposa amarilla
Terias deva chilensis

ID: WS 1.75 in (4.5 cm). Pale yellow with a brown patch on the apex of the forewing. Larvae feed on the mimosa tree, *Cassia stipulacea*. Very common. Slow flier. Some place this species in the genus *Eurema*.

RANGE: Central Chile, from Copiapó to Aconcagua. In scrub on Andean slopes around 5500 ft (1700 m) elevation.

SUBFAMILY PIERINAE: WHITES

Eroessa Butterfly
Mariposa eroesa
Eroessa chilensis

ID: WS 1.75–2 in (4.5–5 cm). Greenish-white. Forewings have a conspicuous, orange transverse band and dark brown wingtips. Lives in *Nothofagus* forest clearings, appearing in spring to feed on red, pink or white flowers of plants such as Chilco (*Fuchsia magellanica*) and Mora (*Rubus* sp.).

RANGE: ENDEMIC. Local on the coast from Maule to Aisén, and in the foothills of Cautín, Osorno and Llanquihue.

Mariposa del quintral
Mathania leucothea

ID: WS 1.5 in (3.75 cm). Milky white overall.

RANGE: Coquimbo to Valdivia. Common in gardens and near Quintral (*Tristerix* sp.), an epiphytic plant on which it lays its eggs.

Large White
Mariposa blanca de la col
Pieris brassicae

ID: WS 2.75 inches (7 cm). White. FEMALES have two black spots and a black streak on the forewings. MALES lack forewing spots. Undersides of wings yellowish with black flecking in both sexes. Lays masses of yellow eggs on underside of cabbage leaves and other brassicas. Caterpillar is pale green with black smudges, a yellow line along the back and sides, and short white hairs. Adults feed on flower nectar. INTRODUCED agricultural pest; native to Eurasia.

RANGE: Coquimbo to Valdivia. In vegetable gardens, roadsides, towns.

Andean Foothills White
Mariposa blanca preandina
Tatochila theodice

ID: WS 2.5 in (6.25 cm). White, with black markings, especially on forewings. FEMALES are darker and more golden in color than the MALES.

RANGE: Arica to Valdivia. Common around flowers and blossoming trees on mountain slopes and gullies.

Common White Tatochila
Mariposa mercedes
Tatochila mercedis

ID: WS 2–2.5 in (5–6.25 cm). White, with black markings. Hindwings white with a few black spots.

RANGE: Arica to Magallanes. Common in a wide variety of habitats.

RELATED SPECIES: The following genera are very similar to *Tatochila*. Most MALES are white with blackish markings and designs. FEMALES are darker than males.

Hypsochila species are small and generally greyish in both sexes. MARIPOSA DE WAGENKNECT, *H. wagenknecti*, is common in foothill areas from Coquimbo to Santiago. PAMPAS WHITE, MARIPOSA BLANCA DE LA ESTEPA, *H. argyrodice*, is uncommon on the Patagonian steppe.

Phulia and *Intraphulia* species occur at high elevations up to 16,000 ft (5000 m). MARIPOSITA BLANCA ANDINA, *Phulia nimphula*, is common in the Andes Range from Arica to Santiago. FULIA DE PANTANO, *Intraphulia ilyodes*, is white with grey marks. Common in high Andean *bofedales* and marshes from Arica to Antofagasta.

TRUE BUTTERFLIES 97

Quintral

Mariposa del quintral
Mathania leucothea
Coquimbo–Valdivia
1.5 in (3.75 cm)

♀ **Large White**
Mariposa blanca de la col
Pieris brassicae
Coquimbo–Valdivia
2.75 in (7 cm)

Eroessa Butterfly
Mariposa eroesa
Eroessa chilensis
Maule–Aisén
1.75–2 in (4.5–5 cm)

Bicolor Hairstreak
Licena de dos colores
Eiseliana bicolor
Atacama–Biobío
1 in (2.5 cm)

♀ / ♂ **Andean Foothills White**
Mariposa blanca preandina
Tatochila theodice
Arica–Valdivia
2.5 in (6.25 cm)

♀ / ♂ **Common White Tatochila**
Mariposa mercedes
Tatochila mercedis
Arica–Magallanes
2–2.5 in (5–6.25 cm)

Scrub-Hairstreak
Licena tornasol común
Strymon eurytulus
Atacama–Chiloé
1 in (2.5 cm)

Grey Ministreak
Licena invasora
Ministrymon azia
Arica–Atacama
0.5–1 in (1.25–2.5 cm)

Quebrada Ministreak
Licena de la quebrada
Ministrymon quebradivaga
Arica–Tarapacá
1 in (2.5 cm)

♂ **Tamarugo Blue**
Licena del tamarugo
Leptotes trigemmatus
Arica–Santiago
0.75 in (2 cm)

Chilean Blue
Licena morena
Pseudolucia chilensis
Atacama–Santiago
0.75 in (2 cm)

Dwarf Blue
Licena enana
Itylos titicaca
Arica–Antofagasta
0.5 in (1.25 cm)

Monarch Butterfly, Monarcha
Danaus erippus
Arica–Biobío
3.5 in (8.75 cm)

Astragalus sp.

FAMILY LYCAENIDAE
HAIRSTREAKS & BLUES
Lycaenids are small butterflies, commonly colored blue, grey, brown or coppery above, with metallic spots on the hindwings. Sexes may differ in coloration and the wing underside may differ from the dorsal surface.

SUBFAMILY THECLINAE: HAIRSTREAKS

Hairstreaks have small tails and bright eyespots on the hindwings, creating a "false head" at the rear to divert predators. Their larvae are closely associated with ants.

Scrub Hairstreak
Licena tornasol común
Strymon eurytulus
ID: WS 1 in (2.5 cm). Variable in color. Most are lead-grey with a violet iridescence; top of abdomen is yellow. MALES have a black spot on the wings. This is one of the most common lycaenids seen in central Chile in the early spring. Swift, darting flight. Readily attracted to flowers. Sometimes sunbathes with wings open.
RANGE: Atacama to Chiloé, in woodland, fields, gardens.
RELATED SPECIES: LICENA DE ATACAMA, *Strymon crambusa*, is grey with no metallic spots; wings bear a dark spot or band. Rare on the Atacama coast near Caldera.

Grey Ministreak
Licena invasora
Ministrymon azia
ID: WS 0.5–1 in (1.25–2.5 cm). Tiny, with small tails. Dorsal face of wings grey, with a blue iridescence and a few orange metallic spots. Underside of wings have a narrow postmedian line of orange bordered with cream. Rapid, darting flight over the tops of shrubs. Adapted for living in arid places. Females lay eggs on flower buds of caterpillar host plants such as *Prosopis* mesquites and other spiny shrubs, especially those near watercourses.
RANGE: Arica to Atacama, and north to sUSA. Thorn scrub and matorral.

Quebrada Ministreak
Licena de la quebrada
Ministrymon quebradivaga
ID: WS 1 in (2.5 cm). Bronze, with an orange spot on the hindwings. Flits above treetops.
RANGE: Valleys of Arica and Tarapacá.

Bicolor Hairstreak, Licena de dos colores
Eiseliana bicolor
ID: WS 1 in (2.5 cm). Grey, with large patches of orange on forewings and hindwings.
RANGE: Atacama to Bíobío. Common near flowers and flowering shrubs.
RELATED SPECIES: LICENA DE WAGENKNECHT, *Heoda wagenknecti*, is grey with a large spot of orange on wings. Widespread in a variety of habitats. Atacama to Coquimbo. LICENA NEVADA, *Heoda nivea*, is brown. Andean foothills from Coquimbo to Aisén.

SUBFAMILY POLYMMATINAE: BLUES

Blues are very small butterflies that are mostly blue above and mottled buff and brown below.

Dwarf Blue, Licena enana
Itylos titicaca
ID: WS 0.5 in (1.25 cm). Violet-blue with distinct black wing margins edged by a row of black and white spots. No tails on hindwings. Ventral side of hindwings have a waved post-median band.
RANGE: Arica to Antofagasta; also Peru, Bolivia. In *Astragalus* milk vetch on Puna steppe, and in *bofedales* and *Polylepis* groves above 10,000 ft (3300 m).

Tamarugo Blue, Licena del tamarugo
Leptotes trigemmatus
ID: WS 0.75 in (2 cm). MALES are blue. FEMALES brown with a slight blue iridescence. Ventral side of wings are marbled light brown and cream, with three black spots on the hindwings. Larvae, which live in association with ants, feed on buds, flowers and leaves of *Prosopis tamarugo*, a tree cultivated for fodder in the Atacama Desert. The larvae are a major food source for the Tamarugo Conebill. Adults are considered beneficial

insects because they fertilize the tamarugo flowers when bees are absent.

RANGE: Arica to Santiago.

Pseudolucia Blues
Pseudolucia spp.

ID: WS 0.75–1 in (2–2.5 cm). The 21 *Pseudolucia* species in Chile come in a broad range of colors, ranging from blue to brown to silver, often with orange, white or brown patterns and an overlay of blue to silver iridescence. FEMALES and MALES differ in color or markings in most species.

LICENA MORENA, *Pseudolucia chilensis*. Males are grey-blue with small orange spots on the hindwing. Females have a larger orange patch on the wings. Ventral face of forewings are orange and hindwings grey. Atacama to Santiago.

LICENA CELESTE, *Pseudolucia collina*. Males are blue to sky blue. Females are brown with orange spots. Often seen resting on the ground, or flying around flowers and shrubs in open areas in the foothills from Coquimbo to Ñuble.

LICENA CONFUSA, *Pseudolucia lyrnessa*. The males are pale plumbeous blue with a dark wing margin. Females are darker with a large orange spot on the hindwings. Perches on the ground. Coquimbo to Biobío.

The following species are called **NABOKOV BLUES**, in reference to Vladimir Nabokov, Russian-American author of *Lolita*, and also a lepidopterist who studied the Chilean blues.

AURELIAN BLUE, *Pseudolucia aureliana*. Both sexes are deep lustrous blue with checkered fringes. Ranges in the Atacama mountains. Named from "The Aurelian," a short story in which Pilgrim, an ardent butterfly collector, is unable to fulfill his dream of journeying to the tropics.

CHARLOTTE'S BLUE, *Pseudolucia charlotte*. Males are azure with orange; females brown with orange. Ranges in the Patagonian areas of Argentina and Chile. Named for Lolita's mother, Charlotte.

LICENA DE LOS HAZE, *Pseudolucia hazeorum*. Males are lustrous indigo with wide, black to grey bands. Females are brown with orange streaks on the forewings. Common in the Andes above 6500 ft (2000 m). "Haze" refers to the blue's dark wing bands as well as the infamous Lolita and her mother, Charlotte Haze.

WHITAKER'S BLUE, *Pseudolucia whitakeri*. Large, pale lustrous blue from Patagonia. Named for G. Warren Whitaker, an avid reader of Nabokov novels and practicing New York attorney who in 1993 provided the "Nabokovian names."

ZEMBLA BLUE, *Pseudolucia zembla*. Males lustrous azure with a narrow black margin. Females' forewings are yellow-orange, hindwings brown. Named after the mythical kingdom in *Pale Fire*; found in the Andes.

FAMILY NYMPHALIDAE: BRUSH-FOOTED BUTTERFLIES
SUBFAMILY DANAINAE: MILKWEED BUTTERFLIES

MILKWEED BUTTERFLIES
Monarch Butterfly, Monarcha
Danaus (plexippus) erippus

ID: WS 3.5 in (8.75 cm). Large, brown to orange-brown butterfly. Wings have white-dotted black margins and dark veins. Larvae feed on milkweed leaves (*Asclepia* sp.), ingesting substances that make them toxic to predators; adults retain the protective poisons. Adults sip nectar from milkweed flowers, thus fertilizing the plant. The female Monarch lays her eggs on milkweed plants, usually not more than one egg per leaf. About the size of the head of a pin, the egg hatches in 3 to 4 days.

The South American Monarch, *Danaus erippus*, is a sister species to *D. plexippus* of North America and to *D. chleophile* of the Caribbean. Lepidopterists hypothesize that the Monarch evolved in Central America and n South America. The recession of the ice sheets about 12,000 years ago may have encouraged *D. plexippus* to migrate north and *D. erippus* to reach its present range in South America. Unlike the northern species, South American monarchs do not migrate.

RANGE: Arica to Biobío. Common in fields, grasslands, gardens.

SUBFAMILY SATYRINAE: SATYRS

SATYRS

Most satyrs are drab colored. Most adults are colored brown or grey and have eyespots (ocelli) on both the upper and lower faces of the wings. They live in woodland and scrub. They have a fast, erratic flight and are seen most often at dawn and dusk. The larvae have a forked tail and a thin, elongated shape that tapers on both ends. Larvae feed at night, mainly on grasses. Adults feed on flower nectar. Satyrs produce only one brood annually and overwinter as larvae.

Silver Satyr
Mariposa plateada
Argyrophorus argenteus
ID: WS 1.75–2 in (4.5–5 cm). Dorsal face of wings have a mercury-like iridescence often compared to a shiny silver dollar. Ventral forewings are orange and silver with a black spot; hindwings dotted with dark brown over cream. Females are duller; wings have a brown margin. Very fast flight.
RANGE: Coquimbo to Aisén, in a wide variety of habitats.
RELATED SPECIES: *Argyrophorus penai*. Rare resident in the mountains of Antofagasta.

Common Chilean Satyr
Satírido negro común
Cosmosatyrus chilensis
ID: WS 1.75 in (4.5 cm). Dark brown, with a marbled pattern on the ventral face of the hindwings. Ventral forewings are orange in the distal area and have a dark eyespot. One of the most common butterflies of Chile.
RANGE: Atacama to Magallanes.
RELATED SPECIES: MARIPOSA DEL COIRÓN, *Cosmosatyrus leptoneuroides*, is dark brown. Inhabits high altitude grasslands from Coquimbo to Magallanes. SATÍRIDO DE OCELO BLANCO, *Fanula leocognele*, is dark brown with one white eyespot on the ventral side of the forewing. Ranges in the High Andes from Tarapacá to Ñuble. SATÍRIDO DE LA ESTEPA PATAGÓNICA, *Fanula patagonica*, is dark brown; wing underside has white spots, with a band of white on the hindwing. Ranges on the steppes of Aisén.

Starry Satyr
Satírido estrellado
Chillanella (Tetraphlebia) stelligera
ID: 1.75 in (4.5 cm). Dark brown, with faint reddish spots on the upperwings. Underside of wings have a dark eyespot with two white dots. Hindwings have a series of white dots in the wing margin. NOT ILLUSTRATED.
RANGE: Coquimbo to Valdivia.
RELATED SPECIES: SATÍRIDO DE FRANJA GRIS, *Tetraphlebia germaini*, is brown with small reddish patches on the wings. Underside of the hindwing has a pale greyish band. Santiago to Ñuble in the foothills and high mountains.

Ochre-banded Satyr
Satírido de banda ocre
Neosatyrus ambriorix
ID: 1.75 in (4.5 cm). Brown overall, with a large light red eyespot on the hindwings. The underside of the forewings have a dark eyespot with two white dots. Undersides of the hindwings have white dots along the outer margin. NOT ILLUSTRATED.
RANGE: Valparaíso to Valdivia.

Janiriodes Satyr
Satírido confuso
Neomaenus janiriodes
ID: WS 1.75 in (4.5 cm). Dorsal face of wings is coffee-colored, with darker brown patches and a faint black spot at the wing apex. Ventral face of forewings is brown with an orange patch and a large black eyespot bearing two white dots.
RANGE: Coquimbo to Valdivia. Common in a variety of habitats.

Monachus Satyr
Satírido monacal
Neomaenas monachus
ID: WS 1.75 in (4.5 cm). Dorsal face of wings brown with a reddish wash. Ventral face of

TRUE BUTTERFLIES 101

Common Chilean Satyr, Satírido negro común
Cosmosatyrus chilensis
Atacama–Magallanes
1.75 in (4.5 cm)

Silver Satyr, Mariposa plateada
Argyrophorus argenteus
Coquimbo–Aisén
1.75–2 in (4.5–5 cm)

Janiriodes Satyr, Satírido confuso
Neomaenus janiriodes
Coquimbo–Valdivia
1.75 in (4.5 cm)

Andean Silverspot, Mariposa dione
Dione glycera
Arica–Tarapacá
2.25 in (5.75 cm)

Monachus Satyr, Satírido monacal
Neomaenus monachus
Coquimbo–Aisén
1.75 in (4.5 cm)

Pale Satyr, Satírido pálido
Auca pales
Santiago–Magallanes
2 in (5 cm)

Four-eyed Lady, Mariposa colorada
Vanessa carye
Arica–Magallanes
Easter Island, Juan Fernández
2 in (5 cm)

Variegated Fritillary, Mariposa hortensia
Euptoieta claudia
Coquimbo–Valdivia
2 in (5 cm)

Yramea Fritillary, Mariposa pintada
Yramea cytheris
Santiago–Magallanes
2 in (5 cm)

Snout Butterfly, Mariposa común del trópico
Lybytheana carinenta
Coast of Linares
1.75 in (4.5 cm)

wings is reddish brown, with a dark longitudinal band.

RANGE: Coquimbo to Aisén.

RELATED SPECIES: SATÍRIDO ROJIZO, *Neomaenas fractifascia*, is brown with red spots. Ventral face is mottled white and brown. Common from Ñuble to Valdivia in places with bamboo thickets.

Pale Satyr
Satírido pálido
Auca pales

ID: WS 2 in (5 cm). Brown overall with a reddish wash. Dark spot at apex of the upperwing. The underwing has an orange patch with an eyespot enclosing two white dots. Like other satyrs, pale satyrs inhabit woodland and dense scrub. They fly close to the ground in erratic patterns. Towards dusk, they can be found perching on decomposing fruit or directly on the ground. Often seen fluttering around flowers.

RANGE: Common. Santiago to s Argentina.

RELATED SPECIES: COCTEI SATYR, *Auca coctei*, is brown, with one to two dark eyespots on the wings. Coquimbo to Aisén.

Matorral Satyr
Satírido grande del matorral
Elina montroli

ID: WS 1.75 in (4.5 cm). Warm brown overall, with reddish patches and a large black eyespot on the dorsal face of the upperwing. Underside of the forewing has a large red eyespot in the shape of a figure-8, with two white dots edged in black.

RANGE: From Valparaíso to Valdivia, in matorral.

Satírido Danzarino
Elina vanessoides

ID: WS 1.75 in (4.5 cm). Brown overall, with irregular patches of red, orange and white on the underside of the wings. The dorsal face of the forewing has black spots at the apex.

RANGE: Concepción to Isla Chiloé, in *Nothofagus* forest.

Satírido del Sotobosque
Nelia nemyroides

ID: 1.75 in (4.5 cm). Brown with faint reddish spots. Wing underside bears a characteristic pattern, with a small, black eyespot on the forewing and a multi-colored pattern on the hindwings. Common in *Chusquea* bamboo understory. NOT ILLUSTRATED.

RANGE: Cachapoal to Llanquihue.

SUBFAMILY HELICONIINAE: FRITILLARIES

Andean Silverspot, Mariposa dione
Dione glycera

ID: WS 2.25 in (5.75 cm). Dorsal face reddish with thick, black veins. Underside of the hindwings has striking silver spots. Larvae feed mainly on Passion Flower (Passifloraceae). Adults sometimes rest in groups on low vegetation.

RANGE: Arica and Tarapacá. Open and deforested areas, villages and towns, and the mid-elevation valleys.

Yramea Fritillary
Mariposa pintada común
Yramea cytheris

ID: WS 2 in (5 cm). Orange with black spots. Often seen resting on the ground.

RANGE: Santiago to Magallanes.

RELATED SPECIES: MARIPOSA PINTADA DE LA ALTURA, *Yramea lathonioides,* is pale orange with black spots. Atacama to Magallanes, in foothills and mountains. MARIPOSITA PINTADA CHICA, *Yramea modesta,* is pale orange with black spots. Uncommon in the High Andes from Coquimbo to Llanquihue.

Variegated Fritillary
Mariposa hortensia
Euptoieta claudia hortensia

ID: WS 2 in (5 cm). Pale orange-brown with black patches, spots and veins.

RANGE: Coquimbo to Valdivia.

SUBFAMILY NYMPHALINAE: TRUE BRUSHFOOTS

Four-eyed Lady, Mariposa colorada
Vanessa carye

ID: WS 2 in (5 cm). Smaller sister species to the Painted Lady *(Vanessa cardui)* of North

America. Colored reddish-orange with black patches. White dots on the forewing. Four eyespots on the dorsal hindwings. Ventral face of wings is muted in color. Larvae feed on nettles and mallows.
RANGE: Arica to Magallanes; Easter Island and Juan Fernández. Widespread in South America in a variety of habitats, including towns and cities.
RELATED SPECIES: MARIPOSA COLORADA DE PHILIPPI, *Vanessa terpsichore*, is very similar to, but paler than *V. carye*. Ventral face of wings colored in earth tones, with a large reddish patch on the forewings. Common from Coquimbo to Magallanes.

SUBFAMILY LIBYTHEINAE: SNOUT BUTTERFLIES
Snout Butterfly
Mariposa común del trópico
Lybytheana carinenta
ID: WS 1.75 in (4.5 cm). Brown with orange patches on both forewing and hindwing, and a few white spots on the forewings. Long, projecting mouthparts.
RANGE: Local in coastal Linares.

SUPERFAMILY CASTNIOIDEA
FAMILY CASTNIIDAE
GIANT BUTTERFLY MOTHS
Castniidae is a small family of butterfly moths found in the Neotropics, Australia and Southeast Asia. They are mid-sized to large, and usually have drab, cryptically-marked forewings and brightly colored hindwings. They have clubbed antennae and fly by day. They are often mistaken for butterflies, and some earlier classification systems grouped them with butterflies or skippers. A single species occurs in Chile.

Castnid Butterfly Moth
Mariposa del chagual
Castnia psittachus
ID: WS 5 in (12.5 cm). Forewings are dark grey to golden brown with two whitish bands. Hindwings are dark in the discal area and bear reddish spots on the outer margin. Occurs in areas having chagual bromeliads (*Puya* spp.).
RANGE: Coast of central Chile.

SUBORDER HETEROCERA
MOTHS
Moths generally have plumper, more haired bodies than butterflies. At rest, moths usually hold their wings open. Moths are protected from entanglement in spider webs by their ability to shed scales at the point of contact with the orb and flutter loose. Most moths have a curved spine or bristle called a frenulum on the inner part of the hindwing. This structure helps hold the wings together in flight. Most moths fly at night and are attracted to lights. Their antennae are often feathery or threadlike and usually lack the clubbed tip found in butterflies. Moth larvae spin silken cocoons, or pupate on the ground or in underground chambers.

Moths produce potent PHEROMONES— aromatic chemicals that induce mating. The male moth's antennae are covered by chemical receptors so sensitive they can be triggered by a single pheromone molecule, thus enabling the male to easily find a mate.

Moth families present in Chile include:
FAMILY COSSIDAE: CARPENTERWORM MOTHS are fairly large, strong-flying moths. Like the larvae of *Chilecomadia moorei* moths (shown here), larvae of this family bore into roots or trunks of woody plants to pupate.

FAMILY NOCTUIDAE: Adult OWLET MOTHS (Noctuinae, Acronyctinae, Plusiinae, Catocalinae) are stout-bodied with moderately narrow forewings and fan-shaped hindwings that are usually hidden under the forewings when folded. A few species are brightly-colored diurnal species, but most are cryptically-colored, nocturnal moths. The thick-bodied, hairless larvae are called CUTWORMS because they can cut off young plants at ground level. They emerge at night from leaf shelters or debris on the ground.

FAMILY LASIOCAMPIDAE: In Chile, there are 14 species of LAPPET MOTHS in the genera *Macromphalia, Euglyphis, Bombyx* and *Porthetria*. These moths are tan to brown in color and have stout, hairy bodies. Their larvae, often called TENT CATERPILLARS, rest in silky webs that they spin in tree crotches. They emerge from the tents to feed on the leaves of their host tree.

FAMILY GEOMETRIDAE: The GEOMETER MOTHS have thin bodies and broad, delicate, pale brown marbled wings, which they fold in a flat, deltoid shape. Geometer, meaning "earth measurer," refers to the way the larvae draw the rear of the body up to the front legs, forming a loop before extending the body again. The larvae are thus known as inch-worms, measure worms, span worms or loopers. *Chlorotimandra viridis, Aconcagua fessa, Apicia valdiviana, Coironalia cruciferaria* and *Coironalia denticulata* are species that occur in Chile.

FAMILY ARCTIIDAE: ARCTIID MOTHS have a tymbal organ on the body. The organ's membranes can be vibrated to produce ultrasonic sounds. They also have ultrasonic hearing that is used in finding mates.

Many arctiid moths retain distasteful or toxic chemicals from their host plants, and some species manufacture their own poisonous chemicals. They advertise these defenses with bright colors, postures, odors or ultrasonic vibrations. The BELLA MOTH, *Utetheisa ornatrix*, is a diurnal moth that ranges from North America east of the Rockies into Brazil, Argentina and Chile. The larvae and adults are protected against predators by alkaloids they gather from their host plants. When the adults mate, they pass along the defensive chemical to the egg. Males also derive a pheromone from the alkaloid and emit it from a pair of extrusive brushes during courtship.

FAMILY SPHINGIDAE: SPHINX MOTHS are large, extremely muscular moths. They are often mistaken for hummingbirds because of their rapid wingbeats and habit of hovering in front of flowers as they feed. The SPHINX MOTH, or MONROY, *Hyles annei*, occurs in north and central Chile and Bolivia. The large, stout larvae hold the body erect in a sphinx-like position and have a prominent horn or spine at the rear end of the body. The larvae are large and the thick body has a large posterior spine. Adults have a very long proboscis that can be uncoiled from within the head to retrieve nectar from long, tubular flowers. They are most active at dusk and dawn, and on some moonlit nights, hundreds of adults will gather to feed at flowers.

FAMILY SATURNIIDAE: Saturniidae include some of the most beautiful and largest moths—the emperor and silk moths. They are broad-winged with stout, short bodies and feathery antennae. The larvae are not haired, but are usually armed with bumps or branched spines, which can cause a skin rash like that caused by nettles. Pupation occurs underground or in a silken cocoon.

Most silk moth adults do not feed. They have only vestigial mouthparts and live on food the larvae have stored in their bodies. Since they have a limited supply of energy and food, adults live only a few days and exist only to reproduce. When a female moth emerges from the cocoon, she remains at the site and emits a pheromone that attracts males. Mating takes place within a day of emergence. The female then flies away to lay her eggs, which hatch from one to two weeks later.

The 19 species of Chilean saturniids can be found from Coquimbo to Magallanes. *Adetomeris, Cinommata, Ormiscodes* and *Polythysana* species are small, day-flying moths whose larvae have branched spines. The subfamily Cercophaninae includes endemic species in the genera *Cercophana, Microdulia* and *Neocercophana*. These are large, very beautiful moths that spend the day in the foliage of woodland trees and shrubs that act as host plants for their larvae. These spectacular moths can also be seen on stone walls, resting on mottled areas that bear colors similar to their own.

REPTILES AND AMPHIBIANS

ORDER TESTUDINES
TURTLES

There are no land turtles in Chile, but four sea turtle species are found in Chilean waters.

- Sea turtles have a top shell called a CARAPACE and a lower shell called a PLASTRON.

- Most sea turtles have a bony carapace covered with horny plates called SCUTES. The leatherback is an exception—it's carapace is made of cartilage with an underlying layer of small bones.

- Unlike terrestrial species, sea turtles can't retract their head and limbs into their shell.

- Sea turtles lack teeth. They chew with their jaws. The green sea turtles have finely serrated jaws suited for feeding on sea grasses and marine algae. Loggerheads and ridleys have strong jaws adapted for crushing and grinding hard prey such as crabs or mollusks. The leatherbacks have fine, scissor-like jaws used for feeding on jellyfish, tunicates and other soft organisms.

- The sea turtle's long paddle-like flippers are used for swimming. Foreflippers are used for propulsion; hind flippers serve as rudders.

- At maturity, a male sea turtle develops a long, thick tail. His reproductive organ is housed at the base of his tail.

- After mating, female sea turtles migrate from their offshore feeding grounds to sandy beaches where they lay their eggs. They deposit the eggs in deep holes dug out with their hind flippers.

- The soft-shelled turtle eggs hatch underground and the young must dig themselves to the surface and enter the sea independently.

SUPERFAMILY CHELONIOIDEA
SEA TURTLES

Sea turtles are cold-blooded, air-breathing reptiles that inhabit warm and temperate oceans of the world. They are larger than, and different from, land turtles in that the limbs are modified into flippers and the head and limbs cannot be retracted into the shell. Male sea turtles seldom come ashore. Adult females must return to land to lay their eggs, and often migrate long distances between their oceanic feeding grounds and coastal nesting beaches.

FAMILY CHELONIIDAE: SUBFAMILY CHELONIINAE

Green Turtle, Tortuga verde
Chelonia mydas

ID: 2.5–3.6 ft (0.8–1.12 m). WT 150–410 lbs (68–186 kg). The largest individual ever collected was 5 ft (1.5 m) long and weighed 871 lbs (395 kg). The carapace is smooth and can be shades of black, grey, green, brown, and yellow. The plastron is pale yellow to cream. Adult green turtles feed almost exclusively on sea grass and algae. This diet is thought to give them a greenish colored fat, from which they take their name. They reach sexual maturity at 20 to 50 years of age. At maturity, the females leave their benthic feeding grounds and migrate to their natal beaches, often travelling hundreds of miles each way. They return to lay eggs every two to four years. When the hatchlings emerge from the nest, they swim to offshore waters where they are believed to live for several years, feeding close to the sea surface on a variety of planktonic plants and animals. Juveniles later move to deepwater foraging grounds near the coast and begin to feed solely on plant matter. ENDANGERED.

RANGE: Arica to Chiloé; occasional farther south. Visitor to Easter Island. Occurs in warm oceans along continental coasts and islands between 30°N–30°S latitudes. In austral summer, green turtles feed in the warm waters off the mouth of the Río Loa, between Iquique and Antofagasta.

Leatherback
Tortuga laúd
Dermochelys coriacea
Coast of Central Chile
4–8 ft (1.2–2.4 m)

Loggerhead, Tortuga boba
Caretta caretta
Arica–Coquimbo
3 ft (1 m)

Green Turtle, Tortuga verde
Chelonia mydas
Arica–Chiloé; Easter Island
2.5–3.6 ft (0.8–1.12 m)

Olive Ridley Tortuga verde
Lepidochelys olivacea
Arica–Valparaíso
2.5 ft (0.75 m)

FAMILY CHELONIIDAE: SUBFAMILY CARETTINAE

Loggerhead Turtle, Tortuga boba
Caretta caretta
OTHER NAMES: Cabezona, Caguama.
ID: 3 ft (1 m). WT 250 lbs (113 kg). Large head. Reddish-brown carapace is slightly heart-shaped and covered by angled, horny scutes—hard scales that cover the shell. The plastron is generally pale yellowish. Neck and flippers are brown to reddish-brown on top and yellowish on the sides and bottom. Powerful jaws enable loggerheads to feed on hard-shelled, bottom dwelling invertebrates. Coral reefs, rocky seabeds and shipwrecks are often used as feeding areas. Loggerheads reach sexual maturity at about 35 years of age. They nest on ocean beaches and occasionally on estuarine shorelines with suitable sand. THREATENED.
RANGE: Uncommon to rare between Arica and Coquimbo. Widespread in subtropical waters of the Atlantic, Pacific and Indian Oceans. Occurs hundreds of miles out to sea and in bays, salt marshes, ship channels and mouths of large rivers.

Olive Ridley, Tortuga verde
Lepidochelys olivacea
ID: 2.5 ft (0.75 m). WT 100 lbs (45 kg). Carapace is pale olive, the plastron yellowish. Feeds on jellyfish, snails, crabs and some algae. Groups can sometimes be seen basking in the sun at the sea surface, which allows them to maintain their body temperature.
RANGE: Rare pelagic from off the north and central coast of Chile between Valparaíso and San Antonio.

FAMILY DERMOCHELYIDAE

Leatherback Sea Turtle
Tortuga laúd
Dermochelys coriacea
ID: 4–8 ft (1.2–2.4 m). WT 800 lbs (365 kg). Largest living turtle; the largest on record weighed 2019 lbs (916 kg). The barrel-shaped body tapers at the rear to a blunted point. No visible carapace. The carapace is made up of hundreds of irregular bony plates that form seven longitudinal ridges, covered with bluish-black, leathery skin. Back may appear brown when seen in the water. White to pinkish-white bottom shell. Pink patch on top of the head. Front flippers are longer than any other marine turtles, and can measure 8 ft (2.5 m) in adults. Feeds on jellyfish, tunicates, and other soft-bodied sea animals and plants. ENDANGERED.
RANGE: Uncommon pelagic caught by fishermen off the c Chile coast. Breeds in the West Indies, Florida, ne coast of South America, Senegal, Natal, Madagascar, Sri Lanka and Malaysia.

> ORDER SQUAMATA
> ## LIZARDS, GECKOS AND SERPENTS
> About 90 species of lizards and serpents occur in Chile. These vertebrate animals share the following features:
> - A body covered with epidermal scales
> - Most lizards have paired limbs, usually with five toes, adapted for climbing, running or paddling. Limbs are absent in snakes and some lizards
> - A well-ossified (bony) skeleton
> - Respiration by lungs, not gills
> - A three-chambered heart in most, with two aortic arches that carry blood from the heart to the body
> - Cold-bloodedness
> - Internal fertilization
> - Most species lay eggs (oviparous)

SQUAMATA: SUBORDER LACERTILIA
LIZARDS AND GECKOS

There are more than 3700 known species of lizards and many more are being discovered each year. Most of us get only fleeting glimpses of these elusive reptiles, but they are widespread in tropical and temperate regions of the world at altitudes ranging from sea level to 16,000 ft (4900 m).

Most lizard species are small, with the snout to vent (SV) length averaging 2–4 in (5–10 cm). This measurement excludes the length of the tail because many specimens secured for identification have a missing or attenuated tail. A lizard's tail is designed to break off easily when seized by a predator, after which the tail regenerates.

This juvenile Southern Grumbler *(Pristidactylus torquatus)* is barely as long as an index finger.

INFRAORDER IGUANIA
FAMILY IGUANAIDAE
IGUANID LIZARDS

This is a diverse group of lizards that were formerly classed in many different families. The group is distinguished by having the frontal bones of the head fused to each other. Most have moveable eyelids and an ear opening on each side of the head.

SUBFAMILY TROPIDURINAE: GENUS LIOLAEMUS
NEOTROPICAL GROUND LIZARDS

Liolaemus is a very large genus of neotropical ground lizards with about 170 species distributed mainly in Chile and Argentina. The snout–vent measurement of most species is 2–3.5 in (5–8.75 cm), and the tail is typically as long as, or longer than, the body. Most are polymorphic (have many different forms). They are often cryptically patterned with spots, lines and bands, and a few have bold body patterns colored in red, blue, yellow and green. Most have coarse body scales; a few are very spiny in appearance. They have a distinct head and neck, and well-developed limbs and toes. Most are insectivorous. They ambush their prey and capture it with their tongue. Some species are oviparous, others are viviparous (the embryo develops in the mother's body rather than in the egg). Most are terrestrial, but two Chilean species—*Liolaemus tenuis* and *Liolaemus pictus*—live in trees.

Brilliant Lizard, Lagartija rayada nortina
Liolaemus alticolor
ID: SV 1.75 in (4.5 cm). Back is greenish-brown, with a black ventral line and two pale lateral bands that are bordered in black. Omnivorous, diurnal and viviparous.
RANGE: Arica to Tarapacá. In tola scrub on the Altiplano; to 13,000 ft (3960 m).

Dusky Lizard, Lagartija parda
Liolaemus bellii (altissimus)
ID: SV 2.25–3 in (5.5–8 cm). Dusky grey to brown, with longitudinal rows of dark spots edged with pale grey.
RANGE: Volcán El Morado and Andes near Santiago; 6550–9950 ft (2000–3000 m).

Andean Lizard, Lagartija andina
Liolaemus andinus (molinai)
OTHER NAMES: Molina's or Schmidt's Lizard.
ID: SV 3 in (7.5 cm). Tail is shorter than the snout–vent length. Grey, with an ochre rib and spine pattern on the back.
RANGE: Antofagasta. On the Altiplano above 13,000 ft (4000 m).

Buerger's Lizard, Lagartija de Buerger
Liolaemus buergeri
ID: SV 2.5 in (6.25 cm). Sooty brown.
RANGE: Maule to Biobío. In the Andes, around 9850 ft (3000 m).

Chilean Lizard, Lagartija chilena
Lagartija de cabeza verde
Liolaemus chiliensis
ID: SV 3–3.75 in (8–9.5 cm). Brownish-grey body, with green head. Scaly. Oviparous.
RANGE: Coquimbo to Los Lagos; 1000–3900 ft (300-1200 m).

Cyan Lizard, Lagartija de vientre azul
Liolaemus cyanogaster
ID: SV 2.5 in (6.25 cm). Color ranges from a green body with brownish tail to a brown body with tan longitudinal stripes and bright green highlights on sides and face. Vent is usually cyan.
RANGE: Concepción to Chiloé; adjacent Argentina. In a variety of habitats.

Fabian's Lizard, Lagartija de Fabián
Liolaemus fabiani
OTHER NAME: Yañez's Lizard.
ID: SV 3 in (7.5 cm). Beautiful beaded pattern of black, cream and sulphur yellow.
RANGE: Salar de Atacama. On salt flats.

Fitzinger's Lizard, Lagartija de Fitzinger
Liolaemus fitzingeri
ID: SV 3 in (7.5 cm). Heavy-bodied. Grey to bluish; rust-colored patches on the back.
RANGE: Southern Chile and Patagonia.

Brown Lizard, Lagartija oscura
Liolaemus fuscus
ID: SV 2 in (5 cm). Brown with two pale longitudinal lines along each side. Oviparous.
RANGE: Coquimbo to Biobío; Argentina; 1540–4250 ft (500-1300 m).

Gravenhorst's Lizard
Lagartija de Gravenhorst
Liolaemus gravenhorsti
ID: SV 2.5 in (6.25 cm). Brown with a longitudinal dull ochre line running down each side from the neck to the base of the tail. Vent is golden brown. Named after Johann Gravenhorst (1777–1857), a German naturalist at the University of Breslau, Poland.
RANGE: Valparaíso to Santiago; 1540–4250 ft (500–1300 m).

Wreath Lizard, Lagartija lemniscatus
Liolaemus lemniscatus
ID: SV 1.75–2.25 in (4.5–5.5 cm). A slender, long tailed lizard. Polymorphic. Pale brown with pale side stripes, or pale brown sides with dark brown and lead grey stripes on the back. Oviparous.
RANGE: Coquimbo to Los Lagos; Argentine Patagonia; 800–4600 ft (250–1400 m).

Leopard Lizard, Lagartija leopardo
Liolaemus leopardinus
ID: SV 3 in (7.5 cm). Light brown; camouflaged by mottled greenish spots on its back when on lichen-encrusted rocks.
RANGE: Central Chilean Andes outside Santiago. On large rocky outcrops.

Magellanic Lizard, Lagartija magellánica
Liolaemus magellanicus
ID: SV 2.5 in (6.25 cm). Coarse body scales. Light brown to grey, patterned with dark brown rectangles on back, sides and tail.
RANGE: Aisén, Magallanes, Tierra del Fuego. Most southern reptile of the Americas.

Mountain Lizard
Lagartija de los montes
Liolaemus monticola
ID: SV 2.25–2.75 in (5.75–7 cm). Extremely variable. Common form has a brown back, with black spots and two whitish longitudinal lines. Sides are blackish, with white and brown spots. Feet and tail are brown with small black spots. Vent is pale grey. Feeds on insects, especially ants. Perches on small rocks, often at the edge of woodland.
RANGE: El Maule, Valparaíso, to Santiago; Andes; 1150–7900 ft (350–2400 m).

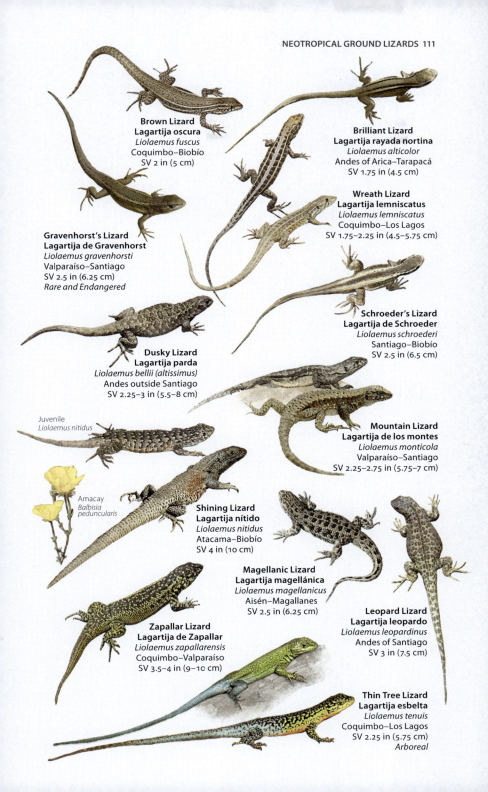

Black-headed Lizard
Lagartija de cabeza negra
Liolaemus (Ctenoblepharis) nigriceps
ID: SV 2.5 in (6.25 cm). Black head; body grey with rust or gold.
RANGE: Andes of Atacama; nw Argentina.

Many-spotted Lizard
Lagartija de mancha
Liolaemus nigromaculatus
ID: SV 2.25–2.75 in (5.75–7 cm). Numerous pale spots on a dark body.
RANGE: Antofagasta to Coquimbo; sandy coastal terraces and matorral, in vegetation such as Coronilla del fraile *(Encelia canescens)* or Hierba del salitre *(Frankenia chilensis)*; 250–3950 ft (80–1200 m).

Blackish-green Lizard
Lagartija negro verdosa
Liolaemus nigroviridis
ID: SV 2.5–3 in (6.25–7.5 cm). Blackish body, with white spots on the back and sides, some tinted greyish-green.
RANGE: Valparaíso to Santiago; between 3600–7900 ft (1100–2400 m).

Shining Lizard, Lagarto nítido
Liolaemus nitidus
ID: SV 4 in (10 cm). Adult brownish black on the back, with rust and white scales on the sides. Juvenile has bands of black and white scaling down the back. Insectivorous. Oviparous. VULNERABLE.
RANGE: Atacama to Biobío. In the Coastal Range and Andes, on rocky slopes with matorral vegetation such as Yellow Daisy *(Haplopappus parvifolius)*, Amacay *(Balbisia peduncularis)*, Quisco cactus *(Copiapoa carrizalensis)* or Coironcillo grass *(Stipa tortuosa)*; 1650–7550 ft (500–2300 m).

Paulina's Lizard, Lagartija de Paulina
Liolaemus paulinae
ID: SV 1.25 in (3.2 cm). Small, with small feet. Back is light brown; underparts are grey with reddish tints. Inhabits scrub with Cachiyuyo saltbush *(Atriplex atacamensis)*. Feeds on insects, small beetles and flies.
RANGE: Found only in Calama, Antofagasta.

Painted Tree Lizard
Lagartija pintada
Liolaemus pictus
ID: SV 3 in (7.5 cm). Polymorphic. Common form is colored cyan, with a wide dark brown band and delicate black lines down the back. Underside is grey, with reddish tints on the sides. Tail has black transverse bands. Arboreal. Feeds on insects supplemented with flower nectar and fruit.
RANGE: Maule to Los Lagos and Chiloé. In wooded areas.

Braided Lizard, Lagartija
Liolaemus platei
ID: SV 2.5 in (6.25 cm). Dark, with a plated pattern of black and brown, edged on each side by golden longitudinal lines.
RANGE: Antofagasta to Coquimbo; sandy or gravel soils; on low rocks or in succulent vegetation such as *Nolana, Heliotropium, Pleocarpus* and *Opuntia*. Said to feed on flowers of *Copiapoa hasseltoniana* cactus around Paposo, Antofagasta.

Schroeder's Lizard
Lagartija de Schroeder
Liolaemus schroederi
ID: SV 2.5 in (6.25 cm). Pale tan, with rows of brown bands on the back and tail.
RANGE: Santiago to Biobío. On rocky coasts and in the coastal mountains above 3600 ft (1100 m).

Thin Tree Lizard
Lagartija esbelta
Liolaemus tenuis
ID: SV 2.25 in (5.75 cm). Long-tail. Brightly colored. Arboreal. Males are colored in bright cyan, chartreuse and yellow, often with black spotting on back and head. Females have muted colors, and are always found within the confines of a colonized tree or fence. Lays eggs in communal nests. In one case, about 400 eggs that had been covered with blackberry leaves were found on top of an adobe fence. Feeds on insects.
RANGE: Coquimbo to Los Lagos. Lives almost exclusively at the base of, or in the foliage of trees; 650–5900 ft (200–1800 m).

Zapallar Lizard, Lagarto de Zapallar
Liolaemus zapallarensis
ID: SV 3.5–4 in (9–10 cm). Black with bright yellow scales on back and sides.
RANGE: Coquimbo to Valparaíso; sea level to 1650 ft (500 m).

SUBFAMILY TROPIDURINAE: GENUS MICROLOPHUS
PACIFIC IGUANIDS
Atacama Lava Lizard
Corredor de Atacama
Microlophus atacamensis
OTHER NAME: Atacamen Pacific Iguana.
ID: SV 2.5–4.75 in (6.25–12 cm). Males have a larger snout-vent length, hindlimb and head than females. Dark grey with variable pale grey to greenish-grey mottling on the back. Sides are blackish. Related to the Lava Lizard of the Galapagos. Northern coastal populations are often seen foraging in the intertidal zone for marine invertebrates or algae; lizards in the southern and inland areas feed on terrestrial prey. Adults and subadults can be aggressive towards juveniles. Females select larger males for mating, and larger males have larger or better territories.
RANGE: Atacama Desert. Common on dark coastal rocks. Fewer observations inland, but this may be due to similarity of *M. tarapacensis*.
RELATED SPECIES: CORREDOR DE ARICA, *Tropidurus heterolepis*, is greenish brown, with white spots on the back and a black spot near the mouth. White vent. Feeds on invertebrates and algae on the Arica coast. DESERT LIZARD, CORREDOR DE TARAPACÁ, *Microlophus tarapacensis*; tamarugo groves in Tarapacá. *Microlophus quadrivittatus* and *M. yanezi*; Arica.

Corredor de Pica, Corredor de Tereza
Microlophus theresioides
ID: SV 2.5–4.75 in (6.25–12 cm). Pale grey with delicate white spotting on the back. Orange ring around the eye. Males have a blue and yellow trait.
RANGE: Desert around Pica in Tarapacá.

GENUS PHRYNOSAURA
DRAGON LIZARDS
Lagarto Dragón de Reiche
Phrynosaura reichei
ID: SV 2.5 in (6.25 cm). Pale golden brown with darker brown spotting on the head and body. Inhabits hyper-arid desert areas and spends most of the day under the salt crust to avoid excessive dessication. Said to feed only on wind-borne insects.
RANGE: RARE. Arica to Antofagasta.
RELATED SPECIES: DRAGON DE OÍDO CUBIERTO, *Phrynosaura audituvelata*; RARE from Arica to Tarapacá. *P. manueli*; RARE at Diego de Almagro, Atacama. *P. torresi*; Calama only.

GENUS PHYMATURUS
MOUNTAIN LIZARDS
Phymaturus is a small group of mid-sized lizards found in the Andes of Argentina and Chile and the central Patagonian Plateau. These lizards have a robust body, short legs and a spiny tail. Most species are dark in color, but some have bright orange, yellow, or green patches. They are usually found in areas with large boulders and rock crevices. All species are viviparous.

High Mountain Lizard, Matuasto
Phymaturus flagellifer
OTHER NAMES: *Centrura flagelifera*, *Phymaturus palluma*.
ID: SV 3–5 in (7.5–12.5 cm). Wide, flattened body. Variable skin patterns, often marked with green or yellow. Greenish-brown tail with brown spots on the sides. Omnivorous. Viviparous. VULNERABLE.
RANGE: Santiago to Maule; also Argentina; 3950–11,500 ft (1200–3500 m).
RELATED SPECIES: *Phymaturus vociferator*; RARE in the High Andes of Biobío. Makes loud noises when disturbed.

GENUS DIPLOLAEMUS
PATAGONIAN IGUANIDS
These South American lizards have large, triangular heads and strong jaws. They feed on insects and other small invertebrates. The genus is also placed in the Leiosauridae.

Leopard Grumbler
Diplolaemus leopardinus
ID: SV 2–3.75 in (5–9 cm). Large, triangular head. Brown with dark brown patches that form bands down the back and sides.
RANGE: Local in Lonquimay Valley, Araucanía; 3500–6500 ft (1000–2000 m).
RELATED SPECIES: DARWIN'S GRUMBLER, *Diplolaemus darwinii*; Magallanes; sea level to 2300 ft (0–700 m). BIBRON'S GRUMBLER, *Diplolaemus bibronii*; Aisén to Magallanes; sea level to 3500 ft (0–1000 m).

SUBFAMILY POLYCRINAE: GENUS PRISTIDACTYLUS
PRIMITIVE ANOLES
Pristidactylus is a genus of terrestrial South America lizards. In Chile, they range in the forests and woodlands of the central and southern regions. Most have a dark collar on the underside of the neck. They feed on insects and other small invertebrates. This genus is also placed in the Leiosauridae.

Southern Grumbler, Gruñidor del sur
Pristidactylus torquatus
OTHER NAMES: Forest Lizard, Lagarto de bosque. *Torquatus* is Latin for "wearing a twisted necklace or collar."
ID: SV 2.5–4.25 in (6.25–11 cm). Robust. Large head and strong feet. Back is reddish with large grey patches. Vent is greenish-yellow. Lives under shade trees where it feeds mainly on beetles that it cuts with its strong jaws. Breeds in summer. Females lay 5 to 6 eggs in the sand.
RANGE: Maule to Los Lagos, in open woodland and matorral.
RELATED SPECIES: *Pristidactylus valeriae*; Altos de Cantillana, Valparaíso. *P. alvaroi*; Cerro El Roble, Santiago. *P. volcanensis*; El Volcán, in the Andes near Santiago.

FAMILY TEIIDAE
WHIPTAILS AND TEGUS
These lizards are distinguished by an elongated body, pointed head, well-developed limbs, and long neck, trunk and tail. They have granular scales on the back and large, rectangular ventral plates.

Chilean Iguana, Iguana chilena
Callopistes maculatus (palluma)
ID: SV 5–6.5 in (12.5–16.5 cm). Brown back with four rows of black dots edged with white. Vent is reddish in males and pale yellow in females. Females lay eggs in underground burrows. Diurnal.
RANGE: Antofagasta to Maule. Rocky coasts, quebradas and matorral, often in succulent vegetation such as *Nolana, Heliotropium, Pleocarphus* and *Opuntia*; sea level to 1650 ft (0–500 m).

FAMILY SCINCIDAE
SKINKS
The large scales that cover the head and body of skinks are actually bony plates covered with skin. Many species, but not all, have movable eyelids. The lower eyelid is the one that closes over the eye, and some species have a clear window in the lower eyelid that allows vision even when it is closed. Most skinks are active during the day.

Snake-eyed Skink
Moko Uri-uri, Lagarto negro
Cryptoblepharus poecilopleurus
OTHER NAME: *Ablepharus boutoni*. Snake-eyed refers to the lack of moveable eyelids.
ID: SV 2 in (5 cm). Slender, elongated body is blackish, with cyan and gold metallic highlights. Two pale lines extend along the sides from the head to the tail. Moves using lateral undulation. Diurnal. Insectivorous. Oviparous. Lays two yellow eggs.
RANGE: Easter Island and tropical Pacific.

INFRAORDER GECKOTA
FAMILY GECKONIDAE
GECKOS
Geckos are characterized by large, often lidless eyes with vertical pupils. The nearly transparent body skin is covered with fine, beaded scales. They have enlarged toe pads with numerous setae (stiff hairs), which act like suction cups and enable them to climb on vertical surfaces or cling to ceilings. Geckos are generally nocturnal or active at twilight. They are sometimes active during

LIZARDS, GRUMBLERS, DRAGONS, IGUANAS AND SKINKS

Corredor de Pica
Microlophus theresioides
Desert in Tarapacá
SV 2.5–4.75 in (6.25–12 cm)

Atacama Lava Lizard
Corredor de Atacama
Microlophus atacamensis
Atacama Desert coast
SV 2.5–4.75 in (6.25–12 cm)

High Mountain Lizard
Matuasto
Phymaturus flagellifer
Santiago–Maule
SV 3–5 in (7.5–12.5 cm)

Chilean Iguana
Iguana chilena
Callopistes maculatus
Antofagasta–Maule
SV 5–6.5 in (12.5–16.5 cm)

Phymaturus vociferator
Rare in Andes of Biobío
SV 4 in (10 cm)

Lagarto Dragón de Reiche
Phrynosaura reichei
Desert of Arica–Tarapacá
SV 2.5 in (6.25 cm)

Southern Grumbler
Gruñidor del sur
Pristidactylus torquatus
Maule–Los Lagos
SV 2.5–4.25 in (6.25–11 cm)

Lagarto Dragón
Phrynosaura manueli
Rare in Atacama
SV 2.25 in (5.75 cm)

Darwin's Grumbler
Lagartija patagónica
Diplolaemus darwinii
Magallanes
SV 2–4 in (5–10 cm)

Pristidactylus volcanensis
El Volcán, Santiago
SV 2–3.75 in (5–9 cm)

Snake-eyed Skink
Moko Uri-uri
Cryptoblepharus poecilopleurus
Easter Island
SV 2 in (5 cm)

Leopard Grumbler
Diplolaemus leopardinus
Lonquimay Valley, Araucanía
SV 2–3.75 in (5–9 cm)

Mourning Gecko
Moko Uru-uru Kahu
Gekko polinésico
Lepidodactylus lugubris
Easter Island
SV 2 in (5 cm)

Chilean Marked Gecko
Salamanqueja del Norte Chico
Homonota gaudichaudii
Antofagasta–Coquimbo
SV 1–3 in (2.5–7.5 cm)

Leaf-toed Gecko
Salamanqueja del Norte Grande
Phyllodactylus gerrhopygus
Arica–Antofagasta
SV 1–3 in (2.5–7.5 cm)

the day inside buildings, in dense shade, or in other subdued light. They typically lay two eggs with hard, durable, calcareous shells that resist dehydration. This feature may account for their successful dispersal on logs and vegetation carried by ocean currents as well as incidental transport by both early and modern man.

Chilean Marked Gecko
Salamanqueja del Norte Chico
Homonota gaudichaudii
ID: SV 1–3 in (2.5–7.5 cm). Tan to greyish, with irregular dark lines and patches.
RANGE: Antofagasta to Coquimbo; Bolivia. Found along the desert coast; often around Copao cactus (*Eulychnia* sp.).
RELATED SPECIES: DARWIN'S MARKED GECKO, *Homonota darwinii*; Patagonia. D'ORBIGNY'S MARKED GECKO, *Homonota dorbignii*; Aconcagua to Valparaiso; mainly coastal. COQUIMBO MARKED GECKO, *Homonota penai*; Atacama to Coquimbo; in the interior desert; 5000–7900 ft (1500–2400 m).

Leaf-toed Gecko
Salamanqueja del Norte Grande
Phyllodactylus gerrhopygus
ID: SV 1–3 in (2.5–7.5 cm). Tan, brown, or pinkish back. Dark spots on the back; the dorsal granular scales are interspersed with tubercles (small bumps). Underparts are buff with a whitish vent. Vertical pupils. Immovable eyelids. Leaf-like toe pads. Fragile tail breaks off very easily. Lives under rocks, in abandoned buildings or in homes where it walks and runs on walls and ceilings. Nocturnal. Feeds on insects. Makes insect-like chirps. Lays one to two white eggs.
RANGE: Arica to Antofagasta, mainly in Azapa Valley, the Pica Oasis, and Mamiña Valley; sea level to 9000 ft (2750 m).
RELATED SPECIES: PERU LEAF-TOED GECKO, *Phyllodactylus inaequalis*; Mamiña Oasis (inland from Iquique), on the Antofagasta coast, and in w Peru.

Mourning Gecko
Moko Uru-uru Kahu, Gekko polinésico
Lepidodactylus lugubris
ID: SV 2 in (5 cm). Smooth skin. Pale buff to brown, with a dark brown, wavy chevron pattern on the back. Black bar runs along each side of the head from the snout. Can change color to suit surroundings. Makes a loud chirping noise *chik-chik-chik-chik*. Active in low light inside houses, under foliage, and at twilight. The female's eggs do not require fertilization by a male (a process known as parthenogenesis); consequently populations may all be female.
RANGE: Easter Island (Rapa Nui) and trans-Pacific. Widespread in natural habitats and in close association with humans.

COLUBRID AND SEA SNAKES

Chilean Slender Snake
Culebra de cola corta
Tachymenis chilensis
Atacama–Los Lagos
24 in (60 cm)

Yellow-bellied Sea Snake
Culebra de cola corta
Pelamis platurus
Easter Island
18–25 in (45–64 cm)

Long-tailed Green Racer
Culebra de cola larga
Philodryas chamissonis
Atacama–Biobío
72 in (185 cm)

Elegant Racer
Philodryas elegans
Arica–Tarapacá
77 in (195 cm)

SUBORDER SERPENTES: FAMILY COLUBRIDAE
COLUBRID SNAKES

Colubrid snakes are referred to as "typical snakes." They comprise the largest family of serpents with over 2000 species worldwide. Most are medium-sized, lack a pelvic girdle and lack vestigial hind limbs. The left lung is either absent or greatly reduced.

Long-tailed Green Racer
Culebra de cola larga
Philodryas chamissonis

ID: Heavy bodied snake, to about 72 in (185 cm) long. Brown with yellowish longitudinal stripes that are edged with black lines. Aggressive and graceful. Very active; moves easily in bushes and trees. Hunts for small reptiles, birds, rodents and rabbits, killing them mainly through constriction. Mildly venomous; the venom contains an anticoagulant that induces prolonged bleeding. Venom flows from the back teeth of the upper mandible. No serious threat to humans.
RANGE: ENDEMIC. Atacama to Biobío; in coastal desert and Mediterranean zone.
RELATED SPECIES: ELEGANT RACER, *Philodryas elegans*. 77 in (195 cm). Coastal and inland desert of Tarapacá; 0–10,000 ft (0–3300 m). SCHMIDT'S RACER, *P. tachimenoides*. Arica, in Camarones, Lluta and Azapa Quebradas. SIMON'S RACER, *P. simonsii*. Arica.

Chilean Slender Snake
Culebra de cola corta
Tachymenis chilensis

ID: 24 in (60 cm). Pale brown, with a longitudinal whitish band edged with a thin black line on each side. Feeds on frogs and lizards. Venomous. Venom contains a neurotoxin that affects the nervous system. No serious threat to humans.
RANGE: Atacama to Los Lagos; also Peru; sea level to 6550 ft (0–2000 m).
RELATED SPECIES: PERU SLENDER SNAKE, *Tachymenis peruviana*. High Andes of Arica and Tarapacá; Peru, Bolivia, nw Argentina.

FAMILY HYDROPHIIDAE
SEA SNAKES
Yellow-bellied Sea Snake
Pelamis platurus

ID: 18–25 in (46–64 cm) in the e Pacific; to 45 in (114 cm) elsewhere. Narrow, elongated, flattened head. Flattened body and tail. Blackish-brown back with bright or pale yellow sides and underside; may be all yellow or yellow with a narrow black stripe on the back. Black spots or bars on tail. Not aggressive. Small fangs on front of upper jaw. Venom yield low. Eats small, surface-dwelling fish and eels. Forms large congregations at sea, possibly for breeding.
RANGE: Easter Island. Widespread in the Indo-Pacific Ocean.

> CLASS AMPHIBIA
> ## AMPHIBIANS
> Amphibia derives from the Greek *amphi* meaning "both" and *bios* meaning "life." Amphibians usually live in freshwater when young, then change to forms that can live on land. Their metamorphosis involves the gills becoming lungs, fins becoming legs, and the diet changing from vegetarian to a carnivorous one.
>
> Amphibia includes toads and frogs, which are in the order Anura. Adult toads are terrestrial, have dry warty skin, and they hop. Frogs are mainly aquatic, have smooth slick skin, and they leap.
>
> Most amphibians share the following features:
> - Bony skeleton
> - Head joins directly to the trunk, with no intervening neck
> - Large eyes located on top of head
> - Large mouth with an extendable tongue
> - Skin lacks scales and has many glands; some may be poison glands
> - Adults develop from tailed tadpoles
> - Gills are external in the larval form
> - Respiration is through the lungs, skin and gills, either separately or in combination, in various life stages
> - Three-chambered heart
> - Cold-bloodedness—a condition where the body temperature varies with the environment
>
> About one third of the world's amphibian species are threatened with extinction. A widespread fungal disease called chytridiomycosis is one cause behind their decline.

ORDER ANURA
TOADS AND FROGS

Chile has about 60 species of toads and frogs. Many are relatively rare or restricted to a single locality. Some species' populations are declining due to habitat destruction or disease, others for unknown reasons.

Toads and frogs in the order Anura have the head joined directly to the trunk and a short vertebral column. Forelimbs are short. Hindlimbs are long and are used for jumping and swimming. The eyes are large and on top of the head. Superficial ear membranes lie behind the eyes. Adults have no tail. Toads and frogs are primarily nocturnal. Most spend the day resting under logs or leaves, or hiding in damp burrows. They emerge from their shelters at night to hunt for insects and other small invertebrate prey.

Anurans lay eggs, have external fertilization and develop from tailed tadpoles. Males are usually smaller than females, and have vocal sacs. During the spring mating season, groups of males join in nocturnal chorus in order to attract females. If a male is successful in enticing a receptive female, he climbs onto her back and clings to her as he fertilizes her eggs.

Most toads and frogs shed their eggs directly into the water where they hatch into long-tailed tadpoles equipped with external gills. After a varying period of time—sometimes a year or more—skin grows over the gills, the tail absorbs into the body, and an adult frog or toad emerges.

In the case of Darwin's Frog, the female deposits her eggs into leaf litter. When the larvae inside the eggs begin to move, the adult male takes them up into his mouth and incubates them in his vocal sac. The young emerge from the male's mouth in their adult form.

FAMILY BUFONIDAE
TRUE TOADS

Toads are squat-bodied, tailless, terrestrial amphibians. Their dry, warty skin reduces water loss and allows survival in arid areas. They have horizontal pupils and prominent bony ridges called cranial crests on top of the head. They also have wartlike structures called PAROTID GLANDS behind the eyes—a feature that distinguishs true toads from all other tailless amphibians. The glands and warts secrete a fatty, white, toxic substance that acts as a deterrent to predators. True toads have no teeth. They have a long tongue attached to the front of the lower jaw that can be extended to catch prey. The toad's short, powerful legs are suited for crawling and hopping. Toads copulate while floating on the water surface. The male, who is normally smaller than the female, clings to the female's back, fertilizing the strings of eggs as they pass into the water.

South American toads formerly classed in the genus *Bufo* have recently been placed in a new genus, *Chanus*.

Concepción Toad, Arunco
Chaunus (Bufo) arunco
OTHER NAMES: *Bufo chilensis,* Sapo de Rulo, Sapo de Secano, Gen-co (Mapuche).
ID: 2.5–4 in (6.25–10 cm). A large toad with a big head. Glandular skin with prominent, conical warts. Color and color pattern are variable. The back is normally pale grey, with irregular dark patches. The underside is cream, at times with blackish spots. Feet and digits are sometimes washed with rose, and the soles of the feet can be tinted yellow. JUVENILES are greyish, often with yellow-orange limbs and sometimes with red spots on the body.

These toads occupy semi-arid habitats and hide in small holes or under rocks during the daytime. Adults feed mainly on insects. They seek out shallow bodies of freshwater for copulation and egg laying. Long strings of eggs are deposited directly into the water upon fertilization (Aug–Oct). The black tadpoles are free swimming. VULNERABLE.
RANGE: Central Chilean dry steppe from Coquimbo to Concepción. Found from coast to mountains; near streams, rivers, reservoirs; sea level to 4900 ft (0–1500 m).

Atacama Toad, Vallenar Toad Sapo del desierto
Chaunus (Bufo) atacamensis
ID: 2–3 in (5–7.5 cm). Males and females are the same size. Large, angular head is more than one-third of body length. Males are yellow to greenish-yellow with dark blurry patches; female greyish. Skin is relatively smooth and almost free of callosities (bumpy growths). Lives under rocks near oases and streams. Reproduction takes place in freshwater ponds, livestock tanks, streams and rivers. Long strings of eggs are deposited directly into the water. VULNERABLE.
RANGE: ENDEMIC. Coastal Atacama and around the Ríos Huasco and Copiapó; isolated populations near Paposa in Antofagasta; 800–8200 ft (250–2500 m).

Red-spotted Toad, Sapo
Chaunus (Bufo) rubropunctatus
ID: 2–2.5 in (5–6.25 cm). Males are smaller than females. Dark grey to dark olive, with whitish bands and reticulations and a few rust-colored spots. Fairly smooth skin with rounded glandular bumps. Small and heavy bodied. Large head, with a short neck. Eyes placed well to the sides of the head. Prominent parotid glands. Short digits. Adults live in small holes or under bushes, logs or stones during the day. Forms large aggregations in breeding season. Breeding occurs in shallow temporary ponds adjacent to rivers, reservoirs and lakes. VULNERABLE.
RANGE: Biobío to Los Lagos; also Argentina. In wet to dry *Nothofagus* forest; 650–2635 ft (200–800 m).

Warty Toad, Sapo espinosus
Chaunus (Bufo) spinulosus
OTHER NAMES: Sapo de rulo, Andean Spiny Toad, Huanuco Toad, Capillococha Toad.
ID: 2–3 in (5–7.5 cm). Uniformly brown or greenish-brown, often with small, irregular, dark blotches on the female. Fairly small head with close-set eyes. Long anterior legs. Small parotid glands. Many rounded and pointed bumps on the back and digits. Nocturnal, but sometimes seen in daytime on cloudy and rainy days or during mating season. Breeding takes place in temporary ponds, Altiplano lagoons and slow flowing streams. VULNERABLE.
RANGE: Arica to Valparaíso; Peru, Bolivia; also Argentine Patagonia *(C. s. papillosus)*. Common in cultivated fields around Arica and the Río Loa, in ravines and scrub in the High Andes, and on the Altiplano

near Volcán Licanbur and the Volcán Taito geysers; sea level to 14,750 ft (500–4500 m).

Patagonian Toad, Eden Harbor Toad
Chaunus (Bufo) variegatus
ID: 2 in (5 cm). Males smaller than females. Short neck. Brown to greenish, with pale dorsal streaks. Underside white, with black spots. No visible eardrum. Oval parotid glands at eyes. Skin on the male's legs is dotted with prominent, rounded callosities (bumpy growths). Male sometimes emits peeping calls. Occupies cold, wet forests, bogs and Magellanic tundra; often found under logs in southern *Nothofagus* forest. Reproduces in shallow temporary pools and swamps. Fairly rare in Chile.
RANGE: Laguna del Laja in Biobío to Isla Wellington in Magallanes; also s Argentina; sea level to 6500 ft (0–2000 m).

FAMILY BATRACHOPHRYNIDAE
HELMETED WATER TOADS
Helmeted Water Toad, Chilean Toad
Rana chilena gigante
Caudiverbera caudiverbera
OTHER NAMES: Gay's Frog, Chilenischer Helmkopffrosch.
ID: MALES 5 in (12.5 cm). FEMALES 10 in (25 cm). Robust body. Large head, with a short, rounded snout. Small eyes with vertical pupil. Smooth skin, with elongate pustules on the back. Breeding males have black nuptial growths on the inner surfaces of the thumbs. Fingers are moderately short and unwebbed; toes are about one-half webbed. Back is dull brown with faint, paler, irregular markings; underside is greyish-white. Iris is dull bronze. Active by day and night. When threatened, these toads inflate the lungs, elevate the body, open the mouth, lunge and bite. Feeds on aquatic insect larvae, fishes, frogs, and some small birds and mammals. During breeding season (Sep–Oct), eggs are laid in clumps in shallow water of ponds; clutches consist of a globular mass of 800 to 1600 eggs, which hatch about twenty days after deposition. The tadpoles develop in ponds, with the metamorphosis taking about two years. Adults live 10 to 15 years. There is some trapping of this species for human food and efforts have been made to establish artisanal raniculture.
RANGE: Coquimbo to Los Lagos. Primarily aquatic in large, deep ponds, lakes and rivers; sea level to 1650 ft (0–500 m).

False Toads
Telmatobufo spp.
This group includes *Telmatobufo venustus, T. australis* and *T. bullocki,* which range in s Chile and Argentina. The SAPO HERMOSO, *T. venustus,* is so rare that in 1999 it was found in the Andean forests of Maule and Biobío for the first time in over 100 years.

FAMILY LEIUPERIDAE
FOUR-EYED FROGS
Prominent glandular bumps on the hips of this group of frogs give the appearance of an extra set of eyes, thus the common name, Four-eyed Frogs.

Chile Four-eyed Frog
Sapito de cuatro ojos
Pleurodema thaul
ID: 2 in (5 cm). Polymorphic. Base color is cream to tan or olive; large, dark brown or black ovals edged with cream decorate the back and legs. A pale longitudinal band runs down the center of the back. Conspicuous eye-like glands on the hips. Adults are terrestrial, hiding in vegetation, and under logs and rocks. Makes repeated chirping sounds around breeding ponds in spring. Prefers shallow water for egg-laying.
RANGE: Atacama to Los Lagos; Argentina. Abundant in sclerophyll and *Nothofagus* forest; also found in grasslands, urban areas and other altered habitats.
RELATED SPECIES: MARBLED FOUR-EYED FROG, *Pleurodema marmoratum,* is locally common on open Puna and Altiplano above 12,750 ft (3900 m) in Chile, Bolivia and Peru. GREY FOUR-EYED FROG, *Pleurodema bufoninum,* occurs on steppes from Biobío to the Strait of Magellan and into Argentine Patagonia.

TOADS AND FOUR-EYED FROGS

Concepción Toad, Arunco
Chaunus (Bufo) arunco
Coquimbo–Concepción
2.5–4 in (6.25–10 cm)

Warty Toad, Sapo espinosus
Chaunus (Bufo) spinulosus
Arica–Valparaíso
2–3 in (5–7.5 cm)

Red-spotted Toad, Sapo
Chaunus (Bufo) rubropunctatus
Biobío–Los Lagos
2–2.5 in (5–6.25 cm)
Nothofagus forest

Atacama Toad, Sapo del desierto
Chaunus (Bufo) atacamensis
Antofagasta–Atacama
2–3 in (5–7.5 cm)
Desert oases, streams

**Patagonian Toad, Eden Harbor Toad
Sapo variegado**
Chaunus (Bufo) variegatus
Forest; Biobío–Magallanes
2 in (5 cm)

Grey Four-eyed Frog
Pleurodema bufoninum
Biobío–Magallanes
2 in (5 cm)

**Chile Four-eyed Frog
Sapito de cuatro ojos**
Pleurodema thaul
Atacama–Los Lagos
2 in (5 cm)

Four-eyed frogs are named for the bump on their hips, which gives the impression that they have an extra set of eyes.

Sapo hermoso
Telmatobufo venustus
Andes; Maule–Biobío
2 in (5 cm)
Recently rediscovered in Chile

**Helmeted Water Toad, Chilean Toad
Rana chilena gigante**
Caudiverbera caudiverbera
Coquimbo–Los Lagos
5–10 in (12.5–25 cm)

Juvenile

Helmeted water toads are the largest Chilean amphibian. Tadpoles are about 6 in (15 cm) long before they lose their tail. Adult males are about 5 in (12.5 cm) long and adult females are normally twice that size.

FAMILY CERATOPHRYIDAE, SUBFAMILY BATRACHYLINAE

WOOD FROGS

Male wood frogs chorus in austral autumn (Jan–May), calling from the water's edge or from under vegetation, fallen logs and rocks. Eggs are laid in clusters of 100 to 150 and are fertilized on damp soil under logs and rocks, where embryonic development takes place. In rainy season, these areas flood and the tadpoles develop in the flood water. Adults of most species climb trees.

Marbled Wood Frog, Sapo
Batrachyla antartandica
ID: 1–2 in (2.5–5 cm). Yellow with black and brown marbling. Eggs are laid on the ground under logs or moss.
RANGE: Valdivia to Los Lagos; s Argentina. Occupies wet, temperate to cold *Nothofagus* forest, bogs, wetlands in forests, shorelines of ponds, marsh-fringed lakes and irrigated farms and gardens.

Grey Wood Frog, Sapo
Batrachyla leptopus
ID: 1.75 in (4.5 cm). Greyish-brown, smooth, slick skin, with irregular dark grey patches. Underside is white with fine black dots. Occupies temperate to subantarctic rainforests, bogs and wetlands in forests, shores of ponds, and lakes surrounded by swamps. Males call from hollows found under moss near streams. Adults have been observed climbing *Nothofagus* trees and exhibiting parental care behavior.
RANGE: Biobío to Los Lagos, and possibly to the Strait of Magellan; also s Argentina. In temperate *Nothofagus* forest; 165–3300 ft (50–1000 m).

Nibaldo's Wood Frog
Sapo de Nibaldo
Batrachyla nibaldoi
ID: 1.75 in (4.5 cm). Brown with darker brown bands on sides and legs similar to the Banded Wood Frog. Occupies steppe habitat in valleys surrounded by forests of *Nothofagus antartica, Nothofagus betuloides* and *Drimys winteri*. Often found under logs, rocks and shrubs.
RANGE: Temperate rainforest on eastern slopes of the Andes in Los Lagos, and at Laguna San Rafael National Park and Las Guaitecas National Reserve in Aisén.

Banded Wood Frog, Sapo
Batrachyla taeniata
ID: 1.75 in (4.5 cm). Brown, with darker brown and pale bands on sides and legs. Occupies a broad range of climates and habitats ranging from the matorral and espinal to the Valdivian rainforest. Lives around temporary or permanent, shallow ponds that are surrounded by swamps and bogs. Populations in central Chile inhabit relict forests or marshes in *Nothofagus* forest. Males call from under bushes, and eggs are laid under logs and in the leaf litter.
RANGE: Coquimbo to Los Lagos; Neuquén to the lower Río Negro, Argentina. Occurs in a wide variety of habitats.

FAMILY CERATOPHRYIDAE; SUBFAMILY TELMATOBINAE

WATER FROGS

Water frogs occur in streams in the Andes of South America, from Ecuador to Chile and Argentina. These frogs average about 1.75 in (4 cm) in length.

Marbled Water Frog
Telmatobius marmoratus
ID: 1.75 in (4.5 cm). Greyish green, with dark spots. An aquatic species, living under stones in small streams and slow-flowing rivers. Reproduction occurs in the water. The large tadpoles are free-swimming.
RANGE: High Andes of ne Chile, s Peru, Bolivia and nw Argentina.
RELATED SPECIES: ZAPAHUIRA WATER FROG, *Telmatobius zapahuirensis,* is a semi-aquatic frog found in streams and small rivers in the High Andes. *Telmatobius vilamensis* and *Telmatobius pefauri* are fairly common in montane rivers in the High Desert, mainly around Río Vilama and the road between San Pedro de Atacama and the El Tatio Geyser. *Telmatobius fronteriensis* has been recorded from streams around the town of Ollague in Antofagasta.

FROGS 123

Marbled Wood Frog
Batrachyla antartandica
Valdivia–Puerto Montt
1–2 in (2.5–5 cm)

Banded Wood Frog
Batrachyla taeniata
Coquimbo–Los Lagos
1.75 in (4.5 cm)

Nibaldo's Wood Frog
Sapo de Nibaldo
Batrachyla nibaldoi
Los Lagos–Aisén
1.75 in (4.5 cm)

Grey Wood Frog
Batrachyla leptopus
Biobío–Los Lagos
1.75 in (4.5 cm)

Marbled Water Frog
Telmatobius marmoratus
High Andes of Arica–Tarapacá
1.75 in (4.5 cm)
Mountain streams

Grey morph

Chiloé Ground Frog
Eupsophus calcaratus
Biobío–Aisén
1.75 in (4.5 cm)

Russet morph

Nahuelbuta Ground Frog
Eupsophus nahuelbutensis
Nahuelbuta
1.75 in (4.5 cm)

Daytime colors

Emerald Forest Frog
Hylorina sylvatica
Biobío–Aisén
2–3 in (5–7.5 cm)

Rosy Ground Frog
Eupsophus roseus
Maule–Aisén
1.75 in (4.5 cm)

Nighttime colors

Valdivia Ground Frog
Eupsophus vertebralis
Biobío–Chiloé
1.75 in (4.5 cm)

Cabreria Spiny-chest Frog
Alsodes barrioi
Nahuelbuta
2 in (5 cm)

Darwin's Frogs sport many different color patterns but can always be identified by the long pointed snout.

Black Spiny-chest Frog
Sapo arriero
Alsodes nodosus
Valparaíso–Maule
2–3 in (5–7.5 cm)

Darwin's Frog
Sapito vaquero
Rhinoderma darwinii
Concepción–Aisén
1–1.5 in (2.5–3.75 cm)
Austral forests

FAMILY CYCLORAMPHIDAE; SUBFAMILY ALSODINAE
GROUND FROGS

In Chile, these small ground frogs live in wet areas in the *Nothofagus* forest. They average 1.75 in (4.5 cm) long. Most are brown in color, with a dark band running through the eye. In austral spring, males call from holes or burrows at the edge of forest streams. Larval metamorphosis takes place in small water-filled holes and tunnels in the ground near streams or flooded ground.

Chiloé Island Ground Frog
Eupsophus calcaratus
ID: Lives around swamps and riverbanks in humid *Nothofagus* forest. Free-swimming tadpoles develop in water-filled holes in the ground. Over much of its range, *Eupsophus calcaratus* is sympatric with the Grey Wood Frog, *Batrachyla leptopus*.
RANGE: Biobío to Aisén in Chile; adjacent Argentina. Near rivers and in wet forest.

Nahuelbuta Ground Frog
Eupsophus nahuelbutensis
ID: Lives under logs and rocks in temperate *Nothofagus* forest and lays eggs in small, terrestrial water-filled holes on hillsides.
RANGE: Locally common in the Nahuelbuta Range; 2950–4900 ft (900–1500 m).

Rosy Ground Frog
Eupsophus roseus
ID: Dark pinky-mauve with black markings. Lives under logs near swamps or streams in wet *Nothofagus* forest. Deposits eggs in water-filled holes on hillsides.
RANGE: Locally common from Maule to the Chonos Archipelago and Aisén; also in the Río Negro region of Argentina.

Valdivia Ground Frog
Eupsophus vertebralis
ID: Brown, with a creamy line on the back. Lives under logs and rocks near streams in temperate *Nothofagus* forest. Deposits eggs in water-filled holes on hillsides.
RANGE: Biobío to Chiloé.

RELATED SPECIES: The CONTULMO GROUND FROG, *Eupsophus contulmoensis* is black with yellow lines, spots and vermiculations. It lives under logs and rocks in *Nothofagus* forest. Known only from Contulmo in Malleco Province.
MOCHA ISLAND GROUND FROG, *Eupsophus insularis*, lives under logs in the mixed temperate forest on Mocha Island, off the central Chilean coast.
EMILIO'S GROUND FROG, *Eupsophus emiliopugini*, has a brown back with an iridescent gold line from snout to vent; sides and underside rosy-red. Terrestrial in humid forests with cold streams. Larval development takes place in water-filled cavities on the ground. Adults live under logs or in small holes at the edges of forest streams. In the breeding season males call from the small holes by day. Females deposit eggs inside the holes. Known from La Picada, Osorno Province, and Isla Kent, s Chile; also Lago Puelo National Park, Argentina.

FAMILY CYCLORAMPHIDAE; SUBFAMILY ALSODINAE
EMERALD FOREST FROGS

These beautiful frogs occupy humid forests from Valdivia to the Chonos Archipelago, Chile, and adjacent Argentina.

Emerald Forest Frog
Hylorina sylvatica
ID: 2–3 in (5–7.5 cm). Females are slightly larger than males. Males are more brightly colored. At night, both males and females are dark green; during the day they turn an emerald green with two iridescent copper bands. Eyes have a vertical, elliptical pupil. Tadpoles are light brown on top and dark brown below; there is dark ring around the nostrils and a rhomboidal spot between the eyes. In non-breeding season, these frogs live under fallen trunks or in leaf litter in *Nothofagus* forest. Mating and egg laying occur in austral summer (Dec–Jan) in open areas next to lakes and lagoons. Males congregate along the edge of water bodies,

and call in chorus before mating. The fertilized eggs sink and form a gelatinous mass in shallow water at the shoreline. The tadpoles emerge after about 10 days. Metamorphosis occurs at the end of one year.

RANGE: Forested areas from the Cordillera de Nahuelbuta to Laguna San Rafael; also in Nahuel Huapi and Los Alerces National Parks in sc Argentina.

FAMILY CYCLORAMPHIDAE; SUBFAMILY ALSODINAE
SPINY-CHEST FROGS

Black Spiny-chest Frog, Sapo arriero
Alsodes nodosus
ID: 2–3 in (5–7.5 cm). Robust. Blackish-olive back, at times with grey or metallic highlights or irregular spots. Skin is rough and spiny on the underside and chest. Locally common in temperate scrub and in seasonal and permanent streams, where it breeds. Tadpoles move to small backwater ponds where they undergo metamorphosis. Feeds on insects and larvae. ENDANGERED.

RANGE: Valparaíso to Maule; also Mendoza, Argentina. In forest and ravines with ample vegetation and freshwater.

RELATED SPECIES: CABRERIA SPINY-CHEST FROG, *Alsodes barrioi*, is found in the Nahuelbuta Range, under logs or rocks near mountain streams in *Nothofagus dombeyi* and *Araucaria* forest. VANZOLINI'S SPINY-CHEST FROG, *Alsodes vanzolini*, inhabits small patches of coastal *Nothofagus* forest. *Alsodes verrucosus* and *Alsodes australis* are known from the Aisén and Magallanes.

FAMILY CYCLORAMPHIDAE: SUBFAMILY CYCLORAMPHINAE
MOUTH-BROODING FROGS

Members of this family lay their eggs on land. Tadpoles complete their development in the vocal sacs of the male *Rhinoderma darwinii* or are carried to the water in the mouth of the male *Rhinoderma rufum*.

Darwin's Frog, Sapito vaquero, Narigon
Rhinoderma darwinii
ID: 1–1.5 in (2.5–3.75 cm). *Rhinoderma*, meaning "rhinoceros-nosed," refers to the fleshy, proboscis-like extension at the tip of the snout, which gives the head a triangular appearance. Color and pattern are extremely variable. These frogs may be green, gold or brown, and often have striped hindlimbs.

The female Darwin's frog deposits about forty large, unpigmented eggs in leaf litter. When the larvae inside the eggs begin to move, the adult male ingests the eggs and incubates them in his vocal sacs. Larvae develop inside his throat and emerge after metamorphosis. Populations are declining for unknown reasons; some possible causes are habitat destruction, pollution, climate change or disease. VULNERABLE.

RANGE: Biobío to Aisén; adjacent Argentina. Western slopes of the Andes, Central Valley and Coastal Range; temperate and subantarctic forests, on shaded stream banks.

RELATED SPECIES: The only other member of the family Cycloramphidae, *Rhinoderma rufum*, was last seen in Chile in 1978 and is POSSIBLY EXTINCT.

METAMORPHOSIS IN FROGS AND TOADS
- A tadpole forms within the egg
- Gills are replaced by lungs or other respiratory organs
- The skin develops glands to avoid dehydration
- Eyelids form and an eardrum develops to lock in the middle ear
- Hind legs and forelegs form, and the tail absorbs into the body
- The frog or toad emerges from the water

BIRDS OF A *feather*

> There are about 10,000 living species of birds in the world, divided into some 23 orders, 142 families and 2057 genera. They share these characteristics:
> - Feathers
> - Bony beak with no teeth
> - Forelimbs modified as wings
> - Walk on two legs (bipedal)
> - Lay eggs (oviparous)
> - Light, strong skeleton
> - Hollow bones
> - Four-chambered heart
> - High metabolic rate
> - Warm-blooded

What makes birds so unique? The answer is their feathers. Feathers separate birds from all other living creatures.

Feathers provide a number of services for birds. They shield them from ultraviolet light and act as insulation, allowing birds to maintain a body temperature of around 104°F (40°C).

Feathers also supply a bird with color, an important factor in sexual display, camouflage and mutual identification. Feather color comes from two main sources—the pigments within the feather or refraction of light. Melanins and porphyrins are pigments that are manufactured in a bird's body. Melanins provide grey, tan, brown and black colors. Porphyrins give mainly browns, but also some reds and greens. Red, orange, yellow and pink colors come from carotenoids, which must be obtained from a bird's food. Blues, greens and some other iridescent colors are produced when light refracts off minute structures on the feather surface.

Feathers do not grow randomly on a bird's body. They grow in orderly rows called tracts, with one row of feathers overlapping the next like house shingles.

Feathers come in varied shapes, with each type having a specific function. Soft, fluffy down feathers provide insulation and allow chicks to withstand wide temperature fluctuations when parents are absent from the nest. Contour feathers hug the adult bird's body, acting as streamlined insulation and waterproofing. The wing primaries and to some extent the tail feathers allow a bird to control lift and direction when airborne.

Feathers are uniquely adapted to suit the needs of each species. For example, snipes have stiff outer tail feathers that are vibrated to make an odd drumming sound during their aerial winnowing display. Owls have very soft wing feathers, which allow them to fly silently in pursuit of prey. Penguin feathers, on the other hand, are stiff and densely packed; they provide waterproofing and insulation so penguins can stay warm in their cold water environment.

A Note on Classification

Until recently, birds were classed mainly by similar physical and behavioral characteristics. The DNA hybridization experiments of Charles Sibley and Jon Ahlquist now allow scientists to determine which birds have a true evolutionary relationship with common ancestors and which evolved from different ancestors, but developed similar structures in response to similar lifestyles—a process called CONVERGENT EVOLUTION. This book attempts to blend the traditional taxonomic classification with the Sibley-Ahlquist system, which has been adopted by the South American Checklist Committee (SACC), a subcommittee of the American Ornithologists' Union (AOU). Discrepancies between the two methods are noted under the family descriptions.

The Art of Birdwatching

Novice birders are usually amazed when a seasoned pro identifies a bird in a single glance. This ability to quickly identify a bird comes with practice and time, but it is an observational skill that is open to all.

PARTS OF A BIRD

It involves knowing what features to look for and how to tie that observation to a particular bird species.

The first step to becoming a proficient birdwatcher is obtaining a good pair of binoculars. They don't have to be big, expensive or high-powered. A small pair of binoculars with a 7- to 8-power of magnification is easy to hold steady in the field and will let you see all of the important features that lead to identification.

What are the most important features to note? Many experienced birders have a mental list of questions that they run through when they sight a new species. Everyone has his or her personal mantra, but here are a few you may want to incorporate into your own litany.

SIZE: How big is it? Small as a sparrow, the size of a robin, or as large as a hawk?

COLOR: What is the bird's overall color? Is the plumage mottled, drab, or are there brightly colored markings on the head, wings, rump or tail?

SHAPE: What is the shape of the bill? Is it sharp and pointed like a woodpecker's, thin and curved like a curlew's, or short and conical like a sparrow's? Are the wings short and broad or long and pointed? Is the tail long or short, narrow or broad, forked or square?

FLIGHT: Does the bird fly in a straight line like a crow or zigzag near to the ground like a snipe? Does it continually flap its wings in flight, or does it flap and glide like a pelican? Does it soar effortlessly on stiff wings like an albatross, or circle high in the sky like a flock of vultures riding a thermal?

MOVEMENT: Does the bird hop or walk, or does it run restlessly from place to place?

BEHAVIOR: Does it skulk in the shrubbery? Does it perch high in the treetops, in low bushes, out in the open on bare branches or rocky outcrops? Does it bob its tail, flick its wings or call when perched?

DISTRIBUTION: Is the bird normally found in this geographical location and habitat? It is more likely that you will see a species common to the area rather than a rarity.

Now you are ready to pick out a matching illustration in your field guide. You may not find one that is an exact match. Birds exhibit different plumages at different ages and seasons, and it is virtually impossible to illustrate all of these variances and still keep a guide portable. So field guides present a generic study of a real-life bird, usually illustrating the optimal plumage of an adult male, adult female and juvenile.

If you will be doing some birdwatching while you are in Chile, you may want to supplement the material in this book with Jaramillo's *Birds of Chile*, an in-depth guide that illustrates and describes the subspecies and rarities. The book is available in both English and Spanish.

STRUTHIONIFORMES: Ratites

Ratites are large, flightless birds of Gondwanian origin, most of them now extinct. Ostriches, emus, cassowaries, rheas and kiwis are in this order. These birds have no keel on their breastbone (sternum). They nest on the ground and incubation of the eggs is undertaken mostly or entirely by the male.

FAMILY RHEIDAE
RHEAS
Rheas have long soft feathers, long necks, short wings, and long legs with 3-toed feet. They feed mainly on vegetation, insects and small vertebrates.

Lesser Rhea, Ñandú
Pterocnemia pennata
OTHER NAMES: Darwin's Rhea, Avestruz, Suri, Choike, Chenqué, Ñandú petizo, Nandou, Darwinnandu.
ID: 39 in (100 cm). Brownish-grey, with white-tipped lateral feathers. Underparts pale grey. Bill dark horn. Long yellow legs. Rheas can run at speeds up to 37 miles per hour (60 km/hr). To flee danger they run in zigzag patterns or squat in vegetation so they are not noticed. In breeding season, a male uses wing-fluttering displays and deep calls to attract hens. Several hens can mate with a successful male, and deposit a collective total of 20 to 30 white eggs in his scrape (ground nest). The male incubates the eggs for 40 days, and when all are hatched, he leads the chicks away from the nest. He tends the fledglings for several months, keeping them together with whistling calls. If some chicks stray away, another male with his own young will often adopt the lost chicks. NEAR THREATENED.
RANGE: Arica–Parinacota to Atacama; Aisén and Magellanes; introduced to Tierra del Fuego; also Argentina, Bolivia.
SUBSPECIES: The AVESTRUZ DE MAGALLANES or DARWIN'S RHEA, *P. p. pennata*, inhabits the grassy steppes of s Chile and s Argentina. The SURI or PUNA RHEA, *P. p. tarapacensis*, occurs in n Chile on the Altiplano grasslands and salares above 10,000 ft (3500 m).

TINAMIFORMES: Tinamous

Tinamous are an ancient order of ground-dwelling birds that live in the forests and grasslands of Central and South America. They are closely related to the ratites.

FAMILY TINAMIIDAE
TINAMOUS
The tinamou has a small head with a thin decurved bill, a long slender neck, a heavy body, short wings and tail, sturdy legs, and three front toes and one backward pointing toe, which is elevated or absent. Tinamous are capable of weak but swift flight for short distances. Their cryptic coloration makes them hard to see in vegetation, and one is alerted to their presence by their mellow, whistling and trilling calls. They feed on plant matter, insects and small vertebrates.

Tinamous have a breeding pattern similar to that of ratites. At the beginning of the mating season, a male establishes a territory where he will mate with several hens. After copulation, a hen lays 3 to 4 glossy, brightly colored eggs in the male's nesting scrape. She then departs to mate with and lay eggs for a subsequent male. The male incubates the eggs for 17 to 21 days, and cares for the brood for two months or more.

Chilean Tinamou, Perdiz chilena
Nothoprocta perdicaria
OTHER NAMES: Chilesteisshuhn, Tinamou perdrix.
ID: 11.5 in (29 cm). Upperparts greyish-brown with black and white spots and lines of dark cinnamon. Throat and abdomen whitish. Neck, breast and flanks brownish-grey. Upper bill horn; lower bill yellow. Legs yellow. Clutch is 5 to 8 wine-colored eggs laid in a nest of grass, hidden in vegetation.
RANGE: ENDEMIC to Chile. Atacama to Los Lagos; introduced to Easter Island. Scrub, grassland, grain fields, and at forest edge in s Chile; sea level to 2000 ft (0–6500 m).
SUBSPECIES: PERDIZ COMÚN, *N. p. perdicaria*, of c Chile has a grey breast. PERDIZ DEL SUR, *N. p. sanborni*, ranges from Maule to Los Lagos; it has a brown breast.

RHEA, TINAMOUS AND QUAIL

Lesser Rhea, Ñandú
Pterocnemia pennata
Arica–Atacama
Aisén–Magellanes
39 in (100 cm)

California Quail, Codorniz
Callipepla californica
Atacama–Los Lagos
Juan Fernández
10 in (25 cm)
Introduced

Chilean Tinamou
Perdiz chilena
Nothoprocta perdicaria
Atacama–Los Lagos
11.5 in (29 cm)
Introduced to Easter Island

Rhea chick in bunchgrass

Elegant-crested Tinamou
Perdiz copetona
Eudromia elegans
Aisén
16.5 in (42 cm)

Andean Tinamou
Perdiz cordillerana de Arica
Nothoprocta pentlandii
Rare in Arica–Tarapacá
11 in (28 cm)

Tola
Baccharis sp.

Patagonian Tinamou
Perdiz austral
Tinamotis ingoufi
Aisén–Magellanes
14 in (36 cm)

Puna Tinamou
Perdiz de la puna
Tinamotis pentlandii
High Andes of Arica–Atacama
17 in (43 cm)

Ornate Tinamou
Perdiz cordillerana
Nothoprocta ornata
High Andes of Arica–Tarapacá
14 in (36 cm)

Ornate Tinamou, Perdiz cordillerana
Nothoprocta ornata
OTHER NAMES: Pisaca, Perdiz de cerro, Tinamou orné, Pisaccasteisshuhn.
ID: 14 in (36 cm). Upperparts brown with black and buff vermiculations. Breast grey with fine, pale barring. Lower breast and flanks tawny; abdomen buff. Crown black, spotted with buff. Long tail. Nests on sandy soil in tola vegetation. Clutch is 4 to 5 glossy, wine-colored eggs.
RANGE: Arica–Parinacota to Tarapacá; Peru, Bolivia. Altiplano above 10,000 ft (3000 m).

Andean Tinamou
Perdiz cordillerana de Arica
Nothoprocta pentlandii
OTHER NAMES: Pentland's Tinamou, Perdicita de la sierra, Inambú serrano chico, Keu, Andensteisshuhn, Tinamou des Andes.
ID: 11 in (28 cm). Small. Greyish-brown on back, with black spots and dun barring. Flanks barred grey and black. Crown and nape blackish. Forehead, sides of head and lower neck bluish-grey. Chin and abdomen buff. Upper breast spotted white.
RANGE: Andean pastures and grain fields of Ecuador and Argentina. Recorded in 1948 at Socoroma, Tarapacá; no recent records.

Puna Tinamou, Perdiz de la puna
Tinamotis pentlandii
OTHER NAMES: Pentland's Tinamotis, Kiula, Pisaca, Punasteisshuhn, Tinamou quioula.
ID: 17 in (43 cm). Grey with yellow streaks and spots. Lower belly chestnut. Bold black and white stripes on the head and hindneck. Lacks a hind toe. Clutch is 5 to 8 yellowish-green eggs with white surface grains. Nests on sandy ground in tola vegetation. Flute-like call *kewla-kewla-kewla*. VULNERABLE.
RANGE: Arica-Parinacota to Atacama; Peru, nw Argentina, Bolivia. Altiplano grasslands and scrubland above 11,500 ft (3500 m).

Patagonian Tinamou, Perdiz austral
Tinamotis ingoufi
OTHER NAMES: Ingouf's Tinamotis, Patagoniensteisshuhn, Tinamou de Patagonie.
ID: 14 in (36 cm). Back and breast bluish-grey, spotted ochre and black. Abdomen and primaries rufous. Head and neck white, with black longitudinal stripes. No hind toe. Clutch is 5 to 8 yellowish-green eggs. Feeds on *Gaultheria* and *Berberis*.
RANGE: Extremely RARE from Aisén to the Strait of Magellan; common in s Argentina on grassy steppe with calafate scrub.

Elegant-crested Tinamou
Perdiz copetona
Eudromia elegans
OTHER NAMES: Martineta, Perlsteisshuhn, Tinamou élégant.
ID: 16.5 in (42 cm). Long, thin, upcurled black crest. Spotted black and tan on back. Black and tan barring on chest. Two white stripes from eye to neck. Feeds on alfalfa leaves, small insects and leaves of perennial thorny shrubs. Nests in cover of perennial shrubs. Clutch is 8 to 10 deep green eggs.
RANGE: Restricted to Chile Chico in Aisén; Argentina. Semi-arid grasslands, scrub, agricultural fields; 650–1300 ft (200–400 m).

GALLIFORMES: Gallinaceous Birds
FAMILY ODONTOPHORIDAE
NEW WORLD QUAIL
Quail are terrestrial gamebirds with short, rounded wings and short, strong legs. They have a short, thick bill; the upper mandible hangs over the tip of the lower.

California Quail, Codorniz
Callipepla californica
OTHER NAMES: Tococo, Schopfwachtel.
ID: 10 in (25 cm). Stocky, with a squared head and very short bill. Bluish-grey breast and nape; abdomen brown with white lines and speckles. MALE's face and throat dark brown edged with white; FEMALE's is plain. Prominent, forward-curving crest. Forms large family groups called coveys, which forage on the ground. Lays 10 to 18 speckled brown eggs in a ground scrape. Both parents look after the young. INTRODUCED to Chile in 1870 and to Juan Fernández in 1912.
RANGE: Atacama to Los Lagos. Common in grassland, matorral and villages.

ANSERIFORMES: Waterfowl

Anseriformes includes the swans, geese and ducks. They are characterized by webbed feet that aid in swimming. The modified tongue acts as a suction pump to draw water in at the tip of the wide, flattened bill and expel it from the sides and rear; fine filtering plates called lamellae trap small particles that are licked off and swallowed. Waterfowl eat a variety of freshwater plants and invertebrates taken from the water surface or while diving; some species eat grain, grasses and seaweed. In most species, the male is more brightly plumaged than the female.

FAMILY ANATIDAE, SUBFAMILY DENDROCYGNINAE
WHISTLING-DUCKS

These ducks are named for their whistling calls. They have long legs and necks. They are gregarious, forming large flocks that roost in trees. Both sexes have the same plumage. All have black underwings. Three vagrant species have been recorded in Chile.

FULVOUS WHISTLING-DUCK, or PATO SILBÓN, 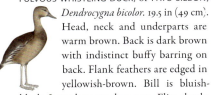 *Dendrocygna bicolor*. 19.5 in (49 cm). Head, neck and underparts are warm brown. Back is dark brown with indistinct buffy barring on back. Flank feathers are edged in yellowish-brown. Bill is bluish-black. Long legs are slate-grey. Flies slowly on short wings with head down-turned. Emits a two-syllable whistling call *pwe-twee*. Records from the O'Higgins and Santiago Regions in open fields near fresh water.

WHITE-FACED WHISTLING-DUCK, *Dendrocygna viduata*. 19 in (48 cm). Face and foreneck white; back of head and neck and band across throat black. Back brown, feathers pale edged. Rump, tail and center of underparts are black. Chest is chestnut. Sides of body are barred black and white. Recorded at the Huechun Reservoir outside the city of Santiago.

BLACK-BELLIED WHISTLING-DUCK, *Dendrocygna autumnalis*. 21 in (53 cm). Face and upper neck grey; white eyering. Bright orange-red bill and legs. Lower breast black. Back rufous. White wing patch. Recorded at La Unión, Los Lagos.

FAMILY ANATIDAE, SUBFAMILY ANSERINAE
SWANS

The two South American swan species have white plumage patterned with black. They have fleshy pink to reddish legs.

Coscoroba Swan
Cisne coscoroba
Coscoroba coscoroba

OTHER NAMES: Cisne blanco, Coscorobaschwan, Coscoroba blanc. Name is derived from the four-syllable call, *cos-co-RO-va*.
ID: 35–45 in (90–115 cm). Goose-like. White plumage, except for black tips to the outer six primary feathers. Red iris. Red bill and pink legs. Lacks the black lores that other swans have. Feeds on grass, aquatic plants, mussels and fish. Nest is a bulky mound of vegetation, lined with soft grass and down; nests on islets, in reedbeds, or in grass near the water. The female incubates the eggs while the male defends the nest and fledglings. These swans can live to 20 years of age.
RANGE: Resident in the Los Lagos Region; winters north to Valparaíso; uncommon Aisén to Magallanes. Ranges in Argentina, Falklands, Paraguay, Uruguay, s Brazil. On fresh and brackish lakes, lagoons, canals.

Black-necked Swan
Cisne de cuello negro
Cygnus melancoryphus

OTHER NAMES: Thula, Kaum, Schwarzhalsschwan, Cygne à cou noir. The genus is named for the Cygnus constellation, which resembles a long-necked bird in flight.
ID: 40–49 in (102–124 cm). White body; black neck and head. Blue-grey bill with red caruncles (fleshy growths) at base. Flesh-colored legs. Feeds on aquatic vegetation, insects and fish spawn, taken with neck and head extended underwater. Lays 4 to 8 eggs in a bulky pile of aquatic plants placed in reedbeds on the lakeshore or on small islets. White cygnets often ride on a parent's back.
RANGE: Atacama to Tierra del Fuego; also Argentina, Falklands, s Brazil; vagrant at Juan Fernández and Antarctic Peninsula. Lakes with reedbeds, marine fjords, brackish lakes.

FAMILY ANATIDAE: SUBFAMILY TADORNINAE

SHELDGEESE, STEAMER-DUCKS AND TORRENT DUCKS

Members of the subfamily Tadorninae are found in South America. They are intermediate between true geese and ducks.

SHELDGEESE: These geese have stocky legs, thick necks and short bills with prominent lamellae. In flight, the wings of most species show dark primaries and have an iridescent speculum edged with white. Most graze on grass and some feed on seaweed.

Andean Goose, Piuquén
Chloephaga melanoptera
OTHER NAMES: Guayata, Andengans, Ouette des Andes.
ID: 29–32 in (75–80 cm). Males are larger than females. White body, with black wings and tail. Red bill. Red legs. Nests (Nov) at very high elevations on the Altiplano. Lays 5 to 10 eggs in a ground scrape hidden in sparse hillside vegetation near water.
RANGE: Arica to Maule; also s Peru, Bolivia, nw Argentina. Resident on the Altiplano in Andean wetlands *(bofedales)* and grasslands *(pajonales)*; 10,000–16,500 ft (3000–5000 m); some birds descend to the Central Valley lowlands in winter.

Ashy-headed Goose, Canquén
Chloephaga poliocephala
OTHER NAMES: Cauquén real, Ouette à tête grise, Graukopfgans.
ID: 20–22 in (50–55 cm). Head and neck grey; breast and upper back are coppery-chestnut. Body sides have white and black barring; center of abdomen white. Black tail. Black primaries; green speculum; white secondaries and wing coverts. Black bill. Gregarious, grazing in mixed groups with upland geese and domestic ducks. Nests in down-lined mounds hidden in long grass, or sometimes in hollows of burned tree trunks or branches.
RANGE: Biobío to Magallanes; winters north to Maule; Argentina and the Falklands. Fields, lakes, rivers, estuaries and wet meadows *(mallines)* in *Nothofagus* forest.

Upland Goose, Caiquén
Chloephaga picta
OTHER NAMES: Ganso, Lesser Magellan Goose, Magellangans, Ouette de Magellan.
ID: 23–26 in (60–66 cm). MALE has white head and rump; rest of plumage barred black and white, or barred only on flanks, depending on subspecies. Iridescent green speculum, white lesser wing coverts and secondaries; dark primaries. FEMALE is like female *C. rubiceps*, but larger, darker and more coarsely barred on the flanks; center of abdomen is always barred; vent is white. Breeds in great numbers on the semiarid pampas of s South America. Nest is a down-lined depression set in long grass. Clutch is 5 to 8 eggs. Often seen grazing among sheep on ranches.
RANGE: Southern Chile, from Los Lagos to Magallanes; Argentina and the Falklands. Semi-arid open plains, farmland, and coasts of channels and bays.
SUBSPECIES: CAIQUÉN DE MAGALLANES, *C. p. picta*. Los Lagos to Cape Horn. Males have barred breasts. CAIQUÉN DE LAS MALVINAS, *C. p. leucoptera*. Tierra del Fuego, Patagonia and the Falklands. This subspecies is larger and males have unbarred breasts.

Ruddy-headed Goose, Canquén colorado
Chloephaga rubidiceps
OTHER NAMES: Avutarda colorada, Shoti, Rottkopfgans, Ouette à tête rousse.
ID: 20 in (50 cm). Head and neck drab cinnamon. Abdomen and upper back are finely barred in rufous, grey and black. Black tail. Wings have an iridescent green speculum, white lesser wing coverts and secondaries, and black primaries. Black bill.
RANGE: Magallanes; Argentina and the Falklands. Seasonal on inundated grasslands around the Strait of Magellan. Flocks arrive in s Chile in September, nest in October, and leave for Patagonia in March or April. Increasingly RARE, possibly due to illegal hunting of this species on its Argentine wintering grounds.

Kelp Goose, Caranca
Chloephaga hybrida
OTHER NAMES: Avutarda blanca, Carauca, Cagüa, Kelpgans, Ouette marine.
ID: 22–25 in (55–65 cm). Marked sexual dimorphism. All white plumage of MALE conspicuous. Bill black with a flesh-colored spot around the nostrils. Yellow legs. FEMALE is cryptically colored in brown and black, with coarse white barring on breast, flanks, and abdomen. Lower back, rump, tail and lower abdomen white. Crown and nape dull greyish-brown; forehead, face, throat and neck blackish-brown. Green speculum; white lesser wing-coverts and secondaries; dark primaries. Bill pink. Legs yellow. Feeds heavily on green marine algae (*Ulva* sp.) Usually seen in pairs.
RANGE: Resident from Los Lagos to the Strait of Magellan; less common south of the Strait; winters north to Araucanía; rare on Atlantic coast of Tierra del Fuego; common in the Falklands. On rocky coasts.

STEAMER-DUCKS: These heavy-bodied ducks have short wings, broad bills, and very large legs and feet. They move across the water while flapping the wings, producing a wake resembling that of a paddlewheel steamer.

Flightless Steamer-Duck
Quetru no volador
Tachyeres pteneres
OTHER NAMES: Pato vapor, Brassemer cendré, Magellan-Dampfschiffente.
ID: 31–33 in (78–83 cm). WT to 14 lb (6 kg). Grey overall. Mottled bluish-grey on the back, breast and flanks. Lower breast and abdomen white. Very short wings with a white speculum. Pale postocular line. Bill yellow-orange with black tip and orange caruncle at base. Flightless. When alarmed, propels itself over the water using wings and large feet, attaining speeds up to 10 knots (11.5 mi/hr). Feeds on mollusks, crustaceans and small fishes, taken in shellfish banks or kelp beds. Nests from Chiloé south in dense coastal forest and on islets with sparse vegetation.
RANGE: Valdivia to Tierra del Fuego; also Staten Island, Argentina. Sheltered rocky seacoasts and coastal islands; exclusively marine; never found on inland lakes.

Flying Steamer-Duck, Quetru volador
Tachyeres patachonicus
OTHER NAMES: Pato vapor volador, Brassemer de Patagonie, Langflügel-Dampfschiffente.
ID: 26–28 in (65–70 cm). Much smaller and less than half the weight of the Flightless Steamer-Duck, with longer wings and tail. MALES are grey, with a pale grey to whitish head. Strong, stout, yellow-orange bill has a black tip and blue-grey area around the nostrils. Pale postocular line. FEMALES are brownish on head and neck. Often reluctant to fly, preferring to propel itself through the water like the Flightless Steamer-Duck. Nests in long grass or low vegetation on small islands.
RANGE: Resident from Biobío to Tierra del Fuego; also s Argentina and the Falklands; on inland lakes, seacoasts and channels; sea level to 5000 ft (0–1500 m).

TORRENT DUCKS: These small ducks have an elongate body, a long stiff tail, and claws at the joints of the wings. They are found along fast-flowing rivers where they swim against strong currents with ease. They use their narrow, flexible bill to pick food from the cracks and crevices of submerged rocks.

Torrent Duck, Pato cortacorrientes
Merganetta armata
OTHER NAMES: Chilean Torrent Duck, Pato correntino, Pato forzudo, Sturzbachente, Merganette des torrents.
ID: 16–18 in (40–46 cm). Slender with a long, stiff-feathered tail. Bill and legs are red. Wings show a green speculum bordered by white bands. MALE has a white head with long black lines running from head to neck, and a tawny breast and abdomen. FEMALES are rust-colored with a grey crown, nape and back. Male emits a high-pitched whistle, which is audible over the sound of rushing water. Nests in burrows and rock crevices along fast flowing rivers.

RANGE: Arica to Tarapacá and Atacama to Magallanes; e South America. Fast-flowing rivers; 1000–13,750 ft (300–4200 m).
SUBSPECIES: PATO CORTACORRIENTES, *M. a. armenti*, ranges in sc Chile. The males have black flanks and a black bar under the eyes. The CHULYRIMPI, or PATO CORTACORRIENTES DEL NORTE, *M. a. berlepschi*, ranges in the Andes of n Chile and Peru. Males have streaked flanks and lack the dark bar under the eyes.

FAMILY ANATIDAE, SUBFAMILY OXYURINAE
STIFF-TAILED DUCKS
Except for the Black-headed Duck, members of this subfamily have a large, wide bill. The long, stiff tail feathers are held cocked when the bird is at rest. These ducks occupy bodies of freshwater and forage underwater for aquatic plants and invertebrates.

Andean (Ruddy) Duck
Pato rana de pico ancho
Oxyura ferruginea
OTHER NAMES: Peruvian Ruddy Duck, Pato pitroco, Pato pimpollo, Pato pana, Schwarzkopf-Ruderente, Érismature des Andes.
ID: 17–19 in (42–48 cm). Adult breeding MALE is chestnut, with a black head and neck, and a broad-tipped, bright blue bill. Steeply-sloped forehead. Stiff tail feathers usually are held cocked while swimming. FEMALES and JUVENILES are brown, with pale facial patches and lead-colored bills. The Andean ducks construct bulky nests of floating vegetation in rushes and reedbeds. The clutch is 7 to 12 extremely large, rough-shelled eggs, which the adult covers with down when it leaves the nest.
RANGE: Arica to Magallanes; Argentina. Ponds and lakes in the Andes to 15,000 ft (4600 m). Some birds winter on freshwater lakes and streams at lower elevations.

Lake Duck, Pato rana de pico delgado
Oxyura vittata
OTHER NAMES: Argentine Blue-billed Duck, Pato tripoca, Pata pimpollo, Bindenruderente, Érismature ornée.
ID: 16–18 in (40–46 cm). Adult breeding MALES are chestnut, with a black head and neck, and a narrow-tipped, bright blue bill. Separated with difficulty from the Andean Duck by smaller size, narrower bill tip, more rounded head and forehead, and tendency to swim with tail floating in the water. FEMALES are mottled brown with two white lines extending from nape to bill below the eyes. Clutch of 3 to 5 eggs are laid in nests similar to those of Andean ducks.
RANGE: Atacama to Isla Chiloé; local and uncommon in Aisén and Magallanes. Ranges in temperate South America on lowland lakes edged with dense vegetation; sea level to 3300 ft (1000 m).

Black-headed Duck
Pato rinconero
Heteronetta atricapilla
OTHER NAMES: Pato de cabeza negra, Kuckucksente, Hétéronette à tête noire
ID: 14–16 in (35–40 cm). A dark, slender duck that swims low in the water. MALE is dark brown with a black head and warm brown flanks. In breeding season, the long, narrow bill is blue-grey with a red base; bill is dark grey in non-breeding plumage. FEMALE is dark brown, with mottling on sides of face and flanks. Parasitic in nesting habits, habitually laying its eggs in nests of other ducks and waterbirds, including pochards, coots, ibis and night-herons.
RANGE: Local to uncommon from Valparaíso to Osorno, Los Lagos; Argentina, Paraguay, Uruguay and s Brazil. Inhabits cattail lakes and *Scirpus* reedbeds; to 2000 ft (600 m).

FAMILY ANATIDAE, SUBFAMILY ANATINAE
DIVING AND DABBLING DUCKS
These gregarious ducks live on freshwater lakes, ponds, estuaries and marshes.

DIVING DUCKS: Diving ducks are so named because they feed by diving for seeds of aquatic plants, insects and small mollusks. Their legs are set to the rear of the body. This helps propel them underwater, but makes them ungainly on land.

Rosy-billed Pochard, Pato negro
Netta peposaca

OTHER NAMES: Pato picazo, Rosenschnabelente, Nette demi-deuil.

ID: 21–23 in (53–57 cm). MALE has a bright pink, black-tipped bill. Head, neck and breast are iridescent purple-black. Back is black; sides finely-barred grey. Vent white. White wing stripe. Yellow legs. FEMALE is warm brown with a white vent, white wingbar, dark crown, pale throat, pale eyeline, grey bill and yellow legs. Dives and also dabbles when feeding. Nests in rushes, reeds or long grass around lakes. Clutch is 10 to 14 pale, greenish-white eggs laid in a nest of fresh vegetation lined with down, which is pulled over the eggs when the adult leaves the nest.

RANGE: Uncommon on lakes and rivers, Valparaíso to Osorno, Los Lagos. Winters north to the Atacama Region; summer visitor in e Aisén and Magallanes. Widespread from Brazil to s Argentina.

DABBLING DUCKS: These ducks dabble (tip up their bottoms) as they feed in shallow water on submerged aquatic vegetation. They rarely dive. The legs are placed towards the center of their bodies. They walk well on land and some species feed on land as well. The color of the bill, head and wings offer good clues to identifying similar species.

Crested Duck, Pato juarjual
Lophonetta (Anas) specularioides

OTHER NAMES: Pato crestón, Schopfente, Canard huppé.

ID: 20–24 in (50–60 cm). Grey and brown, with a dark crest that hugs the back of the neck. Long pointed tail. Speculum rosy-bronze, edged by an iridescent purplish-black band and a narrow white trailing edge. Yellow or red eye, depending on the subspecies. This species is intermediate between shellducks and river ducks.

RANGE: Arica to Cape Horn; also Peru, Bolivia, Argentina and the Falklands. On lakes, ponds, rivers, and marine coasts; sea level to 15,000 ft (0–4600 m).

SUBSPECIES: The red-eyed PATO JUARJUAL DEL SUR, *L. s. specularioides*, is found on mountain lakes, open plains and rocky seacoasts from Maule to Cape Horn. The yellow-eyed PATO JUARJUAL DEL NORTE, *L. s. alticola*, is common in wet areas around lagoons and salt flats in the High Andes from Arica to Maule.

Yellow-billed Pintail
Pato jergón grande
Anas georgica spinicauda

OTHER NAMES: Chilean Pintail, Brown Pintail, Pato maicero, Spitzschwanzente, Canard à queue pointue.

ID: 19–21 in (48–54 cm). Brown plumage spattered with dusky spots; whitish throat is sometimes spotted black. Bill yellow with black culmen and tip. Neck is long and slender. Pointed tail. Green speculum edged with tan bands. Feeds on seeds and native aquatic plants such as Luchecillo (*Elodia chilensis*). Sometimes feeds in rice fields and also eats river snails. Lays 4 to 10 eggs on a bare scrape near water. Covers eggs with down and grass when absent from nest.

RANGE: Common from Arica to Magallanes, and throughout South America; summer visitor in southern part of range. Vagrant in South Shetland Islands, Antarctica. Rivers, ponds, marshes, marine coasts; sea level to 13,000 ft (0–4000 m).

Speckled Teal
Pato jergón chico
Anas flavirostris

OTHER NAMES: South American Greenwing Teal, Chilean Teal, Pato barerro, Pato barcino, Andenente, Sarcelle tachetée.

ID: 15–17 in (38–43 cm). Dark head and short neck are finely mottled black and brown. Back is spotted with brown. Breast whitish with black spots. Pale unspotted flanks. Speculum metallic green and black, bordered by light brown bands. Bill yellow with black culmen and tip. Blue-grey legs. Gregarious, often seen in groups of 10 to 20 on ponds, small coastal lagoons and around human habitation.

DUCKS 137

Torrent Duck
Pato cortacorrientes
Merganetta armata
Arica–Tarapacá
Atacama–Magallanes
16–18 in (40–46 cm)

Andean Duck
Pato rana de pico ancho
Oxyura ferruginea
Tarapacá–Magallanes
19 in (48 cm)

Lake Duck
Pato rana de pico delgado
Oxyura vittata
Atacama–Los Lagos
18 in (46 cm)

Black-headed Duck
Pato rinconero
Heteronetta atricapilla
Valparaíso–Los Lagos
15 in (38 cm)

Crested Duck
Pato juarjual
Lophonetta specularioides
Tarapacá–Magallanes
24 in (60 cm)

Rosy-billed Pochard
Pato negro
Netta peposaca
Valparaíso–Los Lagos
23 in (57 cm)

Steamer-ducks stir up a wake as they paddle across the water.

Flightless Steamer-Duck
Quetru no volador
Tachyeres pteneres
Valdivia–Magallanes
33 in (83 cm)

Flying Steamer-Duck
Quetru volador
Tachyeres patachonicus
Biobío–Magallanes
27 in (70 cm)

RANGE: Arica to Tierra del Fuego. Widespread in South America and the Falklands. Freshwater ponds, river deltas, sheltered marine coasts.
SUBSPECIES: The smaller subspecies, PATO JERGÓN CHICO, *A. f. flavirostris*, of the central and southern lowlands nests on the ground in vegetation near water. In forested zones, it may place its nest in the fork of trees. PATO JERGÓN CHICO DEL NORTE, or HUANCAYO, *A. f. oxyptera*, of the Andean Altiplano above 13,500 ft (3500 m), is larger and has a more slender bill, less spotted underparts and paler back. It nests in holes in banks or escarpments.

White-cheeked Pintail, Pato gargantillo
Anas bahamensis
OTHER NAMES: Greater Bahaman Pintail, Bahamaente, Canard des Bahamas.
ID: 19–20 in (48–51 cm). A long-necked, brown duck with a conspicuous white area on the sides of the face and neck. Blue-grey bill has red or orange marks at the base of the upper bill. Iridescent green speculum with a pale brown band in front and black band behind. White pointed tail.
RANGE: RARE BREEDING MIGRANT between Coquimbo and Los Lagos. Nests in valleys near Curicó, Maule. NON-BREEDING MIGRANT in Arica and Magallanes. More common east of the Andes north to the Bahamas on seacoasts and freshwater or brackish lakes; sea level to 3250 ft (0–1000 m).

Silver Teal, Pato capuchino
Anas versicolor
OTHER NAMES: Silberente, Sarcelle bariolée.
ID: 16–17 in (40–43 cm). Dark brown cap, or *capuchón*, extends to beneath the eye; cheeks and neck buff. Back brown; breast buff with dark brown spots; flanks coarsely barred black and white; rump and vent finely barred black and white. Iridescent green speculum with white lines. Bill is blue with a yellow patch on either side of upper bill. Gregarious, flocking in marshy or flooded areas around rivers and lakes.
RANGE: Valparaíso to Magallanes; Bolivia; s Brazil to Argentina and the Falklands. Wetlands near rivers and small lakes; sea level to 3250 ft (0–1000 m).
SUBSPECIES: The smaller PATO CAPUCHINO, *A. v. versicolor*, ranges from Valparaíso to Isla Chiloé. PATO CAPUCHINO AUSTRAL, *A. v. fretensis*, which is found from Valdivia to Tierra del Fuego, has coarse dark barring on the abdomen and flanks.

Puna Teal, Pato puna
Anas puna
OTHER NAMES: Pato puneño, Pato argentino, Punaente, Sarcelle du puna.
ID: 17–19 in (45–49 cm). Large hyacinth-blue bill with black culmen. Separated from *Anas versicolor* by blacker cap, creamy-white cheeks, and finer black and white barring on flanks, vent and tail. FEMALE has brown underparts with very faint or no barring on tail and vent. Inhabits lakes, lagoons and salares on the Puna. Builds its nest in coarse vegetation near water. Clutch is 6 large, cream-colored to pinkish eggs.
RANGE: Arica to Antofagasta; also Peru, Bolivia and nw Argentina. Resident on the Altiplano and Puna, on lakes and rivers above 13,000 ft (3000 m).

Cinnamon Teal, Pato colorado
Anas cyanoptera
OTHER NAMES: Pato carmelito, Zimtente, Sarcelle cannelle.
ID: 16–19 in (41–48 cm). MALE is colored deep cinnamon, with black vent and rump. Pale blue scapulars, green speculum, white underwing coverts, dark primaries. Red eye. Black broad-tipped bill. Yellow legs. FEMALE warm brown with darker brown spots. Lays a clutch of 6 to 12 cream-colored eggs in a nest built among rushes.
RANGE: Locally common from Tarapacá to Los Lagos. MIGRANT in Arica and Magallanes. Separate breeding populations in North and South America. Inhabits small freshwater lakes, ponds and marshes; sea level to 15,000 ft (0–4600 m).
SUBSPECIES: PATO COLORADO, *A. c. cyanoptera*, the smaller subspecies, ranges from Copiapó

DABBLING DUCKS 139

Dabbling ducks forage by upending in shallow water and reaching for submerged aquatic vegetation

Silver Teal, Pato capuchino
Anas versicolor
Valparaíso–Magallanes
15.5–17 in (40–43 cm)

White-cheeked Pintail, Pato gargantillo
Anas bahamensis
Arica, Coquimbo–Los Lagos, Magallanes
20 in (51 cm)
Rare

Puna Teal, Pato puna
Anas puna
Arica–Antofagasta
17.5–19 in (45–49 cm)

Speckled Teal, Pato jergón chico
Anas flavirostris
Arica–Magallanes
15–17 in (38–43 cm)

Yellow-billed Pintail, Pato jergón grande
Anas georgica
Arica–Magallanes
19–21 in (48–54 cm)

Red Shoveler, Pato cuchara
Anas platalea
Atacama–Magallanes
20–22 in (51–56 cm)

Spectacled Duck, Pato anteojillo
Speculanas specularis
O'Higgins–Magallanes
18–21 in (46–54 cm)

Cinnamon Teal, Pato colorado
Anas cyanoptera
Arica–Los Lagos, Magallanes
15–19 in (38–48 cm)

Chiloé Wigeon, Pato real
Anas sibilatrix
Atacama–Magallanes
17–21 in (43–54 cm)

to the Strait of Magellan. PATO COLORADO DE LA PUNA, *A. c. orinomus*, occurs in the Andes from Arica to Antofagasta. The female has a very dark face and neck.

Spectacled Duck, Pato anteojillo
Speculanas specularis
OTHER NAMES: Bronze-winged Duck, Pato perro, Kupferspiegelente, Canard à lunettes.
ID: 18–21 in (46–54 cm). Brown, with dark back, warm brown flanks. Dark bronzy-green wings; rosy-violet speculum. Head dark chestnut with a white crescent-shaped neck band and white oval patch in front of eye. Black bill. Yellow legs. Call is a hoarse, dog-like bark. Nests on islets in fast-flowing rivers. Lays 4 to 5 eggs in a down-lined nest built in long grass. NEAR THREATENED.
RANGE: Biobío to Magallanes; s Argentina; winters north to Santiago. Fast-flowing rivers in breeding season; lakes and ponds in winter; sea level to 5000 ft (0–1500 m).

Chiloé Wigeon, Pato real
Anas sibilatrix
OTHER NAMES: Pato overo, Chilepfeifente, Canard de Chiloé.
ID: 17–21 in (43–54 cm). White forehead and cheeks conspicuous against iridescent blackish-green head and neck. Bill is blue-grey with dark tip. Feathers of breast and back are black edged with white. Flanks tawny. White rump. White wing coverts edged with iridescent green bands. Dark legs. Males sound a 2- to 3-note whistling call. Gregarious, flocking on open water near center of lakes. Clutch is 5 to 8 creamy white eggs laid in a nest sited on dry ground among long grass, often far from water.
RANGE: Mouth of the Río Huasco, Atacama, to Tierra del Fuego; also Argentina and the Falklands. Winters to Brazil, Paraguay and Uruguay. Vagrant in Antarctica. Wetlands, lakes and rivers.
RELATED VAGRANT: BLUE-WINGED TEAL, *Anas discors*, has a dark grey head with a white crescent in front of the eye; speculum green; sky blue wing coverts. Two records from Coquimbo and Santiago.

Red Shoveler, Pato cuchara
Anas platalea
OTHER NAMES: Argentine Shoveler, Fuchslöffelente, Canard spatule.
ID: 20–22 in (51–56 cm). Large spatulate bill is adapted for filtering plankton and probing in muddy lake bottoms. MALE has mottled brown head; dark back and vent; rufous flanks have black spots; circular white patch on rear flanks. White eye. White wingband separates the iridescent green speculum from sky blue wing coverts. FEMALE brown, with dark brown spotting. Nests in dry areas near estuaries and coastal lagoons. Lays 5 to 8 creamy white eggs.
RANGE: Valparaíso to Chiloé; winters north to Atacama; summer visitor to Aisén and Magallanes. Widespread in South America. Marshes, brooks, estuaries, muddy lakes; sea level to 2000 ft (0–600 m).

INTRODUCED DUCKS

Muscovy Duck, Pato criollo
Cairina moschata
OTHER NAMES: Canard musqué, Greater Wood Duck, Moschusente.
ID: 26–33 in (66–84 cm). WT to 12 lb (5 kg). Black with iridescent green and purple on wings and back; white wingband; bill barred black and pink. Domesticated birds have variable plumage, often with a white head and red caruncle at base of a grey to pink bill. Forms flocks of 6 to 15 individuals in forested areas near wetlands. Roosts in tree hollows or on top of palms. Omnivorous, feeding on termites and other insects, tadpoles, small reptiles, aquatic vegetation and grain. Voice is a harsh *quack*.
RANGE: Domesticated muscovies have naturalized in Maule around Talca and Curicó. Feral in tropical South America in forest areas near ponds, reservoirs and dams.

Tule Bullrush
Scirpus californicus

White-tufted Grebe, Pimpollo
Podiceps rolland
Arica–Magallanes
10.2 in (26 cm)

Podiceps o. juninensis
Arica–Antofagasta
10.5 in (27 cm)

Silvery Grebe Blanquillo
Podiceps occipitalis
Antofagasta–Magallanes
10.5 in (27 cm)

Pied-billed Grebe, Picurio
Podilymbus podiceps
Atacama–Magallanes
12.2 in (31 cm)

Great Grebe, Huala
Podiceps major
Atacama–Magallanes
27–31 in (70–78 cm)

PODICIPEDIFORMES: Grebes

In the Sibley-Ahlquist taxonomic system, the order Ciconiiformes (Storks and Allies) now encompasses Podicipediformes (Grebes).

FAMILY PODICIPEDIDAE
GREBES

Grebes are freshwater diving birds. They have long necks, pointed bills, short wings and rudimentary tails. They have large feet, with broad lobes on the toes and small webs connecting the front three toes. The feet are placed far back on the body, making grebes graceful on water, but ungainly on land.

Most grebes are black or dark grey on the back, and white or mottled-brown below. In breeding season, most have conspicuous ear tufts, which pale in winter. The grebe's plumage is dense and waterproof. They can adjust their buoyancy by pressing their curved feathers against the body, and one can observe them swimming low in the water with just the head and neck exposed.

Grebes lay fairly small, biconical eggs on floating nests of aquatic vegetation. The eggs have an outer layer of calcium phosphate, which allows them to breathe when wet. The incubation period is about 23 days. The young can swim soon after hatching but are carried on the back of the parents for several weeks, except during dives.

Grebes often eat their own feathers and feed them to their young. This may reduce vulnerability to gastric parasites or perhaps slow down the process of digestion, thereby helping the bird's gizzard to process fish bones and debris. Feathers and other indigestible matter are later regurgitated.

Great Grebe, Huala
Podiceps major
OTHER NAMES: Guala, Macá grande, Grand grèbe, Magellantaucher. The Chilean name is derived from the loud plaintive call *waa-oooo-looo*, similar to that of a loon.
ID: 27–31 in (70–78 cm). Large with long neck and long, pointed, slightly-upturned bill. Back dark grey to black; whitish below. Front of neck rufous. Black erectile crest on crown. White wingbar. Almost exclusively aquatic. Comes ashore only if injured or ill. Courtship display is elaborate. Pairs face

one another on the water, dip their beaks, and then swim side by side, with frequent change of direction. Pairs make a floating platform nest of aquatic vegetation on which 3 to 5 elliptical, pale blue eggs are laid. First nesting occurs in October, with a second nesting attempted in February. Groups of 10 to 15 adults forage together, diving after small fishes, crustaceans and other aquatic organisms.

RANGE: Bahía Salada to Tierra del Fuego; s Brazil, Paraguay, Uruguay, and Argentina. Lowland lakes, rivers, estuaries, seacoast.

White-tufted Grebe, Pimpollo
Podiceps rolland

OTHER NAMES: Chilean Grebe, Pollollo, Hualita, Chulyumpi, Macá común, Grèbe de Rolland, Rollandtaucher.

ID: 10.2 in (26 cm). BREEDING PLUMAGE: Black head, neck and back. White ear tufts. White wingbar. Flanks are rufous. NON-BREEDING PLUMAGE: Brown neck; pale ear patch; buffy flanks. Juvenile has dark lines on face. Shy and rather secretive, diving quickly when alarmed and rising with only its head and neck above the surface. Nests (Sep–Dec), laying 4 to 6 eggs on floating platforms in reeds, especially in tule *(Scirpus)*, which is common around freshwater lakes and marshes throughout the Americas.

RANGE: Arica to Magallanes; also Peru, s South America, Falklands. Inhabits lakes, ponds, Andean salares, streams; sea level to 14,500 ft (0–4500 m). Flocks are occasional along marine coasts from March to May and September to November.

Silvery Grebe, Blanquillo
Podiceps occipitalis

OTHER NAMES: Crested Grebe, Pollollo, Hualita, Macá plateado, Grèbe aux belles joues, Inkataucher.

ID: 10.5 in (27 cm). Ashy-grey head, throat and back with whitish underparts. Dark cap. Yellow ear tufts (pale grey in non-breeding plumage). Thin, upturned bill. Bright red eyes. Call is a high-pitched *chiop*. Breeds around lowland lakes, building a floating nest of aquatic plants in reedbeds. The clutch is 4 to 6 blue eggs. Migratory; winters in flocks on large lakes.

RANGE: Atacama to Tierra del Fuego; also s Argentina and the Falklands. On lakes from sea level to 3250 ft (0–1,000 m). Flocks are occasional off sea coasts from March to June and September to November.

SUBSPECIES: BLANQUILLO DEL NORTE, *Podiceps occipitalis juninensis*. 10.5 in (27 cm). Black cap. Pale grey ear tufts; throat and upper neck completely white. Plumage remains the same all year. Anchors nest of floating vegetation to aquatic plants. Clutch is 1 to 3 eggs. Non-migratory. Lives on lakes and ponds in the High Andes from Arica to Antofagasta; 11,500–14,500 ft (3500–4500 m).

Hooded Grebe
Pimpollo tobiano
Podiceps gallardoi

ID: 10.2 in (26 cm). Similar to the Silvery Grebe. Lower face black; white forehead; chestnut-colored erectile crest. VAGRANT. Recent records from lakes and ponds in lowland Chile. Breeds in sw Argentina on lagoons on the high Patagonian plateau.

Pied-billed Grebe
Picurio
Podilymbus podiceps

OTHER NAMES: Pollollo, Macá pico grueso, Grèbe à bec bigarré, Bindentaucher.

ID: 12.2 in (31 cm). Heavy-bodied. Dark brown upperparts; white undertail. Stubby greyish-yellow bill is encircled by a black band (bill lacks black band in non-breeding plumage). Usually silent, but occasionally utters a clucking call *kuk-kuk*. Solitary, or seen in small groups of 3 to 4 individuals, often swimming within floating vegetation. Nests (Sep–Nov) in reedbeds. Lays 4 to 8 dull white eggs on a floating platform of rushes that is anchored to reeds or overhanging marsh vegetation.

RANGE: Atacama to Magallanes and Tierra del Fuego. Common in the Americas on lowland lakes, ponds and rivers.

SPHENISCIFORMES: Penguins

Penguins are flightless seabirds that evolved from flighted birds about 45 million years ago. The 16 to 19 living species of penguins live in the cold oceans and currents of the Southern Hemisphere, and nine species occur in Chilean waters. The order Sphenisciformes may soon be placed under Cinconiiformes.

FAMILY SPHENICIDAE

PENGUINS

Penguins are insulated from the cold by dense, scalelike feathers enclosing a thick layer of blubber. Their wingbones are fused into paddle-like flippers.

They can swim underwater at speeds over 25 mi per hour (40 km/hr), using flippers for propulsion and feet as rudders. They alternate swimming underwater with short leaps through the air—a movement called PORPOISING. They use this technique to breathe without losing swimming speed and to escape marine predators. Penguins swim on the sea surface with only their head, neck and part of the back showing.

On land, penguins walk upright on short legs set to the rear of the body. The waddling gait similar to a toddler's may be the origin of their Chilean soubriquet, *pajaros niños*, meaning "birds that resemble children." In the Antarctic, penguins use their flippers to push themselves along the snow and ice on their belly—a method of locomotion known as TOBOGGANING.

Penguins nest in colonies on sparsely populated seacoasts and islands. At the breeding grounds they communicate with vocalizations and ritual movements called DISPLAYS. The displays range from intricate and intimate bows and head wags of mated pairs, to loud brays and flipper waves that males make when claiming a territory. Mates are said to recognize each other's calls, and young will come out of a CRÈCHE (a huddle of chicks) to feed when they hear a parent's call. Pairs that have successfully raised a brood generally remain mated for life. Most species seek out the same patch of ground or burrow as the previous season.

The Emperor and King Penguins are exceptions. They are not tied to a particular nesting location because they lay and incubate their single egg on their feet.

The males of most species assume the bulk of the incubation and brooding tasks, fasting for long periods while the females forage at sea and recoup from egg laying. Later, when the chicks can thermoregulate, both parents feed the chicks. At the end of the breeding season, normally after the young have fledged, the adults undergo an annual molt—a process in which feathers are shed to make way for new plumage. During this stressful time, they remain on shore and do not eat.

Penguins face predation by birds, marine and land mammals, and humans. Although the former practice of rendering penguins for lamp oil is long past, these birds are now threatened by oil spills, entanglement in fishing nets, overfishing of prey species, and unrestricted human activities around nesting colonies.

GENUS *SPHENISCUS*: The Magellanic and Humboldt penguins are the most common penguins of continental Chile. They are sometimes called SOUTH AMERICAN JACKASS PENGUINS because of their braying calls. They nest in burrows when soil conditions permit. They lay 2 eggs at 4-day intervals and incubate the eggs for about 40 days.

Humboldt Penguin
Pingüino de Humboldt
Spheniscus humboldti

OTHER NAMES: Peruvian Penguin, Manchot de Humboldt, Humboldt-Pinguin. Named in honor of German naturalist Alexander Humboldt who described this species.

ID: 26 in (65 cm). HT 15 in (38 cm). WT 9 lb (4 kg). Black back and face; white supercilium curls around ear coverts. Eyes are reddish-brown. A single black chestband runs across the white chest (this feature separates them from Magellanic penguins). Pink fleshy area at base of the stout, black bill. Chicks have dark greyish-brown down.

They feed on anchovetas, sardines, squid and crustaceans at depths of 200 ft (60 m).

Humboldt penguins nest in burrows dug into guano, or on bare ground deep in sea caverns. Nesting colonies are situated on top of high sea cliffs, often amid stands of cactus. Mating follows the molting period. There are two breeding periods—April to May and September to October. Two eggs are laid 2 to 4 days apart. Both adults share in the incubation and brooding. The chicks remain in the nest for about 12 weeks until they fledge. The young forage along the coast until they return to their natal colony at about 2 years of age.

Dogs, foxes and caracaras prey on adult Humboldt penguins as well as their eggs and chicks. At sea, adults are taken by fur seals, sharks and toothed whales. Current population in Chile is estimated at 8000 breeding pairs, with the largest colonies at Chañaral and Pan de Azucar National Park in Atacama. VULNERABLE.

RANGE: Pelagic in the Humboldt Current. Nests on coasts and islands from Isla Foca, Peru, to Algorrobo, Valparaíso (5°S–33°S) with isolated colonies occurring south to the Islas Punihuil (42°S) in Los Lagos.

Magellanic Penguin
Pingüino de Magallanes
Spheniscus magellanicus

OTHER NAMES: Pingüino patgónico, Manchot de Magellan, Magellan pinguin.

ID: 26–28 in (65–70 cm). HT 17 in (43 cm). Black above; white below. Two black chestbands. White supercilium curls around ear coverts. Extensive pink fleshy area around eye and across lores. CHICKS are brownish-grey above, creamy white below.

The breeding cycle begins in September when pairs excavate their burrows in the tussock and coastal heath. In October the female lays one egg in the burrow, then lays another about four days later. Normally only the first hatchling survives; two chicks are reared only when enough food is available. Chicks make their first forays outside the burrows at 30 days of age. They are fed by both adults who forage in coastal waters. Adults leave the colony in the morning, and return with food later the same day. After the chicks fledge at 9 to 17 weeks, the adults undergo a three-week molt, then abandon the colony until the next breeding season. Marine and land mammals are natural predators. The practice of using penguins as crab bait, overfishing, and uncontrolled human activities around nesting colonies are other threats. NEAR THREATENED.

RANGE: Islas Chañaral, Atacama, to Tierra del Fuego and Islas Diego Ramírez; also Argentina and the Falklands. Fjords and offshore islands with tussock grass or small shrubs. Occasional at Juan Fernández.

GENUS *EUDYPTES*: Erect-crested penguins sport bright yellow or orange head plumes. Their heavy beaks are suited for crushing crustaceans and capturing squid, krill and fish. They lay two eggs of unequal size 4 to 5 days apart. The first egg is considerably smaller, takes longer to incubate, and is rarely successful.

Rockhopper Penguin
Pingüino de penacho amarillo
Eudyptes chrysochome

OTHER NAMES: Pingüino real, Kalanina, Gorfu sauter, Felsenpinguin. Rockhopper refers to the two-footed hops these birds make as they move up and down paths worn into the rockface of the nesting colony.

ID: 20–24 in (50–60 cm). HT 14 in (35 cm). Black head, neck and back; white below. Narrow yellow supercilium with fine, drooping, yellow plumes at sides of head. Reddish-brown bill. Red eyes. Legs and feet pink. Aggressive, showing little fear of people, birds or large animals. The main prey species are krill, amphipods, copepods, isopods, squid and fishes taken at depths to 325 ft (100 m).

Rockhoppers nest in colonies situated on top of sea cliffs. Pairs return to the same breeding site each year in October. Two eggs of unequal size are laid in November.

PENGUINS 145

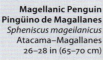

Magellanic Penguin
Pingüino de Magallanes
Spheniscus magellanicus
Atacama–Magallanes
26–28 in (65–70 cm)

Magellanic penguins nest in burrows dug in loose soil.

Humboldt Penguin
Pingüino de Humboldt
Spheniscus humboldti
Arica–Los Lagos
26 in (65 cm)

Chinstrap Penguin
Pingüino antártico
Pygoscelis antarctica
Antarctica
27–30 in (68–76 cm)

Rockhopper Penguin
Pingüino de penacho amarillo
Eudyptes chrysochome
Aisén–Magallanes
20–24 in (50–60 cm)

Macaroni Penguin
Pingüino macaroni
Eudyptes chrysolophus
Magallanes–Antarctica
27.5 in (70 cm)

Adelie Penguin
Pingüino de Adélie
Pygoscelis adeliae
Antarctica
27–28 in (68–70 cm)

Gentoo Penguin
Pingüino papúa
Pygoscelis papua
Magallanes–Antarctica
29–35 in (74–90 cm)

Emperor Penguin
Pingüino emperador
Aptenodytes forsteri
Fast ice of Antarctica
39–51 in (100–130 cm)

King Penguin
Pingüino rey
Aptenodytes patagonicus
Magallanes–Subantarctic islands
33–37 in (85–95 cm)

146 BIRDS

Rockhoppers lay two eggs but usually raise only one chick—the one that hatches from the larger egg.

The male assumes most of the incubation and brooding duties, remaining on the nest fasting while the female returns to the nest with food for the chicks. Once the offspring begin to crèche with other young, both parents forage for the chicks until they fledge at 10 weeks of age. The adults then undergo a 25-day molt before they abandon the colony. VULNERABLE.

RANGE: Aisén to Magallanes and the Islas Diego Ramírez; also Argentina, Falklands, South Georgia. Highly pelagic in subantarctic waters in non-breeding season.

Macaroni Penguin, Pingüino macaroni
Eudyptes chrysolophus

OTHER NAMES: Pingüino de frente dorada, Gorfou macaroni, Goldschopfpinguin. The name Macaroni refers to orange plumed hats worn in the 18th-century by members of London's Macaroni Club. The name was popularized in the lyrics of *Yankee Doodle Dandy*—"He stuck a feather in his hat and called it Macaroni."

ID: 27.5 in (70 cm). HT 18 in (46 cm). Black head, neck and back; white below. Golden yellow plumes extend from the center of the forehead and sweep backwards above the red eyes. Bill is reddish-brown with a pink fleshy gape. Pink legs. They feed on crustaceans, squid and fish.

Macaroni penguins nest (Oct–Jan) in colonies on rocky subantarctic coasts. In the South Shetlands, pairs sometimes nest in the middle of chinstrap penguin colonies. After the chicks fledge (Feb–Mar), the adults undergo an annual 25-day molt on land, after which they abandon the colony and spend the winter at sea. VULNERABLE.

RANGE: Magallanes; UNCOMMON on Islas Desolation and Diego Ramírez; RARE at Islas Noir and Deceit. Widespread pelagic in subantarctic waters when not breeding.

GENUS *PYGOSCELIS*: Adelie, chinstrap and gentoo penguins are called BRUSH-TAILED PENGUINS. They nest in large colonies in the Antarctic and Subantarctic The three species share food resources by having different breeding schedules and feeding at varied depths and distances from shore. The saying that "Chinstraps charge, Adelies stand their ground, and Gentoos flee" captures the very different temperaments of the three pygoscelid species.

Adelie Penguin, Pingüino de Adélie
Pygoscelis adeliae

OTHER NAMES: Pingüino de ojo blanco, Manchot Adélie, Adelie-Pinguin. French Captain Jules Dumont d'Urville named this species for his wife, Adélie, while in command of the *Zeleé* (1837-41).

ID: 27–28 in (68–70 cm). WT 5–10 lb (2–4 kg). Black head, neck and back; white underparts. White ring around the eye. Bill brick red. CHICKS have a dark grey head and silver-grey down, which molts to brown.

Adelies feed on krill taken about 30 mi (50 km) from shore at depths of 250 ft (75 m), and often feed in pack ice. The nesting season (Sep–Jan) begins as the males make their way across the ice toward the Antarctic coast. They reclaim former nesting sites and wait for returning mates. After courtship and copulation, the female lays 1 to 2 eggs on a high mound of pebbles. Males, who have already fasted for several weeks, take on the first incubation shift, fasting for two more weeks before females relieve them at the nest. As soon as the chicks crèche with other young, both of the parents forage at sea and return daily with food. They call their chick out of the crèche, relying on the offspring's ability to recognize its parent's voice and chase after the adult while begging for food. The

Adult penguins have to brood their chicks during the first weeks of life to keep them warm. Once a chick can thermoregulate, it joins other young birds in a crèche, which frees both parents to forage for food for the chicks.

Gentoo chick at 3 weeks

Chinstrap chick at 5 weeks

Adelie chick at 7 weeks

feeding chase leads closer to the shoreline each day, thus orienting the chicks toward the sea, which they must soon enter alone.

The adult Adelies abandon the colony and molt on the pack ice at the end of January. The fledglings eventually plunge into the icy surf. They must find food on their own and avoid being eaten by leopard seals or orcas. Only about 10 percent of the chicks survive these threats, and very few live to 12 years of age.

RANGE: Circumpolar in Antarctic pack ice. Nests along the coast of Antarctica, the Antarctic Peninsula, the South Shetlands, South Orkneys, South Sandwich, Bouvet, Balleny and Peter I Islands.

Chinstrap Penguin, Pingüino antártico
Pygoscelis antarctica
OTHER NAMES: Pingüino de barbijo, Manchot à jugulaire, Kehlstreifpinguin. Chinstrap refers to the narrow black band that crosses the white throat.
ID: 27–30 in (68–76 cm). Black back; white underparts. Crown and back of head black; sides of head and neck white. Narrow black band from ear to ear across throat. CHICKS have greyish down. Chinstraps feed mainly on krill taken some 20 mi (32 km) from shore at depths of 200 ft (60 m).

The chinstrap breeding cycle begins in late October when adults return to their natal colony to search out mates and compete for nesting sites. Waves of cacophonous brays *ah-kak-KAUK ah-kak-kauk* resound through the colony. Reunited pairs cement their bond through head-weaving displays called SNAKE-NECKING. Males wage serious and sometimes bloody battles to retain a favored mate or nest location. Pairs build a domed nest of rocks and pebbles (often pilfered from a neighbor's nest) on which they lay 1 to 2 white eggs. Midway through the nesting season one can see long lines of "off-duty" parents with krill-stained breasts waddling to the shore. There they meet incoming groups sporting gleaming white and black plumage. Adults begin to molt by late February. They fast during this two-week period, thus weaning the chicks. Chinstraps winter at sea beyond the pack ice.
RANGE: Pelagic at the Antarctic ice edge in winter. Nests on the Antarctic Peninsula to 64°S and on the Scotia Arc islands. Rare at Bouvet, Heard, Balleny, Peter I. One record at Isla Nueva, Magallanes.

Gentoo Penguin, Pingüino papúa
Pygoscelis papua
OTHER NAMES: Pingüino de vincha, Eselspinguin, Manchot papou. Gentoo, a Falkland term for Hindu refers to the white turban-like swath on the top of the head.
ID: 29–35 in (74–90 cm). Third largest penguin. Docile and confiding. Slate-black head and back; white underparts. Wide

white band across the crown of the head. White eyering. Bill is coral-red with a black tip. Legs are reddish. CHICKS are dark grey above with pearl grey underparts.

Gentoos have the longest breeding cycle of the pygoscelids—up to seven months in the Subantarctic. They incorporate plant matter into their nests whenever possible. Gentoos pilfer nesting materials from their neighbor's mound in a most "genteel" way, stealing lichens, pebbles and feathers with an innocent air and then presenting the booty to their mate with a courtly bow. Two eggs is the normal clutch, and males and females take turns in incubating the eggs. Chicks are brooded for 28 days, after which both parents forage near shore for fish and krill taken at 450 ft (135 m) depths. Gentoos undergo a 3-week molt (Jan–Mar, depending on latitude). Mated pairs stay near their breeding grounds throughout the year. NEAR THREATENED.

RANGE: Uncommon in Magallanes; resident in Chilean Antarctica in ice-free areas to 65°S. Circumpolar in the Subantarctic. Large colonies in the Falklands, on Macquarie Island, and islands in the s Indian Ocean.

GENUS *APTENODYTES*: This genus contains the largest living penguins, the king and emperor penguins. Both species lay and incubate their single egg on the feet, rather than on a nest. These penguins have long slender bills for catching fish and squid. They are deep divers, with the emperor penguins recorded making 18-minute dives to depths of 870 ft (265 m).

King Penguin, Pingüino rey
Aptenodytes patagonicus
OTHER NAMES: Königs-Pinguin, Manchot royal.
ID: 33–37 in (85–95 cm). HT 30 in (76 cm). ADULTS have a greyish-blue back, black head and white front. Oval orange ear patches are connected by yellow bands to orange upper breast. Black bill with rose or orange stripe at the base of the bill. JUVENILES have white ear patches and pale pink bill stripe. CHICKS are covered with shaggy, cinnamon-brown down. The adults remain near the breeding colony all year. Mated pairs attempt to raise 2 broods over a 3-year period. The first egg is laid in November and the chick fledges about a year later. The adults then molt and go to sea to feed. Another egg is laid the next February. This egg hatches just as food supplies dwindle and the chick requires up to 13 months to fledge. Another attempt is made at laying in March of the third year. This egg seldom survives.

RANGE: Occasional in Magallanes where the species possibly breeds. Nests on subantarctic and antarctic coasts. Circumpolar in the Southern Ocean.

Emperor Penguin, Pingüino emperador
Aptenodytes forsteri
OTHER NAMES: Manchot empereur, Kaiserpinguin.
ID: 39–51 in (100–130 cm). HT 33 in (84 cm). ADULTS have a bluish-grey back and cream-colored underparts. Black cheeks, chin and throat. Yellow semicircular patch on side of neck (patch is whitish in JUVENILES). Long, decurved, black bill, with a thin line of orange, rose or purple on lower bill. CHICKS are pale grey with a dark grey helmet.

Emperor penguins nest on the fast ice (ice permanently attached to land) at the onset of austral winter in June. The female lays a single egg, transfers it to the male's feet and leaves to feed at sea, which may be as far as 60 mi (100 km) away. Hatching coincides with the female's return about 64 days later. Males then make their way to the sea to take their first nourishment in three months, having lost up to half their body weight. Once the males return, both parents alternate feeding the chicks. Older chicks are left to huddle in crèches. Adults molt in January. Fledglings and parents then move to the disintegrating ice edge and drift off to sea on the ice floes.

RANGE: Fast ice and ice floes around Antarctica. RARE in Chilean Antarctica; there is a small nesting colony at Margarita Bay (67°52'S) on the Antarctic Peninsula.

The external tubular nostrils of procellariids have earned them the common collective name "tubenose."

Black-browed Albatross | Kermadec Petrel | Broad-billed Prion

Southern Giant-Petrel | Christmas Shearwater | Wilson's Storm-Petrel

PROCELLARIIFORMES: Tube-nosed Birds

Procellariiformes, which may soon be placed with the Cinconiiformes, includes the albatrosses, petrels, shearwaters, prions, storm-petrels and diving-petrels. These birds have external tubular nostrils. They are highly pelagic and most come to land only to breed. They lay a single egg, experience a long period of immaturity, and have a long life span. Most exude a musty smell.

Procellariids are referred to as "tubenoses" because of their external tubular nostrils. Albatrosses have a small nasal tube on each side of the upper mandible, while the others have tubular nostrils united on top of the bill. The nostrils exude excess salt, which is removed from the body by a gland at the base of the bill. The salty waste drips out of the nostrils, or is forcibly ejected in some species. The nasal tubes open to an enlarged olfactory lobe of the brain, which may help birds to locate food and the nesting burrow. Tubenoses store oil extracted from marine prey in the stomach. The oil is rich in Vitamin A and serves as a food cache for adults and chicks, who experience long periods of fasting. Some birds spit out the smelly oil in defense, striking presumed predators with excellent marksmanship.

FAMILY DIOMEDEIDAE

ALBATROSSES

Albatrosses are the world's largest seabirds. They are distinguished by a strong, hooked bill with tubular nostrils on both sides of the upper mandible, long narrow wings, a short tail and large webbed feet.

The albatrosses can be divided into three groups: the GREAT ALBATROSSES, which have wingspans of about 10 ft (3 m); the MOLLY-MAUKS, which have wingspans averaging 7 ft (2.2 m); and SOOTY ALBATROSSES whose wingspans average 6.5 ft (2 m).

Of the 21 to 24 recognized living species, all but three range in the Southern Hemisphere. Those species are restricted to the North Pacific Ocean, distanced from their southern relatives by the windless doldrums that encircle the equator. This geographic separation is an indication of the albatross's dependence on the wind to fly.

On calm days, albatrosses have to patter across the water surface and flap awkwardly to become airborne. But on windy days, they simply open their wings and let the air currents lift them from the waves. They climb into the wind, stall out at an altitude where drag and body weight slow ascent, then bank leeward and plummet down gaining momentum. They glide across the ocean surface taking maximum advantage of the uplift of individual waves before climbing into the wind again. This energy-efficient method of flight is called DYNAMIC SOARING. With little perceptible movement of their wings, albatrosses can approach and easily round an ocean-going ship making 14 knots. Effortless flight allows these birds to cover long distances when foraging for food, especially during breeding and adolescence, when the foraging range of most species covers thousands of miles of ocean.

Albatrosses feed at night while swimming on the ocean surface where they prey on squid, fish and krill. They also follow ships for garbage and marine prey churned up in the wake. They attend fishing trawlers, and are attracted to the baited hooks of longlines, which results in the incidental hooking and drowning of thousands of albatrosses each year. Feral cats, rats and degradation of nesting habitat are other factors that threaten their survival.

Most albatrosses spend their adolescence exploring the vast open ocean. Young birds sometimes return to their natal colony where they "practice" albatross courtship rituals and begin to select a mate. Once successful nesting is achieved—usually at 9 to 10 years of age—pairs mate for life and may continue to breed on the same site for several decades. The parents alternate incubating their single white egg and brooding and feeding the chick. Because it takes up to nine months to fledge a chick, most albatross species nest every other year.

Literary references to these seabirds often express the belief that albatrosses are the reincarnation of drowned seamen. Samuel Coleridge's epic poem "Rime of the Ancient Mariner," published in 1798, relates how a storm blew the Ancient Mariner's ship into the ice around Antarctica. No living thing was seen until...

> At length did cross an Albatross,
> Through the fog it came;
> As it had been a Christian soul,
> We hailed it in God's name.

To the crew's chagrin, the Ancient Mariner killed the albatross with an arrow. Their ship drifted, was becalmed, and all hands perished except for the Ancient Mariner who was condemned to a life of wandering the world seeking atonement.

A beautiful eulogy to lost mariners composed by the Chilean poet Sara Vial is engraved on a stone monolith seated next to the Albatross Monument at Cape Horn.

> *Soy el Albatros que te espera*
> *en el final del mundo.*
> *Soy el alma olvidada de los marineros*
> *muertos que cruzaron el Cabo de Hornos*
> *desde todos los mares de la tierra.*
> *Pero ellos no murieron en las furiosas olas.*
> *Hoy vuelan en mis alas, hacia la eternidad,*
> *en la última grieta de los vientos antárticos.*

> I am the albatross who awaits you
> at the bottom of the world.
> I am the lost soul of mariners
> from all the world's oceans
> who perished while rounding Cape Horn.
> But they did not die in the storm-tossed waves.
> Today they fly on my wings, for all eternity,
> in the final embrace of the antarctic winds.

The Albatross Monument at Cape Horn

WANDERING ALBATROSSES (GENUS *DIOMEDEA*): The species *Diomedea exulans* recently has been split into: Wandering Albatross *(Diomedea exulans)*, Antipodean Albatross *(Diomedea antipodensis)*, Gibson's Albatross *(Diomedea gibsoni)*, and Tristan Albatross *(Diomedea dabbenena)*. The Wandering and Antipodean species occur in Chilean seas.

Wandering Albatross, Albatros errante
Diomedea exulans
OTHER NAMES: Snowy Albatross, Albatros viajero, Carnero del Cabo, Grand albatros, Albatros hurleur, Wanderalbatros.
ID: 42–53 in (107–135 cm). WS 100–138 in (305–350 cm). Largest albatross, weighing up to 16 pounds (7.25 kg). Progressive whitening occurs in 7 stages, allowing identification of intermediate plumages. ADULT "SNOWY" MALES are entirely white except for black primaries and a narrow black margin along the secondaries. ADULT FEMALES are smaller than males and retain their dark breeding cap into maturity. A few black outer tail feathers may be present on the otherwise white tail. Bill and legs are pink. FIRST YEAR PLUMAGE birds are chocolate brown with a white face and white underwings. IMMATURES whiten first on the belly, flanks, saddle, rump and center of the upperwing. As the head, body and tail whiten, the white patches on the upperwing also increase in area, forming a diagnostic wedge on the dark upperwing. The white wedge gradually expands forward on the upperwing until it is mostly white.

Albatrosses nest in colonies on flat grasslands of subantarctic islands. They generally make their first breeding attempt at eight years of age. Once mated, the pair returns to the same nesting site of previous years. When pairs arrive at the nesting grounds (Oct–Nov) they renew their bond by engaging in elaborate courtship rituals. The female lays a single egg in late December. The egg is incubated for 75 to 80 days and the chick hatches in April. Both parents feed it throughout the austral winter on a diet of fish, squid and carrion. The chick is fed daily at first, then weekly, as parents make foraging flights as long as 3750 mi (6000 km). They stop feeding the chick when it begins to molt its juvenile down at about 278 days of age. The chick fledges after it loses enough weight to become airborne.

The parent birds abandon the colony and spend the following year at sea, sometimes circling the globe before returning to their colony. Satellite telemetry trackings made by Jouventin and Weimerskirch in 1989 show that wandering albatrosses fly up to 560 mi per day (900 km/day) at air speeds of 50 mi per hour (80 km/hr) and can travel over 9300 mi (15,000 km) when foraging.

These magnificent seabirds can live to 80 years of age. But adults are susceptible to drowning when striking at longline baited hooks, and chicks perish when fed debris ingested by adults at sea. VULNERABLE.
RANGE: Valparaíso to Magallanes. Circumpolar in the Southern Ocean. Pelagic in cold currents and especially in the open ocean south of 40°S latitude.

Antipodean Albatross
Albatros de las Antipodas
Diomedea antipodensis
OTHER NAME: Albatros des Antipodes.
ID: 43 in (110 cm). ALL STAGES show white and brown plumage with little white on the upperwing. Pink bill. Adult MALES have a white back with chocolate-brown wavy lines. White neck; dark crown. Underparts white. Undertail coverts buff. Underwing white with dark primaries. FEMALES are darker and more rust-colored than males. Brown of the crown extends to the nape and around the neck in a loose collar, setting off the pale face and throat. IMMATURES resemble first-year wandering albatrosses. Feeds on cephalopods and fish. Mortalities result from drownings at hooks of the longline tuna fishery and predation by feral pigs and cats at nesting colonies. VULNERABLE.
RANGE: Uncommon visitor offshore south and central Chile. Breeds in the Antipodes,

Campbell and Auckland Islands (NZ). Nests on coastal ridges, slopes and plateaus, usually amid tussock or shrubs. Non-breeding birds disperse over the Tasman Sea and South Pacific east to coastal Chile, and possibly throughout the Southern Ocean.

ROYAL ALBATROSSES: *Diomedea epomophora* recently has been split into the Southern Royal Albatross, *Diomedea epomophora*, and Northern Royal Albatross, *Diomedea sanfordi*. Both have a black cutting edge on a pink bill. White tail lacks black feathers except in juvenile plumage.

Southern Royal Albatross
Albatros real del sur
Diomedea epomophora

OTHER NAMES: Pájaro carnero, Albatros royal, Königsalbatros.
ID: 42–48 in (107–122 cm). WS 120–138 in (305–350 cm). Plumage whitens in 5 stages. ALL STAGES show a light pink bill with a black cutting edge on upper mandible and flesh-colored legs. In JUVENILES the head, neck, rump and underparts are white; the white mantle is flecked with black; the dark brown upperwing has white flecks on coverts; and the white tail is tipped in blackish-brown. As birds mature, the back and tail become white, and, starting at leading edge near shoulder, the upperwing coverts become increasingly white.

Feeds mainly on squid and fish, supplemented by salps, crustaceans and carrion. Nests on tussock grassland slopes, ridges, and plateaus in New Zealand. Breeding is biennial if a chick is successfully reared.

Mortality factors include feral pigs and cats that take eggs and chicks, the spread of *Dracophyllum* scrub into breeding habitat, and drownings at longlines. **VULNERABLE**.
RANGE: Uncommon pelagic over the continental shelf from Valparaíso to Magallanes. Nests on New Zealand's Auckland Islands, Campbell Island, and South Island. Non-breeders disperse to open ocean waters off New Zealand and the coast of South America, and may be circumpolar.

Northern Royal Albatross
Albatros real del norte
Diomedea sanfordi

OTHER NAME: Albatros royal du Nord.
ID: 42–48 in (107–122 cm). WS 120–138 in (305–350 cm). Similar to the Southern Royal Albatross. Two plumage stages. ALL STAGES show a light pink bill with a black cutting edge on the upper mandible and have flesh-colored legs. MATURE birds are white, with completely dark upperwings, except for a white triangle in the inner leading edge. JUVENILE STAGE is like the first stage of the Southern Royal Albatross.

Feeds on cephalopods, fish, salps, crustaceans and carrion. Nests on flat summits of New Zealand islands. **ENDANGERED**, mainly due to storms in 1985 that degraded habitat at the nesting colonies in the Chathams.
RANGE: Uncommon pelagic off the central Chile coast from Valparaíso to Los Lagos. Nests on New Zealand's Chatham Islands, South Island and Enderby Island. Non-breeding birds are known to disperse to Chilean and Argentine continental shelf waters and may be circumpolar in the Southern Ocean.

MOLLYMAUKS: Sailors and whalers called the smaller albatrosses MOLLYMAUKS, which derives from the Dutch word meaning "foolish gull." These albatrosses have white underparts, a white rump, and dark-colored upperwings, mantle and tail. Bill color and varying patterns of grey on the head are the best clues to identification. Like the larger albatrosses, mollymauks are susceptible to the effects of longline fishing and many are classed as Vulnerable or Endangered.

Black-browed Albatross
Albatros de ceja negra
Thalassarche melanophris

OTHER NAMES: Albatros ojeroso, Albatros à sourcils noir, Schwarzbrauenalbatros.
ID: 35 in (8 cm). WS 88.5 in (225 cm). WT 7–12 lb (3–5 kg). Conspicuous slate-grey eyebrow. ADULTS have a white head, body and rump; black upperwings, mantle and tail. Under-

wings are white with a broad dark leading edge and narrow dark trailing edge. Bill is yellow with an orange or pink tip. JUVENILES are like adults, but have a dark-tipped grey bill that gradually lightens to olive-brown. A grey wash on the nape and lower neck creates a broad collar or hood, similar to that of juvenile grey-headed albatrosses.

Nests annually in dense colonies situated on cliff tops and steep hillsides where there is constant wind for takeoff and landing. Normally returns to the same breeding site and partner each season. A single egg is laid on a high pillar of mud, guano and grass. Incubation is about 72 days. Both parents feed the chick, making foraging flights taking several days and extending hundreds of miles. Fledglings go to sea in early April, about 17 weeks after hatching.

Feeds on krill, fish, cephalopods, salps and jellyfish taken from the sea surface or by plunge-diving from heights of up to 30 ft (9 m). Follows ships in low flight, searching for waste, kitchen scraps or prey organisms churned up in the wake. Known to live 30 years or more. NEAR THREATENED.

RANGE: Common off the entire Chilean coast, and in fjords and canals. Circumpolar in the Southern Ocean, from the pack ice north to the Tropic of Capricorn. Nests (Oct–Apr) at Islas Diego Ramírez, Noir and Evout; also Falklands, South Georgia and other subantarctic islands.

Grey-headed Albatross
Albatros de cabeza gris
Thalassarche chrysostoma
OTHER NAMES: Graukopfalbatros, Albatros à tête gris, Pájaro carnero, Albatros cabecigrís.
ID: 32 in (81 cm). WS 87 in (220 cm). ADULTS have a bluish-grey head with a paler crown and a dark eyebrow that passes through the eye. Bill is black with narrow yellow bands on the top and underside of the bill. Mantle, upperwing and tail blackish. Rump and underparts white. Underwing white with irregular black margins. JUVENILES are dark versions of adults, with dark underwings and a black bill. The head is more uniformly dark grey than similar juvenile Black-browed Albatross.

Breeds biennially beginning at 7 years of age. Arrives in September at colonies on steep coastal slopes to engage in courtship rituals and reunite with mate. Lays a single egg in October in a conical nest of mud, lined with grasses. The male incubates the egg for the first 70 days—almost the total incubation period. The chick takes up to 4 days to chip out of the egg. The female broods the chick and both parents feed it. Fledging of chicks and departure from the colony takes place in mid-May. Adults that have successfully raised a chick spend the next year circling the Southern Ocean before returning to their breeding colony.

Feeds on squid, fish and crustaceans; chicks are also fed eel-like lampreys. Recent satellite tracking of the grey-headed albatrosses at Diego Ramírez, south of Cape Horn, indicates these birds forage deep in polar waters to 67°S, and can fly more than 5000 mi (8000 km) in one foraging flight.

Approaches ships but does not usually follow them. Can live to 36 years of age. Low numbers, low reproductive rate and proficiency at stealing bait, leaves them open to adverse effects of longline fishing. VULNERABLE.

RANGE: Uncommon pelagic in cold currents off s Chile from Los Lagos to Magallanes; circumpolar in the Southern Ocean. Nests at Diego Ramírez, South Georgia, other subantarctic islands.

Pacific (Buller's) Albatross
Albatros de Buller
Thalassarche platei
OTHER NAMES: Buller-albatros, Albatros de Buller, Albatros du Pacifique. *Thalassarche platei* was split from *Thalassarche bulleri* and nominated for species status in 1998.
ID: 30 in (80 cm). WS 83 in (210 cm). Underparts and rump white. Underwing white with broad dark leading edge. Mantle, upperwing and tail dark grey. Head grey

with paler forehead. Black bill with broad yellow stripe on the top of the bill and a yellow-orange stripe on the lower mandible. The Pacific Albatross differs from Buller's in that the forecrown is silvery-grey rather than white, the hood is darker, and the dark supercilium extends two-thirds of the way across the lores and merges into the dark grey bill base. The extent of yellow on the bill and its smaller size separates the adult Pacific Albatross from the adult Grey-headed Albatross. JUVENILES resemble adults, except that they have a dark-tipped, olive-brown bill. VULNERABLE.

RANGE: Irregular pelagic visitor between Arica and Maule. Nests on the Chatham Islands, New Zealand, then spreads across the South Pacific Ocean as far east as the Humboldt Current.

Salvin's (Grey-backed) Albatross
Albatros de Salvin
Thalassarche salvini

OTHER NAMES: Shy Albatross, White-capped Albatross, Bounty Mollymauk, Weisskappenalbatros, Albatros de frente blanca. Considered a subspecies of the Shy Albatross, *Thalassarche cauta,* by some.

ID: 37 in (95 cm). WS 98 in (250 cm). Largest mollymauk. ADULT has a steel grey mantle, head, neck and tail; forehead and crown are whitish. Underparts and rump white. Underwing is white with narrow dark margins and a dark "thumbprint" on the leading edge of the wing where it meets the body. Bill is grey with a yellow tip and base. Adult plumage is achieved after 4 or 5 years. JUVENILE bill is grey with a black tip. As the birds mature, the side plates and top of the bill turn pale greyish-horn and the tip turns yellow. SUBADULTS have a grey hood of variable darkness. VULNERABLE.

RANGE: Arica to Los Lagos. Common over continental slope areas. Breeds annually (Oct–Apr) on New Zealand's Snares and Bounty Islands. Non-breeders range widely, reaching the Humboldt Current and the Indian Ocean.

Chatham Island Albatross
Albatros de las Chathams
Thalassarche erimita

ID: 35 in (90 cm). WS 87 in (220 cm). Slightly smaller than Salvin's Albatross, with a proportionally shorter bill. ADULTS differ from Salvin's in having a solid banana-yellow bill and a uniformly dark grey hood that lacks an obvious white cap. The grey hood is darker than that of Salvin's, and it contrasts sharply with the white chest and white underparts. Mortality factors include oil spills, disease, and storms that often destroy nesting sites in the Chatham Islands. CRITICALLY ENDANGERED.

RANGE: Small numbers occur from Arica to Los Lagos, usually with Salvin's. Breeds annually (Sep–Apr) on The Pyramid, a rock stack in the Chatham Islands, New Zealand. Non-breeding birds disperse into the South Pacific Ocean, west to Tasmania and east to the Humboldt Current (Apr–Jul).

SUBSPECIES: Considered a subspecies of the Shy Albatross, *Thalassarche cauta,* by some.

Light-mantled Albatross
Albatros oscuro de manto claro
Phoebetria palpebrata

OTHER NAMES: Carnero negro, Pastor, Albatros fuligineux à dos clair, Albatros tiznado, Graumantel-Russalbatros. Called "Blue Bird" by sealers because its back looks blue in strong light. *Phoebetria* honors the Greek goddess Phoebe (Artemis), untamed spirit of the natural world.

ID: 31–35 in (85–93 cm). WS 90–94 in (230–240 cm). ADULT dark sooty-grey with pale greyish back. Distinctive white crescent around the back of the eye. Bill black with a pale blue stripe on lower mandible. Long pointed wings often held bent at the elbow in flight. Wedge-shaped tail. JUVENILE like adult, with a pale grey collar.

Feeds mainly on squid and krill, taken by plunge-diving or feeding on the ocean surface; also feeds on fish and carrion. Breeds biennially, in single pairs or very small colonies of up to fifteen nests situated

on cliffs. The nest is a low mound of mud and vegetation, usually lined with grass. Courtship involves elaborate ritual dances, often accompanied by a shrill two-noted call *PEE-ow*. The single egg is incubated for 70 days by both parents, with the male taking the first 11-day shift after laying. After hatching the chick is brooded for 20 days until it is able to thermoregulate. Both parents then forage at sea, bringing food to the chick about every three days. Chicks fledge at about five months and spend the next 7 to 10 years at sea before returning to the natal colony. Adults spend a year at sea following breeding. THREATENED.
RANGE: Uncommon pelagic from Los Lagos to Magallanes. Circumpolar in the Southern Ocean as far south as the pack ice edge. Nests on subantarctic islands.
RELATED SPECIES: SOOTY ALBATROSS, *Phoebetria fusca*. Recorded in waters south of Cape Horn. Nests on islands in the South Atlantic Ocean. Separated from the Light-mantled Albatross by its dark back.

Waved Albatross
Albatros de las Galápagos
Phoebastria irrorata
OTHER NAMES: Galapagos albatross, Albatros ondulado, Galapagosalbatros.
ID: 34–37 in (85–93 cm). ADULT has a white head and neck, washed with ochre on the crown and nape. Chestnut-brown upperparts. Upperwing, back and tail brown, with a narrow white crescent at the base. Upper breast white; rest of underparts are barred with fine, dark wavy lines. Underwing pale grey, with browner axillaries, and brown around margins. Yellow bill. Bluish feet project beyond tail in flight. JUVENILE is like adult but with a whiter head.
  Feeds on fish, squid and crustaceans. Also known to scavenge on the regurgitated food of other birds. Mortality factors include drowning on longlines, disease, and illegal overfishing of feeding grounds. VULNERABLE.
RANGE: Records from Arica to Antofagasta in El Niño years. Breeds (Mar–Jan) on Española in the Galapagos and Isla de la Plata off Ecuador. Breeding adults fly east–southeast to Peruvian coastal upwellings to forage. Non-breeding birds range in continental shelf waters off Ecuador and Peru.

FAMILY PROCELLARIIDAE
PETRELS AND SHEARWATERS
Procellariidae comprises twelve genera and about fifty-five species of oceanic birds, including fulmarine petrels, gadfly petrels, prions, larger petrels and shearwaters. They vary in size from the large giant-petrels to the diminutive prions. These seabirds have nostrils united in a single tube on top of the bill. Their clutch is a single white egg.

FULMARINE PETRELS: These petrels have heavy, deeply-grooved, hooked bills for grasping and holding marine prey.

Southern (Antarctic) Giant-Petrel
Petrel gigante antártico
Macronectes giganteus
OTHER NAMES: Stinker, Black Molly, White Nellie, Southern Giant Fulmar, Carnero negro, Quebranta huesos, Fardelon, Jote de mar, Abanto-marino antártico, Pétrel géant, Süd-Riesensturmvogel.
ID: 34–39 in (86–99 cm). WS 72–81 in (185–205 cm). ADULTS are mottled sooty and brown, with a pale grey head and a green-tipped, flesh-colored bill. Eyes are dark or pale grey. The white morph, the "White Nellie," appears in about 5 percent of Antarctic birds. FIRST-YEAR birds are dark brown with yellowish bill and dark brown eyes. SUBADULTS show a progressive whitening of the head and upper breast. Separated from the albatrosses by stockier body, shorter wings and massive bill with tubes united on top of the upper mandible. Adults are separated from the Northern Giant-Petrel by the green-tipped, flesh-colored bill, whiter head, and pale leading edge of the upperwing. JUVENILES closely resemble Northern Giant-Petrel juveniles.
  Omnivorous, gregarious feeders, often forming large, noisy groups taking fish,

squid, offal and carrion from the surface of the water. They also prey on penguin chicks and eggs, dead or injured seabirds, and seal placentas and carcasses at pupping grounds. Follows ships and fishing vessels in large groups.

Nests in ice-free coastal areas, on rocky bluffs, open flats or offshore rocks of the Subantarctic and Antarctic regions. Pairs tend to return to the same nesting site every breeding season. A single white egg is laid on a low mound of vegetation or rocks in August. One or the other parent must continually sit on the nest to protect the egg or young chick from the potentially fatal cold and predation by brown skuas. Giant-petrels defend their eggs and small chicks by regurgitating and hurling food and stomach oils at predators if they are disturbed. Chicks fledge in February and immediately go to sea. They spend their early years roaming the Southern Ocean. VULNERABLE.

RANGE: Common from Arica to Tierra del Fuego, and south to Antarctica. Follows the Humboldt Current north in winter to within six degrees of the equator. Casual visitor to Easter Island and Juan Fernández. Breeds on the Antarctic continent, Antarctic Peninsula and subantarctic islands circumpolar.

Northern Giant-Petrel
Petrel gigante subantártico
Macronectes halli
OTHER NAMES: Hall's Giant-Petrel, Giant Fulmar, Nelly, Stinker, Pétrel de Hall, Hallsturmvogel, Abanto-marino subantártico.
ID: 32–37 in (81–94 cm). WS 71–79 in (180–200 cm). ADULTS are dark grey-brown, whitish on the face and chin, and mottled white on the head, neck and breast. The plumage becomes paler and more mottled as they age. The underwing is grey-brown with a dark leading edge; silvery-grey at base of the secondaries and inner primaries. Adults have a conspicuous pale grey iris, whereas juveniles have a dark iris. The bill is horn-colored with a reddish tip, a feature that separates this species from the Southern Giant-Petrel. JUVENILES are dark brown, developing a white face and capped appearance with age.

Scavenges and preys on seal pups, seal placentas, and penguin and albatross eggs and chicks. Feeds heavily on fish in the winter months. Northern giant-petrels arrive at breeding colonies in August or September. Males assume the larger share of incubating the egg and brooding the chick. Chicks fledge in late February. Eggs and chicks can be lost by desertion, trampling by adults and skua predation. NEAR THREATENED.

RANGE: RARE off n Chile; UNCOMMON from Valparaíso to Magallanes. Casual at Easter Island and Juan Fernández. Nests on South Georgia and subantarctic islands between 46°S–54°S. Ranges at sea from the e South Atlantic to w South Pacific.

Southern Fulmar
Petrel plateado
Fulmarus glacialoides
OTHER NAMES: Silver-grey Fulmar, Cape Dove, Fardela blanca, Fulmar antarctique, Silversturmvogel.
ID: 18–20 in (46–50 cm). WS 47 in (120 cm). Bluish-grey above; white below. Upperwing grey, darkening at wingtips, and with a white triangular patch at base of primaries. Bill is pink with a dark blue nasal tube and dark grey tip. Sexes are alike and there is no seasonal variation in plumage. Can be mistaken for a seagull.

Nests on rocky ledges of steep cliffs on the Antarctic coast. Adults return to their breeding colonies in October and begin to nest in November. The female lays only one egg each breeding season. Skua predation and extreme weather conditions are significant causes of egg and chick mortality. Chicks fledge in late March. Adults and young move north away from the pack ice, often reaching 10°S latitude in the cold currents of the Southern Ocean. Often flies, rests and feeds in large flocks,

A Northern and Southern Giant-Petrel investigate a carcass in the shallows.

especially in association with Cape Petrels. Feeds at night at the surface of the ocean on krill, other crustaceans, squid and fish.

RANGE: Pelagic from Arica to Magallanes and south to Antarctica. Visitor at Juan Fernández and San Félix y San Ambrosio. Circumpolar in the Southern Ocean. Nests in Antarctica, the South Sandwich, South Orkney, South Shetland, South Georgia, Bouvet, and Peter I Islands.

Antarctic Petrel
Petrel antártico
Thalassoica antarctica

OTHER NAMES: Damero oscuro, Pétrel antarctique, Weissflugelsturmvogel.

ID: 16–18 in (40–46 cm). WS 41 in (104 cm). Chocolate brown above and white below. White rump. Broad white band on the trailing edge of upperwing. Tail is white with a dark brown tip. The solid brown upperwing with a solid white subterminal wing band separates the Antarctic Petrel from the Cape Petrel.

Antarctic Petrels are gregarious at sea, roosting on icebergs in flocks comprising hundreds of birds. They feed on krill, pteropods, amphipods, cephalopods and small fishes. Adults arrive at the breeding colonies in Antarctica between October and November. Clutch is a single egg laid in crevices and on bare ledges of rocky cliffs in areas free of ice and snow. Chicks fledge in January.

RANGE: Lives and nests in the Antarctic. Generally restricted to pack ice, icebergs and ice floes. Irregular visitor to Tierra del Fuego and Cape Horn. Vagrant at Valdivia. Occasional in Australia and New Zealand.

Cape Petrel
Petrel moteado
Daption capense

OTHER NAMES: Pintado Petrel, Cape Pigeon, Damero, Tablero, Damier du Cap, Kapsturmvogel, Kaptaube.

ID: 15–16 in (38–40 cm). WS 32–36 in (81–91 cm). Back and upperwings are blackish-brown with conspicuous white spots and patches. Tail is white with black terminal band. The underwing is white with black margins. Bill, legs and feet are black.

Feeds on krill, squid and small fish; also scavenges on carcasses. Flocks follow ships and boats to take scraps and offal. Large flocks often rest on the water near ice floes. Starts breeding at about five years of age. Nests colonially on rocky ledges in the Antarctic and Subantarctic. One white egg is laid in November or early December.

RANGE: Arica to Magallanes. Follows cold currents as far north as the subtropics after nesting. Casual at Easter Island. Circumpolar in the Southern Ocean.

Snow Petrel
Petrel de las nieves
Pagodroma nivea

OTHER NAMES: Lesser Snow Petrel, Schneesturmvogel, Pétrel des nieges.

ID: 12–14 in (30–35 cm). WS 31 in (79 cm). White with black eyes and a black bill. Legs and feet are bluish-grey. Feeds on fish, squid, other mollusks and krill; also feeds on seal placentas and carcasses of dead seals, whales and penguins. Normally does not follow ships. Flies low over the ice, but very high over land to avoid predators such as skuas. Flocks are often seen sitting on icebergs.

Snow Petrels nest in loose colonies on cliffs, usually near the sea, but also inland. Some birds remain at the colony all year, but the main nesting period is from mid-September to March. The nest is a pebble-lined scrape in a deep rock crevice with overhanging protection. A single white egg is incubated for 41 to 49 days. The chick is brooded for eight days and remains in the nest for an additional seven weeks. The main causes of egg and chick mortality are skua predation and severe weather early in the nesting season.

RANGE: Circumpolar, usually near pack ice and ice floes. Breeds on South Georgia and other subantarctic islands, on the Antarctic Peninsula and the Antarctic continent.

GADFLY PETRELS (GENUS *PTERODROMA*): Gadfly petrels do not follow in ships' wakes. They are most commonly seen at a distance as they wheel over the open ocean in rapid, erratic flight. The *Pterodroma* petrels can be separated into dark-backed forms and those having a light grey back with a dark open-M across the back and wings. The latter closely resemble prions and blue petrels.

DARK-BACKED PTERODROMAS
Kermadec Petrel, Fardela negra de Juan Fernández
Pterodroma neglecta
OTHER NAMES: Fardela del día, Pétrel des Kermadec, Kermadecsturmvogel.
ID: 15 in (38 cm). WS 35.75 in (91 cm). Large gadfly-petrel with light, dark and intermediate morphs (different morphs may be separate subspecies). All forms have a white patch on underwing primaries and white primary shafts. All have short black bills, fleshy-pink legs and fleshy-pink feet with black webs. LIGHT MORPH: grey head, smoky brown upperparts, white underparts. Dark brown underwing with white patch at base of primaries. Similar to light morph Herald Petrel, which has a more extensive underwing patch and dark breastband. DARK MORPH: uniform dark brown except for white patch on underwing. Easily confused with dark morph of the Herald Petrel. INTERMEDIATE MORPH: dark head and breastband with a white throat and belly; or dark head and neck with rest of underparts pale ashy brown; or completely dark with white marbling on chest and belly.
RANGE: Nests (Oct–Feb) at Easter Is., San Félix y San Ambrosio, and Masatierra and Santa Clara, Juan Fernández Archipelago; also other South Pacific islands. Occasional along the Chilean mainland coast.

Herald Petrel, Fardela heraldica
Pterodroma arminjoniana
OTHER NAMES: Tahio, Südtrinidadsturmvogel, Wappensturmvogel, Pétrel hérault.
ID: 14.25 in (36 cm). WS 35.5 in (90 cm). Similar to the Kermadec Petrel. White underwing patches extend in an irregular line from base of primaries to axillaries. Black primary shafts. Irregular, dark breastband in the light morph. Black bill. Flesh-colored legs and feet; dark toes and webs. Light morphs, and less commonly dark plumaged birds, occur on Easter Island.
RANGE: Light morph, *P. a. heraldica*, nests on Easter Island. Other morphs are widespread in the subtropical South Pacific.

Phoenix Petrel, Fardela de fénix
Pterodroma alba
OTHER NAMES: Phönixsturmvogel, Pétrel à poitrine blanche.
ID: 13 in (33 cm). WS 32.75 in (83 cm). Sooty-brown upperparts. Underparts white except for a dark band across upper breast. Inconspicuous white throat. Underwing dark sooty-brown. Legs and feet flesh-colored; toes and webs dark. VULNERABLE.
RANGE: Uncommon pelagic at Easter Island. Ranges in the tropical Pacific Ocean.

Great-winged Petrel, Fardela de alas grandes
Pterodroma macroptera
ID: 16 in (41 cm). WS 40.2 in (102 cm). Like the Kerguelen Petrel, but larger and with a pale grey forehead, face and neck. Tail is long and slightly wedge-shaped. NOT ILLUSTRATED.
RANGE: RARE PELAGIC in Cockburn Channel, Magallanes, and possibly along the entire s Chile coast. Nests on subantarctic islands of the Atlantic and Indian Oceans.

Kerguelen Petrel, Fardela de Kerguelen
Aphrodroma brevirostris
OTHER NAMES: Kerguelensturmvogel, Pétrel de Kerguelen.
ID: 14 in (36 cm). WS 32.75 in (82 cm). Dark grey. Underside of primaries is pale silver. Long pointed wings; short body and tail. Large, rounded head. Bill and legs black. Formerly classed as a *Pterodroma*, now thought to be related to fulmarine petrels.
RANGE: Highly pelagic, from the edge of the Antarctic pack ice to subantarctic waters. RARE PELAGIC to Drake Passage and

Mehuin, Valdivia; may range between these points. Nests on subantarctic islands of the Atlantic and Indian Oceans.

PALE-BACKED PTERODROMAS

Cook's Petrel, Fardela blanca de Cook
Pterodroma cooki
OTHER NAMES: Cooksturmvogel, Pétrel de Cook.
ID: 10 in (26 cm). WS 26 in (66 cm). Pale grey back with a dark open-M across back and wings. Black tail tip. Forehead and lores white, mottled with grey. Black patch around eyes. Black bill. Underparts white. Underwing white with a dark margin, wider on leading edge. Legs pale blue. ENDANGERED.
RANGE: Non-breeding pelagic visitor to the Chilean coast from Arica to Valparaíso. Nests in New Zealand (Oct–Apr).

Masatierra Petrel
Fardela blanca de Masatierra
Pterodroma defilippiana
OTHER NAMES: De Filippi's Petrel, Pétrel de Defillippe, Juan Fernandez-Sturmvogel.
ID: 10 in (26 cm). WS 26 in (66 cm). Pale grey back with a dark open-M across back and wings. Separated with difficulty from Cook's Petrel by stockier build, grey half-collar, contrasting face, black eye patch, much heavier bill, longer tail, and lack of dark tail tip. VULNERABLE.
RANGE: Nests (Jul–Nov) at San Félix y San Ambrosio and Isla Masatierra, Juan Fernández Archipelago. Pelagic visitor to the Chilean coast from Atacama to Biobío.

Mottled Petrel
Fardela moteada
Pterodroma inexpectata
OTHER NAMES: Pétrel de Peale, Regensturmvogel.
ID: 13 in (33 cm). WS 29 in (74 cm). Back grey with indistinct, dark open-M across back and wings. Hindcrown and area around eyes dark grey, contrasting with mottled grey forecrown and white face. Underparts white, except for a variable dark grey area on lower breast and belly. Underwing white,

with a dark grey leading edge, and a black diagonal stripe forming an incomplete open-M. Short, black bill. Legs and feet flesh-colored; black toes. NOT ILLUSTRATED.
RANGE: Uncommon pelagic off Magallanes in Drake Passage. Nests in New Zealand sector; migrates to the North Pacific.

Stejneger's Petrel, Fardela de Masafuera
Pterodroma longirostris
OTHER NAMES: Masafuera Petrel, Fardela blanca chica, Stejnegersturmvogel, Pétrel de Stejneger.
ID: 10 in (26 cm). WS 26 in (66 cm). Pale grey back with a dark open-M across back and wings; trailing edge of wing dark brown. Forehead, lores and forecrown white; rest of crown, nape and tail brownish-black. Dark hindneck extends onto sides of breast to form a partial collar. Underparts white. Underwing white with black trailing edge and short diagonal black line from bend of wing. Black bill. Feet lilac-blue with brown webs. VULNERABLE.
RANGE: Nests (Dec–Mar) on Isla Masafuera, Juan Fernández Archipelago. Pelagic off the n Chilean coast. Ranges in warm temperate Pacific waters as far as Japan.

Juan Fernández Petrel
Fardela blanca de Juan Fernández
Pterodroma externa
OTHER NAMES: White-necked Petrel, Petrel de Salvin, Salvinsturmvogel.
ID: 17 in (43 cm). WS 37.75 in (96 cm). Greyish-brown above, white below, with a long dark tail. Pale grey back with a darker open-M across the back and wings. Crown, nape, mantle and shoulders grey; rump paler grey. Forehead and face white. Underparts white. Underwings have a narrow, black anterior margin and a short, diagonal black line from the bend of the wing. Black bill. Legs and feet flesh-colored with black webs and toes. VULNERABLE.
RANGE: Nests (Dec–Mar) on Isla Masafuera, Juan Fernández Archipelago. Visitor to the Chilean coast from Arica to Maule. Pelagic in tropical and subtropical Pacific waters.

White-headed Petrel
Fardela de frente blanca
Pterodroma lessoni
OTHER NAMES: Petrel à tête blanche, Weisskopfsturmvogel.

ID: 17 in (43 cm). WS 43 in (109 cm). White head and underbody. Dark smudge through the eye. Back, rump and tail pale grey. Dark open-M across back. Underwing dark. Short, stout black bill. Legs and feet are fleshy-pink; distal part of toes and webs are dark. NEAR THREATENED.

RANGE: Pelagic records from Drake Passage and w Strait of Magellan; possible vagrant to Valdivia. Nests on subantarctic islands of New Zealand and the s Indian Ocean.

PRIONS (GENUS *PACHYPTILA*): Whalers saw prions feeding on matter stirred up by cetaceans and called them "whalebirds." Prions skip across the water with legs extended as they feed. They scoop up prey and force water through sieve-like lamellae along the bill edge. Their flight is low and fast; they sometimes dip into a wave in flight. Prions are blue-grey with a dark, open-M across the upper wing and back. Species can be identified at sea by observing the head color and extent of the nuchal collar.

Antarctic Prion, Petrel-paloma antártico
Pachyptila desolata
OTHER NAMES: Dove Prion, Pétrel de la Desolation, Taubensturmvogel.

ID: 11 in (27 cm). WS 24 in (61 cm). Largest prion. Bill is moderately wide when viewed from above; bill edges are almost straight, not curved. Small lamellae cannot be seen when bill is closed. At sea, white chin and dark half-collar are distinctive. Gregarious, with flocks of hundreds commonly seen at sea. Feeds on krill and other crustaceans, small cephalopods and polychaete worms. Feeds by running along the surface of the water with wings outstretched and the bill submerged in the water like a scoop. Also takes prey from the water surface in flight or while swimming, or sometimes makes shallow foraging dives. Nests on exposed cliff ledges, in hollows under boulders, or in short burrows dug into soft grass-covered slopes. Single egg is laid in December and is incubated by both parents for 45 days. Chicks fledge in March, after which adults and fledglings move north into temperate waters for the winter. Predators at the nest include skuas and gulls.

RANGE: Nests on islands off the Antarctic Peninsula, on South Georgia, Iles Crozet, Iles Kerguelen, Heard, Macquarie, Auckland and Scott Islands. Occasional in Magallanes (summer); Antofagasta to Valdivia (winter). Circumpolar in the Southern Ocean.

VAGRANTS: THIN-BILLED PRION, *Pachyptila belcheri*, has a narrow, shallow bill. Slim and pale body. Broad white supercilium. Fast, erratic flight. Recorded in Drake Passage and off Antofagasta. Nests in the Falklands and some subantarctic islands of the Indian Ocean. SALVIN'S PRION, *Pachyptila salvini*, has a wide bill with convex edges; lamellae visible when bill is closed. Ranges in subantarctic Indian Ocean; recorded at Antofagasta and Cape Horn. BROAD-BILLED PRION, *Pachyptila vittata*, of the South Atlantic, has a wide bill with convex edges that allow the lamellae to show at the bill base. FAIRY PRION, *Pachyptila turtur*, is smaller and lacks a distinctive head pattern. Nests in the Falklands and subantarctic islands in the s Atlantic and Indian Oceans. Recorded off Arica and Easter Island.

BLUE PETREL, WHITE-CHINNED PETREL, GREY PETREL: These seabirds are intermediate between petrels and shearwaters.

Blue Petrel
Petrel azulado
Halobaena caerulea
OTHER NAMES: Whalebird, Blausturmvogel, Pétrel bleu.

ID: 12 in (28 cm). WS 23 in (58 cm). Blue-grey above, with dark open-M across the back and wings. Underparts white. Square tail with a conspicuous, white, terminal tailband. Forecrown is mottled grey and white. Crown, nape and sides of head dark

PETRELS AND SHEARWATERS

Grey Petrel
Fardela gris
Procellaria cinerea
Rare off Magallanes
19 in (48 cm)

Flesh-footed Shearwater
Fardela negra de patas pálidas
Puffinus carneipes
Rare off Juan Fernández
18 in (42 cm)

Christmas Shearwater
Fardela de Pascua
Puffinus nativitatis
Easter Island
15 in (38 cm)

Pink-footed Shearwater
Fardela blanca
Puffinus creatopus
Arica–Aisén
Juan Fernández
19 in (48 cm)

Manx Shearwater
Fardela atlántica
Puffinus puffinus
Rare off Magallanes
13.5 in (34 cm)

Great Shearwater
Fardela capirotada
Puffinus gravis
Rare off Magallanes
21 in (53 cm)

Sooty Shearwater, Fardela negra
Puffinus griseus
Arica–Magallanes
16–18 in (40–46 cm)

Juan Fernandez Petrel
Fardela blanca de Juan Fernández
Pterodroma externa
Juan Fernández
Arica–Maule
17 in (43 cm)

At sea, the White-chinned Petrel can be mistaken for a first year Giant-Petrel or a Westland Petrel

Buller's Shearwater
Fardela de dorso gris
Puffinus bulleri
Antofagasta–Maule
18 in (46 cm)

Westland Petrel
Fardela de Nueva Zelanda
Procellaria westlandica
Rare off Arica–Magallanes
20 in (51 cm)

White-chinned Petrel
Fardela negra grande
Procellaria aequinoctialis
Arica–Magallanes
Subantarctic
20–23 in (51–58 cm)

grey; incomplete dark collar. Bill black. Legs and feet pale blue with grey webs. Separated from prions by the dark hood and white tail tip.
RANGE: Valparaíso to Drake Passage. Nests at the Islas Diego Ramírez, south of Cape Horn. Circumpolar pelagic in the Southern Ocean, especially around the Antarctic Convergence.

White-chinned Petrel
Fardela negra grande
Procellaria aequinoctialis
OTHER NAMES: Shoemaker, Cape Hen, Pétrel à menton blanc, Weisskinn-Sturmvogel. Sealers thought the clacking sounds of nesting white-chinned petrels sounded like a cobbler at work—hence, the name Shoemaker.
ID: 20–23 in (51–58 cm). WS 55 in (140 cm). Large, brownish-black petrel. Pale yellow to ivory bill; plate edges are narrowly lined with black. White feathering on the chin varies in size and is sometimes absent. Black legs. Feeds on fish and squid in the open ocean and sometimes follows ships to scavenge food. Solitary at sea. Powerful flight, with slow, purposeful wing beats interspersed with long glides. This petrel can be mistaken for a first year Giant-Petrel, a Sooty Albatross or a Sooty Shearwater. They are the largest burrow-nesting petrels, and construct an unusual saucer-shaped nesting platform deep within the burrow. **VULNERABLE**.
RANGE: Uncommon pelagic along the entire Chilean coast; common in subantarctic waters. Nests on islands in the southern oceans from 30°S to 60°S. Disperses north to upwellings such as the Humboldt Current.

Compare the White-chinned Petrel's ivory bill with the Westland Petrel's pale yellow and black bill.

RELATED SPECIES: The WESTLAND PETREL, *Procellaria westlandica*, is a regular, but uncommon visitor to the Chilean coast. Separated from the White-chinned Petrel by its black-tipped bill and smaller size. Nests in New Zealand. **VULNERABLE**.

Grey Petrel, Fardela gris
Procellaria cinerea
OTHER NAMES: Graustsurmvogel, Puffin gris. Pediunker, the common name for this bird on the South Atlantic island of Tristan de Cunha, is derived from its call.
ID: 19 in (48 cm). WS 47.25 in (120 cm). Upperparts ash-grey; darker on the crown, tail and wings. Underparts white, except for the grey undertail coverts and flanks. Bill pale green to horn. Legs rose-grey. Sometimes accompanies pods of cetaceans. Feeds at night on the sea surface, mainly on bioluminescent marine organisms.
RANGE: RARE PELAGIC off the Chilean coast. Circumpolar in subantarctic waters. Pelagic to 60°S and the Antarctic ice in the New Zealand-Australian sector in summer.

SHEARWATERS (GENUS *PUFFINUS*): Shearwaters have long, slender bills with external nasal tubes. They arc and bank on stiff, bowed wings, and plunge dive on coastal shoals and banks to catch prey.

Sooty Shearwater, Fardela negra
Puffinus griseus
OTHER NAMES: Muttonbird, Yegua, Doña, Petrel fuligineux, Dunkel-Sturmtaucher. Muttonbird is a New Zealand name that refers to fledgling birds the Maori people take from the burrow and prepare for human consumption.
ID: 16–18 in (40–46 cm). WS 37 in (94 cm). Sooty brown above, mouse brown below. Pale underwing coverts. Black bill and feet. Can fly at speeds up to 45 mi per hour (74 km/hr). Forms flocks of thousands that skim the sea surface. Feeds on krill and other marine organisms taken in plunge dives; the birds use their wings to propel themselves under the water. Nests in deep

burrows dug into soft sandy soils. Adults return to the nesting colony at dark after feeding at sea during the day; this reduces the risk of predation by skuas and gulls. Parent birds convert the ingested marine prey into an energy-rich oil before feeding it to the young. The last feeding of oil prior to fledging can sustain a chick for up to three weeks.

RANGE: Arica to Magallanes. Nests in s South America (Sep–Apr), New Zealand and Tasmania. Transequatorial migrant to the North Pacific and Arctic Ocean north of Alaska.

RELATED SPECIES: FLESH-FOOTED SHEARWATER, *Puffinus carneipes*. 19 in (48 cm). Separated from the Sooty Shearwater by its pale legs, feet and bill. Occasional visitor to Juan Fernández from waters of Australia and New Zealand, where it nests. One record from the Golfo de Penas off Aisén.

Pink-footed Shearwater
Fardela blanca
Puffinus creatopus

OTHER NAMES: Fardela de la noche, Rosafuss-Sturmtaucher, Puffin à pieds roses.

ID: 19 in (48 cm). WS 30.25 in (99 cm). Dark brownish-grey upperparts blend smoothly into white belly. Sides of neck, lower belly and flanks mottled. Underparts are sometimes barred or completely grey. Dark undertail coverts. Underwing white with irregular grey margins. Bill yellow to pink with dark tip. Legs flesh.

This species was first described from the California coast. Nesting colonies were found on Isla Masatierra, Juan Fernández, in 1913 and on Isla Mocha in 1932. The burrows were all sited on forested slopes from sea level to 1500 ft (450 m) elevation. Burrows vary in length from 6–10 ft (2–3 m) and end in a rounded nesting chamber.

RANGE: Pelagic from Arica to Chiloé, and along the Pacific continental shelf of the Americas. Found in coastal waters around the nesting colonies on Isla Mocha (38°S) and in the Juan Fernández Archipelago.

Christmas Shearwater
Fardela de Pascua
Puffinus nativitatis

OTHER NAMES: Weihnachtssturmtaucher, Puffin de la Nativité.

ID: 15 in (38 cm). WS 28.25 in (72 cm). Small, dark brown shearwater with a black bill and dark legs.

RANGE: Nests at Easter Island and Sala y Gómez (Nov–Apr). Tropical Pacific.

Buller's Shearwater
Fardela de dorso gris
Puffinus bulleri

OTHER NAMES: Graumantel-Sturmtaucher, Puffin de Buller.

ID: 18 in (46 cm). Dark M-pattern across a grey-brown back. White underparts. Slate grey bill. Dark cap. Pale grey bands on dark upperwings. Long, pointed tail.

RANGE: Irregular visitor to coast of central Chile (Jul–Oct). Migrant along the Pacific coast of North America, the Aleutians and Hawaii. Nests in New Zealand.

RELATED SPECIES: GREAT SHEARWATER, *Puffinus gravis*, is separated from Buller's by the solid grey back and wings. Rare pelagic off Cape Horn and Tierra del Fuego. Nests on islands in the s Atlantic.

Manx Shearwater
Fardela atlántica
Puffinus puffinus

OTHER NAMES: Puffin des Anglais, Schwarzschnabel-Sturmtaucher.

ID: 13.5 in (34 cm). WS 33 in (84 cm). Black above; white underparts.

RANGE: RARE but regular pelagic visitor to Cape Horn and Tierra del Fuego. Nests in the North Atlantic; migrates to the South Atlantic (Oct–Jan).

RELATED SPECIES: LITTLE SHEARWATER, *Puffinus assimilis*. 11 in (28 cm). Dark upperparts, white below. Separated from the Manx Shearwater by smaller size, shorter and more rounded wings, and extensive white on underwings. Ranges in the s Indian and s Atlantic Oceans. Recorded off Chiloé.

FAMILY HYDROBATIDAE
STORM-PETRELS

Storm-petrels are the smallest seabirds, averaging 7–8 in (18–20 cm) in length and 1–2 oz (26–58 g) in weight. They are called Sea Swallows *(Golondrinas de mar)* because they resemble swallows as they fly across a ship's wake in a low, zigzag pattern.

Their distinctive posture when feeding is reflected in the family name Hydrobatidae, which means "water-walker." Storm-petrels face into the wind with outstretched wings, extend their long legs, and patter across the ocean surface in search of plankton and bits of fat, oil and carrion. George Edwards, an 18th-century English naturalist and artist wrote of the storm-petrels: "They flutter so near the Surface of the Water that they seem to walk on it, for which Reason...they are called Peterils, because they imitate Peter's walking on the Sea."

A storm-petrel's nostrils are united in a single nasal tube on the bill. Drops of saline solution secreted by a gland at the base of the bill are ejected through the tubes as the bird faces into the wind. The nasal tube is attached to the olfactory lobe, which may heighten their sense of smell. Storm-petrels are thought to use their keen sense of smell to locate their nesting burrow by its distinctive musky odor and to find food at sea. The latter is almost certainly true, for if one throws a bucket of fish offal onto the surface of the ocean, storm-petrels appear out of nowhere and begin to feed.

Storm-petrels nest in burrows and rock crevices on scree slopes and rocky hillsides. They lay a single white egg.

Wilson's Storm-Petrel
Golondrina de mar
Oceanites oceanicus

OTHER NAMES: Bailarín, Gallito, Petrel de las tormentas, Mother Carey's Chickens, Océanite de Wilson, Buntfuss-Sturmschwalbe.
ID: 7 in (18 cm). WS 16.1 in (41 cm). Sooty brown body with a paler brown band across the greater wing coverts. The rump and sides of the vent are white. Short, rounded wings and square tail. Black bill. Black legs project beyond tail; feet are black with yellow webs.

These little seabirds feed on krill, small cephalopods, fish and carrion in typical storm-petrel fashion—by running along the surface of the water with wings outstretched and bill submerged in the water to scoop up food from the surface. They readily follow ships and attend trawlers to feed on scraps and discarded waste. Attracted by lights of ships at anchor, they often fly into the bulkheads at night; they are unable to escape a ship in the absence of wind and will remain motionless in the gutters until the vessel gets underway.

Wilson's storm-petrels arrive at nesting burrows in the Southern Hemisphere in November or December. Egg-laying occurs in mid-December and the parents incubate the eggs for 39 to 48 days. They feed their chick for up to 52 more days, then abandon the nest and the fledgling. Young that escape the gauntlet of predatory skuas and gulls waiting at the burrow entrance set out on their northward journey independent of their parents. They join migrating flocks of storm-petrels, which can number in the several thousands. Antarctic populations leave their southern breeding grounds in March or April and fly across the equator to the n Atlantic, n Indian and n Pacific Oceans. Non-breeders will often remain in northern waters for the following year, but breeding birds will complete a return migration and many will be on their Southern Hemisphere nesting grounds by the next November.

RANGE: Arica to Antarctica. Pelagic and coastal, in polar to tropical waters.
SUBSPECIES: *O. o. chilensis* nests on islands around Cape Horn and migrates north along the Pacific coast to the latitude of c Peru. *O. o. exasperatus* nests on antarctic and subantarctic islands, and migrates across the equator to the oceans of the Northern Hemisphere.

STORM-PETRELS 169

Dorsal view of Wilson's and Elliot's storm-petrels

Wilson's Storm-Petrel
Golondrina de mar
Oceanites oceanicus
Arica–Antarctica
7 in (18 cm)

Elliot's Storm-Petrel
Golondrina de mar chica
Oceanites gracilis
Arica–Maule
6.5 in (16 cm)

Wedge-rumped Storm-Petrel
Golondrina de mar peruana
Oceanodroma tethys
Arica–Antofagasta
8 in (20 cm)

Black-bellied Storm-Petrel
Golondrina de mar de vientre negro
Fregetta tropica
Magallanes
8 in (20 cm)

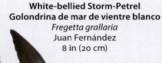

White-bellied Storm-Petrel
Golondrina de mar de vientre blanco
Fregetta grallaria
Juan Fernández
8 in (20 cm)

Hornby's (Ringed) Storm-Petrel
Golondrina de mar de collar
Oceanodroma hornbyi
Arica–Coquimbo
9 in (23 cm)

Grey-backed Storm-Petrel
Golondrina de mar subantártica
Garrodia nereis
Magallanes–Antarctica
7 in (18 cm)

Markham's Storm-Petrel
Golondrina de mar negra
Oceanodroma markhami
Arica–Valparaíso
9 in (23 cm)

Polynesian Storm-Petrel
Golondrina de mar de garganta blanca
Nesofregetta fuliginosa
Easter Island
10 in (26 cm)

Elliot's (White-vented) Storm-Petrel
Golondrina de mar chica
Oceanites gracilis
OTHER NAMES: Danzarín, Gallito, Bailarín, Elliotsturmschwalbe, Océanite d'Elliot.
ID: 6.5 in (16 cm). WS 16 in (40 cm). Brownish-black. White rump, vent and center of abdomen. Square tail. Black bill. Long black legs; feet black with yellow webs and black web margins.
RANGE: Pelagic in the Humboldt Current. Arica to Valparaíso, and north to Peru. Nesting sites undetermined; nests found near La Serena on Isla Chungungo (30°S).

Grey-backed Storm-Petrel
Golondrina de mar subantártica
Garrodia nereis
OTHER NAMES: Graurücken-Sturmschwalbe, Océanite néréide.
ID: 7 in (18 cm). WS 15.4 in (39 cm). Dark ashy-grey upperparts with a pale grey rump and shoulders. Faint, pale grey band on dark upperwings. White below; underwing white with black trim. Square grey tail with black terminal band. Black bill and legs. Nests in tussock grass pedestals in the Falklands, and in burrows on subantarctic islands in the Southern Ocean.
RANGE: At sea off Cape Horn, Islas Diego Ramírez and Isla Chiloé. Highly pelagic in cold subantarctic waters. Circumpolar.

White-bellied Storm-Petrel
Golondrina de mar de vientre blanco
Fregetta grallaria
OTHER NAMES: Fardelita, Océanite à ventre blanc, Weissbauch-Sturmschwalbe.
ID: 8 in (20 cm). WS 18 in (46 cm). Upperparts brownish-black with white rump. Throat, upper breast and undertail coverts black; rest of underparts white. Underwing white with broad black margins. Square tail. Black bill and legs. Nests in rock crevices and boulders at the base of sea cliffs.
RANGE: Pelagic in temperate to tropical seas. Rare in the Subantarctic. Nests (Dec–Jan) at Juan Fernández, San Félix y San Ambrosio, and on islands in temperate oceans.

Black-bellied Storm-Petrel
Golondrina de mar de vientre negro
Fregetta tropica
OTHER NAMES: Petrel de las tormentas, Schwarzbauch-Sturmschwalbe, Océanite à ventre noir.
ID: 8 in (20 cm). WS 18 in (46 cm). Dark brown head and upperparts appear black at sea. White rump. Underparts white with a black line extending from throat to the vent (seen with difficulty when bird banks in flight). Broad black margins to white underwing. Square tail.
RANGE: Pelagic off Cape Horn and the Antarctic Peninsula. Breeds circumpolar in Antarctic and Subantarctic. Rare pelagic in tropical waters.

Polynesian (White-throated) Storm-Petrel
Golondrina de mar de garganta blanca
Nesofregetta fuliginosa
OTHER NAMES: Weisskehl-Sturmschwalbe, Océanite à gorge blanche.
ID: 10 in (26 cm). WS 20 in (51 cm). Dark brown back with white rump. Throat and belly white. Dark pectoral band. Long legs and slightly-forked tail. Separated from other storm-petrels by its larger size, bounding flight and long-tailed appearance. VULNERABLE.
RANGE: Pelagic around Easter Island and Isla Sala y Gómez, where it nests. Coastal in tropical and warm temperate waters around breeding sites on islands in the central Pacific.

Wedge-rumped (Galapagos) Storm-Petrel
Golondrina de mar peruana
Oceanodroma tethys
OTHER NAMES: Gallito, Bailarín, Océanite téthys, Galapagoswellenläufer.
ID: 8 in (20 cm). WS 18 in (45 cm). Brownish-black. White wedge-shaped rump and sides of vent. Pale underwing coverts. Slightly forked black tail. Black bill and legs.
RANGE: Pelagic far offshore in warm, deep waters from Arica to Antofagasta, and north to Mexico. Nests (May–Jul) in the Galapagos and islands off the Peruvian coast.

Diving-petrels, or Yuncos, fly low with a rapid whirring of wings, often pitching into the water a short distance away from their takeoff point.

Common Diving-Petrel
Yunco de los canales
Pelecanoides urinatrix
Los Lagos–Magallanes
7 in (18 cm)

Magellanic Diving-Petrel
Yunco de Magallanes
Pelecanoides magellani
Los Lagos–Magallanes
8 in (20 cm)

Peruvian Diving-Petrel
Yunco
Pelecanoides garnotii
Arica–Los Lagos
9 in (23 cm)

Markham's Storm-Petrel
Golondrina de mar negra
Oceanodroma markhami

OTHER NAMES: Sooty Storm-Petrel, Russwellenläufer, Océanite de Markham.
ID: 9 in (23 cm). WS 19 in (50 cm). Entirely brownish-black. Forked tail.
RANGE: Pelagic in the Humboldt Current from Arica to Valparaíso and north to Peru. Nesting grounds undetermined.

Hornby's (Ringed) Storm-Petrel
Golondrina de mar de collar
Oceanodroma hornbyi

OTHER NAMES: Océanite de Hornby, Kragenwellenläufer.
ID: 9 in (23 cm). Grey above, with dark grey cap and white forehead. Grey pectoral band. White underparts. Underwing grey. Deeply-forked tail. Black bill and legs.
RANGE: Pelagic in the Humboldt Current; Arica to La Serena, Coquimbo, and north to Ecuador. May nest in the coastal desert.

FAMILY PELECANOIDIDAE
DIVING-PETRELS

Diving-petrels are black and white in color. The body is stocky with short wings, short neck and short tail. The stubby, hooked bill has a short nasal tube with upward-facing nostrils. Their flight is low with a rapid whirring of wings. They can fly through the crest of a wave, propelling themselves with their wings. Diving-petrels are colonial burrow nesters, laying a single white egg. They feed on krill and copepods.

Peruvian Diving-Petrel
Yunco
Pelecanoides garnotii

OTHER NAMES: Pato yunco común, Garnot-Lummensturmvogel, Puffinure de Garnot.
ID: 9 in (23 cm). WS 13 in (34 cm). Black above, white below. Dark breast band extends from sides of neck. Legs and feet bright blue with dark grey webs. ENDANGERED.
RANGE: Arica to Los Lagos and north along the Peruvian coast. Pelagic inshore in the Humboldt Current.

Magellanic Diving-Petrel
Yunco de Magallanes
Pelecanoides magellani

OTHER NAMES: Pato yunco, Puffinure de Magellan, Magellan-Lummensturmvogel.
ID: 8 in (20 cm). WS 12.5 in (32 cm). Similar to *P. garnotii* but smaller, with a crescent-shaped white patch and a narrow black spur on the sides of the neck.
RANGE: Common in canals and fjords from Chiloé to Cape Horn; also s Argentina.

Common Diving-Petrel
Yunco de los canales
Pelecanoides urinatrix

OTHER NAMES: Coppinger's Diving-Petrel, Puffinure plongeur, Lummensturmvogel.
ID: 7 in (18 cm). Similar to *P. garnotii*, but with a grey breastband and indistinct white crescent on cheek. Cobalt-blue feet and legs.
RANGE: Chiloé to Diego Ramírez, where it nests. Widespread in temperate and subantarctic waters between 35° S–55° S latitudes.

PELECANIFORMES: Pelicans and Allies

This diverse order includes the tropicbirds, boobies, pelicans, cormorants and frigatebirds. These birds are good fliers and swimmers. They dive after fish from the air or from the water surface. They have large hooked bills, short legs and webbed feet with four toes joined by webs. The unfeathered throat, or gular pouch, is distensible. This feature is obvious in pelicans whose pouch expands as it fills with fish and water during feeding and in male frigatebirds who inflate their bright red pouch to attract a mate.

FAMILY FREGATIDAE

FRIGATEBIRDS

Frigatebirds are tropical seabirds that soar effortlessly on long, narrow wings that are held in a bent W-shape. They open and close their deeply forked tails in flight. Their plumage is not completely waterproof, so they use their long, hooked bill to pick food from the ocean surface without landing on the water. They also pirate food from other seabirds, harrassing terns and boobies in flight until they disgorge their food.

Great Frigatebird
Ave fragata grande
Fregata minor

OTHER NAMES: Bindenfregattvogel, Frégate du Pacifique.

ID: 37 in (93 cm). MALE is black with a brown band on the upperwing and a red gular sac that is inflated during courtship. FEMALE is black with a white throat and chest. JUVENILE is dark brown with a white head that is washed with cinnamon.

RANGE: Easter Island and Sala y Gómez, where it nests (Dec–Apr). Tropical oceans.

FAMILY PHAETHONTIDAE

TROPICBIRDS

Tropicbirds occur throughout the tropical oceans. They are colored black and white, and have greatly elongated central tail feathers. They have large heads, short necks and long, pointed wings. Bills are moderately long, heavy and sharply pointed. They plunge dive to catch fish and cephalopods. Tropicbirds nest in small caves or rocky crevices and lay a single white egg.

Red-billed Tropicbird
Ave del trópico de pico rojo
Phaethon aethereus

OTHER NAMES: Rotschnabel-Tropikvogel, Phaéton à bec rouge.

ID: 39 in (98 cm) with tail feathers. White, with finely barred upperparts. Black line through eye. Red bill. Elongated central tail feathers are white. JUVENILES have a yellow bill, some black patches on the head, and central tail feathers are short or absent.

RANGE: Pelagic from Arica to Valparaíso. Nests (Oct–Apr) at Chañaral in Atacama. Pelagic records from open ocean between Valparaíso and Juan Fernández.

Red-tailed Tropicbird
Ave del trópico de cola roja
Phaethon rubricauda

OTHER NAMES: Rotschwanz-Tropikvogel, Phaéton à brins rouges.

ID: 31 in (78 cm) with tail feathers. ADULTS are white, at times with a pink tinge on the mantle. Black eyeline. Bill red. Central tail feathers red. JUVENILES are white with fine barring on upperparts. Black nuchal collar. Central tail feathers absent. The black bill of fledglings turns to orange as they age.

RANGE: Nests (Oct–Apr) at Easter Island and Sala y Gómez. Ranges in the tropical Indo-Pacific Ocean.

White-tailed Tropicbird
Ave del trópico de cola blanca
Phaethon lepturus

OTHER NAMES: Weissschwanz-Tropikvogel, Phaéton à bec jaune.

ID: 31 in (78 cm) with tail feathers. ADULTS are white, with a black eyebrow and conspicuous black markings on wings. White central tail streamers. Bill greenish-yellow to rosy-orange. JUVENILES are white with fine black barring on upperparts.

RANGE: Non-breeding visitor to Easter Island and Juan Fernández. Widespread in tropical oceans.

FAMILY SULIDAE
BOOBIES

Boobies have torpedo-shaped bodies, long wings, strong conical bills and long, wedge-shaped tails. They fly in formation—lines of birds, one behind another, alternately flapping and gliding. They feed by diving from heights of up to 100 ft (30 m) and then pursuing their prey underwater. They nest in colonies on sea cliffs or in trees near fresh water and lay 1 to 3 white eggs.

Peruvlan Booby, Piquero
Sula variegata
OTHER NAMES: Guanotölpel, Fou varié.
ID: 29 in (74 cm). ADULT head, neck and underparts white. Back has fine brown and white, wavy lines. Long, pointed tail. Wings brown with coverts edged white. Bill blue-grey. Feet pale blue-grey. JUVENILES brown with varying amounts of white. A major guano producer of Peru and n Chile.
RANGE: Arica to Los Lagos; also Peru and Ecuador. On rocky seacoasts and offshore islands in the Humboldt Current. Bulk of population moves south in March and April, returning north in September.

Masked Booby, Piquero blanco
Sula dactylatra
OTHER NAMES: Maskentölpel, Fou masqué.
ID: 32–36 in (81–92 cm). ADULT white with black primaries, secondaries and tail. Bill is yellow. Bare facial skin is greyish-black. Legs are grey-green. JUVENILES have varying amounts of brown. SUBADULTS have brown feathering on back, wings and neck.
RANGE: San Félix y San Ambrosio, Sala y Gómez, and Easter Island. Widespread in tropical waters around breeding colonies.

Blue-footed Booby
Piquero de patas azules
Sula nebouxii
OTHER NAMES: Fou à pieds bleus, Blaufuss-Tolpel.
ID: 31 in (80 cm). Dark blue bill. Bright blue feet. Back of head and neck finely striped in brown and white. Back mottled brown and white, with a white patch on the back of the nape. White rump. Underparts white. Wings and tail brown; tail of this species longer than other boobies.
RANGE: Occasional at coastal Antofagasta. Ranges in tropical and warm temperate waters along the Pacific coast of South America from Mexico to Peru.

Brown Booby, Piquero café
Sula leucogaster
OTHER NAMES: Piquero pardo, Fou brun, Braun-Tolpel.
ID: 25–29 in (64–74 cm). ADULT upperparts, neck, head and upper breast chocolate brown. Lower breast and abdomen white. Yellow bill. Pale green feet. JUVENILES are dark brown with light brown on the lower breast and abdomen.
RANGE: RARE. Recorded at Sala y Gómez, Pisagua, and the n Chilean coast between Arica and Antofagasta. Widespread in shallow inshore waters of tropical oceans.
RELATED VAGRANT: RED-FOOTED BOOBY, *Sula sula*. 28 in (71 cm). Red feet and legs. BROWN MORPH, which can be confused with the Brown Booby, is entirely brown, with a yellow tint to the crown and hindneck. WHITE MORPH is white overall with dark brown primaries and secondaries. Vagrant at Sala y Gómez. Widespread in tropical oceans of the world.

FAMILY PELECANIDAE
PELICANS

Pelicans are very large, fish-eating birds. They have a long, straight, hooked bill and a large, distensible gular pouch.

Peruvian Brown Pelican, Pelícano
Pelecanus thagus
OTHER NAMES: Alcatraz, Huajache, Braun-Pelikan, Pélican thage.
ID: 60 in (152 cm). WS 98 in (248 cm). One of the largest flying birds. Long bill with a hooked tip. The conspicuous gular sac is used as a scoop net for catching fish. Long, rounded wings. Short, stout legs with large, webbed feet. Drab brown overall. Head

and neck are chestnut brown. White on forehead extends behind the eye and to the upper breast. Yellow color on the bare skin around the eyes becomes more intense in breeding season. JUVENILES are brown with a paler belly. These birds nest in colonies on islands, islets and headlands, and have a clutch of 2 to 3 white eggs.

RANGE: Marine coasts and coastal islands from Arica to Los Lagos; also Peru. Accidental in Tierra del Fuego.

FAMILY PHALACROCORACIDAE
CORMORANTS

Cormorants are long-necked, long-billed, diving birds. Most feed on fish. They live along rivers, seacoasts and coastal islands. The eyes, bills and bare facial skin are often brightly colored, especially in nuptial plumage. Bills are long, thin and hooked at the tip. Body and neck are elongated, the tail long and stiff-feathered. Legs are short and feet are webbed. Birds often stand with their wings spread out to dry. Cormorants nest colonially. The clutch is 2 to 4 white or pale aqua, calcareous eggs. Tree-nesting species build a nest of sticks; ground nesters build a simple conical nest of mud augmented with seaweeds.

Guanay Cormorant, Guanay
Phalacrocorax bougainvillii
OTHER NAMES: Cholo, Pato de mar, Guano-Scharbe, Cormoran de Bougainville. The species name honors French explorer Louis Antoine de Bougainville (1729–1811).
ID: 30 in (76 cm). ADULT is black with a white throat, breast and belly. Red facial skin. Green eyering. Bill is flesh-colored with a reddish base. Legs are fleshy-pink. NUPTIAL PLUMAGE shows fine white plumes under the eye and on the neck. JUVENILES are drab grey with a paler belly.

This "Billion-dollar Bird" is the most important guano-producing seabird and the most abundant seabird species of Peru and n Chile. Overfishing of the anchoveta (*Engraulis ringens*) and the effects of El Niño events cause tremendous fluctuations in population numbers. NEAR THREATENED.
RANGE: Coast and coastal islands from Arica to Los Lagos; center of dispersal is the Chincha and Lobos Islands of Peru.

Red-legged Cormorant, Lile
Phalacrocorax gaimardi
OTHER NAMES: Red-footed Shag, Pato lilo, Cormoran de patas coloradas, Chuita, Buntscharbe, Cormoran de Gaimard.
ID: 30 in (76 cm). Dark grey with paler grey underparts; wings spotted white. White oval patch on both sides of neck. Facial skin orange-red. Bill yellow with an orange base. Red-orange legs. JUVENILES are dark brown with faint white patches on the sides of the neck. NEAR THREATENED.
RANGE: Arica to Tierra del Fuego; Peru, Argentina. Found on rocky seacoasts and coastal islands.

Neotropic Cormorant, Yeco
Phalacrocorax brasilianus
OTHER NAMES: Olivaceous Cormorant, Black Cormorant, Cuervo, Biguá, Olivenscharbe, Cormoran vigua.
ID: 23–29 in (58–73 cm). ADULT is black. Brown bill. Black legs. BREEDING PLUMAGE shows fine white plumes on the sides of the face, throat and neck, and dark yellow facial skin. JUVENILES are dark brown; very young birds have whitish underparts.
RANGE: Arica to Cape Horn, and from the s USA through South America. Marine coasts, lakes, rivers.
SUBSPECIES: The YECO NEGRO AUSTRAL, *P. b. hornensis*, ranges along the Beagle Channel and in the Cape Horn islands.

Imperial Cormorant, Cormorán imperial
Phalacrocorax atriceps
OTHER NAMES: Magellanic Blue-eyed Shag, King Shag, Blauaugenscharbe, Cormoran impérial.
ID: 29 in (75 cm). Upperparts black with green, blue and violet iridescence. Underparts white. Yellow-orange nasal caruncle. Cobalt-blue eye ring. Horn-colored bill.

Pale red or orange legs. Occurs on seacoasts, channels and islands, as well as on inland bodies of water.
RANGE: O'Higgins to Magallanes.
SUBSPECIES: BLUE-EYED SHAG, CORMORÁN IMPERIAL, *P. a. atriceps*, has a white patch on the center of the back and white wingband. White on the sides of the face arches up behind eye. Ranges from Isla Mocha (38° S) to Diego Ramírez. The KING CORMORANT, CORMORÁN IMPERIAL DE LAS MALVINAS, *P. a. albiventer*, lacks any white markings on the back or wings. The black of the head and the white of the throat forms a horizontal line across the cheeks. Ranges from the Strait of Magellan to Cape Horn, the Patagonian coast, and the Falklands.

Antarctic Blue-eyed Shag
Cormoran antártico
Phalacrocorax bransfieldensis
OTHER NAME: Antarctic Cormorant.
ID: 30 in (76 cm). Similar to, but larger than *Phalacrocorax atriceps*. The upperparts are iridescent black; underparts white. White wingband and white patch on back. Yellow-orange nasal caruncle. Cobalt-blue eye ring. Grey to horn-colored bill. Pale red legs.
RANGE: Coast and coastal archipelagos of the Antarctic Peninsula, south to 65° S.

Rock Cormorant
Cormorán de las rocas
Phalacrocorax magellanicus
OTHER NAMES: Magellan Cormorant, Coimio, Cormoran de Magellan, Felsenscharbe.
ID: 27 in (68 cm). ADULT head, neck and rump are iridescent blue-back. Back and wings iridescent green. Breast and belly white. Orange facial skin. Small white ear patch. Prenuptial crest of satiny plumes on crown. JUVENILES are dull black with paler mottling on ventral area; similar to juvenile Neotropic Cormorant.
RANGE: Valdivia to Islas Diego Ramírez; casual at Talcahuano and Valparaíso; also Falklands and Atlantic coast of s Argentina. Seacoasts, channels and fjords.

CICONIIFORMES: Storks and Allies
This order presently encompasses the herons, egrets, bitterns, storks, ibises, spoonbills and flamingos—fish-eating birds that have long legs for wading in shallow water. Recent DNA hybridization has revealed that the order includes many other, seemingly unrelated bird families.

FAMILY ARDEIDAE
HERONS, EGRETS AND BITTERNS
Herons and egrets are large, long-legged, slender birds with long bills, short tails and large, broad wings. They fly with their necks pulled into an S-shape and with legs extended beyond their tail. They live in marshes and around small lakes, rivers and brooks. They are colonial nesters, and lay a clutch of 3 to 6 sky-blue or light green eggs.

Bitterns are shorter and squatter than herons. They are known for their skulking behavior and their habit of remaining motionless with the head and bill pointed skyward when alarmed. Their presence in the dense reedbeds they inhabit is often revealed only by their deep booming call.

Cocoi Heron, Garza cuca
Ardea cocoi
OTHER NAMES: White-necked Heron, Cuca, Pillo, Garza mora, Garzón, Cocoireiher, Héron cocoi.
ID: 47 in (120 cm). Largest heron in Chile. Crown and nape black. Rest of head, neck and underparts white. Back and wing coverts bluish-grey. Wings and tail black. Yellowish bill and legs. Solitary.
RANGE: Antofagasta to Magallanes. Seen most often between Concepción and Puerto Montt in flooded lowlands in rural areas and near rivers and ponds. Widespread in South America.

Great Egret, Garza grande
Ardea alba
OTHER NAMES: White Egret, Garza mayor, Silberreiher, Grande aigrette
ID: 34 in (85 cm). White, with a yellow bill and black legs and feet. Large with a long

CORMORANTS

Red-legged Cormorant
Lile
Phalacrocorax gaimardi
Arica–Magallanes
30 in (76 cm)

Neotropic Cormorant
Yeco
Phalacrocorax brasilianus
Arica–Magallanes
23–29 in (58–73 cm)

Imperial Cormorant
Cormorán imperial
Phalacrocorax atriceps
Maule–Magallanes
28 in (72 cm)

Antarctic Blue-eyed Shag
Cormorán antártico
Phalacrocorax bransfieldensis
Antarctica
30 in (76 cm)

Blue-eyed Shag
Cormorán imperial
Phalacrocorax a. atriceps

King Cormorant
Cormorán imperial de las Malvinas
Phalacrocorax a. albiventer

Guanay Cormorant
Guanay
Phalacrocorax bougainvillii
Arica–Los Lagos
30 in (76 cm)

Rock Cormorant
Cormorán de las rocas
Phalacrocorax magellanicus
Los Lagos–Magallanes
27 in (68 cm)

thin neck. Gregarious. Roosts in trees. Occurs around lakes, ponds, rivers, brooks and inundated fields.
RANGE: Common from Arica to Tierra del Fuego. Worldwide distribution.

Snowy Egret, Garza chica
Egretta thula
OTHER NAMES: Garcita, Aigrette neigeuse, Schmuckreiher.
ID: 23 in (58 cm). White. Long white plumes on head, breast and rump in breeding plumage. Bill black with yellow at base. Legs black with a greenish-yellow line up the back; yellow feet. Gregarious. Lives near lakes, ponds, rivers, brooks and inundated fields.
RANGE: Common from Arica to Chiloé. Accidental around the Strait of Magellan. Worldwide distribution.

Cattle Egret, Garza boyera
Bulbulcus ibis
OTHER NAMES: Kuhreiher, Héron gardeboeufs.
ID: 20 in (51 cm). White. Yellow-orange bill. Short, fairly thick neck. BREEDING PLUMAGE shows carmel-colored plumes on crown, breast and rump. Legs greyish to yellow. JUVENILES are white with grey legs. Forages near cattle and other livestock.
RANGE: Arica to Isla Navarino, Magallanes; vagrant in Chilean Antarctica. Spread from Africa to South America in the 1870s and now ranges across the Americas. Meadows and ranches, especially around livestock.

Little Blue Heron, Garza azul
Egretta caerulea
OTHER NAMES: Blaureiher, Aigrette bleu.
ID: 22 in (56 cm). Slate-grey, with chestnut head and neck. Blue bill with black tip. Blue-green legs. JUVENILES white, usually with black-tipped primaries. Juveniles can be separated from the adult Snowy Egret by bill and leg color, and lack of long plumes on the head and breast.
RANGE: Coastal Arica to Tarapacá; s USA to South America. Lakes and wetlands.

Black-crowned Night-Heron, Huairavo
Nycticorax nycticorax
OTHER NAMES: Huadra, Banda, Bruja, Nachtreiher, Bihoreau gris.
ID: 22 in (56 cm). Back and rump black with metallic-green sheen; underparts grey or whitish. Grey wings. Long dark bill. Short, flesh-colored legs. Red eyes. Two to three white coronal plumes. JUVENILES streaked grey and tan. Call is a guttural *quok*.
RANGE: Common throughout Chile near rivers, brooks, flooded pastures and marine coasts. Worldwide distribution.
SUBSPECIES: The dusky HUAIRAVO COMÚN, *N. n. obscurus*, ranges from Arica to the Diego Ramirez Islands. The paler HUAIRAVO DEL NORTE, *N. n. hoactli*, occurs on the Altiplano of n Chile; it has a light cream face and throat, and pale grey underparts.

Stripe-backed Bittern, Huairavillo
Ixobrychus involucris
OTHER NAMES: Pygmy Bittern, Totorero, Garza amarillo, Cuerpo sin alma, Mirasol chico, Streifendommel, Blongios varié.
ID: 13 in (33 cm). Small and slender. Tawny body with black crown and nape. Dusky streaks on back. Flight feathers are dark grey with tan trailing edge and yellowish-brown at bend of wing. Greenish-yellow bill and legs. Largely nocturnal, secretive and well camouflaged. When alarmed it freezes with its head and long, sharp beak pointed upward. Clutch is 1 to 3 grape-green or bilious yellow eggs laid on a flimsy platform of twigs anchored to two reeds. Feeds on small frogs, fishes, mollusks and aquatic larvae.
RANGE: Coquimbo to Chiloé, Los Lagos, and across South America in reedbeds along edges of rivers, ponds and marshes.

VAGRANT HERONS: TRICOLORED HERON, *Egretta tricolor*. Records from Coquimbo and Arica. GREEN-BACKED HERON, *Butorides striatus*. Coquimbo, Valparaíso and the mouth of the Lluta River in Arica. EASTERN REEF EGRET, *Egretta sacra*. Easter Island and reefs of the eastern South Pacific islands.

HERONS, EGRETS AND BITTERNS

FAMILY THRESKIORNITHIDAE
IBISES

Ibises are gregarious residents of swampy forests and flooded areas. They have thin, decurved bills that they use to probe for food in shallow water or wet soil. They fly with necks extended. Ibises lay 2 to 3 eggs.

Black-faced Ibis, Bandurria
Theristicus melanopis
OTHER NAMES: Buff-necked Ibis, Weisshalsibis, Schwarzzügelibis, Ibis mandore.
ID: 29 in (74 cm). Stocky and brightly plumaged. Head and neck ochre; chestnut forehead, crown and nape. Bare black skin around the eyes, lores and throat. Long, decurved bill is black with horn-colored tip. Wings grey, with black flight feathers. Stout, reddish legs. Loud, clanking call. Feeds on frogs, salamanders, worms, insects and other aquatic life. Nests communally in groups of 10 to 30 pairs. Builds a large nest of twigs and vegetation in a variety of situations ranging from treetops to cliff ledges to reedbeds. Eggs are white with tiny brown spots.
RANGE: Antofagasta to Magallanes; Peru, s Argentina. Meadows, marshes, cultivated and newly plowed fields; sea level to 9850 ft (0–3000 m).
SUBSPECIES: The BANDURRIA COMÚN, *T. m. melanopis*. Antofagasta to Tierra del Fuego. BANDURRIA DE LA PUNA, *T. m. branickii;.* Known historically from the High Andes of Arica-Parinacota; may no longer occur there.

White-faced Ibis, Cuervo de pantano
Plegadis chihi
OTHER NAMES: Gallareta, Cuervillo, Glossy Ibis, Brillensichler, Ibis à face blanche.
ID: 23 in (57 cm). Shining chestnut head, neck and underparts; Back, wings and tail have a bronzy-green iridescence. Band of white around base of bill and behind eye. Long decurved bill. JUVENILES are dark green above and whitish below with some bronze on neck. Forms large flocks that fly in formation from one feeding ground to the next. Nests in dense reedbeds around lakes and rivers. Lays a clutch of dark blue-grey eggs in a nest of twigs and rushes laid atop a high platform of trodden reeds.
RANGE: Antofagasta to Valdivia. Widespread in the Americas. Ponds and marshes; sea level to 2600 ft (0–800 m).

Puna Ibis, Cuervo de pantano de la puna
Plegadis ridgwayi
OTHER NAMES: Andean Glossy Ibis, Yanahuiki, Punaibis, Schmal-Schnabelsichler, Ibis de Ridgway.
ID: 24 in (61 cm). Black with green and purple metallic highlights. Separated from the White-faced Ibis by its larger size and underparts, which are fulvous with a slight purplish sheen; also lacks the white band around the bill. JUVENILE has white and black streaks on head and neck, and is difficult to separate from *P. chihi*.
RANGE: Arica to Tarapacá. Uncommon on lakes and marshes of the Altiplano at Parinacota and Lake Chungará. A few birds descend to the coastal wetlands. More common in Peru, Bolivia, and Argentina, on the Altiplano to 16,500 ft (5000 m).

FAMILY PHOENICOPTERIDAE
FLAMINGOS

Flamingos breed in large colonies situated on low islands in brackish estuaries and alkaline lakes. Nesting is sporadic and the colony is easily disturbed by changes in water level or the activities of predators. The nest is a truncated cone of mud and salt muck with a saucer-like depression on the top. The normal clutch is one, or rarely two, chalky-white eggs. Chicks are covered in greyish down. A few days after hatching, chicks group into crèches *(parvadas)*, which are tended by a few adults. Flamingos feed on diatoms, tiny mollusks, crustaceans and algae that live in highly saline water. They hold the thick, curved bill upside down in the shallows. The lamellae on the bill edge act to filter out food. Flamingos are usually silent when feeding, but call to each other in flight with a goose-like honking. They fly with their long neck and legs extended.

Chilean Flamingo
Flamenco chileno
Phoenicopterus chilensis
OTHER NAMES: Guaichete, Chileflamingo, Flamant du Chili.
ID: 39.5 in (100 cm). Pale pink body; wing coverts and some back feathers are pale red. Black primaries. Bill is pale yellow at the base; distal half is black. Legs are pale blue, with red knees and red feet. This species has a hind toe, which is visible on close observation. Pale eye. JUVENILES have a dull grey head, neck and breast, and a white abdomen. Back and wing coverts have dusky spots. White tail. Highly migratory. NEAR THREATENED.
RANGE: Arica to Magallanes; Peru, Bolivia, Argentina, s Brazil, Paraguay, Uruguay. On salt lakes and brackish estuaries; sea level to 15,750 feet (0–4800 m).

Andean Flamingo
Parina grande
Phoenicoparrus andinus
OTHER NAMES: Pariguana, Tococo, Anden-Flamingo, Flamant des Andes.
ID: 45 in (115 cm). Pale rose body feathers. Lower neck and breast vinous. Base of bill is yellow with a red spot; distal part of the bill is black. Legs are pale yellow; 3-toed feet lack a hind toe. Eyes are dark red. Exclusively a high altitude species. VULNERABLE.
RANGE: Arica to Atacama; nw Argentina, w Bolivia, s Peru. Shallow saline lakes on the Puna; 8200–15,750 ft (2500–4800 m). Nesting records at Surire, Huasco and Coposa in Tarapacá and at Ascotan and Salar de Atacama in Antofagasta.

James' (Puna) Flamingo
Parina chica
Phoenicoparrus jamesi
OTHER NAMES: Churruro, Pariguana, Flamant de James, Kurzschnabel-Flamingo. Species is named for the British business tycoon Berkeley James. He sponsored Charles Rahmer who collected specimens of this species at Isluga in 1886. Nothing more was heard about the species until 1956, when Chilean naturalists A. W. Johnson, Bryan Johnson and W. R. Millie travelled 3100 mi (5000 km) trying to locate this flamingo in the Andes of n Chile. Unsuccessful in finding the birds in Chile, they pressed on and discovered the first known nesting colony of James' Flamingo at the Laguna Colorada in Bolivia.
ID: 35.5 in (90 cm). Smallest of the highland flamingos. Relatively short neck and legs. Pale pink body with contrasting reddish-pink head, breast, neck and tertials. Yellow bill with lower one-third black; small red patch on bend of upper mandible. Dark pinkish mask around dark eye. ADULT legs and 3-toed feet are red. JUVENILES have grey legs with red feet. NEAR THREATENED.
RANGE: Arica to Atacama; also Bolivia, Peru, Argentina. Salt lakes and ponds on the Puna; 9800–15,750 ft (3000–4800 m).

VAGRANT SPOONBILLS AND STORKS: ROSEATE SPOONBILL, ESPÁTULA, *Ajaja ajaja*. Historical records at Valparaíso, Colchagua and near Santiago. WOOD STORK, CIGÜEÑA DE CABAZA PELADA, *Mycteria americana*. Recorded at the mouth of the Lluta River, Arica, and near Santiago. MAGUARI STORK, PILLO, *Euxenura maguari*. Records from central and southern Chile.

FAMILY CATHARTIDAE
NEW WORLD VULTURES
Condors and American Vultures are now thought to be related to the order of storks, Ciconiiformes. Although this is not universally accepted, most ornithologists believe it to be accurate based on morphological, behavioral and DNA evidence.

The cathartids feed almost exclusively on carrion. Their heads are unfeathered—an adaptation to feeding habits where the head is introduced into body cavities of dead animals, many badly-decayed. The hooked bill and talons are relatively weak, and these birds are unable to rip apart a recently killed animal. The bill has a perforated nostril and lacks the nasal septum present in Old World Vultures. These birds

NEW WORLD VULTURES

Andean Condor

Andean Condor Cóndor
Vultur gryphus
Arica–Magallanes
39–48 in (100–122 cm)

Turkey Vulture Jote de cabeza colorada
Cathartes aura
Arica–Magallanes
24–30 in (62–76 cm)

Turkey Vulture

Black Vulture

Black Vulture Jote de cabeza negra
Coragyps atratus
Atacama–Magallanes
22–29 in (56–74 cm)

have difficulty taking off without wind to lift them up. The wings are long, wide and flat—well-suited to circling or "kettling" high in thermals and updrafts. They nest in caves, on cliff ledges, or on the ground under thick vegetation. The normal clutch is 1 to 3 eggs.

Andean Condor, Cóndor
Vultur gryphus

OTHER NAMES: Buitre, Andenkondor, Manqué.
ID: 39–48 in (100–122 cm). **WS** 108–122 in (274–310 cm). **WT** 25 lb (11.5 kg). Largest flighted landbird. MALE has a red, naked head with a fleshy dark red or black crest and a white ruff (nuchal collar). The rest of plumage is black with a conspicuous white area on the upperwings. The wings are rectangular with eight long "fingers" on each wing. FEMALE is similar to the male but lacks the head crest. JUVENILES are dark brown and lack the white ruff and white wing patch.

Condors are superb gliders, flapping their wings only during takeoff and landing. They locate food mainly by sight, descending in wide concentric circles toward the carrion and then approaching on foot. On the northern coast, they feed on dead seal pups and placentas. They also feed on dead lambs on the Patagonian steppe. Condors roost and nest in caves, hollows and ledges of steep cliffs, laying a clutch of 1 to 2 white eggs in September or October. Parents tend chicks for several months and breed every other year. NEAR THREATENED.

RANGE: Arica to Magallanes; sea level to 16,500 ft (0–5000 m). Resident throughout the Andes, especially where ravines are edged by cliffs and rocky ledges.

Black Vulture, Jote de cabeza negra
Coragyps atratus
OTHER NAMES: Queluy, Zopilote, Gallinazo cabeza negra, Rabangeier, Urubu noir.
ID: 22–29 in (56–74 cm). WS 52–63 in (133–160 cm). Black, with whitish patch on underside of wing tips. Bare skin of head and throat is black and wrinkled. Short tail. Flies on flat wings; does not rock and tip in flight like the Turkey Vulture. Soars then gives a series of rapid wing beats in what is said to resemble a Spanish dance known as the Jota (thus, the name Jote). Feeds on carrion and refuse. Tends to congregate around garbage dumps, stockyards and abattoirs. Clutch of 2 large, white eggs with lilac or red spots is laid in early spring, on bare ground in a cave or on a cliff ledge.
RANGE: Common from Atacama to Aisén; ranges from s USA through South America. Lowlands; anywhere there are dead animals or refuse; sea level to 6500 ft (0–2000 m).

Turkey Vulture, Jote de cabeza colorada
Cathartes aura
OTHER NAMES: Gallinazo, Camaronero, Queluy, Truthahngeier, Urubu à tête rouge, Vautour, Zopilote aura, Aura cabecirroja. Gallinazo means "like a red cockscomb."
ID: 24–30 in (62–76 cm). WS 63–72 in (160–182 cm). ADULTS are blackish-brown with a red, naked head. JUVENILES have a brown head. Long, narrow tail. Two-toned underwing with a lighter trailing edge. Holds wings at a dihedral angle in flight, with wingtips lifted above the body; rocks from side to side in the wind. Usually seen singly or in pairs except when congregating around a carcass. Locates carrion by sight and smell. Nests in caves and abandoned mine shafts in the north, and on bare ground in dense vegetation in southern ravines.
RANGE: Open terrain from Arica to Cape Horn, and throughout North and South America; sea level to 8000 ft (0–2500 m).
RELATED VAGRANT: LESSER YELLOW-HEADED VULTURE, *Cathartes burrovianus*; one record from Vallenar in the Atacama Region.

FALCONIFORMES: Birds of Prey
Falconiformes includes raptors such as hawks, eagles, ospreys and falcons.

FAMILY PANDIONIDAE
OSPREYS
Osprey, Aguila pescadora
Pandion haliaetus
OTHER NAMES: Fischadler, Balbuzard pêcheur, Gavilán pescador.
ID: 23 in (59 cm). Head, neck, breast and abdomen white; dark lines on crown. Dark brown line from eye to neck. Upperparts brown. Tail darkly barred. Eye is yellow in ADULTS, red in JUVENILES. Feeds entirely on fish. Has a reversible outer toe and sharp, pointed spicules on the bottom of the feet to grasp and hold prey.
RANGE: Uncommon; Arica to Valdivia. One of the most widespread birds in the world, found on all continents except Antarctica. Lives on seacoasts and around freshwater lakes and rivers.

FAMILY ACCIPITRIDAE
KITES, ACCIPITERS AND HAWKS
This family includes kites, accipiters and hawks—raptors with strong, sharp talons and fairly long tail. The bill is short, curved, and has a covering called a "cere" at the base of the bill. The wings are wide and rounded, and are held flat in flight. In most cases the female is larger than the male. There are many color phases, and immature birds are substantially different than adults.

White-tailed Kite, Bailarín
Elanus leucurus
OTHER NAMES: Weissschwanzaar, Gleitaar, Élanion à queue blanche, Élanion à queue blanche, Milano coliblanco.
ID: 14–17 in (35–43 cm). Female is smaller than the male. ADULT has pale grey back and white forehead, sides of head and underparts. Large black patch on the upperwing surface and a smaller black mark on wing's underside. Black eyeline. Red iris. Legs are yellow. Tail is slightly forked. JUVENILE is pale golden-brown with white mottling on

the back. Underparts are brown, feathers edged with cinnamon. Tail is white with a narrow, dark subterminal band. Readily identified by its habit of hovering (kiting) while hunting for small mammals.

RANGE: Atacama to Chiloé. Ranges from sw USA to South America in open grasslands and plains, scrubland and marshes.

Chilean Hawk, Peuquito
Accipiter chilensis

OTHER NAMES: Bicolored Hawk, Chilean Goshawk, Gavilán chileno, Chilesperber, Zweifarbensperber, Épervier bicolore.

ID: ♂ 15 in (38cm). ♀ 16.5 in (42 cm). Sexes are alike except for size. Slender-bodied with short, rounded wings and a long, barred tail. Dark grey above; underparts grey with narrow, transverse white bars. Tail is grey with six dark bars and a whitish terminal band. Rufous stockings. Yellow eyering and iris. Greenish-yellow legs. JUVENILE is dark grey above with a slightly rufous nape. Underparts cream with black stripes. Stockings are barred brownish-grey and black. Tail has conspicuous barring. Swift and agile flight. Able to pursue and overtake small birds, even in heavy timber. Nests (Oct) in a large, rounded mass of twigs, branches and grass set into a fork of a tall tree situated in the center of the woods. The clutch is 3 to 4 white eggs spotted with yellow or green.

RANGE: Valparaíso to Tierra del Fuego; one record at Fray Jorge, Coquimbo. Migrates to higher elevations in summer. Inhabits open areas at the edge of dense woodland, especially in Roble *(Nothofagus obliqua)*.

Cinereous Harrier, Vari
Circus cinereus

OTHER NAMES: Grauweihe, Busard bariolé.

ID: ♂ 15 in (39 cm). ♀ 19 in (48 cm). Body is slender with long wings. The pale, erectile facial disk and slight ruff gives these birds an owlish look. MALE is bluish-grey except for the abdomen and flanks, which are barred white and pale rufous. FEMALE is dark brown above; lined white and light rufous below. JUVENILE is similar to the female, with pale rufous on the underparts. Characteristic slow, hesitating flight, with frequent aerial ballets. Found in open country, including cultivated land, where it hunts for rats, mice, birds, reptiles, insects and frogs. Nests (Nov–Dec) on a mound of grasses, reeds and rushes piled on the ground in marshes, wet meadows and grain fields. Clutch is 3 to 4 pale blue eggs.

RANGE: Locally common from Arica to Tierra del Fuego; more numerous in central Chile. Ranges widely in sw South America and the Falklands. In cattail marshes and agricultural fields; sea level to 13,000 ft (0–4000 m).

VAGRANT ACCIPITER: LONG-WINGED HARRIER, *Circus button*. 20.5 in (52 cm). Purplish-black above. Forehead and facial disk white; neck black. Throat, breast and abdomen white. Open fields and marshes. Historical records in central Chile; ranges in eastern South America.

Black-chested Buzzard-Eagle, Aguila
Geranoaetus melanoleucus

OTHER NAMES: Chilean Buzzard, Calquín, Agula, Buse aguia.

ID: 24–30 in (60–76 cm). Largest hawk in Chile. Broad wings and short, broad tail. ADULT has a black head, throat and breast. The abdomen is white, finely lined with black. Stockings are white with fine blackish lines. Mantle and forward edge of upperwings are black; trailing edge of upperwing is ashy black. FEMALE is larger, with a rufous wash on the secondaries and rump. JUVENILE is dark chestnut above; breast is tawny and spotted with black; stockings are tawny with black bars.

Feeds on rabbits, hares, rats, snakes, foxes, newborn lambs and other small mammals. Swoops down on its prey, carries it off in its sharp talons, and kills it instantly with its sharp bill and claws. Nests on cliff ledges or in high trees. The nest, which is reused from year to year if not disturbed, is a bulky structure of twigs lined with mammal hair.

Clutch is 2 white eggs that are spotted with greyish-brown.

RANGE: Arica to Tierra del Fuego. Widespread along the Andes Range, mainly in semi-arid habitats. Occurs at forest edge in s Chile and in desert oases in n Chile; sea level to 13,000 ft (0–4000 m).

Harris's Hawk
Peuco
Parabuteo unicinctus

OTHER NAMES: Bay-winged Hawk, One-banded Buzzard, Peuco castellano, Peuco gallinero, Wüsten-bussard, Buse de Harris.
ID: 18–23 in (45–59 cm). ADULTS are dark brown above with some rufous feathering on the back and a prominent rufous patch on the wings. The underparts are brownish-grey with some feathers edged in golden brown or white. Throat is white with black stripes. Stockings barred yellow-brown and rufous. Tail dark grey; base and terminal band white. Bluish-grey bill; yellow cere. Yellow legs. JUVENILE has buffy underparts streaked with black. Dark grey above with golden mottling. Tail grey with darker barring, and whitish at base and tip.

Harris's hawks hunt in family groups comprised of a pair, with a dominant female and several helpers. The hawks sight their quarry from the air, then land and attempt to flush it from its hiding place. When one of the group catches the prey, it covers the animal with its wings—a behavior known as MANTLING. These hawks feed mainly on mice, rats, reptiles and lizards, but can also take prey as large as a rabbit. They also raid chicken coops and dovecotes, which makes them unpopular with ranchers.

Pairs are normally monogamous, except where food is abundant, in which case polyandry is the norm. The pair is often joined by others of the family group, who help with building the nest, incubation of eggs, feeding of the chicks, and defense. These hawks breed year round, and can produce 2 to 3 clutches in a year. The nest is a platform of twigs, sticks and vegetation lined with mosses and grasses set in a tree about 15 ft (5 m) above the ground. Clutch is 2 to 4 eggs. Both parents share in the 35 day incubation period. Chicks fledge at about 40 days of age, and remain around the nestting area for several months.

RANGE: Common from Arica to Aisén, from the Andean precordillera to the coast, in open country with brush-covered slopes. Ranges from sw USA to South America to about 42°S latitude.

Variable Hawk
Aguilucho
Buteo polyosoma

OTHER NAMES: Red-backed Buzzard, Ñancu, Rotrücken-bussard, Buse tricolore.
ID: 20–22 in (45–62 cm). WS 50–56 in (113–151 cm). Plumage varies with age and there are light, melanistic and rufous morphs. The field mark common to all is the white, finely-barred tail with a black subterminal band. MALES are typically slate grey with darker wings and entirely white underparts; some males may be entirely slate grey. FEMALES have a rust-colored back. The head and wings may be slate grey or dark grey. Underparts may be white, deep rust, or black and deep rust. JUVENILES are streaked with brown and ochre, and have black wingtips. These hawks feed on rats, mice, other small mammals, birds, reptiles and snails. They build a bulky nest of sticks on cliff ledges or build their nest in trees in densely forested areas.

RANGE: Arica to Tierra del Fuego; also Juan Fernández. Ranges from Colombia to Argentina and the Falklands.

SUBSPECIES: AGUILUCHO, *B. p. polyosoma*, ranges from Arica to Tierra del Fuego. The JUAN FERNÁNDEZ HAWK, AGUILUCHO DE MAS AFUERA, *B. p. exsul*, is found on Isla Masafuera (Alejandro Selkirk) in the Juan Fernández Archipelago. It is larger, has white-tipped feathers on a bluish-grey back, and has white underparts. Neither sex has any rufous on the back.

RELATED VAGRANT: PUNA HAWK, AGUILUCHO

DE LA PUNA, *Buteo poecilochrous*. Larger than the similar Variable Hawk. One record in Chile at Caritaya in the Arica-Parinacota Region. The normal range extends from Colombia to nw Argentina. Always occurs in the mountains, never on the seacoast.

Rufous-tailed Hawk
Aguilucho de cola rojiza
Buteo ventralis
OTHER NAMES: Red-tailed Buzzard, Peuco negro, Magellanbussard, Buse de Patagonie.
ID: 18–22 in (45–57 cm). WS 50 in (125 cm). Uncommon and not well-known. Large, with rounded wings and typical *Buteo* tail. Polymorphic. TYPICAL MORPH has a dark brown back, pale throat, and rufous chest with dark streaks that form bands across the chest and abdomen; the tail is rufous above and cream below, with eight to ten dark, narrow, transverse bars on both top and underside. In flight, this morph shows pale cinnamon wing linings with a dark patch on the leading edge. The MELANISTIC MORPH is brownish black above and below; the leading edge of the underwing is dark brown, the trailing edge whitish; the tail is dark with darker barring above, and white with dark barring below. The FERRUGINOUS MORPHS show rufous on the face, chest and mantle. JUVENILES are dark-backed. The underparts are white with black striations on the head and flanks. Tail is ash grey with thin grey bars. Underwings are pale with a dark leading edge. Builds a nest from thick branches in tall trees.
RANGE: Maule to Tierra del Fuego and Isla Navarino, Magallanes; also w Argentina; in the *Nothofagus* forests of the Patagonian Andes, and in low growth in burned scrub; sea level to 5000 ft (0–1500 m).

White-throated Hawk
Aguilucho chico
Buteo albigula
OTHER NAMES: Lesser Buzzard, Weisskehlbussard, Buse à gorge blanche.
ID: 16–18 in (40–46 cm). WS 37 in (93 cm). Short-bodied, short-tailed. Straight trailing edge on the wings and a flat wing profile. Blackish-brown above; white below with dark on flanks. White throat is conspicuous against the dark helmet of the head. White stockings with rufous bars. Black bill with a yellow cere. Top of tail dark brown with numerous indistinct black bars; underside of tail white with fine dark barring. JUVENILE similar, with wing coverts finely-edged pale rufous; tan-and-black barred stockings. First described by R. Philippi in 1899. Subsequently misidentified from a few scattered specimens. Now known to be a RARE, but regular summer visitor and breeder. Leaves Chile in the autumn and migrates north along the Andes.
RANGE: Atacama to Los Lagos (summer visitor); Columbia to Argentina (resident). Encountered in clearings in *Nothofagus* woodland; sea level to 6500 ft (0–2000 m).

FAMILY FALCONIDAE
FALCONS AND CARACARAS
Members of this family have long, thin, pointed wings. They have a buoyant flight and rarely soar. Falcons and caracaras eat small mammals, birds, snakes, amphibians, crustaceans, mollusks and insects. They nest in trees or on hillsides and lay a clutch of 2 to 6 red-speckled, creamy-white eggs.

Chimango Caracara
Tiuque
Milvago chimango
OTHER NAMES: Chimango Carrion Hawk, Chimangokarakara, Caracara chimango.
ID: 15.7 in (40 cm). ADULT has a tawny back with dark brown wings and pale patches on rump and primaries. Underparts lighter with rufous tint to breast; abdomen buffy. Tail finely lined in cream and brown; wide, brown subterminal band. JUVENILE is paler brown and lacks brown tailband.

Noisy groups can be found scavenging on the ground at open markets, in garbage dumps, agricultural fields being plowed for cultivation, and other open habitats. Feeds indiscriminately on grubs, larvae, caterpillars, frogs, crabs, small fish and

BUTEO HAWKS 189

White-throated Hawk

**Harris's Hawk
Peuco**
Parabuteo unicinctus
Antofagasta–Los Lagos
18–23 in (45–59 cm)

Adult Harris's Hawk

Juvenile Harris's Hawk

**White-throated Hawk
Aguilucho chico**
Buteo albigula
Atacama–Los Lagos
16–18 in (40–46 cm)

Melanistic morph

Rufous morph

Typical adult Rufous-tailed Hawk

**Rufous-tailed Hawk
Aguilucho de cola rojizo**
Buteo ventralis
Los Lagos–Magallanes
18–22 in (45–57 cm)

Typical morph

Rufous female Variable Hawk

Typical female Variable Hawk

Typical male Variable Hawk

Typical male Variable Hawk

Grey morph male Variable Hawk

**Variable Hawk
Aguilucho**
Buteo polyosoma
Arica–Magallanes
20–22 in (45–62 cm)

Rufous female Variable Hawk

carrion. Can breed twice a year. Nest is a bulky structure of sticks lined with grass, moss, wool fibers, and bits of cloth or string. Nest is set in the upper branches of low trees, or may be hidden in the grass in treeless habitats.

RANGE: Atacama to Tierra del Fuego; also Argentina, Brazil, Paraguay and Uruguay. INTRODUCED to Easter Island. Found in almost all habitats within its range; sea level to 5900 ft (0–1800 m).

SUBSPECIES: TIUQUE, *Milvago c. chimango*, ranges from Atacama to Concepción and Aisén to Magallanes. Introduced to Easter Island. The dark-backed TIUQUE DEL SUR, *M. c. temucoensis*, ranges from Ñuble to Chiloé and on the coasts of Aisén and Magallanes. Breast is ochre-brown, and there is heavy barring on the breast and abdomen. The largest chimango, TIUQUE DE TIERRA DEL FUEGO, *M. c. fuegiensis*, ranges in forested areas of Tierra del Fuego.

Southern Caracara, Carancho, Traro
Caracara plancus

OTHER NAMES: Carancho Carrion-Hawk, Crested Caracara, Huaro, Taro, Karakara, Caraira, Quelele, Totache, Caracara huppé, Caracara du Nord.

ID: 19–24 in (49–61 cm). WS 120 cm (47 in). Large, long-legged raptor. Appears dusky overall; upper part of head black, flat-crowned and crested; cream to buffy on throat and cheeks. Back and breast dusky with creamy barring. White primary patches. White tail with fine brown bars and black terminal band. Bare facial skin red. Bill yellow with blue base and orange cere. Legs pale yellow. JUVENILES are lighter on back and are streaked below; face and legs paler than adult. The call is a percussive rattle *krak-karak*, which sounds like a stick being beaten on a hollow branch.

Aggressive and merciless hunter of rats and other small mammals, young birds and bird eggs, snakes, frogs, grubs and newborn lambs. Often seen at carrion with vultures. Builds a large nest of sticks in tall trees, grassy ledges of low bluffs, and in dense shrubbery. The clutch is 2 to 3 red-spotted, cream-colored eggs.

RANGE: Arica to Cape Horn; more common in s Chile. Ranges to Bolivia, Argentina, Paraguay, and Uruguay. Open fields, sheep ranches, woodland; sea level to 16,400 ft (0–5000 m).

Mountain Caracara
Carancho cordillerano
Phalcoboenus megalopterus

OTHER NAMES: Andean Caracara, Tiuque cordillerano, Matamico blanco, Guarahuan, Chinalinda, Caracara montagnard, Berg-karakara.

ID: 20–22 in (52–56 cm). Glossy black on head, back and breast; rest of underparts white. Long wings reach tail tip when at rest. Upperwing coverts, primaries and secondaries black; underwing coverts white. Black tail has white at base and tip. Bare facial skin reddish. Bill pale blue with reddish base. Legs orange-yellow. JUVENILES are uniformly rufous with creamy uppertail coverts. Nests on cliff ledges, laying 2 to 3 eggs on the bare ground or in a shallow nest made of mud.

RANGE: Arica to Maule; also Argentina, Bolivia, Peru, Ecuador, Colombia. Andean wetlands and grasslands, especially near cliffs; 5000–16,400 ft (1500–5000 m); descends to the coast in the northern part of its range.

White-throated Caracara
Carancho cordillerano del sur
Phalcoboenus albogularis

OTHER NAMES: Carancho negro, Tiuque cordillerano del sur, Caracara à gorge blanche, Weisskehlkarakara.

ID: 21–22 in (53–55 cm). All white underparts and yellow facial skin separate this species from the Mountain Caracara. Nests on cliff ledges in the rugged mountains of the Fuegian region.

RANGE: Biobío to Tierra del Fuego, and adjacent Argentina. Occupies cold Andean steppe; 1650–8200 ft (500–2500 m).

CARACARAS AND FALCONS 191

Peregrine

Aplomado

Kestrel

Aplomado Falcon
Halcón perdiguero
Falco femoralis
Arica–Maule, Magallanes
14–18 in (36–45 cm)

American Kestrel
Cernícalo
Falco sparverius
Arica–Magallanes
10 in (25 cm)

Striated Caracara

Peregrine Falcon
Halcón peregrino
Falco peregrinus
16–18.5 in (38–47 cm)
Arica–Magallanes

Pallid Falcon, Halcón palido
Falco peregrinus
Magallanes
17 in (43 cm)
Rare pale morph peregrine

Southern Caracara

Southern Caracara
Carancho, Traro
Caracara plancus
19–24 in (49–61 cm)
Arica–Magallanes

White-throated Caracara

Mountain Caracara
Carancho cordillerano
Phalcoboenus megalopterus
Arica–Maule
20–22 in (52–56 cm)

White-throated Caracara
Carancho caracara del sur
Phalcoboenus albogularis
Los Lagos–Magallanes
21–22 in (53–55 cm)

Mountain Caracara

Striated Caracara
Carancho negro
Phalcoboenus australis
Magallanes
24.5 in (62 cm)

Chimango Caracara
Tiuque
Milvago chimango
Atacama–Magallanes
15.75 in (40 cm)

Chimango Caracara

Striated Caracara, Carancho negro
Phalcoboenus australis

OTHER NAMES: Forster's Caracara, Johnny Rook, Tiuque cordillerano austral, Matamico, Falklandkarakara, Caracara austral.
ID: 24.5 in (62 cm). ADULT is blackish-brown with pale striations on nape, throat, neck and breast. Stockings and lower abdomen rufous. Pale patch at base of primaries. Black tail with terminal white band. Facial skin and legs orange-yellow. JUVENILE is smoky-brown with buff spotting. Tail is golden-brown. Facial skin and legs light grey. Unusually tame and curious. Takes birds and chicks by running and snatching them. Also feeds on insects, mollusks, carrion, and excreta of seals and penguins. NEAR THREATENED.
RANGE: Uncommon along the channels and rocky, outer coasts of Magallanes, and on islands south of the Beagle Channel, Tierra del Fuego and Staten Island. Fairly common in the Falklands.

Peregrine Falcon, Halcón peregrino
Falco peregrinus

OTHER NAMES: Duck Hawk, Gavilan, Wanderfalke, Faucon pèlerin. Peregrine means "wanderer," an apt name since the boreal-nesting peregrine makes one of the longest migrations of any North American bird—a round trip of 15,500 mi (25,000 km) in a single year.
ID: ♂ 16 in (38 cm). ♀ 18.5 in (47 cm). Powerfully built. Long-winged and narrow-tailed. ADULT has black hood, black "teardrop" and white ear crescent. Cream-colored forehead and chest. Abdomen and flanks are cream with dark grey barring. Back is slate-grey. Blue bill with a yellow cere. Yellow eye ring. Yellow legs and feet. JUVENILES have a pale rufous nuchal collar and tan underparts, strongly spotted black except on the throat.

Peregrines hunt birds by dropping down on them from high above in a spectacular stoop, often attaining speeds of 70 mi per hour (112 km/hr) in direct pursuit of prey. The peregrine strikes its prey with its talons, killing it instantly and dropping it to the ground. Sounding a shrill *whek-whek-whek*, the peregrine swoops upward in a wide arc, then returns to pick up the prey and fly off with it.
RANGE: Arica to Tierra del Fuego; sea level to 12,500 ft (0–3800 m); vagrant on Juan Fernández. Occurs on oceanic islands and all continents except Antarctica.
SUBSPECIES: HALCÓN PEREGRINO BOREAL, *F. p. anatum*, is a summer visitor from North America, ranging from Arica to Valdivia. HALCÓN PEREGRINO AUSTRAL, *F. p. cassini*, is a resident breeder ranging from Atacama to Tierra del Fuego. It is darker, with a facial pattern that lacks the white ear patch and has a buffy chest. The PALLID FALCON, HALCÓN PÁLIDO, *F. p. kreyenborgi*, is a rare, pale grey and buff subspecies found in Magallanes, ranging from Puerto Natales to Tierra del Fuego and s Patagonia.

Aplomado Falcon, Halcón perdiguero
Falco femoralis

OTHER NAMES: Halcón azulado, Faucon aplomado, Aplomadofalke.
ID: 14–18 in (36–45 cm). Lead-grey on the back and crown, with a black "teardrop" on the cheeks. Eyeline and cheeks pale cinnamon. Ochre-cinnamon underparts are paler on the breast and rufous-tinted on the abdomen and stockings. Sometimes has black and white barring on the flanks and vent. Long, dark grey tail with 6 to 7 white bands. Dark grey bill with yellow cere. Yellow legs.

The Aplomado feeds on tinamous, small birds, and occasionally on young chickens. It takes its prey in low and fast flight, striking and killing with its talons before carrying off the prey. This falcon nests in low trees in central Chile and in tall cacti in the north.
RANGE: Arica to Maule, and Magallanes; desert, open fields, agricultural land and Patagonian steppe; sea level to 12,500 ft (0–3800 m). Widespread from sw USA through South America.

SUBSPECIES: The HALCÓN PERDIGUERO, *F. f. pichinchae*, ranges from Arica to Maule. The smaller and paler HALCÓN PERDIGUERO AUSTRAL, *F. f. femoralis*, is found only in the Magallanes Region.

American Kestrel, Cernícalo
Falco sparverius
OTHER NAMES: Sparrow Hawk, Halconcito, Cernícalo chitero, Buntfalke, Crécerelle d'Amérique.
ID: 10 in (25 cm). MALE's head is chestnut and blue-grey. The white cheeks have two "teardrops." The mantle (upper back) is rufous with transverse black bars. Wings are blue-grey. The throat is white; underparts are buff, with brown streaks on flanks. Rufous tail has a black subterminal band. FEMALES and JUVENILES are streaked reddish-brown on the underparts; the tail is finely-barred with black. Females are larger than males.

The American Kestrel preys mainly on insects and mice, and occasionally takes small birds. Perches on telephone wires or bare tree branches, or hovers over open fields, watching for any movement in the grass. Once it spots its quarry, it kills the prey in a lightening dive and then carries it off to be eaten at leisure. Kestrels lay their eggs in hollows of tree branches and cacti, in holes in embankments and stone walls, or on rafters in barns. They make no real nest, but lay the clutch of 3 to 6 eggs on the bare substrate.
RANGE: Arica to Tierra del Fuego; also Juan Fernández and Desventuradas. Widespread in North and South America in a variety of open habitats.
SUBSPECIES: CERNÍCALO, *F. s. cinnamominus*. Atacama to Tierra del Fuego. CERNÍCALO DEL NORTE, *F. s. peruvianus*. Valleys and oases in Arica and Tarapacá. CERNÍCALO DE JUAN FERNÁNDEZ, *F. s. fernandensis*. Juan Fernández and the Islas Desventuradas.
VAGRANT: LAUGHING FALCON, *Herpetotheres cachinnans*. One record at Camarones Gorge, Arica. Ranges in tropical and subtropical forests of the Americas.

GRUIFORMES: Rails and Allies
FAMILY RALLIDAE
RAILS, GALLINULES AND COOTS
These aquatic birds inhabit marshes and ponds edged with dense vegetation. Rails tend to be solitary and hide in marsh vegetation. Coots and gallinules are more gregarious and will swim out in the open. Most species are somber-hued. They have a relatively small head with a laterally-compressed bill and frontal shield. The large feet have lobed toes. Reluctant fliers, they are good swimmers and divers, and are able to walk and run through reedbeds with great stealth. They feed on aquatic plants.

Austral Rail, Pidén austral
Rallus antarcticus
OTHER NAMES: Antarctic Rail, Râle austral, Magellanralle.
ID: 8 in (20 cm). Back streaked tan and black. Throat and face pale grey; breast and abdomen darker slate grey. Wings black; wing coverts rufous with black spots. Flanks are barred black and white. Upper mandible bright red; lower bill dark red. Yellow-orange iris. Cocks and flicks tail. Very secretive. VULNERABLE.
RANGE: Magallanes. Historical records in marshes and wet fields at Santiago, Llanquihue and Magallanes. Recently rediscovered in *Scirpus* marshes in areas where the Patagonian forests and grasslands meet.

Black Rail, Pidencito
Laterallus jamaicensis salinasi
OTHER NAMES: Chilean Black Crake, Burrito cuyano, Tagüita de Salinas, Râle noir, Schieferralle.
ID: 6 in (15 cm). Smallest rail in Chile. Head lead-grey. Hindneck, nape and upper mantle drab olive-chestnut (dotted with white in young birds). Rest of upperparts and wings olive brown with narrow white transverse bars. Underparts lead grey; flanks barred black and white. Short, dull green bill. Greenish legs. Red iris. Nests in November or December. Clutch of 4 to 7 red-spotted, white eggs are laid in a nest of

marsh grass lined with softer grasses. The nest is built on the ground and is well-hidden in the rushes and long grass. Very difficult to see due to its small size and secretive habits. NEAR THREATENED.

RANGE: Atacama to Los Lagos, and throughout the Americas in sedge marshes and wet or flooded fields.

Plumbeous Rail, Pidén
Pardirallus sanguinolentus
OTHER NAMES: Common Rail, Gallineta común, Cotuta, Râle à bec ensanglanté, Grauralle.
ID: 15 in (38 cm). Olive-brown back; lead-grey underparts. Long bill is grass green, with blood red color at the base of the lower bill and sky blue at the base of the upper mandible. Legs and feet red. Iris purplish-red. Remains within the cover of vegetation in midday, but is often seen in the open at other times. Terrestrial; very reluctant to swim. Feeds on insects, larvae, worms and some plant matter. Nests (Oct–Dec) in a loose pile of grass placed on the ground in heavy vegetation. The clutch is 4 to 6 red-spotted, tan-colored eggs.
RANGE: Arica to Magallanes; s Argentina, Peru. Wetlands and ponds with dense vegetation; sea level to 9850 ft (0–3000 m).
SUBSPECIES: LANDBECK'S RAIL, *R. s. landbeckii*; Atacama to Aisén. SIMON'S RAIL, *R. s. simonsi*; oases in Arica, Tarapacá and Antofagasta. MAGELLAN RAIL, *R. s. luridus*; Strait of Magellan to Tierra del Fuego; larger and with a rufous tint to the back.

Spot-flanked Gallinule, Tagüita
Gallinula melanops
OTHER NAMES: Chilean Little Waterhen, Pollona pintada, Pitroca, Gallareta ligas rojas, Gallinule à face noire, Maskenpfuhlhuhn.
ID: 11–12 in (27–30 cm). Forehead and crown dark grey. Rest of head, neck and breast pale grey, fading to white on belly and undertail. Flanks olive-brown with round, white spots. Back, rump, top of tail and wings are drab olive, with a chestnut wash on the wing coverts. Bill and frontal shield are dull green. Red iris. More secretive than coots, but less so than rails. Often seen swimming amid floating vegetation at the edge of lakes and slow-flowing rivers. They are excellent divers, attaining depths of 26 ft (8 m) when foraging for aquatic vegetation. Rather than taking flight, they run over the surface of the water when alarmed. Nests (Oct) in a partially roofed mound of dry rushes. The nest is set slightly above the waterline in the rushes or set directly on the wet ground. Clutch is 4 to 8 off-white eggs with reddish-brown spots. The bitter-tasting flesh of this species has afforded it some protection from hunters.
RANGE: Atacama to Los Lagos. Widespread from se Brazil to Bolivia and Argentina. Placid waters of rivers, lakes, lagoons, inlet estuaries and other wetlands; sea level to 2300 ft (0–700 m).

Common Moorhen, Tagüita del norte
Gallinula chloropus
OTHER NAMES: Garman's Gallinule, Tagüita grande, Llagareta, Gallinule poule-d'eau Teichralle.
ID: 14 in (36 cm). Slate-colored overall. Darker grey on the head, brownish-olive on back and slightly paler below (birds on the Altiplano are larger and blacker). Conspicuous white flank streaks and white vent. Scarlet red frontal plate; bill bright red with a yellow-green tip. Green legs with red tibia (the "garters"). Long toes lack the typical scallop-shaped lobes. The nest is a bulky mound of reeds and rushes, placed in thick vegetation in or at the edge of shallow water. Clutch is 6 to 17 buff-colored eggs marked with fine, dark brown speckling.
RANGE: Arica to Coquimbo. Widespread in the Americas. In marshes, ponds, estuaries, lakes; sea level–15,500 ft (0–4700 m).

White-winged Coot, Tagua chica
Fulica leucoptera
OTHER NAMES: Weissflügel-Blässhuhn, Foulque leucoptère.
ID: 17 in (43 cm). Blackish overall. Rump

RAILS, GALLINULES AND COOTS 195

Austral Rail
Pidén austral
Rallus antarcticus
Magallanes
8 in (20 cm)
Rare

Spot-flanked Gallinule
Tagüita
Gallinula melanops
Atacama–Los Lagos
11–12 in (27–30 cm)

Black Rail
Pidencito
Laterallus jamaicensis
Atacama–Los Lagos
6 in (15 cm)

Common Moorhen
Tagüita del norte
Gallinula chloropus
Arica–Coquimbo
14 in (36 cm)

Plumbeous Rail
Pidén
Pardirallus sanguinolentus
Arica–Magallanes
15 in (38 cm)

Andean Coot
Tagua andina
Fulica ardesiaca
Arica–Tarapacá
16–18 in (40–46 cm)
Altiplano

Red-gartered Coot
Tagua común
Fulica armillata
Coquimbo–Magallanes
20 in (51 cm)

Red-fronted Coot
Tagua de frente roja
Fulica rufifrons
Atacama–Los Lagos
Magallanes
17 in (43 cm)

White-winged Coot
Tagua chica
Fulica leucoptera
Arica–Magallanes
17 in (43 cm)

Tasselweed
Ruppia filifolia

Horned Coot
Tagua cornuda
Fulica cornuta
Arica–Antofagasta
24 in (62 cm)
Altiplano

Giant Coot
Tagua gigante
Fulica gigantea
Arica–Antofagasta
25 in (64 cm)
Altiplano

is black in the center and white on the sides. White tips to the secondaries are visible in flight. Rounded, lemon yellow frontal shield. Bill yellow to pale yellow, without red tones. Legs green. Eyes red. Widespread and common from the coast to the High Andes. Nests in the reedbeds in lowland areas; at higher elevations it builds a floating nest anchored to aquatic weeds. The clutch is 4 to 9 light brown eggs with many fine, dark spots.

RANGE: Arica to Magallanes; Bolivia to Tierra del Fuego. In marshes, ponds and lakes; sea level to 8200 ft (0–2500 m).

Red-gartered Coot, Tagua común
Fulica armillata

OTHER NAMES: Armillatahuhn, Foulque à jarretières.

ID: 20 in (51 cm). Dark slate-grey body with a black head and neck. Bill and moderately-pointed frontal shield are yellow with a red "strap" at junction of shield and bill base. Green legs with red tibia (garters). Most common coot of lowland lakes and rivers. Nests (Oct–Jan), building a floating platform of dry rushes with a built up rim of damp reeds. Clutch is 4 to 8 light brown eggs with dark brown to reddish spots. The Black-headed Duck *(Heteronetta atricapilla)* parasitizes nests of this coot.

RANGE: Coquimbo to Magallanes; se Brazil to n Argentina; marshes, ponds and lakes; sea level to 8200 ft (0–2500 m).

Red-fronted Coot, Tagua de frente roja
Fulica rufifrons

OTHER NAMES: Foulque à front rouge, Rotstirnblässhuhn.

ID: 17 in (43 cm). Head and neck black; body sooty-grey. Elongated, pointed dark red frontal shield; bill is lemon yellow with a red base. Cocks tail, showing white undertail coverts. Uncommon. Tends to remain near cover of marsh vegetation.

RANGE: Atacama to Los Lagos; also Magallanes; se Brazil to Argentina and Falklands. Marshes and ponds edged with dense vegetation; sea level to 3500 ft (0–1,000 m).

Andean Coot, Tagua andina
Fulica ardesiaca

OTHER NAMES: Peruvian Coot, Foulque ardoisée, Andenblässhuhn.

ID: 16–18 in (40–46 cm). Black overall, with very little white on the undertail coverts. Green legs. Whitish bill with yellow sides and a greyish tip. Bulbous, deep red frontal shield. The bill and frontal shield fade to white in winter, a possible reason why this coot was previously mistaken for the American Coot *(Fulica americana)*.

RANGE: Arica to Antofagasta, and adjacent areas of the High Andes. Altiplano lakes, lagoons and bofedales; 11,000–17,000 ft (3500–5000 m). A few birds may descend to lower altitude wetlands and slow-flowing rivers around Arica.

Giant Coot, Tagua gigante
Fulica gigantea

OTHER NAMES: Ajoya, Foulque géante, Reisenblässhuhn.

ID: 25 in (64 cm). Largest coot in Chile, and the only coot with red legs and feet. Black overall. Yellow frontal shield; dark red bill; upper bill has a white central band and a pale yellow tip. Nests in August and again in November on Altiplano lakes. Builds a huge 10-ft (3-m) wide, conical platform nest from strands of aquatic vegetation such as tasselweed, *Ruppia filifolia,* which is also a preferred food plant. The nest is placed in the open some distance from shore and is anchored to subsurface plants. A cavity in the center of the nest holds the 3 to 5 pale olive-grey eggs. Eggs and chicks can fall prey to Andean gulls and culpeo foxes take adult birds that are grazing on shore.

RANGE: Arica to Antofagasta; also Bolivia, Peru. Lakes and lagoons on the Altiplano; 13,000–15,000 ft (4000–4600 m).

Horned Coot, Tagua cornuda
Fulica cornuta

OTHER NAMES: Choika, Foulque cornue, Rüsselblässhuhn.

ID: 24 in (62 cm). Head and neck black; rest of body dark slate-grey. Undertail coverts grey. Bill is yellow-green to orange with a black upper edge. No frontal shield. A long, shaggy, black caruncle hangs down from the forehead. Legs greenish-yellow.

The Horned Coot builds its large nest on a conical pile of stones built up from the lake bottom about 100 ft (30 m) from shore. The base of the nest may be 13 ft (4 m) in diameter. Mated pairs have been observed picking up stones from the shore or lake bottom and carrying them one by one in their bill to the nesting site. Once the foundation is in place, the pair gather aquatic plants and pile them on top of the stone foundation. Nesting vegetation often includes tasselweed, *Ruppia filifolia,* which is also a preferred food plant. A cavity in the center of the nest holds the 3 to 5 pale eggs. Pairs reuse their nest for many years. NEAR THREATENED.

RANGE: Arica-Parinacota to the headwaters of the Río Huasco in Atacama; also Bolivia, nw Argentina. RARE on Altiplano lakes and lagoons having stony bottoms; 10,000–14,000 ft (3000–4300 m).

VAGRANT RAILS: SPOTTED RAIL, *Pardirallus maculatus.* Single record from the Juan Fernández Archipelgo. PURPLE GALLINULE, *Porphyrula martinica.* Recorded at the Pica Oasis in Tarapacá and at Pan de Azucar National Park.

CHARADRIIFORMES: Shorebirds, Gulls, Terns

This is a large order of wading, swimming and diving birds that live in diverse habitats— inland marshes and lakes, coastal waters, beaches and meadows. They are united mainly by anatomical characteristics of the palate, syrinx and muscles. All have a tufted oil gland. Most have eleven primaries. The dense, often waterproof plumage is colored in shades of black, white and brown. Sexes are alike. All species except the seedsnipes are carnivorous.

Recent phylogenetic data suggests that there are new relationships between families in this order, particularly the close blood ties of the very dissimilar Thick-knee, Sheathbill and Magellanic Plover.

FAMILY CHARADRIIDAE
LAPWINGS AND PLOVERS

This is a family of small to medium-sized brown, grey, or black and white waders that inhabit open, bare areas of coasts, lakes, ponds, rivers, marshes and fields. They nest on the ground and feed on insects earthworms, mollusks and small crustaceans. These birds run across open areas, then stop abruptly before moving on. Their calls are melodious whistles. Plovers and lapwings are distinguished by a large rounded head, short thick neck, and short tail. The eyes are positioned at the sides of the head, giving them a broad field of vision. Most species have a short, fairly stout bill that is swollen at the tip, except for the Diademed Sandpiper-Plover and Tawny-throated Dotterel, which have a long, thin, sandpiper-like bill. Lapwings have broad, rounded wings, and some lapwings have a sharp spur at the bend of the wing that is used for territorial sparring. The long, narrow wings of plovers are suited for sustained migratory flight.

Southern Lapwing, Queltehue
Vanellus chilensis
OTHER NAMES: Chilean Lapwing, Treile, Tero-Tero, Vanneau téro, Bronzekiebitz.
ID: 14 in (36 cm). Black forehead, lores, foreneck and breast. Head grey with a short, thin crest. Back olive-grey with a bronzy-green iridescence on the shoulders. Belly is white. Tail white with a black subterminal band. Bill pink with a black tip. Red eyes. Pink legs. In flight, a conspicuous white crescent can be seen on the upperwing contrasts with the black primaries and secondaries. Underwings are white with a broad black trailing edge.

Typically found in fields and wetlands, Southern Lapwings also inhabit meadows, parks and gardens in urban areas. They feed mainly on insects and thus are very beneficial to agriculture. Lapwings function as round-the-clock sentries, alerting everyone and everything to perceived danger with a strident metallic call, *kradeeer-kradeeer.*

Queltehue nest in early July—midwinter in the Southern Hemisphere. The nest is a ground scrape covered with dry grass. The clutch is 3 to 4 large pyriform (pear-shaped) eggs, which are greenish-brown with dark blotches. Chicks feed independently a few hours after hatching. The cryptic coloration of their down renders them nearly invisible to the naked eye.

RANGE: Atacama to Magallanes. Vagrant at Juan Fernández and Islas Desventuradas. Common in meadows and wet cultivated fields throughout South America; sea level to 7200 ft (0–2200 m).

SUBSPECIES: QUELTEHUE, *V. c. chilensis*, is resident from Atacama to Chiloé; accidental in the Juan Fernández Archipelago. The smaller QUELTEHUE AUSTRAL, *V. c. fretensis*, ranges from Aisén to Tierra del Fuego.

Andean Lapwing
Queltehue de la puna
Vanellus resplendens

OTHER NAMES: Leque-Leque, Anden-Kiebitz.
ID: 12.5 in (32 cm). Grey head and neck. Grey chest ends in a dark line, which separates it from the white abdomen. Back greenish. Bill yellow to rose with black tip. Separated from the Southern Lapwing by smaller size, lack of black on the head, throat and chest, and preference for high-altitude wetlands. Clutch is 3 to 4 finely-spotted eggs, laid in a ground scrape lined with grasses.

RANGE: Locally common on the Puna from Arica to Antofagasta, and in Ecuador, Peru, Bolivia and Argentina. Two sight records from the mouth of the Lluta River near Arica. Inhabits damp fields, lakeshores and edges of ponds above 11,500 ft (3500 m).

American Golden Plover
Chorlo dorado
Pluvialis dominica

OTHER NAMES: Lesser Golden Plover, Chorlo pampa, Pluvier bronzé, Amerikanischer Goldregenpfeifer.
ID: 10.25 in (26 cm). An irregular migrant to Chile, where it appears in NON-BREEDING PLUMAGE. Back feathers dusky with flecks of gold and yellow. Dark crown contrasts with the whitish supercilium. Underparts creamy with fine lines of grey on breast and flanks. Black bill. Blackish legs. In late March, birds begin to show the black underparts of breeding plumage. Occupies a variety of habitats in migration, including lawns, fields, open grasslands, estuaries and beaches. Feeds almost exclusively on seeds.

RANGE: Breeds on the Arctic tundra. Birds that migrate south along the Atlantic coast spend the austral summer (Sep–Mar) on the grasslands of Brazil, Uruguay, Argentina and se Chile. A few birds migrate down the Pacific coast to the beaches and grasslands of Arica and Tarapacá.

Black-bellied Plover, Chorlo ártico
Pluvialis squatarola

OTHER NAMES: Grey Plover, Pollo de mar grande, Pollo cabezón, Pluvier argenté, Kiebitzregenpfeifer.
ID: 11 in (28 cm). Austral summer visitor to coastal Chile, where it appears in NON-BREEDING PLUMAGE. Upperparts and breast finely speckled in ivory and grey. Throat, belly and rump are white. White wing-stripe and rump. Black axillaries (wing pits) visible in flight. Black bill and legs. In late March, birds begin to show the black underparts of breeding plumage.

RANGE: Arica to Concepción (Oct–Apr) and the coasts of Ecuador and Peru. Sandy beaches, estuaries and mudflats. Breeds on the Arctic tundra. Migrates via Central America and along the Pacific coast of South America. Some immature birds may overwinter in Chile.

Semipalmated Plover
Chorlo semipalmado
Charadrius semipalmatus

OTHER NAMES: Pollito de mar, Pluvier semi-palmé, Amerikanischer Sandregenpfeifer.
ID: 7 in (17.5 cm). Austral summer visitor to coastal Chile, where it appears in NON-BREEDING plumage. Brown back. Forehead and supercilium white. White nuchal collar and throat. Brown breastband. Abdomen

PLOVERS, LAPWINGS AND DOTTERELS 199

and belly white. Bill black with yellow at the base. Legs yellow. Breeding birds have a black breastband and black facial markings. The similar Collared Plover lacks the white hindneck and is not present on the coast in austral summer.

RANGE: Coastal Arica to Valparaíso, with a few birds reaching Los Lagos and Magallanes. Boreal breeder on the Canadian and Alaskan tundra. Migrates south through Central America to the Galapagos and along both coasts of South America to Patagonia.

Killdeer, Chorlo gritón
Charadrius vociferus

OTHER NAMES: Peruvian Killdeer, Pluvier kildir, Keilschwanz-Regenpfeifer.

ID: 10 in (25 cm). Brown above, white below, with a white nuchal collar and two black breastbands. White forehead and postocular supercilium. Black forehead bar. Black bill. Legs flesh-colored. In flight, the tawny rump and white wing stripe are distinctive. Lanky, with slender wings. Call is a ringing *kill-dee, kill-deer*. Larger than the Two-banded Plover and with a longer tail.

RANGE: RARE at Arica on the stony banks of the Lluta River. This Peruvian subspecies of the Killdeer ranges in coastal Peru from Piura to Tacna.

Rufous-chested Dotterel
Chorlo chileno
Charadrius modestus

OTHER NAMES: Chilean Dotterel, Winter Plover, Chorlo negro, Chorlo de invierno, Pluvier d'Urville, Rotbrust-Regenpfeifer.

ID: 9 in (22 cm). Upperparts brown with a white forehead, white supercilium and white outer tail feathers. Throat is grey. In BREEDING PLUMAGE the breast is rich chestnut with a posterior black band. The breast plumage molts to dark brown in non-breeding season. Rest of underparts white. Runs rapidly across the ground and is a strong flier that sounds its two-note *pu-wee* in flight. Nests in s Chile, mainly in damp upland areas along the Golfo de Corcovado, the Strait of Magellan and the Beagle Channel. Lays a clutch of two darkly mottled eggs in a shallow hollow on top of dry moss or cushion plants. The male diverts attention from the nest by showing itself to an intruder and drawing close before flying away. Most of the population moves north in April to winter on the rocky coasts and mudflats of nc Chile and Argentina before returning to the breeding grounds in September.

RANGE: Antofagasta to Magallanes; also Argentina and the Falklands. Resident in southern Chile; winter visitor in the north.

Two-banded Plover
Chorlo de doble collar
Charadrius falklandicus

OTHER NAMES: Patagonian Sand Plover, Pollito de mar, Pluvier des Falkland, Falkland-Regenpfeifer.

ID: 7.5 in (19 cm). Resembles a small Killdeer. BREEDING ADULT is brown above and white below, with two black breastbands and black lines dividing the white face and neck from the rufous crown. JUVENILES lack the black and cinnamon markings. Black bill and legs. Nests (Nov–Jan) in wetlands of the Fuegian region, then migrates north to the coastal beaches and estuaries of central Chile and Argentina.

RANGE: Antofagasta to Magallanes; also Uruguay, s Argentina and the Falklands.

Snowy Plover
Chorlo nevado
Charadrius alexandrinus peruviana

OTHER NAMES: Kentish Plover, Angelito, Pluvier neigeux, Seeregenpfeifer.

ID: 6 in (15 cm). Pale brown above, white below. White neck collar. Tawny crown and nape. Black forehead bar and black postorbital stripe. Incomplete black breastband. Brown replaces black markings on immatures and non-breeding birds. Black bill. Grey legs. Feeds on sand fleas in the tidal zone; behaves much like a Sanderling as it prods the sand behind a receding wave and runs back as the next wave breaks. A clutch of 2 to 3 sand-colored eggs is laid in

September and again in January in a scrape in the sand above the high tide mark.
RANGE: Pacific coast from Chiloé to Arica and north to Peru. The only resident plover on the sandy beaches of northern Chile and most numerous plover farther south along the coast.

Collared Plover, Chorlo de collar
Charadrius collaris
OTHER NAMES: Azara's Sand-Plover, Pluvier d'Azara, Schlankschnabel-Regenpfeifer.
ID: 6.25 in (16 cm). Brown above, white below. Crown and ear coverts cinnamon. ADULT has a black breast band and forehead bar. Fairly long, black bill. Pink legs. JUVENILES have a dark brown, broken breastband and brown forehead bar. Found on coastal beaches and estuaries in austral winter (Apr–Aug). Moves inland in September to nest on sand spits and pebble islets in rivers and streams.
RANGE: Uncommon from Valparaíso to Los Lagos; widespread from Mexico through South America east of the Andes. Winters on the sc Chilean coast; nests inland; sea level to 3300 ft (0–1000 m).

Puna Plover, Chorlo de la puna
Charadrius alticola
OTHER NAMES: Chorlo serrano, Chiuche, Pluvier du puna, Punaregenpfeifer.
ID: 7 in (17.5 cm). Stocky plover of the High Andes. Upperparts are pale brownish-grey. White below. Tawny crown and neck. White face edged by black forehead bar, which continues down sides of head and onto the breast where it forms an incomplete collar. Lower breastband is complete and is grey to brown. Black bill and legs.
RANGE: Puna from Arica to Atacama, and adjacent nw Argentina, w Bolivia, s Peru; 7875–16,400 ft (2400–5000 m).

Diademed Sandpiper-Plover
Chorlito cordillerano
Phegornis mitchellii
OTHER NAMES: Camayo, Pluvier des Andes, Diademregenpfeifer. The word diademed derives from the Greek *diadema,* meaning "regal headband of the Persian kings."
ID: 7.5 in (19 cm). A "must see" species for birders visiting Chile. Stocky plover with a long, sandpiper-like, black bill. Black head and face with a crisp white diadem. Rufous hindneck. Brown back. Upper breast white; lower breast and flanks white with fine black vermiculations. Yellow legs. JUVENILES lack black markings and have a rufous and brown barred back.
Lives in pairs on the edge of high altitude bogs, lakes and streams. Feeds on aquatic insects picked from the water surface or from aquatic plants. Call is a penetrating and melancholy whistled *kweeew.* Nests in a twig-lined depression in shingle and sand spits. Eggs are colored light olive-buff with black and dark brown spots and blotches. Confiding, but may abandon its territory if frequently disturbed. NEAR THREATENED.
RANGE: Arica-Parinacota to Maule; also Peru, Bolivia and Argentina. Localized and resident in the High Andes; 6500–16,500 ft (2000–5000 m).

Tawny-throated Dotterel
Chorlo de campo
Oreopholus ruficollis
OTHER NAMES: Slender-billed Plover, Pollo de campo, Pachurrón, Talulo, Pluvier oréophile, Orangekehl-Regenpfeifer.
ID: 11.5 in (29 cm). Slender plover that stands tall. Back is dark brown, heavily streaked with gold. Long neck and crown are grey. Pale buff supercilium; black line through the eye. Throat is tawny to bright rufous. Underparts cream with a prominent black patch in the center of the abdomen. Long, slender, sandpiper-like bill. Pink legs and feet with very short toes.
Runs in a stop and start fashion. Forms flocks of 10 to 30 individuals that are silent and inconspicuous when on the ground, restless and active before they burst into flight with a loud, tremulous whistled *wheeoo.*
RANGE: Two highly migratory populations. One group ranges from Arica to Valparaíso,

the other in e Magallanes. Birds in n Chile nest both on the coast and on the dry Puna to about 15,000 ft (4575 m); they are thought to descend to the semi-arid hillsides of the Central Valley. Southern birds nest in the grasslands of eastern Magallanes and then most migrate to the pampas of Argentina and Uruguay.

FAMILY HAEMATOPODIDAE
OYSTERCATCHERS
These are large, gregarious shorebirds that live and nest on sandy and rocky coasts. Their plumage is either all black or strongly pied with black above, white below. They have a long, red, blunt, knife-like bill that is used for prying mollusks off rocks. They also use the bill to dig out crustaceans and worms from sandy beaches and tidal flats. Their call is a resonant piping whistle.

American Oystercatcher
Pilpilén
Haematopus palliatus
OTHER NAMES: Peru Oystercatcher, Huîtrier d'Amérique, Braunmantel–Austernfisher.
ID: 17 in (44 cm). Head, neck and breast are slate-black. Brown back. Black tail. Abdomen and belly white. Wings show a broad white stripe from the inner secondaries to the outer greater coverts. Carmine red bill with a yellow tip. Pink legs. Found mainly on sandy beaches. When alarmed the bird will fly out over the water, calling *pheeoo*, then land a short distance down the beach. Clutch is 2 to 3 black-spotted, stone-colored eggs that are laid on the ground in the sand dunes.
RANGE: Arica to Chiloé. Widespread on the coasts of the Americas on sandy beaches and coastal mudflats.

Magellanic Oystercatcher
Pilpilén austral
Haematopus leucopodus
OTHER NAMES: Fuegian Oystercatcher, Fil-Fil, Pilpilén overo, Tero real, Huasito, Huîtrier de Garnot, Magellan-Austernfisher.
ID: 18 in (45 cm). Shining metallic black plumage. Scarlet red bill. Pale pink legs. These birds seem to call incessantly in the long days of austral summer, continually making a high-pitched, plaintive repeated whistle. Clutch is 1 to 2 dark-colored eggs laid directly on the coastal rocks or on marshy ground of the interior.
RANGE: Chiloé to Cape Horn; s Argentina, Falklands. On sandy beaches, rocky islets, muddy estuaries and grasslands; sea level to 2000 ft (0–600 m).

Blackish Oystercatcher
Pilpilén negro
Haematopus ater
OTHER NAMES: Ostrero, Huîtrier noir, Russ-Austernfisher.
ID: 18 in (45 cm). Head, neck and underparts black. Back wings and tail dark sooty brown. Reddish-orange bill. Legs are fleshy pink. Usually seen singly or in pairs. Clutch is 1 to 2 pale eggs laid on the bare ground, usually on stony beaches.
RANGE: Arica to Cape Horn; also Peru, s Argentina, Staten Island and the Falklands. Recorded in Juan Fernández. On offshore islets and rocky coastal beaches.

FAMILY RECURVIROSTRIDAE
AVOCETS AND STILTS
These are long-legged, long-billed wading birds that live around water. The front toes are partially webbed and the hind toe is vestigial or absent. These are strong flying birds with long, pointed wings. They feed on small crustaceans, mollusks, insects, larvae and other aquatic organisms.

Andean Avocet
Caití
Recurvirostra andina
OTHER NAMES: Avocette des Andes, Anden-Säbelschnábler. Caití mimics the Avocet's frequently sounded call notes *kiéet-kiéeti*.
ID: 18 in (45 cm). Head and underparts white; wings, tail and center of the back black. Pale grey legs. Dark grey, slender, upturned bill. Feeds by sweeping its bill from side to side as it wades in the marshes

204 BIRDS

A white-backed stilt will often build its nest on clumps of aquatic plants such as Sosa.

and salt lakes of the Puna. Feeds in groups of 15 to 20 birds, sometimes with flamingos. Nests in September and again in January, laying a clutch of 3 to 4 eggs in a ground scrape set amid coarse lakeside vegetation.
RANGE: Puna zone of the High Andes from Arica to Atacama; adjacent Peru, Bolivia and Argentina; on saline lakes and ponds; 8200–16,500 ft (2500–5000 m).

White-backed Stilt
Perrito
Himantopus melanurus
OTHER NAMES: Southern Stilt, Black-tailed Stilt, Échasse à queue noire, Stelzenläufer. Perrito refers to the dog-like yapping call, *kwaap-kwaap*.
ID: 16.5 in (42 cm). Extremely long red legs. Plumage is pied with a white head, rump, tail and underparts, and black wings, back and hind neck. The straight, slender, black beak has a flattened tip. Forms small, noisy, foraging parties. Feeds by probing in the mud of lowland estuaries, flooded fields and marshes. Breeds in September, often nesting on clumps of aquatic Sosa *(Salicornia* sp.*)* plants. Feigns injury by drooping a wing in order to lead predators from its nest.
RANGE: Huasco Valley, Atacama to Los Lagos; Bolivia and s Brazil to Argentina; in lowland estuaries, marshes and inundated fields; sea level to 2625 ft (0–800 m).

FAMILY BURHINIDAE
THICK-KNEES
This is a family of sandy or grey-brown birds that have large heads and eyes, rather short stout bills, and long legs with thickened tibiotarsal joints or "knees." They have partially webbed feet with three toes. These birds are crepuscular and nocturnal. They live in open, stony and sandy areas, and nest on the ground. They feed on invertebrates, small rodents and frogs.

Peruvian Thick-knee
Chorlo cabezón
Burhinus superciliaris
OTHER NAMES: Alcaraván Peruano, Oedicnème du Pérou, Peruanertriel. *Chorlo cabezón* means "big-headed plover."
ID: 16 in (40 cm). Large, ashy-grey head with a pale eyeline and dark crown stripes. Nape and back ashy-grey; back feathers are edged with black lines and ochre margins. Sandy-grey on the neck and upper chest; lower chest and abdomen cream. Undertail coverts pale cinnamon. Long legs with knobby "knees." Strong fliers. Thick-knees form small flocks that often crouch silently on the ground or stand still in the cover of vegetation by day. They hunt at night, running across fields and beaches, then pausing to snatch up an insect, worm or snail. They lay a clutch of 2 eggs in a scrape on the bare ground.
RANGE: Arica and north to Ecuador. This species was first recorded in Chile in 1851, but until recently was considered accidental. Since 1990 there have been regular sightings of adults and young in the Azapa and Lluta river valleys and estuaries, and also around Arica's horse stables. Lives along arid coasts, in stony scrub, grasslands and agricultural fields; sea level to 1650 ft (0–500 m).

FAMILY CHIONIDAE
SHEATHBILLS
This is a family of white, chicken-like birds that live mainly in the Subantarctic and Antarctic. They have short, stout legs and unwebbed feet. The stout bill is covered by

a horny sheath. Although very different in appearance, sheathbills are closely related to the Thick-knee and Magellanic Plover.

Snowy Sheathbill
Paloma antártica
Chionis alba
OTHER NAMES: American Sheathbill, Greater Sheathbill, Chionis blanc, Grand bec-en-fourreau, Weissgesicht-Scheidenschnabel.
ID: 13–16 in (34–41 cm). These inquisitive, pugnacious birds resemble small, white chickens. The pale yellow bill has a black tip and a thin, bony casing saddling the maxilla like a knife scabbard or sheath. The bare facial skin has fleshy wattles. Legs are grey. A carpal spur on the short wings is used when fighting for territory.

Although typically seen walking or fluttering weakly from place to place, these birds are good swimmers and strong fliers capable of making long migratory flights between southern South America and the Antarctic Peninsula.

Nests (Dec–Jan) on the island of South Georgia, the Scotia Arc islands, and the Antarctic Peninsula to about 65°S. The nest is a messy pile of bones, feathers, eggshells and plant matter that is stuffed into a deep crevice or hole. The clutch of 1 to 4 eggs hatch several days apart.

Sheathbills are indiscriminate scavengers, feeding on refuse, carrion, excrement, seabird eggs, seal placentas and marine organisms. At penguin breeding colonies, pairs work together to distract adults who are feeding their chicks. One of the pair pecks or flutters at an adult penguin until it turns and spills krill from its mouth onto the ground; the mate then snatches up the morsel. Sheathbills are also quick to break open and eat unguarded eggs, or to feed on the remains of chicks taken by larger predators.
RANGE: Magallanes coast, s Argentina and Falklands in winter. SUMMER BREEDING MIGRANT on the Antarctic Peninsula and the coastal archipelagos, where some birds remain over winter.

FAMILY PLUVIANELLIDAE
MAGELLANIC PLOVER
This family contains a single species, the Magellanic Plover, a rare and unique wader that lives only in southern South America.

Magellanic Plover
Chorlo de Magallanes
Pluvianellus socialis
OTHER NAMES: Chorlito ceniciento, Pluvianelle magellanique, Magellanregenpfeifer.
ID: 8 in (21 cm). Upperparts and breast are pale grey; the rest of the underparts are white. Short red legs, black bill and red eyes. Eyes and legs of JUVENILES are yellowish. Feeds on small invertebrates, especially tiny arthropods and midge larvae, picked from the ground or from under pebbles in the manner of a Turnstone. In winter, forages in small flocks along rivers and on the coast, in sheltered bays, lagoons and river mouths. Nests (Sep–Nov) on the open shores of saline lakes with clay or stony shores. Lays two large eggs on the ground; usually only one chick survives. NEAR THREATENED.
RANGE: Local in Magallanes and s Argentina; part of the population migrates north to Argentina's Valdéz Peninsula in winter.

FAMILY SCOLOPACIDAE
SANDPIPERS AND ALLIES
This family of long-winged wading birds are cryptically patterned in brown, grey or black and white. The bill is slender and may be short, long, straight, downcurved or upturned. These species typically inhabit open areas, usually near water, where they feed mainly on invertebrates. Most species that occur in Chile are boreal breeders that migrate to the Southern Hemisphere where they appear in non-breeding plumage.

Hudsonian Godwit
Zarapito pico recto
Limosa haemastica
OTHER NAMES: Chorlo grande, Barge hudsonienne, Hudsonschnepfe.
ID: 15.5 in (39 cm). Long, slightly upturned bill is pink with a black tip. Upperparts

mouse grey. White rump. Black tail. Pale grey breast. White abdomen. Dark grey legs. In late March, before birds migrate north, the breast and abdomen feathers begin to turn rufous and develop dark barring.

RANGE: NON-BREEDING MIGRANT from Arica to Magallanes; seen most often around Isla Chiloé and large bays in Tierra del Fuego. Breeds in the Arctic. Most of the population migrates from James Bay, Ontario, Canada, via the North Atlantic to South America, and reaching Chile, Argentina and the Falklands in late September.

Whimbrel, Zarapito
Numenius phaeopus hudsonicus
OTHER NAMES: Hudsonian Curlew, Perdiz de mar, Perdicilla, Courlis corlieu, Regenbrachvogel.

ID: 17 in (43 cm). Long, decurved black bill. Mottled brown and yellowish-brown, with a dark crown and eyeline setting off the buffy supercilium. Grey legs.

The call on taking flight is a tittering *bibi-bibi-bibi-bi* or a whistled *cur-lew* when in migration. Although the primary diet is marine invertebrates, whimbrels also feed on the Black Crowberry *(Empetrum nigrum)* in preparation for migration in the Canadian Maritimes and coastal Maine. In Tierra del Fuego, they supplement their diet of crustaceans and insects with Red Crowberry, or Mutilla *(E. rubrum)*. The whimbrels carefully pull the berries off a plant with the tip of the bill, then flip the head back to swallow the fruit.

RANGE: Common NON-BREEDING MIGRANT on beaches from Arica to Isla Chiloé; less common in e Magallanes. Two separate migrating populations. Alaskan breeders fly down the Pacific coast as far south as Chiloé. Birds breeding at Hudson Bay, Canada, fly down the Atlantic coast as far south as Tierra del Fuego.

Greater Yellowlegs, Pitotoy grande
Tringa melanoleuca
OTHER NAMES: Chorlo real, Patas amarillas, Grand Chevalier, Grosser Gelbschenkel.

ID: 13 in (33 cm). Upperparts grey with some speckles on the wings. White rump. White underparts. Dark bill is long, slender and very slightly upturned at the tip. Very long, yellow legs.

Ringing call *pee-toy-toy*. Runs about wildly in shallow water, a behavior not seen in the Lesser Yellowlegs that often shares the same pond. Bobs the head when it wades in deeper water. Swings the bill from side to side as it skims off aquatic insects and small crustaceans from the surface of the water.

RANGE: NON-BREEDING MIGRANT from Arica to Magallanes. Breeds in Alaska and Canada, and migrates along both coasts of South America as far south as Tierra del Fuego. Marshes, estuaries, and Andean wetlands; sea level to 15,750 ft (0–4800 m).

Lesser Yellowlegs, Pitotoy chico
Tringa flavipes
OTHER NAMES: Petit Chevalier, Kleiner Gelbschenkel.

ID: 10 in (25 cm). Small, mouse-grey version of the Greater Yellowlegs, with whom it associates. Fine needle-like bill. Long yellow legs. Gives a soft whistling call, *too-too*. Bobs its head as it wades.

RANGE: NON-BREEDING MIGRANT from Arica to Magallanes. Boreal breeder. Migrates along coasts of South America to Tierra del Fuego. Marshes, estuaries, Andean wetlands; sea level to 15,750 ft (0–4800 m).

Willet, Playero grande
Catoptrophorus semipalmatus
OTHER NAMES: Western Willet, Chevalier semipalmé, Schlammtreter.

ID: 13–16 in (33–41 cm). Appears entirely grey until taking flight and revealing the striking black and white wings. White rump. Long, straight, dark bill. Long grey legs. Calls a ringing *pilly-willy-willet* as it takes flight; also sounds a loud *kyaa-yaa*.

RANGE: NON-BREEDING MIGRANT from Arica to Biobío on sandy beaches. Breeds in s Canada and w USA; migrates via Central America to Ecuador, Peru and Chile.

Ruddy Turnstone
Playero vuelvepiedras
Arenaria interpres
OTHER NAMES: Pollo de mar grande, Tournepierre à collier, Steinwälzer.
ID: 10 in (25 cm). Upperparts are brown with black mottling. Face and chest are indistinctly patterned with dark brown and white. White belly and abdomen. Yellow-orange legs. In flight, the conspicuous dark and white pattern is diagnostic. In boreal breeding plumage the upperparts are black and rufous; the black and white pattern of the face and breast show greater contrast. These birds use their wedge-shaped bill to turn over beach stones (thus, their name) when searching for sandhoppers and other small marine organisms.
RANGE: NON-BREEDING MIGRANT from Arica to Magallanes. Seen most often on sandy and rocky beaches in nc Chile. Breeds in the Arctic and winters on coasts of North and South America.

Surfbird
Playero de las rompientes
Aphriza virgata
OTHER NAMES: Tórtola de mar, Bécasseau du ressac, Gischtläufer.
ID: 10 in (25 cm). Stocky, short-legged sandpiper of kelp-covered coastal rocks. Upperparts sooty grey; paler below. Upperwings grey with a white wing stripe. (In boreal breeding plumage the scapulars are rufous.) Tail white with a broad back tip. Throat pale grey, breast sooty grey; rest of underparts white with a few grey streaks. Beak dark grey with some yellow-orange at the lower base. Yellow-green legs. Feeds on mussels, limpets, barnacles, snails, and other invertebrates taken from rocks in the intertidal zone. In Chile, also feeds on the green alga, Luche (*Ulva* sp.).
RANGE: NON-BREEDING MIGRANT from Arica to Aisén and along the Pacific coast of the Americas. In surf zone of rocky beaches. Breeds on the Alaskan tundra.

Spotted Sandpiper, Playero manchado
Actitis macularius
OTHER NAMES: Chevalier grivelé, Drosseluferläufer.
ID: 7.5 in (19 cm). Upperparts bronze-olive. White supercilium; black eyeline. Underparts are white (white with black spots in breeding plumage). Bill yellow with dark grey on the upper mandible and tip. Legs yellow. Walks with its back parallel to ground; bobs of the rear part of its body as it forages for insects.
RANGE: Uncommon NON-BREEDING MIGRANT to the coasts of Arica, Tarapacá, Antofagasta. RARE from Atacama to Los Lagos. Nests in temperate North America and migrates to temperate regions of South America.

Sanderling, Playero blanco
Calidris alba
OTHER NAMES: Pollito de mar, Bécasseau sanderling.
ID: 8 in (20 cm). Upperparts ashy grey. Forehead and face are white. Underparts white. Dark patch at bend of wing; white wing patch shows in flight. Black bill. Black legs. Flies and feeds in flocks, running back and forth on the wet sand in unison with the ebb and flow of the sea.
RANGE: Common NON-BREEDING MIGRANT on sandy beaches from Arica to Aisén. Recorded at Easter Island. Breeds in the Arctic and migrates south to coastal areas in the Northern and Southern Hemisphere.

Red Knot, Playero ártico
Calidris canutus
OTHER NAMES: Bécasseau maubèche, Knutt.
ID: 10 in (25 cm). Stout body. Upperparts grey with dark lines. Uppertail coverts white with brown bars. Underparts white; breast and flanks have brownish speckles and wavy lines (rufous below in boreal breeding plumage). Long, straight, black bill. Short, dull yellow legs. Feeds on mollusks, marine worms, crustaceans and other small invertebrates in migration.

MIGRANT SANDPIPERS 209

Sanderling's plumage in March–April

Sanderling
Playero blanco
Calidris alba
Arica–Magallanes
8 in (20 cm)

Semipalmated Sandpiper
Playero semipalmado
Calidris pusilla
Arica–Tarapacá
6 in (15 cm)

Least Sandpiper
Playero enano
Calidris minutilla
Arica–Tarapacá
5–6 in (13–15 cm)

Spotted Sandpiper
Playero manchado
Actitis macularis
Arica–Atacama
7.5 in (19 cm)

Baird's Sandpiper
Playero de Baird
Calidris bairdii
Arica–Magallanes
7.5 in (19 cm)

Pectoral Sandpiper
Playero pectoral
Calidris melanotos
Arica–Los Lagos
7.5–9.5 in (19–24 cm)

White-rumped Sandpiper
Playero de lomo blanco
Calidris fuscicollis
Arica–Tarapacá
Aisén–Magallanes
7.5 in (19 cm)

Red Knot
Playero ártico
Calidris canutus
Arica–Magallanes
10 in (26 cm)

RANGE: Uncommon NON-BREEDING MIGRANT to the bays, estuaries, mudflats of Tierra del Fuego; RARE in nc Chile. Nests within the Arctic Circle. Alaskan and Canadian Arctic breeders migrate to se South America.

Semipalmated Sandpiper
Playero semipalmado
Calidris pusilla
OTHER NAMES: Bécasseau semipalmé, Sandstrandläufer.
ID: 6 in (15 cm). Dull grey above, whitish below. Short, tubular-shaped black bill. Black legs. Feet are partially webbed, a feature that can be seen on a bird in hand or from observation of its tracks in wet sand.
RANGE: Uncommon NON-BREEDING MIGRANT at Arica on beaches and mudflats. Recorded at Coquimbo and Valparaíso. Breeds in the Arctic and migrates along the Atlantic coast as far south as Argentine Patagonia.

Least Sandpiper
Playero enano
Calidris minutilla
OTHER NAMES: Wiesenstrandläufer, Bécasseau minuscule.
ID: 5–6 in (13–15 cm). Upperparts greyish-brown. Black rump. Outer tail feathers grey. Underparts white, with dark brown streaks across the breast. Short black bill with slightly downturned tip. Yellow-green legs. Tends to crouch with bent legs and belly near the ground.
RANGE: NON-BREEDING MIGRANT at Arica. RARE on coastal mudflats and edges of ponds. Breeds in the Arctic; migrates south as far as Peru and Bahía, Brazil.

White-rumped Sandpiper
Playero de lomo blanco
Calidris fuscicollis
OTHER NAMES: Bécasseau à croupion blanc, Weissbürzel-Strandläufer.
ID: 7.5 in (19 cm). Stocky, with wingtips projecting beyond tail. Sandy grey above with some dark speckling. White supercilium. White rump (seen in flight) separates it from the similar Baird's Sandpiper. Underparts white with streaked chest and flanks. Often feeds with other sandpipers, wading and probing in water of estuaries, river mouths and mudflats.
RANGE: Common NON-BREEDING MIGRANT to Magallanes and e Aisén (Sep–Mar); RARE along the nc Chilean coast. Breeds in the Arctic; migrates east of the Andes Range to Patagonia and Tierra del Fuego; sea level to 1650 ft (0–500 m).

Baird's Sandpiper
Playero de Baird
Calidris bairdii
OTHER NAMES: Pollito de vega, Chorlito lomo negro, Playerito unicolor, Bécasseau de Baird, Bairdstrandläufer.
ID: 7.5 in (19 cm). Slender, with wingtips projecting beyond tail. Upperparts brown with paler streaks. Dark rump, which separates it from the White-rumped Sandpiper in flight. Throat, abdomen and flanks off white. Breast streaked buffy-brown. Thin, straight, black bill. Black legs. Feeds on dry mudflats above the high tide mark.
RANGE: Common NON-BREEDING MIGRANT. Arica to Magallanes; on coastal mudflats, shallow ponds and Andean wetlands. Breeds in the Arctic; migrates as far south as Tierra del Fuego; sea level to 16,500 ft (0–5000 m).

Pectoral Sandpiper
Playero pectoral
Calidris melanotos
OTHER NAMES: Bécasseau à poitrine cendrée, Graubrust-Strandläufer.
ID: 7.5–9.5 in (19–24 cm). Males are much larger than females. Upperparts brown with indistinct dark brown streaking. Streaked brown breast in all plumages. Abdomen and belly white. Fairly long, dark bill droops slightly at tip. Yellowish legs. Solitary birds or small flocks can often be seen probing in mud near shoreline vegetation, both along the coast and inland.
RANGE: Uncommon NON-BREEDING MIGRANT from Arica to Los Lagos; sea level to 1650 ft (0–500 m). Breeds in the Arctic.

PHALAROPES IN NON-BREEDING PLUMAGE

Wilson's Phalarope
Pollito de mar tricolor
Phalaropus tricolor
Arica–Antofagasta
Magallanes
9.5 in (24 cm)

Red Phalarope
Pollito de mar rojizo
Phalaropus fulicaris
Arica–Los Lagos
8.5 in (22 cm)

Red-necked Phalarope
Pollito de mar boreal
Phalaropus lobatus
Arica–Antofagasta
7.5 in (19 cm)

VAGRANT SANDPIPERS: MARBLED GODWIT, *Limosa fedoa*. Recorded at Arica and the Río Aconcagua estuary, Valparaíso.
SHORT-BILLED DOWITCHER, *Limnodromus griseus*. Recorded at Tongoy.
BRISTLE-THIGHED CURLEW, *Numenius tahitiensis*. Recorded at Easter Island.
UPLAND SANDPIPER, *Bartramia longicauda*. Recorded in Antofagasta, Atacama, Santiago.
WANDERING TATTLER, *Heteroscelus incanus*. Recorded in Antofagasta. Possible visitor to Easter Island.
SOLITARY SANDPIPER, *Tringa solitaria*. Recorded at Arica.
WESTERN SANDPIPER, *Calidris mauri*. Recorded in Tarapacá.
STILT SANDPIPER, *Calidris himantopus*. Three records in n Chile.

PHALAROPES: These ocean-going sandpipers have long, pointed wings and a long, thin, straight bill. Females are larger than males, perform a courtship display, and may mate with more than one male. Males assume the nesting duties. In the boreal breeding season phalaropes have red and brown feathers on the neck and underparts. They have grey and white plumage in non-breeding season when they are in Chilean waters. Phalaropes are excellent swimmers. They bob and spin on the water surface as they feed on crustaceans and insects.

Red Phalarope, Pollito de mar rojizo
Phalaropus fulicarius
OTHER NAMES: Grey Phalarope, Phalarope à bec large, Thorshühnchen.
ID: 8.5 in (22 cm). Upperparts grey. Face and neck white; dark patch through the eye extends to cheek. Underparts white; a few birds may show the brick red underparts of boreal breeding plumage when seen off Chile. Fairly short black bill with yellow at the lower base. In flight, the back appears solid grey and the wings have a conspicuous white wingband. Legs are black. Pelagic in offshore upwellings. Migrating flocks arrive off Arica in early September and move down the coast before veering off into the Pacific toward Juan Fernández. Flocks return to offshore Chilean waters in late February or March as they migrate north.
RANGE: Common NON-BREEDING MIGRANT in offshore waters from Arica to Chiloé and in Juan Fernández. Irregular along the mainland coast. Circumpolar breeder on the Arctic tundra. Migrates to the s Pacific and s Atlantic. Recorded at Palmer Station, Antarctica.

Red-necked Phalarope
Pollito de mar boreal
Phalaropus lobatus

OTHER NAMES: Northern Phalarope, Phalarope à bec étroit, Odinshühnchen.

ID: 7.5 in (19 cm). Rarest phalarope in Chile. Similar in non-breeding plumage to the Red Phalarope, but smaller, more compact and thinner-billed. Grey above, white below, with a dark patch through the eye. Tail is black, with white sides and tip. In flight, the white wingbar and white edges on feathers of the back and scapulars are apparent. Jaramillo (2003) notes that flocks tend to congregate along drift lines that mark the meeting of ocean currents.

RANGE: RARE NON-BREEDING MIGRANT to offshore Arica, Tarapacá and n Antofagasta; also recorded at Valparaíso and Magallanes. Nests circumpolar in the Arctic; Alaskan breeders migrate over Pacific waters to the cold currents off Peru and n Chile.

Wilson's Phalarope
Pollito de mar tricolor
Phalaropus tricolor

OTHER NAMES: Phalarope de Wilson, Wilsonwassertreter.

ID: 9.5 in (24 cm). The only phalarope that is regularly seen on brackish ponds on the n Chilean coast and the Altiplano. Slender, long-legged and small-headed with a thin, needle-like bill. Crown, face and back are grey. Underparts are white. Tail is grey with white sides and tip. In flight, the back and wings are entirely grey and the rump is white. Legs are black in breeding season, yellow in migration.

RANGE: NON-BREEDING MIGRANT to salt ponds on the n Chile coast and Andes of n Chile and e Magallanes. Nests near inland lakes in w North America. Migrates along the Pacific coast to sw Peru, then along the Andes to Patagonia and Tierra del Fuego.

SNIPES: The snipes are skulking, cryptically plumaged birds of marshes, bogs and grasslands. Their long, slender bills are sensitive at the tip and are used to probe for worms and grubs. They are known for their nuptial winnowing displays, most often performed at dusk or in early evening. The male shoots upward into the sky, then lets himself fall to earth with half-closed wings and fanned out tail. The vibrating outer tail feathers cause an eerie "drumming" sound. Snipes are most commonly seen when they flush, exploding from cover and launching into a characteristic zigzag flight.

South American Snipe
Becacina
Gallinago paraguaiae magellanica

OTHER NAMES: Magellanic Snipe, Porotera, Bécassine sud-américaine, Azara-Bekassine. Formerly considered a race of the Common Snipe *(Gallinago gallinago)*.

ID: 10–12 in (26–30 cm). Stocky and long-billed with a striped face and striped back. Dark lateral crown stripe, dark eyeline and buff supercilium. Back dark brown with four buffy or golden longitudinal lines. Breast streaked with brown. Rest of underparts white with black barring on the flanks. Short greenish-grey legs. Forages by probing in soft mud. Feeds mainly on insects and earthworms, also plant material. Very rapid, low, zigzag flight when flushed. Nests (July) in wet grasslands in the n Chilean lowlands and peat bogs in the Fuegian regions. Clutch is two olive-green eggs laid on the ground in a well-hidden, grass-lined depression. Chicks are nidifugous, able to leave the nest and feed themselves within a few hours after hatching.

RANGE: Widespread from Coquimbo to Magallanes, and throughout most of South America; also in the Falklands. Inhabits marshes, flooded fields, bogs and grassy wetlands; sea level to 6500 ft (0–2000 m).

Puna Snipe
Becacina de la puna
Gallinago andina

OTHER NAMES: Becacina andina, Bécassine du puna, Punabekassine. Formerly classed as a race of *Gallinago paraguaiae*.

ID: 9 in (23 cm). Separated from the South

American Snipe by smaller size, yellow legs, and distribution in the Altiplano wetlands.
RANGE: Arica to Antofagasta; Peru, Bolivia and Argentina. High altitude bogs and streams; 6500–16,500 ft (2000–5000 m).

Fuegian Snipe
Becacina grande
Gallinago stricklandii
OTHER NAMES: Strickland's Snipe, Cordilleran Snipe, Porotera grande, Avecasina grande, Bécassine de Strickland, Kordillerenbekassine. Named for Hugh Strickland (1811–1853), an English naturalist, geologist and author of ornithological memoirs, who was killed by a train while examining the geological strata along the British rail tracks.
ID: 12–13 in (30–33 cm). Large, dark snipe of the Fuegian boggy forests and grasslands. Brownish-black back has four deep golden-ochre longitudinal stripes. Legs pinkish-grey. Seldom observed in the field. In the Cape Horn islands, it can been heard calling continually at night with a plaintive series of *cheep-cheep-cheep* notes or a louder *char-woo*. Nests at the edge of bogs. Clutch is two olive-buff eggs lightly marked with cinnamon blotches.
RANGE: Chiloé to Magallanes, including the Guaitecas and Chonos Islands; s Argentina and the Falklands. Inhabits the Patagonian steppe and muddy bogs in *Nothofagus* forest clearings; sea level to 2625 ft (0–800 m).

FAMILY THINOCORIDAE
SEEDSNIPES
This South American family comprises only four species, all of which occur in Chile. Seedsnipes are cryptically plumaged, and have plump bodies, long pointed wings, and short legs. They nest on the ground, laying four pyriform eggs per clutch. They are seed-eating birds with the characteristic zigzag flight of snipes—thus, the name seedsnipe.

Rufous-bellied Seedsnipe
Perdicita cordillerana
Attagis gayi
OTHER NAMES: Gay's Seedsnipe, Tortolón, Perdigón, Rotbauch-Höhenläufer, Attagis de Gay. Named after the French naturalist Claudio Gay (1800–1873) who made a vast collection of Chilean flora and fauna and was later made an honorary Chilean citizen and member of the University of Chile.
ID: 11–12 in (29–31 cm). Large ptarmigan-like seedsnipe of the High Andes. Upperparts brownish-grey, with black back feathers edged and lined with ivory and gold. Upper tail coverts pale rufous with black spotting. Throat pale ochre. Grey bill. Rufous breast feathers bear concentric arcs of black. Rest of underparts rufous to cinnamon. Shows pale cinnamon axillaries and underwing coverts in flight. Feeds on rocky slopes and valleys that are watered by melting snow. Nest is a ground scrape, always near water. Hunted locally.
RANGE: Discontinuous distribution in the High Andes from Arica to Aisén; also Bolivia, Argentina. Rocky slopes near the snowline; 8200–16,500 ft (2500–5000 m).

White-bellied Seedsnipe
Perdicita cordillerana austral
Attagis malouinus
OTHER NAMES: Toschti, Attagis de Magellan, Weissbauch-Höhenläufer.
ID: 10–11 in (26–29 cm). Upperparts sandy to rufous; feathers marked with black and rufous spots and lines. Throat and breast greyish to rufous and scalloped with black. Pure white abdomen. Bill is horn-colored with a black tip. Flies in a rapid, erratic manner when flushed, all the while calling *tuwhit-tuwhit-tuwhit*. Nests in the alpine moorland, laying a clutch of four mottled green eggs in a moss and lichen nest set on cushion plants *(Azorella, Bolax)*. Inhabits lowland steppe in winter where it forms small flocks of about fifteen individuals. Flocks tend to feed heavily on Red Crowberry *(Empetrum rubrum)*.
RANGE: Magallanes, Tierra del Fuego; also s Argentina, Staten Island and the Falklands. Alpine moorland to 6500 ft (2000 m) in austral summer; lowland steppe in winter.

Grey-breasted Seedsnipe
Perdicita cojón
Thinocorus orbignyianus
OTHER NAMES: D'Orbigny's Seedsnipe, Corral, Huancho, Puco-puco, Thinocore d'Orbigny, Graubrust-Höhenläufer. Named for French naturalist Alcide D'Orbigny who collected over 10,000 specimens of flora and fauna for the Museum of Paris while in South America between 1826 and 1833.
ID: 8–9.5 in (21–24 cm). Feathers of the back, nape and crown are brown, edged and lined with buff, black and ochre. White throat is encircled with black. Face, neck and breast of the MALE are dove-grey; a narrow black pectoral band divides the grey breast from the white underparts. FEMALE's breast is streaked with brown. Bill is yellowish with a dark tip. Forms small flocks that call to one another with a melodious cooing, *pόoko pόoko*. Nests (Nov, Jan) on semi-arid slopes near the snowline, laying two clutches of white to pinkish eggs. Descends to the foothill valleys in hard winters.
RANGE: Arica to Biobío, and in Magallanes; Argentina, Bolivia, Peru. Inhabits Andean bogs, puna wetlands and grassy riverbanks; 1650–16,500 ft (500–5000 m).

Least Seedsnipe, Perdicita
Thinocorus rumicivorus
OTHER NAMES: Pygmy Seedsnipe, Agachadera, Thinocore de Patagonie, Zwerghöhenläufer.
ID: 6.25–7.5 in (16–19 cm). Sparrow-sized version of the Grey-breasted Seedsnipe. The MALE's black throat margin and breastband are joined by a longitudinal black line, and the back feathers have a greyish appearance overall. The FEMALE's breast is streaked with brown. Gregarious. Forms flocks of 10 to 20 birds that nest in fairly close proximity to one another. Nest is a ground scrape lined with grass or dung that is used to cover the eggs when the parent is off the nest.
RANGE: Discontinuous distribution from Arica to Santiago and Aisén to Magallanes; also Uruguay, Argentina and the Falklands. Occupies marginal habitats along the sea coast, inland, and on the Puna; sea level to 13,000 ft (4000 m).
SUBSPECIES: PERDICITA COMÚN, *T. r. rumicivorus*, is resident on the arid and semi-arid coasts of nc Chile, and a breeding migrant on the Patagonian steppe of e Aisén and e Magallanes. PERDICITA DEL NORTE, *T. r. cuneicauda*, inhabits the arid desert coast and inland valleys of Arica and Tarapacá. PERDICITA BOLIVIANA, *T. r. bolivianus*, lives on the Puna in Arica and Tarapacá.

FAMILY ROSTRATULIDAE
PAINTED-SNIPES
These are reclusive wading birds of reedy marshes. They resemble snipes, but have a downturned bill with a slightly swollen tip. Females are more brightly plumaged and larger than males. Females are polyandrous, taking more than one mate and leaving the rearing of the young to the male.

South American Painted-Snipe
Becacina pintada
Nycticryphes semicollaris
OTHER NAMES: Weissflecken-Goldschnepfe, Rhynchée de Saint-Hilaire.
ID: 7.5–8.25 in (19–21 cm). Brown hood is adorned with a pale supercilium and black crown. When at rest, the white crescents at the sides of the breast appear to join gold-colored lateral lines down the back. Large white patches on the wing coverts. Underparts buffy. Downturned bill is greenish with a burgundy tip. Legs are yellow. Crouches in marsh vegetation when alarmed. Makes no call when flushed, but flies out in a strong and slightly zigzag pattern. Feeds on worms, mollusks, small invertebrates and some plant matter. Nests (Jul) on a small platform of reeds and grass set on swampy ground at the edge of a stream or open pond. Lays two, or exceptionally three, mottled brown and grey eggs. Hunted locally for food.
RANGE: Atacama to Los Lagos; also Brazil to Argentina. Lowland marshes and flooded fields; sea level to 1650 ft (0–500 m).

SNIPES, SEEDSNIPES AND PAINTED-SNIPES

South American Snipe
Becacina
Gallinago paraguaiae
Coquimbo–Magallanes
10–12 in (26–30 cm)

Fuegian Snipe
Becacina grande
Gallinago stricklandii
Los Lagos–Magallanes
12–13 in (30–33 cm)

South American Snipe

Puna Snipe
Becacina de la puna
Gallinago andina
Andes of Arica–Antofagasta
9 in (23 cm)

Fuegian Snipe

South American Painted-Snipe
Becacina pintada
Nycticryphes semicollaris
Atacama–Los Lagos
7.5–8.25 in (19–21 cm)

White-bellied Seedsnipe
Perdicita cordillerana austral
Attagis malouinus
Magallanes
10–11 in (25–29 cm)

Grey-breasted Seedsnipe
Perdicita cojón
Thinocorus orbignyianus
Arica–Biobío
Magallanes
8–9.5 in (21–24 cm)

Rufous-bellied Seedsnipe
Perdicita cordillerana
Attagis gayi
Arica–Aisén
11–12 in (29–31 cm)

Least Seedsnipe, Perdicita
Thinocorus rumicivorus
Arica–Santiago
Aisén–Magallanes
6.25–7.5 in (16–19 cm)

FAMILY STERCORARIIDAE
SKUAS AND JAEGERS

These medium to large brown seabirds are closely related to gulls and terns. They have long, pointed wings and stout, hooked bills. The legs are short and their webbed feet have strong claws. They feed on small mammals and birds, bird eggs, mollusks and carrion when on land. At sea, they feed on fish and other marine organisms, and often resort to pirating food from other seabirds, a behavior known as KLEPTOPARASITISM.

SKUAS: Skuas are large, stocky birds having a stout, hooked bill. They have brown plumage with a diagnostic triangle of white in the wings. They are large, ranging from 18–25 in (46–64 cm) and weighing up to 4 lb (1.8 kg). Skuas are omnivorous. They feed on marine prey, carrion and refuse floating on the sea surface. They also dive on fish and attend trawlers, and prey on seabirds, their chicks and eggs, small mammals and detritus when on land. The species that occur in Chilean waters nest in the polar and subantarctic zones of the Southern Hemisphere. They disperse northward in non-breeding season to spend the austral winter on the open ocean or offshore the continental coast.

Chilean Skua
Salteador chileno
Stercorarius chilensis
OTHER NAMES: Pájaro ladrón, Peuco del mar, Labbe du Chili, Chileskua.
ID: 21–23 in (53–59 cm). Upperparts are brownish-grey, with some gold and rufous speckles on the neck and back. Underparts and underwings are washed with cinnamon. White patch at base of primaries. Bill and legs are dark grey to black. Pirates food from gulls and cormorants, and also preys on their eggs and chicks. Known to seize goslings by the back of the neck, then fly up and drop them from a height of 40 ft (12 m). Breeds (Nov–Mar) in small colonies on the coast and inland in s Chile. Nests on peaty or boggy ground. Clutch is 2 to 3 mottled eggs, which are laid on a loose pile of grass and other plant matter.
RANGE: Mainly coastal from Arica to Magallanes and Islas Diego Ramírez; also Peru, Argentina and s Brazil. Nests south of 37°S latitude in Chile and Argentina, then disperses north along the Pacific and Atlantic coasts.

South Polar Skua
Salteador polar
Stercorarius maccormicki
OTHER NAMES: Labbe de McCormick, Antarktikskua.
ID: 20–22 in (50–55 cm). Smaller and thinner-billed than other skuas. Two main color morphs, with several intermediate phases. DARK MORPH (common on the Antarctic Peninsula) has dark brownish-grey upperparts, brown underparts, and faint golden hackles on the neck. LIGHT MORPH has dark brownish-grey upperparts, dove-grey underparts and head, and gold hackles on neck. All morphs have a white wing patch, black bill and black legs.

Breeds (Nov–Mar) along the Antarctic coast. Nests on the ground. Clutch is 2 to 4 greyish-brown, mottled eggs. Parents feed crustaceans, fish and squid to very young chicks, and later give them carrion and penguin eggs and young.

South Polar Skuas are great ocean wanderers when they are not nesting. A few years ago researcher David Neilson banded a chick on the Antarctic Peninsula in late February. The Danish ornithologist Finn Salmonsen recovered the young bird in Greenland in late July. The record flight of about 9000 mi (14,500 km) was, as Dr. David Parmelee wrote, "one heck of a flight for a baby skua."
RANGE: Circumpolar in coastal waters of the Antarctic in breeding season. Pelagic in non-breeding season, migrating well off the Chilean mainland coast. Adults undertake fairly limited northerly migrations. Juveniles regularly reach the North Atlantic and North Pacific, where they may remain for over a year.

Brown Skua, Salteador pardo
Stercorarius antarcticus lonnbergi
OTHER NAMES: Subantarctic Skua, Sea Hen, Sea Hawk, Labbe antarctique, Labbe brun, Antarktis Skua. *Catharacta*, an alternate skua genus, is Greek for a seabird that swoops down on its prey like an overwhelming torrent of water.
ID: 20–25 in (52–64 cm). Large, dark brown skua with a massive dark bill. Faint golden hackles in breeding season. White patch at base of primaries.

With the onset of austral spring, pairs establish and defend territories at penguin and seabird nesting colonies. They fly over nesting penguins in low-level flights until the general guard is down and it is easy to steal an egg. They dislodge adult penguins from the nest with sharp flying kicks, or peck and probe under them trying to reach the penguin chicks. Skuas are fearless and aggressive around their nest and will attack with unnerving defense tactics. They raise their wings, shriek and fly straight for the eyes. An attack can normally be warded off by waving a substitute target like a hat over one's head and then retreating. But at least one biologist we heard of looked up too late and was knocked out cold by a skua. As he came to, his dazed indignation was sweetened with revenge. There was the skua, two feet away, on the ground and staggering away glassy-eyed.

RANGE: Pelagic throughout the Southern Ocean, wintering off the southern continents. Nests on the Antarctic Peninsula and offshore islands, South Georgia and Heard Island; circumpolar in the Subantarctic.

JAEGERS: Jaegers (pronounced *YAY-gurrs*) breed in the Arctic and migrate to the Southern Ocean. They are smaller than skuas and in breeding plumage have elongated central tail streamers, the shape of which is unique to each species. However, by the time jaegers reach Chilean waters the long tail streamers have been shed and replaced with shorter feathers, making separation of species difficult. They feed on marine organisms and also steal food from other seabirds, using powerful acrobatic flight to overtake their victims.

Parasitic Jaeger, Salteador chico
Stercorarius parasiticus
OTHER NAMES: Arctic Skua, Halcón de mar, Pájaro ladrón, Schmarotzerraubmöwe, Labbe parasite.
ID: 16.5 in (41 cm); 20 in (51 cm) with streamers. A small, slender jaeger with pointed central tail feathers. Seen in non-breeding plumage in Chile. PALE NON-BREEDING ADULT has a brown back, dark cap, cream-colored face, neck and belly, and a faint dark neckband; white patch at base of primaries. INTERMEDIATE and DARK PLUMAGED ADULTS have dusky brown to brownish-black underparts. JUVENILES are cinnamon brown to chocolate overall; the central tail feathers are inconspicuous. Flies with great speed and dexterity, twisting and turning as it pirates food from South American terns, Franklin's gulls and brown-hooded gulls.
RANGE: Pelagic and coastal off the entire Chilean coast (Nov–Mar); fairly common between Valparaíso and Chiloé, especially in bays and harbors. Breeds in the Arctic and migrates down both coastlines of South America.

Pomarine Jaeger, Salteador pomarino
Stercorarius pomarinus
OTHER NAMES: Halcón de mar, Spatelraubmöwe, Labbe pomarin.
ID: 18.5 in (47 cm), or 23 in (58 cm) with streamers. Stocky and barrel-chested jaeger appears in non-breeding plumage in Chile. Central tail feathers are elongated, spoon-tipped and twisted 90 degrees. Wings are broad. Head is large and rounded, with a heavy bill that is pale at the base and black at the tip. PALE NON-BREEDING ADULT is dark brown with a cream-colored neck and belly; underparts are heavily barred; extensive dark cap contrasts with pale base of bill. Dark adults are uncommon. JUVENILES are

brown to dark brown, with strongly barred undertail coverts and a two-toned bill. Flight is powerful and less acrobatic than the Parasitic's as it pirates food from gulls, shearwaters and other large seabirds.

RANGE: Uncommon pelagic (late Oct–Apr) off the n Chile coast. Breeds in the Arctic; migrates along the South America coasts.

Long-tailed Jaeger
Salteador de cola largo
Stercorarius longicaudus

OTHER NAMES: Salteador chico, Labbe à longue queue, Falkenraubmöwe.

ID: 15 in (38 cm), or 23 in (58 cm) with long, pointed streamers. Central tail feathers are shorter in NON-BREEDING PLUMAGE, but still extend beyond the other tail feathers. Non-breeding adults have a light brown back, dark cap, creamy neck and underparts, with an indistinct pectoral band. Underwing is uniformly dark. JUVENILES range from pale grey to greyish-brown. Underwing and tail coverts are barred white. Buoyant flight.

RANGE: Rare to uncommon pelagic off n Chile; seen most often at sea between Valparaíso and Juan Fernández. Breeds in the Arctic; migrates south over the open ocean and well offshore.

FAMILY LARIDAE: SUBFAMILY LARINAE

GULLS

Gulls are mid-sized birds with rounded wings, fairly long legs, and stout bills that turn downward at the tip to form a hook. Most gulls inhabit seacoasts and estuaries. A few species are pelagic, spending most of their life foraging on the open ocean. Some gull species live around inland lakes and ponds, and the unique Grey Gull nests in the Atacama Desert.

Kelp Gull, Gaviota dominicana
Larus dominicanus

OTHER NAMES: Gaviota grande, Cau-Cau, Gaviota cocinera, Cleo, Dominikanermöwe, Goéland dominicain.

ID: 23 in (58 cm). White with black back and wings. Bill yellow with red spot on tip of lower mandible. Yellow legs. JUVENILES are a mottled white with a dark bill. This species is the only seagull that breeds in the Antarctic. Nests (Nov–Dec), laying a clutch of 2 to 3 greenish, spotted eggs. The chicks are well-camouflaged by cryptically patterned greyish-tan down, and hide in cracks and crevices around the colony. They are agile runners and also take to the water when threatened. Groups of adults defend the chicks, flying and calling from overhead until danger is past.

Bill Fraser, an American researcher on the Antarctic Peninsula, noted that the distribution of kelp gull breeding colonies in the Antarctic centers on small marine univalves called LIMPETS. Limpets, which are the main food for kelp gulls in this region, graze on algae growing on rocks in the intertidal zone. The gulls feed on them in the shallows as the limpets move to deeper water on the outgoing tide, when it is easier to pry them loose. The limpets are swallowed whole and regurgitated when the flesh is digested. Piles of limpet shells mark the places where these gulls breed.

RANGE: Coastal and inland. Arica to Magallanes; also Antarctica, the Falklands and South Georgia.

Dolphin Gull, Gaviota austral
Larus scoresbii

OTHER NAMES: Scoresby's Gull, Gaviotilla, Gaviota azulada, Goéland de Scoresby, Blutschnabelmöwe.

ID: 17–18 in (43–46 cm). A beautiful and easily identified gull, especially in adult plumage. Pearl grey head, neck and breast, blackish back, white tail, and rosy red bill and legs. Wings are edged in white. JUVENILES and NON-BREEDING ADULTS have a dark brown head, and the bill is rosy red to horn, tipped with black. Nests (Nov–Dec) on the ground near bodies of water, laying 2 olive-grey eggs on a mound of loose grass.

RANGE: Widespread but uncommon on the coast from Araucanía to Magallanes; also s Argentina and the Falklands.

Band-tailed Gull, Gaviota peruana
Larus belcheri

OTHER NAMES: Belcher's Gull, Simeon, Goéland Siméon, Schwanzbandmöwe.

ID: 20 in (51 cm). BREEDING ADULT has white head and underparts. Upperwings black. Tail white with a black terminal band. Bill yellow with a red tip. ADULT NON-BREEDING is similar except for brown head and pale yellow bill with a red and black tip. FIRST-YEAR BIRDS sport a brown head, mottled brown back and underparts, white tail with terminal dark band, and pale yellow bill with black tip. Preys on seabird chicks and eggs; also feeds on crabs and small fish. Does not usually attend ships. Nests on rocky islets and guano islandså.

RANGE: Common on the seacoast from Arica to Coquimbo; abundant in Peru.

Grey Gull, Gaviota garuma
Larus modestus

OTHER NAMES: Garuma, Mateo, Gaviotín gris, Goéland gris, Graumöwe.

ID: 18 in (46 cm). Mouse-grey plumage; dark wings with a white trim on the secondaries. Bill and legs black. BREEDING ADULT has a whitish head. NON-BREEDING ADULT and JUVENILE has a brown head. Nests inland (Nov–Jan) in the Atacama Desert in rocky areas where very few living plants or animals are able to survive. Nesting adults fly out to feed each day along the coast, which may be as far as 60 mi (100 km) away. Eggs and nestlings are left in the shelter of large rocks until the adults return at dusk with food.

RANGE: Common on the coast from Arica to Valdivia; uncommon south to the Taito Peninsula of Aisén; also Peru and Ecuador.

Brown-hooded Gull, Gaviota cahuil
Larus maculipennis
OTHER NAMES: Gaviota cagüil, Caulle, Gaviota de capucho café, Mouette de Patagonie, Patagonienmöwe.
ID: 15 in (38 cm). Pale grey above, with a white tail and body, and red bill and legs. Upperwing grey with a white wedge on the outer wings; white primaries visible when at rest. BREEDING ADULTS have a dark brown hood and white eye crescents. NON-BREEDERS have a dark ear patch and dark areas around the eye and the crown.

Note that the Franklin's gulls that visit Chile in summer show a partial dark hood whereas breeding brown-hooded gulls have a completely dark head. Non-breeding brown-hooded gulls are also difficult to separate from non-breeding Andean gulls that descend to the coast in winter; both species have white heads in that season.

The brown-hooded gulls have a buoyant flight with slow wingbeats. Their call is a tern-like *keh-keh-keh*. They typically feed along the coast, but also move inland to wet cultivated fields and pastures to feed on grubs. In the southern regions, they frequent abattoirs and freezing plants. They nest (Nov–Dec) colonially in marshes near the seacoast, laying 3 to 4 darkly spotted eggs on floating nests of aquatic vegetation.
RANGE: Arica to Magallanes, and s Atlantic coasts from 10°S in Brazil to Tierra del Fuego and the Falklands.

Andean Gull, Gaviota andina
Larus serranus
OTHER NAMES: Quiulla, Caulle, Chelli, Tiulla, Mouette des Andes, Andenmöwe.
ID: 19 in (48 cm). Pale grey above, white below. Wings are grey, with a white outer wedge that bears conspicuous white oval mirrors edged in black. Legs are black. BREEDING ADULTS have a black hood, white eye crescent, and dark red to black bill. JUVENILES and NON-BREEDERS have a white head and dark ear patch. Juvenile bill is red with a black tip. Preys on eggs and chicks of waterbirds. Breeds (Dec-Jan) around lakes in the High Andes. Lays 2 to 3 deep olive, mottled eggs on floating nests of aquatic plants built far out on the water.
RANGE: Arica to Los Lagos. Occupies the High Andes in summer; large numbers descend to the coast of n Chile in winter.

Franklin's Gull, Gaviota de Franklin
Larus pipixcan
OTHER NAMES: Caulle, Fardela, Mouette de Franklin, Präriemöwe.
ID: 13–15 in (38–43 cm). Occurs in NON-BREEDING PLUMAGE in Chile. Grey above, with a white tail and underbody that often bears a pinkish tint on the abdomen. Dark red bill and legs. Partial dark hood, with white eye crescents and whitish forehead and throat. Mantle and upperwing are grey, with a whitish band separating the grey from the black wing tips.
RANGE: Arica to Aisén. Common NON-BREEDING MIGRANT from boreal breeding grounds to coasts and inland lakes of Chile and Peru.

Swallow-tailed Gull
Gaviota de los Galápagos
Creagrus furcatus
OTHER NAMES: Mouette à queue fourchue, Gabelschwanzmöwe.
ID: 22–24 in (55–60 cm). This large gull breeds in the Galapagos and is pelagic in waters offshore Chile, especially in El Niño years. BREEDING ADULTS have a black head, with red eye crescents and a downturned black bill. White tail is deeply forked. Grey wings bear a large white triangle set off by a black outer wedge similar to Sabine's Gull. NON-BREEDERS have a white head with a black ear patch and a similar wing pattern.
RANGE: Irregular pelagic off the Chilean coast from Arica to Valparaíso.

Sabine's Gull, Gaviota de Sabine
Xema sabini
OTHER NAMES: Schwalbenmöwe, Mouette de Sabine.
ID: 14.5 in (36 cm). Seen in NON-BREEDING

PLUMAGE in Chile. White head, underbody and tail. The black bill sometimes has a yellow tip more typical of breeding plumage. The mantle and upperwing are grey, with a bold white triangle on the inner primaries and secondaries and a black outer wedge on the primaries.
RANGE: Pelagic and coastal migrant off Tarapacá and Antofagasta. Boreal breeder.

VAGRANT GULLS: LAUGHING GULL, GAVIOTA REIDORA, *Larus atricilla*. Several records of adult birds in Arica.

FAMILY LARIDAE: SUBFAMILY STERNINAE
TERNS
Terns are slender-bodied, with long pointed wings, forked tails and short legs. They have a buoyant, rapid flight. Some species make long distance migrations, flying from their Arctic breeding grounds to the Antarctic and back again within the same year. Terns feed mainly on small fishes, which are taken in shallow plunge dives.

Inca Tern, Gaviotín monja
Larosterna inca
OTHER NAMES: Monjita, Zarcillo, Sterne inca, Inkaseeschwalbe. Monja and monjita refer to the white facial plumes, which resemble the stiff white collars worn by nuns *(monjas)* of some religious orders.
ID: 16 in (41 cm). A striking tern. ADULT PLUMAGE is dark slate-grey to black overall, with red bill and red legs. Conspicuous white curling "moustache" extending from the gape to the side of the neck. JUVENILES are slate-grey, with a yellow-tipped, dark grey bill and short moustache. Flies with rapid wingbeats, producing a fluttering flight. Takes small fishes by plunge diving; also feeds on small scraps left by sea lions, gulls and pelicans. Nests in rock crevices, holes in guano mounds, burrows of diving-petrels and penguins, and inside of abandoned barges and boats.
RANGE: Rocky coasts off the Humboldt Current. Resident from Tarapacá to Maule; uncommon south to Chiloé; also Peru.

Peruvian Tern, Gaviotín chico
Sternula lorata
OTHER NAMES: Chirrichi, Chirrín, Churi-Churi, Corbinero, Sterne du Pérou, Peruseeschwalbe.
ID: 9 in (23 cm). Smallest of the Chilean terns. Back and tail are grey. Underparts are white. Black crown and hindneck. Bill yellow-orange with black tip. Legs dull yellow. JUVENILES lack the black crown. Call is a sweetly sounded *chirí–chirí*. Feeds on anchoveta, other small fishes and some krill. Nests (Sep–Dec) along the coast; occasionally nests a few miles inland in the n Chile desert. NEAR THREATENED.
RANGE: RARE on sandy beaches from Arica to Antofagasta and north along the arid littoral of Peru and Ecuador.

South American Tern, Gaviotín sudamericano
Sterna hirundinacea
OTHER NAMES: Chirro, Chibrillo, Chiliula, Gaviotilla, Terrecle, Sterne hirundinacée, Falklandseeschwalbe.
ID: 17 in (44 cm). Most common tern in Chile. Pearl grey back and upperwings. White underparts and tail. Crown and nape black in BREEDING PLUMAGE. Forecrown fades to white in NON-BREEDING PLUMAGE. Vermilion bill and legs. Deeply forked tail is longer than wings when at rest. Feeds in river mouths and estuaries, diving from some height above the water on small fish, crustaceans and aquatic insects. Nests colonially on coastal islands and islets. Breeds throughout the year in its northern range and in the warmer months from Chiloé south. A clutch of 2 to 3 faintly blotched, pale green to white eggs is laid on the ground in a bare scrape.
RANGE: Abundant coastal resident from Arica to Magallanes; also Falklands.

Snowy-crowned Tern, Gaviotín piquerito
Sterna trudeaui
OTHER NAMES: Trudeau's Tern, Chibrillo, Weissscheitel-Seeschwalbe, Sterne de Trudeau.
ID: 11–14 in (28–35 cm). Pearl grey mantle,

faintly mottled brown in winter. Whitish head, rump and underparts. Black eyeline. Bill yellow with subterminal black band. Yellow-orange legs. Feeds on coastal lakes and rivers, taking small, freshwater fishes in plunge dives. Breeds around lakes near the coast, reportedly laying eggs on small, floating nests made from aquatic plants.

RANGE: Uncommon from Atacama to Los Lagos, especially near Valdivia; Argentina, Uruguay, s Brazil. Around freshwater.

Antarctic Tern
Gaviotín antártico
Sterna vittata

OTHER NAMES: Sterne couronnée, Antarktikseeschwalbe.

ID: 16 in (41 cm). Mouse grey above, with a white rump and deeply forked tail. Paler grey below. Bill vermilion. Legs orange-red. Complete black cap in BREEDING PLUMAGE, with forecrown fading to white in austral winter. Lays two eggs (Nov–Feb) in a scrape or hollow lined with small pebbles.

The Arctic Tern, a summer migrant that appears in non-breeding plumage in Chile, can be separated from the breeding Antarctic Tern by its white forecrown.

RANGE: Antarctic Peninsula, South Georgia and subantarctic islands. Some birds winter in the South Atlantic and a few may reach the Cape Horn area in winter months.

Arctic Tern
Gaviotín ártico
Sterna paradisaea

OTHER NAMES: Sterne arctique, Küstenseeschwalbe.

ID: 13–15 in (33–38 cm). Boreal breeder that appears in NON-BREEDING PLUMAGE along the Chilean coast and in the pack ice of the Antarctic Peninsula in austral summer. Pearl grey above, white below. When at rest, the wingtips reach the tips of the deeply forked tail. Similar to the Antarctic Tern and South American Tern, but has an incomplete black breeding cap when in Chilean waters.

RANGE: Antarctic pack ice in austral summer. Uncommon pelagic migrant off the mainland Chilean coast; also the Falklands and South Georgia.

Common Tern
Gaviotín boreal
Sterna hirundo

OTHER NAMES: Sterne pierregarin, Flussseeschwalbe.

ID: 13–15 in (32–38 cm). Occurs in NON-BREEDING PLUMAGE in Chile. Grey back; white underparts. Grey upperwings have a dark wingbar. Crown white; nape black. Black eyeline. Black bill with some red at base. Dark orange to black legs.

RANGE: Uncommon migrant (Nov–Mar) to the coast from Arica to Valparaíso. Boreal breeder.

Elegant Tern
Gaviotín elegante
Sterna elegans

OTHER NAMES: Sterne élégante, Schmuckseeschwalbe.

ID: 17 in (44 cm). Occurs in NON-BREEDING PLUMAGE in Chile. Large, slender tern with a bright orange-yellow bill and a black, shaggy crest. Pearl-grey back. White underparts. Short, dark red to black legs.

RANGE: Arica to Chiloé. Common coastal migrant (Sep–Mar) from breeding grounds in the Gulf of California.

TROPICAL PACIFIC TERNS

Grey Noddy, Gaviotín de San Ambrosio
Procelsterna albivitta

OTHER NAMES: Pacific Grey Ternlet, Bluegrey Noddy, Tubi, Gaviotín grisáceo, Noddi gris, Graunoddi.

ID: 10–12 in (25–30 cm). Small, pale grey tern. Mantle and upperwings grey. Head, neck and underparts whitish-grey. Long notched tail. Dark eyering enclosed by a white crescent. Black bill and legs. Feeds mainly on krill. Nests (Jul–Oct) on rocky ledges of oceanic islands.

RANGE: Easter Island, Sala y Gómez, and San Félix y San Ambrosio. Records from the Juan Fernández Archipelago.

Brown Noddy
Gaviotín de San Félix
Anous stolidus
OTHER NAMES: Tuau, Noddi brun, Noddi.
ID: 17 in (42 cm). Dark brownish-grey, with a whitish crown. Long, wedge-shaped tail. Black bill. Legs black, with yellow-webbed feet. Appears entirely dark in flight. Nests (Dec–Mar) on rocky ledges and beaches.
RANGE: Easter Island, Sala y Gómez, San Félix. Pantropical.
RELATED SPECIES: BLACK NODDY, *Anous minutus*. One record at Sala y Gómez.

White (Fairy) Tern
Gaviotín blanco
Gygis alba
OTHER NAMES: Quía Quía, Gaviotín hada pascuense, Gygis blanche, Feenseeschwalbe.
ID: 12 in (30 cm). White overall, with a ring of black feathers around the eye. Black bill. Legs dark slate-blue. Deeply forked tail. Feeds on small fishes caught as they leap from the water, and also takes small crustaceans and squids. Makes no nest, but lays a single oblong egg on a bare branch or rock. Both parents alternate holding the egg between their legs throughout the entire incubation period. Chicks use their bill and strong claws to cling to their perch to avoid being dislodged by parent birds.
RANGE: Nests (Jul–Oct) on Easter Island and Sala y Gómez; rare or absent outside of nesting season. Widespread in Polynesia.

Sooty Tern, Gaviotín apizarrado
Onychoprion fuscatus
OTHER NAMES: Russseeschwalbe, Sterne fuligineuse.
ID: 17–18 in (43–45 cm). Black above, white below. Forehead white. Black bill and legs. Feeds on small fishes caught as they leap from the water. Rarely dives or swims.
RANGE: Nests (Dec–Feb) on Easter Island, Isla Sala y Gómez, and San Félix y San Ambrosio. Occasional at Juan Fernández. Pelagic in subtropical waters well offshore northern Chile. Vagrant in winter along the Chilean coast.

Grey-backed Tern
Gaviotín pascuense
Sterna lunata
OTHER NAMES: Manutara (Easter Island), Sterne à dos gris, Brillenseeschwalbe.
ID: 14–15 in (35–38 cm). Dark grey mantle, wings and tail. Black crown and eyeline. White forehead, face and underparts. Black bill and legs. Lays a single egg on a scrape in the sand. Separated from the Sooty Tern by its grey mantle.
RANGE: Easter Island (said to nest on Moto Nui); otherwise pelagic. Widespread near breeding islands in the tropical Pacific.

VAGRANT PACIFIC ISLAND TERNS: BRIDLED TERN, *Onychoprion anaethetus*. BLACK TERN, *Chlidonias niger*. SANDWICH TERN, *Sterna sandvicensis*.

FAMILY RYNCHOPIDAE
SKIMMERS

Black Skimmer, Rayador
Rynchops niger
OTHER NAMES: Pico de tijeras, Amerikanischer Scherenschnabel, Bec-en-ciseaux noir.
ID: 18 in (46 cm). Black above, white below, with long pointed wings, short forked tail, very short legs and tiny feet. The most distinctive feature is a large, oddly shaped red and black bill—the bill is flattened laterally and the upper mandible is much shorter than the lower one.

Skimmers feed by flying low over the water with the lower mandible just cutting the surface of the water. As soon as the bill strikes a small fish or other aquatic prey, the upper mandible closes and the prey is swallowed whole. The wake made by the bill's passage may attract small prey to the water surface, especially at dawn and dusk when the water surface is usually still. Skimmers are known to double back after one feeding pass and return to feed in the line of their own wake. Large groups of skimmers often roost on sandbanks of estuaries and rivers.
RANGE: Widespread but fairly uncommon summer visitor to coastal bays and estuaries from Arica to Chiloé.

COLUMBIFORMES: *Pigeons, Doves*
FAMILY COLUMBIDAE
PIGEONS AND DOVES
Pigeons and doves have small heads, short necks and short legs. The bill is soft at the base and hard at the tip, and some have a naked cere at the base of the upper mandible. The plumage often has metallic spots on the wings or a showy iridescent patch at the nape. These birds eat many different kinds of seeds and fruit; some also eat worms, snails and insects. They nest in trees or on the ground in open habitats and lay 1 to 3 white eggs.

Chilean Pigeon, Torcaza
Patagioenas (Columba) araucana
OTHER NAMES: Paloma, Araukaner-Taube, Pigeon du Chili, Kono.
ID: 15 in (37 cm). Head, neck, underparts, mantle and scapulars are vinous-chestnut. Narrow, white, half collar on nape just above an iridescent bronzy-green hindneck. Wing coverts and inner secondaries are dull grey to light bluish-grey. Primaries are blackish-grey with a narrow whitish edge. Tail dark grey with black subterminal band. Orange eyes, with a narrow yellow, pink or purple eyering. Black bill. Coral red legs. FEMALE and JUVENILE are duller overall.

Inhabits *Nothofagus* and *Araucaria* forest, where it usually perches silently in a tree. Infrequently calls an owl-like *hooo-HOO*. Feeds on fruit of trees and shrubs such as Peumo, Lingue, Boldo and Maqui. Flocks gather to feed on bamboo seeds during rare periods of flowering. Nests (Dec–Mar) in loose colonies in forests and bamboo thickets. Lays one egg in a flimsy nest of twigs. The Chilean Pigeon was hunted excessively in the past, and in 1954 the population was decimated by Newcastle disease. Populations have since recovered considerably. PROTECTED SPECIES in Chile.
RANGE: Atacama to the Taitao Peninsula in Aisén; also w Argentina. In lowland woodland and foothill forest; sea level to 4925 ft (0–1500 m).

Rock Dove, Paloma
Columba livia
OTHER NAMES: Felsentaube, Pigeon biset, Domestic Pigeon, Feral Pigeon.
ID: 14 in (36 cm). Variable plumage, often with an iridescent or grey body. White rump and black terminal tail band.
RANGE: Throughout Chile, primarily in urban areas. Introduced to Easter Island and Róbinson Crusoe (Masatierra), Juan Fernández Archipelago. Ranges worldwide.

Pacific Dove, Paloma de alas blancas
Zenaida meloda
OTHER NAMES: West Peruvian White-winged Dove, Paloma cantora, Weissflügel-Taube, Tourterelle à ailes blanches.
ID: 12.5 in (31 cm). Stocky, brownish-grey dove, with conspicuous white bands across wings. Male has an iridescent patch at the sides of the neck. Tail grey, with a black subterminal band and a white terminal band. Black bill. Red legs. Cobalt-blue bare skin around eye.
RANGE: Arica to Coquimbo; also Peru. In riverine woodland, oases, parks, orchards; sea level to 4925 ft (0–1500 m).

Eared Dove, Tórtola
Zenaida auriculata
OTHER NAMES: Maicoño, Cuculí, Ohrflecktaube, Tourterelle oreillarde.
ID: 10.25 in (26 cm). The most common dove of Chile. Rosy-grey overall, with black spots on wings. Small black ear mark. Iridescent patch on neck. Outer tail feathers tipped white. Black bill. Legs coral. Nest is a flimsy stick platform.
RANGE: Widespread in South America in coastal areas, valleys and mountains up to 8200 ft (2500 m).
SUBSPECIES: TÓRTOLA, *Z. a. auriculata*, is common and widespread from Arica to Magallanes. The smaller TÓRTOLA PERUANA, *Z. a. hypoleuca*, is found in ravines in Arica, Camarones, Chaca and Quillagua, and in the tamarugo groves at Salar de Pintados in Tarapacá.

PIGEONS AND DOVES

Picui Ground-Dove, Tortolita cuyana
Columbina picui
OTHER NAMES: Cuculí, Torito, Colombe picui, Picuitäubchen.
ID: 7 in (18 cm). Greyish-brown above, with a grey crown and mantle. Pale tan breast, with a pale buff throat, lower abdomen and undertail coverts. White band on greater wing coverts contrasts with dark primaries. Axillaries and leading edge of underwing are blackish. White outer tail feathers (seen in flight). Pale blue iris. Black bill. Short pink legs. Bobs head as it walks. Confiding. Nests (Sep–Jan) in gardens, orchards, on brush-covered slopes, along stream edges and irrigation ditches. Raises 2 to 3 broods each summer.
RANGE: Atacama to Araucanía, and occasionally to Valdívia; c Argentina. Lowland plains and valleys, farms, gardens, orchards, vineyards; sea level to 4925 ft (0–1500 m).

Croaking Ground-Dove Tortolita quiguagua
Columbina cruziana
OTHER NAMES: Perutäubchen, Colombe à bec jaune. Quiguagua, pronounced as a guttural *key-gwa-gwa*, mimics the frog-like, croaking call of this species.
ID: 6.25 in (16 cm). Pale brown to grey, with a deep carmine wingband. Black spots on wing. Edge of secondary coverts whitish, showing a faint wingband in flight. Axillaries and underside of tail dark grey. Bill yellow to bright orange at base, black at tip. Legs reddish. Makes a flimsy twig and grass nest (Nov–Jan) in orchard trees and bushes or on top of posts.
RANGE: Common in the valleys and oases of Arica and Tarapacá, and north through coastal Peru to Ecuador. Gardens, orchards and scrub; sea level to 4925 ft (0–1500 m).

Bare-faced Ground-Dove Tortolita boliviana
Metriopelia ceciliae
OTHER NAMES: Palomita, Cututa, Cascabelita, Nachtgesicht-Taubchen, Colombe de Cécile.
ID: 6.5 in (17 cm). Upperparts greyish-brown, spotted cream on rump and wing coverts. Bare skin around the eye is reddish-orange. Throat is white; breast light ochre; rest of underparts buffy. Outer tail feathers black with white tips. Rosy legs. Wings make a clapping sound in flight. Nests on cliffs and in stonewalls of towns and villages.
RANGE: Arica to Tarapacá; Peru, Bolivia, nw Argentina. In scrub, cultivated fields, pastures; 7000–13,000 ft (2000–4000 m).

Golden-spotted Ground-Dove Tortolita de la puna
Metriopelia aymara
OTHER NAMES: Culcuta, Palomita dorada, Aymara-Taubchen, Colombe aymara.
ID: 7 in (18 cm). Brownish-grey, with a pale wine tinge to the underparts. Wings spotted iridescent bronzy-gold. Primaries black with rufous at base. Legs pale pink. Copper-colored underwing coverts can be seen in flight. Tends to flock in grassy areas of the dry, open Puna.
RANGE: Uncommon in the High Andes from Arica-Parincota to Coquimbo; also Argentina, Bolivia and s Peru.

Black-winged Ground-Dove Tórtola cordillerana
Metriopelia melanoptera
OTHER NAMES: Culluca, Palomita de alas negras, Weissbugtaubchen, Colombe à ailes noires.
ID: 8–9 in (21–23 cm). Dull grey washed with olive. Black primaries; white patch at bend of wing. Tail black. Patch of orange-colored bare skin in front of the eye. Bill and legs are black.
RANGE: Locally common in the Andes from Arica–Parinacota to Aisén, and the coastal range of Coquimbo; also sw Colombia to s Argentina. In a wide variety of habitats; 3300–13,000 ft (1000–4000 m), at times descending to sea level.

VAGRANT: RUDDY GROUND-DOVE, TORTOLITA ROJIZA, *Columbina talpacoti*. Accidental in Malleco and Rancagua.

Burrowing Parrot Tricahue
Cyanoliseus patagonus
Atacama–Maule
17–19 in (43–49 cm)
Endemic subspecies

Slender-billed Parakeet Choroy
Enicognathus leptorhynchus
Maule–Aisén
16–17 in (41–44 cm)
Endemic

Austral Parakeet Cachaña
Enicognathus ferrugineus
Santiago–Magallanes
14 in (35 cm)

Monk Parakeet, Cotorra
Myopsitta monachus
Introduced to Santiago
13 in (33 cm)

Mountain Parakeet Perico cordillerano
Psilopsiagon aurifrons
Tarapacá–Antofagasta, Santiago
7.25 in (18.5 cm)
High Andes

PSITTACIFORMES: *Parrots*

FAMILY PSITTACIDAE

PARROTS

The parrots that occur in Chile have glossy green plumage often brightened by patches of bright red and yellow. The head is large and the neck short. They have a bare, fleshy cere and a muscular, thumb-like tongue. These birds clamber along branches with great agility, aided by their hooked bills and zygodactylous feet that have two toes directed forward and two aft. They feed on fruit, seeds, nuts, flowers, and sometimes insects and small lizards. They nest in tree holes or in burrows dug into cliff faces.

Burrowing Parrot
Tricahue

Cyanoliseus patagonus byroni
OTHER NAMES: Patagonian Conure, Tricau, Loro barranquero, Grosser Felsensittich, Conure de Patagonie.

ID: 17–19 in (43–49 cm). Upperparts and long tail dark olive-green; rump yellow. Head olive-brown with grey forecrown and white around the eye. White breast band. Abdomen yellow, with streak of red on belly. Blue primaries. Bill dark grey. Yellow legs and pale red feet. Forms gregarious, noisy flocks of 8 to 40 birds that clamber about trees and bushes. Feeds on seeds, berries, nuts, fruits and other vegetable matter, including grain and corn. Roosts in tall trees, nesting burrows, and occasionally on telephone lines near towns. Excavates nesting galleries up to 10 ft (3 m) long in sandstone or limestone cliffs. The parrots fly into the tunnels at full speed, folding their wings back at the last second. The clutch is 2 to 3 eggs. Extinct in much of former range due to trapping for the pet trade and persecution as pests. Chilean populations are estimated at 4000 birds in 12 colonies. **ENDANGERED.**

RANGE: ENDEMIC SUBSPECIES. Discontinuous distribution from Atacama to Maule; in matorral, wooded ravines and agricultural land near nesting cliffs; to 4925 ft (1500 m).

Austral Parakeet
Cachaña
Enicognathus ferrugineus
OTHER NAMES: Austral Conure, Emerald Parakeet, Catita chica, Catita austral, Smaragdsittich, Conure magellanique.
ID: 14 in (36 cm). Dull green overall with metallic-blue sheen on wings. Feathers of crown and upper back spotted with black. Forehead and lores dull red. Red patch on center of abdomen. Tail is reddish-brown faintly tipped with green. Small dark bill. Forms small flocks that forage together in trees and bushes, feeding on seeds, fruit, berries and buds; also forages on the ground on dandelions, grass seeds, roots and bulbous plants. Nests (Dec) in dead tree cavities, or builds a nest of sticks on branches if tree holes are not available. Clutch is 4 to 8 eggs.
RANGE: Santiago to Magallanes. In forests, open woodland and cultivated fields; sea level to 3600 ft (0–1200 m).
SUBSPECIES: CATITA AUSTRAL, *E. f. ferrugineus*, occurs from the Strait of Magellan to Tierra del Fuego, and in s Argentina. The smaller, darker CATITA CHICA, *E. f. minor*, ranges from O'Higgins to Aisén, and in sw Argentina on the e Andean slopes.

Slender-billed Parakeet
Choroy
Enicognathus leptorhynchus
OTHER NAMES: Chilean Conure, Slender-billed Conure, Slight-billed Parakeet, Langschnabelsittich, Conure à long bec.
ID: 16–17 in (41–44 cm). Dark green, with most feathers edged in brown. Forehead, lores, ocular area and abdomen reddish. Primary coverts bluish-green. Tail brownish-red, narrowly tipped with green. Long, slender, pointed upper mandible. Feeds on seeds of wild and cultivated plants such as thistle, corn and wheat, and especially the nuts of Araucaria cones, which it opens with its specialized beak. Remains in large, noisy flocks throughout the year. Migrates seasonally between altitudes and sites. Nests (Nov–Dec) in holes in forest trees sited in ravines or on steep slopes. Clutch is 5 to 6 eggs. Populations have declined drastically due to clearing of forests, excessive hunting and severe outbreaks of Newcastle disease. ENDANGERED.
RANGE: ENDEMIC. Maule to Aisén, including Isla Mocha and Nahuelbuta. In *Araucaria* forests and open or cultivated land; sea level to 6700 ft (0–2000 m).

Mountain Parakeet
Perico cordillerano
Bolborhynchus aurifrons
OTHER NAMES: Golden-fronted Parakeet, Red-billed Parakeet, Margarite's Parakeet, Zitronensittich, Toui à bandeau jaune.
ID: 7.25 in (18.5 cm). Pale green overall, with blue or yellow wash on throat, breast, abdomen and undertail. Wings blue. Tail blue-green. Faint yellow border to forehead. Bill pink or light horn, depending on subspecies. Flesh-colored legs. Forms small flocks of 10 to 30 birds outside of breeding season. Groups wander randomly or make seasonal migrations between locales and latitudes. Feeds on ground in shrub habitat, eating fallen berries and fruit, seeds, buds and other plant material. Sharp call in flight; call otherwise soft and high-pitched. Flight swift and direct. Nests (Oct–Dec) in holes in banks and escarpments.
RANGE: High Andes; Arica-Parinacota to Antofagasta and outside Santiago; sw Peru, w Bolivia and nw Argentina; 8300–11,400 ft (2500–4500 m).
SUBSPECIES: RED-BILLED PARAKEET, PERICO CORDILLERANO, *B. a. rubrirostris*, is found in the Andes outside Santiago, and on eastern slopes of the Andes in Argentina. MARGARITE'S PARAKEET, PERICO CORDILLERANO DEL NORTE, *B. a. margaritae*, ranges from Arica to Antofagasta; it has a conspicuous yellow forehead and yellowish underparts.

Monk Parakeet
Cotorra
Myiopsitta monachus
ID: 13 in (33 cm). Green upperparts, with a grey forehead, throat and breast. Abdomen and undertail coverts yellowish. Long pointed tail. Yellow bill. Flocks readily and builds large communal nests of sticks and twigs on telephone poles and in trees.
RANGE: Escaped cagebird that has established itself around Santiago and recently recorded in Copiapó and Puerto Montt.

Groove-billed Ani
Matacaballos

CUCULIFORMES: Cuckoos
FAMILY CUCULIDAE
CUCKOOS AND ANIS
Groove-billed Ani, Matacaballos
Crotophaga sulcirostris
OTHER NAMES: Riefenschnabel-Ani, Ani à bec cannelé.
ID: 12.5 in (32 cm). Completely black, with a very long tail. Prominent bill is arched, stout and strongly grooved. Prefers weedy fields around livestock. Call is a repeated high-pitched whistle, *PEE-huey*.
RANGE: Restricted to oasis valleys in Arica, Pica and the Quebrada of Tarapacá, with a stray recorded at Peine, se of the Salar de Atacama. Widespread range from s USA to South America.
VAGRANT: DARK-BILLED CUCKOO, CUCLILLO DE PICO NEGRO, *Coccyzus melacoryphus*. Records from the Lluta and Azapa Valleys near Arica.

STRIGIFORMES: Owls
OWLS
Owls have keen sight and hearing and have extremely soft plumage. They have forward directed eyes set in a rounded facial disk, short and strongly curved bills, and short toes with the outer one being reversible. Most are nocturnal hunters. Owls lay round white eggs and most owls nest and roost in trees.

FAMILY TYTONIDAE
BARN OWL
Barn owls are found on every continent except Antarctica. These nocturnal hunters have large heads with forward-facing eyes set in a heart-shaped facial disk.

Barn Owl, Lechuza
Tyto alba
OTHER NAMES: Schleiereule, Effraie des clochers, Cara de mono ("Monkeyface"), Lechuza de los campanarios.
ID: 13–14 in (34–36 cm). Heart-shaped, white facial disk edged with warm brown. Dark eyes. Upperparts are light tawny to blackish-brown with pale spots. Underparts white to dark tawny with darker spots. Primaries and tail barred tawny and black. Short, curved bill with a cere at the base. Feeds mainly on rodents, but will occasionally take other small mammals, reptiles, amphibians and insects. Nocturnal, seeking shelter in tree holes, barns and abandoned buildings by day. When alarmed, shakes the head from side to side while making shrill hisses, whistles and clicking noises. Nests in tree holes, buildings and shallow caves, where it lays 3 to 11 glossy white eggs.
RANGE: Resident in a wide variety of habitats from Arica to Isla Navarino in Magallanes. Distributed worldwide.

FAMILY STRIGIDAE
OWLS
Most owls in the family Strigidae are nocturnal or crepuscular and nest in trees. The Burrowing Owl is an exception—it is diurnal and lays its eggs in underground burrows.

Magellanic Horned Owl, Tucúquere
Bubo magellanicus
OTHER NAMES: Virginiauhu, Grand-duc d'Amérique. Tucúquere is the Chilean approximation of this owl's deep, hollow hooting call, *who-WHOO-kehray*.
ID: 18 in (45 cm). Distinguished by its large size and prominent ear tufts. Overall color greyish-chestnut to pale grey, mottled with darker grey on back and finely barred with tan and black on the chest. White patch at throat. Occupies a wide variety of habitats including Puna, woodland, watered ravines, matorral, agricultural land and Patagonian steppe. Nocturnal. Feeds on rabbits, rats, other small mammals and sometimes birds. Nests in caves or deep fissures in the Andes; nests (Oct) in tall trees in the central regions and in tree holes in the southern rainforests. Clutch is 2 to 3 eggs.
RANGE: Arica–Parinacota to Magallanes; generally restricted to the High Andes in the north, but much more widespread in the south; also Argentina.

Short-eared Owl, Nuco
Asio flammeus
OTHER NAMES: Sumpfohreule, Hibou des marais, Lechuzón de los campos.
ID: 16 in (42 cm). Upperparts dark brown and cream; buffy patch on upperwing is diagnostic in flight. Underparts buff to cream, with dark chestnut longitudinal streaks. White throat. Legs and feet pale yellow. Black ring around eyes; iris yellow. Barely visible, tufted "ears" are set on top of the head. Nocturnal, but sometimes seen in low, slow flight over marshland on overcast days. Feeds on small mammals, birds, reptiles and amphibians. Roosts and nests (Oct–Jan) on the ground in long grass, rushes or reeds. Clutch is 5 to 7 dull white, round eggs.
RANGE: Vallenar, Atacama, to Tierra del Fuego. Resident on Masatierra (Róbinson Crusoe) in Juan Fernández. Distributed worldwide. Found in low swampy ground, lowland marshes, and tail grass near ponds.

Austral Pygmy-Owl, Chuncho
Glaucidium nanum
OTHER NAMES: Chevêchette australe, Araukanerkauz, Caburé.
ID: 20 cm (7.9 in). Small, with a large head, yellow eyes, yellowish-green bill and long tail. Two black "eye spots" on the back of the nape are edged with white. **THREE COLOR MORPHS:** brown, rufous (rare), and grey (uncommon). Chest is streaked with ivory in all morphs. Separated from the very similar Peruvian Pygmy-Owl by its range and streaked rather than spotted crown.

Feeds on small mammals, birds, reptiles and insects, sometimes taking prey larger than itself with its sharp, powerful talons. Nocturnal. Small size makes this owl difficult to spot. Most often located by shrill, half screeching call emitted when setting out to hunt at dusk. In breeding season (Aug–Oct) males sing their nuptial call—an incessant series of metallic *tooks*. Nest is situated in a hole in a tree branch or in a fairly deep hole in an earthen bank. Clutch is 3 to 5 opaque white eggs.
RANGE: Atacama to Magallanes; Argentina. City parks, *Nothofagus* forest, matorral, farmland; sea level to 6500 ft (0–2000 m).
RELATED SPECIES: PERUVIAN PYGMY-OWL, CHUNCO DEL NORTE, *Glaucidium peruanum*, is separated from the Austral Pygmy-Owl by its grey plumage, white-spotted crown, larger eyes, and shorter tail. Lives in desert oases and Andean valleys of Arica, Tarapacá and n Antofagasta; also Peru and Bolivia.

Rufous-legged Owl, Concón
Strix rufipes
OTHER NAMES: Red-legged Owl, Lechuza bataraz, Rollusskauz, Chouette masquée.
ID: 13–15 in (34–38 cm). Dark-eyed owl of dense woods and rainforest. Large dark head, with a rufous to pale grey ocular disk, white eyebrows and white moustache. Back and wings are dark brown with buffy transverse barring. Underparts are lighter; abdomen barred with cream. Pale rufous stockings and toes. Sonorous, hooting call.

OWLS AND NIGHTJARS 235

Barn Owl, Lechuza
Tyto alba
Arica–Magallanes
13–14 in (34–36 cm)

Short-eared Owl, Nuco
Asio flammeus
Atacama–Magallanes
16 in (42 cm)

**Magellanic Horned Owl
Tucúquere**
Bubo magellanicus
Arica–Magallanes
18 in (45 cm)

**Rufous-legged Owl
Concón**
Strix rufipes
Coquimbo–Magallanes
13–15 in (34–38 cm)
Forests

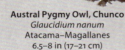

Austral Pygmy Owl, Chunco
Glaucidium nanum
Atacama–Magallanes
6.5–8 in (17–21 cm)

**Band-winged Nightjar
Gallina ciega**
Caprimulgus longirostris
Arica–Aisén
7.5–10.5 in (20–27 cm)

Burrowing Owl, Pequén
Athene cunicularia
Arica–Los Lagos
7–10 in (18–26 cm)

RANGE: Valparaíso to Tierra del Fuego. Uncommon in the northern part of its range; common south of Río Biobío; also Argentina, Peru and the Falklands. Lives in tall, closed canopy *Nothofagus* forest and sometimes in old pine plantations.

SUBSPECIES: CONCÓN, *Strix rufipes rufipes* occurs from Valparaíso to Magallanes. The slightly smaller CONCÓN DE CHILOÉ, *S. r. sanborni*, occurs only on Isla Chiloé.

Burrowing Owl, Pequén
Athene cunicularia

OTHER NAMES: Kanincheneule, Chevêche des terriers, Lechuza de las vizcacheras, Lechuza de los arenales.

ID: 7–10 in (18–26 cm). Long legs. Upperparts brown with creamy spots. Breast, abdomen, and flanks creamy-white with brown bars. Stockings and feathered tarsi light brown. Pale yellow bill. Diurnal and highly terrestrial. Lives year round in rabbit or rodent burrows and is often seen at its burrow entrance. Also perches on rocky outcrops, fence posts or low tree branches. Feeds mainly on small rodents, beetles and other small invertebrates. Call is a scolding *chaak-weet, weet-wit*, or less frequently a plaintive *co-co-róo*. Nests (Oct–Dec) in its roosting burrow. Clutch is 4 to 8 eggs.

RANGE: Arica to Los Lagos, and across s South America. Sandy coastal areas, grasslands, cultivation and airport runways.

CAPRIMUGLIFORMES: Nightjars
FAMILY CAPRIMULGIDAE

NIGHTJARS AND NIGHTHAWKS

These nocturnal or crepuscular birds feed on insects captured in flight. They have cryptic plumage, large eyes and short legs. They have a short bill with a wide base and prominent rictal bristles. They typically roost and nest on the ground. The clutch is 1 to 2 cream-colored eggs.

Band-winged Nightjar, Gallina ciega
Caprimulgus longirostris

OTHER NAMES: Plastilla, Engoulevent à miroir, Spiegelnactschwalbe, Ataja-caminos (Road-blocker). The latter refers to how this bird rests along the road at night, its eyes reflecting the lights of oncoming cars.

ID: 7.5–10.5 in (20–27 cm). Cryptic plumage in various shades of brown and grey, with a rufous patch on the nape and a narrow white collar on the male. Easily identified in flight by the white wingband of the MALE and buff wingband of the FEMALE.

RANGE: Tarapacá to Aisén and Patagonia. Matorral, desert oases, woodland, forest edge, grassland and cultivated fields; sea level to 16,500 ft (0–3800 m).

SUBSPECIES: GALLINA CIEGA, *C. l. bifasciatus*, ranges from Paposo Gorge, Antofagasta, to the Guaitecas Islands and Patagonia. The smaller, darker GALLINA CIEGA DE LA PUNA, *C.l. atripunctatus*, lives on the Puna of Arica, Tarapacá and Antofagasta. The pale plumaged GALLINA CIEGA DE TARAPACÁ, *C. l. decussatus*, is found in Azapa near Arica and in Quillagua, Antofagasta.

VAGRANT: LESSER NIGHTHAWK, GALLINA CIEGA PERUANA, *Chordeiles acutipennis*, has been recorded near Arica and in Antofagasta. Very similar to the Band-winged Nighjar. Best separated by its longer, pointed wings.

APODIFORMES: Swifts
FAMILY APODIDAE

SWIFTS

Swifts are highly aerial birds most often seen in rapid flight high in the sky where they hunt for insects. They have bullet-shaped bodies with long, narrow wings. The bill is short and wide at the base. Legs are extremely short. They lay 1 to 6 white eggs in nests made of plant material and saliva. The superficial resemblance to swallows is a result of convergent evolution.

Andean Swift, Vencejo chico
Aeronautes andecolus

OTHER NAMES: Andensegler, Martinet des Andes.

ID: 5.1 in (13 cm). Upperparts brown with white nape and white rump. Underparts whitish with dusky band across chest.

RANGE: Uncommon resident in the Andes of n Chile; occasional on the coast at Arica,

SWIFTS AND HUMMINGBIRDS

Andean Swift
Aeronautes andecolus
Arica–Tarapacá
5.1 in (13 cm)

Chimney Swift
Chaetura pelagica
Arica–Atacama
5.5 in (14 cm)
Rare

Camarones Gorge and Chusmiza; also in Andes of s Peru, w Bolivia and w Argentina; 1650–16,125 ft (500–4000 m).

Chimney Swift, Vencejo de chimenea
Chaetura pelagica
OTHER NAMES: Schornsleinsegler, Martinet ramoneur.
ID: 5.5 in (14 cm). Upperparts dark sooty-brown. Underparts are pale brown. Long, narrow wings are dark sooty-grey. Square tail has rigid spines formed by feather shafts projecting from tail margin. Seen in greatest numbers at dawn and dusk flying over cultivated fields.
RANGE: RARE SUMMER MIGRANT (Nov–Feb) to the Lluta Valley near Arica and possibly to Calama in Antofagasta and Vallenar in Atacama. Boreal breeder.

FAMILY TROCHILIDAE
HUMMINGBIRDS
Hummingbirds are found only in the Americas. Most have iridescent plumage, and adult males have a bright, iridescent crown and gorget (throat patch). Hummers beat their wings at great speed as they hover in front of a flower. They can fly backward and forward, and up and down, changing direction easily and extremely rapidly. They lay one to two tiny white eggs in a very small, cup-shaped nest. Some hummingbirds enter a state of torpor—a deep sleep with reduced organic functions—when they are subjected to very low temperatures.

Andean Hillstar
Picaflor de la puna
Oreotrochilus estella
OTHER NAMES: Picaflor cordillerano del norte, Anden-Kolibri, Colibri estelle.
ID: 5.1 in (13 cm). MALE has an emerald green throat that is bordered by a black band and edged in iridescent-blue. Chest and abdomen are white, with a chestnut belly stripe. FEMALE is olive-grey on the back, greyish below, with fine speckling on the throat. Central tail feathers dark green; outer tail feathers edged white. Slightly decurved black bill. The Andean Hillstar is one of the high elevation species that enter a state of torpor every night, thus escaping the effects of low night temperatures on the Puna. Nests (Nov–Dec) on a vertical rock face located under an overhang or in a shallow cave. Secures its nest to the rock with a sticky saliva.
RANGE: High Andes of Arica, Tarapacá and Antofagasta. Common in ravines, around villages and in the pre-Puna shrub zone; 10,000–16,500 ft (3500–5000 m).

White-sided Hillstar
Picaflor cordillerano
Oreotrochilus leucopleurus
OTHER NAMES: Colibri à flancs blancs, Weissllanken-Kolibri.
ID: 5.1 in (13 cm). MALE has an emerald green throat, which is bordered by a black band and edged iridescent-blue. Chest and abdomen are snow white with an iridescent, dark blue belly stripe. The back is a dull, greenish-brown. FEMALE is very difficult to separate from the Andean Hillstar female. MIGRATORY through much of its range; most birds leave Chile in March and return from their probable wintering grounds in Argentina in September. Nests (Nov–Dec) on a vertical rock face located under an overhang; secures its nest to the rock with a sticky saliva.
RANGE: Seasonal in the Andes of central and southern Chile from Antofagasta to Aisén; w Argentina. Occurs in dry, rocky ravines;

5000–12,000 feet (1500–3500 m); some birds descend to 1650 ft (500 m) in winter months.

Sparkling Violetear, Picaflor azul
Colibri corruscans
OTHER NAMES: Colibri azul, Veilchenohr-Kolibri, Colibri anaïs.
ID: 5 in (13 cm). Iridescent green, with a narrow, shining, violet-blue band from chin to ear coverts. Large violet-blue patch on center of belly. Strong, fairly straight bill. Conspicuous dark subterminal tail band.
RANGE: Arica to Tarapacá; w Argentina. In eucalyptus around Andean villages at elevations around 10,000 ft (3000 m).

Giant Hummingbird, Picaflor gigante
Patagonas gigas
OTHER NAMES: Picaflor grande, Píngara, Rieser-Kolibri, Colibri géant.
ID: 8–9 in (21–24 cm). Largest hummingbird. Back olive-brown with a cream-colored rump. The MALE's underparts are rufous (brick-red in northern subspecies). FEMALE's underparts are brown. Hovers in front of flowers with slow wingbeats, then darts off in undulating flight, sounding a sharp, high-pitched note. Frequents open hillsides and uncultivated fields, especially those with agave, cacti and thistle plants. Builds a very small nest (Nov–Dec) for this large a hummer, placing it on branches of low trees and shrubs.
RANGE: Arica to Los Lagos.
SUBSPECIES: PICAFLOR GIGANTE DEL NORTE, *P. g. peruviana*, is resident at Putre in Arica-Parinacota, at 10,000 ft (3000 m) elevation; also Ecuador, Peru, Bolivia, nw Argentina. PICAFLOR GIGANTE, *P. g. gigas*, is a breeding summer migrant seen from s Atacama to Araucanía and occasionally to Chiloé; sea level to 12,500 ft (0–3800 m)

Peruvian Sheartail, Picaflor de Cora
Thaumastura cora
OTHER NAMES: Cora-Kolibri, Colibri cora.
ID: 5–6 in (13–16 cm), including male's tail. MALE is metallic-green, with an iridescent rosy-violet throat patch, short bill and extremely long tail. White breast. Grey abdomen, with green on flanks. FEMALE is smaller, with white underparts and a short, white-tipped tail.
RANGE: Oases, wooded ravines and gardens of Azapa and Lluta Valleys near Arica; also Peru; sea level to 1300 ft (0–400 m).

Chilean Woodstar, Picaflor de Arica
Eulidia yarrellii
OTHER NAMES: Yarrel-Kolibri, Colibri d'Arica.
ID: 3 in (8 cm). The smallest hummingbird in Chile. MALE upperparts are iridescent olive-green. Purple-red throat patch. White breast. Abdomen grey, with green or buff on flanks. Long forked tail, often held in a crossed-scissor position. FEMALE is smaller, with white underparts, buffy flanks, and short, white-tipped tail. Populations are in decline for unknown reasons. ENDANGERED.
RANGE: Presently thought to be ENDEMIC to Chile; formerly found in s Peru. Found in gardens and lowland valleys around Arica; occasional in coastal Antofagasta; sea level to 5000 ft (0–1500 m).

Oasis Hummingbird, Picaflor del norte
Rhodopis vesper
OTHER NAMES: Pica-la-rosa, Colibri vesper, Atacama-Kolibri.
ID: 5.3 in (13.5 cm). Upperparts of MALE are metallic olive-green. Rufous rump. Throat rosy-red with amethyst overtones and a metallic-blue border. Underparts white. Long, decurved bill. Forked tail; tips of tail feathers cross when bird is perched. FEMALE lacks iridescent throat and long tail; outer tail feathers have blue-black subterminal band and while tips. Underparts buff.
RANGE: Arica to Atacama; s Peru; in oases, ravines, tamarugo groves, agricultural land and towns; sea level to 5000 ft (0–1500 m).
SUBSPECIES: The PICAFLOR DEL NORTE, *R. v. vesper*, ranges from Arica to Antofagasta. It is said to be common in the citrus groves of Pica. It suspends its bag-like nest from an

HUMMINGBIRDS 239

Sparkling Violetear
Picaflor azul
Colibri coruscans
Arica
5 in (13 cm)

Eucalyptus sp.

Juan Fernández Firecrown
Picaflor de Juan Fernández
Sephanoides fernandensis
Juan Fernández
3.5–4 in (9–11 cm)

Green-backed Firecrown feeding on Tiaque (*Desfontainea spinosa*)

Green-backed Firecrown
Picaflor chico
Sephanoides sephanoides
Atacama–Magallanes
Juan Fernández
3.5–4 in (9–11 cm)

White-sided Hillstar
Picaflor cordillerano
Oreotrochilus leucopleurus
Antofagasta–Aisén
5.1 in (13 cm)

Andean Hillstar
Picaflor de la puna
Oreotrochilus estella
Arica–Antofagasta
5.1 in (13 cm)

Chilean Woodstar
Picaflor de Arica
Eulidia yarrellii
Arica–Antofagasta
3 in (8 cm)

Oasis Hummingbird
Picaflor del norte
Rhodopis vesper
Arica–Atacama
5.3 in (13.5 cm)

Agave sp.

Giant Hummingbird
Picaflor gigante
Patagonas gigas
Arica–Los Lagos
8–9 in (21–24 cm)

Peruvian Sheartail
Picaflor de Cora
Thaumastura cora
Arica
5–6 in (13–16 cm),
including tail

overhanging branch of Pacay *(Inga feuillei)*, a leguminous tree planted for its edible, sweet-pulped, contorted pods. The smaller PICAFLOR DE ATACAMA, *R. v. atacamensis*, occurs at Chañaral in Atacama and at Copiapó in Coquimbo.

Green-backed Firecrown, Picaflor chico
Sephanoides sephanoides
OTHER NAMES: Pingarita, Pinda, Chile-Kolibri, Colibri du Chili.
ID: 3.5–4 in (9–11 cm). Common hummer of central and southern Chile. Upperparts are iridescent bronzy-green. Underparts are pale greyish-brown with brownish flecks; bronzy-green flanks. Iridescent, reddish-orange crown of MALE is difficult to see. FEMALE is smaller, duller colored, and lacks the iridescent crown. Migratory, moving in accordance with the abundance or scarcity of flowers on which it feeds. Enters a state of torpor in cold weather. Builds a hanging nest (Sep–Nov) from moss and lichens and suspends it from a slender branch or fern growing close to water.
RANGE: World's southernmost hummer. Common from Atacama to Tierra del Fuego and sw Argentina; also Isla Masatierra, Juan Fernández. In gardens, fjords, matorral, woodland, agricultural areas; sea level to 6500 ft (0–2000 m).

Juan Fernández Firecrown
Picaflor de Juan Fernández
Sephanoides fernandensis
OTHER NAMES: Juan Fernandez-Kolibri, Colibri robinson.
ID: 3.5–4 in (9–11 cm). MALE is dark brick overall with a metallic golden-red crown. FEMALE's upperparts are shining-green with a metallic blue-green crown. Underparts are white, with throat and flanks spotted metallic-green. ENDANGERED.
RANGE: ENDEMIC to the Juan Fernández Archipelago.

VAGRANT: MOUNTAIN VELVETBREAST, *Lafresnaya lafresnayi*. Green back, throat and breast. Underparts black. One record in the High Andes at Socoroma in Arica-Parinacota.

An Oasis Hummingbird's nest with the leaves and contorted seedpod of Pacay in the background.

CORACIIFORMES: Kingfishers
FAMILY ALCEDINIDAE
KINGFISHERS
The kingfisher has a large head and bill, short neck, short legs and short, rounded wings. These birds feed mainly on fish, which they catch by diving into the water from a low perch. They use their stout bill to excavate nesting holes in riverbanks or escarpments. The clutch is 2 to 7 white eggs. Kingfishers are normally seen singly or in pairs rather than in flocks.

Ringed Kingfisher
Martín pescador
Ceryle torquata
OTHER NAMES: Queté-queté, Külkuchen, Rotbrustfischer, Martin-pêcheur à ventre roux.
ID: 17.5 in (44 cm). Crest and upperparts bluish-grey. White collar. THE MALE has a rufous-chestnut breast and belly. FEMALE is like the male, but has a grey band across the breast. Nests (Oct–Nov) in long burrows dug into banks and escarpments above fresh or salt water. Lays 3 to 5 glossy white eggs in a rounded cavity deep within the burrow. Sister species to the Belted Kingfisher *(Ceryle alcyon)* of North America.
RANGE: Resident from the Río Biobío to the Beagle Channel; occasional north to Colchagua in O'Higgins. Widespread in Central and South America. Around lakes, rivers, bays, channels and fjords.

Green Kingfisher
Martin pescador chico
Chloroceryle americana
OTHER NAMES: Grünfischer, Martin-pêcheur vert, Matraquilla, Camaronero.
ID: 8.25 in (21 cm). Green with white spots above. White below with green speckling on flanks. Wide chestnut breastband on MALE; two green breastbands on FEMALE.
RANGE: Found mainly in the Lluta River Valley near Arica, and occasionally south to Caleta Buena in coastal Tarapacá. These birds represent a Peruvian coastal race of a species that is widespread from Texas through n South America. Lives near rivers and lakes and in coastal areas.

PICIFORMES: Woodpeckers
FAMILY PICIDAE
WOODPECKERS
Woodpeckers are agile climbers. The feet have two toes directed forward and two toes aft. The stiff, pointed tail feathers are used as a brace when perched vertically on tree trunks. The strong, chisel-shaped bill is used to bore into wood and dig into soil. The long, cylindrical tongue is used to extract insects and larvae. Most excavate nesting holes in trees or earthen banks. The clutch is 2 to 8 glossy white eggs.

Chilean Flicker
Pitío
Colaptes pitius
OTHER NAMES: Pitigüe, Pütriu, Bänderspecht, Pic du Chili. Pitigüe and Pitío refer to the bird's loud call, *pitíu-pitíu-pitíu*.
ID: 13 in (33 cm). Forehead, crown and nape are slate-grey; neck and sides of face are buffy. Back is barred brownish-black and tan. Underparts are buff with dusky bars on chest and flanks. Abdomen, rump and underwing shafts are pale yellow. Iris is yellow. Feeds on the ground; preferred food is ants. Nests in holes in earthen banks and escarpments in the northern range; uses holes in forest trees in the south.
RANGE: Locally common from Atacama to Magallanes; also sw Argentina. Inhabits open fields, lightly wooded hillsides and clearings in second growth woodland.
SUBSPECIES: PITÍO, *C. p. pitius*, occurs from Huasco Valley, Atacama, to Lago Llanquihue, Los Lagos. The larger PITÍO AUSTRAL, *C. p. cachinnans*, ranges from Chiloé to the Strait of Magellan; it has wider, more olive barring on breast and flanks.

Andean Flicker
Pitío del norte
Colaptes rupicola
OTHER NAMES: Yaco-yaco, Carpintero de las piedras, Gargacha, Andenspecht, Pic des rochers.
ID: 13 in (33 cm). Forehead, crown and nape slate-grey. Back is barred brownish-black and buff. Buffy rump (seen in flight). Sides of face and underparts pale tawny with a band of black dots across breast. Yellow iris. MALE has a red moustache; FEMALE's is dark slate. Tends to perch on the ground with bill pointing upward. Nests in holes in cliffs and roadway banks.
RANGE: High Andes of Arica and Tarapacá; also Peru, Bolivia, nw Argentina; in Puna grasslands and bofedales; 6000–14,000 ft (1800–4300 m).

Magellanic Woodpecker
Carpintero
Campephilus magellanicus
OTHER NAMES: Carpintero negro, Gallo del monte, Reré Magellanspecht, Pic de Magellan.
ID: 18 in (45 cm). This is a spectacular, large woodpecker of the forests. Shiny bluish-black body with a white "V" on the back (seen when perched). Conspicuous white underwing patch (seen in flight). Yellow iris. MALE has a scarlet-red head and prominent crest that curls upward. FEMALE's head and upward sweeping crest are black; red feathering at base of bill. Often located by its loud, two-note, hammering drum and two-syllable call, *kee-OW*. Excavates nesting holes in snags and stumps of old-growth *Nothofagus* and *Araucaria* trees. Clutch is four glossy white eggs. ENDANGERED.

RANGE: Resident in forests from the Talca Cordillera in O'Higgins to the Beagle Channel in Magallanes; also s Argentina; sea level to 6550 ft (0–2000 m).

Striped Woodpecker
Carpinterito
Picoides lignarius
OTHER NAMES: Carpintero chico, Külalhuayu, Strichelkopfspecht, Pic bûcheron.
ID: 7 in (18 cm). Back is barred black and white; forehead and crown black. MALE's nape is red. Underparts buffy with black striping. Red iris. Shy and inconspicuous; often located by its loud, trilling call. Nests (Oct–Nov) in holes that it excavates in trees and cacti.
RANGE: Coquimbo to Última Esperanza, Magallanes; also Argentina. Found in shade trees in pastures, orchards and farms; also in southern rainforest.

PASSERIFORMES: Perching Birds
PASSERINES
This is the largest order of birds, encompassing about two-thirds of all avian species. All are land birds. They all are able to perch—that is, to alight on a twig or other support and grasp it tightly with three toes bent forward around the perch and one toe aft. Most passerines are relatively small in size. Many have complex vocalizations and for this reason are often called "songbirds."

FAMILY FURNARIIDAE
FURNARIIDS (OVENBIRDS)
Birds in this family are found only in Central and South America. The terms FURNARIID and OVENBIRD refer to the oven-shaped, mud nests constructed by a few members of this group. Most furnariids have drab brown plumage. All are insectivorous. Most lay 2 to 5 white eggs.

The species found in Chile include the miners *(mineros)*, cinclodes *(churretes)*, earthcreepers *(bandurrillas)*, tit-spinetails *(tijerales)*, crag chilias *(chiricocas)*, tree-runners *(comesebos)*, wiretails *(colilargas)*, rushbirds *(trabajadores)*, rayaditos *(rayaditos)*, and canasteros *(canasteros)*.

MINERS (GENUS GEOSITTA): These small passerines inhabit arid and semi-arid areas where they excavate deep nesting holes in caves or earthen banks—a behavior that has earned them their common name "miner." They are pale brown in color, and most have rufous on the wings. In flight, each species shows a unique tail pattern, which is a good clue to identification. The bill is straight or slightly drooping and is dark in color, often with a pale basal area. Miners run or walk over the ground and almost never perch in trees.

Common Miner, Minero
Geositta cunicularia
OTHER NAMES: Caminera común, Caminante, Inasüpü, Pachurra, Pizcarra grande, Patagonienerdhacker, Géositte mineuse.
ID: 6 in (15 cm). Head and mantle cinnamon to greyish-brown. Streaked crown. Light cinnamon supercilium. Wings are brown with a broad rufous band (seen in flight). Tail has a black terminal wedge; tail base and outer tail feathers are pale buff to cream. Buffy to whitish underparts, with a band of brown streaks on the breast. Bill dark; lighter at base. Legs are dark horn.
RANGE: Common, but with discontinuous distribution in arid and semi-arid terrain from Arica-Parinacota to Magallanes; Peru, Bolivia, Argentina, Brazil and Uruguay.
SUBSPECIES: MINERO COMÚN, *G. c. fissirostris*; s Atacama to Llanquihue, Los Lagos. MINERO ARGENTINO, *G. c. cunicularia*; low pampas of Aisén and Magallanes. MINERO DEL NORTE, *G. c. desertícolor*; coastal desert, Arica to Atacama. MINERO CORDILLERANO DEL NORTE, *G. c. titicacae*; High Andes of Arica–Tarapacá. MINERO CORDILLERANO DEL SUR, *G. c. hellmayri*; Araucanía.

Short-billed Miner, Minero austral
Geositta antarctica
OTHER NAMES: Caminera, Géositte à bec court, Feuerland-Erdhacker.
ID: 6 in (15 cm). Similar in color to the Common Miner except for the wings, which lack the bright rufous wingband. Very faint

streaks on breast. Short, straight bill. Tail white, with a black terminal wedge.
RANGE: Strait of Magellan to Tierra del Fuego and s Argentina; moves northward in winter. In lowland fields, grasslands and sandy areas.

Puna Miner, Minero de la puna
Geositta punensis
OTHER NAMES: Pizcarra, Pampero, Géosite du puna, Altiplano-Erdhacker, Caminera de la puna.
ID: 5.5 in (14.5 cm). Paler overall than the Common Miner, with creamy white underparts and no streaking on the breast. Tail is pale cinnamon with a black, inverted-T terminal band.
RANGE: Arica-Parinacota to Atacama; also Bolivia, Peru, nw Argentina, In sandy, arid, sparsely vegetated places on the Puna; 10,000–15,000 ft (3000-4500 m).

Greyish Miner, Minero chico
Geositta maritima
OTHER NAMES: Pachurra, Pampero gris, Südlicher Grauerdhacker, Géosite grise.
ID: 5.5 in (14 cm). Smoky-grey above with a pale cinnamon supercilium. Underparts creamy-white; buff on flanks and undertail coverts. Wings entirely greyish-brown. Tail dark brown; outer tail feathers white. Black legs. Bill is pink with a black tip.
RANGE: Arid shoreline, coastal mountains and fringes of interior deserts; Arica to Atacama; Peru; 1650–9200 ft (500–2800 m).

Creamy-rumped Miner, Minero grande
Geositta isabellina
OTHER NAMES: Caminera morada, Isabellerdhacker, Géosite isabelle.
ID: 7 in (18 cm). Appears to be entirely sandy-brown until in flight when the dull rufous wing patch and creamy-white rump are exposed. Tail is cream with a black terminal wedge. Bill and feet black. Restless and noisy, frequently sounding a high-pitched, metallic *cheet-cheet-cheet*.
RANGE: Uncommon in the Andes from Atacama to Maule; w Argentina. Rocky outcrops, ravines and slopes of mountain valleys above 6500 ft (2000 m).

Rufous-banded Miner, Minero cordillerano
Geositta rufipennis
OTHER NAMES: Pachurra, Caminera grande, Rotschwanz-Erdhacker, Géosite à ailes rousses.
ID: 6.5 in (16 cm). Drab grey above, buffy below, with a striking cinnamon and black wing band. Tail is cinnamon with a subterminal black wedge. Bill and legs black.
RANGE: Antofagasta to Aisén; also Bolivia, Argentina. Usually found above 6000 ft (1000 m) in the Andes, but descends at times to the central coast. In dry, open areas with large outcrops and earthen banks.
SUBSPECIES: MINERO CORDILLERANO, *G. r. fasciata*; s Antofagasta to Araucanía. MINERO CORDILLERANO DE PAPOSO, *G. r. harrisoni*; Paposo Gorge, Antofagasta. MINERO CORDILLERANO AUSTRAL, *G. r. rufipennis*; Aisén.

EARTHCREEPERS (GENUS *UPUCERTHIA*): These are terrestrial, brown-plumaged birds with long, downcurved bills. They hold their tail in a cocked position when running across the ground. They dig nesting holes in banks where they lay 2 to 5 opaque white eggs.

Scale-throated Earthcreeper, Bandurilla
Upucerthia dumetaria
OTHER NAMES: Bandurrita común, Schuppenkehl-Erdhacker, Upucerthie des buissons.
ID: 8 in (21 cm). Upperparts greyish-brown to olive-brown. Underparts tan. Throat and breast feathers are darkly edged, giving a scaly look to the throat and breast. Base of primaries is cinnamon to burnt sienna. Tail dark brown, with pale brown central tail feathers and pale buff tips to the outer tail feathers. Long, decurved, black bill.
RANGE: Antofagasta to Tierra del Fuego; Peru, Bolivia, Argentina. Semi-arid and sometimes sandy areas with brush; sea level to 10,000 ft (0–3000 m).
SUBSPECIES: BANDURRILLA DE LA CORDILLERA, *U. d. hypoleuca*; Antofagasta to Maule.

BANDURRILLA COMÚN, *U. d. saturatior*; Valparaíso to Valdivia. BANDURRILLA DEL SUR, *U. d. dumetaria*; Aisén to Magallanes.

White-throated Earthcreeper
Bandurrilla de Arica
Upucerthia albigula
OTHER NAMES: Upucerthie à gorge blanche, Weisskehl-Erdhacker, Pipo, Lucho-Lucho.
ID: 8.5 in (22 cm). Upperparts dark brown fading to sepia on crown. Buffy supercilium. Center of throat is white. Breast faintly barred. Underparts tan, darker on flanks. Wing coverts and tail mostly cinnamon. Long, decurved bill.
RANGE: Common in native scrub and dry ravines around Putre, Arica-Parinacota; sw Peru; 9850–12,500 ft (3000–3800 m).

Plain-breasted Earthcreeper
Bandurrilla de la puna
Upucerthia jelskii
OTHER NAMES: Buff-breasted Earthcreeper, Pipo, Lucho-Lucho, Bandurrita cordillerano, Bandurrita ocracea, Braunbauch-Erdhacker, Fahlkehl-Erdhacker, Upucerthie de Jelski.
ID: 7.5 in (19 cm). Upperparts and wing coverts pale brown with grey head. Tawny underparts, paler buff on throat. No streaks on breast. Rufous band at base of primaries. Central tail feathers brown; outer tail feathers cinnamon.
RANGE: Altiplano of n Chile, nw Argentina, Bolivia, sw Peru. Rocky, brush-clad slopes near water; 11,500–16,500 ft (3500–5000 m).

EARTHCREEPERS (GENUS *OCHETORHYNCHUS*): These earthcreepers, otherwise placed in *Upucerthia*, have fairly straight bills rather than downcurved ones. They build their nests under boulders or in rock crevices rather than in excavated burrows.

Straight-billed Earthcreeper
Bandurrilla de pico recto
Ochetorhynchus (Upucerthia) ruficauda
OTHER NAMES: Geradschnabel-Erdhacker, Upucerthie à bec droit, Pipo, Lucho-Lucho.
ID: 7.5 in (19 cm). Upperparts brick red; with head and mantle warm brown. White supercilium; rufous auriculars. Throat is white. Rest of underparts are rufous with broad, longitudinal white streaks; rusty margins to feathers on flanks and belly. Secondaries and base of primaries rufous. Tail is rufous with blackish inner barbs. Found singly or in pairs. Runs across rocky terrain, cocking the tail every time it stops.
RANGE: Andes, from Arica-Parinacota to Santiago; Peru, Bolivia, w Argentina. Rocky slopes with native scrub; 8200–12,500 ft (2500–3800 m).
SUBSPECIES: BANDURRILLA DE PICO RECTO, *U. r. ruficauda,* ranges on the Puna from s Tarapacá to Santiago. The paler BANDURRILLA DE PICO RECTO PERUANA, *U. r. montana*, ranges from Parinacota to Peru.
VAGRANT: ROCK EARTHCREEPER, BANDURRILLA DE LAS PIEDRAS, *Upucerthia andaecola*. One specimen from Antofagasta. Similar to the Straight-billed Earthcreeper, but with fine, dark brown scaling on chest.

EARTHCREEPERS (GENUS *EREMOBIUS*): The single species in this genus, the Band-tailed Earthcreeper, is similar to the canasteros in that it builds a nest of sticks in low scrub.

Band-tailed Earthcreeper
Patagón
Eremobius phoenicurus
OTHER NAMES: Bandurilla turca, Annumbi rougequeue, Schwarzschwanz-Erdhacker.
ID: 7.5 in (19 cm). Brownish-grey above. White supercilium. Uppertail coverts and outer tail feathers rufous; rest of tail black. Throat and chest white; abdomen lead-grey; flanks rufous. Bill dark horn, with base of lower mandible yellowish. Legs dark horn. Keeps tail cocked upright when running across the ground. Jaramillo (2003) likens the call to the trilling sound made by a finger running through a comb.
RANGE: Known to occur near the Chilean border since 1940, this species was only recently sighted in Chile near the Atlantic entrance to the Strait of Magellan. Inhabits areas with dense scrub, especially Mata Verde *(Lepidophyllum cupressiforme).*

CHILIA, EARTHCREEPERS AND CINCLODES

Band-tailed Earthcreeper
Patagón
Eremobius phoenicurus
Strait of Magellan
7.5 in (19 cm)

Crag Chilia
Chiricoca
Chilia melanura
Atacama–O'Higgins
7 in (18 cm)

Lepidophyllum cupressiformes

Straight-billed Earthcreeper
Bandurilla de pico recto
Ochetorhynchus ruficauda
Parinacota–Santiago
7.5 in (19 cm)

Grey-flanked Cinclodes
Churrete chico
Cinclodes oustaleti
Antofagasta–Magallanes
Juan Fernández
7 in (17.5 cm)

White-winged Cinclodes
Churrete de alas blancas
Cinclodes atacamensis
Andes; Arica–Santiago
9 in (23 cm)

Bar-winged Cinclodes
Churrete acanelado
Cinclodes fuscus
Arica–Magallanes
7 in (18 cm)

Blackish Cinclodes
Churrete austral
Cinclodes antarcticus
Coastal Magallanes
9 in (23 cm)

Dark-bellied Cinclodes
Churrete
Cinclodes patagonicus chilensis
Valparaíso–Magallanes
8.75 in (22 cm)

Chilean Seaside Cinclodes
Churrete costero
Cinclodes nigrofumosus
Arica–Valdivia
10.5 in (27 cm)

CRAG CHILIA (GENUS *CHILIA*): The single species in this genus, the Chilia, nests in rock cavities and feeds on insects and seeds.

Crag Chilia, Chiricoca
Chilia melanura
OTHER NAMES: Garganta blanca, Rotbürzel-Erdhacker, Chilia des rochers.
ID: 7 in (18 cm). Crown and mantle light brown; rump, upper and undertail coverts rufous. Short, straight, dark bill with pale spot at base. Throat and breast white; rest of underparts pale greyish-brown. Rufous base to blackish primaries and secondaries. Tail rufous with a broad black terminal band. Strong black legs. Cocks tail upright. Restless and active. Seldom flies.
RANGE: ENDEMIC. Atacama to O'Higgins; rocky cliffs and slopes of the c Andes and Coastal Range; 3950–8200 ft (1200–2500 m).
SUBSPECIES: CHIRICOCA, *C. m. melanura*. Valparaíso to O'Higgins. CHIRICOCA DE ATACAMA, *C. m. atacamae*. Atacama.

CINCLODES (GENUS *CINCLODES*): These birds bob and flick their tails as they walk, and have a loud, trilling call. They live near streams and seacoasts, and feed on grubs or small aquatic organisms. They lay their clutch of 2 to 4 white eggs in a grass nest placed in a rock crevice or a hole in a bank.

Dark-bellied Cinclodes, Churrete
Cinclodes patagonicus
OTHER NAMES: Remolinera, Piloto, Cinclode à ventre sombre, Streifenbrust-Uferwipper.
ID: 8.75 in (22 cm). Dark sooty-brown above, greyish-brown below. Long white supercilium. White throat has fine grey barring. Dark breast and upper abdomen are faintly flecked with white; white flecking extends to the lower abdomen of the southern subspecies. Cinnamon wingbar. Outer tail feathers are tipped with buff. Blackish bill. Nests (Sep–Dec) in banks, rodent burrows, rock crevices, clefts in stone walls, holes in tree trunks and on bridge girders.
RANGE: Common from Valparaíso to Tierra del Fuego; sw Argentina. Riverbanks, lakes, coast; sea level to 8200 ft (0–2500 m).
SUBSPECIES: CHURRETE DEL SUR, *C. p. patagonicus*; Golfo de Penas to Tierra del Fuego. CHURRETE, *C. p. chilensis*; Valparaíso to Aisén.

Chilean Seaside Cinclodes
Churrete costero
Cinclodes nigrofumosus
OTHER NAMES: Molinero, Changa, Marisquero, Südlicher Felsuferwipper, Cinclode du ressac.
ID: 10.5 in (27 cm). Largest cinclodes in Chile. Dark sooty-brown. White throat. Breast and abdomen strongly flecked with white. Conspicuous rufous band across the wings (seen in flight). Dark tail, with buffy tips to outer tail feathers. Black bill. Sturdy, dark grey legs. Nests (Aug–Sep) in rock crevices or excavates burrows in earthen banks of bluffs overlooking the sea.
RANGE: Arica to Valdivia; also Peru. Always on the seacoast.

Bar-winged Cinclodes
Churrete acanelado
Cinclodes fuscus
OTHER NAMES: Chiuchihuén, Remolinera parda, Tuiro, Cachirinque, Alcade de aguas, Cinclode brun, Kurzschnabel-Uferwipper.
ID: 7 in (18 cm). Brownish-grey to warm brown above; pale brown below. Pale buff supercilium. Throat white with faint buff flecking. Black bill and black legs. Birds in central and southern Chile have a wide, cinnamon wingband; the Altiplano subspecies, *C. f. albiventris,* has a creamy wingband similar to the White-winged Cinclodes. A confiding species that sometimes nests inside rural homes and barns.
RANGE: Common. Arica to Cape Horn; c South America. Wide variety of habitats.
SUBSPECIES: CHURRETE ACANELADO, *C. f. fuscus*. Atacama to Tierra del Fuego. Highly migratory. Most of the central Chile populations summer in the mountains and descend to the coast in winter. Fuegian populations summer in Chile and disperse

northeast in winter. CHURRETE ACANELADO DEL NORTE, *C. f. albiventris*. Resident on the Altiplano from Arica-Parinacota to Antofagasta; 8200–16,500 ft (2500–5000 m).

Grey-flanked Cincłodes
Churrete chico
Cinclodes oustaleti
OTHER NAMES: Remolinera chica, Oustalet's Cinclodes, Cinclode d'Oustalet, Grauflanken-Uferwipper.
ID: 7 in (17.5 cm). Upperparts dark greyish-brown. Indistinct whitish eyebrow. White throat. Breast and flanks are grey to buff, with pale streaks. Abdomen whitish or buff. Rufous wingbar. Greyish-brown tail, with buff tips to outer tail feathers. Thin, black bill. Dark legs.
RANGE: Antofagasta to Cape Horn; Juan Fernández; w Argentina. Mainland birds live around mountain streams in summer, seacoasts and lowland streams in winter; sea level to 13,125 ft (0–4000 m).
SUBSPECIES: CHURRETE CHICO, *C. o. oustaleti*; Aisen to Antofagasta. CHURRETE CHICO DEL SUR, *C. o. hornensis*, is found in Tierra del Fuego, islands around Cape Horn and the Strait of Magellan; larger, with a longer bill. CHURRETE DE JUAN FERNÁNDEZ, *C. o. baeckstroemii*, is ENDEMIC to Juan Fernández; tinted rufous on sides of abdomen, flanks and undertail coverts.

Blackish Cinclodes, Churrete austral
Cinclodes antarcticus maculirostris
OTHER NAMES: Tussockbird (Falklands), Remolinera negra, Cinclode fuligineux, Russbrauner-Uferwipper.
ID: 9 in (23 cm). Dark smoky brown overall; lighter on the throat and slightly darker on the underwing coverts. Short, heavy black bill; base of lower mandible yellow. Similar to the subspecies, *C. a. antarcticus*, that is common in the Falklands.
RANGE: Uncommon on rocky beaches and coastal moorland on outer islands of the Fuegian Region, islands south of the Beagle Channel and on Diego Ramírez.

White-winged Cinclodes
Churrete de alas blancas
Cinclodes atacamensis
OTHER NAMES: Cinclode à ailes blanches, Schwarzschwanz-Uferwipper, Tuiro-Tuiro, Cachirinque, Remolinera castaña.
ID: 9 in (23 cm). Upperparts rusty-brown, brighter on rump. Grey crown. White supercilium extends back from the eye. Throat white, faintly flecked with black. Breast and center of the abdomen light grey. Flanks and undertail coverts brown. Broad white wingband edged with black. Tail black, with white tips to outer tail feathers. Large size, bright rufous back, and pure white wingband separate it from the Altiplano form of the Bar-winged Cinclodes.
RANGE: Arica-Parinacota to Santiago; Peru, Bolivia, Argentina. Rocky gullies near streams and wet pastures above 8200 ft (2500 m).

WIRETAILS (GENUS *SYLVIORTHORHYNCHUS*): The single species in this genus, Des Mur's Wiretail, is restricted to the temperate rainforests and bamboo thickets of Chile and southwestern Argentina.

Des Mur's Wiretail, Colilarga
Sylviorthorhynchus desmursii
OTHER NAMES: Cola de paja ("Grasstail"), Epu kulen, Chang Kulen, Synallaxe de Des Murs, Fadenschwanzschlüpfer.
ID: 9.5 in (24 cm). A small brown bird with a very long tail—twice as long as the body. Tail has six feathers: two short outer tail feathers, two long medials and two greatly elongated central tail feathers. Upperparts rufous. Underparts tawny to buff. Skulks in dense bamboo and tepú thickets. Easier to locate in spring when it makes its high-pitched, staccato trill, which rises in pitch before descending. Nest is a small ball of dry grass with a hole in one side, usually placed low in dense understory thickets.
RANGE: Valparaíso to n Magallanes, and Andes of sw Argentina. In bamboo thickets and impenetrable underbrush; sea level to 3950 ft (0–1200 m).

RAYADITOS (GENUS *APHRASTURA*): These are small birds of the forest and woodland. They have bare-barbed tail feathers, which give a spine-tailed look. They search tree bark and foliage for insects.

Thorn-tailed Rayadito, Rayadito
Aphrastura spinicauda
OTHER NAMES: Bullicioso, Comesebo chico, Yiqui-Yiqui, Raspatortillas, Synallaxe rayadito, Festland-Stachelschwanzschlüpfer.
ID: 5.5 in (14 cm). Crown and sides of head black; long, wide, golden supercilium. Rest of upperparts dark brown, with rump and uppertail coverts rufous. Underparts white to buffy. Characteristic tail ends in bare shafts; central tail feathers are black; outer tail feathers are black with rufous tips. Bill is short, straight and pointed. A confiding little forest-dweller. Places its nest of small twigs and soft grasses in a crack or crevice between the trunk and bark of a forest tree. Clutch is three large white eggs.
RANGE: Common in forested areas from Fray Jorge, Coquimbo, to Tierra del Fuego; sw Argentina.
SUBSPECIES: RAYADITO COMÚN, *A. s. spinicauda*. Coquimbo to Magallanes. RAYADITO DE ISLA MOCHA, *A. s. bullocki*. Isla Mocha. RAYADITO DE CHILOÉ, *A. s. fulva*. Chiloé to the Chonos Archipelago.

Masafuera Rayadito
Rayadito de Masafuera
Aphrastura masafuerae
OTHER NAMES: Synallaxe de Masafuera, Insel-Stachelschwanzschlüpfer.
ID: 6 in (15 cm). Similar to the Thorn-tailed Rayadito but less richly colored. Most of the plumage is light greyish brown. Off-white supercilium merges into gold at the nape. Wings black, coverts edged with rufous.
RANGE: ENDEMIC to montane fern forests of Isla Masafuera (Alejandro Selkirk) in the Juan Fernández Archipelago.

WREN-LIKE RUSHBIRD (GENUS *PHLEOCRYPTES*): The single species in this genus, the Wren-like Rushbird, inhabits *Scirpus* reedbeds in temperate South America. They differ from all other furnariids in that they lay dark sky-blue eggs instead of white ones.

Wren-like Rushbird, Trabajador
Phleocryptes melanops
OTHER NAMES: Binsenschlüpfer, Synallaxe des joncs. Trabajador ("worker") refers to the amount of effort these birds put into constructing their rounded nest of woven reeds, which is anchored between two reed stems at varying heights above the water.
ID: 5.25 in (13.5 cm). Mantle streaked black, brown and grey. Rump, sides of head and neck light brown. Forehead and crown dark brown with paler striping. Yellowish-white eyeline. Dark wings with chestnut wingbar and chestnut flecking on the wing coverts. Tail brown with black outer tail feathers. Underparts off-white to buff. Brown bill and legs. Often found in the company of the Many-colored Rush-Tyrant *(Tachuris rubrigastra)*. Feeds on insects caught while flitting or hopping from one reed stem to the next. Call is described as a cicada-like whistle followed by the sound of dry sticks being rapidly knocked together.
RANGE: Reedbeds from Arica to Aisén, and in temperate South America.
SUBSPECIES: TRABAJADOR, *P. m. melanops*. Atacama to Aisén. TRABAJADOR DEL NORTE, *P. m. loaensis*. Lives along the Río Loa between Chacance and Quillagua, along the Río San Salvador, and at Chintaguay Oasis in the Quisma Quebrada, Tarapacá.

TREERUNNERS (GENUS *PYGARRHICHAS*): These birds climb up the trunks of forest trees using their stiff tails for support as they search for grubs and insects. They excavate and nest in a hole in decayed or burned trees.

White-throated Treerunner
Comesebo grande
Pygarrhichas albogularis
OTHER NAMES: Carpintero pardo, Pishon-Quillu, Spechttopler, Kleiberbaumspäher, Picotelle à gorge blanche.
ID: 6.3 in (16 cm). Upperparts dark brown

with a rufous rump and tail, which has protruding spines formed by bare shafts. Throat and center of belly white. Brownish-black scaling on abdomen and undertail coverts. Flanks rufous. Dark brown wings; wing-coverts and secondaries edged rufous. White underwing coverts.
RANGE: Forested areas from Valparaíso to Tierra del Fuego.

CANASTEROS (GENUS *ASTHENES*): These are ground-dwelling birds that build large, domed nests of sticks, thus the name canastero ("basketmaker"). Most have a rufous throat patch, but it is not always conspicuous and is not present in all. The tail pattern is a good guide to identification.

Dusky-tailed Canastero, Canastero
Asthenes humilis
OTHER NAMES: Streak-throated Canastero, Bolaria, Taguatera, Canastero pecho rayado, Synallaxe à queue noire, Schwarzschwanzschlupfer.
ID: 6.5 in (16.5 cm). Upperparts smoky brown with a warm brown rump. Throat and breast are greyish-white, with longitudinal dark streaks; cinnamon flanks and undertail coverts. Thin, whitish supercilium. Intense rufous shoulder patch. Tail entirely dark brown. Bill and legs black. Lays two clutches of eggs (Aug, Nov) in a thorn-covered, dome-shaped nest of twigs lined with soft plant matter.
RANGE: Atacama to Biobío; w Argentina. Matorral and semi-arid zones with cactus or Espino *(Acacia caven)*; sea level to 6200 ft (0–2200 m).
SUBSPECIES: CANASTERO, *A. h. humicola*; Atacama to Maule. *A. h. goodalli;* Paposo Gorge in Antofagasta. CANASTERO SUREÑO, *A. h. polysticta*; s Maule to Nahuelbuta.

Cordilleran Canastero, Canastero chico
Asthenes modesta
OTHER NAMES: Chercán de la cordillera, Graslandcanastero, Synallaxe des rocailles.
ID: 6.1 in (15.5 cm). Sandy-brown above. Underparts pale grey with faint creamy streaking. Rufous throat patch. Wings brown with a dull rufous wingband. Tail feathers brown, edged with pale cinnamon. Lives on rocky slopes with scattered brush, and in Andean wetlands in the north.
RANGE: Andes from Arica-Parinacota to O'Higgins; migrant in lowland Aisén and Magallanes. Also Peru, Bolivia, Argentina.
SUBSPECIES: CANASTERO CHICO DEL NORTE, *A. m. modesta*; Arica to Antofagasta; Puna above 13,000 ft (3500 m). CANASTERO CHICO, *A. m. australis*; Atacama to O'Higgins.

Dark-winged Canastero
Canastero del norte
Asthenes (dorbignyi) arequipae
OTHER NAMES: Canastero rojizo, Creamy-breasted Canastero, Fahlbrustcanastero, Synallaxe d'Orbigny.
ID: 6.5 in (16.5 cm). Dark smoky brown above; rump and uppertail coverts rufous. Creamy white throat and belly; undertail and underwing coverts rufous. Wings are dark brown with rufous wing coverts. Tail is blackish-brown, with two rufous outer retrices. Loud, trilling call. Constructs a twig nest (Nov) in large cacti or bushes.

The tail pattern is a diagnostic field mark for the canasteros.

Cordilleran   Canyon   Dark-winged   Sharp-billed   Dusky-tailed   Austral

TIT-SPINETAILS AND CANASTEROS 253

Streaked Tit-Spinetail
Tijeral listado
Leptasthenura striata
Arica–Tarapacá
6.5 in (16.5 cm)

Plain-mantled Tit-Spinetail
Tijeral
Leptasthenura aegithaloides
Arica–Magallanes
6.5 in (16.5 cm)

Canyon Canastero
Canastero de quebradas
Asthenes pudibunda
Putre
7 in (17 cm)

Cordilleran Canastero
Canastero chico
Asthenes modesta
Arica–O'Higgins
Aisén–Magallanes
6.1 in (15.5 cm)

Dark-winged Canastero
Canastero del norte
Asthenes arequipae
Arica–Tarapacá
6.5 in (16.5 cm)

Dusky-tailed Canastero
Canastero
Asthenes humilis
Antofagasta–Araucanía
6.5 in (16.5 cm)

Sharp-billed (Lesser) Canastero
Canastero de cola larga
Asthenes pyrrholeuca
Valparaíso–Aisén
6.5 in (16.5 cm)

Austral Canastero
Canastero del sur
Asthenes anthoides
Valparaíso–Magallanes
6.5 in (16.5 cm)

RANGE: Andes of Arica-Parinacota; Peru, Bolivia, w Argentina. Brush-covered slopes above valleys that have streams and ponds; 8000–12,500 ft (2500–3800 m).

Austral Canastero
Canastero del sur
Asthenes anthoides
OTHER NAMES: Synallaxe austral, Südlicher Flügelspiegelcanastero.
ID: 6.5 in (16.5 cm). The only canastero with a heavily streaked back. Upperparts olive-grey with longitudinal black striations, heavier on head and neck. Chin and throat tawny; breast yellowish-grey; abdomen drab whitish-grey. Rufous wingband and patch at bend of wing. Central tail feathers grey with black shafts; pointed outer tail feathers are dark grey, tipped with buff. Builds a nest of twigs on or near the ground.
RANGE: Los Andes Province, Valparaíso, to Tierra del Fuego. Wet meadows and hillsides. Nests from Concepción south; winter visitor in the north. Also w Argentina.

Sharp-billed (Lesser) Canastero
Canastero de cola larga
Asthenes pyrrholeuca
OTHER NAMES: Canastero chico, Dünnschnabelcanastero, Synallaxe vannier.
ID: 6.5 in (16.5 cm). Wren-like. Long, brown tail with three rufous outer tail feathers. Short, pointed bill. Greyish-brown upperparts; paler below. Wings grey with rufous at the base of the primaries. Faint, pale supercilium. Rufous throat patch is finely dotted black. Nests low in thornless scrub.
RANGE: Los Andes Province, Valparaíso, to Aisén; also Argentina and Bolivia. Semi-arid, sparsely brush-covered Andean mountain slopes to 9850 ft (3000 m).

Canyon Canastero
Canastero de quebradas
Asthenes pudibunda
OTHER NAMES: Canastero peruano, Rostschwanzcanastero, Synallaxe des canyons.
ID: 7 in (17 cm). Warm brown above, with lower back and sides of tail rufous. Rufous wingbar. Reddish throat patch. Underparts are pearl-grey with pale cinnamon flanks.
RANGE: Formerly thought to occur only in the Peruvian and Bolivian Andes. Recently found in the pre-Puna shrub zone around Putre in Arica-Parinacota. Rocky valleys and brush or cactus-covered slopes; 9850–11,800 ft (3000–3600 m).

TIT-SPINETAILS (GENUS *LEPTASTHENURA*): These are tiny, grey or brown birds with ragged, stiff-feathered tails. They flit restlessly in the vegetation, often clinging upside down. They nest in the hollow interior of cacti, in stone walls or abandoned canastero nests. The nest is lined with feathers, which poke out of the entry hole.

Plain-mantled Tit-Spinetail
Tijeral
Leptasthenura aegithaloides
OTHER NAMES: Chuairunca, Tijereta, Siete colas, Cachudito, Coludito, Synallaxe mésange, Zimtspiegel-Meisenschlüpfer.
ID: 6.5 in (16.5 cm). Crown dark rufous with black streaks; white eyebrow. Mantle pale greyish-brown. Throat and upper breast are white; rest of underparts buffy-grey. Wings brownish-grey with rufous on coverts and base of primaries. Long, brown, ragged tail. Often overlooked due to small size and quiet nature. Call is a buzzy chitting or short trill.
RANGE: Arica-Parinacota to Aisén; also Peru to Argentina.
SUBSPECIES: TIJERAL COMÚN, *L. a. aegithaloides*, occurs from Coquimbo to Aisén in parks, open forest, forest edge, matorral. The TIJERAL DEL NORTE, *L. a. grisescens*, is a pale subspecies of the desert oases and valleys from Arica to Atacama; sea level to 4925 ft (0–1500 m). The TIJERAL CORDILLERANO DEL NORTE, *L. a. berlepschi,* has a rufous abdomen and sandy-brown back; Arica-Parinacota to Antofagasta, on the Puna above 9850 ft (3000 m). TIJERAL ARGENTINO, *L. a. pallida*, from Aisén is a pale subspecies with a white crown stripe instead of rufous.

Streaked Tit-Spinetail, Tijeral listado
Leptasthenura striata
OTHER NAMES: Synallaxe strié, Rostspiegel-Meisenschlüpfer.
ID: 6.5 in (16.5 cm). Crown rufous with black streaks; nape pale grey. Mantle streaked olive-brown and yellow. Brown rump. Wings blackish-brown, with a rufous wingbar and pale rufous edge to wing coverts. Throat and breast white with fine black streaks. Abdomen white, feathers edged olive-grey. Long blackish-brown tail.
RANGE: Uncommon in the Andes of Arica-Parinacota, Tarapacá, and Peru. On brush and cactus slopes in the pre-Puna shrub zone; 9850–13,250 ft (3000–4000 m).

FAMILY RHINOCRYPTIDAE
TAPACULOS
Tapaculos are skulking, terrestrial birds of dense forest and brush. The common name Tapaculo means "covered backside," which refers to the habit of running with the tail cocked over the back. Rhinocryptidae means "hidden nose," which gives reference to the fleshy sheath covering the nostrils. Tapaculos are notoriously shy and at the slightest disturbance will dive into a rodent burrow or the underbrush. Their rolling, ringing, ventriloquial calls are normally sounded only when the forest is completely undisturbed. Tapaculos are insectivorous. They scratch the ground like chickens when searching for grubs and other small invertebrates. Some excavate nesting holes in earthen banks or rotting tree stumps; others build a stick nest. The clutch is 2 to 4 pure white, round eggs.

Chestnut-throated Huet-huet
Hued-Hued castaño
Pteroptochos castaneus
OTHER NAMES: Galloreta, Tuta, Teque, Tourco à gorge marron, Braunkehl-Bürzelstelzer.
ID: 9.75 in (24 cm). Forehead, forecrown and eyeline rufous; slate-grey auriculars. Dark slate-grey hindcrown and mantle. Wings dark grey. Rump cinnamon, barred buff and black; uppertail coverts bright rufous; tail slaty black. Throat, neck and upper breast rich chestnut-red. Abdomen, flanks and undertail coverts barred pale rufous and ochre. Bill dark grey. Legs black. Call is a series of low-pitched hoots, *toot-toot-toot*. Excavates nesting holes in steep, heavily vegetated slopes overlooking water or uses cavities in rotting trees.
RANGE: ENDEMIC. O'Higgins to Biobío. In dense old growth forest and forest edge with bamboo thickets; sea level to 4925 ft (0–1500 m).

Black-throated Huet-huet
Hued-Hued del sur
Pteroptochos tarnii
OTHER NAMES: Gallinita, Tuta, Tapacola, Schwarzkehl-Bürzelstelzer, Tourco huet-huet.
ID: 9.75 in (24 cm). Dark rufous forehead and crown; rest of head, nape, neck and mantle slate-grey. Rufous rump. Abdomen rufous, barred black and ochre on the flanks and undertail coverts. Blackish wings, with some of the secondaries and coverts edged rufous. Black tail. Dark grey bill. Black legs. The Araucanian name, Hued-Hued, comes from the call *whét-whét*. Other calls include a sonorous *oop-oop-oop* and a loud, rapid *toot-toot-toot* given when alarmed. Excavates nesting holes in heavily vegetated slopes of watered valleys, or nests under the roots of large, fallen logs, or uses cavities in rotting trees.
RANGE: NEAR ENDEMIC. Biobío to Última Esperanza, Magallanes, including Isla Mocha, Araucanía and e Andean slopes of adjacent Argentina. Dense, old growth rainforest and bamboo thickets; sea level to 4925 ft (0–1500 m).

Moustached Turca, Turca
Pteroptochos megapodius
OTHER NAMES: Turco, Tululagua, Tourco à moustaches, Weissbart-Bürzelstelzer.
ID: 9.75 in (24 cm). Sooty-brown crown, neck, back, wings and tail. Rufous rump. White supercilium, chin and moustache stripe. Throat and breast rufous-brown. Rest of the underparts, including flanks are

white with brown and black scaling. Black bill and legs. Runs rapidly across the ground with tail cocked then abruptly stops, often on a rocky outcrop, to survey the territory. Uses its strong feet and claws to excavate deep nesting burrows (Aug–Oct). Johnson (1965) evocatively describes the Turca's calls as "a series of melodious notes starting high upon the scale and descending note by note" and flute-like notes sounding like "bubbles of water falling, drop by drop, out of an inverted bottle."
RANGE: ENDEMIC. Atacama to Biobío. Dry, rocky slopes with brush; sea level to about 10,000 ft (0–3000 m).
SUBSPECIES: TURCA, *P. m. megapodius*; Coquimbo to Biobío. TURCA DEL NORTE, *P. m. atacamae*; smaller and paler; Atacama.

White-throated Tapaculo, Tapaculo
Scelorchilus albicollis
OTHER NAMES: Tococo, Tourco à gorge blanche, Weisskehltapaculo. This species' musical call, *tá-pa-koo, tá-pa-koo,* has given the tapaculo group their common name.
ID: 7.5 in (19 cm). Upperparts rufous; olive-brown on wings and tail. Lores, eyebrow, and throat whitish. Underparts cream, with dark brown barring.
RANGE: ENDEMIC. Antofagasta to Maule. Dry slopes and ravines with thick brush; open desert scrub in the north; sea level to 4925 ft (0–1500 m).
SUBSPECIES: The TAPACULO, *S. a. albicollis*; Coquimbo to Maule. TAPACULO DEL NORTE, *S. a. atacamae*; Antofagasta to Coquimbo.

Chucao Tapaculo, Chucao
Scelorchilus rubecula
OTHER NAMES: Tricao, Tourco à gorge rouge, Rotkehltapaculo.
ID: 7–7.5 in (18-19 cm). Upperparts dark brown, turning rufous with age. Lores, throat and breast bright rufous; rest of underparts grey with black and white scaling. Seldom seen due to its preference for the darkest, densest parts of the rainforest, often near a stream. Primary call is a loud, explosive series of gobbling notes, *CHU-chu-chu-chu*. Nests on the ground in tree roots or holes in earthen banks having dense vegetation.
RANGE: Maule to Aisén; also w Argentina. Dense forests and bamboo thickets, often near water; sea level to 4925 ft (0–1500 m).
SUBSPECIES: CHUCAO, *S. r. rubecula*; Maule to Aisén; CHUCAO DE LA MOCHA, *S. r. mochae*; Isla Mocha, Araucanía.

Ochre-flanked Tapaculo, Churrín de la Mocha
Eugralla paradoxa
OTHER NAMES: Kittlitz' Babbler, Tutita, Rütri-cu-di-fe, Churrín grande, Mérulaxe à flancs ocre, Rostflankentapaculo.
ID: 6 in (15 cm). Slate-grey above, paler below. Rump, flanks and undertail rufous. Appears flat-headed, with the frontal shield of the thick, chicken-like bill extending to the crown. Call is a rapid, repetitive *check-check-check*. Builds a large, round nest of twigs in thorn trees and bushes (Sep–Dec).
RANGE: NEAR ENDEMIC. Maule to Chiloé; Isla Mocha; Argentina. Bamboo thickets in dense rainforest and forest edge, usually near water; sea level to 3300 ft (0–1000 m).

Magellanic Tapaculo, Churrín del sur
Scytalopus magellanicus
OTHER NAMES: Magellanic Babbler, Andean Tapaculo, Para atrás, Choco, Cholchif, Mérulaxe des Andes, Magellantapaculo.
ID: 4–5 in (10–12 cm). Appears dark sooty-grey overall; darker, almost black, on the head and upperparts. Flanks, wing coverts, vent and primaries dark chestnut to brown (barred brown and black in first-year birds). Some individuals have white feathers on the forecrown. Black bill. Legs dull pink. A variety of calls have been noted: *choo-rín* in the north, *pa-trás* in the south, a harsh *chó-ko* on Chiloé, and a repetitive *tow-chweé, tow-chweé* elsewhere. Nests (Oct–Nov) in crevices between the bark and trunk of trees, or amid roots and vines of fallen trees, or on fern covered banks. Nest is built of root fibers, mosses and lichens, and lined with soft grasses or hair.

TAPACULOS 257

Dusky Tapaculo
Churrín del norte
Scytalopus fuscus
Atacama–Araucanía
5 in (12 cm)
Thickets near water

Magellanic Tapaculo
Churrín del sur
Scytalopus magellanicus
Biobío–Magallanes
4–5 in (10–12 cm)
Bamboo thickets in rainforest
Also High Andean bogs

Chucao Tapaculo
Chucao
Scelorchilus rubecula
Antofagasta–Maule
7–7.5 in (18–19 cm)
Forest, bamboo thickets

Ochre-flanked Tapaculo
Churrín de la Mocha
Eugralla paradoxa
Maule–Chiloé
6 in (15 cm)
Bamboo thickets and brambles

White-throated Tapaculo
Tapaculo
Scelorchilus albicollis
Antofagasta–Maule
7.5 in (19 cm)
Scrub along streams

Moustached Turca
Turca
Pteroptochos megapodius
Atacama–Biobío
9.75 in (24 cm)
Dry, rocky slopes

Chestnut-throated Huet–huet
Hued-Hued castaño
Pteroptochos castaneus
O'Higgins–Biobío
9.75 in (24 cm)
Rainforest

Black-throated Huet–huet
Hued-Hued del sur
Pteroptochos tarnii
Biobío–Magallanes
9.75 in (24 cm)
Rainforest

RANGE: Biobío to Tierra del Fuego, and Andes outside Santiago; Argentina, Falklands. Bamboo thickets, forest ravines near streams; sea level to 9850 ft (0–3000 m).

Dusky Tapaculo, Churrín del norte
Scytalopus fuscus
OTHER NAMES: Chercán negro, Mérulaxe, Dunkelgrauer Tapaculo.
ID: 5 in (12 cm). Northern counterpart of the Magellanic Tapaculo. Separated by its northern range, occurrence in non-forested areas, darker slate plumage and dull yellow legs. Jaramillo (2003) reports the call as a nasal, descending, short trill.
RANGE: Atacama to Biobío; also Argentine Andes. Watered ravines with thickets and brambles; sea level to 6600 ft (0–2000 m).

FAMILY TYRANNIDAE
TYRANT-FLYCATCHERS
Tyrant-Flycatchers are birds of the Western Hemisphere. Most are somberly colored in grey or brown, with notable exceptions in species such as the Vermilion Flycatcher and the Many-colored Rush-Tyrant. Familial characteristics include a slightly flattened, hooked bill with prominent rictal bristles and the habit of flicking the tail. Only a few species such as the Austral Negrito exhibit sexual dimorphism. All are insectivorous, and some extend their diet to fruit, rodents and bird eggs and chicks.

Great Shrike-Tyrant, Mero
Agriornis livida
OTHER NAMES: Zorzal mero, Grand Gaucho, Schwarzschwanz-Hakentyrann.
ID: 10 in (26 cm). Upperparts brown with faint, dark brown streaks on crown. Underparts paler brown, with cinnamon undertail coverts and flanks. Throat white, with heavy black streaking. Black wings. Tail black with white outer tail feathers. Strongly hooked bill; upper mandible black, lower mandible horn. Black legs. Inconspicuous; seldom calls. Avoids wooded and populated areas. Feeds on lizards, frogs, insects, small rodents, bird eggs and chicks. Nests (Oct–Nov) in dense foliage, building a large bulky structure of twigs and grasses lined with animal hair or other soft matter. Clutch is 2 to 4 cream-colored eggs bearing red spots.
RANGE: Atacama to Magallanes; Argentina; open fields and brush-covered slopes; sea level to 6550 ft (0–2000 m).
SUBSPECIES: MERO, *A. l. livida*; Atacama to Valdivia. MERO AUSTRAL, *A. l. fortis*; darker and larger; Aisén.

Grey-bellied Shrike-Tyrant, Mero de Tarapacá
Agriornis microptera
OTHER NAMES: Gaucho, Gaucho argentino, Weissbrauen-Hakentyrann.
ID: 9 in (24 cm). Smaller and paler than the Great Shrike-Tyrant. Undistinguished grey plumage, with pale, faint streaks on the throat and a long, pale supercilium. Tail dark, with little or no white edging.
RANGE: Lluta Valley outside of Arica to San Pedro de Atacama, Antofagasta. Recently recorded in Última Esperanza, Magallanes. More common in Peru, Bolivia, Paraguay, Argentina. Arid brush and tola scrub on Andean slopes and in ravines to 11,500 ft (3500 m).

White-tailed Shrike-Tyrant, Mero de la puna
Agriornis andicola
OTHER NAMES: Huaicho (Aymara), Mero de cola blanca, Gaucho à queue blanche, Weissschwanz-Hakentyrann.
ID: 10 in (26 cm). Paler than the Black-billed Shrike-Tyrant, with whom it shares its habitat. Thick, black bill has a yellowish patch at the base of the lower mandible. White throat, heavily streaked with black. Narrow, creamy-buff line in front of the eye. Abdomen and undertail coverts creamy yellow. Tail is white with two black central tail feathers. VULNERABLE.
RANGE: Andes from Arica-Parinacota to Antofagasta; also Ecuador, Peru, Bolivia, Argentina. RARE in rocky areas and cliffs on the Puna; 11,500–14,750 ft (3500–4500 m).

TYRANTS AND SHRIKE-TYRANTS 259

Black-billed Shrike-Tyrant, Mero gaucho
Agriornis montana
OTHER NAMES: Huaicho, Gaucho à bec noir, Schwarzschnabel-Hakentyrann.
ID: 9 in (23 cm). Dark slate-grey above; pale brownish-grey below. Abdomen is tinted yellowish-brown; creamy undertail coverts. White throat with black streaking. Wings black; secondary feathers edged in white. Central tail feathers black; outer tail feathers mostly white. Bill entirely black, with maxilla ending in pronounced hook. Calls a loud whistling *pweé-twee* at dawn.
RANGE: Locally common from Arica to Biobío; also Colombia to Argentina. Rocky hillsides in high mountains, often near human habitation. Some birds descend to the coast in winter.
SUBSPECIES: MERO GAUCHO, *A. m. leucura*; mountains from Los Andes, Valparaíso, to Río Biobío. MERO GAUCHO DEL NORTE, *A. m. maritima*; paler with white undertail and white tips on central tail feathers; Tarapacá to Coquimbo. MERO GAUCHO BOLIVIANO, *A. m. intermedia*; all white outer tail feathers; High Andes of Arica-Parinacota.

Rufous-webbed Tyrant, Birro gris
Polioxolmis rufipennis
ID: 7 in (18 cm). Small version of the Grey-bellied Shrike-Tyrant, with bright rufous on the underwing coverts and base of tail. Pale iris. Hovers over prey. Frequents groves of Queñoa de altura (*Polylepis tarapacana*).
RANGE: RARE NON-BREEDING MIGRANT in extreme ne Chile. On the Altiplano above 11,500 ft (3500 m).

Chocolate-vented Tyrant
Cazamoscas chocolate
Neoxolmis rufiventris
OTHER NAMES: Gaucho chocolate, Pépoaza à ventre rougeâtre, Hellschulter-Nonnentyrann.
ID: 8.5 in (22 cm). Smoky-grey above with a blackish face. Throat and breast pale smoky grey. Belly, undertail coverts and underwing rufous. Wings cinnamon with whitish leading and trailing edges (seen in flight). Tail black, tipped with white. In Patagonia, where the bird is common, it forms small flocks, often in the company of plovers. Forages for insects on the ground, but readily perches on low bushes and fence posts. Runs across the ground, opening and closing its tail whenever it stops.
RANGE: RARE in Magallanes; nests in Patagonia. In open scrub in the lowland pampas; sea level to 1650 ft (0–500 m).

Fire-eyed Diucon, Diucón
Xolmis pyrope
OTHER NAMES: Pépoaza oeil-de-feu, Feuer-augen-Nonnentyrann, Monjita palomiza, Hurco, Papamosco. Diucón means "large Diuca," a finch of similar color and shape.
ID: 8.25 in (21 cm). A slightly boxy headed, grey flycatcher with a fiery red eye. Upperparts dark grey. Throat white; breast grey; belly and undertail white. Blackish wings, with white edging on secondaries. Tail is light grey, with barb of outer tail feather edged white. Black bill and legs. Call is a soft *psweet*. Perches on low tree branches, posts and wires at forest edge or near cultivated fields, flying out occasionally after insects. Sometimes feeds on wild berries. Nests (Oct–Jan) in small trees or flowering shrubs, building a nest of twigs and grass, lined with mosses and lichens.
RANGE: Atacama to Magallanes; Argentina; woodland and open or shrubby areas.
SUBSPECIES: DIUCÓN, *X. p. pyrope*; Atacama to Tierra del Fuego. DIUCÓN DE CHILOÉ, *X. p. fortis*; Isla Chiloé (on mainland in winter).

GROUND–TYRANTS (GENUS *MUSCISAXICOLA*): Ground-tyrants are long-legged, ground-feeding flycatchers. They have an upright posture and habitually flick their tails and wings. The Spanish name *dormilona* means "sleepyhead" and refers to the habit these birds have of remaining motionless for long periods of time. They all bear similar plumage, differing mainly in the color of the crown and back. A few species are resident in n Chile, but most arrive in spring from countries to the north and then disperse southward along the Andes.

Rufous-naped Ground-Tyrant
Dormilona de nuca rojiza
Muscisaxicola rufivertex
OTHER NAMES: Fraile, Dormilon à calotte rousse, Rotnacken-Grundtyrann.
ID: 6.75 in (17 cm). Upperparts light slate; rump and uppertail coverts blackish. Tail black, with thin white edge to the outer tail feathers. Large patch of reddish-rust on hindcrown and nape. Narrow white supercilium. Underparts whitish, slightly grayer on the neck, breast and flanks; undertail coverts white. Wings dark grey. Runs continually across the ground when feeding, occasionally flying up after insects. Also feeds on berries. Birds that winter along the coast feed on small marine crustaceans. Perches on shrubs and posts.
RANGE: Resident from Arica–Parinacota to n Coquimbo; migrant from Coquimbo to O'Higgins; Peru, Bolivia, Argentina. Pre-Puna scrub in summer; lower elevations in winter; sea level to 14,750 ft (0–4500 m).
SUBSPECIES: DORMILONA DE NUCA ROJIZA, *M. r. rufivertex*; Antofagasta to O'Higgins. DORMILONA DE NUCA ROJIZA DEL NORTE, *M. r. pallidiceps*; Andes of Arica, Tarapacá and Antofagasta; desert coast in winter.

Ochre-naped Ground-Tyrant
Dormilona fraile
Muscisaxicola flavinucha
OTHER NAMES: Napsac, Dormilon à nuque jaun, Gelbnacken-Grundtyrann. *Fraile* refers to the prominent crown patch, which rural people liken to the skullcap once worn by Roman Catholic priests.
ID: 8 in (20 cm). Drab grey above. Greyish-white below, with a rufous wash on the flanks. Lemon yellow patch on hindcrown and nape. White forecrown and lores. Black tail; outer tail feather edged white. Nervously flicks its tail and wings when foraging. Nests (Sep–Jan) in cracks and crevices of rocks and stone walls.
RANGE: BREEDING SUMMER MIGRANT from Arica to Tierra del Fuego. Rocky slopes above watered valleys and wet sites with short grass; 6550–14,750 ft (2000–4500 m), and around 1640 ft (500 m) in the south.
SUBSPECIES: DORMILONA FRAILE, *M. f. flavinucha*; Arica to Los Lagos. DORMILONA FRAILE DEL SUR, *M. f. brevirostris*; Aisén to Cape Horn.

White-browed Ground-Tyrant
Dormilona de ceja blanca
Muscisaxicola albilora
OTHER NAMES: Dormilon à sourcils blancs, Rostkappen-Grundtyrann, Napsac.
ID: 7.25 in (18 cm). Upperparts brownish-grey, tinged with olive; rump and uppertail coverts black. Diffuse dark rufous crown. Black eyeline; white supercilium. Underparts white, merging into pale grey on the neck, chest and flanks. Wings brownish-grey. Tail black, with two outer tail feathers edged in white.
RANGE: BREEDING MIGRANT (Sep–Apr) from Los Andes Province, Valparaíso, to Magallanes; also from Ecuador to Argentina; Andean wetlands and bogs; 4925–13,250 ft (1500–2500 m).

Puna Ground-Tyrant
Dormilona de la puna
Muscisaxicola juninensis
OTHER NAMES: Napsac, Dormilon de Junin, Braunscheitel-Grundtyrann.
ID: 7.25 in (18 cm). Very similar to the White-browed Ground-Tyrant, but has darker grey upperparts, a smaller and darker rufous crown patch and very faint supercilium. Thin, short bill. Occupies wet Puna habitat rather than dry Puna. Nests (Nov–Dec) in holes or crevices in rocks.
RANGE: Resident in bogs in the High Andes from Arica-Parinacota to Tarapacá; Peru, Bolivia and nw Argentina; 13,125–16,400 ft (4000–5000 m).

Black-fronted Ground-Tyrant
Dormilona de frente negra
Muscisaxicola frontalis
OTHER NAMES: Tontito, Dormilon à front noir, Schwarzstirn-Grundtyrann.
ID: 8.1 in (20.5 cm). Upperparts ashy grey

darkening to blackish on the uppertail coverts. Large, conspicuous, black area on the forehead, crown and center of nape. White patch from the eye to the base of the bill. Whitish throat; rest of underparts off white. Black tail, with white outer tail feathers. Long, heavy bill is slightly decurved at tip. Bobs tail. Often nests on rocky slopes overlooking water.

RANGE: Uncommon summer BREEDING MIGRANT from Antofagasta to O'Higgins; nw Argentina; winters in Bolivia and Peru. Occupies arid, rocky barrenland on the Altiplano; 13,250–14,750 ft (2500–4500 m).

Cinereous Ground-Tyrant
Dormilona cenicienta
Muscisaxicola cinereus

OTHER NAMES: Dormilona gris, Dormilon cendré, Graubraun-Grundtyrann.

NOTE: This species is traditionally lumped with the Plain-capped Ground-Tyrant, *Muscisaxicola alpinus*.

ID: 6.75 in (17 cm). Upperparts light smoky grey, with no markings on crown or nape; rump and tail black. Lores and a thin strip above and below eye are white. Underparts white, with a grey wash on the sides of the neck, breast and abdomen. White undertail coverts. Wings darker than back; flight feathers edged black. Black bill and legs.

RANGE: BREEDING SUMMER MIGRANT in the central Andes from Coquimbo to Maule; ranges in Bolivia, Peru, Argentina. Rocky slopes near the snowline; 8200–13,125 ft (2500-4000 m).

White-fronted Ground-Tyrant
Dormilona gigante
Muscisaxicola albifrons

OTHER NAMES: Huacho, Dormilon à front blanc, Weissstirn-Grundtyrann.

ID: 9.5 in (24 cm). Largest of the Chilean ground-tyrants. Upperparts are dark mouse-grey, darkening to black on the rump. Black tail with white outer tail feathers. Dark grey wings. Straight black bill. Center of crown faintly rufous. Forehead and upperpart of lores are white. Base of the lower mandible and chin are white. Underparts are pale grey to white.

RANGE: Uncommon BREEDING MIGRANT in summer in High Andean bogs of Arica and Tarapacá; resident in Peru and nw Bolivia; 13,125–18,375 ft (4000–5600 m).

Dark-faced Ground-Tyrant
Dormilona tontita
Muscisaxicola macloviana mentalis

OTHER NAMES: Dormilona de cabeza obscura, Dormilon bistré, Maskengrundtyrann.

ID: 6.25 in (16 cm). Crown and chin dark brown. Face and lores black. Greyish-brown above, darkening to black on the rump and uppertail coverts. Tail dark brownish-grey, with white outer tail feathers. Greyish-white below. Bill and legs black.

RANGE: Seasonally common from Arica to Magallanes. Breeds (Dec–Jan) in the alpine zone of the southern Andes; descends to the lowlands of nc Chile, nw Argentina, Bolivia and Peru in winter. *M. m. macloviana* subspecies occurs in the Falklands.

Cinnamon-bellied Ground-Tyrant
Dormilona rufa
Muscisaxicola capistratus

OTHER NAMES: Dormilon à ventre roux, Zimtbauch-Grundtyrann.

ID: 7.25 in (18 cm). Upperparts brownish-grey to rufous on back and rump; tail black, with outer tail feathers cream and proximate tail feathers tawny. Forehead, lores and mask black. Crown reddish-chestnut. Throat white; breast buffy-grey; cinnamon on flanks and undertail. Wings and wing coverts brownish-grey, lighter than back. Black bill and legs. Nests (Nov) in holes under rocks and boulders.

RANGE: Antofagasta to Magallanes; also Peru, Bolivia, Argentina. Nests in s Chile and s Argentina on the Patagonian steppe. Populations disperse in winter to the Puna in c Chile and to the Loa and Copiapó Valleys of n Chile. Found from sea level to 1475 ft (0–450 m) in the southern nesting grounds; 9850–14,750 ft (3000–4500 m) in the northern Andes.

GROUND-TYRANTS 263

White-browed Ground-Tyrant
Dormilona de ceja blanca
Muscisaxicola albilora
Antofagasta–Magallanes
7.25 in (18 cm)

Puna Ground-Tyrant
Dormilona de la puna
Muscisaxicola juninensis
Arica–Tarapacá
7.25 in (18 cm)

Rufous-naped Ground-Tyrant
Dormilona de nuca rojiza
Muscisaxicola rufivertex
Arica–O'Higgins
6.75 in (17 cm)

Cinereous Ground-Tyrant
Dormilona cenicienta
Muscisaxicola cinereus
Antofagasta–Maule
6.75 in (17 cm)

Black-fronted Ground-Tyrant
Dormilona de frente negra
Muscisaxicola frontalis
Antofagasta–O'Higgins
8.1 in (20.5 cm)

Dark-faced Ground-Tyrant
Dormilona tontita
Muscisaxicola macloviana
Arica–Magallanes
6.25 in (16 cm)

Ochre-naped Ground-Tyrant
Dormilona fraile
Muscisaxicola flavinucha
Tarapacá–O'Higgins
Aisén–Magallanes
8 in (20 cm)

Spot-billed Ground-Tyrant
Dormilona chica
Muscisaxicola maculirostris
Arica–Magallanes
6 in (15 cm)

White-fronted Ground-Tyrant
Dormilona gigante
Muscisaxicola albifrons
Arica–Tarapacá
9.5 in (24 cm)

Cinnamon-bellied Ground-Tyrant
Dormilona rufa
Muscisaxicola capistratus
Antofagasta–Magallanes
7.25 in (18 cm)

Spot-billed Ground-Tyrant, Dormilona chica
Muscisaxicola maculirostris
OTHER NAMES: Arriero, Mapsac, Dormilon à bec maculé, Schnabelfleck-Grundtyrann.
ID: 6 in (15 cm). Smallest ground-tyrant. Upperparts brownish-grey; head and rump slightly darker. Lores white. Two buffy wingbars. Underparts greyish-buff. Black tail, with white outer tail feathers. Bill is black at tip, pale yellow at base. Nests (Oct–Nov) on brushy hillsides, with the nest hidden in a low shrub or depression among stones. Males engage in nuptial flights similar to those of larks, flying straight up into the air and singing as they descend with tail spread and legs dangling.
RANGE: Resident in the High Andes from Arica-Parinacota to Antofagasta; seasonal at lower elevations; also from Colombia to Argentina; sea level to 12,150 ft (0–3700 m).

D'Orbigny's Chat-Tyrant, Pitajo rojizo
Ochthoeca oenanthoides
OTHER NAMES: Pitajo canela, Graurücken-Schmätzertyrann, Pitajo d'Orbigny. Named after French naturalist Alcide D'Orbigny who discovered the species while on an expedition to South America in 1826–1834.
ID: 6.5 in (16.5 cm). Upperparts sooty brown. Forehead and conspicuous eyebrow white. Greyish-white throat; rest of underparts cinnamon. Wings dark brown with two reddish-brown wingbars. Tail dark brown edged white. Seen alone or in pairs. Perches upright on dead branches or posts, flying down to take insects on the ground and returning to same perch. Flicks wings while calling a repetitive *reeka-teeka*.
RANGE: Uncommon around Putre in Arica-Parinacota and the High Andes of Peru, Bolivia, nw Argentina. In Queñoa de altura *(Polylepis* sp.*)* woodland and steep hillsides near water; 9200–14,750 ft (2800–4500 m).

White-browed Chat-Tyrant, Pitajo gris
Ochthoeca leucophrys
OTHER NAMES: Pitajo à sourcils blancs, Graubauch-Schmätzertyrann.
ID: 6.25 in (16 cm). Dark grey back, tinged rufous on the lower back. Crown and sides of head darker grey. Broad white eyebrow beginning at base of bill and extending to nape; whitish crescent below eye. Throat and breast grey; abdomen white. Wings dark grey with two rufous wingbars. Tail dark grey, with white outer tail feathers. Solitary. Flicks wings and tail. Perches conspicuously on tops of bushes, often around cultivated fields or grassy slopes. Catches insects on the ground or in the air. Call is a piercing *keu-keu*.
RANGE: Fairly common in pre-Puna shrub zone and cultivated fields around Putre in Arica-Parinacota; also in Bolivia, Peru, Argentina; 8200–12,500 ft (2500–3800 m).

Patagonian Tyrant, Viudita
Coloramphus parvirostris
OTHER NAMES: Peutrén, Fío-Fío pardo, Pitajo de Patagonie, Patagonienschmätzertyrann. Call is a plaintive, whistled *tseee*, which has earned it the local name of *viudita*, meaning "widow."
ID: 5.25 in (13.5 cm). Upperparts drab greyish-brown; rump warm brown. Greyish eyebrow extends to form a crescent around the black ear patch. Underparts are dark grey with buff on the belly. Wings dark grey with two cinnamon wingbars. Tail is brownish-grey. Small black bill. Solitary and inconspicuous. In breeding season (Nov–Feb) forages for insects high in the treetops, flying out at infrequent intervals. In winter, sallies out for insects from low perches on shrubs and trees, especially Quillay *(Quillaja saponaria)* and Maitén *(Maitenus boaria)*.
RANGE: Coquimbo to Magallanes; also Argentina. Nests in *Nothofagus* woodland; winters in forested Andean foothills and in gardens of the Central Valley and coast.

White-crested Elaenia, Fío-Fío
Elaenia albiceps
OTHER NAMES: Chiflador, Silvador, Huiro, Weissbauch-Olivtyrann, Élénie à cimier blanc.
ID: 6 in (15 cm). Slender, olive-grey flycatcher, with a white crown-stripe and slight crest.

TYRANT-FLYCATCHERS 265

White-browed Chat-Tyrant
Pitajo gris
Ochthoeca leucophrys
High Andes of Arica
6 in (14.5 cm)

Patagonian Tyrant
Viudita
Coloramphus parvirostris
Coquimbo–Magallanes
5.25 in (13.5 cm)

D'Orbigny's Chat-Tyrant
Pitajo rojizo
Ochthoeca oenanthoides
High Andes of Arica
6.5 in (16.5 cm)

White-crested Elaenia
Fío–Fío
Elaenia albiceps
Arica–Magallanes
6 in (15 cm)

Spectacled Tyrant
Run-Run
Hymenops perspicillata
Coquimbo–Magallanes
6.5 in (16 cm)

Austral Negrito
Colegial
Lessonia rufa
Arica–Magallanes
5 in (12.5 cm)

Warbling Doradito
Pájaro amarillo
Pseudocolopteryx flaviventris
Coquimbo–Valdivia
5 in (12.5 cm)

Many-colored Rush-Tyrant
Siete colores
Tachuris rubrigastra
Antofagasta–Aisén
4 in (10 cm)

Vermillion Flycatcher
Saca-tu-real
Pyrocephalus rubinus
Arica–Tarapacá
5–6 in (13–15 cm)

Dark wings, with two white wingbars. Throat and breast grey; center of abdomen white. Yellow flanks and yellow undertail coverts. Tail dark greyish-brown. Feeds mainly on insects, but will also take berries and seeds. Calls its name *FEeo-FEeo*. Builds a cup-shaped, feather-lined nest of grass, leaves and moss in low bushes.
RANGE: Arica to Tierra del Fuego. Common BREEDING MIGRANT (Sep–Mar); winters east of the Andes. In urban gardens, woodland, orchards and farms.
SUBSPECIES: FÍO-FÍO, *E. a. chilensis*; summer breeding migrant from Atacama to Tierra del Fuego. FÍO-FÍO PERUANO, *E. a. modesta*; white crest and wingbars very faint (may be a separate species). Summer breeding migrant in valleys and oases of Arica and Tarapacá.

Austral Negrito, Colegial
Lessonia rufa
OTHER NAMES: Indio, Mensu cashca, Lessonie noire, Patagoniensporntyrann. The name *Colegial* ("Schoolboy") refers to the brown saddle on the male's back, which resembles the leather book bags of school children.
ID: 5 in (12.5 cm). MALE black with bright cinnamon back. Black bill and legs. FEMALE has brown upperparts that are slightly rufous on the back; greyish-brown underparts. Commonly seen on the ground around swamps, marshes, lakes and rivers, but also perches on fences or low bushes. Forages for insects and larvae by running across the ground in spurts or making short aerial sorties after flying insects. Breeds (Sep–Nov), building a cup-shaped nest of root fibers, twigs and grass on the ground amid marsh grass or low bushes.
RANGE: Arica to Tierra del Fuego; Bolivia, Peru, Argentina, Uruguay, Paraguay, Brazil. Wetlands, lakeshores, pastures, open fields; sea level to 3300 ft (0–1000 m).

Andean (White-winged) Negrito Colegial del Norte
Lessonia oreas
ID: 5 in (12.5 cm). Identical to the Austral Negrito except for the white underside of the primaries and secondaries, which appear as a pale wing flash in flight; also exposes the pale wing patch as it flicks its wings. Usually in pairs or family groups. Perches on grass tussocks and flies out to catch low-flying insects; also makes short runs on the ground after prey. NOT ILLUSTRATED.
RANGE: Local from Arica-Parinacota to Coquimbo; Peru, Bolivia, nw Argentina. In Andean *bofedales* and grassy wetlands; 11,500–14,750 ft (3500–4500 m).

Spectacled Tyrant, Run-Run
Hymenops perspicillata
OTHER NAMES: Pico de plata, Viudita negra de bañado, Ada clignot, Brillendunkeltyrann. Run-Run refers to the snipe-like drumming that males make in nuptial display.
ID: 6.5 in (16 cm). MALE is black, except for white patch on primaries (seen perched and in flight). Pale eye. Bill and fleshy eyering lemon-yellow. Black legs. FEMALE has dark brown upperparts, with feathers edged light brown; underparts buffy with longitudinal black streaks on breast. Primaries rufous with black edging. Wing coverts black. Two buffy wingbars. Black tail feathers edged ochre. Males and females migrate in separate groups, with males arriving first in Chile in September to establish territories. These birds tend to perch conspicuously but silently on reeds, flying up to snatch an insect, then returning to the same vantage point. Nest is a cup of grasses or reeds, lined with feathers or hairs.
RANGE: BREEDING MIGRANT from Coquimbo to Magallanes; winters in Argentina, Bolivia, Brazil, Uruguay. Marshes, swamps, riverine wetlands; sea level to 3950 ft (0–1200 m).

Warbling Doradito
Pájaro amarillo
Pseudocolopteryx flaviventris
OTHER NAMES: Doradito común, Doradite babillarde, Braunrücken-Sumpftyrann.
ID: 5 in (12.5 cm). Upperparts, wings and tail olive-brown; feathers of crown edged rufous. Underparts canary yellow. Shy and silent except for soft, nuptial warbles of the

Pied-crested Tit-Tyrant
Cachudito de cresta blanca
Anairetes reguloides
Arica
4.5 in (12 cm)

Tufted Tit-Tyrant
Cachudito
Anairetes parulus
Antofagasta–Magallanes
4.25 in (11 cm)

Juan Fernández Tit-Tyrant
Cachudito de Juan Fernández
Anairetes fernandezianus
Juan Fernández
5.5 in (14 cm)

Yellow-billed Tit-Tyrant
Cachudito del norte
Anairetes flavirostris
Arica–Tarapacá
4.1 in (10.5 cm)

male. Occurs mainly in reedbeds, but also found in open, damp areas and vegetation along streams and ponds. Weaves its nest (Dec–Jan) in sheltered areas of reedbeds, placing the nest in the fork of stiff-stemmed plants such as dock (*Rumex crispus*) that grow in boggy ground.

RANGE: RARE SUMMER BREEDING MIGRANT; Coquimbo to Valdivia; se Brazil, Uruguay, Paraguay, Argentina. In lowland reedbeds, rushes, marshes and riverbanks.

Many-colored Rush-Tyrant
Siete colores
Tachuris rubrigastra

OTHER NAMES: Matraca, Tyranneau omnicolore, Vielfarben-Tachurityrann.

ID: 4 in (10 cm). Small, colorful, restless bird of rushes and reedbeds. Crown black with a red stripe on the top. The long, yellow eyebrow extends from bill to the side of the neck. Lores, ocular area and ear coverts bluish-grey. Bronzy-green back. Throat and breast white, with a partial black collar across the chest; rest of underparts yellow, with salmon-red undertail coverts. Wings dark brownish-grey with a white wingbar. Tail black with white outer tail feathers. Associates with the Wren-like Rushbird (*Phleocryptes melanops*). Flits from reed to reed, often posing with its head held downward near the water as it searches for insects. Nest (Sep–Dec) is a hollow cone woven of dry, pliable rushes anchored to a single reed stem; nest looks as if it is built of papier-mâché due to the glutinous matter the bird applies to the exterior.

RANGE: Antofagasta to Aisén; Peru, Bolivia, Argentina, Paraguay, Uruguay and Brazil. Reedbeds around lakes, rivers and streams.

SUBSPECIES: SIETE COLORES, *T. r. rubrigastra*; Atacama to Aisén. SIETE COLORES DEL NORTE, *T. r. loaensis*; smaller with a bright white throat and abdomen; bright yellow flanks; Río Loa in Antofagasta.

Vermilion Flycatcher
Saca-tu-real
Pyrocephalus rubinus

OTHER NAMES: Turturpillén, Churrinche, Putilla, Viudita roja, Rubintyrann, Moucherolle vermilion.

ID: 5–6 in (13–15 cm). Sexually dimorphic. ADULT MALE has a vermilion cap and underparts. Mask, upperparts, wings and tail are sooty black. FEMALE is sooty grey above, whitish below, streaked brown on the breast; abdomen, flanks and undertail are rosy-red; underwing coverts and bend of wing are pink. Perches on fence posts, telephone wires, bushes and tree branches. Makes aerial sorties after insects. This bird gets its Chilean name from its faint but often sounded call, *saca-tu-real*. Builds a small nest (Nov) in the crotch of trees, especially in Molle *(Schinus molle)* growing around fields.
RANGE: Local in valleys and foothill oases of Arica and Tarapacá. Ranges from sw USA through Central and South America in semi-arid scrub.

Tufted Tit-Tyrant
Cachudito
Anairetes parulus
OTHER NAMES: Taurillon mésange, Meisentachurityrann, Peshquintún. Torito ("little bull") and Cachudito ("little longhorn") refer to this bird's spiky crest.
ID: 4.25 in (11 cm). Upperparts smoky grey. Head black with recurved crest. White streaking on the forehead, auriculars and sides of head. Underparts pale lemon yellow, faintly streaked black on throat and breast. Black bill and legs. Pale yellow iris. Female has a shorter crest. Call is a soft, musical trill. Forages restlessly for insects in tree foliage and sometimes takes seeds. Builds its tiny, cup-shaped nest (Aug–Nov) in forest clearings and brushy slopes near streams.
RANGE: Antofagasta to Magallanes; w South America; gardens, woodland, scrub.
SUBSPECIES: CACHUDITO, *A. p. parulus*; Antofagasta to Aisén. CACHUDITO AUSTRAL, *A. p. lippus*; darker, with a grey rump and heavier streaking on breast; Magallanes.

Juan Fernández Tit-Tyrant
Cachudito de Juan Fernández
Anairetes fernandezianus
OTHER NAMES: Taurillon de Juan Fernandez, Juan-Fernandez-Tachurityrann, Torito.

ID: 5.5 in (14 cm). Larger and with darker streaking than the Tufted Tit-Tyrant.
RANGE: ENDEMIC to the forests of Isla Masatierra (Alejandro Selkirk), Juan Fernández.

Yellow-billed Tit-Tyrant
Cachudito del norte
Anairetes flavirostris
OTHER NAMES: Torito pico amarillo, Taurillon à bec jaune, Gelbschnabel-Tachurityrann.
ID: 4.1 in (10.5 cm). Like the Tufted Tit-Tyrant but with heavier black streaking on breast; two white, well-defined wingbars; and a flatter, fanlike crest. Black bill; base of mandible yellow-orange. Brown iris.
RANGE: Arica and Tarapacá; Peru, Bolivia, Argentina. Brush-covered slopes and cultivated fields; 3250–12,500 ft (1000–3700 m).

Pied-crested Tit-Tyrant
Cachudito de cresta blanca
Anairetes reguloides
OTHER NAMES: Torito, Taurillon roitelet, Streifenbauch-Tachurityrann.
ID: 4.5 in (12 cm). Like the Tufted Tit-Tyrant but with a pied, two-horned crest and black face and throat. Mantle streaked black and white. Breast heavily streaked in black and white; yellow abdomen. Black wings with 2 white wingbars. Tail feathers black with white terminal tips. Black bill; base of mandible orange-red.
RANGE: Arica and Tarapacá; also Peru. On brush-covered slopes and edges of cultivated fields; sea level to 3250 ft (0–1000 m).

VAGRANT/RARE FLYCATCHERS: SHORT-TAILED FIELD-TYRANT, *Muscigralla brevicauda*; rare at the mouth of the Río Lluta in Arica.
BRAN-COLORED FLYCATCHER, *Myiophobus fasciatus*; Arica and Camarones, Tarapacá.
GREAT KISKADEE: *Pitangus sulphuratus*; Suca Gorge, Tarapacá, and Los Angeles, Biobío.
STREAKED FLYCATCHER, *Myodynastes maculatus*; recorded at Vallenar in Atacama.
EASTERN KINGBIRD, *Tyrannus tyrannus*; Arica, Antofagasta and Valparaíso.
TROPICAL KINGBIRD, *Tyrannus melancholicus*; recorded at Iquique and Santiago.

FORK-TAILED FLYCATCHER, *Tyrannus savana*; recorded at Camarones Gorge, Tarapacá and Lluta Valley, Arica.

YELLOW-BELLIED ELAENIA, *Elaenia flavogaster*; recorded in Azapa Valley, Arica.

CLIFF FLYCATCHER, *Hirundinea ferruginea*; one record at Temuco.

FAMILY VIREONIDAE
VIREOS

The RED-EYED VIREO, VERDERON DE OJOS ROJOS, *Vireo olivaceus*, is a vagrant species in Chile. There is one record from Vallenar, Atacama Region.

FAMILY HIRUNDINIDAE
SWALLOWS

Swallows are fast, tireless fliers capable of making long migrations. They have short necks, streamlined bodies and long, pointed wings. The tail is moderately long and usually forked. The bill is short, flat and wide at the base, and is adapted for catching insects on the wing. The feet and legs are small and weak, and for this reason these birds often select small branches or telephone wires for perching. They descend to the ground when gathering mud or other nesting material. Swallows lay 3 to 7 white or speckled eggs in feather-lined mud nests built in crevices of ravine walls, in natural caves, or under the eaves of buildings.

Chilean Swallow
Golondrina chilena
Tachycineta meyeni

OTHER NAMES: Golondrina de rabadilla blanca, Pilmaiquén, Golondrina azul, Hirondelle du Chili, Chileschwalbe.

ID: 5.25 in (13.5 cm). Upperparts dark metallic blue. Conspicuous white rump. Underparts white, washed grey on flanks and sides of breast. Wings and slightly forked tail are black. JUVENILES lack iridescence but always have a white rump. Builds a mud nest, often under the eaves of houses, and raises 2 to 3 broods of young (Sep–Feb).

RANGE: Atacama to Tierra del Fuego; common resident in central Chile; southern populations winter in Argentina, Bolivia, Paraguay, Brazil. Occurs in almost every habitat; sea level to 8200 ft (0–2500 m).

Blue-and-white Swallow
Golondrina de dorsa negro
Pygochelidon (Notiochelidon) cyanoleuca

OTHER NAMES: Pilmaiquén, Golondrina de rabadilla negra, Golondrina barranquera azul, Hirondelle bleu et blanc, Schwarzsteissschwalbe.

ID: 5 in (12.5 cm). Upperparts entirely dark metallic blue. Underparts white, washed with grey. Wings and tail dusky. Separated from Chilean Swallow by the dark rump. Nests (Oct–Dec) colonially in feather-lined holes in soft banks and slopes near streams; also uses unoccupied holes of the Common Miner *(Geositta cunicularia)* in coastal sand dunes in the north, and holes in forest trees in the south. Common and widespread in Chile.

RANGE: Resident from Arica to Antofagasta; migrant south to Magallanes. Ranges from Costa Rica to Argentina. Occurs around lakes, rivers, inundated fields; sea level to 13,125 ft (0–4000 m).

Andean Swallow
Golondrina de los riscos
Haplochelidon andecola

OTHER NAMES: Andean Cliff Swallow, Golondrina andina, Hirondelle des Andes, Andenschwalbe.

ID: 6 in (15 cm). Upperparts dark bluish-black; uppertail coverts brownish; wings brownish-black. Throat and upper breast ashy, becoming white in center of abdomen; greyish-white undertail coverts. Slightly-forked tail. JUVENILE has a buffy face and throat, and in this plumage can be mistaken for a Barn Swallow. Nests colonially on high bluffs and escarpments overlooking watered valleys. Excavates the nesting hole using the bill to start the hole and then the feet to push away the earth.

RANGE: Altiplano of Arica and Tarapacá; Peru, Bolivia. Often seen around Andean villages; 9850–14,750 ft (3000–4500 m).

Cliff Swallow, Golondrina grande
Petrochelidon pyrrhonota
OTHER NAMES: Hirondelle à front blanc, Fahlstirnschwalbe.
ID: 5–6 in (13–15 cm). Upperparts steel blue with faint white lines on the back. Forehead, nape and rump buffy; crown dark blue. Underparts whitish, with dark chestnut on the throat, cheeks and sides of face. Very slightly forked tail, almost square. Bill and legs black.
RANGE: NON-BREEDING MIGRANT in desert oases of Arica and Tarapacá. Widespread from Alaska to nw Argentina; migrates from its boreal breeding grounds via Cuba and Central America.

Barn Swallow, Golondrina bermeja
Hirundo rustica
OTHER NAMES: Golondrina tijerita, Hirondelle rustique, Rauchschwalbe.
ID: 6-7 in (15–17.5 cm). Upperparts black with bluish sheen. Forehead buff; face and throat cinnamon. Underparts buffy with a narrow, blue-black pectoral band. Wings black with a greenish iridescence. Black, deeply-forked tail has small, white marks on inner web of the tail feathers. Flocks with other swallows. This long distance migrant moves between its boreal breeding grounds and South America each year.
RANGE: NON-BREEDING MIGRANT from Arica to Magallanes. Seen in Chile mainly in March on its northward migration. Occurs worldwide over farmland, towns, wetlands.

Bank Swallow, Golondrina barranquera
Riparia riparia
OTHER NAMES: Sand Martin, Hirondelle de rivage, Uferschwalbe.
ID: 5 in (13 cm). Upperparts and sides of head smoky-brown. Underparts are white with a diagnostic brown band across breast. Wings and forked tail dark brown.
RANGE: NON-BREEDING MIGRANT mainly to northern Chile; recorded frequently as far south as Magallanes. Uncommon summer visitor to lakes, rivers and marshes. Boreal breeder. Ranges worldwide.

Peruvian Martin, Golondrina peruana
Progne murphyi
OTHER NAMES: Golondrina negra, Hirondelle de Murphy, Peruschwalbe.
ID: 6 in (15 cm). ADULT MALE completely black with a bluish sheen. Forked tail. Black bill; brown legs. FEMALE mouse-grey, with some blue sheen on back; throat, breast and flanks smoky-brown; lighter on center of abdomen; undertail coverts white with dark streaks. Glides and soars, and flies higher than swallows.
RANGE: Lluta and Azapa Valleys near Arica; coastal Peru. Rocky outcrops, ravines and farmland on the arid coast.
VAGRANT SWALLOWS: SOUTHERN MARTIN, *Progne elegans*; recorded at Santiago. BROWN-CHESTED MARTIN, *Progne tapera*; recorded at Arica.

FAMILY COTINGIDAE (PHYTOTOMIDAE)
PLANTCUTTERS
These are birds of orchards and gardens. They are named for the habit of cutting buds off trees with their thick, serrated bill. Fruit growers regard this species as a pest.

Rufous-tailed Plantcutter, Rara
Phytotoma rara
OTHER NAMES: Cortarama grande, Kamtrui, Rotschwanz-Pflanzenmäher, Rara à queue rousse.
ID: 7.5 in (19 cm). MALE has grey upperparts with black streaks. Forehead and crown rufous, sometimes with fine, black streaks. Wings black with a white wingbar. Underparts rufous. Prominent rufous tail spots and dark terminal tailband; central tail feathers dark. Stout, conical bill. Red iris. FEMALE like male, but has buff underparts with fine black streaks across the breast. Usually solitary, but seen in pairs or small flocks in breeding season (Oct–Dec). Nests in orchard trees and high bushes. Clutch is 2 to 4 green eggs, sparsely dotted with lilac or brown.
RANGE: Atacama to Magallanes; Argentina. In woodland, brushy fields, orchards and gardens; sea level to 7550 ft (0–2300 m).

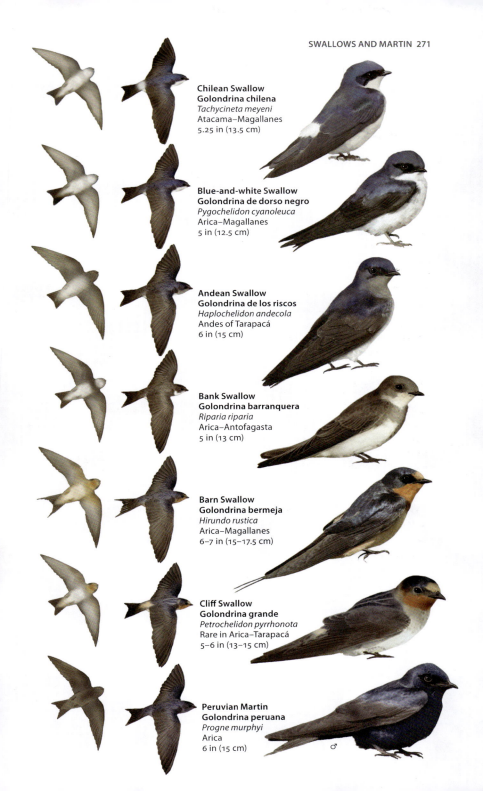

SWALLOWS AND MARTIN 271

Chilean Swallow
Golondrina chilena
Tachycineta meyeni
Atacama–Magallanes
5.25 in (13.5 cm)

Blue-and-white Swallow
Golondrina de dorso negro
Pygochelidon cyanoleuca
Arica–Magallanes
5 in (12.5 cm)

Andean Swallow
Golondrina de los riscos
Haplochelidon andecola
Andes of Tarapacá
6 in (15 cm)

Bank Swallow
Golondrina barranquera
Riparia riparia
Arica–Antofagasta
5 in (13 cm)

Barn Swallow
Golondrina bermeja
Hirundo rustica
Arica–Magallanes
6–7 in (15–17.5 cm)

Cliff Swallow
Golondrina grande
Petrochelidon pyrrhonota
Rare in Arica–Tarapacá
5–6 in (13–15 cm)

Peruvian Martin
Golondrina peruana
Progne murphyi
Arica
6 in (15 cm)

FAMILY TROGLODYTIDAE
WRENS

These small, brown birds have barred wings and short, cocked tails. Their thin, slightly curved bills are adapted for eating insects. They inhabit a variety of habitats and have a rich, melodious song that is amazingly loud for such tiny birds.

Southern House Wren, Chercán
Troglodytes musculus
OTHER NAMES: Chesquén, Ratona, Cucurachero, Troglodyte austral, Hauszaunkönig.
ID: 4.5 in (12 cm). Head and mantle light greyish-brown. Uppertail coverts and tail rufous; tail barred with dark brown. Wings dark brown; rufous outer primaries crossed with small black bars. Underparts pale cinnamon to buff. Flanks and undertail coverts rufous cinnamon. Legs and thin bill are horn colored. Tame and confiding. Harsh scolding note and fast, warbling call. Long nesting season with multiple broods. Male builds several trial nests of twigs and grass placed in holes or nesting boxes; the female selects one for laying her eggs.
RANGE: Common from Arica to Tierra del Fuego. Widespread in North and South America. In scrub, woodland, farmland and near human habitation; sea level to 11,500 ft (0–3500 m).
SUBSPECIES: CHERCÁN COMÚN, *T. m. chilensis*; Atacama to Tierra del Fuego. CHERCÁN DE ATACAMA, *T. m. atacamensis*; paler subspecies; Tarapacá to Coquimbo. CHERCÁN DE ARICA, *T. m. tacellatus*; pale greyish-white underparts and black-barred upperparts; found in valleys near Arica.

Grass (Sedge) Wren, Chercán de las vegas
Cistothorus platensis
OTHER NAMES: Ratona aperdizada, Seggenzaunkönig, Troglodyte à bec court.
ID: 4.25 in (11 cm). Upperparts brownish-grey with black striping on head and black and buff striping on the back. Fine black barring on uppertail coverts. Underparts buff. Wings and tail finely barred black and brown. Bill and legs horn-colored. Secretive and furtive, living exclusively on or near the ground in flooded pastures, reedbeds and grassy riverbanks. Will perch briefly on top of grass stems to investigate an unfamiliar sound such as a birder's *pissst*. Builds a large, rounded, partially roofed nest of grass that is placed on or near the ground.
RANGE: Atacama to Tierra del Fuego. Wide ranging in North and South America and in the Falkland Islands; sea level to 3300 ft (0–1000 m).

FAMILY TURDIDAE
THRUSHES

The Austral Thrush closely resembles the American Robin. It is common south of the desert zone in gardens, parks and farmland. The dark-plumaged Chiguanco occupies the oases, valleys and highlands of northern Chile, Peru, Bolivia and Ecuador. Both have sweet, melodic, whistled songs.

Austral Thrush, Zorzal
Turdus falklandii
OTHER NAMES: Huilque, Merle austral, Magellandrossel.
ID: 9.25 in (23 cm). Upperparts dark olive-grey. Cap and ear coverts blackish, with feathers on forehead edged in brown. Throat streaked with white and black. Rest of underparts buff to pale cinnamon. Wings and tail are dark brown. Bill and legs yellow. FEMALE is paler overall, with a brown head. JUVENILES have a spotted chest. Mainly a ground feeder, it is often seen on lawns as it searches for worms and grubs. Also feeds on snails, fruit and berries. Nest is an open, cup-shaped structure of twigs, grass and mud, set low in dense vegetation.
RANGE: Common in orchards, farmland and gardens from Antofagasta south to Tierra del Fuego; Argentina, the Falklands. Introduced to Juan Fernández.
SUBSPECIES: ZORZAL, *T. f. magallanicus*, ranges from Chañaral, Atacama, to Cape Horn; introduced to Masatierra in Juan Fernández. ZORZAL DE LA MOCHA, *T. f. mochae*, from Isla Mocha off Araucanía, is paler, with a longer, stronger bill.

Chiguanco Thrush, Zorzal negro
Turdus chiguanco

OTHER NAMES: Chiguancodrossel, Merle chiguanco.

ID: 10.25 in (26 cm). MALE upperparts are dark slate-grey to brown, depending on the subspecies. Wings and tail darker than back. Underparts paler, with light brown flecking on throat. Bill and legs bright yellow. FEMALE dull brown with dull yellow bill and legs. JUVENILE has pale brown breast with buffy flecking. Feeds on fruit, grubs and insects. Birds in the Putre area nest in March or April at the end of the "Altiplano winter," when the ground is softer and the grubs more plentiful.

RANGE: Arica to Antofagasta, with records in Santiago, Maule and Biobío; Bolivia, Peru, Ecuador, Argentina. Occurs in dense vegetation around streams, farmland and orchards; sea level to 12,000 ft (0–3600 m).

SUBSPECIES: The ZORZAL DEL NORTE, *T. c. chiguanco*, ranges in highlands of Arica and Tarapacá; males are brown. ZORZAL CUYANO, *T. c. anthracinus*, is uncommon from the Salar de Atacama to Biobío; the males are dark slate-grey.

VAGRANTS: CREAMY-BELLIED THRUSH, *Turdus amaurochalinus*; Vallenar Atacama. VEERY, *Catharus fuscescens*; Lluta Valley, Arica.

FAMILY MIMIDAE
MOCKINGBIRDS

Mockingbirds are characterized by short, rounded wings, a long tail, a slender slightly downturned bill, and long legs. They feed on insects, fruit and seeds. They are known for their beautiful, melodic songs and the ability to mimic the songs of other birds.

Chilean Mockingbird, Tenca
Mimus tenca

OTHER NAMES: Trenca, Moqueur du Chili, Chilespottdrossel.

ID: 10.25 in (26 cm). Upperparts are brown to grey. Feathers of the crown and nape are lightly streaked with black. The wings are black, with the outer primaries and secondaries edged with white. Long, dark brown tail with white patches on the tips of the outer tail feathers. Conspicuous white supercilium. Throat whitish, edged with a dark malar stripe. Underparts pale brownish-grey with dark spots on sides of body. Bill and legs black. A bird of brush-covered slopes. Tends to perch on high branches. Glides from perch to perch with wings and tail fanned out. Builds its nest (Nov–Dec) in the fork of a thorn tree or cactus. The Tenca is the sole seed disperser of Quintral del quisco (*Tristerix aphyllus*), a mistletoe that grows on Quisco cactus.

RANGE: ENDEMIC. Atacama to Los Lagos.

Patagonian Mockingbird
Tenca patagónica
Mimus patagonicus

OTHER NAMES: Calandria gris, Moqueur de Patagonie, Rostflanken-Spottdrossel.

ID: 9.25 in (23 cm). Upperparts mouse grey, with rump tinged with olive. Crisp white supercilium. Wings dark brown, with two white wingbars. Underparts pale grey, with a whitish throat and buffy flanks. Tail is dark grey, with white on outer tail feathers and tip. Separated from Tenca by its southern range, smaller size, and shorter bill and tail. Shy and retiring; keeps to dense shrubbery where it is often overlooked. Sweet, melodic song with phrases of double and triple notes. Nests (Nov–Dec) in bushes or low trees.

RANGE: Summer resident on the pampas of Aisén and Magallanes; also Argentina.

VAGRANT: WHITE-BANDED MOCKINGBIRD, *Mimus triurus*; broad white patches on the wings and tail; cinnamon rump; numerous records in nc Chile.

FAMILY MOTACILLIDAE
PIPITS

These small, terrestrial insect-eaters walk or run over the ground, never hop. They characteristically open and close their tail when alighting. Camouflaged by cryptic plumage, they are almost invisible against the stubble of damp fields. The aerial nuptial ballet of the male has earned these birds the Chilean name, *bailarínes chicos* ("little dancers").

Correndera Pipit
Bailarín chico argentino
Anthus correndera
OTHER NAMES: Caminante, Agachadera, Cachirla pálida, Correnderapieper, Pipit correndera.
ID: 6 in (15.5 cm). Upperparts are streaked brown and buff, with two white "suspenders" on the mantle. Throat is buff; rest of underparts are greyish-white, with black streaks on the breast and flanks. Dark brown wings, flight feathers edged lighter. Tail is dark brown, with white outer tail feathers. Black bill; pale base to mandible. Horn-colored legs; very long, straight hindclaw. Undulating flight, almost always accompanied by a high-pitched *chwiip-chwiip*. White outer tail feathers seen in flight. Flicks tail nervously when alighting. The male's nuptial flight (Oct–Nov) is similar to a lark's, with the bird ascending high into the air, then parachuting back to earth as it sings. Builds an open or semi-roofed, cup-shaped nest of grass on the ground in tall protective vegetation.
RANGE: Common in pastures, marshes, damp meadows, steppe and beaches from Antofagasta to Tierra del Fuego. Widespread in s South America.
SUBSPECIES: BAILARÍN CHICO COMÚN, *A. c. chilensis*; Atacama to Tierra del Fuego; sea level to 3300 ft (0–1000 m). BAILARÍN CHICO DEL NORTE, *A. c. catamarcae*; High Andes of Antofagasta; darker back; longer bill.

Yellowish Pipit
Bailarín chico peruano
Anthus lutescens
OTHER NAMES: Cachirla chica, Savannepieper Pipit jaunâtre.
ID: 5 in (13 cm). Resembles the Correndera Pipit; separated by its range, smaller size and paler, faintly streaked underparts.
RANGE: Uncommon along the arid coast of Arica. Widespread in South America.
VAGRANT: HELLMAYR'S PIPIT, *Anthus hellmayri*; buffy outer tail feathers; hindclaw short and strongly-curved; Araucanía.

FAMILY THRAUPIDAE
TANAGERS AND ALLIES
Thraupidae contains a diverse group of birds, many of which have been placed with the tanagers as a result of DNA analysis. In general, the thraupids are arboreal, short-legged and have bills suitable for feeding on fruit, flower nectar and insects.

Blue-and-yellow Tanager, Naranjero
Thraupis bonariensis
OTHER NAMES: Darwin's Tanager, Llayle, Pichaco, Tangara fourchu, Furchentangare. Naranjero refers to the male's orange breast.
ID: 6 in (16 cm). MALE's head and neck is blue with a black mask. Greenish mantle. Breast is orange. Rump, abdomen and undertail coverts are yellow. Wings and tail bluish-black. Bill dark with whitish mandible. FEMALE is duller in color.
RANGE: Locally common in pre-Puna scrub zone of Arica and Tarapacá; Ecuador, Peru, Bolivia. In wooded ravines and tall trees (*Eucalyptus*, *Schinus*) around villages, farms and pastures; 9850–11,800 ft (3000–3600 m).

Black-throated Flowerpiercer
Comesebo negro
Diglossa brunneiventris
OTHER NAMES: Schwarzkehl-Hakenschnabel, Percefleur à gorge noire.
ID: 5 in (12 cm). Upperparts black. Wings black with ashy-black lesser wing coverts. Underparts reddish chestnut; flanks and underwing coverts light grey. Throat black; cheeks rusty red. Black bill, with a thin, sharp hook at the tip of the upper mandible. JUVENILES are dark grey above, with a tan and black streaked chest and rufous undertail coverts. Feeds on flower nectar taken by piercing the base of the blossom. Forages alone, in pairs or family groups, actively examining tangles and foliage and often hanging upside down.
RANGE: Around Putre in Arica-Parinacota; also Peru, Bolivia. Ravines with flowering shrubs and near villages and farm fields in the pre-Puna scrub zone; 9850–11,500 ft (3000–3500 m).

Cinereous Conebill, Comesebo chico
Conirostrum cinereum
OTHER NAMES: Mielerito gris, Chincheriche, Conirostre cendré, Weissstirn-Spitzschnabel.
ID: 4.5 in (11 cm). Upperparts slate grey with an olive tinge. Whitish forehead and eyebrow. Underparts, throat, breast are white; abdomen and rest of underparts are buffy. Wings black with a white wingbar and a white patch on the secondaries. Tail black. Bill horn. Black legs. Forages for insects in pairs or small flocks in dense foliage. Loud, trilling call.
RANGE: Arica to Tarapacá; Peru. In olive, fig, and tamarugo groves and scrub in oasis valleys; sea level to 11,500 ft (0–3500 m).

Tamarugo Conebill
Comesebo de los tamarugales
Conirostrum tamarugense
OTHER NAMES: Conirostre de Tamarugo, Rotstirn-Spitzschnabel.
ID: 5 in (12 cm). Upperparts dark slate grey. Eyebrow, forehead, throat and breast rusty red. Rest of underparts pale grey, with a yellowish tinge on belly; rufous undertail coverts. Wings and tail are brownish-grey. White patch on primaries. FEMALES and JUVENILES are paler and duller. Nests in tamarugo trees *(Prosopis tamarugo)* on the Pampa del Tamarugal, inland of Iquique, where it feeds on larvae of tamarugo blue butterflies *(Leptotes trigemmatus)*. After the spring breeding season, the main body of birds disperses to the Andean pre-Puna scrub zone. VULNERABLE.
RANGE: Arica-Parinacota to Tarapacá; also sw Peru. In tamarugo groves, oasis valleys, and pre-Puna scrub; sea level to 10,000 ft (3000 m).

Giant Conebill
Comesebo gigante
Oreomanes fraseri
OTHER NAMES: Conirostre géant, Riesenspitzschnabel.
ID: 5.5 in (14 cm). Slate grey above; chestnut below. Cheeks and supercilium are white; eyeline is chestnut. Long, sharply pointed, grey bill. Call is a tinkling *chet-chet-chet*. Lives exclusively in queñoa trees *(Polylepis tarapacana, P. rugulosa)* where it forages for arthropods and insects, often in the company of other passerines.
RANGE: Altiplano of Arica-Parinacota and Peru, Bolivia, Argentina; 9850–13,125 ft (3000–4000 m).
VAGRANT: SUMMER TANAGER, *Piranga rubra*; one record from Antofagasta. CARBONATED FLOWERPIERCER, *Diglossa carbonaria*; one record from Putre.

FAMILY CARDINALINAE
CARDINAL GROSBEAKS
These plump, stocky birds have a thick, strong bill. They are closely related to the Northern Cardinal *(Cardinalis cardinalis)*.

Golden-billed Saltator
Pepitero
Saltator aurantiirostris
OTHER NAMES: Pepitero de corbata, Saltator à bec orange, Goldschnabelsaltator.
ID: 8 in (20 cm). Adult's bill is strong, thick and golden yellow (black in juvenile). Conspicuous black facial disk, bordered by a white throat patch and a broad, white crescent that extends from behind the eye to the neck. Upperparts leaden grey. Chest grey; rest of underparts buff to rufous. Long grey tail, with white on the outer tail feathers (seen in flight). Feeds on the seeds *(pepas)* of various fruits—thus the common name, Pepitero. Perches in full view on the tops of high trees and sings a loud, melodious, finch-like song.
RANGE: Andes of Arica, especially around Putre and Socoroma; c Peru, Bolivia, Brazil, Argentina. Montane woodland and scrub; 9850–11,500 ft (3000–3500 m).

FAMILY EMBERIZIDAE
SPARROWS AND ALLIES
These birds have short, thick, conical bills. Some are brightly colored while others are drab plumaged. Many exhibit sexual dimorphism. Sparrows can be terrestrial or arboreal, and some have sweet songs. Many

of these species are in a state of taxonomic transition due to recent DNA analysis. Some species have been found to be closely related to tanagers; but for now, they are retained in the Emberizidae.

Blue-black Grassquit, Negrillo
Volatinia jacarina
OTHER NAMES: Saltapalito, Jacarini noir.
ID: 5 in (12 cm). ADULT MALE is a glossy blue-black. Wings and tail are brownish-black. The small, conical bill has a dark upper mandible and a pale lower mandible. FEMALE is brown on the back, buff with brown striations below; rufous undertail coverts. Males perform a charming nuptial display, jumping straight up and down while trilling in cadence with the dance. Nests at ground level, attaching its cup-shaped nest to a grass stem or weed.
RANGE: Common around farms, pastures and fields in Arica. Ranges from Mexico to Argentina.

Chestnut-throated Seedeater, Corbatita
Sporophila telasco
OTHER NAMES: Fringilo corbatita, Espiguero corbatón, Sporophile télasco, Braunkehlpfäffchen. Corbatita means "necktie," referring to the chestnut throat of the male.
ID: 5 in (12 cm). MALE upperparts are dark slate-grey, with faint striations on the crown and back. Chestnut throat. Short, thick bill. Wings are blackish, with narrow white wingbars and white bases to the primaries. Tail blackish, with white at tail base. White underparts. FEMALE is brown above, buff below, with faint stripes on the crown, mantle, breast and flanks. Perches on telephone and fence wires.
RANGE: Arica; s Colombia to n Chile. Scrub, farmland, edges of cultivated fields in oasis valleys; sea level to 2000 ft (600 m).

Band-tailed Seedeater, Semillero
Catamenia analis
OTHER NAMES: Fringilo semillero argentino, Spiegelcatamenie, Corbatita azulada chica, Caταménie maculée.
ID: 5 in (12 cm). MALE is slate-grey. Black face contrasts with the short, thick, bright yellow bill. Wings are black with a broad white speculum. Chestnut undertail coverts. Tail black with two white, oval tailspots half-way down the underside of tail. FEMALE upperparts light brown with faint black striations; rump and uppertail coverts are slate-grey with black streaks. Throat and underparts pale grey, with fine, black striations. Center of chest and abdomen are whitish; undertail coverts yellowish.
RANGE: Arica; Colombia, Ecuador, Peru, Bolivia, Argentina. Brush-covered ravines in the pre-Puna shrub zone; 8200–11,500 ft (2500–3500 m).
RELATED VAGRANT: PLAIN-COLORED SEEDEATER, *C. inornata*; Mamiña in Tarapacá.

Band-tailed Sierra-Finch, Platero
Phrygilus alaudinus
OTHER NAMES: Fringilo platero, Pico amarillo, Schwanzfleckenämmerling, Phrygile à queue barrée.
ID: 5.5 in (14 cm). MALE's head, neck and breast are lead-colored; forecrown and face have dark streaks giving the appearance of blackish face. Back brownish with dark streaks. Belly white. Tail black with a broad, white median band, which separates it from the Band-tailed Seedeater. Bright yellow bill and yellow legs. FEMALE's breast is brown with dark brown streaks; lower breast and abdomen whitish. White tail band is narrower than male's. Bill horn-colored. Legs yellow. Walks rather than hops. Feeds on the ground on seeds and plant matter. Reluctant to fly but when it does, the low, undulating flight is accompanied by a double noted call, *tweep-twup*.
RANGE: Coast, Central Valley and Andean foothills from Arica to Valdivia; Ecuador, Peru, Bolivia, Argentina. Pastures and wet meadows; sea level to 8200 ft (0–2500 m).
SUBSPECIES: PLATERO, *P. a. alaudinus*, ranges from Atacama to Valdivia. PLATERO PERUANO, *P. a. bipartitus*; bluish-grey with a white abdomen; found at Putre.

SEEDEATERS AND SIERRA-FINCHES 279

Chestnut-throated Seedeater, Corbatita
Sporophila telasco
Arica
5 in (12 cm)

Band-tailed Seedeater Semillero
Catamenia analis
Arica
5 in (12 cm)

Blue-black Grassquit, Negrillo
Volatinia jacarina
Arica
5 in (12 cm)

Band-tailed Sierra-Finch Platero
Phrygilus alaudinus
Arica–Valdivia
5.5 in (14 cm)

Ash-breasted Sierra-Finch Plebeyo
Phrygilus plebejus
Arica–Antofagasta
4–5 in (11–13 cm)

White-throated Sierra-Finch Cometocino de Arica
Phrygilus erythronotus
Puna of Arica
6 in (15 cm)

Plumbeous Sierra-Finch Pájaro plomo
Phrygilus unicolor
Arica–Magallanes
6.25 in (16 cm)

Red-backed Sierra-Finch Cometocino de dorso castaño
Phrygilus dorsalis
Altiplano of Arica–Atacama
6 in (15 cm)

Mourning Sierra-Finch Yal
Phrygilus fruticeti
Arica–Magallanes
7 in (18 cm)

Mourning Sierra-Finch, Yal
Phrygilus fruticeti
OTHER NAMES: Rara negra, Fringilo negro grande, Fringilo yal, Strauchämmerling, Phrygile petit-deuil.
ID: 7 in (18 cm). ADULT MALE's upperparts slate-grey, with head and mantle streaked with black; young males have black mainly around the bill and chin, and have a heavily streaked back. Throat, side of neck and breast black. Abdomen and undertail white. Wings black with two white wingbars. Bill yellow and legs yellow-brown. Iris light brown. FEMALE's upperparts greyish-brown with faint brown streaks. Auriculars grey. Throat and breast whitish with faint brown streaking; flanks and undertail coverts light brown, streaked with dark brown. Bill and legs flesh-colored. Usually seen in small flocks. In breeding season (Oct–Nov), the males perch on upper branches of bushes and sing a buzzing wheeze in chorus, often ascending to the air in nuptial flight, then fluttering pipit-like down to the ground. Nest is an untidy mass of grasses hidden in long grass.
RANGE: Widespread from Arica to Los Lagos and e Aisén to e Magallanes; Peru, Bolivia, Argentina. Brushy slopes and matorral above 9850 ft (3000 m) in n Chile, descending to sea level in the south.

Plumbeous Sierra-Finch, Pájaro plomo
Phrygilus unicolor
OTHER NAMES: Fringilo plomizo, Diuca cordillerano, Sunichicta, Bleiämmerling, Phrygile gris-de-plomb.
ID: 6.25 in (16 cm). MALE has nondescript plumage; slate-grey overall, with paler grey underparts and whitish undertail coverts. Wings and tail black. FEMALE is light brown, heavily streaked with dark brown to black overall. Although abundant and widespread, both sexes are easily overlooked as their plumage fades into the background of the rocky and brush-clad slopes that they inhabit. Does not flock; forages in pairs. Nests in rock crevices and stone walls.
RANGE: Arica to Magallanes; also sw Peru, Argentina. Rocky and brushy slopes in the Andes; above 8850 ft (2700 m) in n Chile, descending to 1650 ft (500 m) in the south.

Ash-breasted Sierra-Finch, Plebeyo
Phrygilus plebejus
OTHER NAMES: Chicta, Plomito pequeño, Fringilo grisáceo, Aschbrustämmerling, Phrygile plébéien.
ID: 4–5 in (11–13 cm). Small. Inconspicuous. Upperparts ash-grey with dark grey streaks on the back and head. Rump and uppertail coverts dark slate. Wings and tail dusky brown. Breast pale grey; throat whitish; abdomen and undertail coverts white. Greyish-white eyebrow; white semicircular crescent under the eye. Pale brown legs. Bill horn-grey. FEMALE similar to male, but with grey striations on back, breast and flanks. Forages in small flocks, often with plumbeous finches and yellow-rumped siskins.
RANGE: Arica to Antofagasta; s Ecuador to Argentina. Rocky, brush-clad slopes on the Puna; 9850–13,125 ft (3000–4000 m).

Red-backed Sierra-Finch
Cometocino de dorso castaño
Phrygilus dorsalis
OTHER NAMES: Sulte, Fringilo andina, Fringilo de espalda castaña, Phrygile à dos roux, Braunmantelämmerling.
ID: 6 in (15 cm). Stocky, rufous-backed finch of the High Andes. Crown and nape ash-grey. Wing scapulars pale rusty brown. Rump and uppertail coverts slate-grey. Dark wings and tail. Underparts whitish with a pale grey breastband. FEMALE and JUVENILE plumage is more muted; rufous mantle is streaked with dark brown (very similar to a juvenile White-throated Sierra-Finch). Tame and confiding. Seen in small flocks. Male displays by ascending into the air, hovering for a moment and then fluttering to the ground.
RANGE: Rocky slopes adjoining Andean *bofedales* in Antofagasta; uncommon on the Altiplano in Arica–Parinacota; Bolivia, Argentina; 12,500–13,750 ft (3800–4200 m).

White-throated Sierra-Finch
Cometocino de Arica
Phrygilus erythronotus
OTHER NAMES: Fringilo boliviano, Diuca chica, Weisskehlämmerling, Phrygile bicolore.
ID: 6 in (15 cm). Upperparts slate-grey. Throat and upper breast white; lower breast grey; abdomen and undertail coverts are whitish. White streaks under the eyes. Wings and tail blackish. Flanks buffy. Separated from the Red-backed Sierra-Finch by a grey, rather than rufous back. Separated from the Common Diuca-Finch by white flanks, white undertail coverts and absence of white outer tail feathers.
RANGE: Arica-Parinacota; w Bolivia, Peru. Rocky valleys and outcrops on the Altiplano; 12,500–14,750 ft (3800–4500 m).

Patagonian Sierra-Finch
Cometocino patagónico
Phrygilus patagonicus
OTHER NAMES: Quichán, Fringilo chanchita, Phrygile de Patagonie, Magellanämmerling.
ID: 6.25 in (16 cm). MALE has dark grey head, wings and tail; back is washed cinnamon or olive. Rump and underparts are yellow-green; center of abdomen bright yellow; undertail coverts white. FEMALE is dark olive above; pale yellow-green below; belly and undertail coverts whitish. Inhabits dense undergrowth. Nests (Nov–Dec) in tangles and forest detritus in steep-sided, watered valleys, placing its nest low to the ground.
RANGE: Valparaíso to Magallanes. Forest edge, river bottoms with dense vegetation and new growth in forests regenerating from fire; sea level to 4925 ft (0–1500 m).

Grey-hooded Sierra-Finch
Cometocino de Gay
Phrygilus gayi
OTHER NAMES: Grey-headed Sierra-Finch, Fringilo cordillerano, Fringilo amarillo, Chanchito, Cometocino de la cordillera, Cordillerenämmerling, Phrygile à tête grise.
ID: 6.25 in (16 cm). MALE has a dark bluish-grey hood, merging into black lores and area around bill. Rest of upperparts olive-yellow. Breast, upper abdomen and flanks yellow-olive, lighter than the back. Lower abdomen, lower flanks and undertail coverts white. Wings and tail dark brownish-grey. FEMALE has a light grey hood streaked with black; white malar stripe; olive back; underparts olive-yellow; lower abdomen whitish.
RANGE: Atacama to Magallanes; also Peru, Bolivia, Argentina. Inhabits river valleys, open country and desert scrub in both cordilleras, descending to the Central Valley and coast in winter.
SUBSPECIES: COMETOCINO DE GAY, *P. g. gayi*; Atacama to Colchagua, O'Higgins. COMETOCINO DE GAY COSTERO, *P. g. minor*; Antofagasta to Valparaíso. COMETOCINO DE GAY AUSTRAL, *P. g. caniceps*; grassy steppe; Aisén to Magallanes.

Black-hooded Sierra-Finch
Cometocino del norte
Phrygilus atriceps
OTHER NAMES: Black-headed Sierra-Finch, Chuctal, Fringilo cordillerano del norte, Phrygile à tête noire, Kapuzenämmerling.
ID: 6.5 in (16.5 cm). ADULT MALE has jet black hood; bright orange-yellow back and chest. Abdomen and rump are yellow. Undertail coverts are white. FEMALE has more muted colors than the male. Nests (Nov–Jan) in long grass near streams, bushes around rocky outcrops; also nests around villages.
RANGE: Common in the High Andes from the n Chilean border to Coquimbo; Peru, Bolivia, Argentina. Pastures and scrubland on the Puna and Altiplano; 9850–14,750 ft (3000–4500 m).

Common Diuca-Finch
Diuca
Diuca diuca
OTHER NAMES: Siuca, Diuka, Diuca gris.
ID: 6.5 in (16.5 cm). Plump bird with a peaked crown. Slate-grey overall, with a white abdomen and throat. Cinnamon on lower belly; undertail coverts white with cinnamon edging. Wings and tail blackish, the tail with a conspicuous white patch on outer tail feathers. Song, often sounded at

dawn, is a musical, leisurely warble of 4 to 5 notes, with the accent on the final note. Nests (Sep–Feb), often raising 2 to 3 broods a year. The cup-shaped nest is made of grass and root fibers, lined with soft plant material or animal hair.
RANGE: Antofagasta to Magallanes. Introduced to Easter Island. Ranges to s Brazil, Uruguay and Argentina. In fields, hills, ravines, woodland, gardens, town plazas.
SUBSPECIES: DIUCA, *D. d. diuca*; Coquimbo to Magallanes. DIUCA DEL NORTE, *D. d. crassirostris*; Antofagasta to n Coquimbo. DIUCA DE CHILOÉ, *D. d. chiloensis*; Chiloé.

White-winged Diuca-Finch
Diuca de alas blancas
Diuca speculifera
OTHER NAMES: Diuca grande, Spiegeldiuka, Diuca leucoptère.
ID: 7 in (17.5 cm). Stocky. Ashy-grey overall, with a conspicuous white subocular patch. Throat, belly and underwing coverts white. Long, dark grey wings with a large, white speculum. Tail dark grey with white border. Black bill. Lives and nests on the Altiplano. Feeds on the ground among grass tussocks near mountain streams and lagoons.
RANGE: Arica–Parinacota to Tarapacá; also Peru, Bolivia. Around Altiplano *bofedales*; 12,450–16,500 ft (3800–5000 m).

Black-throated Finch, Yal austral
Melanodera melanodera
OTHER NAMES: Canary-winged Finch, Yal verde, Mélanodère à sourcils blancs, Schwarzkehl-Ammerfink.
ID: 6 in (15 cm). Adult MALE has a black face and throat edged with white. Crown, neck and auriculars grey. Back olive-grey and rump olivaceous. Center of underparts yellow; flanks grey; undertail coverts white. Conspicuous yellow wing patch. Center tail feathers olive, outer tail feathers pale yellow, lighter on the tips. FEMALE is streaked buff and brown, with yellow on the outer tail feathers, abdomen and wings.
RANGE: Semi-arid steppe of Magallanes, s Argentina and the Falklands.

Yellow-bridled Finch, Yal cordillerano
Melanodera xanthogramma
OTHER NAMES: Yal de Tierra del Fuego, Yal verde, Zügelammerfink, Mélanodère à sourcils jaunes.
ID: 5.5–7 in (14–17.5 cm). ADULT MALE is similar to the male Black-throated Finch, but with yellow instead of white edging the dark throat and face. Rest of plumage is greyish-blue (no yellow wing patch). FEMALE is greyish-brown, faintly streaked with dark grey; underparts buffy to white with brown streaks. Forages on the ground in small flocks or singly.
RANGE: Rare species of steppes and open, rocky sites in the mountains; Magallanes and s Argentina, and north to Valparaíso in winter; 4900–9850 ft (1500–3000 m).
SUBSPECIES: YAL CORDILLERANO AUSTRAL, *M. x. xanthogramma*; s Magallanes, Tierra del Fuego and Cape Horn. YAL CORDILLERANO, *M. x. ballosi*; Valparaíso to Biobío.

Slender-billed Finch, Pizarrita
Xenospingus concolor
OTHER NAMES: Xénospingue uniforme, Feinschnabelämmerling.
ID: 5 in (12 cm). Upperparts are slate grey; underparts are paler slate, with center of abdomen pale grey. Forehead and lores are black. Wings and tail brownish-grey. Slender, conical, pointed bill is bright yellow. Yellow legs. Female is smaller, with dark brown upperparts. Forages alone or in pairs for insects in the dense riparian thickets of n Chile. Shy. Rarely perches in the open. Cocks tail. VULNERABLE.
RANGE: Arica to Antofagasta; Peru. In riparian thickets, brush around farmland, gardens; sea level to 8200 ft (0–2500 m).

Grassland Yellow-Finch, Chirihue
Sicalis luteola
OTHER NAMES: Misto, Chirigüe, Sicale des savanes, Kurzschnabel-Gilbammer.
ID: 5 in (13 cm). Common and widespread; the only yellow-finch in Chile that has a streaked back. Crown and back olive, with dark brown streaks; rump and uppertail

FINCHES, SIERRA-FINCHES AND DIUCA-FINCHES 283

Black-hooded Sierra-Finch
Cometocino del norte
Phrygilus atriceps
Andes of Arica–Coquimbo
6.5 in (16.5 cm)

Grey-hooded Sierra-Finch
Cometocino de Gay
Phrygilus gayi
Atacama–Magallanes
6.25 in (16 cm)

Patagonian Sierra-Finch
Cometocino patagónico
Phrygilus patagonicus
Valparaíso–Magallanes
6.25 in (16 cm)

White-winged Diuca-Finch
Diuca de alas blancas
Diuca speculifera
Altiplano of Arica
7 in (17.5 cm)

Common Diuca-Finch, Diuca
Diuca diuca
Antofagasta–Magallanes
Easter Island
6.5 in (16.5 cm)

Slender-billed Finch
Pizarrita
Xenospingus concolor
Arica–Antofagasta
5 in (12 cm)

Yellow-bridled Finch
Yal cordillerano
Melanodera xanthogramma
Valparaíso–Magallanes
5.5–7 in (14–17.5 cm)

Black-throated Finch
Yal austral
Melanodera melanodera
Magallanes
6 in (15 cm)

coverts greenish-yellow. Grey cheeks. Forecrown, throat and abdomen yellow, washed with grey on breast and flanks. Wings and tail brown. FEMALE similar, but with muted yellow underparts and a faintly streaked breastband. Forages on the ground for seeds of wild plants growing in open fields and pastures. In spring, flocks often sing their musical, canary-like trills in chorus. Males engage in pipit-like nuptial flights, fluttering into the air and descending to the ground while singing. Long nesting season (Sep–Feb) with 2 to 3 broods of young.
RANGE: Atacama to Aisén, including the Guaitecas Archipelago; s Mexico to n Chile and Argentina. Fields, meadows, matorral, towns; sea level to 6550 ft (0–2000 m).

Patagonian Yellow-Finch
Chirihue austral
Sicalis lebruni
OTHER NAMES: Jilguero patagónico, Sicale de Patagonie, Magellangilbammer.
ID: 5.5 in (14 cm). The only yellow-finch of the Patagonian lowlands. Upperparts grey, faintly mottled in olive. Underparts yellow with greyish flanks; pale yellow undertail coverts. Tail edged with white. FEMALE is greyer than the male. Nests and roosts in holes in rocky gullies and earthen banks.
RANGE: Magallanes to Tierra del Fuego; s Argentina. Semi-arid grassland with rocky ravines; sea level to 1650 ft (0–500 m).

Bright-rumped Yellow-Finch
Chirihue cordillerano
Sicalis uropygialis
OTHER NAMES: Jilguero dorado, Huaicarache, Goldbürzel-Gilbammer, Sicale à croupion jaune.
ID: 5.5 in (14 cm). Upperparts greyish, with an olive-yellow rump. Underparts yellow. Grey cheeks and lores. FEMALE has a streaky crown, a darker back than male and paler yellow underparts. Common on the Altiplano, often seen in large flocks foraging for seeds on the ground. Nests and roosts in cliffs, holes in banks or under house eaves.
RANGE: Arica to Antofagasta; also Peru, Bolivia, Argentina. On slopes, open land, and around livestock corrals and farms; 11,500–14,750 ft (3500–4500 m); some birds descend to lower elevations in winter.

Greater Yellow-Finch
Chirihue dorado
Sicalis auriventris
OTHER NAMES: Chirigüe cordillerano, Jilguero andino, Grand Sicale, Goldbauch-Gilbammer.
ID: 6 in (15 cm). ADULT MALE golden yellow, brighter yellow on belly and vent. Greenish-yellow mantle with grey mottling. Wings and tail greyish; feathers edged in olive-yellow. FEMALE is greyish-brown, with paler grey underparts. Forages on the ground in pairs or small flocks. Occurs in open country, Andean wetlands and near human habitation. Nests (Jan–Feb), often using stone walls as nesting sites.
RANGE: Antofagasta to ne Magallanes; also w Argentina. Rocky slopes and Andean wetlands; 6550–13,125 ft (2000–4000 m) in nc Chile; around 1650 ft (500 m) in the southern regions.

Greenish Yellow-Finch
Chirihue verdoso
Sicalis olivascens
OTHER NAMES: Pajarito amarillo, Chirigüe olivaceo, Sicale olivâtre, Olivbrust-Gilbammer.
ID: 5.5 in (13.5 cm). Greenish-yellow overall. MALE has greenish-olive back and rump, with feathers tipped with grey. Underparts bright yellow-olive. FEMALE is darker than male and has grey flanks. Forages on the ground in pairs or small flocks in bushy to open montane scrub; also around villages. Calls from rocky outcrops or roofs emitting a loud, long, repetitive series of chirps.
RANGE: Andes from Arica to Coquimbo; Peru, Bolivia. Scrubland, fields, villages; 3280–11,800 ft (1000–3600 m).
RELATED SPECIES: PUNA YELLOW-FINCH, *Sicalis lutea*. Male is bright yellow overall, with yellow on wing coverts and rump. RARE in Chile on Altiplano grasslands near Visiviri, ne Arica; 11,500–13,125 ft (3500–4000 m).

Rufous-collared Sparrow, Chincol
Zonotrichia capensis
OTHER NAMES: Copete, Lonco, Mencu toque, Chingolo, Pichirre, Pichuco, Bruant chingolo, Morgenammer.
ID: 5.5–6 in (14–15 cm). An unmistakable sparrow that can be found in all but dense rainforest. Bright rufous half-collar around nape extends to sides of upper breast where it is edged with black. Slightly crested, grey head, with varying number of dark lateral lines depending on subspecies. Upperparts warm brown with darker streaks on the back. Two faint white wingbars. Underparts buffy; breast washed with grey. Bill and legs horn-colored.
RANGE: Arica to Magallanes, and north to Mexico. Abundant in fields, parks, gardens, cities; sea level to 14,750 ft (0–4500 m).
SUBSPECIES: CHINCOL, *Z. c. chilensis*; Atacama to the Islas Guaitecas and n Aisén. CHINCOL DEL NORTE, *Z. c. antofagastae*; smaller; broad dark lines on head; Arica to Antofagasta; sea level to 8000 ft (0–2500 m). CHINCOL AUSTRAL, *Z. c. australis*; largest subspecies; lacks lateral crown bands; in the Andes from Santiago to Aisén; at lower elevations south to Cape Horn. CHINCOL PERUANO, *Z. c. peruviensis*; breast white; Arica; sea level to 11,500 ft (3500 m). CHINCOL ANDINO, *Z. c. sanborni*; pale cinnamon upperparts; Altiplano from Atacama to Valparaíso.

FAMILY PASSERIDAE
OLD WORLD SPARROWS

House Sparrow, Gorrión
Passer domesticus
OTHER NAMES: Moineau domestique, Haussperling.
ID: 6 in (15 cm). ADULT MALE has a grey crown, broad chestnut eyeline that extends to the nape, white cheeks and a black mask and bib. Mantle is streaked with rufous and black; rump grey. Underparts dirty white; flanks grey. Short, thick bill. FEMALE and young have streaked brown upperparts, indistinct head markings and a tan breast.
RANGE: Arica to Tierra del Fuego; Easter Island; Juan Fernández Archipelago. A European species INTRODUCED into Chile in 1904; now common throughout the country around human habitation.

FAMILY FRINGILLIDAE
SISKINS AND ALLIES
Fringillids have short, conical bills adapted for seed-eating. Most are excellent singers, gregarious, and good fliers that migrate in flocks. The female's plumage is usually paler or more muted than the male's.

Black-chinned Siskin, Jilguero
Carduelis barbata
OTHER NAMES: Canario, Cabecita negra de corbata, Chardonneret à menton noir, Bartzeisig.
ID: 5 in (12 cm). MALE has black crown and chin, with a yellow face, yellow supercilium and olive auriculars. Back is olive-yellow, flecked with grey; rump is yellow. Wings are dark grey with two yellow wingbars; a broad yellow bar edged in white on the flight feathers. Tail black; yellow at sides of tail base. FEMALE lacks dark head markings and has grey to muted yellow underparts.
RANGE: Atacama to Magallanes; s Argentina. Common. The only siskin in s Chile and in the c Chile lowlands. Frequents tall trees at forest edge, scrubland, parks, gardens; sea level to 9850 ft (0–3000 m).

Hooded Siskin, Jilguero peruano
Carduelis magellanica
OTHER NAMES: Jilguero de cabeza negra, Magellanzeisig, Chardonneret de Magellan.
ID: 4.25 in (11 cm). MALE has black hood; olive-brown back with brownish streaks; yellow rump. Underparts and sides of neck canary-yellow. Wings black with two yellow wingbars and yellow patch at base of primaries. Tail black, with bright yellow at base of outer tail feathers. FEMALE lacks hood and has muted yellow plumage.
RANGE: Arica. Scrub and low trees in oases and on the pre-Puna; sea level to 12,150 ft (0–3700 m). Widespread in South America.

Thick-billed Siskin, Jilguero grande
Carduelis crassirostris
OTHER NAMES: Jilguero de la puna, Cabecita negra picuda, Chardonneret à bec épais, Dickschnabelzeisig.
ID: 5.5 (14 cm). Separated from the Hooded Siskin by its very thick bill that is swollen at the base of the upper mandible.
RANGE: RARE. Local in *Polylepis* woodland in the High Andes of Arica and on dry, brush-covered slopes in the Andes Range of Santiago and Valparaíso; also Peru, Bolivia, Argentina; 6550–13,125 ft (2000–4000 m).

Black Siskin, Jilguero negro
Carduelis atrata
OTHER NAMES: Telguero, Tintinse, Cabecita negra plomiza, Schwarzzeisig, Chardonneret noir.
ID: 5 in (12 cm). ADULT MALE is black overall, with a bright yellow abdomen and undertail coverts. Bright yellow patch on wing at base of remiges. Tail black, with yellow at sides of tail base. FEMALES and JUVENILES are more brown colored. Forages on the ground or in shrubs, in pairs or flocks. Sometimes perches on telephone wires. Males sing from tops of bushes, posing with wings lowered.
RANGE: Arica to Antofagasta; occasional at Los Andes, Valparaíso, and Colchagua, O'Higgins; also Peru, Bolivia, Argentina. Altiplano; on rocky, brush-covered slopes, in *Polylepis* woodland, farms, gardens and villages; 11,500–16,400 (3500–5000 m).

Yellow-rumped Siskin
Jilguero cordillerano
Carduelis uropygialis
OTHER NAMES: Cabecita negra cordillerano, Canario cordillerano, Kordillerenzeisig, Chardonneret à croupion jaune.
ID: 5 in (13 cm). MALE's head, neck, upperparts black, with some back feathers finely edged with greenish-yellow. Yellow rump; uppertail coverts yellow with black flecks. Tail dark grey; yellow at sides of tail base. Yellow underparts. Broad yellow wingbars on black wings. FEMALES and JUVENILES paler and tinged olive-brown. Nests in scrub near vertical cliffs on the Puna.
RANGE: Andes from Arica to Biobío; Peru, Bolivia, Argentina. Ravines, brush-covered slopes, tola scrub, *Polylepis* woodland and fields; 8200–11,500 ft (2500–3500 m).

YELLOW-FINCHES AND SISKINS 287

Grassland Yellow-Finch
Chirihue
Sicalis luteola
Atacama–Aisén
5.5 in (14 cm)

Bright-rumped Yellow-Finch
Chirihue cordillerano
Sicalis uropygialis
Arica–Antofagasta
5.5 in (14 cm)

Patagonian Yellow-Finch
Chirihue austral
Sicalis lebruni
Pampas of Magallanes
5.5 in (14 cm)

Greenish Yellow-Finch
Chirihue verdoso
Sicalis olivascens
Arica–Coquimbo
5.5 in (14 cm)

Greater Yellow-Finch
Chirihue dorado
Sicalis auriventris
Antofagasta–Araucanía
Magallanes
6 in (15 cm)

♂

Hooded Siskin
Jilguero peruano
Carduelis magellanica
Arica
4.25 in (11 cm)

♂

Thick-billed Siskin
Jilguero grande
Carduelis crassirostris
High Andes of Arica
and Santiago
5.5 in (14 cm)

Yellow-rumped Siskin
Jilguero cordillerano
Carduelis uropygialis
Andes of Arica–Biobío
5 in (13 cm)

Quinoa
Chenopodium quinoa

Black Siskin
Jilguero negro
Carduelis atrata
Altiplano of Arica–Antofagasta
5 in (12 cm)

Matico
Buddeleja globosa

♂

Black-chinned Siskin
Jilguero
Carduelis barbata
Atacama–Magallanes
5 in (12 cm)

FAMILY PARULIDAE
WOOD WARBLERS
These small, arboreal, insectivorous birds occur as vagrants in Chile. The BLACKPOLL WARBLER, *Dendroica striata*, has been recorded at Valdivia and the AMERICAN REDSTART, *Setophaga ruticilla*, near Arica.

FAMILY ICTERIDAE
BLACKBIRDS AND ALLIES
These birds have long, pointed wings and straight, conical, sharply pointed bills. The body and feet are sturdy. Males are usually larger than females, and in some species the females are duller in color than the males. The icterids feed mainly on insects and seeds, and some steal eggs and young from other birds' nests.

Shiny Cowbird, Mirlo
Molothrus bonariensis
OTHER NAMES: Tordo, Vacher luisant, Seidenkuhstärling.
ID: 8 in (20 cm). MALE is black with a blue-violet sheen. Wings and tail black with a green iridescence. Bill and legs black. FEMALE is greyish-brown, with paler underparts, and is smaller than the male. Pairs are usually monogamous. The male bows his head when displaying to the female, and with its body quivering, sings a low, bubbling *purr-purr-purr* followed by a high-pitched, buzzing *ptseee*. A brood parasite; the female lays her rounded, russet-spotted eggs in non-related species' nests, usually ejecting one or more of the host's eggs to make room for her own. Young cowbirds are brooded and fed by the host parents to the detriment of the natural offspring. Once fledged, cowbirds abandon their host parents and assume the lifestyle of their biological parents.
RANGE: This species was possibly introduced or has spread naturally from Argentina into c Chile in recent times. Locally common in Arica and from Atacama to Aisén; Panama to Argentina. Trees and hedgerows around farms, livestock pastures, riparian thickets; sea level to 6550 ft (0–2000 m).

Austral Blackbird, Tordo
Curaeus curaeus
OTHER NAMES: Küren, Tordo negro del sur, Quiscale austral, Stachelkopfstärling.
ID: 10 in (25 cm). Deep, velvety black overall, with a faint, dark blue iridescence on the wings. Pointed feathers on throat give a bearded look. Iris brown. Legs black. Common, noisy and inquisitive. Occurs alone or in small flocks with one bird as leader. Will often sing in chorus. Forages in dense shrubbery for insects and sometimes preys on the eggs or young of other birds. Uses its long, spike-like, black bill for prying food out of tangles and while probing in the ground for insects and larvae. Perchs and roosts in trees or shrubs. Nests (Oct–Dec), building a large, untidy structure of twigs, grass and mud set low to the ground in dense vegetation.
RANGE: Atacama to Tierra del Fuego; s Argentina. Found at forest edge, in trees and hedgerows around farms, and matorral; sea level to 3280 ft (0–1000 m).
SUBSPECIES: TORDO, *C. c. curaeus*; Atacama to the Strait of Magellan. TORDO DE TIERRA DEL FUEGO, *C. c. reynoldsi*; large, with a long, narrow bill; Tierra del Fuego. TORDO DE LOS CANALES, *C. c. recurvirostris*; bill has a bump on the end of the maxilla, forming a spatulate tip; Isla Riesco, Magallanes.

Yellow-winged Blackbird, Trile
Agelaius thilius
OTHER NAMES: Tordo de ala amarilla, Goldschulterstärling, Carouge galonné. Some claim that Trile (pronounced *TREE-lay*) is the origin of Chile's name.
ID: 8 in (20 cm). ADULT MALE entirely glossy black with a yellow patch at the bend of the wing and a yellow underwing. Bill is long and slender, black in the male, dark grey in the female. FEMALE is dark brown with paler streaking, and has a cream-colored supercilium and very faint yellow wing patch. Forages for insects in floating marsh

vegetation, muddy shoreline and adjacent fields. Roosts and nests (Oct–Dec) communally in reed and tule (*Scirpus* sp.) marshes. Builds a cup-shaped nest of dry reeds or rushes and anchors them between two reed stems a foot or two above the water surface. The 2 to 5 eggs are pale buff to pale blue, with many blackish-purple spots and fine, dark scrawls.

RANGE: Atacama to ne Magallanes; Peru to Argentina. Lowland marshes, reedbeds and wetlands; sea level to 3280 ft (0–1000 m).

SUBSPECIES: TRILE, *A. t. thilius*; ranges from Atacama to Los Lagos. TRILE ARGENTINO, *A. t. petersi*; occurs in Chile Chico, Aisén.

Long-tailed Meadowlark
Loica
Sturnella loyca

OTHER NAMES: Loica chilena, Milico, Pecho colorado grande, Sturnelle australe, Langschwanz-Soldatenstärling.

ID: 11 in (28 cm). Upperparts brown with dark streaks. The MALE's throat, chest, and upper abdomen are bright red. Red supercilium fades to white behind the eye. White underwing coverts. FEMALE is pale brown, with a pale red throat and chest.

Lives in pairs or small groups within established territories; sometimes forms large flocks in winter. Nods and bobs as it forages on the ground, taking beetles, larvae, small crustaceans, seeds and small bulbs of wild plants. Perches in the open on fence posts, rocks and tops of shrubbery. Sings, most often in the evening, from an elevated perch with its head thrown back and its throat feathers puffed out. Song is a long, harsh, repetitive *chee-chee-cheerie*.

Nests from spring to summer (Sep–Jan), often raising two broods in a semi-domed, woven grass nest hidden in long grass or other dense vegetation. The female is very furtive when tending her young, never landing near the nest, but alighting on the ground some distance away and stealing quietly through the long grass with her head lowered.

RANGE: Atacama to Magallanes; Argentina, Falklands. Common in farmland, livestock pastures, damp meadows, steppe; sea level to 8200 ft (0–2500 m).

Peruvian Meadowlark
Loica peruana
Sturnella bellicosa

OTHER NAMES: Peruvian Red-breasted Meadowlark, Chate, Sturnelle du Pérou, Weißschenkel-Soldatenstärling.

ID: 9 in (22 cm). Formerly considered a northern subspecies of the Long-tailed Meadowlark. Resembles the Loica, but is smaller, darker on the back and flanks, and has more vividly red underparts. FEMALE is smaller than the MALE and has a streaked crown and feathers of the flanks edged in grey. JUVENILE has a shorter bill and lacks any red on the underparts. Forages on the ground in pairs or family groups. Male performs low, gliding nuptial flights. Song is similar to the Loica's, but with the addition of a harsh *piu-piu-churr*.

RANGE: Local in fertile agricultural valleys and oases around Arica, Tarapacá and Antofagasta; also Peru, Ecuador; sea level to 3280 ft (0–1000 m).

VAGRANT BLACKBIRDS:

WHITE-BROWED BLACKBIRD, *Sturnella superciliaris*; one record in Elqui, Coquimbo.
BOBOLINK, *Dolichonyx oryzivorus*; recorded at Pedro de Valdivia, Antofagasta, and in the Lluta Valley, Arica.
SCREAMING COWBIRD, *Molothrus rufoaxillaris*; one record in Lluta Valley, Arica.
BAY-WINGED COWBIRD, *Agelaioides badius*; one record (1923) at Curicó, Maule.

MAMMALS

> **CLASS MAMMALIA**
>
> Mammals of the world comprise some 46 orders, 152 families, 1200 genera, and 5416 species. Almost all mammals share the following features:
> - Body hair
> - Complete double circulation
> - Four-chambered heart
> - Single-boned lower jaw
> - Mammary glands
> - Bear live young
>
> Mammals can be classed as terrestrial (those that live on land) or marine (those that spend most of their lives at sea).
>
> The following orders of native mammals, excluding the human order Primates, occur in Chile:
> - Didelphimorphia: American Opossums
> - Microbiotheria: Monito del Monte
> - Paucituberculata: Caenolestids
> - Chiroptera: Bats
> - Cingulata: Armadillos
> - Rodentia: Rodents
>   New World Rats and Mice, Chinchillas, Viscachas, Cavies, Degus, Tuco-tucos, Chinchilla Rats, Coypus
> - Carnivora: Carnivores
>   Otters, Grisons, Weasels, Skunks, Foxes, Cats, Seals
> - Artiodactyla: Even-toed Ungulates
>   Camelids, Deer
> - Cetacea: Cetaceans
>   Dolphins, Porpoises, Whales
>
> Old World rabbits, European hares, Old World rats and mice, American minks, American beavers, European deer, wild boars, coatimundis and domesticated dogs, cats, horses and cattle have been introduced to Chile.

Approximately 148 mammal species occur in Chile. Eighteen of these are endemic—that is to say, they are found only in Chile.

Land mammals account for only about 103 of the total species. This is a fairly low number for a country as large as Chile. Argentina, for example, has about 320 species of land mammals, Bolivia 316, and Peru 460. The relative scarcity of land mammals in Chile can be attributed in part to geographical isolation. The High Andes that extend the length of Chile's eastern border, and the hyper-arid Atacama Desert in the north, deter the dispersal of land mammals from the rest of South America. In addition, the vast stretches of ocean separating the outlying territories from the mainland effectively block the expansion of terrestrial mammals into those places.

Many of Chile's land mammals are nocturnal or live in underground burrows, and thus are not easy to observe. Adapting to a nocturnal or subterranean way of life enables animals to avoid the sun's desiccating rays, temperature fluctuations and predation by diurnal hunters such as hawks. Moreover, animals that have been persecuted as pests or have been hunted for their meat or pelt have learned to avoid human contact. To them, man represents a deadly menace. The best places to search for native land animals are in the national parks and reserves where they are protected by law. The services of a knowledgeable guide are invaluable in locating the rarer species.

Marine mammals are much easier to find. Chile's marine precinct harbors great numbers of large whales, dolphins, seals, sea lions, and otters—all of which feast on the bounty of marine organisms living in the cold waters off the Chilean coast. The visitor will be pleased to discover that many coastal cities and parks offer boat excursions with the special purpose of observing marine mammals and seabirds.

More than one-third of Chile's mammals face the threat of extinction. Their decline is the result of habitat destruction, historical exploitation, and competition by exotic species for food and habitat. In the accounts that follow, mammals at risk are indicated by categories set by the World Conservation Union (IUCN) and Convention on International Trade in Endangered Species (CITES). For information on these organizations and their categories, see the glossary on pages 376–377.

TERRESTRIAL MAMMALS

DIDELPHIMORPHIA: American Opossums

These New World marsupials lack a placenta. Young are born in an embryonic state and in most species finish their development in the female's abdominal pouch (marsupium).

FAMILY DIDELPHIDAE, SUBFAMILY DIDELPHINAE

AMERICAN OPOSSUMS

Elegant Fat-tailed Mouse Opossum, Llaca
Thylamys elegans
OTHER NAMES: Southern Mouse Opossum, Comadreja, Marmosa chilena, Yaca, Zierliche Zwergbeutelratte, Marmosa elegante.
ID: 9.5 in (24 cm). Light grey-brown back, paler sides and white belly. Black eyerings extend to the nose. Large naked ears. Long, finely haired, prehensile tail. Fat is stored in the tail for use during winter hibernation. The upper and lower jaws have three pairs of incisors. The first hindfoot digit lacks a nail and is sharply opposed to rest of digits.

Nocturnal. Arboreal. Nests in trees, or in abandoned bird nests, rock crevices and other mammals' burrows. Nest is a spherical mass of moss with a single entry. Females bear two litters of 8 to 15 young, who attach themselves to teats in the female's rudimentary pouch until they have developed. Feeds on arthropods, larvae, small vertebrates, birds' eggs and chicks, and fruit.
RANGE: ENDEMIC to Chile. Coquimbo to Valdivia. Matorral, thorn savanna, forest; sea level to 6500 ft (0–2000 m).
RELATED SPECIES: WHITE-BELLIED FAT-TAILED MOUSE OPOSSUM, *Thylamys pallidior,* ranges in n Chile and Peru to c Argentina.

MICROBIOTHERIA: Monito del Monte

Monito del Monte is the only surviving member of the ancient order Microbiotheria, which is closely related to the Australasian marsupials.

FAMILY MICROBIOTHERIIDAE

MONITO DEL MONTE

Monito del Monte
Dromiciops gliroides
OTHER NAMES: Rata, Colocolo, Chimaihuén Kongoy, Kunwuna, Huenukiki, Chiloë-Beutelratte, Little Mountain Monkey.

ID: 8.5 in (21.5 cm). Thick, woolly fur is fawn to grey on the back; dark grey with whitish patches on sides; pale grey on belly. Face is pale brown with black eyerings and a rufous nape. Small ears. Has a thick, finely-haired, prehensile tail. Fat is stored in the tail base for use during winter hibernation.

Nocturnal. Arboreal. Builds a small, round nest of sticks, bamboo leaves and mosses on branches, amid lianas, bamboo thickets, under rocks and inside of logs. Up to four young develop in the small pouch of the female, and later ride on the mother's back. Feeds on insects, small invertebrates, and sometimes fruit. VULNERABLE.
RANGE: Biobío to Chiloé; also Lago Nahuel Huapi, Argentina. Dense rainforest, especially around *Araucaria, Nothofagus,* and bamboo; sea level to 5000 ft (0–1500 m).

PAUCITUBERCULATA: Caenolestids

Caenolestids occur in western South America in humid places having dense vegetation. These animals lack a marsupial pouch.

FAMILY CAENOLESTIDAE

CAENOLESTIDS

Long-nosed Caenolestid
Comadrejita trompuda
Rhyncholestes raphanurus
OTHER NAMES: Chilean Shrew Opossum, Rincolesta, Chile-Opossummaus, Ratôn runcho coligrueso.
ID: 7.5 in (19 cm). Small, shrew-like marsupial with soft brown fur, thin limbs, small eyes and ears, a long pointed snout and long sensitive whiskers. Short, haired tail is thick at the base and serves as a fat storage organ. Three incisors in the upper jaw, three to four in the lower jaw. First hind digit has a claw. No marsupial pouch. Young attach themselves to the four teats in the groin; there is an isolated fifth teat on the lower belly.

Nocturnal. Terrestrial. Lives in burrows and under fallen logs. Feeds on insects, fungi, seeds, earthworms. VULNERABLE.
RANGE: Chiloé to Osorno, and adjacent Argentina. Forest floor of old growth evergreen forests; sea level to 3725 ft (0–1135 m).

OPOSSUM, MONITO DEL MONTE, CAENOLESTID AND BATS 293

CHIROPTERA: Bats

Bats are flying mammals. Their wings are membranes attached to the body sides, legs and tail. The wings are supported by four to five forelimb digits. The 'thumb' has a sharp nail. Orientation via echolocation is aided by a fleshy prominence in the external ear called the tragus.

FAMILY PHYLLOSTOMIDAE

NEOTROPICAL LEAF-NOSED BATS
Common Vampire Bat, Vampiro común
Desmodus rotundus
OTHER NAMES: Mordedor, Piuchén, Vampirfledermäuse, Chupador.
ID: 3.25 in (8.5 cm). WS 8 in (20 cm). Tiny; body is about the length of a man's thumb. Dark grey to brown, often with an amber wash on the back. Flat nose with a nose leaf, which enhances sonar ability. Large pointed ears. No tail. Young use clawed thumbs in the middle of the wing to cling to the mother's belly fur. Nocturnal. Silent, low flight. Roosts in seaside caves and in rock crevices in the Andean foothills. Can walk rapidly on horizontal or vertical surfaces, using feet and thumbs. Feeds on the blood of horses, burros, cattle, seals, domestic fowl, seabirds and rarely humans. Climbs onto prey using wing nails and shears away the hair or feathers with the teeth. Bites out a circular piece of skin with the upper and lower incisors, then laps the blood, which flows freely due to an anticoagulant in the bat's saliva.
RANGE: Arica to Valparaíso; Mexico to n Argentina; sea level to 6500 ft (0–2000 m).

FAMILY FURIPTERIDAE

SMOKY BATS
Smoky Bat, Murciélago de Schnabel
Amorphochilus schnablii
ID: 3 in (7.6 cm). Crown of head greatly elevated above face. Broad base of funnel-shaped ears cover eyes. Colonial; roosts in large groups in caves and empty buildings. Feeds on nocturnal insects.
RANGE: Arica to Tarapacá; also Ecuador, Peru. Arid seacoast, quebradas, scrub.

FAMILY MOLOSSIDAE

FREE-TAILED BATS
Mexican Free-tailed Bat
Murciélago cola de raton
Tadarida brasiliensis
OTHER NAMES: Murciélago coludo, Guanero, Guano-Fledermaus, Taradide du Brésil.
ID: 4.2 in (10.5 cm). Grey-brown, velvety fur. Large ears, eyes and mouth. Long wings. Tail extends beyond the tail membrane. Roosts in attics and abandoned buildings in noisy colonies, often with *Myotis* bats. Known to hibernate or enter torpor. Feeds on nocturnal insects captured in fast flight, using the tail membrane as a pouch.
RANGE: Arica to Valdivia; s USA through Argentina; sea level to 3250 ft (0–1000 m).

FAMILY VESPERTILIONIDAE

VESPER BATS
Chilean Mouse-eared Myotis
Murciélago orejas de raton del sur
Myotis chiloensis
ID: 3.5 in (8.6 cm). Tiny. Brown. Tail extends to the rear edge of tail membrane. Roosts in caves, tree hollows, rock crevices, buildings, often near lakes and rivers. Drinks from the water surface while in flight. Feeds on insects, using the tail membrane as a pouch in which to manipulate prey. Hibernates.
RANGE: Elqui, Coquimbo to Isla Navarino and Isla Wollaston, Magallanes. Matorral, savanna, moist forest. Most southern bat.
RELATED SPECIES: ATACAMA MYOTIS, *Myotis atacamensis*. Blond fur. Roosts in caves in coastal deserts from Arica to Coquimbo; also Peru; sea level to 7875 ft (0–2400 m).

Big-eared Brown Bat
Murciélago orejón grande
Histiotus macrotus
ID: 4 in (10 cm). Brown. Large ears, which are longer than the head; ears are connected by a low band of skin. Roosts alone or in colonies of thousands of bats, often all the same sex. Feeds on insects taken in agile, slow flight. Relies mainly on echolocation. Projects the ultrasound through the mouth and retrieves the signal with its large ears.

Big Hairy Armadillo
Quirquincho grande
Chaetophractus villosus
Magallanes
17 in (44 cm)

Pichi
Quirquincho pequeño
Zaedyus pichiy
Valparaíso–Magallanes
13 in (33 cm)

Andean Hairy Armadillo
Quirquincho de la puna
Chaetophractus nationi
Arica–Antofagasta
15 in (38 cm)

Tola (*Baccharis tola*)

RANGE: Arica to Biobío; also Peru, Bolivia, Argentina. Attics, rock crevices, abandoned mines; sea level to High Andes.

RELATED SPECIES: SMALL BIG-EARED BROWN BAT, *Histiotus montanus*. Valparaíso to Tierra del Fuego. Widespread in South America in savanna, woodland, all elevations. Roosts in small colonies in empty mine tunnels, caves and attics of old buildings. SOUTHERN BIG-EARED BROWN BAT, *Histiotus magellanicus*. Ranges in s Chile and s Argentina.

Hoary Bat, Murciélago gris
Lasiurus cinereus

OTHER NAME: Eisgraue Fledermaus.
ID: 5 in (12.5 cm). Thick dark brown fur with silver highlights; golden brown fur around face. Most active at dawn and dusk. Insectivorous. Roosts in tree holes or buildings.
RANGE: Arica to Tierra del Fuego; migrates southward and ascends to High Andes in summer. Widespread Canada to Argentina.

Red Bat, Murciélago colorado
Lasiurus blossevillii

OTHER NAMES: Murciélago peludo rojizo, Chauve-souris rousse, Rote Fledermaus. Genus derives from the Greek words *lasios*, meaning "hairy" and *oura*, meaning "tail".
ID: 4 in (10 cm). Soft, dense, brick red to golden fur. Solitary. Migratory. Fast flight. Feeds on nocturnal butterflies and moths, beetles and flies. Female has delayed implantation of sperm, which is stored in the reproductive tract until ovulation occurs. This conserves energy and produces offspring when food is plentiful. Female gives birth to 3 to 4 young, and roosts with them in tree foliage until they are weaned.
RANGE: Coquimbo to Magallanes. Widespread from North America to Argentina. Woodland, orchards; sea level to 5000 ft (0–1500 m).

CINGULATA: Armadillos

In Chile, the order is represented by the hairy armadillos. They have an armor of horny plates joined by flexible skin with projecting hairs.

FAMILY DASYPODIDAE

ARMADILLOS
Andean Hairy Armadillo
Quirquincho de la puna
Chaetophractus nationi

OTHER NAMES: Quirquincho andino, Peludo del altiplano, Peludo mediano de Bolivia, Andenborstengürteltier, Tatou des Andes.
ID: 15 in (38 cm). Carapace grey, with long hairs between plates. Long white hairs on underbody. Nocturnal in summer; diurnal

in winter; may hibernate. Digs and lives in deep burrows. Feeds on insects, maggots, plant roots. Said to kill snakes by jumping on them, using the edge of its carapace to cut them. Hunted as a pest, and for its meat and shell. VULNERABLE; CITES APPENDIX II.
RANGE: Arica to Antofagasta; also Bolivia. Open grasslands of the High Andes, especially in tola scrub on the Altiplano above 11,500 ft (3500 m).

Big Hairy Armadillo, Quirquincho grande
Chaetophractus villosus
OTHER NAMES: Tatou velu, Braunborsten-Gürteltier.
ID: 17 in (44 cm). Carapace grey to rusty brown. Long dark hair between plates. Greyish-pink underbody, sparsely covered with long black hair. Mainly nocturnal. Poor eyesight. Keen sense of smell. Agile runner. Digs and takes refuge in deep, complex networks of burrows. One to three young are born in spring and are reared inside the burrow for several months. Feeds on live and dead animals and plants. Kept as a pet on some rural farms.
RANGE: Magallanes; Bolivia, Argentina. Open fields, steppe, woodland.

Pichi, Piche, Quirquincho pequeño
Zaedyus pichiy
OTHER NAMES: Tatou velu de Patagonie, Zwerggürteltier.
ID: 13 in (33 cm). Carapace dark brown with yellow edges. Tail shield yellow. Pale yellow hair on underparts and between plates. Solitary. Mostly nocturnal. Hibernates. Digs shallow burrows in open areas, at the base of small bushes on sandy soils. When pursued, it anchors itself in its burrow by wedging the serrated edges of the carapace into the surrounding soil. Feeds on insects, worms, carrion, small rodents and lizards, tubers and seed pods of algarrobo trees (*Prosopis* sp.). Hunted for its meat and shell. Kept as a house pet in some rural areas.
RANGE: Local from Valparaíso, to the Strait of Magellan; also Argentina. Andean grasslands and Patagonian steppe.

CARNIVORA: Carnivores
Carnivores are flesh-eating placental mammals. They have strong incisors for biting, canine teeth for piercing meat, and modified cheek teeth called carnassials for shearing flesh. They have claws for seizing prey. In Chile, Carnivora is represented by the mustelids, canids, felids and pinnipeds, the latter of which appear with the marine mammals on pages 329–333.

FAMILY MUSTELIDAE
OTTERS, GRISONS AND WEASELS
Mustelids have elongated bodies and short legs with five-toed, clawed feet. They have a flattened head with a short snout, a well-developed tail and dense fur. Most mustelids are omnivorous, taking a great variety of vertebrate and invertebrate prey. The aquatic otters have adapted to a diet composed almost exclusively of fish.

Marine Otter, Chungungo
Lontra felina
OTHER NAMES: Nutria marina, Gato de mar, Chinchimén, Huallaque, Lobito marino, Gatuna, Lutre marine, Küstenotter.
ID: 33–45 in (83–115 cm). WT 7–13 lb (3.2–5.8 kg). Dark brown back with dark ochre underparts. Separated from the Southern River Otter by the snout hair, which forms a straight line across the nose. Shelters in natural caves along the marine littoral and rests on exposed rocks. Spends much time at sea. Mating takes place in the water. Swims quickly with head out of water. Floats effortlessly on its back, carried by the waves. Feeds on fish, crabs, marine mollusks, and sometimes small birds. Captures prey with front feet. Dives last 15 to 45 seconds. Fewer than 1000 individuals remain in Chile and Peru mainly due to persecution for alleged damage to prawn and crab fisheries. ENDANGERED; CITES APPENDIX I.
RANGE: Arica to Magallanes; also Peru, s Argentina. Along rocky seacoasts.

Southern River Otter, Huillín
Lontra provocax
OTHER NAMES: Lobito patagónico, Lobito de río, Südlicher flussotter, Loutre de Chili.

WEASELS, GRISONS, SKUNKS AND OTTERS 297

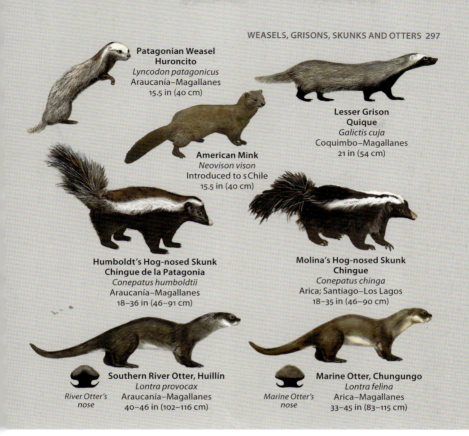

ID: 40–46 in (102–116 cm) Short, dense fur is dark brown above, silvery white below. Flattened forehead. Thick neck. Elongated, cylindrical trunk. Muscular tail is thick at the base, tapering at the tip. Short legs; webbed digits. Ears and nostrils close when swimming and diving. Feeds on fish, shrimp, frogs, crustaceans, mollusks and some small birds. Shelters in coastal rocks, lakeshores and riverbanks. Burrows have one entrance below the water line, the other above ground in the cover of vegetation. Hunted for its pelt. ENDANGERED; CITES APPENDIX I.
RANGE: Araucanía to Magallanes; also s Argentina. Rivers, streams, lakes and sheltered seacoasts with shoreline vegetation.

Patagonian Weasel, Huroncito
Lyncodon patagonicus
OTHER NAMES: Hurón menór patagónico, Zwerggrison.

ID: 15.5 in (40 cm). Smallest mustelid in South America. Slender body. Short legs. Front feet have long, thin nails; soles have four small rounded pads and membranes between the toes. Back greyish-brown with a whitish tinge. Top of the head cream; color extends as a broad stripe on either side to the shoulder. Nape, throat, chest and limbs dark brown. Rest of underparts light brown to grey. Very small ears are concealed by the surrounding fur. Preys on tuco-tucos and cavies (see p. 319) in their burrows. Said to be kept in ranch houses for the purpose of destroying rats.
RANGE: Araucanía to Última Esperanza, Magallanes; also Argentina. In grasslands; sea level to 6500 ft (0–2000 m).

RELATED SPECIES: AMERICAN MINK, *Neovison (Mustela) vison*. Glossy brown fur. Bushy tail. Native to North America. INTRODUCED or has spread from Argentina into s Chile.

Lesser Grison, Quique
Galictis cuja
OTHER NAMES: Cuja, Hurón menor, Kiki, Yaguagumke, Kleingrison.
ID: 21 in (54 cm). **WT** 2.2 lb (1 kg). Very elongated body. Short legs. A white forehead stripe separates the black face and underparts from the grizzled, brownish-grey back. Quick and agile climber. Good swimmer. Active mainly at night. Lives under tree roots or rocks, in hollow logs, or in burrows made by other animals. Emits sharp growling barks when alarmed. Digs family galleries to 15 ft (4 m) long. Omnivorous, feeding on small mammals, birds and bird eggs, reptiles, amphibians, invertebrates and fruit. In colonial times, Chilean ranchers kept lesser grisons as pets or used them to ferret out chinchillas from rock piles.
RANGE: Coquimbo to Los Lagos. Widespread in Central and South America. In forests, open plains, marshes, damp ravines; sea level to 4000 ft (0–1200 m).

FAMILY MEPHITIDAE
SKUNKS
Mephitidae derives from the Latin "mephit" meaning "bad odor." Skunks raise the tail and expel fetid musk from anal scent glands when alarmed.

Molina's Hog-nosed Skunk
Chingue común
Conepatus chinga
OTHER NAMES: Chiñi, Chinke, Aratuya, Añazo, Dakama, Zorrino andino. Named for the Jesuit naturalist Juan Molina (1740–1829) who first described the species.
ID: 18–35 in (46–90 cm). **WT** 5–10 lb (2.2–4.5 kg). Long, thick fur. Black, with a white stripe along each side of the back. Tail hairs black and white. Swollen, unfurred nose. Nocturnal. Excavates deep burrows using long claws; closes the entrance in winter and lives on stored food. Lives in rock piles, hollow logs or burrows made by other animals. Feeds on beetles, spiders, invertebrates, small vertebrates, fruit and bulbs.
RANGE: Andes of Arica and Santiago to Los Lagos; also Peru, Bolivia, Argentina. Open or wooded areas with loose soil; sea level to 8000 ft (0–2500 m).
SUBSPECIES: CHINGUE REAL, *C. c. rex*. Largest subspecies. Tail is entirely black. Hunted locally for its pelt. Resident on the Altiplano to 16,500 ft (5000 m).

Humboldt's Hog-nosed Skunk
Chingue de la Patagonia
Conepatus humboldtii
OTHER NAMES: Zorrino chico patagónico, Patagonischeskunk, Sticktier, Mouffette de Patagonie.
ID: 18–36 in (46–91 cm). **WT** 4–9 lb (2–4 kg). Back is dark rusty-brown to black with two white stripes running from head and along the back. Underparts black. Solitary except in spring breeding season. Nocturnal and crepuscular. Hunted for its pelt. Feeds on roots, spiders, centipedes, amphibians, reptiles, small birds, eggs, small mammals, crabs, and fruits. CITES APPENDIX II.
RANGE: Araucanía to Magallanes; s South America. Grassy areas at woodland edge.

FAMILY CANIDAE
SOUTH AMERICAN FOXES
Foxes have a lithe and muscular body, bushy tail, slender limbs, long slender muzzle and large erect ears. They have 4 digits on the hind feet and 5 on the forefeet. There has been much debate regarding classification of the South American foxes. They are placed alternatively in the genera *Canis, Dusicyon, Pseudalopex* and *Lycalopex*, the latter of which is used here.

Culpeo, Zorro rojo
Lycalopex culpaeus
OTHER NAMES: Fuegian Fox, Zorro colorado, Red Zorro, Lare, Culpeau, Andenschakal. Culpeo is said to stem from the Mapuche *culpem*, meaning "madness," referring to how this fox boldly reveals itself to hunters.
ID: 37–53 in (94–133 cm). **WT** 10–25 lb (4–12 kg). Males are larger than females. The four Chilean subspecies vary in color.

Culpeo
Zorro rojo
Lycalopex culpaeus
Arica–Magallanes
37–53 in (94–133 cm)

Darwin's Fox
Zorro chilote
Lycalopex fulvipes
Los Lagos–Araucanía
25–26 in (63–66 cm)

South American Grey Fox
Chilla
Lycalopex griseus
Atacama–Magallanes
31–36 in (80–92 cm)

In most, the coat is grizzled grey on the back; head and legs are tawny to rufous; the tip and top of the tail are black. Solitary except when breeding. Pairs dig deep dens. Vixen delivers 3 to 5 kits after two months gestation. Omnivorous; feeds on rodents, hares, birds, bird eggs, reptiles and berries. Said to take lambs from ewes by mimicking a playful dog rolling on its back until the ewe loses interest. Hunted for its pelt and as a livestock threat. PROTECTED in Chile.

RANGE: Arica to Magallanes; Ecuador, Peru, Bolivia, Argentina. Ranges widely from arid Andean plains to Patagonian forest; sea level to 16,400 ft (0–5000 m).

South American Grey Fox, Chilla
Lycalopex griseus

OTHER NAMES: Argentine Grey Fox, Zorro gris, Zorro patagónico, Zorro chico, Zorro de la pampa, Nuru, Yeshgai, Renard gris, Argentinische Kampfuchs.

ID: 31–36 in (80–92 cm). WT 5.5–9 lb (2.5–4 kg). Coat brindled grey; paler grey underparts; head rust, flecked with white. Legs pale brown with inconspicuous dark brown or cream stripes. Tail long and bushy with black tip. Black spot on chin. Large ears. Omnivorous, feeding on rodents, birds, lizards, frogs, insects and fruit. Biology similar to the Culpeo. PROTECTED species in Chile, but illegally hunted for alleged depredations to livestock. CITES APPENDIX II.

RANGE: Atacama to Magallanes; Argentina. INTRODUCED to Tierra del Fuego. Inhabits open grassland and foothill forest edge; sea level to 10,000 ft (0–3000 m).

Darwin's Fox
Zorro chilote
Lycalopex fulvipes

ID: 25–26 in (63–66 cm). WT 5–7.3 lb (2.3–3.3 kg). Stocky. Short-legged. Dark grey brindled fur; belly pale grey to cream. Ears rufous. Face greyish with white patches under the chin. Short, dark grey, bushy tail. Solitary. Hunts at night, feeding on insects, small mammals, birds, amphibians, berries and carrion. Formerly known only from a specimen collected by Charles Darwin in 1833. Rediscovered in 1922. Now considered a relict species confined to patches of old-growth Valdivian forest in Los Lagos and Araucanía. CRITICALLY ENDANGERED.

RANGE: Chiloé and Nahuelbuta National Parks. In dense forest and adjacent pastures.

FAMILY FELIDAE, SUBFAMILY FELINAE
FELIDS
Cats are built for hunting. The jaws are powerful, the canine teeth long, and the carnassial teeth well-developed for shearing flesh. The tongue's surface is covered with pointed, recurved papillae that lacerate and hold food in the mouth. The furred feet aid in the silent stalking of prey and the skeleton is specialized for leaping. The five digits on the forefoot and four on the hind foot have sharp retractable claws. Cats have large brains. The pupil of the eye contracts vertically. With the exception of the cougar, classification of the Chilean felids is yet to be determined. Species are provisionally included here in the genus *Leopardus,* with the alternate genera noted in parentheses.

Andean Mountain Cat
Gato montés andino
Leopardus (Oreailurus) jacobitus
OTHER NAMES: Gato lince, Gato montés altiplánico, Aleopardo, Chinchay, Titi, Osjo, Andenkatze, Bergkatze, Chat des Andes.
ID: 45–52 in (115–134 cm). WT 9–15 lb (4–7 kg). Males are larger than females and juveniles. Thick fur is ashy grey with yellowish-brown, irregular blotches arranged in vertical series on the flanks. Rusty to black band of non-erectil fur along the back. Head and face are grey, with white cheeks and lips. Two dark brown lines run across the cheeks. Long, heavy tail is banded with 6 to 9 dark brown or reddish rings. Most active at dusk and dawn. Feeds on chinchillas, viscachas, tuco-tucos, birds and reptiles. Hunted locally for its pelt and for use as a religious icon. CITES APPENDIX I. ENDANGERED.
RANGE: RARE. Arica and Tarapacá; Peru, Bolivia, Argentina. Arid rocky steppe on the Altiplano to 16,000 ft (4900 m).

Pampas Cat
Gato de pajonal
Leopardus (Lynchailurus) pajeros
OTHER NAME: Gato de las pampas.
ID: 32–42 in (83–105 cm). WT 6–13 lb (3–6 kg). Resembles a stocky domestic cat. Color of fur, markings and texture vary greatly with geographic location. Typical pelage shows long, soft, yellowish-brown fur with muted reddish and brown flank marks, and bold striping on the legs. Long hairs on the nape form a dorsal mane. CITES APPENDIX II.
RANGE: Aisén, Magallanes and s Argentina; ranges mainly on the eastern slopes of the Andes. Occurs in a wide variety of habitats, including pampas and reed beds.
RELATED SPECIES/SUBSPECIES: GATO PAJERO. Provisionally classed as *Lynchailurus* sp. or *Oncifelis colocolo pajeros*. Altiplano form of the Pampas Cat. Body fur tawny with rust-colored rosettes arranged in oblique lines on the flanks. Spinal crest of long, erectile fur. Ears colored in black, cream and rufous. Slender tail has 8 reddish, inconspicuous, narrow rings. Complete dark rings on the forelegs. Inhabits steep, rocky valleys on the Altiplano to 16,500 ft (5000 m).

Colocolo
Leopardus (Oncifelis) colocolo
OTHER NAMES: Gato montés, Gato silvestre, Kudmú, Ichu michi, Gato peludo, Gatillo, Osjollo, Chinchay, Osio, Pampaskatze, Chat des pampas. Named by the 18th century Jesuit naturalist Juan Molina after an Araucanian warrior, Colocolo.
ID: 26–40 in (66–102 cm). WT 6–13 lb (3–6 kg). Short, ash blond fur. Rufous or grey elongated spots on the back. Small dark lines from the nape to the shoulders. Reddish-brown rosettes on the flanks and transverse stripes on the legs. Tail has rufous to dark brown rings. Climbs trees and hides in the foliage. Nocturnal. Feeds on birds and rodents. Female dens in grass-lined caves; annual litter is one to three young. Formerly considered the same species as the Pampas Cat; now a separate species. NEAR THREATENED; CITES APPENDIX II.
RANGE: ENDEMIC. In central Chile from Coquimbo to Biobío. In woodland, open grassland, rolling hills with rocky slopes; alpine steppe and subtropical forest on the western Andean slopes.

NATIVE CATS 301

Geoffroy's Cat
Gato montés
Leopardus (Oncifelis) geoffroyi
Los Lagos–Magallanes
26–41 in (66–103 cm)

Silver morph Geoffroy's

Melanistic Geoffroy's

Andean Mountain Cat
Gato montés andino
Leopardus (Oreailurus) jacobitus
Andes of Arica–Tarapacá
45–52 in (115–134 cm)

Melanistic Kodkod

Kodkod, Guigna
Leopardus (Oncifelis) guigna
Biobío–Aisén
23–27 in (59–68 cm)

Pampas Cat
Gato de pajonal
Leopardus (Lynchailurus) pajeros
Aisén–Magallanes
32–42 in (83–105 cm)

Colocolo
Leopardus (Oncifelis) colocolo
Coquimbo–Biobío
26–40 in (66–102 cm)

Cougar, Puma
Puma concolor
Arica–Magallanes
59–98 in (149–250 cm)

Geoffroy's Cat, Gato montés
Leopardus (Oncifelis) geoffroyi
OTHER NAMES: Gato de Geoffroy, Gato de mato, Gato de las salinas, Gato do mato pelo curto, Mbaracayá, Osjo, Geoffroykatze, Chat de Geoffroy. Named for the French naturalist Geoffroy St. Hilaire (1772–1844).
ID: 26–41 in (66–103 cm). **WT** 7–11 lb (3–5 kg). Looks like a small, slender, domestic cat. Highly variable in color, ranging from spotted silvery-grey to ochre to all black; silver morph occurs most often in Chile. Round or elliptical black spots over the entire body; spots unite on the back to form dark lines. Back of each rounded ear is black with a white central spot. Two black streaks on each cheek. Legs have transversal stripes. Tail is ringed towards the tip, spotted near the base. Nocturnal. Hunts on the ground and in trees. Feeds on birds, rats, guinea pigs and other rodents. Annual litter of 2 to 3 young. Once heavily exploited for the fur trade; now protected in most countries. **NEAR THREATENED; CITES APPENDIX I**.
RANGE: Los Lagos to Magallanes; e Andes from Bolivia to Patagonia. Steppe with groves of trees and scrub, rocky scrubland, open woodland, savanna and marshes; sea level to 10,000 ft (0–300 m).

Kodkod, Guigna
Leopardus (Oncifelis) guigna
OTHER NAMES: Güiña, Huiña, Gato pintado, Chat du Chili, Chilenische Waldkatze.
ID: 23–27 in (59–68 cm). **WT** 4.4 lb (2 kg). Smallest wild felid in the Americas. Stocky body. Buffy to brown fur, heavily patterned with small black spots and stripes. Melanism is common. Narrow yellowish lines on head and shoulders. Thick tail is brown with narrow, blackish bands. Large feet are unspotted in c Chilean form, and spotted in southern animals. Arboreal, resting in trees and climbing high when pursued. Dens in bamboo thickets. Constructs a hammock-like nest *(coligüe)* of intertwined branches and lines it with belly hairs. Raises a litter of 5 offspring. Feeds on rabbits, rodents and birds. Raids rural henhouses, killing several chickens, eating only the brains. **VULNERABLE** (deforestation); **CITES APPENDIX II**.
RANGE: Biobío to Aisén, especially in Chiloé and the Guaitecas; sw Argentina. Bamboo thickets in Araucarian and Valdivian rainforests; sea level to 8200 ft (0–2500 m).

Cougar, Puma
Puma concolor
OTHER NAMES: Mountain Lion, Cuguardo, León americano, Chanare, Poghi, Trapial, Haina, Yuninii, Guasaura, Yagua pihtá, Sussuacana, Mitzy, Silberlöwe.
ID: 59–98 in (149–250 cm). **WT** 55–150 lb (25–68 kg). Males are larger than females. Large, lithe and slender, with strong, very muscular limbs, long neck and elongate body. Relatively small head. Hind legs are longer than the front legs, which elevate the rump for jumping. Long, heavy cylindrical tail. Ranges in color from buff to tawny to reddish-brown, with a whitish belly, chin, throat and upper lips. Purrs and gives high-pitched screams. Males have extensive territories that they mark with urine and excrement. A male shares his territory with one or more females, denning in hollows under trees or amid rocks. Feeds on rodents and mammals, including deer and vicuña. Occasionally attacks domestic livestock. Fully protected in Chile. **NEAR THREATENED; CITES APPENDIX I**.
RANGE: Arica to Magallanes, and across the Americas. Woodland, steppe, mountains; sea level to 16,500 ft (0–5000 m).

FAMILY PROCYONIDAE

COATIS

South American Coati, Coatimundi
Nasua nasua
ID: 29–53 in (73–136 cm). **WT** 7–13 lb (3–6 kg). Brown with a long pointed snout and a long, ringed tail.
RANGE: Introduced in 1935 to Isla Masatierra, Juan Fernández, to control rats. Now a pest there; preys on nesting petrels.

ARTIODACTYLA: *Even-toed Ungulates*

Artiodactyla is an order of hoofed mammals that includes camels, deer, pigs and other ruminants. The third and fourth digits bear most of the animal's weight; the toes terminate in hooves, which are flattened on the inner and ventral surfaces.

FAMILY CAMELIDAE

SOUTH AMERICAN CAMELIDS

Camelids expanded from North America into Asia, Africa and South America about two million years ago. They became extinct in North America about 10,000 years ago, but four camelid species survived in South America. These include the wild guanaco and vicuña, and the domesticated llama and alpaca. These lamoid species are characterized by a long thin neck, a small head, and a slender snout with a cleft upper lip. Their hooves are reduced and there are cutaneous pads on the middle digits of each foot. They are grazing and browsing animals. They have a three-chambered ruminating stomach and regurgitate and rechew their food. Lamoids run with a swaying gait with the fore and hind legs of each side moving together. They utter a variety of low and yammering calls. They form harem herds composed of an adult male, several females and their young, which are called *crias*, or in the case of guanacos, *chulengos*.

Guanaco
Lama guanicoe
OTHER NAMES: Luan, Yehoan, Pichua, Nau, Amare.
ID: 73 in (185 cm). SH 43–45 in (110–115 cm). WT 220–265 lb (100–120 kg). Cinnamon body, with a white belly and neck; face is grey or black. Guanacos feed on bunchgrass, shrubs, epiphytes, lichens, fungi and herbs, which provide most of their water needs. They drink only occasionally, although they often stand or lie down in mountain streams and are said to be good swimmers. They can run at speeds of 35 mi per hour (56 km/hr). They lie down to rest, first getting on the front knees and collapsing the hindquarters, then dropping onto the chest with the legs tucked under the body. Guanacos form small, sedentary harem groups that live within a small territory. They use communally shared spots for defecation. Females give birth to a single young *(chulengo)*; gestation is 345 to 360 days. The *chulengo* remains with the female for about a year, at which point the male drives it from his territory. Young females may quickly join another herd, but the immature males live in bachelor herds until they are 4 to 6 years old.

The Incas hunted guanacos for meat, hide and fleece. There were about 30 to 50 million guanacos in South America when Europeans arrived, but their numbers were rapidly reduced by hunters. Today populations stand at an estimated 575,000. Some are killed because it is thought that they compete with domestic sheep for forage, others because their hide is commercially valuable. Pumas are their natural predator. VULNERABLE; CITES APPENDIX II.
RANGE: Arica to O'Higgins and Aisén to Magallanes; Argentina, Peru and Bolivia. Altiplano grasslands and Patagonian steppe; sea level to 14,000 ft (0–4250 m).

Vicugna, Vicuña
Vicugna vicugna
ID: 54–59 cm (138–151 cm). SH 38 in (96 cm). WT 100–120 lb (45–55 kg). Pale cinnamon fur on body, neck and head, with a white belly and a long tuft of white hair on the chest. Long neck, thin legs and a slender build. The lower incisors are ever-growing and have enamel only on one side.

Small family groups remain within the male's territory during the day and ascend to special sleeping territories on the higher slopes at sunset. They graze on perennial grasses and must drink daily—a factor that limits their range. Young often graze while lying prone, with the legs tucked under the body. They dust their fleece by pawing the ground and rolling in the dust. Very shy and constantly alert, they sound a high warning whistle before fleeing danger. They are graceful runners, capable of attaining

29 miles per hour (47 km/hr) at high elevations due to a heart that is 50 percent larger than average for similar-sized mammals.

During the Inca Empire, there were over one million vicuñas. They were rounded up for shearing, and their wool used to make robes for royalty. Vicuñas were caught in enormous traps *(chacos)* made of stakes and rope or boulders. One ancient trap in Lauca National Park is built of volcanic stone slabs measuring 325 ft long by 100 ft wide (100 m x 30 m). The slabs were laid into a ravine and edged with dry stone walls *(pircas)*. Hundreds of people encircled the herd and drove the vicuñas toward the trap, where they were held until they were sheared. Males were killed; the females and crias were set free. The chaco festival took place every four to five years.

After the Spanish conquest, vicuña were hunted relentlessly. By the 20th century herds were decimated and those remaining were pushed onto marginal, high-altitude grasslands. By the 1960s the number of vicuñas in Chile, Argentina, Bolivia, Peru and Ecuador had dropped to fewer than 10,000. In 1975 the five countries signed a collective agreement to protect vicuñas by prohibiting the commercial trade of hides and wool. Some trade is now allowed and cloth woven from the sheared wool of live vicuña can be exported legally. Hunting is also prohibited. Chile created La Reserva Nacional Las Vicuñas, located south of Lauca National Park, to protect vicuña herds. World population is about 125,000.
VULNERABLE; CITES APPENDIX I.

RANGE: Arica to Atacama; Peru, Argentina, Bolivia; Andean *bofedales*; 12,000–15,750 ft (3700–4800 m).

Llama
Lama glama
OTHER NAMES: Hueque, Qawra, Wakaiwa, Chilihueque, Ship of the Andes.
ID: 47 in (120 cm). **SH** 42–47 in (109–120 cm). **WT** 286–340 lb (130–155 kg). Llamas were bred from guanacos over 6000 years ago. They can interbreed with other camelids to produce fertile offspring. Llamas are distinguished by a long neck, long limbs, a rounded muzzle and cleft upper lip. The tips of the large "banana-ears" curve inward. Their fur can be rufous, black or white, or be blotched with contrasting colors. Llamas graze on grasses and low shrubs. They use their protruding lower incisors to clip vegetation against hardened gums.

Family groups consist of about six females, their offspring from the current year, and a single adult male that defends his position by dominance fighting. A dominant male tries to wrestle a challenger to the ground by wrapping his neck around his opponent's and biting his limbs. Dominance is achieved when the opponent has been pushed to the ground and remains lying on its side with the neck lowered and the tail raised.

The Incas found that llamas could carry bags of silver ore in excess of 130 lb (60 kg) for up to 19 miles (30 km) per day at high elevations. This trait is attributed to the llama's hemoglobin, which has a great affinity for oxygen. After the Spanish conquest, entire herds were killed for meat and those remaining were displaced into the high elevation pastures where they are found today. Llamas are now used as pack animals, and locally provide meat for food, hides for shoes and dried excrement for fuel. They are sheared every two years, yielding about 6.5 lb (3 kg) of thick, coarse fleece. Andean farmers have also utilized the male llama's aggressive nature to keep dogs and foxes away from their livestock. By incorporating llamas into sheep or goat flocks, predation drops sharply. The estimated llama population in Chile is 55,000.

RANGE: Arica to Antofagasta; also Bolivia, Peru, Ecuador and nw Argentina. In the Andes; 7500–13,000 ft (2300–4000 m).

Alpaca
Lama pacos
OTHER NAMES: Alpachu, Paqocha.
ID: 45 in (114 cm). **SH** 39 in (90 cm). **WT** 100–170 lb (45–77 kg). Domesticated. Alpacas were selectively bred from vicuñas

about 4000 to 5000 years ago. The alpaca is a graceful, well-proportioned animal with a squarish build, strong legs, small head and short, pointed ears. The tail is held close to the body. The body is covered in thick, soft, long fleece, which can be colored in any of 16 natural shades. A tuft of hair on the head extends over the large eyes, which have long eyelashes and rectangular irises. Alpacas form gregarious herds of up to 300 individuals. Males reach sexual maturity at three years of age, females at two. One male usually mates with ten females. Gestation takes about 345 days, after which the female delivers a single *cria*.

The two main alpaca breeds are known by their Quechua names: HUACAYA and SURI. Huacaya is the most common breed; it has crimped fleece that stands straight out from the body. The rarer Suri has fine, silky hair that hangs in dreadlocks down each side of the body, growing long enough to touch the ground if the animal is not shorn. Fiber from both breeds is valued for its extreme softness, fineness, warmth and strength. Alpacas are usually sheared every two years. Each animal yields about 6 lb (2.5 kg) of raw fleece.

Alpacas were killed in great numbers after the Spanish conquest. Herds were decimated and populations remained low until the value of fleece as a commercial export was realized. Chile's alpaca population now stands at about 30,000 animals.
RANGE: Arica to Antofagasta; Peru, Bolivia. Altiplano; 11,500–16,500 ft (3500–5000 m).

FAMILY CERVIDAE
DEER
Cervids comprise a family of grazing and browsing animals that first appeared in Eurasia over five million years ago. Today, deer occur almost worldwide, including parts of Africa and Australia where they have been introduced. There are presently about 16 genera and 43 species. Species native to Chile include the small forest-dwelling Pudu and two species of microdeer found in the Andes. Common characteristics include bony branching antlers of males that are shed and regrown annually. Except for reindeer, female cervids do not have antlers. The legs are supported on the third and fourth digits, and feet are hoofed. The ruminating stomach has four chambers. There is no gall bladder. The upper canines are either vestigial or absent. The lacrimal glands, which produce tears, are located in a depression in front of the eyes. Most deer are gregarious, living in herds that have complex social organization.

Guemal, Huemul chileno
Hippocamelus bisulcus
OTHER NAMES: South Andean Deer, Huemul del sur, Trola, Shonen, Ciervo andino meridional, Cerf des Andes méridionales, Chilenischer Huemul. Huemul is said to derive from the Mapuche word meaning "to follow another."
ID: 56–68 in (140–170 cm). SH 30–36 in (75–90 cm). WT 110–155 lb (50–70 kg). Males are larger than females and have two-pronged antlers. Thick pelage varies in color from dark brown to golden brown with pale spotting. Anal and inguinal areas white. Large ears. Grey fur around the eyes and nose.

Huemuls (pronounced *whey-MOOLs*) form small, non-territorial family groups composed of a male, his mate and offspring. They feed on grass, new leaves and flowers. Hunting, habitat loss, predation by dogs, and competition for forage from domestic livestock and introduced deer contribute to this species scarcity. They once ranged in the Andes from Santiago south to the Strait of Magellan and in the Argentine highlands. By the early 1970s they had largely disappeared from the area north of Patagonia except in the Nevados de Chillan in Chile and Los Alerces National Park in Argentina. By 1997, only 1500 to 2000 animals remained in protected areas of s Chile and Argentina. ENDANGERED.
RANGE: Mainly in Aisén and Magallanes, with a small population in Los Nevados de

NATIVE AND INTRODUCED DEER 307

Southern Pudu
Pudu
Pudu puda
Maule–Aisén
SH 16 in (40 cm)

Guemal
Huemul chileno
Hippocamelus bisulcus
Biobío–Magallanes
SH 30–36 in (76–90 cm)

Taruca
Huemul del norte
Hippocamelus antisensis
Arica–Tarapacá
SH 30–36 in (76–90 cm)

Fallow Deer
Gamo
Dama dama
Valdivia–Los Lagos
SH 32–40 in (81–101 cm)
Introduced

Red Deer, Elk
Ciervo rojo
Cervus elephus
Biobío–Aisén
SH 30–50 in (70–125 cm)
Introduced

THE HUEMUL AND CHILE'S COAT OF ARMS

Jesuit priest and naturalist Juan Molina described the Huemul to science in 1782. He named it *Equus bisulcus,* a scientific binomial meaning "split-hoofed horse." Thus when Chile adopted the Huemul as its heraldic emblem in 1833, it was drawn on the Coat of Arms as a small, cloven-hoofed horse. Years later it was correctly identified as a deer and was renamed *Hippocamelus,* or "horse-camel." Today it appears with the Andean Condor on the heraldic shield and presidential flag.

Chillán in Biobío; also s Argentina. Grassy hills, scrub, dense forests and places near fresh water; 11,000–16,000 ft (3300–5000 m) in summer; foothill forests and warm, north-facing slopes in winter.

Taruca
Huemul del norte
Hippocamelus antisensis
OTHER NAMES: Guemal, Peruvian Huemul, North Andean Deer, Taruga, Turuka.
ID: 60–68 in (150–170 cm). **SH** 31–36 in (70–90 cm). **WT** 99–143 lb (45–65 kg). Males are larger than females. Stocky, thick, short-legged body. Fur is light brown to grey in color, and consists of coarse brittle hairs with a woolly undercoat. Top of tail is dark brown, the underside white. Throat is pale grey. Dark Y-shaped mark on the forehead and a whitish band around the muzzle. Inside of ears and groin area white. Canines are well-developed in both sexes. Males have short, V-shaped antlers; the front prong is usually shorter than the rear one. Antlers are shed in October and November at the onset of the rainy season. Males are in velvet in December. Births occur in January and February after a gestation of seven months. Young are hidden in vegetation after birth. Tarucas form family herds of 4 to 9 individuals, which are led by an adult female. The herd rests on the hillsides among the rocks by day, then descends to the fertile valleys at night. Some Andean farmers regard the Taruca as a pest since it feeds on the alfalfa grown for domestic livestock. However the Taruca's diet comprises mainly wild sedges, grasses, lichens and mosses. Natural predators include puma and fox. Protected since 1976, but poaching and loss of habitat take a considerable toll.
ENDANGERED; CITES APPENDIX I.

RANGE: Arica-Parinacota to Tarapacá; Peru, Bolivia, Ecuador, nw Argentina. Inhabits mountain slopes and alpine grasslands of the Andean precordillera; 9200–12,800 ft (2800–3900 m).

Southern Pudu, Pudu
Pudu puda
OTHER NAMES: Venadito, Venado, Puyú.
ID: 30–36 in (75–90 cm). **SH** 16 in (40 cm). World's smallest deer. Low-slung body, thick and short legs, slender hooves, small rounded ears, small eyes, and very small external tail. Males have short, spike-like antlers. Hairs of the coat are long, coarse and brittle. Color ranges from buffy agouti to reddish-brown. Fawns are rufous with lines of whitish spots on their back and sides; they achieve adult coloration at the age of three months.

Pudus form small, monogamous family groups. Males are sexually mature at one year of age. They fight by rearing up on their back legs and butting heads. Females build a nest of vegetation where they deliver a single young. Vocalizations include the soft "moo" of the female to her young, and the goat-like bleat of the male. It is said that when a pudu is alarmed, the hairs rise, the body trembles and the eyes fill with tears (in reality, the lacrimal glands open). When pursued, the pudu runs in a zigzag pattern, sometimes climbing tree trunks that are bent over streams or escarpments. Pudus feed on twigs, buds, blossoms, fruits, berries, nuts and acorns of many kinds of trees, shrubs, ferns, vines, and garden vegetables. Natural predators include pumas, kodkods and Darwin's foxes. Adverse human activity has caused their natural range to diminish. Although protected by law, pudus are hunted locally for their hide and meat. VULNERABLE; CITES APPENDIX I.

RANGE: Maule to Aisén; possibly n Magallanes; a large number live on Isla Chiloé; also sw Argentina. Inhabits humid forests, bamboo thickets and woodland; sea level to 5575 ft (0–1700 m).

Red Deer, European Elk, Ciervo rojo
Cervus elaphus

OTHER NAMES: Wapiti, Cerf rouge, Rothirsch.
ID: 66–106 in (165–265 cm). SH 30–50 in (75–125 cm). WT 165–750 lb (75–340 kg). Males (stags) are larger than females (hinds). Males have large antlers with up to eleven points. Reddish-brown, with a white area around the tail. Fawns are spotted. Forms herds of similar age and sex. Old males are solitary. Herds generally remain within their territory, resting by day and feeding at night. Rutting season in Chile is in March. Males butt antlers and roar when fighting for breeding rights. After a gestation of 10 months, the female secludes herself and delivers one to two young. Red deer graze on grass and herbaceous plants from spring to autumn, and browse on low shrubs in winter. The species has spread widely, competing with native deer for food and producing a negative impact on vegetation.
RANGE: INTRODUCED from Europe into Argentina for sport hunting; Red Deer have spread into the montane woodland and forests of Chile from Biobío to Aisén.

Fallow Deer, Gamo
Dama dama

ID: 52–70 in (130–175 cm). SH 32–40 in (81–101 cm). WT 88–220 lb (40–100 kg). Males are larger than females. At 3 to 4 years of age the males develop antlers with broad, palmate areas that measure up to 10 in (25 cm) in width and up to 16 in (39 cm) long. Slim body. Tawny to reddish-brown, with white spots on the back and flanks. Several color variations exist, including albino and melanistic forms. These deer form small herds segregated by sex. Old males are solitary. The rutting period in Chile is in April. Gestation is 8 months. Females bear one, or sometimes two, fawns. Fallow deer are shy and generally keep to dense cover. They are most active at twilight and at night when they graze on grasses and herbaceous plants and browse on leaves and shoots of low shrubs. Fallow deer were INTRODUCED in the 1950s to private preserves in the forests and wooded islands of the Chilean Lake Region. More sedentary than Red Deer, herds tend to stay within their territory and do not spread into the adjacent countryside.
RANGE: Forests and wooded islands from Valdivia to Llanquihue, Los Lagos.

FAMILY SUIDAE

European Wild Boar, Jabalí
Sus scrofa ferus

OTHER NAMES: Sanglier, Wildschwein.
ID: 35–75 in (90–180 cm). SH 22–43 in (55–110 cm). WT 110–775 lb (50–350 kg). Males are larger than females. Males have four continually-growing tusks, one in each jaw quadrant. Females have 6 pairs of teats. Sparse, dark grey to brown coat of coarse, bristle-like hairs. Introduced to Argentina where it interbred with domestic pigs. It has spread into s Chile, where boar hunting is now practiced.
RANGE: Southern Chile. Patagonian forests and scrub, especially in *Nothofagus* forest and reedbeds.

RODENTIA: Rodents

Rodents are numerous in Chile, but because of their small size and furtive habits they are seldom noticed. Rodents have a distinctive dentition: a single pair of upper and lower incisors, and a diastema (a wide space without teeth) between the incisors and molars. Many rodents are fossorial (burrowing) animals. Species that spend most of their lives underground tend to have a short tail, small ears, small eyes and strong claws on the front feet. Those that live in burrows, but forage extensively on the surface, tend to have larger ears and longer tails. Some species are specially equipped to climb trees and rocks; others are specialized for aquatic or semi-aquatic environments.

FAMILY CRICETIDAE, SUBFAMILY SIGMODONTINAE
NEW WORLD RATS AND MICE

Cricetidae is a family of New World rats and mice, which are generally placed in Muroidea—a large, complex superfamily containing over 600 species.

Cricetidae is divided into 3 subfamilies, 12 tribes and 84 genera. The Chilean species can be grouped into 3 to 4 tribes within the subfamily Sigmodontinae:

- AKODONTINI includes the South American field mice and grass mice.
- ORYZOMYINI includes rice rats, spiny mice and marsh rats.
- PHYLLOTINI includes a diverse assortment of mice and rats, many of which live in the High Andes. They have simplified molars well suited for a diet of plants and seeds. *Irenomys*, *Euneomys* and *Reithrodon* species, once in RHEITHRODINI, are now placed here.

TRIBE AKODONTINI: Akodontini is a large tribe (106 species) of small to medium-sized field mice and grass mice that are distributed mainly in the southern half of South America. The akodonts are adapted for terrestrial and semi-fossorial life. The tail is shorter than the head and body length. The ears and eyes are of medium size, and the claws are long. Most species are omnivorous, feeding on fruit, seeds, insects and herbaceous vegetation.

White-bellied Akodont
Ratón ventriblanco
Akodon albiventer

OTHER NAME: White-bellied Grass Mouse. **ID:** 6.25 in (16 cm). Dark grey to olive brown back; white to grey throat, belly and feet. Sparsely-haired tail is dark above and white below. Short ears are well furred. Diurnal. Digs tunnels. Feeds mainly on insect larvae. **RANGE:** Andes of Arica and Tarapacá above 9850 ft (3000 m); at lower elevations in Peru, Bolivia, Argentina. In meadows with thick grass and rocks, and in marshes.

Southern Pericote, Pericote andino
Loxodontomys micropus

OTHER NAME: Southern Big-eared Mouse. **ID:** 8 in (20 cm). Rounded body. Brown to grey upperparts, and white to grey belly. Bicolored tail is shorter than head–body length. Short hind feet. Long whiskers. Large ears. Herbivorous. **RANGE:** Maule to Magallanes; adjacent Argentina. In grasslands and forests with a thick understory; in the Andean pre-cordillera at elevations to 9850 ft (3000 m).

Andean Akodont, Ratón andino
Abrothrix (Chroeomys) andinus

OTHER NAME: Andean Altiplano Mouse. **ID:** 6 in (15 cm). Dense soft fur is light grey to buffy on the back and whitish on the belly. Back of the ears have a white patch and sometimes the entire ears are white. Lips and chin are sometimes white. Digs a system of shallow tunnels about 2 in (5 cm) deep; the tunnels wind between rocks and boulders on sparsely-vegetated slopes. **RANGE:** Arica to Maule; Peru, Argentina; 8200–14,750 ft (2500–4500 m). Also in the matorral of Santiago around 3100 ft (950 m).

Olive-colored Akodont, Ratón olivaceo
Abrothrix olivaceus

OTHER NAMES: Olivaceous Grass Mouse, Ratoncito de hocico amarillo. **ID:** 6.5 in (17 cm). Upperparts greyish-brown, sometimes grizzled with yellow around the muzzle; underparts range from pale grey

ORYZOMYINI AND AKODONTINI RATS AND MICE

Long-tailed Colilargo
Ratón de los espinos
Oligoryzomys longicaudatus
Atacama–Magallanes
8.5 in (22 cm)

White-bellied Akodont
Ratón ventriblanco
Akodon albiventer
High Andes of Arica–Tarapacá
6.25 in (16 cm)

Long-haired Akodont
Ratoncito lanudo
Abrothrix longipilis
Coquimbo–Magallanes
7 in (18 cm)

Andean Akodont
Ratón andino
Abrothrix andinus
Andes of Arica–Maule
6 in (15 cm)

Yellow-nosed Akodont
Ratón hocico bayo
Abrotnrix xanthorhinus
Forests and steppe of
Los Lagos–Magallanes
4.5 in (11.5 cm)

Seeds of Peumo
(*Cryptocarya alba*)

Olive-colored Akodont
Ratón olivaceo
Abrothrix olivaceus
Arica–Magallanes
6.5 in (17 cm)

Southern Pericote
Pericote andino
Loxodontomys micropus
Patagonian Andes of Maule–Magallanes
8 in (20 cm)

Wooly Akodont
Ratón colorado
Abrothrix lanosus
Forests of Magallanes
6.25 in (16 cm)

Sanborn's Akodont
Ratón negruzco
Abrothrix sanborni
Forests of Valdivia–Los Lagos
7 in (18 cm)

Andean Long-clawed Akodont
Ratón topo grande
Chelemys macronyx
Andean forests of Biobío–Magallanes
7 in (18 cm)

Valdivian Long-clawed Mole Mouse
Ratón topo valdiviano
Geoxus valdivianus
Biobío–Magallanes
5.5 in (14 cm)

to brown. Tail is shorter than the body. Mid-sized ears. Mainly terrestrial, but also climbs low bushes and trees. Digs tunnels under rocks and makes runways in dense vegetation. Females build a grass-lined nest hidden by rocks or vegetation, where they can give birth to three litters of 4 to 6 young per year. Abundant in a wide variety of habitats, but generally passes unnoticed due to its habit of remaining immobile when alarmed. Lives in caves, under rocks, in tree roots, or in burrows of coruros (see page 325) and other rodents. A pest in rural houses and farms, where it feeds on grain, cereal crops and flour. Omnivorous; feeds on insects, small invertebrates, newborn of other rodents, and fallen fruit of trees such as *Peumo* and *Belloto*. Populations swell during *ratadas*, the rare flowering and mast seeding of *Chusqea* bamboo, then return to normal when the bamboo dies off.

RANGE: Arica to Magallanes and Tierra del Fuego; Argentina. Grassland, scrub, forests, pastures; sea level to 8200 ft (0–2500 m).

RELATED SPECIES: WELLINGTON AKODONT, *Akodon markhami*, is found only on Isla Wellington, Magallanes.

Long-haired Akodont
Ratoncito lanudo
Abrothrix longipilis

OTHER NAMES: Long-haired Grass Mouse, Ratoncito peludo, Ratón de pelos largos.

ID: 7 in (18 cm). Heavy-bodied and vole-like. Long, shaggy fur is rosy-grey to coffee-colored on the upperparts, with a pale grey belly. Small, thinly-haired ears. Tail is faintly bicolored. Inhabits a wide variety of habitats ranging from scrubland to marshes, fog forests of Fray Jorge and bamboo thickets in Patagonia. In Chile, it is often found near rotting logs, in heavy grass at the base of shrubs, and in rocky ravines with dense vegetation. Active by day and night. Good burrower, building galleries under dense vegetation; usually remains within the burrows during the day. Climbs low shrubs and trees. Diet varies with locale and may include seeds, berries, insects, worms and slugs. Females can give birth 2 to 3 times a year with 6 to 8 offspring in each litter.

RANGE: Coquimbo to Magallanes; also Argentina. In marshes, wet scrubland, rainforests with dense vegetation; sea level to 6500 ft (0–2000 m).

Wooly Akodont, Ratón colorado
Abrothrix lanosus

OTHER NAME: Woolly Grass Mouse.

ID: 6.25 in (16 cm). Cinnamon to olive-brown above; fulvous to white belly. White feet. Bicolored tail. Short, thickly-furred ears.

RANGE: Cool, humid forests of Magallanes and s Argentina.

Sanborn's Akodont, Ratón negruzco
Abrothrix sanborni

OTHER NAME: Sanborn's Grass Mouse.

ID: 7 in (18 cm). Thick, dark brown to iron-grey pelage. Dark, unicolored tail. Active by day and night. Feeds on fungi, spiders and insect larvae. Forest dweller.

RANGE: Valdivia to Los Lagos, including Llanquihue and Chiloé; wc Argentina.

Yellow-nosed Akodont
Ratón hocico bayo
Abrothrix xanthorhinus

OTHER NAME: Laucha de nariz amarilla.

ID: 4.5 in (11.5 cm). Small, short-tailed brown mouse with varying amounts of golden to rust-colored fur on the snout, top of the legs and sides of the tail. Omnivorous; feeds on insects, seeds and grass.

RANGE: Los Lagos to Magallanes and Tierra del Fuego. Patagonian forests and steppe; most common in marshy areas and grasslands edged by *Nothofagus-Drimys* forest.

RELATED SPECIES: HERSHKOVITZ'S AKODONT, *Abrothrix hershkovitzi*. Occurs on Magellanic steppe and coastal forests of islands around Cape Horn.

LONG-CLAWED MOLE MICE: Rodent species in the genera *Geoxus* and *Chelemys* have very long claws, short tails, small eyes, and dense, mole-like fur.

Valdivian Long-clawed Mole Mouse
Ratón topo valdiviano
Geoxus valdivianus
OTHER NAMES: Long-clawed Akodont, Rata topo cordillerano, Ratón topo de la selva, Ratón topo pardo.
ID: 5.5 in (14 cm). Shrew-like, short-tailed mouse of the southern rainforests. Velvety, short fur colored olive brown to black, or washed with reddish-brown. Small eyes; very small ears; pointed nose. Large feet, with claws that are longer than the digits. Spindle-shaped body is adapted to move in small tunnels. Exceptional burrower. Excavates burrows in the moist forest soil, leaving them briefly to forage at night. Maintains runways near rotting logs and dense *Berberis* undergrowth. Feeds mainly on worms and grubs, supplemented with vegetation.
RANGE: Biobío to Magallanes, including Isla Chiloé and the Guaitecas; s Argentina. In *Saxegothaea* bamboo in *Nothofagus* forests, and in tussock grass, marshes and wet meadows; sea level to the timberline.

Andean Long-clawed Akodont
Ratón topo grande
Chelemys macronyx
OTHER NAME: Andean Long-clawed Mouse.
ID: 7 in (18 cm). Stout-bodied, short-tailed mouse, with elongated front claws and dense fur that nearly conceals the small ears. Blackish to coffee-colored upperparts contrast sharply with greyish-white sides and belly. Bicolored tail. Excavates a network of tunnels in the deep, moist soils of montane *Nothofagus pumilio* forest. Feeds on grass seeds, fruit, fungi, spiders and earthworms.
RANGE: Biobío to the Strait of Magellan, and adjacent Argentina. In Patagonian forests; foothills to the timberline.
RELATED SPECIES: The LARGE LONG-CLAWED AKODONT, *Chelemys megalonyx*, occurs in sc Chile. Separated from *Chelemys macronyx* mainly by its paler incisors. Endangered.
RATÓN TOPO DEL ESTRECHO DE MAGALLANES, *Chelemys delfini*, occurs around the Strait of Magellan.

TRIBE ORYZOMYINI: Members of this tribe have a tail that is longer than the head and body length. Because they require ample fresh water for drinking, they live in wetland and marsh habitats.

Long-tailed Colilargo
Ratón colilargo
Oligoryzomys longicaudatus
OTHER NAMES: Long-tailed Pygmy Rice Rat, Colilargo común, Coludo, Ratón chileno de cola larga, Lauchita de los espinos, Ratón de los arrozales, Ratón de los espinos.
ID: 8.5 in (22 cm). Upperparts buffy to ochre, finely lined with black. Belly is pale grey. Long, thinly-haired tail is bicolored, with white on the underside. Long hind feet.
Inhabits a wide variety of habitats, from cloud forest to open brush and roadsides with berry and rosebush brambles. Crepuscular. Highly arboreal, running, jumping, and climbing on bushes and tree branches, or scurrying beneath dense, thorny bushes. Solitary. Reaches sexual maturity within a few months. Females bear 2 or 3 litters of 3 to 5 offspring. Nests in trees, or uses abandoned bird nests.
Feeds mainly on seeds, but also takes worms and insects. Colilargo populations increase when quila bamboo (*Chusquea* sp.) flowers and produces seed at the end of a 15- to 40-year cycle, an event known as mast seeding *(ratada)*. When the bamboo dies off, the number of rice rats falls to a normal level. The Colilargo can transmit the Hanta virus, which can cause serious respiratory disease in humans.
RANGE: Atacama to Magallanes; adjacent Argentina; sea level to 6500 ft (2000 m).
RELATED SPECIES: PATAGONIAN COLILARGO, *Oligoryzomys magellanicus*, occurs in s Chile and Argentina.

TRIBE PHYLLOTINI: Phyllotini is a diverse group in terms of external appearance. The tail may be long or short, and the fur ranges from buff to dark brown to black-and-white. Members of this group all have simplified molars for chewing plants and seeds and have a hairy heel. Almost half of the Phyllotini species live in the High Andes.

Andean Mouse
Rata andina
Andinomys edax
ID: 10.2 in (26 cm). Stocky body with long, soft, dense fur colored brown above, grey below. Bicolored tail is shorter than head and body length. Short hind feet. Large ears. Long whiskers. Nocturnal. Arboreal. Most often seen in dense brushy thickets along mountain streams. Builds a straw-lined nest in holes in tree branches. Feeds entirely on plant matter. Breeds at the end of dry season (Oct–Nov) so that young are born when spring rains produce abundant plant growth.
RANGE: Andes of Arica and Tarapacá; Peru, Bolivia, nw Argentina. Scrub along watercourses; 5900–16,500 ft (1800–5000 m).

Bolivian Pericote
Ratón orejudo
Auliscomys boliviensis
OTHER NAME: Puna Mouse.
ID: 9 in (22 cm). Stout, with a fairly short tail, long ragged fur, and very big ears. Buff and tan on the back, with a creamy white vent. Tuft of yellowish hair in front of each ear. Soles of hind feet are black. Diurnal. Feeds on plant matter and seeds, often near viscacha colonies and tuco-tuco burrows.
RANGE: Altiplano of Arica-Parinacota; s Peru and w Bolivia. On rocky slopes with sparse vegetation, rock slides, stone walls, and near tuco-tuco and viscacha colonies; 10,000–16,500 ft (3000–5000 m).
RELATED SPECIES: LOFTY PERICOTE, PERICOTE ANDINO, *Auliscomys sublimis*. Small and vole-like. Has a shorter tail and smaller ears than *Auliscomys boliviensis*. Lives in open areas with bunchgrass and rocks, near tuco-tuco and viscacha colonies. Altiplano of Chile, Peru, Bolivia, Argentina; 13,000–19,700 ft (4000–6000 m)—one of the highest elevations recorded for a mammal of the Western Hemisphere.

Graceful Laucha
Lauchita andina
Calomys lepidus
OTHER NAME: Andean Vesper Mouse.
ID: 4.5 in (12.5 cm). Resembles the House Mouse, *Mus musculus*. A tiny herbivorous mouse, with dense tan to brown grizzled fur on the back and a white to grey belly. Short, buff-colored tail.
RANGE: Arica to Antofagasta; Peru, Bolivia, nw Argentina. Grasslands on the Altiplano; 9850–16,500 ft (3000–5000 m).

Altiplano Chinchilla Mouse
Laucha chinchilla, Achallo
Chinchillula sahamae
ID: 10.2 in (26 cm). Chinchilla-like pelage of thick, soft, silky fur. Striking coloration. Upperparts are grey and black; underparts are snow white. Hips and rump are white edged with black. Whitish tail is fully haired. Large ears. Broad feet. Nocturnal. Herbivorous. People of the Altiplano use its fur to make ceremonial robes, each of which may contain 150 pelts.
RANGE: Arica-Parinacota and Tarapacá; also s Peru, sw Bolivia. Rocky sites, around stone walls and viscacha dens on the Altiplano above 13,000 ft (4000 m).

Altiplano Laucha
Ratoncito de pié sedoso
Eligmodontia puerulus
OTHER NAMES: Highland Desert Mouse, Ratón del altiplano, Laucha colilargo bayo, Achucus.
ID: 7 in (17 cm). Small, pale buff mouse with a white belly. Long, hind legs. Spade-shaped hind feet have hairy cushions on the soles. Inhabits semi-arid areas with sandy soil and open vegetation. Feeds mainly on seeds, especially *Prosopis* and *Berberis*; also eats insects. Stores food. Requires very little water and can drink salt water. Nocturnal. Digs its own burrows, or uses those of tuco-tucos and other rodents.
RANGE: Arica to Atacama. In areas of open sand and low bushes on the Puna and Altiplano above 9850 ft (3000 m).

PHYLLOTINI AND REITHRODONT RATS AND MICE

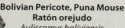

Bolivian Pericote, Puna Mouse
Ratón orejudo
Auliscomys boliviensis
Altiplano of Arica-Parinacota
9 in (22 cm)

Graceful Laucha
Lauchita andina
Calomys lepidus
Altiplano grasslands of Arica–Antofagasta
4.5 in (12.5 cm)

Altiplano Laucha
Ratoncito de pié sedoso
Eligmodontia puerulus
High Andes of Arica–Atacama
7 in (17 cm)

Altiplano Chinchilla Mouse
Laucha chinchilla, Achallo
Chinchillula sahamae
High Andes of Arica–Tarapacá
10.2 in (26 cm)

Andean Mouse
Rata andina
Andinomys edax
High Andes of Arica–Tarapacá
10.2 in (26 cm)

Red-nosed Neotomys
Ratón ebrio
Neotomys ebriosus
High Andean wetlands of Arica–Tarapacá
8 in (20 cm)

Patagonian Leaf-eared Mouse
Lauchon orejudo austral
Phyllotis xanthopygus
Arica–Magallanes
9 in (22 cm)

Large-footed Irenomys
Rata arborea chilena
Irenomys tarsalis
Forests of Biobío–Aisén
11.5 in (29 cm)

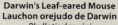

Darwin's Leaf-eared Mouse
Lauchon orejudo de Darwin
Phyllotis darwini
Coast of Coquimbo–Los Lagos
9 in (22 cm)

Hairy-soled Coney Rat
Rata conejo
Reithrodon auritus
Open grasslands of Aisén–Magallanes
9.5 in (24 cm)

Tierra del Fuego Euneomys
Rata sedosa fueguina
Euneomys chinchilloides
Maule–Magallanes
8.1 in (21 cm)

RELATED SPECIES: WESTERN PATAGONIAN LAUCHA, *Eligmodontia morgani*, ranges from Aisén to the Strait of Magellan, and into s Argentina on gravel plains, rocky slopes and in semi-arid scrub.

Darwin's Leaf-eared Mouse
Lauchón orejudo de Darwin
Phyllotis darwini

OTHER NAMES: Darwin's Pericote, Pericote orejudo de Darwin, Lauchita de Darwin, Pericote panza gris.

ID: 9 in (22 cm). Long tail, big ears and big eyes. Long, silky, coffee-colored fur, darker on the back than on the belly. Nocturnal. Arboreal. Climbs well. Generally solitary, but will sometimes form small colonies. Burrows and shelters under rocks by day, and sometimes enters farm houses. In Chile, the diet is herbivorous in spring and granivorous in summer; also feeds on insects. Seldom drinks, but requires some drinking water. Females bear 4 to 8 young in a rounded nest made of intertwined plant fibers built in shrubs and cacti.

RANGE: Coast of wc Chile from Coquimbo to Los Lagos; in areas of low scrub and tamarugo groves. Once thought to range throughout the Andes, now recognized as a geographically restricted species.

RELATED SPECIES: The newly-defined species *P. limatus*, *P. magister* and *P. osgoodi*, range from Peru south into Bolivia and n Chile.

Patagonian Leaf-eared Mouse
Lauchón orejudo austral
Phyllotis xanthopygus

OTHER NAMES: Yellow-rumped Pericote, Lauchón orejudo andino.

ID: 9 in (22 cm). Greyish brown with a buffy to tawny wash on the rump. Nocturnal. Lives in rocky outcrops. Forages in open areas with little vegetative cover where it is open to predation by raptors and foxes.

RANGE: Andes from Arica to Magallanes, north of the Strait of Magellan, and Peru to s Argentina. Occupies almost the entire altitudinal range of Chile from sea level to 18,375 ft (0–5600 m).

Large-footed Irenomys
Rata arborea chilena
Irenomys tarsalis

OTHER NAMES: Chilean Climbing Mouse, Ratón de las quilas, Laucha arborea, Colilargo oreja negra.

ID: 11.5 in (29 cm). Mid-sized and slender, with a very long, penicillate tail and large hind feet. Large eyes. Dense, soft fur is brownish-black with cinnamon wash. Ears are black. Grooved upper incisors. Lives in the dense rainforests of the southern Andes. Climbs trees. Feeds on seeds, leaves and fungi; eats quila bamboo seeds and may experience population outbreaks when the bamboo has a mast seeding *(ratada)*.

RANGE: Temperate rainforests from Biobío to Aisén, including Isla Chiloé and the Guaitecas; also s Argentina; sea level to 3600 ft (0–1100 m).

Hairy-soled Coney Rat, Rata conejo
Reithrodon auritus

OTHER NAMES: Ratón conejo, Bunny Rat.

ID: 9.5 in (24 cm). Large, with a short tail, big eyes and big furry ears. Long, soft fur is buff-grey to brown on the back, golden on the sides, and blackish on the crown; belly is yellowish to pale buff. Inhabits grassy areas, where it excavates its own communal burrows or occupies those of tuco-tucos and armadillos. Builds a nest of plant fibers and sheep's wool in a burrow, under fallen tree trunks or amid rocks. Feeds at night on grass, tuberous rhizomes and roots. Said to eat its own weight in grass each day.

RANGE: Patagonian sector of Aisén and Magallanes; c Argentina through Tierra del Fuego. Inhabits grassy steppe, cultivated fields, pastures, stony hillsides and sandy coasts; sea level to 1970 ft (0–600 m) in Chile; to 9850 ft (3000 m) in Argentina.

Red-nosed Neotomys, Ratón ebrio
Neotomys ebriosus

OTHER NAMES: Andean Swamp Mouse, Ratón andino de los pantanos.

ID: 8 in (20 cm). Stocky body. Tip of muzzle bright cinnamon-orange. Grizzled greyish-brown above; chest and sternal band dirty brown; belly white to grey. Long guard hairs. Short tail is well-furred and bicolored, brown above and grey to buffy below. Feet grey to buffy, sometimes with rufous on the ankles. Broad incisors; upper incisors have a narrow groove at the outer corner. Shelters under isolated rocks. Active by day and night.

RANGE: Andes of Arica-Parinacota; s Peru, Bolivia, nw Argentina. In grasslands and brush-clad steppe, often near streams and marshes, above 8200 ft (2500 m).

Tierra del Fuego Euneomys
Rata sedosa fueguina
Euneomys chinchilloides
OTHER NAMES: Patagonian Chinchilla Rat, Ratón sedoso chinchilloides, Ratón peludo castaño.

ID: 8.1 in (21 cm). Vole-like in form, with a short tail and long, soft fur. Upperparts are dark grey varied with black and reddish-brown, underparts are buffy to grey. Small ears are heavily furred in black. Long, thick whiskers. Feet are white to cream and have thickly cushioned soles. Furred tail is bicolored. Inhabits sandy areas with rocks, grass and brush; also occurs in Ñirre forests *(Nothofagus antarctica)* and areas of glacial retreat. Agile climber. Females give birth to 4 to 8 offspring per litter.

RANGE: Maule to Magallanes and Tierra del Fuego. Grassland, forest, brush, sand, barren slopes; sea level to 5250 ft (0–1600 m).

RELATED SPECIES: LARGE EUNEOMYS, *Euneomys mordax*, occurs in the Andes from Santiago to Araucanía and adjacent Argentina at elevations to 9850 ft (3000 m). The buffy-grey *Euneomys noei* occurs in the Andean foothills around Santiago.

FAMILY CHINCHILLIDAE
CHINCHILLAS AND VISCACHAS

These stocky, rabbit-like rodents inhabit the Andes of Chile, Argentina, Peru and Bolivia. They have very luxurious, dense fur, which they keep clean by taking dust baths. They have long whiskers. The furred tail is shorter than the head–body length. The hind legs are long and strong; the front feet are short. These rodents are herbivores. They have long gestation periods and give birth to precocius young that are able to feed themselves almost immediately.

Mountain Viscacha, Vizcacha
Lagidium viscacia
OTHER NAMES: Rock Squirrel, Vizcacha de montana, Chinchillán, Pilquén.

ID: 26 in (67 cm). WT 3.3 lb (1.5 kg). Rabbit-sized rodent with long, thick fur, long ears and large eyes. Fur is agouti grey and brown on the upperparts, sometimes with patches of cream to black; belly is pale yellow to tan. Fur undergoes seasonal molts, known locally as *pelechas*. The long, penicillate tail is haired to the tip, with the longest hairs on the upper surface. The tail is held in a semi-curled position when resting and fully extended when moving about. The forefeet are short; the long hind feet allow them to climb and jump with great agility.

Viscachas live in colonies in boulder strewn areas of the Andes and shelter in rock crevices and fissures. They are diurnal, spending much of the day sunbathing on the rocks or dust bathing. Alarm call is a sharp whistle. Feeds exclusively on plant matter, and requires little or no water for drinking. Markings from the dark-colored, concentrated urine can be seen around the colony. Reaches sexual maturity at 7 months of age. Females have one litter per year and give birth to a single offspring.

Natural predators include foxes and cats. Protected in Chile, but illegal hunting has dramatically reduced numbers in central and southern regions. VULNERABLE.

RANGE: Andes from Arica-Parinacota to Última Esperanza in Magallanes; Bolivia, s Peru, w Argentina. In arid, rugged, rocky areas; 2000–16,500 ft (600–5000 m).

RELATED SPECIES: The larger WOLFFSOHN'S MOUNTAIN VISCACHA, or CHINCHILLA ANARANJADA, *L. wolffsohni*, is golden-brown with a bushy tail and short black ears; it ranges in Magallanes and sw Argentina. The NORTHERN MOUNTAIN VISCACHA, *L. peruanum*, ranges from c Peru to n Chile.

CHINCHILLAS: The first chinchillas exported from Chile went to the London Zoo in 1820 and the Hamburg Zoo in 1865. Commercial breeding began in 1918 after Mathias F. Chapman, an American engineer for the Anaconda Copper Mining Co., obtained permits to collect chinchillas in the Andes. Chinchilla numbers had been so thinned by overhunting by that time that it took a team of 23 men three years to find eleven suitable animals. It took the men another year to slowly bring the animals down from the Andes and acclimate them to their new surroundings. The chinchillas were carried by ship to California, and by the time they arrived in Los Angeles in February of 1923, the first young had been born on board. This was the beginning of the chinchilla farming and chinchilla pet trade in the USA.

Long-tailed Chinchilla
Chinchilla chilena
Chinchilla lanigera
OTHER NAMES: Chinchilla de cola larga.
ID: 14.25 in (37 cm). Silvery-grey, dense, silky fur. Large rounded ears and eyes. Very long whiskers. Tail is well-furred, especially on the upper surface. Lives in communal burrows and crevices among rocks, on hillsides with sandy soils, and under large bushes, often sharing their tunnels with mice or degus. Feeds on seeds, leaves, stems and bulbs of Chagual *(Puya berteroniana)*, the fruit of cacti or shrubs such as *Bridgesia incisifolia* and needlegrass *(Nassella chilensis)*. Females are the dominant sex. They mate in austral winter and bear a single young after a gestation of 111 days. Chinchillas were hunted for their valuable fur toward the end of the 19th century; nearly half a million pelts per year were exported from the ports of Coquimbo and Vallenar. Today only remnant populations remain in the wild. **PROTECTED** since 1929. **VULNERABLE**; CITES APPENDIX I.

RANGE: ENDEMIC to Chile. Most wild chinchillas are restricted to Coquimbo at Las Chinchillas Reserve in the Choapa Valley, ne of Illapel; 3600–5575 ft (1100–1700 m).

Short-tailed Chinchilla, Chinchilla andina
Chinchilla brevicauda
ID: 14 in (36 cm). Grey, slightly crimped fur. Similar to, but more compact than the Long-tailed Chinchilla with a thicker neck and shoulders, shorter tail and smaller ears. Gestation period is about 128 days. Severe human persecution has drastically reduced the range and habitat. Predation by foxes, competition from other rodents, and the small viable population also influence their chances of survival in the wild. **CRITICALLY ENDANGERED.**
RANGE: RARE. Andes of Arica–Antofagasta; s Peru, Bolivia, nw Argentina. Grasslands and rocky outcrops above 10,825 ft (3300 m).

FAMILY CAVIIDAE
CAVIES, GUINEA PIGS AND CUIS
In Chile, this group of South American rodents is represented by wild cavies and domesticated guinea pigs—also commonly called cavies after their scientific name, or cuis (pronounced *COO-eez*) after their Spanish name. In general, the body is stout and elongated with an extremely reduced or vestigial tail. The large head is shortened frontally. Eyes and ears are large. There are four toes on the forefeet and three on the hind feet. Molars are ever-growing.

GUINEA PIGS: The domestic guinea pig is commonly kept as a pet in many countries and is widely used in scientific research. Guinea pigs may have been named for their pig-like, squealing vocalizations. The word "guinea" may derive from the guinea, a gold coin that was the price of the animal when it was first marketed in England. It may also refer to Guyana, the country from which they were first shipped to Europe, or it may possibly refer to Guineamen, the slave traders who were among the first to carry cuis from South America to England.

CAVIES, TUCO-TUCOS, CHINCHILLAS AND VISCACHAS

Domestic Guinea Pig, Cuy
Cavia porcellus
Arica–Tarapacá
12 in (30 cm)

Guinea pigs come in many colors including warm brown, grey, black and pied.

Montane Guinea Pig Cavy, Cuy serrano
Cavia tschudii
Andes of Arica–Tarapacá
8.5–10.5 in (22–27 cm)

Southern Mountain Cavy Cuy chico
Microcavia australis
Lowlands of Magallanes
7.5–9 in (19–23 cm)

Common Yellow-toothed Cavy Cuy de dientes amarillos
Galea musteloides
Andes of Arica–Tarapacá
6.5–9.5 in (17–24 cm)

Tawny Tuco-tuco Tuco-tuco de Atacama
Ctenomys fulvus
Arica–Atacama
12.5 in (32 cm)
Desert oases

Maule Tuco-tuco Tuco-tuco de Maule
Ctenomys maulinus
Maule–Valdivia
11.5 in (29 cm)
Forest edge

A Magellanic Tuco-tuco (*Ctenomys magellanicus*) at its burrow entrance, showing its prominent orange teeth.

Highland Tuco-tuco Tuco-tuco de la puna
Ctenomys opimus
Arica–Tarapacá
12 in (30 cm)
Altiplano and Puna

Short-tailed Chinchilla Chinchilla andina
Chinchilla brevicauda
Andes of Arica–Antofagasta
14 in (36 cm)

Bridgesia incisifolia

Viscachas can often be seen sunbathing outside their den with the tail extended and eyes closed.

Long-tailed Chinchilla Chinchilla chilena
Chinchilla lanigera
Coquimbo
14.25 in (37 cm)

Mountain Viscacha, Vizcacha
Lagidium viscacia
Andes of Arica–Magallanes
26 in (67 cm)

The ancestor of the domestic guinea pig is probably the wild Montane Guinea Pig, or Cuy serrano *(Cavia tschudii)*. The Incas selectively bred this animal to show a wide range of colors. They also raised it for use in sacred rites. After Spanish conquest, the clergy tried to suppress all rituals involving guinea pigs, but the animal continued to figure in Altiplano ceremonies. In one ritual, a black guinea pig was rubbed over the naked body of a patient to detect disease. If it squealed while being passed over the body, it was thought that it found the point of disease and would absorb the sick spirits. The animal was then offered a selection of medicinal herbs, and the plant it selected was considered an appropriate remedy for the human patient. The animal was then killed and its intestines examined to find the possible cause of disease.

Today guinea pigs are kept by the people of the High Andes as a source of meat and an item of barter. A mated pair is a typical household gift to newlyweds, guests or children. The rodents are usually kept in the household kitchen, where they are allowed to run around freely. Adobe hutches *(cuyeros)* are provided for shelter. Women and children are the primary caregivers, charged with collecting the feed, cleaning the floor and maintaining the *cuyeros*.

Montane Guinea Pig, Cavy, Cuy serrano
Cavia tschudii
OTHER NAMES: Wild Guinea Pig, Cobaye.
ID: 8.5–10.5 in (22–27 cm). Stocky body with extremely short or no tail. Short, unfurred ears. Short legs. Feet are armed with sharp claws. Pelage is coarse and long, with a ruff of neck hairs. In Chile, the coat is colored pale agouti brown on the back, with a white to cream belly.

Cuis inhabit moist grasslands with scattered rocks. They feed at dawn and dusk on grass and leaves. They form small groups of 5 to 10 individuals. Groups sometimes merge with others giving the impression of a large colony. They dig their own burrows or occupy other animals' burrows. Females can reproduce at the age of two months. Gestation is 60 to 70 days, and litter size averages 1 to 4 young.
RANGE: Andes of Arica and Tarapacá; Peru, Bolivia, Argentina. Wet meadows with scattered rocks; 6560–12,465 ft (2000–3800 m).

Common Yellow-toothed Cavy Cuy de dientes amarillos
Galea musteloides
OTHER NAMES: Conejo moro, Cuy común, Cobaye à dents jaunes.
ID: 6.5–9.5 in (17–24 cm). Silky fur. Back is greyish-brown; paler grey underparts. Big eyes and ears. Digs communal burrows with many levels and entrances, which are often covered with grass; also occupies burrows of viscachas, armadillos and tuco-tucos. Will share runways and engage in social grooming with the Southern Mountain Cavy. Vocalizations include a *churr*, tooth chatter, and a so-called "rusty gate" alarm call. Females are the dominant sex. They can give birth at one month of age and can have about seven litters a year. Gestation is 53 days; litter size is one to five young.
RANGE: Arica-Parinacota and Tarapacá; also s Peru, n Argentina, Paraguay. On brush-covered Andean slopes, grasslands, fields, rocky areas; 11,500–16,500 ft (3500–5000 m) in Chile; lower elevations elsewhere.

Southern Mountain Cavy, Cuy chico
Microcavia australis
ID: 7.5–9 in (19–23 cm). Small. Upperparts yellowish-grey to agouti brown; underparts grey to cream. Ring of light hair around eye. Short ears and short stout claws. Diurnal. Lives in semi-arid scrubland. Uses runways through brush and open areas. Shelters in a shallow depression dug under a bush; sometimes digs shallow burrows, or uses those of viscachas or armadillos. Climbs bushes and trees to feed on leaves and other plant material. Very seldom drinks water, presumably obtaining sufficient water from food. Males are non-territorial, but can be aggressive toward other males. Females, especially mothers and daughters, forage

together. Females can produce up to five litters per year. Gestation is 54 days. Males pursue females, sometimes following with their nose at the female's rump. Vocalizations include twitters and alarm shrieks. Farmers regard cuis as pests that destroy crops and create holes hazardous to horses. Natural predators include lesser grisons and foxes.

RANGE: Magallanes; s Argentina. Lowlands in semi-arid brushland, riparian habitats, under fallen forest trees, along cultivated fields, and in rock piles.

RELATED SPECIES: ANDEAN MOUNTAIN CAVY, *Microcavia niata*. Recently recorded in the Andes of n Chile; normal range is in se Peru and w Bolivia.

FAMILY CTENOMYIDAE
TUCO-TUCOS

This family of large, burrowing rodents is endemic to South America, ranging from the western lowlands of Peru to Tierra del Fuego, with discontinuous distribution into e Brazil. The vernacular name, Tuco-tuco, derives from their call, which is sounded in their burrows. The call is described as a 10- to 20-second, bubbling *tuc-tuc-tuc* that increases in tempo toward the end.

The Tuco-tuco has a robust, cylindrical body, with a large head, small external ears, small eyes set near the top of the head, and a short thinly-haired tail. Legs are short and muscular. Comb-like bristles on the hind feet are used to groom the fur.

Tuco-tucos prefer dry, sandy soils for a burrow, which consists of a long main tunnel with several entrances and secondary underground runs that may or may not lead to the outside. They excavate the burrow by loosening soil with the clawed forefeet and sweeping the soil out with the hind feet. The main burrow is dug to a food source. This allows the animal to forage a short distance from the tunnel entrance and quickly return with food to the safety of the burrow. The prominent orange-colored incisors are used to clear roots and plant matter from around the entrance holes. Although only a single male or several females will occupy a burrow, either sex will share its den with lizards, mice or cuis. Females give birth to an annual litter of 1 to 7 young in a grass-lined nesting chamber located below the main tunnel. Gestation is about 102 to 120 days. Newborn are able to fend for themselves shortly after birth. Ranchers believe that tuco-tucos damage crops and compete for forage with livestock.

Tawny Tuco-tuco
Tuco-tuco de Atacama
Ctenomys fulvus

OTHER NAMES: Atacama Tuco-tuco, Tuco-tuco del tamarugal, Tuco-tuco coludo.

ID: 12.5 in (32 cm). Buff-colored shaggy fur. Sometimes has black on the face. Small ears. Short tail is colored buff and brown. Feeds on bulbs, roots and leaves. Excavates many long tunnels under preferred food sources. Tunnels are expanded when the vegetation is depleted and long paths of bare ground indicate where the vegetation was stripped. Plugs and unplugs its burrow with earth in order to maintain a steady burrow temperature of 72°F (22°C), while the temperature of the desert experiences great thermal oscillation.

RANGE: Arica to Atacama; also Argentina.

SUBSPECIES: TUCO-TUCO DEL TAMARUGAL, *C. f. robustus*, occurs at Pica in Tarapacá. TUCO-TUCO DE ATACAMA, *C. f. fulvus*, occurs in mountain desert oases having well-drained sandy soils from Arica to Atacama; 3600–12,150 ft (1100–3700 m).

Highland Tuco-tuco
Tuco-tuco de la puna, Tujo tujo
Ctenomys opimus

OTHER NAME: Puna Tuco-tuco.

ID: 12 in (30 cm). Long silky fur; brown to buffy-grey on the back, paler on the sides and belly, and blackish on the head. Incisors are bright orange-yellow. Remains underground for most of the day; most surface activity takes place in early morning.

RANGE: High Andean steppe of Arica and

Tarapacá; s Peru, sw Bolivia, nw Argentina. On slopes with sparse vegetation and sandy or stony soil; 8200–16,500 ft (2500–5000 m).

Maule Tuco-tuco, Tuco-tuco de Maule
Ctenomys maulinus
ID: 11.5 in (29 cm). Light brown to dark olive-brown, mole-like fur. Tuft of white hairs at tail tip. Populations vary in color in relation to the color of soil around their burrows.
RANGE: Maule to Valdivia; also Neuquén, Argentina. Grassy or brush-covered slopes; volcanic soils; in *Araucaria* and *Nothofagus* forest; 2950–6560 ft (900–2000 m).

Magellanic Tuco-tuco
Tuco-tuco de Magallanes
Ctenomys magellanicus
OTHER NAMES: Tuco-tuco magellánico.
ID: 11 in (27.5 cm). Geographical races vary in color from pale grey to black, some with a cinnamon vent. Excavates long galleries in the Patagonian pampas, where it feeds on the plant roots and bulbs. Mounds of loose soil at tunnel entrances, and the drumming and hammering sounds coming from the subterranean galleries, are good clues to locating a colony. This animal was an important food source for the Ona tribe of Tierra del Fuego. Sheep ranching on the pampas has led to the disappearance of many tuco-tuco colonies. VULNERABLE. NOT ILLUSTRATED.
RANGE: Aisén to Tierra del Fuego. On the Patagonian steppe, in open meadows with dense grass and low bushes; from sea level to 500 ft (0–150 m).

FAMILY OCTODONTIDAE
OCTODONTS

Octodonts are rat-like, ground-dwelling or burrowing herbivores that inhabit the Andes of South America. They have dense, silky hair with a well-developed undercoat. Octodonts are grey or brown except for the Coruro, which is black. Members of this group have a large head, pointed nose, long whiskers, and large rounded ears. The legs are short. The forefeet have four digits, the hind feet five, and the toes end in sharp, curved claws. The tail is penicillate (haired, with the hairs growing longer closer to the tip and ending in a tuft). The strong incisors are bright orange in color and the molars' grinding surfaces are shaped roughly like a figure eight.

Degu, Degu común
Octodon degus
OTHER NAMES: Ratón cola de trompeta, Ratón de las pircas, Ratón de los cercos, Mulita, Bari, Arten Gewöhnlicher Degu.
ID: 10.5 in (27 cm). Smallest degu. Diurnal. Soft underfur with long guard hairs is colored warm brown above and cream on the belly. Large head. Large eyes and ears. Pale orange incisors. Long, thinly-haired, penicillate tail with a black tuft at the tip.

Degus live in colonies in the sclerophyll woodland. They do not hibernate. They dig communal galleries having multiple entries that are hidden by bushes and low trees such as Espino *(Acacia caven)* or Litre *(Lithraea caustica)*. The tunnels have separate latrine areas, nesting chambers, and storage areas where food is cached for winter. Females attain sexual maturity in their first year and give birth to an annual litter of 6 to 8 young.

Sticks, stones and droppings deposited at the burrow entrance serve as territorial markers. The degus also communicate in high-pitched whistles and growling noises. They climb shrubs in search of seeds and plant matter. They do not eat fruit because they are sugar-intolerant and unable to metabolize fructose. Degus raise their tail as they run along paths in the vegetation. The long tail is easily shed. If a predator grabs the tail, the skin and fur strips off, leaving behind bare bone. The bone withers, falls off and does not regrow.

Degus are threatened by free-roaming livestock that trample burrows, forcing the colonies deep into undisturbed vegetation. Once regarded as a food source by the Mapuches, degus are now bred in captivity and kept as pets in several countries.
RANGE: ENDEMIC to Chile. West slopes of

the Andes between Vallenar, Atacama, and Curicó, Maule. In sclerophyll woodland and matorral to 5900 ft (1800 m).

Bridges's Degu, Degu de los matorrales
Octodon bridgesi
OTHER NAMES: Degu de Bridges, Wald-Degu.
ID: 12.5 in (32 cm). Dark grey to agouti-brown above, with a tan vent and white spots in the groin and armpit area. Straight tail with a black tuft of short hairs at the tip. Moves with its tail dragging behind on the ground. Forefeet have a rudimentary fifth toe; hind feet have granulated soles. Large head, large eyes and well-developed ears. Emits shrill alarm calls. Herbivorous. Said to damage plantation-grown pines. VULNERABLE.
RANGE: RARE. Range has diminished within the last decade, and is now restricted to three discrete populations in the Andean foothills from Coquimbo to Araucanía; also occurs in Neuquén Province, Argentina. Inhabits forests and rocky sites; sea level to 3950 ft (0–1200 m).
RELATED SPECIES: PACIFIC DEGU, *Octodon pacificus*, a newly described species similar to *Octodon bridgesi*, occurs on Isla Mocha. MOON-TOOTHED DEGU, *Octodon lunatus*, has a chestnut back and black-tipped tail. It is identified by the moon shape of the last maxillary molar. Ranges in the coastal mountains of Coquimbo and Valparaíso.

Mountain Degu, Chozchoz
Rata cola pincel
Octodontomys gliroides
OTHER NAME: Long-tailed Octodon.
ID: 12 in (31 cm). The chozchoz (plural chozchoris) has big ears, large eyes and a long, penicillate tail. Pearl grey to brown above; belly and feet white. Nocturnal. Climbs rocks. Likes to dust bathe. Does not dig burrows, but lives in hollows among rocks, in caves, and at the base of cacti and shrubs. Feeds on cactus fruit in summer and pods from leguminous plants in winter. Piles of legume pods often indicate a burrow.
RANGE: High Andes of Arica and Tarapacá; Bolivia, nw Argentina. Open, arid habitats with cacti, brush and rocks; 6500–16,500 ft (2000–5000 m).

Coruro
Spalacopus cyanus
OTHER NAMES: Eastern Mole, Cururo, Curucho, Chululo, Cureita, Cuyeita, Topo occidental, Topos.
ID: 7.5 in (19 cm). Soft, glossy black fur. Stocky cylindrical body, with small ears, small eyes, and a short, sparsely-haired tail. Feet have strong claws used for burrowing. Large incisors are long, broad, and strongly protruding; they assist in excavation of burrows. Molars are ever-growing and have crowns with an 8-shaped pattern.

The Coruro builds complex communal burrows, some hundreds of feet long. Some tunnels lead to entrance holes, others to plant and bulb storage chambers. Feeds mainly on the tubers and roots of Huilli (*Leucoryne ixiodes*), which supplies most water needs. Active by day and night, but seen above ground mainly when excavating soil or sun bathing. Vocalizations include a series of 3 or 4 sharp trills or a bubbling *tloc-tloc-tloc*, sounded when pushing soil to the surface. Females give birth to 2 to 3 offspring once or twice a year in the spring and summer months.
RANGE: Locally common from Atacama to Biobío. Separate coastal and Andean populations. Grassy areas with scattered shrubs, in moist, sandy soils and wet stream banks; sea level to 11,150 ft (0–3400 m).
SUBSPECIES: *S. c. maulinus* is ENDANGERED.

Chilean Rock Rat, Tunduco
Aconaemys fuscus
OTHER NAME: Rata de los pinares.
ID: 9 in (22.5 cm). Small-bodied, short-tailed and small-eared. Large sharp claws. Large prominent incisors. Typical pelage is rich dark brown above, rufous to whitish below, with a brown, furred tail; some subspecies are dark brown in color, with a bicolored tail, black above, white below. Tunducos are generally associated with the *Araucaria*

forests and pine nuts *(piñones)*, but also inhabit *Nothofagus* forests and cleared land. They dig long tunnels under bushes near the soil surface. The tunnels have many entrance holes, which are connected by runways shielded by vegetation. Tunducos lead a subterranean life, appearing above ground only when gathering seeds and nuts. They store plant matter in underground chambers for use in winter when snow often covers the burrow entrances.

RANGE: High Andes from Maule to Los Lagos; also adjacent Argentina.

RELATED SPECIES: SAGE'S ROCK RAT, *Aconaemys sagei*. Agouti brown fur and bicolored tail. A recently discovered species found in Malleco, Araucanía, and in Neuquén, Argentina. PORTER'S ROCK RAT, *Aconaemys porteri*. Occurs from Volcán Villarica to Puyehue in Los Lagos, and in Neuquén, Argentina. In forests to 6500 ft (2000 m).

FAMILY ABROCOMIDAE

CHINCHILLA RATS

Abrocomidae comprises a family of mid-sized rodents that have stiff hairs projecting over the nails of the three central digits of the hind feet. These rats have short limbs, a pointed snout, large ears, and a fairly short and tapering tail. Members of this family live in the Andes, from s Peru to n Argentina.

Bennett's Chinchilla Rat
Ratón chinchilla común
Abrocoma bennetti

OTHER NAMES: Ratón chinchilla de Bennett, Bori, Chinchillón, Ratón arboreo.

ID: 14 in (35.5 cm). Dense, long, luxurious, greyish-brown fur like that of a chinchilla. Large ears and large eyes. Furred, muscular tail. Short legs, with four digits on the fore feet and five on the hind feet. Strictly nocturnal. Agile rock climber; also climbs bushes in search of food. Feeds on grass, herbs, seeds, and the roots and bark of shrubs. Digs shallow burrows, often under rocks, in densely-vegetated, rocky places; also shares burrows of degus, tunducos and chinchillas. The burrows can be detected by the strong smell of their viscous, reddish-brown urine and piles of feces. Females give birth twice a year to litter of 1 to 6 young. Chinchilla rats were formerly hunted for their pelts.

RANGE: Common. Coquimbo to Biobío. In rocky areas with dense brush; sea level to 8200 ft (0–2000 m).

RELATED SPECIES: The ASHY CHINCHILLA RAT, *Abrocoma cinerea*, is colored silver-grey. It is smaller and has a much shorter tail than *A. bennetti*. It lives in small colonies, and digs narrow tunnels at base of boulders and shrubs in arid rocky zones in the High Andes of n Chile, Peru and Bolivia, to elevations of 16,500 ft (5000 m).

FAMILY MYOCASTORIDAE

COYPUS

Coypus, also known as Nutrias, are native to temperate marshes, rivers and streams in South America. They have been introduced to North America, Europe and Africa.

Coypu, Nutria, Coipo
Myocastor coypus

OTHER NAMES: Quiyi, Luu, Longu.

ID: 34 in (86 cm). **WT** 9–11 lb (4–5 kg). Chile's largest native rodent. Fur appears cinnamon-colored overall, but consists of a soft, dense, dark grey underfur and long, coarse, reddish-brown guard hairs. Tip of muzzle and chin are white. Body is highly arched; head is squared. Short ears. Small eyes are located toward the top of the head, long whiskers and short neck. Incisors are broad and orange-colored. Long, rounded, tapering, sparsely-haired tail. The legs are short; hind feet are longer than fore feet. Four of the five digits on each posterior foot are webbed. The forefeet have four long unwebbed digits and a vestigial thumb.

Mainly nocturnal. Feeds on aquatic vegetation supplemented with crustaceans and garden crops. Digs a simple burrow with a nesting chamber at the edge of marshes,

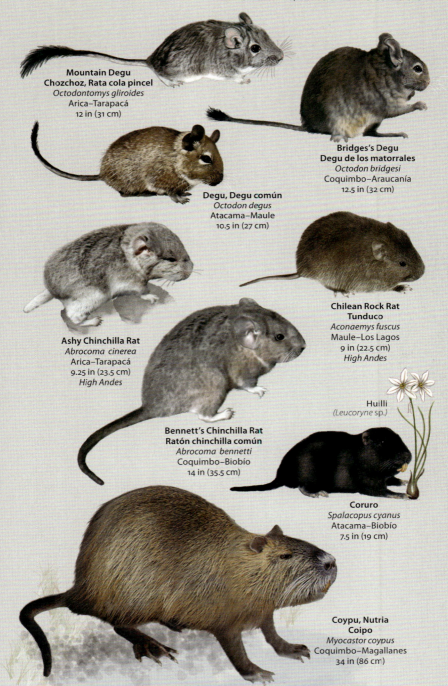

river banks and estuaries of glacial-fed streams. Also constructs nesting platforms made of large piles of reeds and sedges set in the marsh vegetation. Females give birth in austral spring and summer, and can have two litters per year, each consisting of 2 to 11 young. Females have four pairs of mammae located far up the sides of the body, so the young do not have to submerge to suckle.

The dense, soft pelt is highly valued in the Argentine fur trade. Furriers remove the stiff guard hairs from the pelt, exposing the velvety underfur. PROTECTED in the National Parks of Chile.

RANGE: Coquimbo to Magallanes; s Brazil, Paraguay, Uruguay, Bolivia, Argentina. In areas with permanent water and aquatic or semi-aquatic vegetation. In southern Chile and Tierra del Fuego they occur in the bays of coastal islands and estuaries of glacier-fed streams.

INTRODUCED RODENTS
FAMILY CASTORIDAE
BEAVERS
American Beaver, Castor
Castor canadensis
ID: 46.5 in (116 cm). WT 40 lb (18 kg). Large, robust, aquatic rodent with a broad, horizontally-flattened, scaly tail and fully-webbed hind feet. The fur is rich chestnut-brown on the back and sides. Underparts are paler and often have a silver sheen.

Beavers live in lodges (mounds of mud and sticks built in shallow water) and also dig burrows in muddy banks of ponds and rivers. Both of these structures have an underwater entrance. Beavers also build sizeable dams of sticks and logs from trees they have felled by chewing with their prominent front teeth. The purpose of the dam is to provide deep enough water to permanently cover their burrow or lodge entrance. The habit of felling trees for their dams causes flooding and can drown trees growing on the riverbanks. Beavers also kill young saplings by nibbling at the bark and shoots, which are their main food items.

Beavers were introduced to Tierra del Fuego in 1946 by Argentine fur breeders. When the fur industry declined, many of the beavers were abandoned and escaped into the wild. They have now spread north of the Strait of Magellan into the Andean forests of s Chile and have colonized many of the Fuegian islands.

RANGE: Magallanes and s Argentina. Native to North America.

FAMILY CRICETIDAE
MUSKRATS
Common Muskrat, Rata almizclera
Ondatra zibethicus
ID: 18–25 in (45–64 cm). WT 2–4 lb (1–2 kg). Thick, rich brown underfur, overlaid with coarse guard hairs; belly silvery. The long, black tail is naked, scaly, and flattened from side to side—a feature which immediately distinguishes it from the beaver. The front feet and hind feet are 5-toed, although the inner toe of the front foot is so small that it rarely shows in the tracks. The hind feet are partially webbed. Muskrats build large, conical mounds of matted marsh vegetation in shallow water of marshes and ponds and also burrow into earthen banks; both have underwater entrances. They feed on aquatic vegetation, clams, frogs and fish. Muskrats were introduced from Canada to Tierra del Fuego in 1948 by fur traders.

RANGE: Marshes and ponds in Tierra del Fuego and Navarino Island in Magallanes.

FAMILY MURIDAE
OLD WORLD MICE AND RATS
House mice and roof rats arrived in Chile in the 17th century in the holds of Spanish ships. Norway rats also arrived in ships, but in the 19th century.

House Mouse, Laucha
Mus musculus
OTHER NAMES: Ratón casero, Westliche Hausmaus, Souris domestique.
ID: 7 in (18 cm). Brownish-grey above, white to grey or pale yellow below. Soft dense fur. Large, rounded ears. Bulging eyes in a

INTRODUCED RODENTS, RABBITS AND HARES

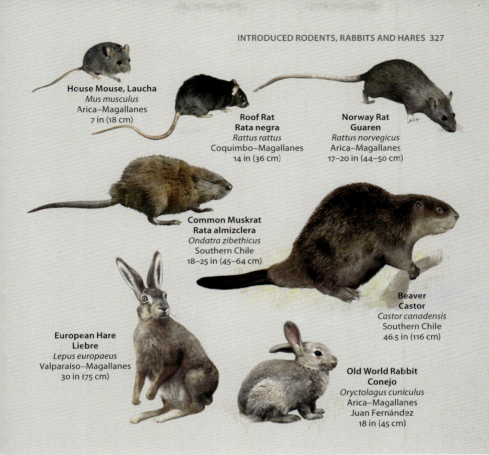

House Mouse, Laucha
Mus musculus
Arica–Magallanes
7 in (18 cm)

Roof Rat, Rata negra
Rattus rattus
Coquimbo–Magallanes
14 in (36 cm)

Norway Rat, Guaren
Rattus norvegicus
Arica–Magallanes
17–20 in (44–50 cm)

Common Muskrat, Rata almizclera
Ondatra zibethicus
Southern Chile
18–25 in (45–64 cm)

Beaver, Castor
Castor canadensis
Southern Chile
46.5 in (116 cm)

European Hare, Liebre
Lepus europaeus
Valparaíso–Magallanes
30 in (75 cm)

Old World Rabbit, Conejo
Oryctolagus cuniculus
Arica–Magallanes
Juan Fernández
18 in (45 cm)

small head. Has one pair of chisel-shaped incisors with hard yellow enamel on front surfaces. Scaly tail is about the same length as the body. Mainly nocturnal. Makes nests of shredded material. Females have 3 to 6 litters per year, each with 3 to 8 young. The young are born with closed eyes, which open after 13 days.
RANGE: Arica to Magallanes. Found around human habitation around the world.

Roof Rat, Rata negra
Rattus rattus
OTHER NAMES: Black Rat, Alexandrian Rat, Fruit Rat, Ship Rat.
ID: 14 in (36 cm). The tail is longer than the combined head–body length. Slender, dark brown to black rat with a very long, hairless tail. Ears are large and nearly hairless. Nose and muzzle are pointed. Large, prominent eyes. Nocturnal. Poor swimmer. Feeds on animal and plant matter, especially fruit. Forages for food in elevated areas both indoors and outdoors. Excellent climber, often using trees and utility lines to reach food and enter buildings. Nests in attics under buildings, in trees, piles of rubbish or timber, and sometimes in shallow burrows.
RANGE: Coquimbo to Magallanes. Introduced to the Americas. Native to Asia.

Norway Rat, Guaren
Rattus norvegicus
OTHER NAMES: Rata noruega, Pericote, Rata de acequia, Brown Rat, Grey Rat, House Rat, Wharf Rat, Sewer Rat, Water Rat.
ID: 17–20 in (44–50 cm). The tail is shorter than the combined head–body length. Fur color varies from greyish-brown to pure grey, pure black or reddish-brown. The

underparts are grey to pale yellow. Nose and muzzle are blunt. Small eyes. Naked ears are held close to the head. Naked, scaly tail is dark on top with a paler underside. Mainly nocturnal. Lives communally with other rats in cellars, tunnels and long galleries. Omnivorous. Can eat a third of its weight in 24 hours. Requires abundant drinking water. Poor climber, but a good swimmer able to cross wide rivers in migration. Females bear two litters of 5 to 21 young annually. Young are suckled for a month, and are capable of reproducing within 80 days.
RANGE: Arica to Magallanes. Occurs in urban areas worldwide, in cellars, sewers, tunnels and burrows.

INTRODUCED LAGOMORPHS

Hares and rabbits are lagomorphs. These animals have long ears, well-developed hindlimbs, a very short tail and a unique dental formula. They have a pair of incisors in the lower jaw. They are born with 3 pairs of upper incisors, but lose the outer tooth on each side as they age. The incisors are ever-growing and are completely covered by enamel. Lagomorphs are herbivores, eating only plant matter. They retrieve and swallow their wet droppings, thus allowing the digestive system to reprocess the food for added nourishment.

FAMILY LEPORIDAE

European Hare, Liebre
Lepus europaeus

ID: 30 in (75 cm). In 1880, a German consul introduced European hares to Argentina, and from there the animals spread across the Andes into Chile. Fur is tan to brown with a reddish stain on the neck. Very long ears and long, muscular legs. Sits upright. Lives above ground. Digs shallow burrows on rare occasions. Uses tree hollows to shelter from wind and rain. Forages at night. Sleeps by day, waking at the slightest noise. Remains immobile when alarmed, then runs in a zigzag pattern to elude predators. Male hares engage in frenzied battles in the mating season. Females can bear 4 to 5 litters per year, each with 2 to 4 young (young hares are called leverets in Europe). During the one-month gestation period, without assistance from the male, the female prepares a bed in the grass and vegetation where she delivers and suckles her young. Females are very sensitive to disturbances around the nest and will abandon the leverets if sufficiently alarmed.
RANGE: Valparaíso to Magallanes. In fertile, wooded plains to 6500 ft (2000 m).

Old World Rabbit, Conejo
Oryctolagus cuniculus

ID: 18 in (45 cm). Introduced from Spain at the beginning of the 19th century. Greyish brown. Tail is dark on the top and white underneath. Long oval ears. Digs and lives in burrows that have separate living and birthing chambers. Sleeps in the burrow by day, and emerges to forage with other rabbits at night along established runways. Remains immobile when alarmed, then runs in a zigzag pattern to the shelter of the burrow. Females bear 5 to 7 litters per year, each with 6 to 12 young (young rabbits are known as coneys in Europe). Both parents tend the offspring for several weeks until the young are independent.
RANGE: Lives at woodland edge and areas with sandy or soft soils in the Camarones Quebrada near Arica, from Coquimbo to Valdivia, and in Magallanes. Introduced to Juan Fernández Archipelago.

A beaver-chewed stump with lichens and anemones

MARINE MAMMALS

This section of the guide includes the seals, sea lions, porpoises, dolphins and whales that occur in Chilean waters. Excepted is the Marine Otter, which also makes the ocean its home for all or part of its life. It has been described and illustrated with the terrestrial carnivores for purposes of comparison with the River Otter.

CARNIVORA: SUBORDER CANIFORMIA
PINNIPEDS

Pinnipeds are amphibious aquatic carnivores whose front and hind limbs are flippers. The digits are fully webbed and, with the limbs, are modified to form paddles. The hind limbs are used for propulsion when swimming.

FAMILY OTARIIDAE

FUR SEALS AND SEA LIONS

There are two groups of otariids—fur seals and sea lions. Fur seals have a coat of guard hairs that are backed by a dense, short underfur. Sea lions are so named for the adult male's thick mane and lion-like roar.

Otariids evolved from bear-like animals in the Miocene Epoch about 23 million years ago. They have small external ear flaps called pinnae; long, sparsely-haired foreflippers; and large hind flippers that can be rotated forward beneath the body. Females have two pairs of teats. Males are often five times heavier than females. The male's testes are contained in an external scrotum. Males arrive at breeding grounds ahead of the females to acquire territory. Shortly after coming ashore, females who are pregnant from the previous year give birth to a single pup. Females often mate again within a few days of giving birth, but continue to nurse their newborn pup for several weeks.

South American Fur Seal
Lobo de dos pelos
Arctocephalus australis
OTHER NAMES: Lobo fino, Falkland Fur Seal.
ID: ♂ 6.25 ft (1.9 m). WT 440 lb (200 kg). ♀ 4.5 ft (1.4 m). WT 110 lb (50 kg). Stocky body, long pointed snout and large pinnae. MALES are dark brown, and have a grizzled mane. FEMALES are dark grey or brown on the back and paler on face and chest. In the warmer parts of their range, these seals haul out in caves and on steep, rocky slopes that offer shade for part of the day. They hunt at night, diving to depths of 100 ft (30 m) after fish, cephalopods and crustaceans.

Breeding season in the Southern Hemisphere is October through January. Males defend territories, but do not maintain harems. Females begin to mate at four years of age. Gestation is about 350 days, including a 45-day delayed implantation. Females bear a single pup, which is covered with fine black hair. Females mate a few days after giving birth, but continue to feed their pup for up to a year. Marine predators include sharks and orcas. Vampire bats are said to suck blood from pups. Prehistoric canoe people of the Chilean fjords hunted these animals for food and pelt. From the 1700s through the 1900s, fur seals were hunted for their luxurious fur and to make lamp oil. They are now PROTECTED throughout their range; only Uruguay maintains a fur seal hunt. There are about 40,000 South American fur seals in Chile, mostly in the southern regions.
RANGE: Rocky coasts of Chile, from Arica to Magallanes; also c Peru and s Brazil to Tierra del Fuego and the Falklands.

Juan Fernández Fur Seal
Lobo de Juan Fernández
Arctocephalus philippii
OTHER NAMES: The species name honors R. A. Philippi of the Santiago Natural History Museum who collected the first specimen on Masatierra in 1864. The common name honors the 16th-century Spanish navigator Juan Fernández, who discovered this seal.
ID: ♂ 6.8 ft (2.1 m). WT 308 lb (140 kg). ♀ 5 ft (1.5 m). WT 110 lb (50 kg). Long pointed snout. MALE has a heavy mane with golden-tipped guard hairs that contrast with dark brown pelage. Pups are born in

November and December. Females mate a week after delivering pups, but continue to nurse their offspring for up to ten months. During lactation, females make extended foraging trips of 12 to 25 days, ranging as far as 300 mi (500 km) offshore. Diet includes lanternfish, squid and other cephalopods. Herds haul out at base of sea cliffs. This species was thought to be extirpated by 19th-century sealers. But in 1965, a colony of 200 seals was discovered on Masafuera. A PROTECTED species, but a few are taken in illegal kills by fishermen. Natural predators include sharks and killer whales.

RANGE: ENDEMIC. Juan Fernández Archipelago and San Félix y San Ambrosio.

Antarctic Fur Seal
Lobo marino gracil
Arctocephalus gazella

OTHER NAMES: Lobo antártico, Otarie antarctique, Südliche pelzrobbe. The species name honors the German ship *SMS Gazelle* that carried the first specimen to Europe from the Kerguelen Islands.

ID: ♂ 6.25 ft (1.9 m). WT 440 lb (200 kg). ♀ 4.5 ft (1.4 m). WT 88 lb (40 kg). MALES are grey to brown on the back and have a dense, grizzled mane on a thick neck and chest. Snout is relatively short and blunt. FEMALES are brown on back, paler below. PUPS are black. Males can be very aggressive and bite like a dog. Moves quickly on land and can climb steep hills. Feeds on krill, squid and deepwater fishes. The species was almost exterminated by sealers of the 18th and 19th centuries. Populations have recovered and today about 1.8 million Antarctic fur seals breed at South Georgia alone.

RANGE: Subantarctic islands with rocky or sandy beaches and tussock meadows.

South American Sea Lion
Lobo de un pelo
Otaria flavescens

OTHER NAMES: Southern Sea Lion, León marino austral, Lobo chusco.

ID: ♂ 9 ft (2.8 m). WT 660–750 lb (300–340 kg). ♀ 7.2 ft (2.2 m). WT 315 lb (144 kg). ADULT MALES have a massive neck, broad head with an upturned muzzle, and a golden mane. Adult males defend territories above the high-tide line and maintain harems of 3 to 10 females. FEMALES are dark brown or blond, but appear almost black when first emerging from the water. They are smaller than males, with a smaller head and no mane. NEWBORN PUPS are shiny black on the back, ash blond on the belly; fur turns brown to reddish-brown with age. Diet includes pelagic larval stages of rock lobster, fish and jellyfish, taken at depths of 1000 ft (300 m) or less.

The early indigenous people of South America hunted sea lions for food and pelt and used the hides in boat construction. Commodore J. Byron of the *HMS Dolphin* discovered this species in the early 1800s. It was subsequently hunted for pelt, meat and oil until 1907 when sealing stopped. A regulated hunt for pups resumed in Chile in 1976. Fishermen regard the sea lion as a pest and competitor for fish, and sometimes kill those following their boat.

RANGE: Entire Chilean coast; also coastal South America from Peru and s Brazil to Tierra del Fuego and the Falklands.

PINNIPEDIA: FAMILY PHOCIDAE
TRUE OR EARLESS SEALS

Phocids are descended from the otter-like mammals of the Miocene. Unlike the otariids, these seals lack external ears and the hind limbs cannot be turned under the body to assist movement on shore. On land, they move by hunching their backs and wriggling from side to side. In swimming, the hind flippers move in a side-to-side sculling motion. Fish, krill and other marine invertebrates provide the main diet. The leopard seal also preys on penguins. The lactation period (the length of time a female nurses her pup) is less than 50 days. Most of the Chilean phocids occur on subantarctic oceanic islands or ice floes off Antarctica; only the Southern Elephant Seal strays regularly to the Chilean mainland.

FUR SEALS, SEA LIONS AND TRUE SEALS

Crabeater Seal, Foca cangrejera
Lobodon carcinophagus
OTHER NAMES: Krabbenfresser, Crabier. *Carcinophagus* means "eater of crabs," but these seals feed mainly on krill.
ID: 6.5–8.5 ft (2–2.6 m). **WT** 495 lb (225 kg). Unspotted pelage of dark grey to cream dorsally, shading to silver or cream below. Narrow upturned muzzle. Postcanine teeth have lobed cusps designed to filter krill from mouthfuls of seawater. When the tongue presses against the palate, it forces out the water through the closed jaws, leaving the krill in the seal's mouth. The body often has gashes on sides from attacks of leopard seal sand orcas. Females bear a single pup in October. The female, her mate and pup remain together on the ice floes for two weeks or more, with copulation taking place before the parents and young separate. Molt occurs in January, during which time the seals continue to swim and feed. Populations are estimated at about ten million.
PROTECTED under the Antarctic Treaty.
RANGE: Pack ice off coastal Antarctica, the Antarctic Peninsula and Ross Sea. Wanders to South Africa, Australia, New Zealand and southern South America.

Leopard Seal, Leopardo marino
Hydrurga leptonyx
OTHER NAMES: Léopard de mer, Seeleopard.
ID: 10–12 ft (3–3.6 m). **WT** 595–990 lb (270–450 kg). Large reptilian-like head with a large mouth. Slender, tapering body. Dark, oily-grey back; pale grey belly; sides have random dark and light leopard-like spots. Vocalizes from under the ice. Omnivorous. Diet includes krill, cephalopods, fish and penguins taken in waters near breeding colonies. Will attack crabeater seals and known to strike at humans walking on ice floes. Natural predators are killer whales. World population is estimated at 200,000.
RANGE: Coasts and pack ice of Antarctica and subantarctic islands. Wanders to South Africa, Australia, New Zealand and Tierra del Fuego; recorded at Buenos Aires, and the Austral and Cook Islands.

Weddell Seal, Foca de Weddell
Leptonychotes weddellii
OTHER NAMES: Phoque de Weddell, Weddell-Robbe. Named for British Captain James Weddell who discovered the species on an Antarctic sealing voyage in the 1820s.
ID: 9–11 ft (2.7–3.3 m). **WT** 880–1300 lb (400–600 kg). Grey to greyish-blond coat, with paler spots and streaks on the flanks and underparts. Rotund body with small head and dog-like muzzle. Large brown eyes and a mouth that appears to be smiling.

Powerful canine and incisor teeth are used to keep breathing holes open in sea ice. Very vocal underwater. Copulation takes place in the water, under the ice. Females nurse their pup for 50 days with breast milk that averages 60 percent fat. Feeds on ice fish, cephalopods, krill, other crustaceans, taken on 15-minute dives to 1300 ft (400 m).
RANGE: Fast ice of Antarctica. Hauls out on pack ice and beaches of the Antarctic Peninsula. Vagrant at South Georgia, South Orkneys, Juan Fernández and Patagonia.

Ross Seal, Foca de Ross
Ommatophoca rossi
OTHER NAMES: Big-eyed Seal, Singing Seal, Phoque de Ross, Ross-Robbe. Named for Sir James Clark Ross who secured specimens on the 1839 British Antarctic Expedition.
ID: 7.5 ft (2.3 m). **WT** 460 lb (210 kg). Females are larger than males. Small broad head, large eyes, short snout, small mouth and teeth, thick neck. Long flippers. Back dark grey to dark brown; paler fur on chest and belly streaked with grey. Greyish-brown to reddish-brown parallel streaks descend from the face and lower jaw. May be scarred on neck from fighting with one another or from orca or leopard seal attacks.

Ross seals typically lift their head and neck, and point the muzzle skyward when alarmed; this position is also used when making chugging and siren-like vocalizations. Feeds on squid, krill and fishes, taken at night.
RANGE: Circumpolar in the fast ice and consolidated pack ice around Antarctica.

Southern Elephant Seal, Elefante marino
Mirounga leonina
OTHER NAMES: Foca elefante del sur, See-Elefant, Phoque éléphant.
ID: ♂ 16.6 ft (5 m); WT to 11,000 lb (5000 kg). ♀ 6.5–10 ft (2–3 m); WT 2000 lb (900 kg). Largest seal in the world. ADULT MALES have an inflatable trunk-like snout, which resonates vocalizations. Brown or dark grey coat of short stiff hairs. Flexible body; can bend backwards and touch its tail with its head. The large eyes have pigments similar to deep-sea fishes; these may aid sensing prey taken at depths to 2650 ft (800 m).

The males come ashore in August to compete for breeding rights with loud roars and posturing. Only 3 percent of the largest males are likely to breed in a season. Pregnant females arrive in September and October, and deliver pups about a week after hauling out. Pups are born with a lanugo of fine black body hair, which molts to light brown. Females nurse pups with extremely rich milk for 23 days, then abandon them. They mate and return to sea to forage until the next breeding season. Pups remain on shore for 50 more days, losing about 70 percent of their body mass before going to sea to feed independently. These seals shed patches of skin in a 4-week annual molt, during which time they fast and huddle together on beaches and in wallows.

Southern elephant seals were killed and rendered into oil in the 1800s, and from 1909 to 1965 on South Georgia. They are now protected south of the Antarctic Convergence under the Antarctic Treaty. Their population is estimated at 750,000.
RANGE: Subantarctic islands, islands off the Antarctic Peninsula, and on pack ice; small numbers occur in s Argentina and at Ainthworth Bay, Tierra del Fuego.

CETACEA: Cetaceans
Cetaceans are streamlined, almost hairless, entirely aquatic mammals. The forelimbs are modified to form paddle-like fins without visible digits. Hind limbs are absent. The pelvis is vestigial. The horizontal tail fin (fluke) is used for propulsion. The skull has nasal openings (blowholes) set far back on the dorsal surface. The smaller species are called porpoises or dolphins; the larger species are called whales. Two suborders occur in Chilean waters: Mysticeti (baleen whales) and Odontoceti (toothed whales, porpoises, dolphins).

SUBORDER MYSTICETI
Mysticeti includes those whales that have a double blowhole and baleen (keratinous sheets that hang like curtains from the roof of the mouth). Baleen whales ingest zooplankton by swimming with their mouths open and gulping seawater. Comb-like structures at the tips of the baleen sheet filter the zooplankton from the water.

FAMILY BALAENIDAE
RIGHT WHALES
These whales are characterized by a large head with a long, thin, arched rostrum and a bowed lower jaw. Most species lack a dorsal fin and have no throat grooves. The name Right Whale originated with whalers who considered this species the "right" whale to catch because they floated when killed and yielded a lot of oil.

Southern Right Whale
Ballena franca austral
Eubalaena australis
OTHER NAMES: Ballena de sur, Baleine australe. Closely related to and formerly regarded as the same species as the North Atlantic Right Whale, *E. glacialis*.
ID: 56 ft (17 m). WT 100 tons (90,000 kg). Males are smaller than females. The robust body is grey to dark grey in color with variable white patches, especially on belly. Extremely large head, which can be more than one-fourth of the body length. No dorsal fin. Conspicuous growths called callosities form on the narrowly arched

rostrum, bowed lower jaw, chin, and above the eyes. Each side of the upper jaw is lined with 220 to 260 black baleen plates that are up to 9 ft (2.7 m) in length. Flippers are wide and fan-shaped, with smooth margins. Flukes are broad with smooth contours.

Raises flukes on longer dives. Ejects air and vapor in a V-shaped blow through blowholes set at right angles to each other. Actively breaches, lob-tails and flipper-slaps. Also engages in "sailing," where a whale hangs vertically upside down in the water, "standing" on its head, with its tail flukes in the air. Small groups move through patches of copepods and krill with their mouths agape, filtering prey through the baleen (skim feeding). Vocalizations include moans and burping noises. Roger Payne, who studied breeding right whales at Valdés Peninsula, Argentina, from 1971 to 2000, observed that females will mate with more than one male in succession or even mate with two males simultaneously. Females give birth to a single calf every 3 to 5 years after a year-long gestation. Their life expectancy is thought to exceed 70 years.

Almost exterminated by the 1900s, right whales were granted protection in 1935. However, illegal catches in 1951 and 1970 reduced remaining populations to the point that numbers are unlikely to fully recover. World population now stands between 1500 and 4000. ENDANGERED; CITES APPENDIX I.

RANGE: Maule to Tierra del Fuego; circumpolar in the Southern Ocean. Migratory, wintering (Apr–Nov) in coastal waters of the southern continents and spending the austral summer feeding near Antarctica.

FAMILY NEOBALAENIDAE
PYGMY RIGHT WHALE
Pygmy Right Whale
Ballena franca pigmea
Caperea marginata
OTHER NAMES: Baleine pygmée, Zwergglattwal. John Gray, curator of the British Museum's Zoology Department, described this species in 1846.

ID: 21 ft (6.4 m). WT 1455 lb (3200 kg). Smallest of the baleen whales and the only right whale with a dorsal fin. The short, sickle-shaped dorsal fin is set behind the mid-back. Dark grey above, paler below. Some individuals bear two chevrons along the sides, one above the flipper, the other midway down the body. Dark, narrow, rounded flippers. Broad, notched flukes. Arched jaw, with 213 to 230 yellowish-white baleen plates, sometimes edged with black, in each side of the upper jaw. There is a pair of shallow throat grooves. Inconspicuous, small blow. Known to feed on copepods and krill. Mostly solitary or in pairs. Virtually indistinguishable at sea from the Antarctic Minke, unless the head and arched jawline are visible.

RANGE: Temperate waters of the Southern Ocean; recorded in s Chile and Argentina.

FAMILY BALAENOPTERIDAE
RORQUALS
Rorqual whales include the world's largest mammal—the blue whale. These whales have a streamlined body with a distinct dorsal fin set behind the midpoint of the back. The throat is wrinkled in deep longitudinal folds, or pleats. Fast and active lunge feeders, they can open their jaws very wide and distend their throat to take in huge mouthfuls of water and plankton when feeding. Most species feed in polar seas in summer and migrate to tropical breeding grounds where they typically fast. Rorqual whales can live up to 50 years.

Humpback Whale, Jorobada
Megaptera novaeangliae
OTHER NAMES: Yubarta, Rorcual jorobado, Baleine à bosse, Buckelwal.

ID: 56 ft (17 m). WT 45 tons (40,000 kg). Southern Hemisphere whales are black above, white below with 14 to 35 ventral pleats extending back to the navel or beyond. Variable amount of white on flippers and flukes. Small humped dorsal fin is set back toward tail. Extremely long flippers with

RIGHT WHALES AND HUMPBACK WHALES 335

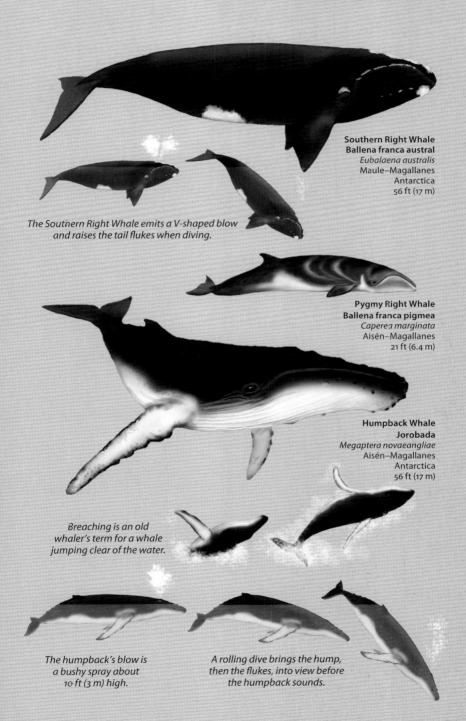

Southern Right Whale
Ballena franca austral
Eubalaena australis
Maule–Magallanes
Antarctica
56 ft (17 m)

The Southern Right Whale emits a V-shaped blow and raises the tail flukes when diving.

Pygmy Right Whale
Ballena franca pigmea
Caperea marginata
Aisén–Magallanes
21 ft (6.4 m)

Humpback Whale
Jorobada
Megaptera novaeangliae
Aisén–Magallanes
Antarctica
56 ft (17 m)

Breaching is an old whaler's term for a whale jumping clear of the water.

The humpback's blow is a bushy spray about 10 ft (3 m) high.

A rolling dive brings the hump, then the flukes, into view before the humpback sounds.

tubercles on leading edge. Broad knobbed rostrum and head. Mouth has 270–400 black baleen plates. Ejects air and vapor in a round, bushy blow about 10 ft (3 m) high. Raises flukes when diving. Individual whales can be identified by unique pattern on underside of tail. Breaches, lob-tails and flipper-slaps. Blows bubble nets or bubble clouds to trap prey. Forms small, unstable groups. Humpbacks do not feed in the breeding season, but subsist on fat reserves stored in the blubber. Males sing long, complex songs in breeding season. Females have a single calf after a year of gestation; the calf remains with the female for one to two years. Highly exploited in the 1900s. VULNERABLE; CITES APPENDIX I.

RANGE: Antarctic Peninsula populations migrate between summer feeding grounds off Antarctica and winter breeding grounds off the west coast of Central America. Ranges in all oceans, mainly along coasts and over the continental shelf.

Antarctic Minke Whale
Ballena enana sin mancha blanca
Balaenoptera bonaerensis

OTHER NAMES: Piked Whale, Südlicher Zwergwal, Minkewal. Said to be named for the 18th-century Norwegian whaler Minke who harpooned so many cetaceans that all whales became known as "Minke's whales."
ID: 35 ft (10.7 m). WT 10 tons (9,100 kg). Dark grey dorsally; white ventrally, with streaks or chevrons of grey on the lateral surface. Small body. Falcate (sickle-shaped) dorsal fin is set well back toward tail. Pointed head with a prominent median ridge. The 50 to 70 short throat pleats extend just past the flippers. From 200 to 300 pairs of black baleen plates. Inconspicuous, diffused blow appears simultaneously with the dorsal fin. Does not raise flukes when diving. Spyhops with its head above water. Seldom breaches. Swims singly or in pairs. Feeds mainly on krill. Emits mechanical vocalizations similar to submarine sonar. Japan harvests minke whales for scientific purposes and for meat.

RANGE: Coastal and offshore waters of the Southern Hemisphere from 10°S to the Antarctic ice edge. Migrates between summer feeding grounds around Antarctica and winter grounds in tropical waters.

Dwarf Minke Whale
Ballena enana
Balaenoptera acutorostrata subsp.

OTHER NAMES: Rorcual menor, Little Piked Whale, Petit rorqual.
ID: 26 ft (7.8 m). WT 7 tons (6400 kg). Small sleek body, with a falcate (sickle-shaped) dorsal fin and sharply pointed head. Dark grey to black above, white to cream-colored below. Bright white flipper band is visible when animals are near the surface. About 200 to 300 pairs of whitish baleen plates. Usually emits no visible blow. Does not raise flukes when diving. Behavior and social organization poorly known. Considered either a Southern Hemisphere species or a subspecies of the Northern Minke Whale.

RANGE: Southern Hemisphere waters from 10°S latitude to the Antarctic ice edge.

Sei Whale
Ballena boreal
Balaenoptera borealis

OTHER NAMES: Rorcual mediano, Rorqual de Rudolphi, Seiwal, Coalfish Whale. Sei (pronounced "sigh") refers to the sei whales' arrival off the Norwegian coast at the same time as *seje (sei)* pollack fish.
ID: 64 ft (19.5 m). WT 50 tons (45,000 kg). Dark grey above. Pale grey belly. Often bears oval scars from bites of cookie-cutter sharks or lampreys. Single rostral ridge. The 300 to 410 baleen plates on each side of jaw are black with a white inner fringe. Falcate (sickle-shaped) dorsal fin rises at a steep angle from the back and is visible when the whale emits a tall columnar blow up to 10 ft (3 m) high. Forms small, fast swimming, unstable groups of 2 to 5 individuals. Submerges quietly, without arching back or raising flukes. When feeding, tends to dive and surface in a predictable manner, remaining just below

RORQUAL WHALES 337

The sei, fin and minke whales rarely raise their flukes when diving.

Sei Whale
Ballena boreal
Balaenoptera borealis
Arica–Magallanes
64 ft (19.5 m)

Sei and fin whales emit high columnar blows.

Fin Whale
Rorcual común
Balaenoptera physalus
Arica–Magallanes
89 ft (27.1 m)
Left lower jaw is black

A minke whale spyhopping, exposing its piked snout.

Antarctic Minke Whale
Ballena enana sin mancha blanca
Balaenoptera bonaerensis
Arica–Magallanes
Antarctic
35 ft (10.7 m)

Blue Whale
Ballena azul
Balaenoptera musculus
Arica–Magallanes
110 ft (33.3 m)

Dwarf Minke Whale
Ballena enana
Balaenoptera acutorostrata subsp.
Arica–Magallanes
Antarctic
26 ft (7.8 m)

the surface between breaths. Feeds on krill, copepods and fish. Sei whales were hunted so severely in the mid-20th century that numbers remain depleted. Protected since 1979. ENDANGERED.

RANGE: Occurs in open oceans worldwide. Movements poorly understood; thought to be migratory between summer feeding grounds at high latitudes and winter grounds in the tropics and subtropics.

RELATED SPECIES: BRYDE'S WHALE, *Balaenoptera edeni*, has 3 longitudinal rostral ridges. Occurs in all oceans between 40°N and 40°S.

Fin Whale
Rorcual común
Balaenoptera physalus

OTHER NAMES: Finner, Common Rorqual, Razorback, Finnwal.

ID: 89 ft (27.1 m). WT 130 tons (120,000 kg). Second largest species of whale. Body is dark grey to brownish-black above, white below; grey chevrons behind the head. Right lower lip and jaw are white; left jaw is black. Right front baleen plates white to cream; rest of baleen is blackish-olive. Streamlined body. Pointed head. Flukes broad and triangular. Backward-sloping dorsal fin set well toward tail; fin is visible during or shortly after blow. Blow is a slim inverse cone 13–19 ft (4–5.8 m) high. Does not raise flukes when diving. Can dive to depths of over 800 ft (250 m) when hunting for fish and squid. Very fast swimmers with maximum speeds up to 20 miles (32 km) per hour. Makes very loud, low-frequency vocalizations that can carry for several miles underwater. Heavily exploited in the 1950s and 1960s. Protected since 1976. ENDANGERED; CITES APPENDIX I.

RANGE: Offshore Chile and in open ocean worldwide.

Blue Whale
Rorcual azul
Balaenoptera musculus intermedia

OTHER NAMES: Sibald's Rorqual, Sulphurbottom, Rorqual bleu, Blauwal.

ID: 110 ft (33.3 m). WT 200 tons (180,000 kg). Largest whale and world's largest mammal. Immense bluish-grey body with pale grey mottling; diatom films on the belly surface often give a sulphur-yellow tinge to the belly. Broad, flat, uniformly blue, U-shaped head, with a prominent ridge from snout to blowholes. Slender columnar blow to about 29.5 ft (9 m) high. About 55 to 88 long throat pleats; 260 to 400 black baleen plates on each side of mouth. Long, pointed flippers. Small, triangular dorsal fin is seen only when diving, is located well back towards flukes. Raises flukes when diving; broad flukes have a straight trailing edge and a prominent notch. Does not breach. Usually seen alone or in pairs. Very loud, low-frequency vocalizations can carry over a hundred miles underwater. Feeds by lunging into schools of krill. The largest individuals can consume 6 tons (5500 kg) of krill per day. Females give birth to a single calf every 2 to 3 years. A nursing calf can gain up to 200 lb (90 kg) per day; the calf remains with the female for 8 months. There are records of hybridization between fin whales and humpback whales.

Blue whales were almost exterminated in the 1900s. More than 360,000 blue whales were killed in the Southern Hemisphere alone. The species has been PROTECTED since 1965. About 450 animals are known from the Southern Ocean, and a few hundred to a thousand in the North Atlantic. In the summer of 2003, the nursing and feeding grounds of the Blue Whale, and possibly the Pygmy Blue Whale, were discovered in the Gulf of Corcovado and on the west coast of Chiloé. ENDANGERED; CITES APPENDIX I.

RANGE: Coastal and continental shelf waters off Chile, and in open ocean worldwide. Separate northern and southern populations have complex seasonal movements; those in the Southern Hemisphere range from about 45°S to the pack ice of Antarctica.

RELATED SUBSPECIES: The poorly known subspecies, the PYGMY BLUE WHALE *(B. m. brevicauda)* is smaller and does not range as deeply into polar waters as the Blue Whale.

SUBORDER ODONTOCETI

The porpoises, dolphins and whales in this suborder have teeth and a single blowhole.

FAMILY PHOCOENIDAE
PORPOISES

Porpoises are small and stocky. They have a rounded or conical head that lacks a distinct beak. Most have a short, triangular dorsal fin, a narrow tail fin with a shallow notch, short flippers, and spade-shaped teeth. They live in small groups and feed on fish, squid and marine invertebrates.

Spectacled Porpoise
Marsopa de anteojos
Phocoena dioptrica
OTHER NAME: Marsouin de Lahille.
ID: 5.5–6.5 ft (1.7–2 m). WT 110–185 lb (50–84 kg). Bluish-black upperparts contrast with white sides and belly. White line around the eyes and mouth gives the look of spectacles. Dark line extends from the mouth to small, rounded flippers. MALES have a large, rounded dorsal fin, FEMALES a triangular fin. Beak is short or non-existent. Black lips. Solitary or forms small, inconspicuous groups. Known from a few strandings and sightings. CITES APPENDIX II.
RANGE: Magallanes, especially in the Beagle Channel. Ranges in cold-temperate coastal waters of e South America and subantarctic islands; possibly circumpolar.

Burmeister's Porpoise, Marsopa spinosa
Phocoena spinipinnis
OTHER NAMES: Black Porpoise, Burmeister-Schweinswal, Marsouin de Burmeister.
ID: 5–6 ft (1.5–1.8 m). WT 110–154 lb (50–70 kg). Dark grey to black; pale grey on belly and chin. Dorsal fin rises at a shallow angle, is set well back toward tail, and has tubercules (bumps) at leading edge. Blunt head. Beakless, upturned mouth. Black line from chin to broad, rounded flippers. Forms herds of 1 to 8 individuals. Feeds on hake, anchoveta, squid, krill and mollusks. ENDANGERED (estimated 500 individuals remain). CITES APPENDIX II.
RANGE: Shallow coastal waters of Chile and Peru; also s Brazil to Tierra del Fuego.

FAMILY DELPHINIDAE
DOLPHINS, PILOT WHALES & ORCAS

Members of this family are small to mid-sized cetaceans. They are characterized by a distinct beak, conical teeth and a large, falcate (sickle-shaped) dorsal fin set at the mid-back. Many species in this group are threatened by incidental kills in fishing nets. Moreover, they are also killed for use as crab bait, food or oil.

Chilean Dolphin, Delfín chileno
Cephalorhynchus eutropia
OTHER NAMES: Black Dolphin, Delfín negro, Dauphin noir du Chili, Chile-Delphin.
ID: 4–5 ft (1.2–1.5 m). WT 100–132 lb (45–60 kg). Small and stocky, with a short beak that merges imperceptibly with the broad, flat forehead. Black, except for white patches on the throat, in the axillaries and around the anus; dark band between the flippers. Appears all black in the water. Dorsal fin low and rounded. Forms groups of 2 to 15 or more. Shy and wary of approach. Diet includes fish, cephalopods and crustaceans.
RANGE: Very few sightings, most on the west coast of s Chile from 30° S to 55° S. In cold, shallow, inshore waters and channels.

Commerson's Dolphin, Tonina overa
Cephalorhynchus commersonii
OTHER NAMES: Piedbald Dolphin, Delfín blanco, Commerson-Delphin, Dauphin de Commerson. Named after the French 18th-century botanist Philibert Commerson who discovered this species.
ID: 4.5–5.5 ft (1.4–1.7 m). WT 110–145 lb (50–66 kg). Small and stocky. Blunt head with little or no beak. Low, rounded dorsal fin. Cape-like whitish band encircles the body, contrasting with black head, flippers, lower back and tail. White throat patch. Small, active groups often approach small boats in shallow waters and swim along side. Said to sometimes swim upside down. Feeds on benthic fish, squid and shrimp.
RANGE: Magallanes and shallow coastal waters of the Falklands; also the Kerguelens and South Georgia.

Peale's Dolphin, Delfín austral
Lagenorhynchus australis
OTHER NAMES: Blackchin Dolphin, Delfín griseo blanco, Dauphin de Peale, Peale Delphin. Named for Titian Peale, naturalist on the *USS Vincennes*, who illustrated this dolphin off the Patagonian coast in 1839.
ID: 6.5–7 ft (2–2.1 m). WT 250 lb (115 kg). Stocky body. Pointed, falcate dorsal fin. Dark grey to black with lighter shading on the flanks and a white flank patch behind fin. Curved light grey stripe angles forward from the ventral side and flank narrowing to a single line that ends near the dorsal fin. Pale grey patch on the throat has a thin dark line underneath. Double black eyering extends toward the snout. Separated from the similar Dusky Dolphin by dark flippers, white axillary patch, single white stripe from tailstock, and blackish stripe below the pale flank. Forms groups of 5 to 30 individuals. Frequently bowrides, leaping high into the air and falling sideways into the water with a loud splash. Feeds on fish and cephalopods taken in kelp beds, along rocky coasts, estuaries and at riptide entries to fjords. CITES APPENDIX II.
RANGE: Valparaíso to the Strait of Magellan and Tierra del Fuego. Common in cool to temperate coastal waters, bays and inlets of s South America and the Falklands.

Dusky Dolphin, Delfín oscuro
Lagenorhynchus obscurus
OTHER NAMES: Fitzroy's Dolphin, Dauphin sombre, Schwarzdelphin. The name "Fitzroy's Dolphin" dates to Charles Darwin's 1832 description of a Dusky Dolphin caught off Patagonia, which he named for Robert FitzRoy, commander of the *HMS Beagle*.
ID: 6–7 ft (1.8–2.1 m). WT 250–310 lb (115–140 kg). Body color pattern is complex, with the dark back fading into a light grey, irregular thoracic patch and white abdomen. Flanks are marked with spikes of light grey that split into two ascending blazes. Bicolored dorsal fin is pointed and falcate. Short but distinct beak. White chin patch; black genital patch. Fine dark line from flipper to eye, which is set in a small dark patch. Congregates in herds of 20 to 300 individuals. Herds are closely knit, with members coming to the aid of others entangled in fishing nets or experiencing stress or injury. Fast, energetic bowriders that perform acrobatic tumbling leaps. Feeds on a variety of fish and squid.
RANGE: Entire Chilean coast and temperate coastal waters of the Southern Ocean.

Hourglass Dolphin, Delfín cruzado
Lagenorhynchus cruciger
OTHER NAMES: Dauphin crucigère, Stundenglas-Delphin. First described by French zoologists Jean Réné Quoy and Jean Paul Gaimard in 1822.
ID: 5.5–6 ft (1.7–1.8 m). WT 220–264 lb (100–120 kg). Stocky body is sharply demarcated in black and white, with a conspicuous white hourglass marking on sides. White belly. White, hook-shaped mark below the black flank patch near the genital aperture. Dorsal fin strongly falcate. Small, compact black beak. Avid bowriders. Large groups feed near the surface, taking mainly fish, squid and crustaceans. CITES APPENDIX II.
RANGE: Southern Chile and cold waters in the Southern Ocean between 45°S and 65°S latitude. Southernmost dolphin.

Short-beaked Common Dolphin Delfín común
Delphinus delphis
OTHER NAMES: Saddleback Dolphin, Bec d'oie, Gemeiner Delphin.
ID: 7–8.5 ft (2.1–2.6 m). WT 180–300 lb (82–136 kg). Dark brownish-grey back with a tall, slightly falcate dorsal fin; dark cape forms a distinctive 'V' below the dorsal fin. Tan or pale buff thoracic patch (may appear cream); light grey, streaked tailstock forms an hourglass pattern that crosses below dorsal fin. Belly white. Stripe from chin to flipper sometimes meets gape. Black mask or bridle extends from the eyes across the beak and forehead. Forms large, active schools that roll and arch out of the water or zigzag just beneath the water surface,

PORPOISES AND DOLPHINS

Spectacled Porpoise, Marsopa bicolor
Phocoena dioptrica
Magallanes
5.5–6.5 ft (1.7–2 m)

Burmeister's Porpoise, Marsopa spinosa
Phocoena spinipinnis
Arica–Magallanes
5–6 ft (1.5–1.8 m)

Commerson's Dolphin, Tonina overa
Cephalorhynchus commersonii
Magallanes
4.5–5.5 ft (1.4–1.7 m)

Chilean Dolphin, Delfín chileno
Cephalorhynchus eutropia
Los Lagos–Magallanes
4–5 ft (1.2–1.5 m)

Peale's Dolphin, Delfín austral
Lagenorhynchus australis
Valparaíso–Magallanes
6.5–7 ft (2–2.1 m)

Dusky Dolphin, Delfín oscuro
Lagenorhynchus obscurus
Arica–Magallanes
6–7 ft (1.8–2.1 m)

Short-beaked Common Dolphin, Delfín común
Delphinus delphis
Arica–Biobío
7–8.5 ft (2.1–2.6 m)

Hourglass Dolphin, Delfín cruzado
Lagenorhynchus cruciger
Los Lagos–Magallanes
5.5–6 ft (1.7–1.8 m)

Striped Dolphin, Delfín azul
Stenella coeruleoalba
Arica–Atacama
8–9 ft (2.4–2.7 m)

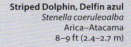

Pantropical Spotted Dolphin, Delfín pardo
Stenella attenuata
Arica–Atacama
5.25–8.5 ft (1.6–2.6 m)

often while making squealing calls. Ardent bowriders. Forms groups to herd small schooling fishes, which are taken at night anywhere from near the surface to depths of 130 ft (40 m). CITES APPENDIX II.

RANGE: Offshore waters of nc Chile; oceanic in the temperate and tropical Pacific; also North Atlantic, Mediterranean, Black Sea.

Southern Right Whale Dolphin
Delfín liso
Lissodelphis peronii

OTHER NAMES: Tonina sin aleta, Dauphin aptère austral, Südlicher Glattdelphin. First described by François Peron, naturalist on the 1800 French *Geographe* Expedition.

ID: 6.5–9.5 ft (2–3 m). WT 132–220 lb (60–110 kg). Very slender body with a curving pattern of black above and white below. No dorsal fin. Beak is short but distinct. Small, recurved flippers are white with a black trailing edge. Narrow tail stock. Small flukes are white below, dark grey above. Forms large schools of 30 to 1000 individuals, often in association with dusky dolphins and pilot whales. Wary of ships; schools flee in a concentrated formation, while making smooth, high, arching leaps. Biology relatively unknown. Thought to feed on squid and fish, especially lanternfish. CITES APPENDIX II.

RANGE: Pelagic in deep, cold currents from Atacama to Magallanes; also cool temperate to polar waters of the Southern Ocean to about 64°S latitude.

Bottlenose Dolphin, Tonina común
Tursiops truncatus

OTHER NAMES: Delfín mular, Grand Dauphin, Grosser Tümmler.

ID: 6.2–12 ft (1.9–3.75 m). WT up to 1300 lb (600 kg). Stocky grey dolphin. Short thick beak has a sharp demarcation between the beak and melon (rounded forehead). Tall, falcate dorsal fin set at mid-back. Light to dark grey on the back and sides, fading to white or buff on the belly, which is occasionally spotted. Group size of coastal populations is usually less than 20, but herds of several hundred occur offshore, often in association with spotted and Risso's dolphins, and pilot and humpback whales. Feeds on inshore benthic fishes, eels, sharks, rays, hermit crabs and pelagic fishes such as sardines, anchoveta and hake. Attends fishing trawlers. Feeds cooperatively on schooling fish. Individuals will also chase fish onto mudbanks. Dives to depths of 2000 ft (600 m). Said to aid human swimmers in distress. CITES APPENDIX II.

RANGE: Arica to Santiago. Mainly coastal, but also occurs in open ocean in temperate and tropical seas worldwide.

Striped Dolphin, Delfín azul
Stenella coeruleoalba

OTHER NAMES: Blue-white Streaker, Longsnout, Estenela listada, Dauphin bleu-et-blanc, Blauweisser Delphin, Suji-iruka.

ID: 8–9 ft (2.4–2.7 m). WT 220–286 lb (100–130 kg). Dark grey or dark brown on back, white to pinkish on belly. Dark spike behind the dorsal fin extends forward. Black stripes from eye to anus and eye to flipper. Light grey spinal blaze from head to falcate dorsal fin sometimes present. Long, slender beak. Forms large schools of 100 to 500 individuals, often in association with Yellowfin Tuna. Feeds on squid and small pelagic fishes, especially lanternfish. CITES APPENDIX II.

RANGE: Pelagic in deep offshore waters from Arica to Coquimbo; also tropical to temperate oceans worldwide.

Pantropical Spotted Dolphin
Delfín pardo
Stenella attenuata

OTHER NAMES: Spotter, Delfín pintado, Estenala moteada, Dauphin tacheté de pantropical, Schlankdelphin, Arari-iruka.

ID: 5.25–8.5 ft (1.6–2.6 m). WT up to 265 lb (120 kg). Body slender and streamlined. Dorsal fin is narrow, falcate and pointed. Distinct crease separates the long thin beak from the melon. Lips and tip of beak are white. Dark dorsal cape and grey flanks and belly have varying amounts of spotting.

DOLPHINS, PILOT WHALES AND ORCAS

Bottlenose Dolphin
Tonina común
Tursiops truncatus
Arica–Maule
6.2–12 ft (1.9–3.75 m)

Risso's Dolphin
Delfín gris
Grampus griseus
Arica–Magallanes
12.5 ft (3.8 m)

Southern Right Whale Dolphin
Delfín liso
Lissodelphis peronii
Biobío–Magallanes
6.5–9.5 ft (2–3 m)

The rounded forehead or "melon" of cetaceans such as the Pilot Whale contains a mass of waxy material thought to focus acoustic signals.

Long-finned Pilot Whale
Piloto
Globicephala melas
Arica–Magallanes
15.5–21 ft (4.7–6.3 m)

False Killer Whale
Orca falsa
Pseudorca crassidens
Arica–Maule
16–20 ft (4.6–6 m)

Adult male Orcas have a dorsal fin that can be 10 ft (3 m) high.

Killer Whale
Orca
Orcinus orca
Biobío–Magallanes
23–30 ft (6–9.1 m)

Two types occur in the eastern tropical Pacific. COASTAL SPOTTED DOLPHINS range near the Pacific coast; they have a robust body and beak, and heavy spotting that nearly covers the dark grey cape. OFFSHORE SPOTTED DOLPHINS range more than 20 mi (30 km) from the Pacific shore and in open ocean worldwide; they have a slender beak and smaller body, with slight to moderate spotting. Both types are fast swimmers, engaging in acrobatics and bowriding, except in tuna fishing grounds where they are wary. Forms large herds in association with yellowfin and skipjack tunas, spinner dolphins, and other pelagic predators of epipelagic fish and squid. Fishermen use this knowledge to locate tuna. As a result, the incidental kill of dolphins in tuna nets is high, especially in the eastern tropical Pacific. CITES APPENDIX II.

RANGE: Arica to Maule, and tropical oceans worldwide.

RELATED SPECIES: EASTERN SPINNER DOLPHIN, *Stenella longirostris orientalis*. 7.2 ft (2.2 m). Dark grey cape, light grey sides and belly. Dark eye-to-flipper stripes. Dark lips on long, thin beak. Dorsal fin erect, falcate to triangular. Spins and turns in the air many times before falling back to the water. Ranges in the tropical Pacific from Baja California south to 10°S off Peru; ACCIDENTAL in Chile.

Risso's Dolphin, Delfín gris
Grampus griseus

OTHER NAMES: Grampus, Falso calderón, Delfín de Risso, Rundkopf-delphin, Dauphin de Risso, Hana gondo kujira.
ID: 12.5 ft (3.8 m). WT 880 lb (400 kg). Robust, heavily-scarred, dark grey to pale grey body. Blunt head has vertical crease in front of melon, and lacks a distinct beak; mouthline slopes upward. Two to seven pairs of teeth at front of lower jaw; usually none in upper jaw. Flippers long, pointed, and recurved. Dorsal fin tall and falcate. Forms mid-sized herds that surface slowly and occasionally breach or bowride. Feeds on squid and crustaceans. May hybridize with *Tursiops truncatus*. CITES APPENDIX II.

RANGE: Deep oceanic and continental slope waters off Chile, and similar tropical and temperate waters in both hemispheres.

Long-finned Pilot Whale, Piloto
Globicephala melas

OTHER NAMES: Calderón, Pothead, Blackfish, Globicéphale commun, Grindwal.
ID: ♂ 21 ft (6.3 m). WT 5000 lb (2300 kg). ♀ 15.5 ft (4.7 m). WT 2900 lb (1300 kg). Dark brownish grey to black, with a pale anchor-shaped patch on the throat, breast and belly. Pale saddle on back behind dorsal, and whitish blaze above and behind eye. Bulbous melon. Low, wide-based dorsal fin is set far forward. Long pointed flipper with prominent elbow. Eight to thirteen teeth in each tooth row. Forms gregarious pods of 20 to 100 individuals that forage in broad ranks, sometimes with other cetaceans, and raft on the ocean surface when at rest. Diet includes squid and mackerel taken at depths of 600–1600 ft (200–500 m). Prone to mass strandings. CITES APPENDIX II.

RANGE: Coastal Chile and cool temperate oceans of the Southern Hemisphere and North Atlantic Ocean.

Killer Whale, Orca
Orcinus orca

OTHER NAMES: Schwertwal, Orque.
ID: 23–30 ft (7–9.1 m). WT to 16,000 lb (7257 kg). Stocky black body with white patches on belly, lower jaw and under tail flukes. Greyish saddle on mid-back behind dorsal fin. White patches of the Antarctic populations are often discolored by a thin brown layer of diatoms. Ten to twelve large oval teeth in each jaw. Flippers are large and paddle-shaped. Dorsal fin is tall with a wide base; female's curves backwards; male's is triangular. Dorsal fin may be 10 ft (3 m) high in ADULT MALES, and 3 ft (1 m) high in FEMALES. Travels in pods. Sometimes raises flukes when diving. Known to launch coordinated assaults on large and small marine mammals. CITES APPENDIX II.

RANGE: Biobío to Magallanes and the pack ice of Antarctica; also oceans worldwide.

Pygmy Sperm Whale
Cachalote pigmeo
Kogia breviceps
11.5 ft (3.5 m)

Sperm Whale, Cachalote
Physeter catodon
Arica–Magallanes
36–60 ft (11–18.3 m)

Profile of a sperm whale dive — a bushy blow forward and to the left, a show of the dorsal fin and crenulations, and a final raising of the tail flukes.

False Killer Whale, Orca falsa
Pseudorca crassidens

OTHER NAMES: Blackfish, Dickzachniger, Faux orque, Okikondo.
ID: ♂ 20 ft (6 m). ♀ 16 ft (5 m). WT up to 3000 lb (1360 kg). Black, with a small grey patch extending from chin to chest. Long, tapered head with no beak. Tall, erect, falcate dorsal fin. Hump on leading edge of flippers. Seven to twelve large conical teeth in both jaws. Forms fast-swimming groups of 10 to 30 individuals. Diet includes fish and cephalopods. Known to attack and kill smaller cetaceans. Occasionally bowrides. Said to take bait and fish from longlines of commercial fishing boats. Prone to mass strandings. CITES APPENDIX II.
RANGE: Arica to Maule. In temperate and tropical oceans worldwide between 50°N and 50°S latitude.

FAMILIES PHYSETERIDAE & KOGIIDAE
SPERM WHALES

The sperm whales have large teeth in the underslung lower jaw. The head contains an organ called a "case" that contains spermaceti, a waxy oil once used as a base for candles, cosmetics and lubricants.

Sperm Whale, Cachalote
Physeter catodon

OTHER NAMES: Ballena esperma, Pottwal, Makko kijira.
ID: ♀ 60 ft (18.3 m). WT 60 tons (57,000 kg). ♂ 36 ft (11 m). WT 26 tons (24,000 kg). Largest toothed whale. Black to brownish-grey, with white patches around the mouth and belly. Wrinkled skin on anterior body. Distinctive, huge, squared head. Narrow underslung jaw; 20 to 26 pairs of conical teeth in the lower jaw fit into sockets in upper jaw. Flippers wide and spatulate. Low, rounded dorsal fin. Series of crenulations (bumps) on the dorsal ridge of the tailstock. FEMALES often have calluses on the dorsal hump. There is an S-shaped blowhole at the front of head; the round blow projects up to 16 ft (5 m) forward and to the left. May surface and blow for over an hour. Raises broad, triangular flukes before diving to depths of 10,500 ft (3200 m) after squid, octopus, rays, sharks and bony fishes. Forms large herds of up to 50 individuals, which segregate into nursery groups of adult females, offspring and a courting male, or bachelor groups of mature, non-breeding males displaced from the maternal herd.

Groups often bask motionless at the sea surface. Every 4 to 6 years, females bear a single calf that they nurse for 2 years. Sperm whales were exploited in factory ship whaling in the 20th century and in the Yankee whaling era of the 1800s. (Herman Melville's novel *Moby Dick* was based on a sperm whale attack on a whaling ship off Isla Mocha, Chile.) Whales were harvested for spermaceti, which was a source of wax for candles and a high-temperature lubricant. Ambergris distilled from the whales' intestines was used as a perfume fixative. Tooth ivory was used for scrimshaw carving, and whalebone for corsets. CITES APPENDIX I.

RANGE: Occurs in ice-free oceans, in deep offshore waters or over narrow continental shelves that slope sharply into the abyss.

Pygmy Sperm Whale, Cachalote pigmeo
Kogia breviceps

OTHER NAMES: Zwergpottwal, Cachalot pygmée, Zaru kaburi.

ID: 11.5 ft (3.5 m). WT 900 lb (410 kg). Dark bluish-grey back; pale to white below; belly may have a pinkish tone. Pale bracket mark called the "false gill" between the eye and the flipper. Shark-like head with a narrow, underslung lower jaw. Lower jaw has 12 to 16 pairs of long, sharp, fang-like teeth that fit into sockets in the toothless upper jaw. Flippers are set high on the sides near the head. Small falcate dorsal fin at mid-back. Small groups of up to ten individuals often bask motionless at sea surface. Feeds on squid, benthic crustaceans and fish. Other behavior poorly documented. Rarely seen at sea. CITES APPENDIX II.

RANGE: Recorded at Juan Fernández and off mainland Chile. Normally ranges seaward of the continental shelf in tropical and temperate oceans worldwide.

RELATED SPECIES: DWARF SPERM WHALE, *Kogia simus*. 8.75 ft (2.7 m). Seven to twelve pairs of sharp lower jaw teeth; three pairs in upper jaw. Rarely seen. Recorded off Chile in deep water over the continental shelf. Occurs in tropical and temperate oceans.

FAMILY ZIPHIIDAE
BEAKED WHALES

Beaked whales are mid-sized cetaceans with pointed snouts, a crescent-shaped blowhole, and a pair of short throat grooves. The dorsal fin is set far back on the body. Small flippers fit into depressions on the sides. Flukes are not notched. Back usually bears scratch marks. Dives to depths of 1000 ft (300 m) and spends little time at the surface. Feeds mostly on squid. One or two pairs of functional teeth erupt in the lower jaw of males only, except for *Berardius* and *Tasmacetus*, in which females also have teeth. Rarely seen. Stranded specimens can be identified by dental formula (page 348).

Arnoux's Beaked Whale, Zifio marsopa
Berardius arnuxii

OTHER NAMES: Southern Fourtooth Whale, Ballena nariz de botella, Béradien d'Arnoux, Ballenato de Arnoux, Südlicher Schwarzwal. Named after M. Arnoux, ship's surgeon on the French corvette *Rhin*, who discovered a skull on a New Zealand beach in 1846.

ID: 32 ft (9.8 m). Slate grey or brown, often scarred with pale lines and circular marks; belly paler, with irregular white patches. Small melon on head. Crescent-shaped blowhole has an almost vertical frontal surface from which a tubular snout projects. Short, slightly falcate dorsal fin. Large unnotched triangular flukes sometimes raised when diving. Pair of V-shaped throat grooves. Pair of triangular teeth and a small secondary pair at the tip of the lower jaw; lower teeth erupt outside the closed mouth of BOTH SEXES. Feeds on squid and deep-sea fishes. Forms herds of 6 to 50 individuals. Shy of boats.

RANGE: Aisén to Magallanes. Circumpolar around Antarctica and the southern continents. May enter pack ice and remain close to the ice edge in summer.

Cuvier's Beaked Whale, Zifio común
Ziphius cavirostris

OTHER NAMES: Goosebeaked Whale, Ziphius, Ballena de Cuvier, Cuvier-Schnabelwal,

BEAKED WHALES 347

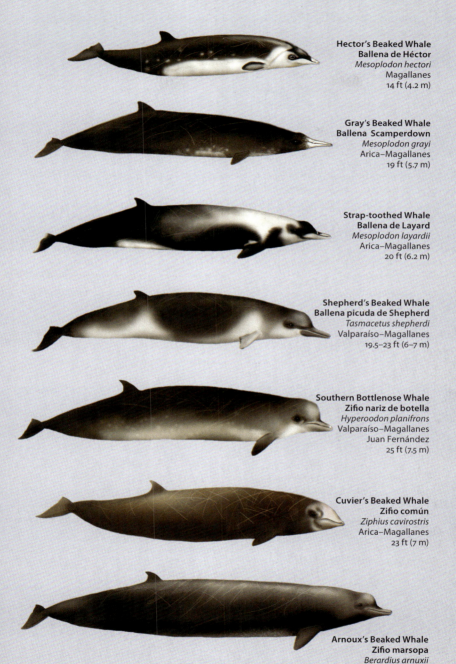

Hector's Beaked Whale
Ballena de Héctor
Mesoplodon hectori
Magallanes
14 ft (4.2 m)

Gray's Beaked Whale
Ballena Scamperdown
Mesoplodon grayi
Arica–Magallanes
19 ft (5.7 m)

Strap-toothed Whale
Ballena de Layard
Mesoplodon layardii
Arica–Magallanes
20 ft (6.2 m)

Shepherd's Beaked Whale
Ballena picuda de Shepherd
Tasmacetus shepherdi
Valparaíso–Magallanes
19.5–23 ft (6–7 m)

Southern Bottlenose Whale
Zifio nariz de botella
Hyperoodon planifrons
Valparaíso–Magallanes
Juan Fernández
25 ft (7.5 m)

Cuvier's Beaked Whale
Zifio común
Ziphius cavirostris
Arica–Magallanes
23 ft (7 m)

Arnoux's Beaked Whale
Zifio marsopa
Berardius arnuxii
Aisén–Magallanes
32 ft (9.8 m)

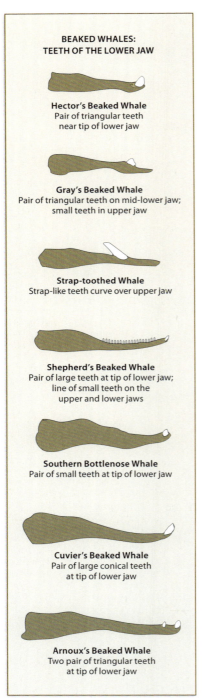

Akago kujira. Named for Parisian paleontologist Georges Cuvier who described this species in 1804 from a fossil skull.

ID: 23 ft (7 m). Tan or pale rusty brown (Indo-Pacific) or dark slate grey (Atlantic) with paler areas on head and belly. Blunt melon, which is whitish in adult males, slopes to a poorly-defined, stout beak. Dark patches around eyes. Robust body, often bearing linear scars from intraspecific fighting and pale oval marks from bites of cookie cutter sharks or lampreys. Small falcate dorsal fin is set well back on body. Small flippers can be tucked into a slight depression along the body. **ADULT MALES** have a single pair of forward-pointing conical teeth at the tip of the lower jaw. Solitary, or in small groups of 2 to 7 individuals. Feeds on deep sea squid supplemented by pelagic fishes and crustaceans. Avoids boats. Frequently strands. A mass stranding of twelve Cuvier's beaked whales in the Mediterranean in 2001 coincided with a NATO military test of acoustic systems for submarine detection. Whale mortality may have been caused by resonance in the whales' cranial airspaces that tore apart delicate tissues, or by acute bends caused by the whales' rapid rise to the surface as they fled the sound.

RANGE: Off the entire Chilean coast, and in temperate and tropical oceans worldwide. Pelagic; rarely found close to shore, except over submarine canyons or narrow continental shelves with deep coastal waters.

Shepherd's Beaked Whale
Ballena picuda de Shepherd
Tasmacetus shepherdi

OTHER NAMES: Tasman Beaked Whale, Tasmacète, Shepherdwal. Named in honor of G. Shepherd, Curator of the Wanganui Museum, New Zealand, who collected the type specimen from Ohawe Beach in 1933.

ID: 19.5–23 ft (6–7 m). Dark grey cape and hood, with a whitish ventral field. Cigar-shaped body with falcate dorsal fin set about two-thirds of the way back from the prominent long beak. **BOTH SEXES** have two large teeth at the tip of the lower jaw and 17 to 29 pairs of small teeth lining both the upper and lower jaws. Very little is known about this whale. The stomach contents of stranded animals suggest that they feed mainly on benthic and deepwater fish.

RANGE: May be circumpolar in offshore Southern Hemisphere temperate waters. Known from a few stranded specimens in the Juan Fernández Archipelago, Tierra del Fuego and the Peninsula Valdés, Argentina; also Tristan da Cunha, South Africa, New Zealand, and Australia.

Southern Bottlenose Whale
Zifio nariz de botella
Hyperoodon planifrons

OTHER NAMES: Ballena nariz de botella del sur, Hyperoodon austral, Südlicher Entenwal.

ID: 25 ft (7.5 m). Robust. Tan to greyish-brown body, sometimes discolored by a thin layer of phytoplankton. Falcate dorsal fin. Bulbous or squared forehead, pale in some individuals. Short, dolphin-like beak. MALES have a single pair of conical teeth at the tip of the lower jaw, rarely visible in live animals. Raises triangular flukes when diving. After long dives, remains on the surface for about 10 minutes, blowing every 30 to 40 seconds. Forms pods of 5 to 25 individuals. Feeds mainly on squid.
CITES APPENDIX I AND II.

RANGE: Circumpolar in deep cold waters of the Southern Ocean south of 29°S. Recorded at Valparaíso, Chile, and the Antarctic ice edge in austral summer.

Gray's Beaked Whale
Ballena Scamperdown
Mesoplodon grayi

OTHER NAMES: Zifio de Gray, Mésoplodon de Gray, Gray-Zweizahnwal, Baleine à bec de Gray. Scamperdown is a New Zealand beach where an early specimen stranded. Gray was a famous 19th-century British taxonomist.

ID: 19 ft (5.7 m). WT 2400 lb (1100 kg). Dark grey to dark brown, with pale patches on the underside. Slender body, with a small, falcate dorsal fin. Small melon on head. Long, slender beak whitens in maturity. Raises white snout out of the water as it surfaces. ADULT MALES have a pair of erupting triangular teeth mid-way along the mouthline. Both sexes have 17 to 22 small teeth on each side of the upper jaw. Known mainly from strandings.

RANGE: Circumpolar in temperate waters of the Southern Ocean. Records from the Strait of Magellan, Peru, Argentina, Falklands, South Africa, Australia, New Zealand.

Hector's Beaked Whale
Ballena de Héctor
Mesoplodon hectori

OTHER NAMES: Zifio de Héctor, Baleine à bec d'Hector, Hector Schnabelwal.

ID: 14.4 ft (4.4 m). Dark grey to brown; pale grey underside. Scratches and scars are common on the flanks. Dark patches around eyes and on the melon. Long beak with a small, flat, roughly triangular tooth exposed on either side of the ADULT MALE's lower jaw near the tip. Feeds on squid.

RANGE: Possibly circumpolar in temperate Southern Hemisphere oceans. Strandings recorded at Isla Navarino, Chile; Argentina, Falklands, South Africa, New Zealand.

Strap-toothed Whale
Ballena de Layard
Mesoplodon layardii

OTHER NAMES: Layard-Zweizahnwal, Mésoplodon de Layard, Baleine à bec de Layard.

ID: 20 ft (6.2 m). Boldly marked. Dark grey body and facial mask. Throat and front half of beak white. White band behind eye joins pale grey cape. Pale around the urogenital opening. Single pair of straplike teeth of the ADULT MALE curve over the upper jaw, preventing it from fully opening. Small groups bask at the surface on calm, sunny days. Does not raise flukes when diving, but sinks quietly beneath the surface, then rises and blows again about 500 ft (150 m) away. Feeds on squid.

RANGE: Circumpolar in cool to temperate waters of the Southern Ocean. Records at Isla Navarino and the Strait of Magellan.

WHERE TO SEE WILDLIFE

Chile's Forestry and Parks Unit, CONAF, administers 31 national parks, 48 national reserves and 15 national monuments. These represent 54,000 sq mi (140,000 sq km) of land, or 19 percent of Chile's territory. These and the many city, provincial, and private parks offer splendid opportunities for wildlife observation. Only a few locations are described here, but any of the Chilean parks are worth exploring. Chile has an excellent internal airline network and tourist infrastructure, making it possible for one to visit a number of wildlife sites and a variety of habitats within a two to three week period.

ARICA–PARINACOTA REGION
Arica

LOCATION: Pacific seaboard, about 12.5 mi (20 km) south of the Peru–Chile border.
TERRAIN: Arica is situated on the Pacific coast at the mouth of the Río San José and Azapa Quebrada. The massive promontory of Morro de Arica lies to the south. To the north are pampas watered by the Río Lluta. The great Atacama Desert and the Andes Mountains lie to the east.
CLIMATE: Coastal desert with overcast and fog. Little to no rainfall. Average temperature is 65°F (18°C).
VEGETATION: Flowering shrubs and palms in the city; fruit trees and crops in the quebradas; candelabra cactus in the desert.
BIRDS: (CITY, QUEBRADAS, PAMPAS) Peruvian Thick-knee, Chilean Woodstar, Peruvian Sheartail, Oasis Hummingbird, Burrowing Owl, Blue-and-white Swallow, Pacific Dove, Eared Dove, Croaking Ground-Dove, Rock Dove, Vermilion Flycatcher, Short-tailed Field-Tyrant, House Wren, Groove-billed Ani, Chestnut-throated Seedeater, Slender-billed Finch, Blue-black Grassquit, House Sparrow, Rufous-collared Sparrow, and Peruvian Meadowlark.

(COASTAL, PELAGIC) Humboldt Penguin, Black-browed Albatross, Salvin's Albatross, Southern Giant-Petrel, White-chinned Petrel, Pink-footed Shearwater, Buller's Shearwater, Sooty Shearwater, Wilson's, Elliot's and Markham's Storm-Petrel, Peruvian Diving-Petrel, Peruvian Pelican, Peruvian Booby, Guanay Cormorant, Red-legged Cormorant, Chilean Skua, Grey Gull, Band-tailed Gull, Kelp Gull, Franklin's Gull, Sabine's Gull, Pomarine Jaeger, Parasitic Jaeger, Peruvian Tern, South American Tern, Elegant Tern, Inca Tern, Ruddy Turnstone, Surfbird, Red-necked Phalarope, American Oystercatcher, Blackish Oystercatcher, and Chilean Seaside Cinclodes.
MAMMALS: Mexican Free-tailed Bat, Big-eared Brown Bat, Vampire Bat, Marine Otter, Southern Sea Lion.
REPTILES: *Microlophus quadrivittatus*, *Microlophus yanezi*, Warty Toad, Leaf-toed Gecko, Elegant Racer, Schmidt's Racer.
BUTTERFLIES: Long-tailed Skipper, Grey Ministreak, Quebrada Ministreak, Common White Tatochila, Southern Dogface, Four-eyed Lady, Monarch Butterfly.

Lauca National Park and UNESCO Biosphere Reserve

LOCATION: On the Altiplano, 90 mi (145 km) east of Arica. The town of Putre lies west of the park and south of Nevados de Putre, which rises to 18,000 ft (5500 m).
SIZE: 532 sq mi (1379 sq km).
TERRAIN: Treeless tableland lying above 11,500 ft (3500 m) and surrounded by snow-capped volcanoes, four of which are over 19,850 ft (6050 m) high. Melting snows of the Parinacota and Pomerape volcanoes feed Lago Chungará, one of the world's highest lakes lying at 14,366 ft (4379 m) elevation.
CLIMATE: High Andean steppe. Semi-arid. Most rain and snow falls in summer (Dec–Feb) in the "Altiplano winter." Cold nights and cool, partly cloudy days.
VEGETATION: Puna (High Andean floral communities) with cacti, *Polylepis*, llareta, tola, bunchgrass. Wildflowers (Mar–May). Pre-Puna shrub zone (alpine vegetation) with flowering trees and shrubs. Crops such as quinoa and alfalfa around towns.

BIRDS: (LAUCA) Lesser Rhea, Puna Tinamou, White-tufted Grebe, Silvery Grebe, Black-crowned Night-Heron, Puna Ibis, Chilean Flamingo, Andean Flamingo, James' Flamingo, Andean Goose, Crested Duck, Puna Teal, Andean Ruddy Duck, Speckled Teal, Yellow-billed Pintail, Andean Condor, Variable Hawk, Mountain Caracara, Aplomado Falcon, Giant Coot, Puna Plover, Diademed Sandpiper-Plover, Andean Lapwing, Andean Avocet, Greater Yellowlegs, Pectoral Sandpiper, Wilson's Phalarope, Neotropic Cormorant, Grey-breasted Seedsnipe, Rufous-bellied Seedsnipe, Andean Gull, Andean Flicker, Plain-breasted Earthcreeper, Puna Miner, Cordilleran Canastero, Bar-winged Cinclodes, White-winged Cinclodes, Andean Negrito, Black-billed Shrike-Tyrant, D'Orbigny's Chat-Tyrant, White-fronted and Rufous-naped Ground-Tyrant, Giant Conebill, Andean Swallow, Plumbeous Sierra-Finch, Red-backed Sierra-Finch, Ash-breasted Sierra-Finch, White-winged Diuca-Finch, and Black Siskin.

(AROUND PUTRE) Ornate Tinamou, Rufous-bellied Seedsnipe, Grey-breasted Seedsnipe, Andean Hillstar, Sparkling Violetear, Giant Hummingbird, Andean Swift, Variable Hawk, Bare-faced Ground-Dove, Black-winged Ground-Dove, Streaked Tit-Spinetail, Canyon and Dark-winged Canastero, Straight-billed Earthcreeper, Plain-breasted Earthcreeper, White-throated Earthcreeper, White-browed Chat-Tyrant, Yellow-billed Tit-Tyrant, Black-billed Shrike-Tyrant, Tamarugo Conebill, Cinereous Conebill, Golden-billed Saltator, Blue-and-yellow Tanager, Black-throated Flowerpiercer, Black-hooded and Mourning Sierra-Finch, Greenish Yellow-Finch, Band-tailed Seedeater, and Hooded Siskin.

MAMMALS: Vicuña, Guanaco, Alpaca, Llama, Taruca, Viscacha, Andean Hairy Armadillo, Andean Cat, Puma, Culpeo Fox, Mountain Degu, Highland Tuco-tuco, Yellow-toothed Cavy, White-bellied Akodont, Altiplano Chinchilla Mouse, Andean Mouse, Bolivian Pericote, Altiplano Laucha.

REPTILES: Brilliant Lizard, *Liolaemus jamesi*, *L. enigmaticus*, *L. signifer*, *L. pleopholis*, *L. tacnae*, Peru Slender Snake.
AMPHIBIANS: Warty Toad, Zapahuira and Marbled Water Frog, *Telmatobius pefauri*.
BUTTERFLIES: Dwarf Blue, Andean Foothills White.

WITHIN THE PARK: The archaeological site of ALERO DE LAS CUEVAS (BC 9500–8000) lies at the west entry to Lauca. Nearby is a CHACU, an Incan stone trap used for capturing vicuñas. Viscacha can be seen sunbathing on rock piles *(roquerios)* near the road. Highland Tuco-tuco are found near the chacu.

CHUCUYO VILLAGE was built to service pre-Columbian caravan traffic moving between the gold mines of Potosí, Bolivia, and Arica. Giant Coot, Puna Snipe, Andean Avocet, Puna Tinamou and Lesser Rhea are often seen in the surrounding wetlands.

The Aymara ceremonial village of PARINACOTA (meaning "Place of Flamingos") has *bofedales* where flamingos, Andean Avocet, Puna Plover, Diademed Sandpiper-Plover, and alpacas and llamas are often seen. The CONAF Visitor Center is also located here. The 17th-century adobe church, rebuilt in 1789, is a National Monument.

LAGUNAS COTACOTANI (meaning "Place of Small Lakes") comprises a series of interconnecting turquoise ponds. Water from Lake Chungará seeps down through the lava beds into the lagunas. Water from the ponds discharges into the tiny Río Desaguadero, which feeds the Parinacota *bofedal*, which becomes the headwaters of the Río Lauca.

LAKE CHUNGARÁ is one of the world's highest lakes and one of the most beautiful. The movement of innumerable waterbirds on the lake create ever-changing reflections of snow-capped volcanos.

SERVICES: Camping, picnic sites. Hotels, restaurants and park offices in Putre. Open all year. Most bird tours visit Oct–Nov.
ADVISORY: Acclimate at lower altitude. Move slowly to avoid high altitude sickness. Carry sunscreen, sunglasses, rain gear, warm clothing, food and water.

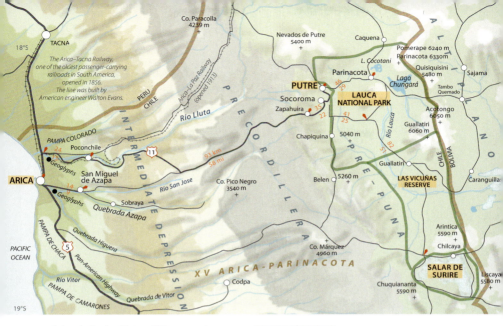

Salar de Surire Natural Monument

LOCATION: On the Altiplano at 13,776 ft (4200 m); 78 mi (126 km) s of Putre; 49 mi (79 km) n of Colchane.

TOTAL AREA: 61 sq mi (159 sq km).

TERRAIN: Intensely white salt flat and saline lagoons with climate, vegetation and flora similar to that of Lauca National Park.

BIRDS: Lesser Rhea (Suri), three species of flamingos, Tawny-throated Dotterel, Puna Snipe, Rufous-webbed Tyrant, Grey-bellied Shrike-Tyrant, Puna Yellow-Finch, Thick-billed Siskin, Red-backed Sierra-Finch.

MAMMALS: Vicuña, Culpeo Fox, Andean Hairy Armadillo, Viscacha, Yellow-toothed Cavy, Altiplano Chinchilla Mouse, Altiplano Laucha and the *Conepatus chinga rex* subspecies of Molina's Hog-nosed Skunk. The rare Andean Mountain Cat and Andean Pampas Cat *(Gato pajero)* have been seen several times at dusk at Salar de Surire.

SERVICES: Open all year. Campsites and *refugio*; no potable water. Four-wheel drive is suggested. Carry sunscreen, sunglasses, rain gear, warm clothing, hiking boots, sleeping bags, water and food. Move slowly to avoid altitude sickness.

NEARBY PARK: LAS VICUÑAS NATIONAL RESERVE protects the wild vicuña herds and other native fauna of Chile.

TARAPACÁ REGION
Iquique

LOCATION: The city lies on a narrow littoral plain on the Pacific seacoast at 20°13' S.

TERRAIN: Beaches flank the tidal pools of the Cavancha Peninsula. Gigantic dunes to 1970 ft (600 m) high rise behind the city.

CLIMATE: Arid coast with frequent fog. No rain. Average temperature is 65°F (18°C).

VEGETATION: Cacti and grasses. The coastal hills s of Iquique have lomas formations at 3280 ft (1000 m) with assemblies of cacti and *Tillandsia landbeckii* bromeliads.

BIRDS: Humboldt Penguin, Sooty Shearwater, Peruvian Diving-Petrel, Peruvian Pelican, Peruvian Booby, Neotropic Cormorant, Guanay Cormorant, Red-legged Cormorant, Little Blue Heron, Black-crowned Night-Heron, Cattle Egret, Turkey Vulture, Peregrine Falcon, Blackish Oystercatcher, migrant shorebirds, Black Skimmer, Grey Gull, Band-tailed Gull, Kelp Gull, Franklin's Gull, Sabine's Gull, South American, Elegant and Inca Tern, Eared Dove, Pacific Dove, Cinereous Ground-Tyrant, Chilean Seaside Cinclodes, Rufous-collared Sparrow.

MAMMALS: Southern Sea Lion, Marine Otter, Striped Dolphin, Short-beaked Common Dolphin, Bottlenose Dolphin, Long-finned Pilot Whale.

REPTILES: Green Sea Turtle, Olive Ridley, Loggerhead, Lagarto Dragón, *Microlophus quadrivitattus,* Leaf-toed Gecko.
SERVICES: Boats trips to see seabirds and marine mammals leave from the fishing pier, which is also a good spot to photograph gulls, terns, pelicans and sea lions.
OTHER ATTRACTIONS: Iquique is the gateway to ISLUGA NATIONAL PARK, 155 mi (250 km) to the east. Total area is 675 sq mi (1747 sq km). Average elevation is 6900 ft (2100 m) with-Volcán Isluga rising to 17,552 ft (5350 m). Wildlife is similar to Lauca's. Campsites and thermal baths are available. Trails lead to Laguna Arabilla (flamingos) and the ancient fortified city of Pukará.

ANTOFAGASTA REGION
Antofagasta
LOCATION: Pacific coast at 23°39'S.
TERRAIN: The port occupies a narrow strip of coast backed by the Coastal Range.
CLIMATE: No rain. Coastal desert with frequent fog. Warm, sunny afternoons.
VEGETATION: *Eulychnia iquiquensis, Copiapoa* cacti and other desert plants can be viewed at the LA CHIMBA NATIONAL RESERVE.
BIRDS: Peruvian Pelican, Grey Gull, Kelp Gull, Brown-hooded Gull, Franklin's Gull, Inca Tern, Turkey Vulture, Eared Dove, Rock Dove, Barn Swallow, House Sparrow.
MAMMALS: Southern Sea Lion.
REPTILES: Green Sea Turtle (rare), Braided Lizard, Peru Leaf-toed Gecko.
FISH AND SHELLFISH: Anchoveta, Mackerel, Corvina, Congrío, Scallops, Oysters, Loco (False Abalone) and Piure (Sea Squirt) are offered for sale at the open-air fish markets.
NEARBY ATTRACTIONS: LA PORTADA NATURAL MONUMENT ("The Gateway"), n of Antofagasta, is a natural arch 140 ft (43 m) high, formed by marine erosion and composed of black andesite and marine sedimentary rock with exposed fossil shells.

Salar de Atacama at Los Flamencos
LOCATION: Salar de Atacama is a part of the vast Los Flamencos National Reserve. San Pedro de Atacama, the town nearest the Salar, is 120 mi (190 km) ne of Antofagasta; 57 mi (92 km) e of Calama.
TERRAIN: High Andean intermontane basin with enormous salt pans and saline ponds. Fertile oases along the Río Loa.
CLIMATE: Warm, sunny days; cold nights. Hyper-arid in most areas; only the High Andean sectors receive precipitation during the "Altiplano winter" (Dec–Feb).
VEGETATION: Cardón and other cacti, grasses including *Atriplex* sp., *Distichlis spicata, Tessiaria absinthioides, Ephedra breana, Baccharis petiolata, Frankenia meyenianna*. Trees include *Prosopis* mesquites growing at the north end of the Salar and Algarrobo blanco, Pimiento and Chañar in towns.
BIRDS: (AROUND THE SALARES) Lesser Rhea, Andean, Chilean Flamingo, James' Flamingo, Andean Gull, Puna Plover, Andean Avocet, Condor, Variable Hawk, Burrowing Owl, Rufous-naped Ground-Tyrant, Common Miner, Andean Negrito. (AROUND OASES) Horned Owl, Blue-and-white Swallow, Black-winged Ground-Dove, Golden-spotted Ground-Dove, House Wren, Chiguanco Thrush, Greenish Yellow-Finch, Rufous-collared Sparrow.
MAMMALS: Chilla, Culpeo, Vicuña, Viscacha, Coruro, Bolivian Pericote, Altiplano Laucha.
REPTILES: (LOS FLAMENCOS) Fabian's Lizard, Black-headed Lizard, Andean Lizard, *Liolaemus constanzae, L. hajeki, L. filiorum, L. barbarae, L. multicolor, L. erguetae, L. puritamensis*, Dragón de oído cubierto, *Phrynosaura erronea*, Peru Slender Snake. (CALAMA) Leaf-toed Gecko, Paulina's Lizard, Corredor de Pica, *Phrynosaura torresi*.
AMPHIBIANS: Warty Toad, Water Frog.
IN THE RESERVE: SALAR DE ATACAMA is a salt pan covering 1158 sq mi (3000 sq km) and lying at 7545 ft (2300 m). Lithium, borax, potassium and other salts are mined there. Waters of Río San Pedro feed the saline lagoons. The area supports a variety of birds, including flamingos. The VALLEY OF THE MOON *(Valle de Luna)* is a salt basin lying sw of San Pedro. The valley and the sharply-crested cliffs edging it are the remains of

an ancient lake bottom whose sedimentary strata were folded into a vertical position and eroded by wind and water. Streaks of rose, orange and lavender color the escarpment when lit by the setting sun.

LAGUNAS MISCANTI Y MIÑIQUES lie south of Socaire amid rolling hills and volcanos. The rich, varied fauna includes flamingos, Horned Coot and Lesser Rhea. TARA, AGUAS CALIENTES and PUJSA salares lie five hours e of San Pedro. They comprise salt basins and lagoons set amid rolling plains covered in bunchgrass and tola scrub.

SERVICES: Park offices, lodging, auto, bike and horse rentals are in San Pedro de Atacama. No lodging, camping or food in the park. Park ranger's office is in Toconao, 24 mi (38 km) s of San Pedro. There are hiking and riding trails to popular areas such as the Valley of the Moon.

OASIS TOWNS: SAN PEDRO DE ATACAMA stands on the Río San Pedro, the largest river of the Salar de Atacama. Mummies and Atacameño pottery predating the Inca conquest can be seen in the LE PAIGE MUSEUM founded by the Belgian Jesuit priest Gustave Le Paige in 1955. At the museum entrance is a small cactus garden. The IGLESIA DE SAN PEDRO, built in 1745, has a ceiling made from large rafters of Algarrobo, inset with cactus panels. Similar construction is found in the old adobe church at CHIU CHIU, which lies at the fertile junction of the Ríos Salado and Loa. The rafters at Chiu Chiu are made of Chañar, the doors from flattened skeletons of Cardón tied with leather strips. Near Calama is the CHUQUICAMATA COPPER MINE, which produces 47 percent of Chile's copper and also mines sulphur.

ATACAMA REGION
Pan de Azúcar National Park

LOCATION: Seacoast at the border of the Antofagasta and Atacama Regions; 120 mi (194 km) n of Copiapó. Access is via a secondary road off Highway 5.

TOTAL AREA: 169 sq mi (438 sq km).

TERRAIN: A sugarloaf-shaped island gives the reserve its name. The adjacent coast is backed by quebradas and low peaks (2625 ft/ 800 m) of the Coastal Range. There are beaches at Laguna Blanca and Los Piqueros.

CLIMATE: Semi-arid, with oceanic influence and frequent morning coastal fog. Average temperature is 64°F (18°C). Warm, sunny, summer days. Scant winter rain.

VEGETATION: Cacti include *Copiapoa cinerea* and *Neoporteria* sp. Drought tolerant plants, including *Nolana, Heliotropum, Euphorbia* and *Tetragonia*. Wildflowers bloom in years with adequate rainfall.

BIRDS: Humboldt Penguin, Peruvian Booby, Peruvian Pelican, Inca Tern, Guanay Cormorant, Red-legged Cormorant, Band-tailed Gull, Kelp Gull, Grey Gull, Variable Hawk, Kestrel, Blue-and-white Swallow.

MAMMALS: Guanaco, Culpeo Fox, Southern Sea Lion, Marine Otter.

REPTILES: Braided Lizard, Atacama Lava Lizard, Many-spotted Lizard, *Liolaemus bisignatus, L. silvai, L. velosoi*, Chilean Iguana, *Phrynosaura manueli*, Long-tailed Racer.

AMPHIBIANS: Chile Four-eyed Frog.

SERVICES: Visitors can hire guides for sport fishing and scuba diving, and boats to view marine wildlife at Fishermen's Cove. Roads and trails run through the park and to a bay vista point. Cabins, campsites, potable water, showers, mini-market. Entry fee.

Nevado Tres Cruces National Park

LOCATION: High Andes, on the Puna de Atacama; 124 mi (200 km) e of Copiapó.

TOTAL AREA: 228 sq mi (591 sq km).

TERRAIN: Puna at 12,140 ft (3700 m) lying beneath the dormant stratovolcano complex of Nevado Tres Cruces at 22,142 ft (6749 m) and Ojos del Salado, the world's highest active volcano at 22,615 ft (6893 m). Salar de Maricunga and the saline lagoons of Laguna Santa Rosa and Laguna del Negro Francisco are famous for flamingos.

CLIMATE: High desert. Mild days; cold nights.

VEGETATION: High Andean steppe, with bunchgrass, cacti, tola scrub.

BIRDS: 62 species, with Andean Flamingo,

Horned Coot, Andean Goose, Crested Duck.
MAMMALS: Vicuña, Guanaco, Culpeo Fox.
REPTILES: *Liolaemus isabelae, L. patriciaiturrae, L. rosenmanni, L. melanopleurus.*
AMPHIBIANS: Warty Toad.
SERVICES: Spartan CONAF huts with beds, bathrooms and kitchen. Carry drinking water, food, gas for cooking, sleeping bags.

Llanos de Challe National Park

LOCATION: Coastal desert of Atacama near Carrizal Bajo; 31 mi (50 km) nw of Huasco; 50 mi (80 km) nw of Vallenar.
TOTAL AREA: 176 sq mi (457 sq km).
TERRAIN: Coastal mountains; highest point is Cerro Negro at 3115 ft (950 m); the central plain and quebradas open onto the white sand beach of Carrizal Bajo.
CLIMATE: Coastal desert with fog.
VEGETATION: ENDEMIC *Copiapoa carrizalensis* cacti and other desert plants grow in lomas formations created by the *camanchaca* fog. The park lies within the Flowering Desert where Añañuca, Pata de guanaco, Lirio de campo, Malvilla, Suspiro and the ENDEMIC Lion's Claw or Garra de león *(Leontochir ovallei)* bloom in springs of abundant rain.
BIRDS: 56 species includes Chilean Flamingo, White-winged Coot, Black-necked Swan, Andean Condor, Peregrine Falcon.
MAMMALS: Guanaco, Chilla Fox, Culpeo Fox.
REPTILES: Braided Lizard, Shining Lizard, Many-spotted Lizard, Atacama Lava Lizard, Chilean Iguana, Chilean Marked Gecko, Long-tailed Racer.
AMPHIBIANS: Atacama Toad.
SERVICES: Self-guided tour routes for autos. Hiking trails to see *Copiapoa carrizalensis* and lomas formations on Cerro Negro.

Humboldt Penguin National Reserve

LOCATION: Islas Chañaral, Damas, Choros and Gaviota lie 4 mi (10 km) off the coast. Boat landing is prohibited.
TOTAL AREA: 33 sq mi (86 sq km).
CLIMATE: Semi-arid, with oceanic influence and frequent morning fog. Average annual temperature is 64°F (18°C).
VEGETATION: Copiapoa and Copao cacti.
BIRDS: Humboldt Penguin, Peruvian Booby, Peruvian Pelican, Inca Tern, Red-legged Cormorant, Guanay Cormorant, Band-tailed Gull, Kelp Gull, Black Vulture, Turkey Vulture, Blackish Oystercatcher, Common Diuca-Finch, Chilean Seaside Cincloides.
MAMMALS: Southern Sea Lion, Marine Otter. Bottle-nosed Dolphin at Isla Choros; mouse opossums occur on the island's rocks where they feed on crustaceans.
REPTILES: Green Turtle, *Liolaemus melaniceps*, Chilean Slender Snake.
SERVICES: Boat tours to see the seabirds and marine mammals can be arranged at Caleta Punta de Choros (weather-permitting).

COQUIMBO REGION

Fray Jorge National Park and UNESCO World Biosphere Reserve

LOCATION: Desert coast; 94 mi (150 km) s of La Serena; 56 mi (90 km) w of Ovalle.
TOTAL AREA: 37 sq mi (96 sq km).
TERRAIN: Altos de Talinay rises to 2187 ft (666 m) from the coastal desert plain.
CLIMATE: Semi-arid steppe with frequent overcast and morning fog.
VEGETATION: Relict Valdivian-type forest at higher elevations, with Canelo, Boldo, Olivillo, Tepa, ferns and lianas that are watered by the coastal fog. Espinillo, Guayacán, Uvilla *(Ribes)* and cacti edge the roads near the park entrance. Añañuca, Azulillo and other desert wildflowers can be seen in springs that provide adequate rainfall.
BIRDS: Chilean Tinamou, California Quail, Horned Owl, Barn Owl, Black-chested Buzzard-Eagle, Variable Hawk, White-throated Tapaculo, Chilean Mockingbird, Long-tailed Meadowlark, Common Diuca-Finch, Black-chinned Siskin. Migrant shorebirds at the Río Limarí estuary.
MAMMALS: Molina's Hog-nosed Skunk, Puma, Culpeo Fox, Guanaco, Southern Sea Lion, Marine Otter.
REPTILES: Braided Lizard, Zapallar Lizard, Shining Lizard, Chilean Iguana, Chilean Marked Gecko, Long-tailed Racer.

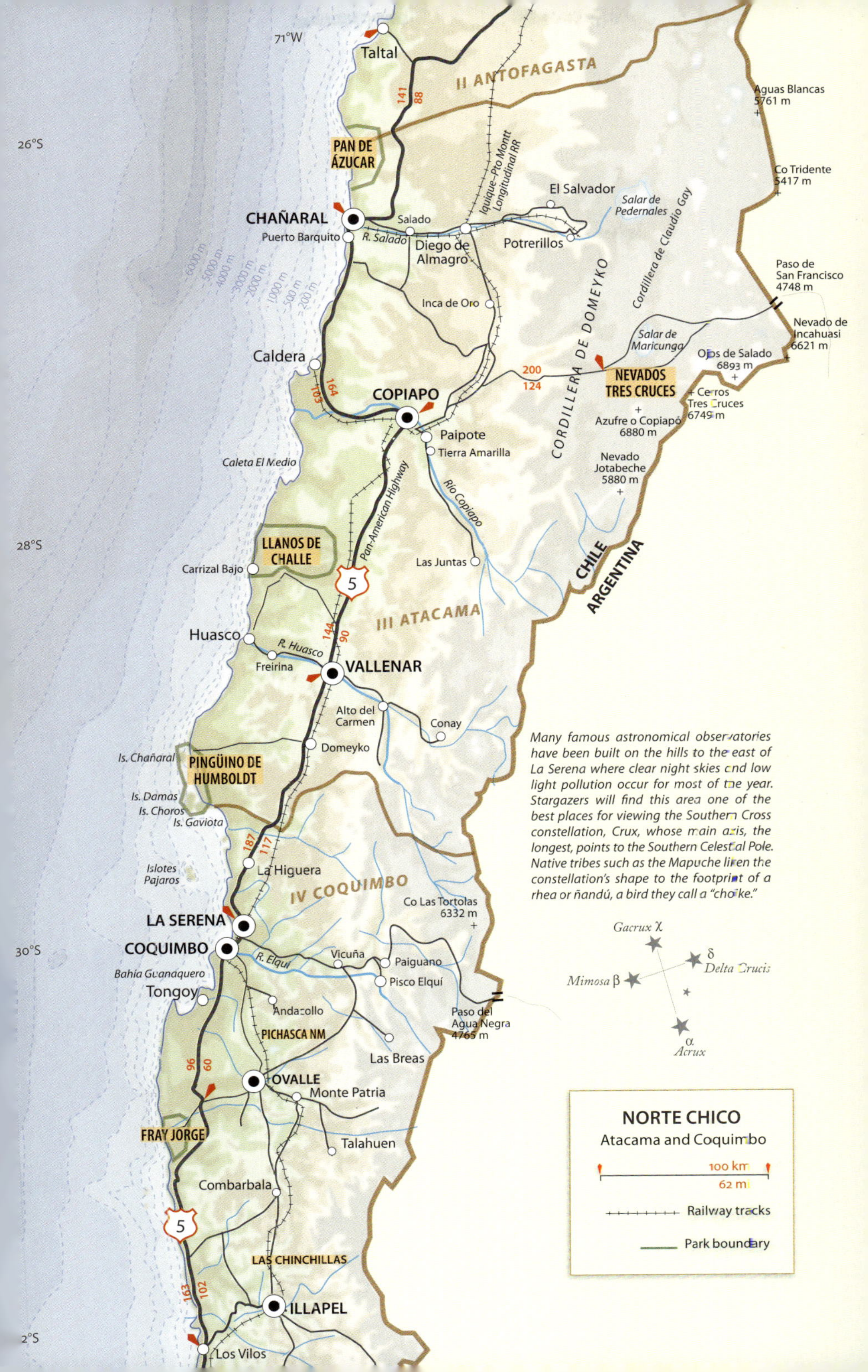

NORTE CHICO
Atacama and Coquimbo
100 km
62 mi
Railway tracks
Park boundary
Many famous astronomical observatories have been built on the hills to the east of La Serena where clear night skies and low light pollution occur for most of the year. Stargazers will find this area one of the best places for viewing the Southern Cross constellation, Crux, whose main axis, the longest, points to the Southern Celestial Pole. Native tribes such as the Mapuche liken the constellation's shape to the footprint of a rhea or ñandú, a bird they call a "choike."
Gacrux χ
δ Delta Crucis
Mimosa β
α Acrux
71°W
26°S
28°S
30°S
II ANTOFAGASTA
III ATACAMA
IV COQUIMBO
CHILE
ARGENTINA
Taltal
PAN DE ÁZUCAR
CHAÑARAL
Puerto Barquito
Salado
R. Salado
Diego de Almagro
El Salvador
Potrerillos
Salar de Pedernales
Cordillera de Claudio Gay
Iquique–Pto Montt Longitudinal RR
Inca de Oro
Aguas Blancas 5761 m
Co Tridente 5417 m
Paso de San Francisco 4748 m
Nevado de Incahuasi 6621 m
Ojos de Salado 6893 m
Salar de Maricunga
CORDILLERA DE DOMEYKO
NEVADOS TRES CRUCES
Cerros Tres Cruces 6749 m
Azufre o Copiapó 6880 m
Nevado Jotabeche 5880 m
Caldera
COPIAPO
Paipote
Tierra Amarilla
Río Copiapó
Caleta El Medio
Pan-American Highway
Las Juntas
LLANOS DE CHALLE
Carrizal Bajo
5
Huasco
R. Huasco
Freirina
VALLENAR
Alto del Carmen
Conay
Domeyko
Is. Chañaral
PINGÜINO DE HUMBOLDT
Is. Damas
Is. Choros
Is. Gaviota
Islotes Pajaros
La Higuera
Co Las Tortolas 6332 m
LA SERENA
COQUIMBO
R. Elqui
Vicuña
Paiguano
Pisco Elquí
Bahía Guanaquero
Tongoy
Andacollo
PICHASCA NM
Paso del Agua Negra 4765 m
Las Breas
OVALLE
Monte Patria
FRAY JORGE
Talahuen
Combarbala
LAS CHINCHILLAS
ILLAPEL
Los Vilos
6000 m
5000 m
4000 m
3000 m
2000 m
1000 m
500 m
200 m

AMPHIBIANS: Chile Four-eyed Frog.

SERVICES: The CONAF offices and nature center are 3 mi (5 km) from the entrance. Campground has stoves, firewood, picnic tables, running water, restrooms. Housekeeping units may be available at the administrator's house. The 6-mi (10-km) *Bosque Hidrofilo* interpretive trail for wildlife observation is best in spring. No food or petrol in the park. Entry fee. Open 0900 to 1800 Thur–Sun and holidays (Dec–Mar); Sat–Sun and holidays (Apr–Nov).

VALPARAÍSO REGION

La Campana National Park and Unesco World Biosphere Reserve

LOCATION: 37 mi (60 km) w of Valparaíso; 100 mi (160 km) n of Santiago. Access to Ocoa is by unpaved road off Highway 5. Granizo and Cajón Grande are accessed by unpaved road from Olmué.

TOTAL AREA: 30 sq mi (80 sq km).

TERRAIN: Mountains, valleys and ravines in the Coastal Range. Highest peaks are Cerro El Roble at 7217 ft (2200 m) and La Campana at 5997 ft (1828 m).

CLIMATE: Mediterranean climate moderated by proximity to the sea; coastal fog. Warm, dry summers; cool, rainy winters.

VEGETATION: Ocoa Valley contains one of the last remaining CHILEAN PALM forests. ALPINE-LIKE STEPPE occupies rocky slopes on the peaks; flora includes bunchgrasses, sedges and low shrubs such as Yerba blanca and Colliguay. NOTHOFAGUS FOREST with *Nothofagus obliqua* var. *macrocarpa* occurs in scattered relictual stands on south-facing slopes; typical flora includes Radal, Maqui, Lilén, barberry and currants. FOG FOREST, which occupies seaward slopes and ravines watered by the coastal *camanchaca* fog, contains Patagua, Canelo, Maqui, Repu, Luma, Northern Belloto, Mayu, epiphytes and bromeliads. SCLEROPHYLLOUS FOREST occupies south-facing slopes below 3280 ft (1000 m). Flora includes Peumo, Boldo, Northern Belloto, Lilén, climbing vines and thickets of *Chusquea cumingii* bamboo.

MATORRAL vegetation with Espino, Algorrobo, Litre, Quillay, Maitén, Quisco and Chagual grows in open, disturbed sites at lower elevations.

BIRDS: Chilean Tinamou, Chilean Hawk, Variable Hawk, American Kestrel, Black-chested Buzzard-Eagle, Harris' Hawk, Chimango Caracara, Chilean Pigeon, Black-winged Ground-Dove, Picui Ground-Dove, Giant Hummingbird, Green-backed Firecrown, Chilean Flicker, Striped Woodpecker, Rufous-legged Owl, Austral Pygmy Owl, Chilean Swallow, Chilean Mockingbird, White-throated Tapaculo, Dusky Tapaculo, Moustached Turca, Fire-eyed Diucon, Plain-mantled Tit-Spinetail, Tufted Tit-Tyrant, Des Murs' Wiretail, Crag Chilia, Thorn-tailed Rayadito, Dusky-tailed Canastero, Rufous-tailed Plantcutter, Grey-hooded Sierra-Finch, and Common Diuca-Finch. (The SENDERO LOS PEUMOS trail to Cerro Penitentes is best for specialty and endemic birds.)

MAMMALS: Culpeo, Chilla, Molina's Hog-nosed Skunk, Lesser Grison, Viscacha, Degu.

REPTILES: Mountain Lizard, Chilean Lizard, Schröeder's Lizard, Wreath Lizard, Thin Tree Lizard, Long-tailed Racer, Slender Snake *(Tachymenis coronellina)*.

AMPHIBIANS: Helmeted Water Toad, Chile Four-eyed Frog.

WITHIN THE PARK: (OCOA) Trail through the Chilean Palm forest passes along the bank of the Río Rabuco to the Cascada La Cortada. (GRANIZO) The SENDERO EL ANDINISTA trail ascends to the summit of Campana where Charles Darwin took in the view in 1834. Allow a full day for the steep, rocky climb and descent; wear good hiking boots and carry food and water. SENDERO LOS PEUMOS ascends Cerro Penitentes for birdwatching. (CAJÓN GRANDE) Trails to Portezuelo Ocoa, La Poza del Coipo and El Plateau.

SERVICES: Lodging, food in nearby towns. Park has campsites, restrooms, showers, and riding and hiking trails to the major park attractions. CONAF park office is in Olmué. Open daily 0900–1900 (Sep–Apr). Open weekends and holidays 0900–1800 (May–Aug). Entry fee.

NEARBY ATTRACTIONS: The port of QUINTERO (n of Valparaíso) is a departure point for pelagic trips to the Humboldt Current. Seabirds include Humboldt Penguin, Black-browed Albatross, Grey-headed Albatross, Buller's Albatross, Northern Royal Albatross, Salvin's Albatross, Southern Giant-Petrel, Southern Fulmar, Cape Petrel, White-chinned Petrel, Westland Petrel, Masatierra Petrel, Pink-footed Shearwater, Sooty Shearwater, Wilson's Storm-Petrel, Peruvian Diving-Petrel, Red Phalarope, South American Tern, Inca Tern, Chilean Skua, Parasitic Jaeger.

El Yali National Reserve

LOCATION: Coast of San Antonio Province; 24 mi (38 km) s of Santo Domingo.
TOTAL AREA: 2 sq mi (5 sq km).
TERRAIN: Salt marshes, estuary, sand dunes and beach.
CLIMATE: Mediterranean, with coastal fog.
VEGETATION: Meadows and matorral along the beach. Thorn trees and sclerophyllous forest composed of Boldo, Lilén and Molle grow inland of the beach; exotic eucalyptus and pines at Laguna Matanzas.
BIRDS: El Yali is among the most important wetlands in nc Chile for waterbirds and waders with more than 115 species, including the Chiloé Wigeon, Yellow-billed Pintail, White-cheeked Pintail, Black-headed Duck, Great Grebe, Red-gartered Coot, Great Egret, Cocoi Heron, Stripe-backed Bittern, White-faced Ibis, Black-faced Ibis, Black-necked Swan, Coscoroba Swan, Brown-hooded Gull, Rufous-chested Dotterel.
REPTILES: Green Sea Turtle, Olive Ridley, Leatherback, Schröeder's Lizard, Shining Lizard, Mountain Lizard, Chilean Lizard, Thin Tree Lizard, Long-tailed Racer, Slender Snake *(Tachymenis coronellina)*.
AMPHIBIANS: Helmeted Water Toad, Chile Four-eyed Frog.
SERVICES: Inquire about entry permits and hours at the CONAF center in Viña del Mar or at the park entry office.
NEARBY RESERVES: The reservoir at LAGO PAÑUELAS RESERVE, s of Valparaíso, attracts birds such as the Lake Duck, Black-headed Duck, Cinereous Harrier, Striped Woodpecker, Chilean Flicker, Chilean Mockingbird, Dusky-tailed Canastero, Warbling Doradito, Patagonian Tyrant, Long-tailed Meadowlark. It is also a good fishing spot for Pejerry *(Odonthestes bonariensis)*.
LAGUNA PERAL RESERVE, n of San Antonio, is known for White-tufted Grebe, Silvery Grebe, Plumbeous Rail, Stripe-backed Bittern, Black-headed Duck, Lake Duck, Black-necked Swan, Neotropic Cormorant, Collared Plover, White-backed Stilt, Common Tern, Arctic Tern, Many-colored Rush-Tyrant, Rufous-tailed Plantcutter, Austral Blackbird.

SANTIAGO METROPOLITAN REGION
El Yeso Reservoir

LOCATION: In the Mediterranean Andes, 56 mi (90 km) e of Santiago, the last 20 mi (33 km) of which is uphill and unpaved.
TERRAIN: Montane canyon reservoir lying at about 7500 ft (2300 m) on the Río Yeso, which flows into the Río Maipo.
CLIMATE: Alpine. Warm and dry in summer; cold, wind and snow in winter.
VEGETATION: Cactus and scrub at lower elevations. Bogs and barren land around the reservoir and river. Wildflowers in spring.
BIRDS: ENDEMICS include the Moustached Turca, Diademed Sandpiper-Plover, Dusky-

tailed Canastero, Crag Chilia, Magellanic Tapaculo, and Chilean Mockingbird. Also Andean Condor, Black-chested Buzzard-Eagle, Variable Hawk, Mountain Caracara, Andean Goose, Mountain Parakeet, White-sided Hillstar, Grey-breasted Seedsnipe, Black-winged Ground-Dove, Chilean Flicker, South American Snipe, Scale-throated Earthcreeper, Rufous-banded Miner, Bar-winged Cinclodes, Grey-flanked Cinclodes, Lesser Canastero, Great Shrike-Tyrant, Ochre-naped, Cinereous, Rufous-naped, Black-fronted and White-browed Ground-Tyrant, Grey-hooded, Mourning, Band-tailed and Plumbeous Sierra-Finch, Greater Yellow-Finch, Yellow-rumped Siskin, Diuca-Finch.
MAMMALS: Puma, Culpeo Fox.
REPTILES: Mountain Lizard, Dusky Lizard, *Liolaemus ramonensis*, Matuasto Lizard.
AMPHIBIANS: Warty Toad.
SERVICES: No services. Carry food and water. Entry permit required.
OTHER RESERVES: RÍO CLARILLO RESERVE is in the Andean precordillera, 28 mi (45 km) se of Santiago. Peumo, Litre, Quillay, Canelo and Lingue grow on slopes along the river. Picnic area, restrooms, nature center, and trails to see the Chilean Pigeon and Chilean Iguana. FUNDO YERBA LOCA RESERVE, 15.5 mi (25 km) e of Santiago on the road to the Farellones ski area, has montane deciduous forest and birds such as Dusky Tapaculo.

O'HIGGINS REGION
Río de los Cipreses National Reserve
LOCATION: 31 mi (50 km) e of Rancagua via Presidente Eduardo Frei Montalva (Copper) Highway to Coya mining village; then 3 mi (5 km) to Termas de Cauquenes and 9 mi (15 km) on unpaved road. (1.5 hour drive).
TOTAL AREA: 142 sq mi (369 sq km).
TERRAIN: Waterfalls, lagoons and glaciers in the Andean precordillera. Río Los Cipreses flows through a long, narrow valley edged by mountains, the highest of which is El Palomo at 15,912 ft (4850 m).
CLIMATE: Warm summers; cool winters with 31–59 in (800–1500 mm) of rain and snow.
VEGETATION: Peumo, Litre and Quillay grow along the river valley. Cordilleran Cypress grows at higher elevations.
BIRDS: Burrowing Parrots (Tricahues) can be seen at dusk when flocks return to roost at Las Loreras on the Río Cachapoal cliffs. Also Andean Condor, Black-chested Buzzard-Eagle, Torrent Duck, Upland Goose.
MAMMALS: Culpeo, Chilla, Puma, Guanaco.
REPTILES: Chilean Lizard, Mountain Lizard, Shining Lizard, Wreath Lizard, Thin Tree Lizard, *Pristidactylus volcanensis*, Long-tailed Racer.
AMPHIBIANS: Chile Four-eyed Frog.
SERVICES: CONAF center, thermal baths, old mining sites, trails, picnic area, lodging. Archeological sites and petroglyphs at La Piedra del Indio, Carrizal, Cotón, Agua de la Vida and Rincón de los Guanacos.

MAULE REGION
Radal Siete Tazas National Reserve
LOCATION: 62 mi (100 km) ne of Talca; 34 mi (55 km) e of Molina on unpaved road.
TOTAL AREA: 20 sq mi (51 sq km).
TERRAIN: Andean precordillera, with peaks and crags to 7040 ft (2146 m). Park is known for its scenic beauty, pristine forests and the Siete Tazas ("Seven Cups") waterfalls that pour from ancient basaltic rocks on the Río Claro. The Ríos Campo, Toro and Radal flow along the park's eastern boundary.
CLIMATE: Mediterranean-montane. Warm, dry summers; cold, snowy winters.
VEGETATION: Deciduous forest with Roble, Hualo, Coigüe and Ñirre. Avellano, Laurel, Long-leafed Mañio, Quillay, Litre, Peumo. Cacti and Chagual on arid slopes. Cordilleran Cypress at higher elevations.
BIRDS: Torrent Duck, Andean Condor, Peregrine Falcon, Black-chested Buzzard-Eagle, White-tailed Kite, Variable Hawk, Magellanic Woodpecker, Burrowing Parrot, Austral Parakeet, Chilean Pigeon, Chilean Mockingbird, Austral Thrush.
MAMMALS: Llaca, Monito del Monte, Pudu, Puma, Colocolo, Kodkod, Culpeo Fox, Chilla Fox, Molina's Hog-nosed Skunk.

REPTILES: Thin Tree, Shining and Chilean Lizard, Chilean Iguana, Long-tailed Racer.

AMPHIBIANS: Chile Four-eyed Frog, Spiny-chest Frog *(Alsodes hugoi)*.

SERVICES: CONAF visitor center, picnic area, hiking trails. Privately-owned campground and hosteria (hotel). Entry fee.

Vilches–Altos del Lircay Nature Reserve

LOCATION: 41 mi (66 km) e of Talca; 27 mi (44 km) s of San Clemente.

TOTAL AREA: 64 sq mi (167 sq km).

TERRAIN: Forested valley of the Río Lircay in the Andean precordillera.

CLIMATE: Mediterranean.

VEGETATION: Hualo, Raulí, Laurel, Arrayán, Cordilleran Cypress.

BIRDS: Andean Condor, Burrowing Parrot, Magellanic Woodpecker, California Quail.

REPTILES: Southern Grumbler, Buerger's Lizard, Long-tailed Racer.

AMPHIBIANS: Grey Four-eyed Frog, Concepción Arunco Toad.

ARTHROPODS: Tarantula.

SERVICES: All day trek to the basaltic El Enladrillado plateau. Horseback riding, kayaking. Archaeological site. Pets and fires not allowed. Entry fee.

OTHER RESERVES IN MAULE: Stands of rare and endangered tree species can be seen at the EL MORRILLO NATURE SANCTUARY, FEDERICO ALBERT NATIONAL PARK and the LOS BELLOTOS DEL MELADOS, LOS QUEULES, and LOS RUILES National Reserves.

BIOBÍO REGION

Nevados de Chillán Biological Corridor

Nevados de Chillán is located about 250 mi (400 km) s of Santiago; 25 mi (40 km) e of Chillán. The entire area has been subject to intensive logging, the introduction of non-native trees and mammals, land privatization and construction of hydroelectric dams and natural gas pipelines. The Nature Conservancy and its Chilean partners are attempting to connect existing reserves such as Huemules del Niblinto and Laguna de Laja with private properties to allow forest regeneration and free movement of native wildlife.

Los Huemules del Niblinto Reserve

LOCATION: In the Andes e of Chillán and s of Nevados de Chillán and Río Ñuble.

TOTAL AREA: 37 sq mi (96 sq km).

CLIMATE: Mediterranean–montane. Warm dry summers; cool, wet winters with snow at higher elevations.

TERRAIN: Forested river valleys and ravines in the Andean precordillera. Río Neblinto originates in the Nevados de Chillán, an active volcano that rises to 10,538 ft (3212 m).

VEGETATION: Second-growth woodland with deciduous *Nothofagus*, Ulmo, Guindo Santo, Maitén, Lleuque and Radal enano *(Orites myrtodea)*. Northernmost Araucaria groves. Bamboo, Puya, Mitique, Copihue, orchids. Wet meadows *(mallines)* with dense, high grass. Cordilleran Cypress in the mountains.

BIRDS: 49 species including Andean Condor, Chilean Hawk, Magellanic Woodpecker, Chilean Pigeon, Rufous-legged Owl, Green-backed Firecrown, Thorn-tailed Rayadito, White-crested Elaenia.

MAMMALS: 26 species, including the ENDANGERED Huemul (an estimated 60 individuals in the reserve), Monito del Monte, Culpeo, Chilla, Puma, Kodkod, Colocolo, Molina's Hog-nosed Skunk, Grison, Pudu, Viscacha, Long-haired Akodont, Olivaceous Akodont, Bridge's Degu, and introduced rabbits.

REPTILES: Painted Tree and Thin Tree Lizard, High Mountain Lizard, Southern Grumbler, Long-tailed Racer, Chilean Slender Snake.

AMPHIBIANS: Sapo Hermoso *(Telmatobufo venustus)*, seen in 1999 for the first time in 100 years. Warty Toad.

SERVICES: Food and lodging in Chillán.

Laguna del Laja National Park

LOCATION: In the Andes; 132 mi (212 km) se of Concepción; 53 mi (86 km) e of Los Ángeles on the unpaved Antuco road.

TOTAL AREA: 45 sq mi (116 sq km).

CLIMATE: Warm, dry summers; 85 in (2170 mm) of rain and snow, most in winter.

TERRAIN: Andean lake edged with lava flows from Volcán Antuco (11,762 ft/3585 m).
BIRDS: Chestnut-throated Huet-huet, Spectacled Duck, Aplomado Falcon, Andean Condor, Mountain Caracara, Great Shrike-Tyrant, Scale-throated Earthcreeper, Yellow-bridled Finch.
REPTILES: Buerger's Lizard, *Liolaemus chillanensis, L. araucaniensis, L. hermannunezi, L. lineomaculatus, L. kriegi, Phymaturus vociferator, Diplolaemus sexcinctus,* Chile Slender Snake.
AMPHIBIANS: Grey Four-eyed Frog.
SERVICES: Trails. Entry fee.

ARAUCANÍA REGION
Nahuelbuta National Park

LOCATION: In the Coastal Cordillera, 83 mi (132 km) nw of Temuco; 22 mi (35 km) w of Angol via unpaved road.
TOTAL AREA: 26 sq mi (68 sq km).
TERRAIN: Mountains of the Nahuelbuta Range; highest peak is Piedra el Águila at 5248 ft (1600 m).
CLIMATE: Mediterranean. Warm summers. Long rainy season; annual rainfall 39–59 in (1000–1500 mm); snow in mountains.
VEGETATION: Mixed forest with Araucaria (some over 1000 years old), Lenga, Coigüe, Ñirre, Canelo, Notro, Colihue bamboo.
BIRDS: Chilean Tinamou, White-throated Hawk, Rufous-tailed Hawk (rare), Chilean Hawk, Rufous-legged Owl, Green-backed Firecrown, Striped Woodpecker, Magellanic Woodpecker, Chilean Mockingbird, Slender-billed Parakeet, Austral Parakeet, Dark-bellied Cinclodes, Correndera Pipit, Black-throated Huet-huet, Chucao, Ochre-flanked and Magellanic Tapaculo, White-throated Treerunner, Thorn-tailed Rayadito, Plain-mantled Tit-Spinetail, Tufted Tit-Tyrant, Patagonian Tyrant, Fire-eyed Diucon, Patagonian Sierra-Finch, Austral Blackbird.
MAMMALS: Puma, Pudu, Darwin's Fox.
REPTILES: Southern Grumbler, Chile Lizard, Cyan Lizard, Wreath Lizard, Painted Tree Lizard, Thin Tree Lizard, Long-tailed Racer, Chilean Slender Snake.

AMPHIBIANS: Darwin's Frog, Rosy Ground Frog, Nahuelbuta Ground Frog, Chile Four-eyed Frog, Helmeted Water Toad, Grey Wood Frog, Banded Wood Frog.
SERVICES: Campsites, picnic area, restrooms. Marked hiking and horseback riding trails. No food or lodging in park. Entry fee.

Conguillio–Los Paraguas National Park

Paraguas means "umbrellas," referring to the shape of mature Araucaria trees.

LOCATION: In the Andes, 93 mi (148 km) ne of Temuco. Laguna Captrén entry is 17 mi (28 km) se of Curacautin; main entry at Lago Conguillio is 3 mi (5 km) beyond that point. A dirt road in the park continues south for 18 mi (30 km) to Melipeuco.
TERRAIN: Lakes, lagoons, rivers and old-growth Araucaria forest in the midst of lava flows from the active Volcán Llaima that rises to 10,250 ft (3125 m). Lava flows created dams on many of the rivers, creating Lago Conguillio, Laguna Captrén, Laguna Verde and Laguna Arcoiris (Rainbow Lake).
CLIMATE: Rainy temperate with Mediterranean influence. Annual precipitation is 78–98 in (2000–2500 mm), with snow in winter. Average temperature is 59°F (15°C) in summer; 43°F (6°C) in winter.
VEGETATION: Araucaria trees (some over 1200 years old) and old-growth Coigüe and Lenga. Ferns and grasses are colonizing the more recent lava flows.
BIRDS: Ashy-headed Goose, Andean Duck, Speckled Teal, Flying Steamer-Duck, Pied-

billed Grebe, Plumbeous Rail, Southern Caracara, White-throated Hawk, Magellanic Woodpecker, Rufous-tailed Plantcutter, Chucao, Ochre-flanked Tapaculo.

MAMMALS: Puma, Kodkod, Culpeo Fox.

REPTILES: Painted Tree Lizard, Thin Tree Lizard, Leopard Grumbler, Chile Slender Snake.

AMPHIBIANS: Darwin's Frog.

TRAILS: LAS ARAUCARIAS trail from the main entry has informative placards placed along the forest trail (allow one hour). The 3-mi (5 km) LOS CARPINTEROS trail from the main entry winds through Araucaria, Coigüe and Lenga forest to Laguna Captrén, passing a giant Araucaria whose trunk diameter is 6.5 ft (2 m). The one-mile (2-km) LAGUNA CAPTRÉN trail encircles the lake and allows for birdwatching and fly fishing. The 6-mi (10-km) SIERRA NEVADA trail leads through forested areas to a ridge for views of Lago Conguillio, Volcán Llaima and glaciers (allow 5 to 6 hours). A short trail from the park road leads to an old colonial house near the LAGUNA ARCOIRIS. The SENDERO DE LOS GLACIARES extends a short distance up the slopes of Volcán Llaima. LAS VERTIENTES trail climbs past an area of subterranean springs to Truful–Truful ("Spring to Spring") where an interpretive center describes the area's geology and hydrology.

SERVICES: Visitor center, campsites, cabins, market, restrooms, picnic area, boat rental, first aid station and ski area (winter).

NEARBY PARKS: MALALCAHUELLO NATIONAL RESERVE, lies n of Conguillio within sight of Volcán Lonquimay. TOLHUACA NATIONAL PARK, is 21 mi (34 km) n of Curacautín.

Villarica National Park

LOCATION: About 5 mi (8 km) se of Pucón; 75 mi (120 km) se of Temuco.

TOTAL AREA: 243 sq mi (630 sq km).

TERRAIN: Forests, caves, rivers, waterfalls. Volcán Villarica rises to 9338 ft (2847 m).

CLIMATE: Warm summers with 70°F (22°C) temperatures. Cold winters. Annual precipitation is 98–137 in (2500–3500 mm).

VEGETATION: Araucaria and Lenga in the higher elevations; Raulí, Coigüe, Hualo and Long-leafed Mañío in the lower sectors.

BIRDS: Great Grebe, Chiloe Wigeon, Black-headed Duck, Torrent Duck, Red-gartered Coot, Black-chested Buzzard-Eagle, Chilean Hawk, Cinereous Harrier, Peregrine Falcon, Slender-billed Parakeet, Magellanic Woodpecker.

MAMMALS: Monito del Monte, Puma, Pudu, Chilla, Culpeo, Coypu, Grison, Molina's Hog-nosed Skunk, Southern River Otter.

REPTILES: Painted Tree Lizard, Chilean Lizard, *Liolaemus araucaniensis*, Chilean Slender Snake.

AMPHIBIANS: Darwin's Frog.

SERVICES: Campsites, restrooms, thermal pools, trails. Guided treks to the snow-rimmed crater of Volcán Villarica.

NEARBY PARKS: HUERQUEHUE NATIONAL PARK, located 22 mi (35 km) ne of Pucón, has waterfalls, lagoons, forests of old-growth Coigüe and Araucaria. Birdlife includes Andean Duck, Chucao Tapaculo, Magellanic Woodpecker, Black-throated Huethuet. Tours are also available at the privately-owned CAÑI SANCTUARY, which safeguards old-growth Araucaria and Coigüe forests.

LOS LAGOS REGION
Puyehue National Park

LOCATION: 188 mi (189 km) ne of Puerto Montt; 50 mi (80 km) e of Osorno.

TOTAL AREA: 386 sq mi (1000 sq km).

TERRAIN: Rugged montane wilderness created by glaciation and volcanic activity. Dense rainforests, rivers and waterfalls.

CLIMATE: Cool and rainy. Daytime high summer temperatures average 64°F (18°C); winter highs average 46°F (8°C).

VEGETATION: Lowlands have dense stands of Coigüe, Ulmo, Olivillo and Tineo with an understory of mosses, ferns, lichens and *Chusquea* bamboo, and wetland meadows *(mallines)* with tall grass, rushes, Ñirre and Guaitecas Cypress. Higher up there is Tepa, Mañío, Magellanic Coigüe and Lenga, which is beautiful in autumn color.

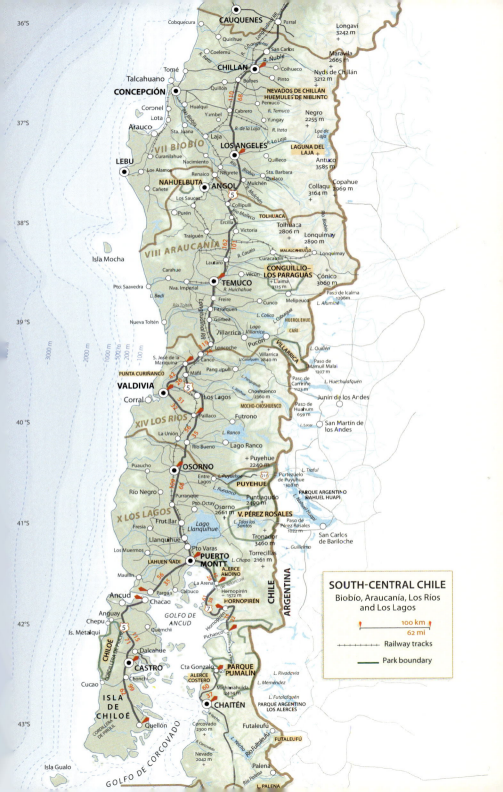

BIRDS: Chilean Tinamou, Great Grebe, Flying Steamer-Duck, Torrent Duck, Spectacled Duck, Rufous-tailed Hawk, White-throated Hawk, Chilean Hawk, Magellanic and Striped Woodpecker, Slender-billed Parakeet, Austral Parakeet, Chilean Pigeon, Green-backed Firecrown, Austral Pygmy Owl, Black-throated Huet-huet, Magellanic, Chucao and Ochre-flanked Tapaculo, Rufous-tailed Plantcutter, Bar-winged and Dark-bellied Cinclodes, White-throated Treerunner, White-browed Ground-Tyrant, Patagonian Tyrant, Tufted Tit-Tyrant, Des Murs' Wiretail, Yellow-bridled Finch, Patagonian Sierra-Finch, Black-chinned Siskin.

MAMMALS: Puma, Chilla, Grison, Coypu, Kodkod, Molina's Hog-nosed Skunk.

BUTTERFLIES: Eroessa Butterfly, Little Yellow Terias, Bicolor Hairstreak, Starry Satyr, Yramea Fritillary, Chilean Skipper.

REPTILES: Painted Tree Lizard, Cyan Lizard, Chile Slender Snake.

AMPHIBIANS: Patagonian Toad, Darwin's Frog, Emerald Forest Frog, Chile Four-eyed Frog, Grey Wood Frog, Banded Wood Frog.

WITHIN THE PARK: The ANTICURA sector has trails through the forest for wildlife observation; the highway to Argentina skirts the lowland rainforest and Río Gol Gol. The CONAF office, campsites and other services are at AGUAS CALIENTES. The ski slopes on Volcán Casablanca (6527 ft, or 1990 m) are in the ANTILLANCA sector, which also has birding, geological and botanical sites.

SERVICES: Rustic cabins and hotels, campsites, picnic areas, restrooms, hiking trails, hot springs and a ski center (winter).

Vicente Pérez Rosales National Park

LOCATION: About 51 mi (82 km) ne of Puerto Montt. A car ferry crosses Lago Todos los Santos linking Petrohué with Puella and Bariloche in the Argentine lake district.

TOTAL AREA: 969 sq mi (2510 sq km).

TERRAIN: Evergreen rainforest, snow-capped volcanoes, deep blue lakes carved by glaciation, and the Saltos de Petrohué that cut into and cascade over black volcanic rock.

CLIMATE: Cool and rainy; annual precipitation is 98–157 in (2500–4000 mm); snow in the higher elevations.

VEGETATION: Gallery forests around Laguna Cayutué contain Canelo, Coigüe, Patagua and Pitra. The shores of Lago Todos Los Santos have stands of Olivillo mixed with Ulmo, Tiaca and Coigüe. At 650–3280 ft (200–1000 m) are the old-growth Coigüe forests with Ulmo, Tepa and Tineo and an understory of Tepu, Mutilla, Copihue and bamboo. Alerce occurs above 3000 ft (900 m). Lenga occupies the upper tier of tree growth and appears in dwarf form at the snowline. Trees around the Salto de Petrohué are placarded with common and scientific names.

BIRDS: 100 species, including Torrent Duck, Flying Steamer-Duck, Ashy-headed Goose, Great Grebe, Red-gartered Coot, Black-chested Buzzard-Eagle, Southern Caracara, Green-backed Firecrown, Chucao Tapaculo, Magellanic Woodpecker, Des Murs' Wiretail.

MAMMALS: 30 species, including Monito del Monte, Long-nosed Caenolestid, Kodkod, Pudu, Geoffroy's Cat, Puma, Chilla Fox, Culpeo Fox, Grison, Southern River Otter.

REPTILES: Painted Tree Lizard, Cyan Lizard, Chile Slender Snake.

AMPHIBIANS: Patagonian Toad, Darwin's Frog, Emerald Forest Frog, Chile Four-eyed Frog, Grey Wood Frog, Banded Wood Frog.

FISH: Rainbow and Brown Trout.

SERVICES AND ACTIVITIES: Rangers, visitor

center, trails. Fishing, swimming, kayaking, rafting, skiing, mountaineering, trekking, thermal baths. Entry fee.

Isla Chiloé and Chiloé National Park

When the Mapuches drove the Spanish north of the Río Biobío in 1598, a small colony of 200 Spaniards on Chiloé were cut off from the mainland. The colony was isolated for almost 250 years; throughout the 17th century, only one ship a year brought supplies to the island from Lima. Intermarriage with the native Mapuches, Caucahues and Chonos resulted in a unique mestizo culture that is still very much alive on Chiloé.

LOCATION: 56 mi (90 km) sw of Puerto Montt; access is via road and a ferry across Canal Chacao. The national park lies in the nw part of the island. Access is a secondary road off the Pan American Highway, which ends its long journey through the Americas at Quellón at the southern tip of Chiloé.

TOTAL PARK AREA: 166 sq mi (431 sq km).

TERRAIN: Cordillera de Piuche and Cordillera de Pirulil rise in the western part of the island. They slope gradually into the eastern valleys and wetlands, and finally slip beneath the waters of the Golfo Ancud.

CLIMATE: The Pacific seacoast is cool, with strong winds and a heavy annual rainfall of 120 in (3000 mm). The eastern sector, which is sheltered by the Coastal Range, has less rain and wind, frequent overcast, and an average temperature of about 50°F (10°C).

VEGETATION: Evergreen forest with Olivillo, Coigüe, Luma, Arrayán, Tepu and Alerce, the latter growing in isolated stands above 1950 ft (600 m). The eastern sector has some native forest and scrubland. Land around the settlements has been planted to orchards and crops.

BIRDS: (CASTRO) Chimango Caracara, Black and Turkey Vulture, Rock Dove, Green-backed Firecrown, Blue-and-white Swallow, Fire-eyed Diucon, White-crested Elaenia, Rufous-tailed Plantcutter, Common Diuca-Finch, House Sparrow. (FOREST) Chucao Tapaculo, Black-throated Huet-huet, Des Murs' Wiretail, Slender-billed Parakeet. (WETLANDS) Black-necked Swan, Flightless Steamer-Duck, Red-gartered Coot, Great Grebe, Trudeau's Tern, Chilean Flamingo, Black-faced Ibis, Cocoi Heron, Snowy Egret, Great Egret, Neotropic Cormorant, Southern Lapwing, Ringed Kingfisher. (COASTAL AND OFFSHORE) Black-browed Albatross, Southern Giant-Petrel, Southern Fulmar, Cape Petrel, Pink-footed Shearwater, Humboldt and Magellanic Penguin, Red-legged, Guanay and Rock Cormorant, Wilson's Phalarope, Baird's Sandpiper, Whimbrel, Greater Yellowlegs, Chilean Skua, Dolphin, Kelp Gull, Brown-hooded Gull, Franklin's Gull, South American Tern.

MAMMALS: Monito del Monte, Long-nosed Caenolestid, Darwin's Fox, Pudu, Marine Otter, Southern Sea Lion, Peale's Dolphin.

REPTILES: Painted Tree Lizard, Southern Grumbler, Chilean Slender Snake.

AMPHIBIANS: Marbled, Grey and Nibaldo's Wood Frog, Helmeted Water Toad, Emerald Forest Frog, Chiloé Ground Frog, Rosy Ground Frog, Valdivia Ground Frog, Darwin's Frog, Spiny-chest Frog.

SERVICES: Campsites at CHEPU (n park entry) and the park ranger post; hostel at Anguay. A rough coastal trail leads south to near the Isla Metalqui sea lion colony. Campsites and guard post at CUCAO (south park entry). Trails run north and south along the coastal sand dunes. Entry fee.

Alerce Andino National Park

LOCATION: 23 mi (46 km) e of Puerto Montt.

TOTAL AREA: 152 sq mi (393 sq km).

TERRAIN: Rugged montane wilderness, with lakes and Alerce forests. Highest peak is Volcán Calbuco rising to 6569 ft (2003 m).

CLIMATE: Rainy and cool. Annual precipitation is 129–177 in (3300–4500 mm); snow in winter. Temperature averages 59°F (15°C) in summer, 44°F (7°C) in winter.

VEGETATION: Virgin forest above 1300 ft (400 m); Alerce, Coigüe de Chiloé, Magellanic Coigüe, Lenga, Mañío, Tineo, Canelo and Tepa, lianas, mosses, and bamboo.

BIRDS: Upland Goose, Chiloe Wigeon,

Condor, Chilean Hawk, Magellanic Woodpecker, Black-throated Huet-huet, Ringed Kingfisher, Chilean Pigeon.
MAMMALS: Monito del Monte, Pudu, Chilla Fox, Puma, Kodkod, Molina's Hog-nosed Skunk, Viscacha.
REPTILES: Southern Grumbler, Painted Tree Lizard, Thin Tree Lizard, Cyan Lizard, Chile Slender Snake.
AMPHIBIANS: Patagonian Toad, Darwin's Frog, Emerald Forest Frog, Chile Four-eyed Frog, Grey Wood Frog, Banded Wood Frog.
FISH: Peladilla (Farionela), Percatrucha, and introduced Brown and Rainbow Trout.
SERVICES: Rangers, nature center, refugios. Trails are suited for hikers in good physical condition. Four-wheel drive recommended. No food or hotels in the park. Entry fee.
NEARBY PARKS: HORNOPIREN NATIONAL PARK in the Patagonian Andes of Palena Province, 65 mi (105 km) from Puerto Montt, offers a magnificent forested landscape with lakes, volcanoes, rocky areas and glaciers.

Parque Pumalín

American Douglas Tompkins, founder of the outdoor retail company North Face and longtime devotee of the Patagonian Andes, purchased 1158 sq mi (300,000 ha) of land in Palena Province in the 1990s. In 2002 he donated his land to the Pumalín Foundation with the intent of ultimately turning the area into a Chilean national park.

LOCATION: Palena Province; 88 mi (142 km) se of Puerto Montt; 36 mi (58 km) n of Chaitén. A direct ferry from Puerto Montt to Caleta Gonzalo operates year round. In summer, Caleta Gonzalo can be accessed by ferry from Hornopiren, the rest of the year via the Austral Highway from Chaitén.
TOTAL AREA: 1158 sq mi (3000 sq km).
TERRAIN: Rugged montane wilderness, with river valleys and pristine forests extending up to the glaciers of the Patagonian Andes.
CLIMATE: Cool. Annual rainfall is 98–157 in (2500–4000 mm); snow at higher elevations.
VEGETATION: Siempreverde forest with Alerce, Lenga, Guaitecas and Cordilleran Cypress.
BIRDS: 71 bird species including Magellanic Penguin, Neotropic, Guanay and Imperial Cormorant, Ashy-headed Goose, Torrent Duck, Black-necked Swan, Black-faced Ibis, Chilean Flamingo, Condor, Turkey Vulture, Variable Hawk, Cinereous Harrier, Chimango Caracara, Southern Caracara, White-tailed Kite, Skimmer, Dolphin Gull, Kelp Gull, Franklin's Gull, Southern Lapwing, Magellanic Woodpecker, Chilean Flicker, Green-backed Firecrown, Austral Parakeet, Slender-billed Parakeet, Austral Pygmy Owl, Chilean Swallow, Chucao, Black-throated Huet-huet, Thorn-tailed Rayadito, Dark-bellied Cinclodes, White-throated Treerunner, Dark-faced Ground-Tyrant, Austral Negrito, Fire-eyed Diucon, White-crested Elaenia, House Wren, Austral Thrush, Grey-hooded and Mourning Sierra-Finch, Grassland Yellow-Finch.
MAMMALS: (IN THE PARK) Chilean Mouse-eared Myotis, Big-eared Brown Bat. Monito del Monte, Culpeo Fox, Grison, Molina's Hog-nosed Skunk, Puma, Kodkod, Huemul, Pudu, Long-tailed Colilargo, Valdivian Long-clawed Mole Mouse, Olive-colored Akodont, Southern Pericote, Large-footed Irenomys, Coypu, Southern River Otter. Introduced Rabbit, Hare, Mink, Wild Boar. (GOLFO DE ANCUD) Southern Sea Lion, Marine Otter, Chilean Dolphin, Peale's Dolphin, Orca.
REPTILES: Painted Tree Lizard.
AMPHIBIANS: Patagonian Toad, Grey Wood Frog, Marbled Wood Frog, Nibaldo's Wood Frog, Banded Wood Frog, Chiloé Ground Frog, Chile Four-eyed Frog, Darwin's Frog.
TRAILS: SENDERO DE LOS ALERCES offers an easy hike to stands of old-growth Alerce. SENDERO CASCADA is a 3-hour hike through the forest to a waterfall. SENDERO TRONADOR is a 1.5 hour ascent to a suspended bridge overlooking a mountain lake and waterfall.
SERVICES: Campsites, cabins, visitor center, cafeteria, handicraft mart, picnic area at Caleta Gonzalo. Fly fishing. Boat excursions to the sea lion rookery. No entry fee.
ADVISORY: Bring water bottles, flashlight, rain gear and equipment designed for rain.

AISÉN REGION

Laguna San Rafael National Park and UNESCO World Biosphere Reserve

LOCATION: East of the Taito Peninsula and north of the Golfo de Penas. Boat access.
TOTAL AREA: 6725 sq mi (17,420 sq km). One of Chile's largest parks. Includes most of the Northern Ice Field.
CLIMATE: Oceanic cold temperate to polar due to elevation; rain in lowlands throughout the year; snow on peaks in winter.
TERRAIN: Deep fjords, marine channels, islands, glaciers, snowfields and mountains.
VEGETATION: Guaitecas Cypress, Coigüe, Coigüe de Chiloé, Coigüe de Magallanes, Lenga, Mañio, Canelo, Notro, Calafate, Fuchsia, Chaura and Tepa. Bogs and marsh vegetation at Laguna San Rafael.
BIRDS: Black-browed Albatross, Common Diving-Petrel, Fuegian Snipe, Magellanic Oystercatcher, Black-necked Swan, Kelp Goose, Flightless Steamer-Duck, Flying Steamer-Duck, Yellow-billed Pintail, Imperial Cormorant, Neotropic Cormorant, Kelp Gull, Chilean Skua, South American Tern, Condor, Turkey Vulture, Black-chested Buzzard-Eagle, Chucao Tapaculo, Black-throated Huet-huet, Green-backed Firecrown, Dark-bellied Cinclodes, Patagonian Sierra-Finch.
MAMMALS: Pudu, Huemul, Puma, Kodkod, Culpeo, Marine Otter, Southern Sea Lion.
ATTRACTIONS: San Quintín and San Rafael Glaciers. Laguna San Rafael icebergs. Mount San Valentín rising to 13,315 ft (4058 m).
REPTILES: Fitzinger's Lizard, *Liolaemus lineomaculatus*, Darwin's and Bibron's Grumbler.
AMPHIBIANS: Marbled Wood Frog, Grey Four-eyed Frog, Darwin's Frog, Spiny-chest Frog *(Alsodes australis, A. monticola)*.
SERVICES: CONAF office and ranger posts. Rustic campsites, restrooms. Boat ramp. Hiking permits. Entry fee.

Queulat National Park

LOCATION: Patagonian Andes of Aisén, 112 mi (180 km) s of Chaitén, Los Lagos; 103 mi (165 km) n of Coihaique.
TOTAL AREA: 595 sq mi (1541 sq km).
CLIMATE: Oceanic cold temperate; annual precipitation to 160 in (4000 mm); winter snow.
TERRAIN: Mountainous, with deep glacial valleys, rocky slopes, lakes, waterfalls, thermal baths. Highest peak is Alto Nevado at 8383 ft (2555 m).
VEGETATION: Siempreverde and Patagonian Andean forest types, with Lenga, Coigüe de Magallanes, Coigüe de Chiloé, Maitén enano, Michay blanco, Tineo, Tepa, Luma, Canelo, Coicopihue, ferns, lianas, bamboo.
BIRDS: Upland Goose, Black-necked Swan, Andean Condor, Austral Parakeet, Ringed Kingfisher, Magellanic Woodpecker, Chilean pigeon, Chucao, Black-throated Huet-huet.
MAMMALS: Pudu, Kodkod, Puma, Culpeo, Southern River Otter, Southern Sea Lion.
REPTILES: Fitzinger's Lizard, *Liolaemus lineomaculatus, Liolaemus bibroni*, Darwin's Grumbler, Bibron's Grumbler.
AMPHIBIANS: Darwin's Frog, Grey Four-eyed Frog, Marbled Wood Frog, Spiny-chest Frog *(Alsodes australis, A. coppingeri, A. monticola, A. verrucosus)*.
SERVICES: Visitor center, campsites, potable cold water, trails to the lakes, waterfalls and glaciers. Rustic cabin at Ventisquero entry; Puyuhuapi Lodge adjacent to park.
NEARBY RESERVES: LAGO ROSELOT, LAGO CARLOTA, LAGO LAS TORRES and MAÑIHUALES NATIONAL RESERVES contain Siempreverde forest. Birds include Condor, Black-chested Buzzard-Eagle, Chucao Tapaculo, Austral Thrush, Austral Blackbird, Austral Parakeet. Mammals include Puma, Culpeo, Coypu, Pudu, Humboldt's Hog-nosed Skunk, Pichi, Long-tailed Colilargo and introduced Red Deer, American Mink and Old World Rabbit.

Río Simpson National Reserve

LOCATION: Aisén; entry at the 37 km post on the Coihaique–Puerto Aisén highway.
TOTAL AREA: 160 sq mi (416 sq km).
CLIMATE: Oceanic cold temperate; rainy.
TERRAIN: Rugged; deep valleys and ravines; peaks to 6165 ft (100–1880 m).
VEGETATION: Siempreverde forest type, with

Coigüe, Tepa, Canelo, Notro and Fuchsia. Matorral and deciduous forest with Ñirre, Lenga and Calafate at higher elevations.
BIRDS: Condor, Black-chested Buzzard-Eagle, Kestrel, Ringed Kingfisher, Chucao, Austral Thrush, Austral Blackbird, Austral Parakeet.
MAMMALS: Humboldt's Hog-nosed Skunk, Puma, Culpeo, Pudu, Coypu, introduced Old World Rabbit and American Mink.
REPTILES: Magellanic Lizard, Fitzinger's Lizard, Darwin's and Bibron's Grumbler.
AMPHIBIANS: Marbled Wood Frog, Grey Four-eyed Frog, Darwin's Frog, Spiny-chest Frog *(Alsodes australis, A. coppingeri, A. monticola, A. verrucosus).*
INSECTS: Midges. Carry repellent.
SERVICES: Famous for trout and salmon fly fishing. Nature center. Campsites, restrooms, showers and refugio.
NEARBY ATTRACTIONS: East of Coihaique are the COIHAIQUE and TRAPANANDA RESERVES and DOS LAGUNAS NATURAL MONUMENT. Vegetation is transitional between the deciduous forests of the Patagonian Andes and the grasslands of the Patagonian steppe. Fauna includes Black-necked Swan, Red-gartered Coot, Black-chested Buzzard-Eagle, Southern Caracara, Magellanic Woodpecker, Chilean Flicker, Austral Parakeet, Chucao Tapaculo, Austral Thrush, Austral Blackbird, Puma, Culpeo Fox, Humboldt's Hog-nosed Skunk and Pichi.
CERRO CASTILLO NATIONAL RESERVE, located south of Coihaique, contains cold, rugged steppe dominated by basalt-pinnacled Cerro Castillo at 7612 ft (2320 m). The reserve is mainly deciduous Lenga forest. Birdlife includes Condor, Black-chested Buzzard-Eagle, Austral Parakeet, and Austral Thrush. Mammals include Huemul, Guanaco, Geoffroy's Cat, Puma, Culpeo, Pichi, Humboldt's Hog-nosed Skunk, Long-tailed Colilargo.

Lago Jeinimenii National Reserve
LOCATION: 40 mi (65 km) s of Chile Chico.
TOTAL AREA: 622 sq mi (1611 sq km).
CLIMATE: Cold steppe.

VEGETATION: Patagonian steppe vegetation and deciduous forest with Lenga, Ñirre, Calafate, Chaura and Notro.
BIRDS: Andean Condor, Black-chested Buzzard-Eagle, American Kestrel, Ringed Kingfisher, Chucao, Austral Thrush, Austral Blackbird, Austral Parakeet.
MAMMALS: Humboldt's Hog-nosed Skunk, Pichi, Chilla Fox, Puma, Geoffroy's Cat, Huemul, Guanaco, Long-tailed Colilargo, Patagonian Laucha.
REPTILES: Bibron's Grumbler, Magellanic Lizard, *Liolaemus bibroni, L. lineomaculatus, L. kolenghi, L. scolaroi, L. zullyi.*
AMPHIBIANS: Grey Four-eyed Frog and the rare *Atelognathus jeinimenensis.*
OTHER ATTRACTIONS: CUEVA DE LAS MANOS (Cave of the Hands) in the ne park sector has cave paintings of Tehuelche origin.
SERVICES: Campsites with restrooms and potable water. Trails and guard posts.
OTHER RESERVES: LAGO COCHRANE (TAMANGO) NATIONAL RESERVE is located 3.5 mi (6 km) ne of Cochrane. This small, lakeside reserve is forested with Lenga, Ñirre, Magellanic Coigüe and Notro. Many of the birds and mammals of Lago Jeinimenii are also found here. Services in the reserve include campsites, refugios, restrooms, showers, hiking trails and ranger guided treks in springtime to view huemuls.

Bernardo O'Higgins National Park
LOCATION: Canal Baker, Aisén, to Puerto Natales, Magallanes; 48°S–51°38′S. Access is by boat from Pto. Natales or Pto. Montt.
TOTAL AREA: 13,625 sq mi (35,259 sq km); the largest protected area of Chile.
TERRAIN: Deep fiords, dense rainforests, and spectacular glaciers. Includes most of the Southern Ice Field and the PÍO XI (BRÜGGEN) GLACIER, the largest glacier of the South Hemisphere outside of Antarctica. Pío XI's ice face is 250 ft (75 m) high, and ice falling from the glacier into the fjord can generate waves over 33 ft (10 m) high.
CLIMATE: Cold and rainy year round. Annual precipitation 141–157 in (3600–4000 mm).

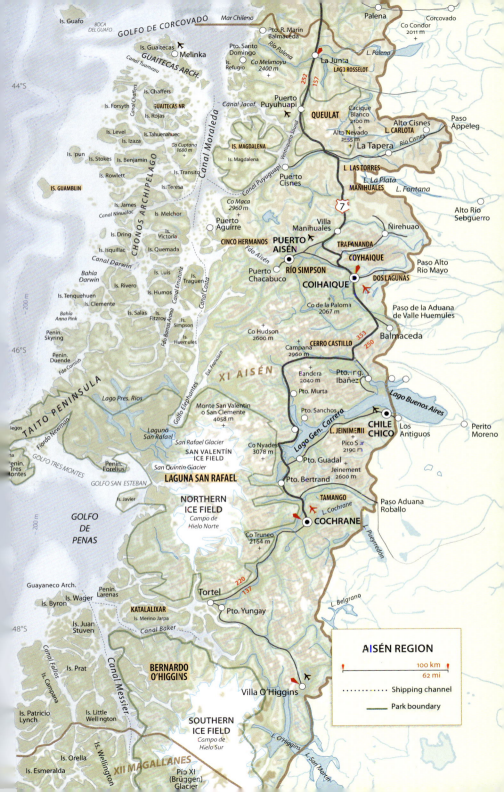

Annual median temperature is 48°F (9°C).
VEGETATION: Magellanic Coigüe forest, with Magellanic moorland and bogs in the lowlands; Lenga, Ñirre, *Gunnera*, fachine and *Blechnum* ferns at higher elevations.
BIRDS: Magellanic Penguin, Black-browed Albatross, Southern Giant-Petrel, Cape Petrel, Magellanic Diving-Petrel, Rock and Imperial Cormorant, Chilean Skua, South American Tern, Upland Goose, Crested Duck, Black-necked Swan, Condor, Turkey Vulture, Chucao Tapaculo, Ringed Kingfisher, Austral Thrush, Austral Parakeet, Green-backed Firecrown, Dark-bellied Cinclodes, Bar-winged Cinclodes, Black-chinned Siskin.
MAMMALS: Huemul, Kodkod, Puma, Long-tailed Colilargo. Marine Otter, Southern Sea Lion, Southern Fur Seal.
REPTILES: Fitzinger's Lizard, Magellanic Lizard, *Liolaemus lineomaculatus, L. escarchadosi, L. bibroni,* Darwin's and Bibron's Grumbler.
AMPHIBIANS: Grey Four-eyed Frog, Spiny-chest Frog *(Alsodes australis, A. verrucosus).*
SERVICES: No services in the park. CONAF guard posts at Villa O'Higgins and Caleta Tortel, and a fishing village at Puerto Eden.

MAGALLANES REGION
Punta Arenas
LOCATION: 53°09′S 70°55′W. Port city on the nw shore of the Strait of Magellan, across from Isla Grande de Tierra del Fuego.
TERRAIN: Punta Arenas ("Sandy Point") lies at the junction of the Patagonian Andean forests and the Patagonian steppe. Forested hills rise behind the town. A stony beach runs along the Strait of Magellan.
CLIMATE: Cool and windy; 40 in (1000 mm) of rain and snow.
VEGETATION: Fields, streams and riparian woodland lie on the town outskirts. To the east lie the flat, grassy pampas and wetlands. Forested areas to the sw contain Lenga, Ñirre, Magellanic Coigüe, Canelo and Notro.
BIRDS: (CITY) Chimango Caracara, Austral Thrush, Rock Dove, House Wren, Black-chinned Siskin, House Sparrow, Rufous-collared Sparrow. (WATERFRONT) Black-browed Albatross, Southern Giant-Petrel, Imperial and Rock Cormorant, Chilean Skua, Dolphin, Kelp and Brown-hooded Gull, South American Tern, Crested Duck, Yellow-billed Pintail, Correndera Pipit, Bar-winged Cinclodes. (WOODLAND, FIELDS) Tufted Tit-Tyrant, Fire-eyed Diucon, Austral Negrito, Dark-faced Ground-Tyrant, Thorn-tailed Rayadito, White-crested Elaenia, Patagonian Sierra-Finch, Grassland Yellow-Finch, Long-tailed Meadowlark. (AIRPORT ENVIRONS) Lesser Rhea, Black-necked Swan, Upland Goose, Chiloé Wigeon, Black-chested Buzzard-Eagle, Kestrel, Southern Caracara.
MAMMALS: Chilla Fox, Culpeo Fox, Woolly Akodont, Western Patagonian Laucha.
REPTILES: Magellanic Lizard.
AMPHIBIANS: Grey Four-eyed Frog, Patagonian Toad.
NEARBY RESERVES: LAGUNA DE LOS CISNES NATURAL MONUMENT lies across the Strait near Porvenir. Birds include Black-necked Swan, Coscoroba Swan, Flightless Steamer-Duck, Magellanic Plover, Austral Canastero.

LOS PINGUINOS NATURE RESERVE lies about 22 mi (35 km) n of Punta Arenas, access is by rubber boat excursion. Isla Marta and Isla Magdalena have Magellanic Penguin and cormorant colonies (Oct–Mar), a sea lion rookery, lighthouse and interpretive center describing early navigation of the Strait.

SENO OTWAY PENGUIN COLONY lies 40 mi (65 km) n of Punta Arenas. Fauna includes Magellanic Penguin (summer), Two-banded Plover, Southern Lapwing, White-rumped Sandpiper, Baird's Sandpiper, Whimbrel, Blackish Oystercatcher, Magellanic Oystercatcher, and Chilla Fox.

Torres del Paine National Park and UNESCO World Biosphere Reserve
LOCATION: 223 mi (360 km) nw of Punta Arenas on a partially paved road; 70 mi (113 km) n of Puerto Natales on gravel road.
TOTAL AREA: 1000 sq mi (2590 sq km).
TERRAIN: Spectacular scenery with grassy meadows, winding rivers, waterfalls, lakes,

forest, glaciers and the rugged, majestic granite pillars of Torres del Paine rising to 9184 ft (2800 m).
CLIMATE: Trans-Andean and polar due to elevation. Spring and summer offer the best weather and less variable conditions.
VEGETATION: Lenga and Magellanic Coigüe forest; grasses, Calafate, Fachine, orchids.
BIRDS: 105 species, including Lesser Rhea, Chilean Flamingo, Black-faced Ibis, Andean Condor, Southern Caracara, Black-chested Buzzard-Eagle, Black-necked Swan, Austral Parakeet, Upland Goose, Ashy-headed Goose, Red-breasted Meadowlark, Least Seedsnipe.
MAMMALS: 25 species, including Guanaco, Armadillo, Chilla, Culpeo, Puma.
REPTILES: Magellanic Lizard, Fitzinger's Lizard, *Liolaemus lineomaculatus*, *L. bibroni*, Darwin's Grumbler, Bibron's Grumbler.
AMPHIBIANS: Grey Four-eyed Frog, Spinychest Frog *(Alsodes australis, A. verrucosus)*.
SERVICES: Hotels, camps, refugios, fishing, mountain climbing, kayaking, rafting and wildlife observation. Clearly marked trails lead to Zapata, Dickson, Grey and Francés Glaciers, to the base of Torres del Paine, Lago Paine and Laguna Verde, and to many wonderful nearby sites. The PAINE CIRCUIT (for hardy hikers only) circles the Paine Massif; allow 7 to 10 days for the trek.

The Beagle Channel

LOCATION: The channel runs on an east-west axis at about 54°S latitude. It separates the shores of mainland s Chile and Tierra del Fuego from the islands to the south.
TERRAIN: Rugged mountainous fjords, with aretes, cirques, hanging valleys, tidewater glaciers, stony strands. The marine channel is about 150 mi (241 km) long and 3 mi (5 km) wide at its narrowest point.
CLIMATE: Cool to cold, with frequent drizzle and overcast throughout the year.
VEGETATION: Pristine Magellanic rainforest with Lenga, Magellanic Coigüe, Canelo, Notro, *Poa* grass, *Usnea* lichens, mistletoe, and Darwin's Bread. Many wildflowers and orchids in the warmer months. Sundews and hard cushion plants in boggy sites. *Macrocystis* kelp grows in the waters of coves and sheltered bays.

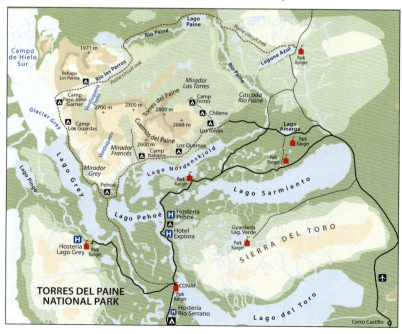

BEAGLE CHANNEL AND CAPE HORN 375

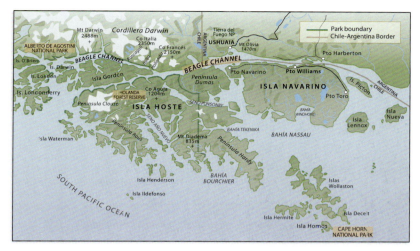

BIRDS: Magellanic Penguin, Black-browed Albatross, Southern Giant-Petrel, Common Diving-Petrel, Magellanic Diving-Petrel, Rock Cormorant, Imperial Cormorant, Kelp Goose, Upland Goose, Crested Duck, Flightless Steamer-Duck, Flying Steamer-Duck, Chilean Skua, Dolphin Gull, Kelp Gull, South American Tern, Condor, Turkey Vulture, Green-backed Firecrown, Austral Parakeet, Austral Thrush, Austral Negrito, Fire-eyed Diucon, Blackish Cinclodes, Dark-bellied Cinclodes, Bar-winged Cinclodes.

MAMMALS: Southern Sea Lion, Southern Fur Seal, Marine Otter, Spectacled Porpoise.

BUTTERFLIES: Common White Tatochila.

REPTILES: Magellanic Lizard, *L.sarmientoi*.

AMPHIBIANS: Patagonian Toad, Grey Four-eyed Frog.

MOLLUSKS/CRUSTACEANS: Chitons, Limpets, Giant Mussel, Sea Urchins, Centolla Crab.

OTHER ATTRACTIONS: ALBERTO DE AGOSTINI NATIONAL PARK, 80 mi (129 km) se of Punta Arenas, contains the Darwin Cordillera, its ice fields and tidewater glaciers that flow down into the Beagle Channel. The park is named after the Italian Salesian missionary, geographer and mountaineer Alberto María de Agostini (1893–1960) who climbed many peaks in this range. PUERTO WILLIAMS is a seldom-visited gem with abundant birdlife and some of the last Yahgan descendants.

Cape Horn National Park

LOCATION: Isla Hornos at 55°59′ S; the most southern point of South America.

TERRAIN: Small, high island with steep sea cliffs and a prominent headland.

CLIMATE: Cool to cold; subject to frequent storms and high winds.

VEGETATION: Magellanic moorland, with *Poa flabellata*, *Blechnum penna-marina*, *Gunnera magellanica*, *Gaultheria mucronata*, *Empetrum rubrum*, *Hebe elliptica*, *Berberis* sp., *Senecio* sp., *Acaena magellanica*, dwarf *Nothofagus antarctica*, and *Juncus* rushes. *Macrocystis* kelp fills the landing cove.

BIRDS: Magellanic Penguin, Plumbeous Rail, Striated Caracara, Turkey Vulture, Thorn-tailed Rayadito, Austral Thrush, Dark-bellied Cinclodes. (OFFSHORE) Wandering Albatross, Southern Royal Albatross, Black-browed Albatross, Grey-headed Albatross, Southern Giant-Petrel, Cape Petrel, White-chinned Petrel, Sooty Shearwater, Magellanic Diving-Petrel.

MAMMALS: Southern Sea Lion, Southern Fur Seal, Marine Otter.

SERVICES: A steep wooden staircase climbs from the rocky landing beach to the plateau. At the top is a meteorological station where the chief officer will often cachet passports. There is also a lovely wooden chapel, the impressive Albatross Monument and Cape Horn Captains' Monument.

GLOSSARY

altiplano. Geographical formation and unique ecosystem of the Andean intermontane basin that lies above 11,500 feet (3500 m) elevation.

anticyclone. A weather system with high atmospheric pressure at its center, around which air slowly circulates in a clockwise (Northern Hemisphere) or counterclockwise (Southern Hemisphere) direction, e.g., the Southeastern Pacific Anticyclone, which is associated with calm, dry weather over northern Chile.

aquatic. Relating to animals or plants that live or grow in or near water.

archipelago. A group of islands.

austral. Of or relating to the south, in particular the Southern Hemisphere, e.g., austral summer. Antonym for BOREAL, e.g., relating to the north.

blowhole. The nostril of a cetacean on the top of its head that is used for breathing and for ejecting air and vapor in what is called a "blow."

broad-leaved. Of a tree or plant having relatively wide, flat leaves rather than needles.

bowriding. The behavior in which a cetacean, usually a dolphin, swims at the front of a boat, surfing or riding on the vessel's pressure wave.

carnivore. A flesh-eating animal.

channel. A stretch of water between two landmasses that lie close to one another. In Chile, channel *(canal)* usually signifies a marine passage deep enough for ships.

circumpolar. Distributed around one of the geographic poles within polar latitudes, e.g., between 60°S–90°S or 60°N–90°N.

CITES. The Convention on International Trade in Endangered Species of Wild Fauna and Flora is an agreement between governments that regulates international trade in wild animals and plants. Species of concern are listed in three CITES Appendixes: Appendix I bans all international trade. Appendix II monitors and regulates international trade. Appendix III monitors trade bans of individual governments.

climate. The condition of the atmosphere or weather over a long period of time, e.g., a Mediterranean climate typically has warm, dry summers and moderately cool, wet winters.

cold-blooded. Having a body temperature that fluctuates with that of the environment.

CONAF. *Corporacion Nacional Forestal,* the Chilean Forestry Service.

continental shelf. The area of seabed around a continent where the sea is relatively shallow compared with the open ocean.

convergent evolution. The development of similar external characteristics in unrelated organisms as each adapts to a similar way of life.

crèche. A group of young animals, especially penguins, gathered in one place for protection.

current. A body of water moving in a definite direction, especially through a surrounding body of water in which there is less movement, e.g., the Humboldt (Peru) Current.

deciduous. Of a tree or shrub that sheds its leaves annually. Contrast with PERENNIAL.

desert. Dry, barren land that receives less than 10 in (254 mm) of precipitation annually.

DNA-hybridization. A technique of measuring the degree of genetic similarity or divergence between organisms by comparing molecules of DNA (deoxyribonucleic acid).

ecosystem. A community of living plants and animals, plus their physical environment.

elevation. Height above sea level.

El Niño. Abnormal sea surface temperatures and atmospheric pressures that result from changes in the trade winds in the tropical and equatorial Pacific region. The event occurs at 2 to 7 year intervals. It usually begins around Christmas, and is so named for El Niño, the Spanish name for the Christ Child. Also known as the El Niño Southern Oscillation Cycle (ENSO).

Endangered. IUCN category indicating that an organism faces a very high risk of extinction in the wild based on evidence such as greatly diminished population size or geographic range. Organisms assessed to be at lesser risk of extinction are categorized as VULNERABLE or THREATENED.

endemic. A plant or animal restricted to a certain country or area. Contrast with NATIVE.

fauna. Animals of a particular region or habitat.

flora. Plants of a particular region or habitat.

food chain. A hierarchical series of organisms each dependent on the next as a source of food. A system of interlocking and interdependent food chains is called a FOOD WEB.

front. A meteorological term indicating the boundary of an advancing mass of air, e.g., the South Polar Front.

genus. A principal taxonomic category that ranks above species and below family, and is denoted by a capitalized Latin name that is written in italics, e.g., *Lama.* Contrast with SPECIES.

glacier. A slowly moving mass or river of ice formed by the accumulation and compaction of snow on mountains.

habitat. The natural home or environment of an animal or plant that is defined by physical factors of the environment, such as climate, soils, and landform.

herbivore. An animal that feeds on primary producers, mainly green plants.

hibernation. The resting or dormant state in which some animals pass the winter.

ice. Frozen water. LAND-ICE is frozen freshwater. SEA-ICE is frozen salt water. PACK ICE is an expanse of large pieces of floating ice driven together into a nearly continuous mass. FAST ICE is ice permanently attached to land.

iceberg. Large pieces of ice that have calved (broken off) from an ice shelf or glacier.

ice shelf. A thick sheet of ice that floats on the sea surface but is permanently attached to land.

intertidal zone. The area of a seashore that is covered at high tide and uncovered at low tide.

IUCN. The World Conservation Union; an international organization that evaluates the status of world flora and fauna, and publishes their findings in the Red List of Threatened Species. Animals and plants are assessed as Critically Endangered, Endangered, Vulnerable, Threatened, or of Least Concern.

lamellae. Gill-like membranes along the edge of the bill of some waterfowl and seabirds that filter small food prey from water.

latitude. The distance in degrees on the earth measured from the equator, running horizontally. Lines of latitude are described as North or South of the equator; they are parallel to each other. Latitude is usually expressed in degrees and minutes, e.g., 30°41'S latitude. The South Pole lies at 90°S latitude and the Tropic of Capricorn, which defines the southern limit of the tropics, lies at 23°30'S latitude.

longitude. The angular distance in degrees on the earth measured East and West from the Prime Meridian in Greenwich, England; usually expressed in degrees and minutes, e.g., 71°35'W longitude. Lines of a certain degree of longitude are called meridians. Meridians run vertically over the earth and thus are not parallel; they converge at the North and South Poles.

marine. Of, found in, or produced by the sea.

molt. A periodic loss and regrowth of feathers, fur or outer skin.

morph. A variant form of an animal or plant.

native. An animal or plant indigenous to a place, but not restricted to that place. Contrast ENDEMIC.

Neotropics. Biogeographical region comprising most of Central America and South America.

oviparous. Producing young by means of eggs that hatch after the parent lays them.

pelagic. Of or relating to the open ocean, e.g., a pelagic seabird that spends most of its life on ocean waters beyond the continental shelf.

perennial. A plant that remains leafy throughout the year. Same as evergreen, or siempreverde.

plate tectonics. A theory of global-scale dynamics involving the movement of many rigid plates of the earth's crust.

plateau. An area of relatively level, high ground.

polymorphic. Occurring in different forms.

precipitation. Rain, snow, sleet, or hail that falls to the ground.

puna. (Geographic) Arid intermontane plateau that lies south of the Altiplano in the High Andes. (Biological) Ecosystem found in arid sectors of the High Andean plateau.

rainforest. A luxuriant, dense, evergreen forest found in areas with consistently heavy rainfall.

salt flat. Flat, arid land covered with a layer of salt.

seismic. Of or relating to earthquakes or other vibrations of the earth and its crust.

sexual dimorphism. Differences in form, size or color that distinguish males (♂) from females (♀) of a species of organism.

Southern Hemisphere. The half of the world that lies south of the equator, extending to the South Pole.

Southern Ocean. The ocean region composed of the southern portions of the Atlantic Ocean, Indian Ocean, and Pacific Ocean. The Southern Ocean extends from the coast of Antarctica north to 60°S latitude, which coincides with the Antarctic Treaty Limit.

species. A group of living organisms consisting of similar individuals capable of exchanging genes or interbreeding. Species is the principal natural taxonomic unit, ranking below genus and denoted by a Latin binomial that is written in italics, e.g., *Lama glama*. The abbreviation "sp." indicates that the species is unknown or unidentified, e.g., *Viola* sp.

steppe. A large area of flat, treeless grassland, also called a savanna or plain in North America, or a pampa in South America. In the strict botanical definition, it corresponds to plant communities composed of perennial herbs, grasses and low, woody shrubs.

strait. A narrow passage of water connecting two seas or two large bodies of water.

subspecies. A taxonomic category that ranks below species, usually a fairly permanent geographically isolated race. Subspecies are designated by a Latin trinomial, e.g., *Zenaida auriculata hypoleuca*. Contrast with SPECIES.

taxonomy. The classification of organisms in an ordered system that indicates natural relationships.

terrestrial. Relating to an animal that lives on land or in the ground, or a plant that grows on land or in the soil.

tola. A word applied collectively to the low shrubs with small resinous or pubescent leaves that grow on the Altiplano and the Puna

torpor. A state of motor and mental inactivity with a partial insensibility.

trade wind. A wind blowing steadily toward the low-pressure zone at the equator from the northeast in the Northern Hemisphere or from the southeast in the Southern Hemisphere, especially at sea.

viviparous. Bringing forth live young that have developed inside the parent's body.

warm-blooded. Able to maintain a constant body temperature by metabolic means.

weather. The climatic conditions over a brief period of time, at a certain place and time of year.

wingspan. The distance from the left wingtip to the right wingtip of any winged creature.

SPANISH–ENGLISH DICTIONARY

Spanish	English
acantilado	cliff
altiplano	Andean high plateau
alto	high
arbol	tree
archipiélago	archipelago
arena	sand
arroyo	gully
bahía	bay
bajo	low
ballena	whale
bofedales	boggy grasslands
bosque	forest, woodland
bosque húmido	rainforest
Cabo	Cape (point of land)
caducifolio	deciduous
caleta	cove
camanchaca	coastal fog
campo	field, countryside
campo de hielo	ice field
canal	channel
caracoles	seashells
cascada	waterfall
cerro	mount, hill
chingue	skunk
colina	hill
conejo	rabbit
cordillera	mountain range
corriente	current
costa	coast, seaboard
cueva	cave
culebra, serpiente	snake
delfín	dolphin
depresión	basin, valley
desiérto	desert
embalse	dam, reservoir
ensenada	hidden cove or bay
esclerófilo	sclerophyll (vegetation)
espinal	spiny forest
estáncia	ranch
estepa	steppe, pampa
estero	stream
estrecho	strait
estuario	estuary
faldeo	mountainside, slope
fiordo	fjord
flor	flower
gato	cat
gaviota	seagull
golfo	gulf
hoja	leaf
humedal	marsh, wetland
invierno	winter
isla	island
jardín	garden
lagartija, lagarto	lizard
lago, laguna	lake, lagoon
laurifólio	laurel-leaved
litoral	seashore
llano	flat plain
lomas	foggy coastal slopes
mallines	wetland meadows
mamífero	mammal
mariscos	shellfish
matorral	scrubland
mar	sea, ocean
mariposa	butterfly
meseta	plateau
montaña	mountain
monte	mount
morro	steep promontory
murciélago	bat
ñadi	seasonal bog
naturaleza	nature, natural history
nevado	snow-capped peak
orilla	water's edge, riverbank
otoño	autumn
pájaro	bird
pajonal	scrubland, brush
pampa	grassy plain, savanna
pantano	marsh, swamp
paso	mountain pass
pato	duck
pastizal	pasture
pescado, pez	fish
piscicultura	fish farming
planifólio	broad-leaf (deciduous)
playa	beach
pollilo	moth
portezuelo	pass, border crossing
precordillera	foothills
primavera	spring
puerto	port, harbor
puna	Andean plateau or habitat
punta	point of land
quebrada	deep, wide river gorge
rana	frog
ratón	mouse
refugio	rustic shelter, hut
río	river
roble	*Nothofagus* beech tree
roca	rock
salar	salt flat
salto	waterfall
sapo, sapito	toad, frog
sendero	trail
seno	sound (body of water)
siempreverde	evergreen, perennial
sierra	hill, ridge, slope
sotobosque	undergrowth, understory
témpano de hielo	ice floe, iceberg
terma	thermal waters
tierra	land, earth
torre	tower
tortuga	turtle
totora	reed, rush
valle	valley
vega	swampy meadow, marsh
ventisquero	snowfield, glacier
verano	summer
zorro	fox

BIBLIOGRAPHY

Abbott, R. Tucker, and S. Peter Dance. 1982. *Compendium of Seashells*. California: Odyssey Publishing.
Araya, Braulio, and Guillermo Millie. 1986. *Guia de Campo de las Aves de Chile*. Santiago: Editorial Universidad.
Araya, Braulio, and Sharon Chester. 1993. *The Birds of Chile: A Field Guide*. Santiago: Latour.
Bailey, L.H. 1938. *Manual of Cultivated Plants*. New York: The Macmillan Company.
Campos, Hugo. *Mamíferos Terrestres de Chile*. CONAF. Valdivia: Marisa Cúneo Ediciones.
De la Peña, Martín, and Maurice Rumboll. 1998. *Birds of Southern South America and Antarctica*. Princeton: Princeton University Press.
Donoso., Claudio. 2005. *Arboles Nativos de Chile: Chilean Trees*. Valdivia: Marisa Cúneo Ediciones.
_____. 2005. *Arbustos Nativos de Chile: Chilean Bushes*. Valdivia: Marisa Cúneo Ediciones.
Fjeldså, Jon, and Niels Krabbe. 1990. *Birds of the High Andes*. Zoological Museum, University of Copenhagen.
Goodall, Rae Natalie Prosser. 1979. *Tierra del Fuego*. Ushuaia, Argentina: Ediciones Shanamaiim.
Goodson, Gar. 1988. *Fishes of the Pacific Coast: Alaska to Peru*. California: Stanford University Press.
Harris, Graham. 1998. *A Guide to the Birds and Mammals of Coastal Patagonia*. Princeton: Princeton Univ. Press.
Harrison, Peter. 1983. *Seabirds: An Identification Guide*. Kent: Croon Helm Ltd.
Hechenleitner, V. P., and Martin Gardner. 2005. *Plantas Amenazadas del Centro-Sur de Chile*. Universidad Austral de Chile and the Royal Botanic Garden of Edinburgh.
Heyerdahl. Thor. 1958. *Aku-Aku: The Secret of Easter Island*. Chicago: Rand McNally.
Hoffmann, Adriana. 2005. *Flora Silvestre de Chile: Zona Araucana*. 5th ed. Santiago: Eds. Fundación Claudio Gay.
_____. 1979. *Flora Silvestre de Chile: Zona Central*. 2nd ed. Santiago: Ediciones Fundación Claudio Gay.
Hoffmann, Adriana, and M.K. Arroyo, F. Liberona, M. Muñoz, J. Watson. 1998. *Plantas Altoandinas en la Flora Silvestre de Chile*. Santiago: Ediciones Fundación Claudio Gay.
Jaramillo, Alvaro. 2003. *Birds of Chile*. Princeton: Princeton University Press.
Johnson, A. W. 1965. *The Birds of Chile and Adjacent Regions of Argentina, Bolivia and Peru*. 2 vols. Buenos Aires: Platt Establecimientos Gráficos S.A.
Mabberley, D. J. 1990. *The Plant-Book: A Portable Dictionary of the Higher Plants*. UK: Cambridge University.
Moore, D. M. 1983. *Flora of Tierra del Fuego*. Anthony Nelson, UK, and Missouri Botanical Garden, USA.
Muñoz Schick, Melica. 1980. *Flora del Parque Nacional Puyehue*. Santiago: Editorial Universitaria, S.A.
Murphy, Robert C. 1936. *Oceanic Birds of South America*. New York: American Museum of Natural History.
Nowak, Ronald M. 1999. *Walker's Mammals of the World*. 6th ed. Baltimore: Johns Hopkins University Press.
Paynter, Raymond A. 1988. *Ornithological Gazeteer of Chile*. Cambridge: Harvard University.
Redford, Kent H., and John F. Eisenberg. *Mammals of the Neotropics: The Southern Cone*. Chicago: University of Chicago Press.
Reeves, Randall R., and Brent Stewart, Phillip Clapham, James Powell. 2002. *National Audubon Society Guide to Marine Mammals of the World*. New York: Alfred A. Knopf.
Rodriguez, Roberto, and Oscar Matthei, Max Quezada. 1983. *Flora Arbórea de Chile*. Chile: Univ. de Concepción.
Strange, Ian J. 1992. *A Field Guide to the Wildlife of the Falkland Islands and South Georgia*. London: Harper Collins.
Turismo y Communicaciones S.A. 1992. *Chile: A Remote Corner on Earth*. Chile: Empresas Cochrane.
Wheatley, Nigel. 1995. *Where to Watch Birds in South America*. Princeton: Princeton University Press.
Wilson, D. E., and D. M. Reeder (eds). 2005. *Mammal Species of the World*. Baltimore: Johns Hopkins Univ. Press.
Wilcox, Ken. 1996. *Chile's Native Forests: A Conservation Legacy*. California: Ancient Forests International.

WEB SITES

Alto Andino Nature (Flora and fauna of n Chile). *http://birdingaltoandino.com/nature-Arica.htm*
AMNH Amphibian Species of the World. *http://research.amnh.org/herpetology/amphibia/*
Aves de Chile (Birds). *http://www.avesdechile.cl*
CephBase (Cephalopods). *http://www.cephbase.utmb.edu/*
Chilean Mollusks. *http://www.geocities.com/moluscoschilenos/*
ChileFlora.com. *http://www.chileflora.com/*
Classification of the bird species of South America. *http://www.museum.lsu.edu/~Remsen/SACCBaseline*
Conchas y Caracoles de Chile (Mollusks). *http://pagina.de/conchas*
Enciclopedia de la Flora Chilena (Plants). *http://www.florachilena.cl/*
Insectos de Chile (Butterflies). *http://www.insectos.cl/mariposas/* and *http://www.entomologia.cl*
Le Jardin Botanique Alpin du Lautaret (Plants). *http://www.ujf-grenoble.fr/JAL/chili*
Project Gutenberg (Darwin's *Voyage of the Beagle*) *http://www.gutenberg.org/etext/944*
Reptile Database. *http://www.reptile-database.org/*
Taxonomy and System Naturae. *http://www.taxonomy.nl/taxonomicon/Default.aspx*
World Wildlife Fund Ecoregions. *http://www.worldwildlife.org/science/ecoregions/neotropic.cfm*

INDEX OF SCIENTIFIC NAMES

Abrocoma *bennetti* 324, 325; *cinerea* 324, 325
Abrothrix *andinus* 310; *hershkovitzi* 312; *lanosus* 312; *longipilis* 312; *olivaceus* 310; *sanborni* 312; *xanthorhinus* 312
Acacia *caven* 41, 42, 83
Acaena sp. 61
Accipiter *chilensis* 185, 186
Aconaemys *fuscus* 323, 325
Actitis *macularius* 208
Adelomelon *ancilla* 29
Adesmia sp. 38, 39, 65, 83
Adetomeris *erythrops* 92, 105
Aeronautes *andecolus* 236, 237
Aextoxicon *punctatum* 46, 47, 53, 86
Agelaioides *badius* 290
Agelaius *thilius* 288, 289
Agriornis *andicola* 258, 259; *livida* 258, 259; *micropetra* 258, 259; *montana* 259, 260
Ajaja *ajaja* 182
Akodon *albiventer* 310, 311
Alsodes *barrioi* 125; *nodosus* 123, 125; *vanzolini* 125
Alstroemeria *ligtu* 51; *magnifica* 37; *spathulata* 37
Ameghinomya *antiqua* 25
Amomyrtus *luma* 53, 54, 84; *meli* 84
Amorphochilus *schnablii* 293, 294
Anairetes *fernandezianus* 267, 268; *flavirostris* 267, 268; *parulus* 267, 268; *reguloides* 267, 268
Anas *bahamensis* 138; *cyanoptera* 138; *discors* 140; *flavirostris* 136, 139; *georgica* 136, 139; *platalea* 139; *puna* 139; *sibilatrix* 139, 140; *versicolor* 138, 139
Andinomys *edax* 314, 315
Anemone *decapetala* 62, 63
Anous *stolidus* 224, 227
Anthus *correndera* 273, 275; *lutescens* 273, 275
Aphrastura *masafuerae* 250, 251; *spinicauda* 250, 251
Aphriza *virgata* 207, 208
Aphrodroma *brevirostris* 161, 163
Aptenodytes *forsteri* 145, 148; *patagonicus* 145, 148
Araucaria *araucana* 47, 51, 73
Arctocephalus *australis* 329, 331; *gazella* 330, 331; *philippii* 17, 329, 331
Ardea *alba* 176, 179; *cocoi* 176, 179
Arenaria *interpres* 207, 208
Argobuccinum *ranellieformi* 29
Argonauta *nodosa* 26, 29
Argopecten *purpuratus* 23
Argopteron *aureipennis* 93, 94
Argyrophorus *argenteus* 100, 101
Aristolochia *chilensis* 93, 95
Aristotelia *chilensis* 47, 48, 66, 79

Arjona *patagonica* 64, 65
Armeria *maritima* 61
Asio *flammeus* 234, 235
Asteranthera *ovata* 57
Asthenes *anthoides* 253, 254; *arequipae* 252, 253; *humilis* 252, 253; *modesta* 252, 253; *pudibunda* 253, 254; *pyrrholeuca* 253, 254
Athene *cunicularia* 235, 236
Atriplex *atacamensis* 112
Attagis *gayi* 213, 215; *malouinus* 213, 215
Auca *coctei* 102; *pales* 101, 102
Auliscomys *boliviensis* 314, 315; *sublimis* 314
Austrocedrus *chilensis* 47, 49, 73
Azara *celastrina* 80; *integrifolia* 79; *petiolaris* 43, 79; *serrata* 79
Azorella *compacta* 38, 39, 86
Baccharis *magellanica* 63; *petiolata* 354
Baccharis *speciosa* 39, 88
Balaenoptera *acutorostrata* 336, 337; *bonaerensis* 336, 337; *borealis* 336, 337; *musculus* 337, 338; *physalus* 337, 338
Balbisia *peduncularis* 112
Bartramia *longicauda* 211
Bathybembix *macdonald* 28
Batrachyla *antartandica* 122, 123; *leptopus* 123, 124; *nibaldoi* 122, 123; *taeniata* 122, 123
Battus *polydamus* 93
Beilschmiedia *berteroana* 76; *miersii* 41, 43, 76
Belgica *antarctica* 20
Berardius *arnuxii* 346, 347
Berberis *buxifolia* 63, 76; *corymbosa* 66; *darwinii* 51, 77; *empetrifolia* 50, 63, 77; *ilicifolia* 61, 77; *trigona* 50, 51, 77
Blechnum *cycadifolium* 66; *hastatum* 57; *penna-marina* 61
Boehmeria *excelsa* 66, 67
Bolax *gummifera* 62, 87
Bolborhynchus *aurifrons* 232
Brama *australis* 23
Broussonetia *papyrifera* 69
Browningia *candelaris* 35, 37, 87
Bubo *magellanicus* 234, 235
Bufo See *Chaunus*
Bulbulcus *ibis* 178, 179
Burhinus *superciliaris* 203, 204
Buteo *albigula* 188, 189; *poecilochrous* 188; *polyosoma* 17, 187, 189; *ventralis* 188, 189
Butleria *flavomaculata* 93, 94
Butorides *striatus* 178
Caesalpinia *spinosa* 35, 36, 83
Cairina *moschata* 140
Calandrinia *compacta* 38, 39

Calceolaria *biflora* 63; *uniflora* 64, 65
Caldcluvia *paniculata* 53, 54, 56, 80
Calidris *alba* 208; *bairdii* 210; *canutus* 208; *fuscicollis* 210; *himantopus* 211; *mauri* 211; *melanotos* 210; *minutilla* 210; *pusilla* 210
Calliostoma *chilena* 28
Callipepla *californica* 129, 130
Callopistes *maculatus* 114, 115
Callorhinchus *callorhinchus* 23
Calomys *lepidus* 314, 315
Caltha *sagittata* 62, 63
Calyptrea *trochiformes* 27, 29
Campephilus *magellanicus* 241, 242
Cancer *edwardsii* 25
Caperea *marginata* 334, 335
Caprimulgus *longirostris* 235, 236
Caracara *plancus* 190, 191
Caranx *georgianus* 17
Carduelis *atrata* 286; *barbata* 286; *crassirostris* 286; *magellanica* 286; *uropygialis* 286
Caretta *caretta* 107
Carex *magellanica* 65
Castnia *psittachus* 103, 105
Castor *canadensis* 326, 327
Catamenia *analis* 278, 279; *inornata* 278
Cathartes *aura* 184; *burrovianus* 184; *fuscescens* 274
Catoptrophorus *semipalmatus* 206
Caudiverbera *caudiverbera* 120
Cavia *tschudii* 319, 320
Cellana *ardosidea* 17, 28
Centauria *chilensis* 37
Cephalorhynchus *commersonii* 339, 341; *eutropia* 339, 341
Cercophana *venusta* 105
Cervus *elaphus* 307, 309
Ceryle *torquata* 240, 241
Cestrum *parqui* 43
Chaetodon *litus* 15
Chaetophractus *nationi* 295; *villosus* 295, 296
Chaetura *pelagica* 237
Champsocephalus *gunnari* 22
Charadrius *alexandrinus* 199, 200; *alticola* 199, 201; *collaris* 199, 201; *falklandicus* 199, 200; *modestus* 199, 200; *semipalmatus* 198, 199; *vociferus* 199, 200
Chaunus *arunco* 119, 121; *atacamensis* 119, 121; *rubropunctatus* 119, 121; *spinulosus* 119, 121; *variegatus* 120, 121
Cheilopogon *rapanouiensis* 15
Chelemys *macronyx* 311, 313
Chelonia *mydas* 106, 107
Chenopodium *quinoa* 38, 39
Chilecomadia *moorei* 42, 103
Chilia *melanura* 247, 248
Chiliotrichum *diffusum* 62, 63, 88

INDEX OF SCIENTIFIC NAMES 381

Chillanella stelligera 100
Chinchilla brevicauda 318, 319; lanigera 318, 319
Chinchillula sahamae 314, 315
Chionis alba 203, 205
Chiton magnificus 25
Chloephaga hybrida 134; melanoptera 132; picta 132; poliocephala 132; rubidiceps 132
Chloraea magellanica 64, 65
Chloroceryle americana 241, 242
Chlorotimandra viridis 104
Chordeiles acutipennis 236
Choromytilus chorus 25
Chorus giganteus 29
Chuquiraga oppositifolia 38, 39
Chusquea culeou 50, 51, 89; quila 47, 48, 89
Cilus gilberti 23
Cinclodes antarcticus 247, 249; atacamensis 247, 249; fuscus 247, 248; nigrofumosus 247, 248; oustaleti 247, 249; patagonicus 247, 248
Circus cinereus 185, 186
Cistanthe grandiflora 37
Cistothorus platensis 272, 273
Coccyzus melacoryphus 233
Codonorchis lessonii 62, 63
Colaptes pitius 242; rupicola 241, 242
Colias flaveola 95, vauthierii 93, 95
Colibri coruscans 238, 239
Colletia hystrix 41, 43
Colliguaja interrima 48; odorifera 41
Colobanthus quitensis 20, 70
Colocasia escuelenta 69
Coloramphus parvirostris 264, 265
Columba livia 228, 229
Columbina cruziana 229, 230; picui 229, 230; talpacoti 230
Concholepas concholepas 25
Conepatus chinga 297, 298, 353
Conirostrum cinereum 276, 277; tamarugense 276, 277
Copao coquimbensis 35
Copiapoa 35, 87; carrizalensis 112, 356; cinerea 355
Coprosma pyrifolia 66
Coragyps atratus 183, 184
Corallina officianalis 31
Coralliophila scala 17, 29
Cordia decanara 35, 36
Cordyline terminalis 69
Coscoroba coscoroba 131, 133
Cosmosatyrus chilensis 100, 101
Crassilabrum crassilabrum 29
Creagrus furcatus 221, 222
Crinodendron hookeranum 57; patagua 41, 43, 78
Crotophaga sulcirostris 233
Cryptoblepharus poecilopleurus 16, 114, 115

Cryptocarya alba 41, 43, 46, 76
Ctenomys fulvus 319, 321; magellanicus 322; maulinus 319, 322; opimus 319, 321
Curaeus curaeus 288, 289
Cyanoliseus patagonus 231
Cygnus melancoryphus 131, 133
Cypraea caputdraconis 16, 29; englerti 16, 29
Cyttaria darwinii 58, 59, 78
Dama dama 307, 309
Danaus erippus 97, 99
Daption capense 159, 160
Dasyphyllum diacanthoides 47, 56
Delphinus delphis 340, 341
Dendroceris litoralis 66
Dendrocygna autumnalis 131; bicolor 131; viduata 131
Dendroica striata 288
Dermochelys coriacea 107
Deschampsia antarctica 20, 64, 70
Desfontainea spinosa 59
Desmodus rotundus 293, 294
Dicksonia berteroana 66
Diglossa brunneiventris 275, 277; carbonaria 276
Diloma nigerrima 28
Diomedea antipodensis 151, 153; epomophora 152, 153; exulans 151, 153; sanfordi 152, 153
Dione glycera 101, 102
Dioscorea alata 69
Diplolaemus bibronii 114; darwinii 114, 115; leopardinus 114, 115
Discaria serratifolia 43
Dissostichus eleginoides 23
Distichlis spicata 354
Diuca diuca 283; speculifera 282, 283
Dolichonyx oryzivorus 290
Dosidicus gigas 26
Draba magellanica 64, 65
Drimys confertifolia 66, 67, 74; winteri 41, 46, 47, 50, 51, 53, 54, 55, 59, 60, 74
Dromiciops gliroides 292, 293
Drosera uniflora 61
Durvillaea antarctica 31
Echinopsis atacamensis 35, 36, 87, 354; chiloensis 41, 42, 87
Egretta caerulea 178, 179; sacra 178; thula 178, 179, tricolor 178
Eiseliana bicolor 97, 98
Elaenia albiceps 264, 265; flavogaster 269
Elanus leucurus 184, 185
Eligmodontia puerulus 314, 315
Elina montroui 102; vanessoides 102
Embothrium coccineum 50, 59, 60, 62, 81
Empetrum rubrum 60, 61, 62, 64, 80
Engraulis ringens 23
Enicognathus ferrugineus 231, 232; leptorhynchus 231, 232
Ephedra andina 38, 75; breana 354

Epitonium magellanicum 29
Eremobius phoenicurus 246, 247
Eroessa chilensis 96, 97
Erynnis funeralis 93, 94
Escallonia callcottiae 67; serrata 61
Eschscholzia californica 40
Eubalaena australis 333, 335
Eucryphia cordifolia 47, 53, 80; glutinosa 48, 81
Eudromia elegans 129, 130
Eudyptes chrysochome 144, 145; chrysolophus 145, 146
Eugralla paradoxa 256, 257
Eulidia yarrellii 238, 239
Eulychnia iquiquensis 87, 354
Eulychnia sp. 35
Euneomys chinchilloides 315, 317
Euphausia mucronata 22; superba 22
Eupsophus calcaratus 123, 124; contulmoensis 123, 124; emiliopugini 124; insularis 124; nahuelbutensis 124; roseus 123, 124
Euptoieta claudia 101, 102
Euxenura maguari 182
Fagara mayu 67
Falco femoralis 191, 192; peregrinus 191, 192; sparverius 14, 17, 191, 193
Festuca gracillima 64; magellanica 65; orithophylla 39
Fissurella latimarginata 28; maxima 28
Fitzroya cupressoides 53, 54, 55, 74
Fragaria chiloensis 50
Frankenia meyeniana 354
Fregetta grallaria 169; tropica 170
Fuchsia magellanica 59, 60, 85, 96
Fulica americana 195, 196; ardesiaca 195, 196; armillata 195, 196; cornuta 195, 196; gigantea 195, 196; leucoptera 194, 195; rufifrons 195, 196
Fulmarus glacialoides 158
Galea musteloides 320
Galictis cuja 297, 298
Gallinago andina 212, 215; paraguaiae 212, 215; stricklandii 213, 215
Gallinula chloropus 194, 195; melanops 194, 195
Garrodia nereis 169, 170
Gaultheria antarctica 61, 80; mucronata 80; pumila 61, 80; rigida 66
Gavilea lutea 62, 63
Gelidium chilense 31; lingulatum 30
Gentianella magellanica 64, 65
Genypterus blacodes 23; maculatus 23
Geoffroea decorticans 35, 37, 83, 354
Geositta antarctica 243, 245; cunicularia 243, 245, 269; isabellina 244, 245; maritima 245; punensis 244, 245; rufipennis 244, 245
Geoxus valdivianus 311, 313

382 INDEX OF SCIENTIFIC NAMES

Geranoaetus *melanoleucus* 185, 186
Gevuina *avellana* 47, 81
Gigartina *skottsbergii* 31; *stellata* 31
Girella *albostriata* 17
Glaucidium *nanum* 234, 235; *peruanum* 234
Globicephala *melas* 343, 344
Gomortega *keule* 48, 75
Gracilaria *chilensis* 30, 31
Grampus *griseus* 343, 344
Gunnera *magellanica* 61, 82; *tinctoria* 57, 82
Gygis *alba* 226, 227
Haematopus *ater* 202; *leucopodus* 202, 203; *palliatus* 202, 203
Haliotis *rufescens* 25, 27
Halobaena *caerulea* 163,164
Haloragis *masatierrana* 66
Haplochelidon *andecola* 269, 271
Haplopappus *foliosus* 37; *parvifolius* 112
Hebe *elliptica* 60, 61, 88
Heliopyrgus *americanus* 94
Herpetotheres *cachinnans* 193
Heteronetta *atricapilla* 135, 137, 196
Heteroscelus *incanus* 211
Himantopus *melanurus* 203, 204
Hippocamelus *antisensis* 307, 308; *bisulcus* 306, 307
Hippoglossina *macrops* 23
Hirundo *rustica* 270, 271
Hirundunea *ferruginea* 269
Histiotus *macrotus* 294; *magellanicus* 295; *montanus* 295
Homonota *darwinii* 116; *dorbignii* 116; *gaudichaudii* 116; *penai* 116
Hydrangea *integerrima* 53, 57
Hydrurga *leptonyx* 331, 332
Hylephila *fasciolata* 93, 94
Hyles *annei* 104, 105
Hymenops *perspicillata* 265, 266
Hyperoodon *planifrons* 347, 348
Intraphulia *ilyodes* 96
Irenomys *tarsalis* 315, 316
Itylos *titicaca* 97, 98
Ixobrychus *involucris* 178, 179
Jasus *frontalis* 17
Juania *australis* 66, 67, 88
Jubaea *chilensis* 43, 44, 68, 88
Juncus *scheuchzerioides* 61
Kageneckia *oblonga* 43, 81
Kogia *breviceps* 345, 346
Lactoris *fernandeziana* 66
Lafresnaya *lafresnayi* 240
Lageneria *siceraria* 69
Lagenorhynchus *australis* 341; *cruciger* 341; *obscurus* 340, 341
Lagidium *viscacia* 317, 319
Lama *glama* 304, 305; *guanicoe* 64, 303, 305; *pacos* 304, 305
Lapageria *rosea* 33, 53, 57, 89
Larosterna *inca* 223, 225

Larus *atricilla* 223; *belcheri* 219, 221; *dominicanus* 219, 220; *maculipennis* 221, 222; *modestus* 219, 221; *pipixcan* 221, 222; *scoresbii* 219, 220; *serranus* 221
Lasiurus *blossevillii* 293, 295; *cinereus* 293, 295
Laterallus *jamaicensis* 193, 195
Laurelia *sempervirens* 47, 56, 75
Laureliopsis *philippiana* 47, 49, 53, 54, 75
Legrandia *concinna* 84
Leonthochir *ovallei* 37, 356
Leopardus *colocolo* 300; *geoffroyi* 302; *guigna* 302; *jacobitus* 300, 301; *pajeros* 300, 301
Lepidochelys *olivacea* 107
Lepidodactylus *lugubris* 16, 116
Lepidophyllum *cupressiforme* 64, 65
Leptasthenura *aegithaloides* 253, 254; *striata* 253, 255
Leptonychotes *weddellii* 331, 332
Leptotes *trigemmatus* 97, 98
Lepus *europaeus* 327, 328
Lerodea *eufala* 93
Lessonia *nigrescens* 31; *oreas* 266; *rufa* 265, 266
Leucheria *hahnii* 65
Leucocoryne *ixioides* 37
Limnodromus *griseus* 211
Limosa *fedoa* 211; *haemastica* 205
Liolaemus *alticolor* 108, 111; *andinus* 109, 110; *barbarae* 355; *bellii* 108, 111; *bisignatus* 355; *buergeri* 109, 111; *chiliensis* 109, 110; *constanzae* 355; *cyanogaster* 109, 110; *enigmaticus* 352; *erguetae* 355; *fabiani* 109, 110; *fitzingeri* 109, 110; *fuscus* 109, 111; *gravenhorsti* 109, 111; *hajeki* 355; *isabelae* 356; *jamesi* 352; *lemniscatus* 109, 111; *leopardinus* 109, 111; *magellanicus* 109, 111, 370, 372; *melaniceps* 356; *melanopleurus* 356; *monticola* 109, 111; *nigriceps* 110, 112; *nigromaculatus* 110, 112; *nigroviridis* 110, 112; *nitidus* 111, 112; *patriciaiturrae* 356; *paulinae* 110, 112; *pictus* 108, 110, 112; *platei* 110, 112; *pleopholis* 352, 355; *rosenmanni* 356; *schroederi* 111, 112; *signifer* 352; *silvai* 355; *tacnae* 352; *tenuis* 108, 111, 112; *velosoi* 355; *zapallarensis* 111, 113
Lissodelphis *peronii* 341, 342
Lithodes *antarctica* 25
Lithrea *caustica* 41, 42, 46, 86
Littorina *peruviana* 28
Lobelia *tupa* 66, 67
Lobodon *carcinophagus* 331, 332
Loligo *gahi* 26
Lomatia *ferruginea* 59, 60, 82; *hirsuta* 47, 48, 82
Lontra *felina* 296, 297; *provocax* 297
Lophonetta *specularioides* 136, 137

Lophosoria *quadripinnata* 66
Lottia *ceciliana* 28
Loxechinus *albus* 25
Loxodontomys *micropus* 310, 311
Luma *apiculata* 41, 56, 84
Lupinus sp. 65
Lybytheana *carinenta* 101, 103
Lycalopex *culpaeus* 298, 299; *fulvipes* 299; *griseus* 299
Lynchailurus See *Leopardus*
Lyncodon *patagonicus* 297
Macrocyclis *peruvianus* 53
Macrocystis *pyrifera* 30, 31
Macronectes *giganteus* 156, 159; *halli* 158, 159
Macrouronus *magellanicus* 23
Mathania *leucothea* 96, 97
Maytenus *boaria* 41, 46, 47, 48, 85; *magellanica* 59, 60, 85
Mazzaella *laminarioides* 30, 31
Megabalanus *psittacus* 25
Megaptera *novaeangliae* 334, 335
Melanodera *melanodera* 282, 283; *xanthogramma* 282, 283
Melia *azederach* 69
Merganetta *armata* 134, 137
Merluccius *gayi* 23
Mesodesma *donacium* 25
Mesoplodon *grayi* 347, 349; *hectori* 347, 349; *layardii* 347, 349
Metriopelia *aymara* 229; *ceciliae* 229, 230; *melanoptera* 229, 230
Microcavia *australis* 319, 320
Microlophus *atacamensis* 113, 115; *tarapacensis* 113; *quadrivittatus* 113, 350, 354; *yanezi* 113, 350
Milvago *chimango* 188, 191
Mimus *patagonicus* 273, 274; *tenca* 273, 274; *triurus* 274
Ministrymon *azia* 97, 98; *quebradivaga* 97, 98
Mirounga *leonina* 331, 333
**Misodendrum* sp. 59
Mitraria *coccinea* 57
Molothrus *bonariensis* 288, 289; *rufoaxillaris* 290
Muscigralla *brevicauda* 268
Muscisaxicola *albifrons* 263; *albilora* 261, 263; *capistratus* 263; *cinereus* 263; *flavinucha* 261, 263; *frontalis* 261, 263; *juninensis* 261, 263; *macloviana* 263; *maculirostris* 263, 264; *rufivertex* 261, 263
Mus *musculus* 314, 326, 327
Mutisia *sinuata* 38
Mycteria *americana* 182
Myiophobus *fasciatus* 268
Myiopsitta *monachus* 233
Myocastor *coypus* 324, 325
Myodynastes *maculatus* 268
Myotis *chiloensis* 293, 294
Myrceugenia *fernandeziana* 66, 67, 85; *planipes* 53, 84

INDEX OF SCIENTIFIC NAMES 383

Myrica pavonis 85
Mytilus chilensis 25
Nacella concinna 28
Nasua nasua 302
Nelia nemyroides 102
Neomaenas monachus 102; janiriodes 100, 101; monachus 101
Neoportaria sp. 35
Neosatyrus ambriorix 100
Neotomys ebriosus 315, 317
Neovison vison 297
Neoxolmis rufiventris 259, 260
Nerita mono 16, 28
Nesofregetta fuliginosa 169, 170
Netta peposaca 136, 137
Nodilittorina pyramidalis 16, 28
Nolana paradoxa 37
Nothofagus alessandrii 45, 49, 78; antarctica 45, 50, 54, 62, 63, 78; betuloides 45, 52, 54, 58, 79; dombeyi 45, 46, 47, 49, 50, 55, 78; glauca 45, 46, 49, 78; leonii 45, 78; nervosa 45, 47, 49, 77; nitida 45, 54, 57, 79; obliqua 45, 46,47, 49, 73, 78; pumilio 45, 47, 50, 52, 58, 62, 63, 78
Nothoprocta ornata 129; pentlandii 129, 130; perdicaria 128, 129
Numenius phaeopus 207; tahitiensis 211
Nycticorax nycticorax 178, 179
Nycticryphes semicollaris 214, 215
Oceanites gracilis 169, 170; oceanicus 20, 168, 169
Oceanodroma hornbyi 169, 171; markhami 169, 171; tethys 169, 170
Ochetorhynchus ruficauda 246, 247
Ochthoeca leucophrys 264, 265; oenanthoides 264, 265
Octodon bridgesi 323, 325; degus 322, 325
Octodontomys gliroides 323, 325
Octopus mimus 26
Odontocybiola magellanica 29
Oenothera acaulis 37
Oligoryzomys longicaudatus 311, 313; magellanicus 313
Oliva peruviana 29
Ommatophoca rossi 331, 332
Oncifelis See Leopardus
Ondatra zibetnicus 327
Onychoprion fuscatus 226, 227
Opuntia sp. 35, 87
Orcinus orca 343, 344
Oreailurus See Leopardus
Oreomanes fraseri 276, 277
Oreopholus ruficollis 199, 201
Oreotrochilus estella 237, 239; leucopleurus 237, 239
Orites myrtodea 362
Ormiscodes cinnamomea 105
Oryctolagus cuniculus 327, 328
Otaria flavescens 330, 331
Oxyura ferruginea 135, 137

Oxyura vittata 135, 137
Pachyptila belcheri 164; desolata 163, 164
Pagodroma nivea 159, 160
Pandion haliaetus 184, 185
Panulirus pascuensis 16
Parabuteo unicinctus 187, 189
Paralomis granulosa 25
Parastrephia sp. 39, 88
Pardirallus maculatus 197; sanguinolentus 194, 195
Parribacus perlatus 15
Paschalococos dispersa 68
Passer domesticus 285
Patagioenas araucana 228, 229
Patagonas gigas 238, 239
Pelamis platurus 117
Pelecanoides garnotii 171; magellani 171; urinatrix 171
Pelecanus thagus 173, 174
Perezia recurvata 64, 65
Pernettya See Gaultheria
Persea lingue 41, 46, 47, 56, 76
Petrochelidon pyrrhonota 270, 271
Peumus boldus 41, 43, 75
Phacelia secunda 64, 65
Phaethon aethereus 172, 173; lepturus 173; rubricauda 172, 173
Phalacrocorax atriceps 175, 176, 177; bougainvillii 175, 177; bransfieldensis 176, 177; brasilianus 175, 177; gaimardi 175, 177; magellanicus 176, 177
Phalaropus fulicarius 211; lobatus 211, 212; tricolor 211, 212
Phalcoboenus albogularis 190, 191; australis 191; megalopterus 190, 191
Phegornis mitchellii 199, 201
Philesia magellanica 53, 57, 89
Philodryas chamissonis 117; elegans 117; tachimenoides 117; simonsii 117, 359
Phleocryptes melanops 250, 251, 267
Phocoena dioptrica 339, 341; spinipinnis 339, 341
Phoebastria irrorata 156, 157
Phoebetria fusca 156; palpebrata 155, 157
Phoebis sennae 93
Phoenicoparrus andinus 181, 182; jamesi 181, 182
Phoenicopterus chilensis 181, 182
Phrygilus alaudinus 279; atriceps 281, 283; dorsalis 279, 280; erythronotus 279, 281; fruticeti 279, 280; gayi 281, 283; patagonicus 281, 283; plebejus 279, 280; unicolor 279, 280
Phrynosaura audituvelata 113; manueli 113, 115, 355; reichei 113, 115; torresi 113, 355
Phulia nimphula 96
Phyllodactylus inaequalis 116

Phyllotis darwini 315, 316; xanthopygus 315, 316
Phymaturus flagellifer 113, 115; vociferator 113, 115
Physeter catodon 345
Phytotoma rara 270, 273
Picoides lignarius 241, 243
Pieris brassicae 96, 97
Pilgerodendron uviferum 53, 54, 59, 60, 73
Piranga rubra 276
Pitangus sulphuratus 268
Planaxis akuana 16, 28
Plantago fernandezia 66
Plegadis chihi 180, 181; ridgwayi 180, 181
Pleurodema bufoninum 120, 121; marmoratum 120; thaul 120, 121
Pluvialis dominica 198, 199; squatarola 199; socialis 203, 205
Poa alopecurus 64; flabellata 60, 61
Podanthus mitiqui 43
Podiceps gallardoi 142, major 141; occipitalis 141, 142; rolland 141, 142
Podilymbus podiceps 141, 142
Podocarpus nubigena 54, 55, 56, 74; saligna 46, 56, 74
Polioxolmis rufipennis 259, 260
Polylepis rugulosa 38, 81; tarapacana 38, 39, 81, 350
Polythysana apollina 105; rubrescens 105
Porlieria chilensis 42
Porphyra columbina 31
Porphyrula martinica 197
Prasiola crispa 71
Primula magellanica 64, 65
Prisogaster niger 28
Pristidactylus torquatus 108, 115; valeriae 114; volcanensis 115, 360
Procellaria aequinoctialis 165; cinerea 165; westlandica 165, 166
Procelsterna albivitta 226, 227
Progne elegans 270; murphyi 270, 271; tapera 270
Prosopis alba 35, 36, 37, 83, 354; chilensis 42, 83; tamarugo 35, 83, 98
Prunopitys andina 48, 74
Pseudocolopteryx flaviventris 266
Pseudolucia chilensis 97, 99
Pseudopanax laetevirens 59, 86
Pseudorca crassidens 343, 345
Psidium guajava 69
Pterocnemia pennata 64, 128, 129
Pterodroma alba 161, 162; arminjoniana 161, 163; cooki 162, 163; defilippiana 162, 163; externa 162, 163; inexpectata 162; lessoni 163, 164; longirostris 162, 163; macroptera 161; neglecta 161, 163
Pteroptochos castaneus 255, 257; megapodius 255, 257; tarnii 255, 257
Pudu puda 307, 308

Puffinus *bulleri* 165, 167; *carneipes* 165, 167; *creatopus* 165, 167; *griseus* 165, 166; *nativitatis* 165, 167; *puffinus* 165, 167
Puma *concolor* 301, 302
Puya *berteroana* 41, 42, 89, 103; *chilensis* 41, 42, 89
Pygarrhichas *albogularis* 250, 251
Pygochelidon *cyanoleuca* 269, 271
Pygoscelis *adeliae* 145, 146; *antarctica* 145, 147; *papua* 145, 147
Pyrgus *barrosi* 94; *bocchoris* 93
Pyrocephalus *rubinus* 265, 267
Pyura *chilensis* 24
Quillaja *saponaria* 41, 42, 46, 81
Rallus *antarcticus* 193, 195
Ranunculus *peduncularis* 62
Rattus *norvegicus* 327; *rattus* 326, 327
Recurvirostra *andina* 202, 203
Reithrodon *auritus* 315, 316
Rhaphithamnus *spinosus* 47, 48, 88; *venustus* 66, 67, 88
Rhinoderma *darwinii* 123, 125; *rufum* 125
Rhodophila *phycelliodes* 37
Rhodopis *vesper* 238, 239, 240
Rhyncholestes *raphanurus* 292, 293
Ribes *cucullatum* 50, 51
Riparia *riparia* 270, 271
Robinsonia sp. 66, 67
Rynchops *niger* 226, 227
Salix *chilensis* 41, 80
Saltator *aurantiirostris* 276, 277
Santalum *fernandezianum* 17, 66
Sarcothalia *crispata* 30
Sardinops *sagax* 23
Sarmienta *repens* 57
Saxegothaea *conspicua* 47, 48, 74
Scelorchilus *albicollis* 256, 257; *rubecula* 256, 257
Schinus *latifolius* 41, 42, 86; *molle* 35, 36, 37, 86, 354; *polygamus* 41, 43, 86
Schizanthus sp. 37
Scirpus *californicus* 68, 69, 141
Scomber *japonicus* 23
Scurria *scurra* 28
Scyllarides *roggeveeni* 15
Scytalopus *fuscus* 257, 258; *magellanicus* 256, 257
Senecio *candicans* 61; *magellanicus* 64, 65; *patagonicus* 65
Sephanoides *fernandensis* 66, 67, 239, 240; *sephanoides* 239, 240
Seriola *lalandii* 17
Setophaga *ruticilla* 288
Sicalis *auriventris* 284, 287; *lebruni* 284, 287; *luteola* 282, 287; *olivascens* 284, 287; *uropygialis* 284, 287
Sinum *cymba* 29

Sisyrinchium *patagonicum* 64, 65
Sophora *fernandeziana* 84; *macrocarpa* 43, 84; *microphylla* 84; *toromiro* 68, 69, 84
Spalacopus *cyanus* 323, 325
Speculanas *specularis* 139, 140
Sphagnum *magellanicum* 62
Spheniscus *humboldti* 143, 145; *magellanicus* 144, 145
Sporophila *telasco* 278, 279
Stenella *attenuata* 342, 343; *coeruleoalba* 341, 342
Stercorarius *antarcticus* 217, 218; *chilensis* 216, 217; *longicaudus* 217, 220; *maccormicki* 216, 217; *parasiticus* 217, 218; *pomarinus* 217, 218
Sterna *elegans* 225; *hirundinacea* 223, 225; *hirundo* 224, 225; *lunata* 226, 227; *paradisaea* 224, 225; *trudeaui* 223, 225; *vittata* 224, 225
Sternula *lorata* 223, 225
Stipa *pungens* 39
Strangomera *bentincki* 23
Strix *rufipes* 234
Strombus *maculatus* 29
Strymon *crambusa* 98
Strymon *eurytulus* 97, 98
Sturnella *bellicosa* 289, 290; *loyca* 289, 290; *superciliaris* 290
Sula *dactylatra* 173, 174; *leucogaster* 173, 174; *nebouxii* 173, 174; *sula* 174; *variegata* 173, 174
Sus *scrofa ferus* 309
Sylviorthorhynchus *desmursii* 249, 251
Tachuris *rubrigastra* 250, 265, 267
Tachycineta *meyeni* 269
Tachyeres *patachonicus* 134, 137; *pteneres* 134, 137
Tachymenis *chilensis* 117; *peruviana* 117
Tadarida *brasiliensis* 293, 294
Taraxacum *gilliesii* 64, 65
Tasmacetus *shepherdi* 347, 348
Tatochila *mercedis* 96; *theodice* 96
Tegula *atra* 28
Telmatobius *marmoratus* 122, 123; *pefauri* 122, 352; *vilamensis* 122; *zapahuirensis* 122
Telmatobufo *venustus* 364
Tepualia *stipularis* 53, 54, 56, 59, 85
Terias *deva* 93, 96
Tessiaria *absinthioides* 354
Tetraphlebia *germaini* 100
Thais *chocolata* 29
Thalasoica *antarctica* 159
Thalassarche *bulleri* 154, 157; *cauta* 155; *chrysostoma* 154, 157; *eremita* 155, 157; *melanophris* 152, 157; *salvini* 155, 157
Thalassoica *antarctica* 159, 160

Thamnoseris *lacerata* 14
Thaumastura *cora* 238, 239
Theristicus *melanopis* 180, 181
Thespesia *populnea* 69
Thinocorus *orbignyianus* 213, 215; *rumicivorus* 214, 215
Thraupis *bonariensis* 275, 277
Thylamys *elegans* 292, 293
Thyrsopteris *elegans* 66
Tillandsia *landbeckii* 35, 89, 353
Tinamotis *ingoufi* 129, 130; *pentlandii* 129, 130
Tiostrea *chilensis* 25
Trachurus *symmetricus* 23
Trevoa *trinervis* 41, 42
Trichocereus See Echinopsis
Tringa *flavipes* 206; *melanoleuca* 206; *solitaria* 211
Tristerix *aphyllus* 96, 274
Triumfetta *semitriloba* 69
Troglodytes *musculus* 272
Trophon *geversianus* 29
Tropidurus *heterolepis* 113
Turdus *amaurochalinus* 274; *chiguanco* 273; *falklandii* 272
Turitella *cingulata* 28
Tursiops *truncatus* 342
Tyrannus *melancholicus* 269; *savana* 269; *tyrannus* 268
Tyto *alba* 233, 235
Ugni *candollei* 53, 57, 85; *molinae* 85
Ulva *rigida* 30, 31
Upucerthia *albigula* 245, 246; *andaecola* 246; *dumetaria* 244, 245; *jelskii* 245, 246
Urbanus *dorantes* 94; *proteus* 93
Utethesia *ornatrix* 105
Vanellus *chilensis* 197, 199; *resplendens* 198, 199
Vanessa *carye* 101, 103; *terpsichore* 103
Vicugna *vicugna* 303, 305
Viola *maculata* 63, 64
Vireo *olivaceus* 269
Volatinia *jacarina* 278
Vultur *gryphus* 183
Weinmannia *trichosperma* 47, 53, 54, 55, 56, 80
Xanthochorus *cassidiformis* 29
Xanthoria sp. 71
Xema *sabini* 221, 222
Xenospingus *concolor* 282
Xolmis *pyrope* 259, 260
Yramea *cytheris* 102
Zaedyus *pichiy* 295, 296
Zenaida *auriculata* 228, 229; *meloda* 228, 229
Zerene *caesonia* 93
Ziphius *cavirostris* 346, 347
Zonotrichia *capensis* 285

INDEX OF COMMON NAMES

Abalone Chilean False (Loco) 25, 27
Acaena 61
Aguila 185, 186; pescadora 184, 185
Aguilucho 187, 189; chico 188, 189; de cola rojiza 188, 189; de la puna 188
Akodont Andean 310, 311; Andean Long-clawed 311, 313; Long-haired 311, 312, 362; Olive-colored 310, 311 362; Sanborn's 311, 312; White-bellied 310, 311, 352; Wooly 311, 312, 372; Yellow-nosed 311, 312
Albatros cabeza gris 154, 157; ceja negra 152, 157; de Buller 154, 157; de las Antípodas 151, 153; de Chathams 155, 157; de Galápagos 156, 157; de Salvin 155, 157; errante 151, 153; oscuro 156; oscuro de manto claro 155, 157; real del norte 151, 152; real del sur 151, 152
Albatros Antipodean 151, 153; Black-browed 152, 157, 352, 367, 369, 372, 374; Buller's (Pacific) 154, 157; Chatham Island 155, 157; Grey-headed 154, 157, 375; Light-mantled 155, 157; Northern Royal 151, 152, 359; Salvin's 155, 157, 359; Sooty 156; Southern Royal 151, 152, 375; Wandering 151, 153, 375; Waved 156, 157
Albatross Monument 150
Alberto de Agostini Park 375
Alejandro Selkirk (Is. Masafuera) 17
Alerce 33, 52–55, 74, 77, 366–368
Alerce Andino Park 367
Algae Marine (Seaweed) 30, 31; snow 71; terrestrial 71
Algarrobo blanco 35, 36, 37, 83; chileno 35, 36, 37, 42, 83, 83, 354
Algas marinas 30, 31
Alpaca 304, 352
Alstroemeria 37, 50, 51
Altiplano 8, 38, 87, 88, 350–354
Altiplano (Bolivian) winter 4, 30
Alto Andino 8
Añañuca 37, 356
Anchovy (Anchoveta) 22, 23
Andes Mediterráneos 8, 38
Andes Mountain Range 8
Anémona 62, 63
Ani Groove-billed 233, 350
Antarctica 17–20; flora of 19, 70, 71; marine life 20; birds 20
Antarctic Circle 20
Antarctic Convergence 20
Antofagasta 351, 354
Araucaria 33, 47, 50, 51, 73, 76, 362, 363, 364
Arica 3, 9, 350
Arjona 65
Armadillo Andean Hairy 295, 352, 353; Big Hairy 295, 296; Pichi 295, 296, 369, 370
Aromo de Castilla 79
Arrayán 33, 41, 56, 73, 84, 88, 362

Ave del trópico de cola blanca 172, 173; de cola roja 172, 173; de pico rojo 172, 173
Ave fragata grande 172, 173
Avellano 33, 47, 56, 81, 360
Avestruz 128
Avocet Andean 202, 352, 354
Bailarín 184, 185; chico argentino 273, 275; chico peruano 273, 275
Ballena boreal 336, 337; Cachalote 345; Cachalote pigmeo 346; de Héctor 347, 349; de Layard 347, 349; enana 336, 337; enana sin mancha blanca 336, 337; franca austral 333, 335; franca pigmea 334, 335; Jorobada 334, 335; Orca 343, 344; Orca falsa 343, 345; picuda de Shepherd 347, 348; Piloto 343, 344; Rorcual azul 337, 338; Rorcual común 337, 338; Scamperdown 347, 348; Zifio común 346, 347; Zifio marsopa 346; nariz de botella 348
Balsam Bog 87
Bamboo Colihue (Culeú) 51, 89; Quila 47, 48, 89; Quila enana 89
Bandurilla 244; de Arica 246; de la puna 246; de pico recto 246
Bandurria 180
Barberry 50, 61, 63, 76, 77
Bat Big-eared Brown 293, 294, 350, 368; Chilean Mouse-eared Myotis 293, 294, 368; Vampire 293, 294, 350, 368; Hoary 293, 295; Free-tailed 293, 294, 350; Red 295; Smoky 294
Beagle Channel 8, 13, 374, 375
Beaver American 326, 327
Becacina 212, 215; de la puna 212, 215; grande 213, 215; pintada 214, 215
Beech Southern 45, 77
Bellflower Chilean 33, 89
Belloto de norte 41, 43, 76, 358; del sur 76
Bernardo O'Higgins Park 370
Birro gris 260
Bittern Stripe-backed 178, 179, 359
Blackbird Austral 288, 289, 359, 363, 369, 370; Yellow-winged 288, 289
Blanquillo 141, 142
Boar European Wild 309
Bofedales 38
Boldo 33, 41, 43, 75, 356, 358, 359
Bollén 43, 81
Booby Blue-footed 173, 174; Brown 173, 174; Masked 14, 16, 173, 174; Peruvian 173, 174, 350, 353, 355, 356
Botellita 53, 57
Box Native 60, 88
Bromeliad Ajo dulce 67; Tillandsia 34, 35, 89
Butterflies 90–105; Blues 97, 98, 99, 352; Eroessa 96, 97, 366; Four-eyed Lady 101, 103, 350; Fritillary 101, 366; Hairstreak 97, 98, 366; Ministreaks

97, 98, 350; Monarch 97, 99, 350; Satyr 100–103; Skipperling 93, 94; Skippers 92–95, 350; Snout 101, 103; Sulphur 93, 95; Swallowtail 93, 95; Whites 95–97, 350, 352 375; Yellows 95, 350
Butterfly Moth Castnid 103, 105
Buzzard-Eagle Black-chested 185, 186, 356, 358, 360, 364, 366, 369, 370, 372
Cabbage Tree 67
Cabo de Hornos 7, 11, 150, 376
Cachaña 231, 232
Cachudito 267, 268; de cresta blanca 267, 268; Juan Fernández 267, 268; del norte 267, 268
Cactus Acachaño 37; Candelabra 34, 35, 37, 87; Cardón 35, 36, 87, 354; Chastudo 37; Cholla 37; Copao 35; Copiapoa 35, 87; Eulychnia 34, 35, 87; Opuntia 35, 37, 87; Quisco 41, 42, 87, 358
Caenolestid Long-nosed 292, 293, 366, 367
Caiquén 132, 133
Caití 202, 203
Calafate 50, 51, 62, 63, 76, 369, 374
Calamar común 26
California Poppy 40
Camanchaca fog 4, 30, 34
Canastero 252, 253; Austral 253, 254; Canyon 253, 254, 352; chico 252, 253; Cordilleran 252, 253, 352; Dark-winged 252, 253, 352; de cola larga 253, 254; del norte 252, 253; del sur 253, 254; de quebradas 253, 254; Dusky-tailed 253, 358, 359; Sharp-billed 253, 254, 360
Canelilla 53, 57
Canelo 33, 41, 46, 47, 50–55, 59, 60, 66, 67, 73, 74, 78, 356–374
Canquén 132, 133
Cape Horn 9, 13, 150, 376
Caracara Chimango 6, 188, 191, 358, 367, 368, 372; Mountain 190, 191, 352, 360, 363; Southern 190, 191, 364, 366, 368, 370, 372; Striated 191, 192, 375; White-throated 190, 191
Caracol 27, 28, 29; de bosque 53
Caranca 133, 134
Carancho cordillerano 190, 191; cordillerano del sur 190; negro 192
Carbonillo 35, 36
Carpintero 241, 242
Carpinterito 241, 243
Carza 85
Castor 326, 327
Cat Andean Mountain 300, 301; Colocolo 300, 301; Cougar (Puma) 301, 302; Geoffroy's 301, 302; Kodkod 301, 302; Pampas 300, 301
Cavy 319, 320; Common Yellow-toothed 319, 320, 352, 353; Southern Mountain 319, 320

385

386 INDEX OF COMMON NAMES

Cazamoscas chocolate 259, 260
Central Valley 9, 10
Cephalopods 26
Cernícalo 14, 191, 193
Chacay 43
Chagual 41, 42, 89, 358, 360
Chañar 35, 37, 83, 354
Chascón 31
Chat-Tyrant D'Orbigny's 264, 265, 352; White-browed 264, 265, 352
Chaura 61, 80
Chaurita 61, 80
Chercán 272, 273; de las vegas 272
Chilco 59, 63, 85; de Magallanes 63
Chilia Crag 247, 248, 358, 359
Chilla (fox) 299, 354–374
Chiloé (Is.) 9, 367
Chinchilla andina 318, 319; chilena 318, 319; Long-tailed 318, 319; Short-tailed 318, 319
Chinchilla Mouse Altiplano 314, 315, 352, 353
Chinchilla Rat Bennett's 324, 325; Ashy 324, 325
Chincol 285
Chingue 297, 298; de la Patagonia 297, 298; real 298
Chiricoca 247, 248
Chirihue 282, 287; austral 284, 287; cordillerano 284, 287; dorado 284, 287; verdoso 284, 287
Chiton 25, 27
Chiu Chiu 355
Chorlito cordillerano 199, 201
Chorlo ártico 198, 199; cabezón 204; chileno 199, 200; de campo 199, 201; de collar 199, 201; de doble collar 199, 200; de la puna 199, 201; de Magallanes 203, 205; dorado 198, 199; gritón 199, 200; nevado 199, 200; semipalmado 198, 199
Choroy 231, 232
Chozchoz 323, 352
Chucao 256, 257
Chuncho 234, 235
Chungará Lago 12, 350, 352
Churrete 247, 248; acanelado 247, 248; austral 247, 249; chico 247, 249; costero 247, 248; de alas blancas 247, 249
Churrín de la Mocha 256, 257; del norte 257, 258; del sur 256, 257
Ciervo rojo 307, 309
Cinclodes Bar-winged 247, 248, 352, 360, 372, 375; Blackish 247, 249; Chilean Seaside 247, 248, 350, 353, 356; Dark-bellied 247, 248, 363, 366, 368, 369, 372, 375; Grey-flanked 247, 249, 360; White-winged 247, 249, 352
Ciprés de la cordillera 47, 73; de las Guaitecas 54, 73
Cisne coscoroba 131, 133; de cuello negro 131, 133

Clams 25, 27
Clavel del campo 38, 39
Climate 4, 5
Coastal Mountains 8, 9
Coatimundi, So. American 17, 302
Cochayuyo 31
Codorniz 129, 130
Coicopihue 53, 57, 89
Coigüe (Coihue) 33, 45, 46, 47, 52–55, 58–60, 73, 78, 360–374
Coigüe de Chiloé 33, 45, 54, 55, 57, 79, 367, 369; de Magallanes 33, 45, 59, 79, 369
Col de Juan Fernández 67
Colegial 265, 266; del norte 266
Coliguay 42, 48
Colilarga 249, 251
Colilargo Long-tailed 311, 313, 368, 369, 370, 372
Colocolo 300, 301, 360, 362
Comadrejita trompuda 292, 293
Comesebo chico 276, 277; de los tamarugales 276, 277; gigante 276; 277; grande 250, 251; negro 275, 277
Cometocino de Arica 279, 281; de dorso castaño 279, 280; de Gay 281, 283; del norte 281, 283; patagónico 281, 283
Concón 234, 235
Condor Andean 183, 352–375
Conebill Cinereous 276, 277, 352, 353, 359, 360, 364, 368; Giant 276, 277, 362; Tamarugo 35, 36, 276, 277, 352
Conejo 327, 328
Coney Rat Hairy-soled 315, 316
Conguillio-Los Paraguas 363
Coot Andean 195, 196; Giant 195, 196, 352; Horned 195, 196, 355, 356; Red-fronted 195, 196; Red-gartered 195, 196, 359, 364, 366, 367, 370; White-winged 194, 195, 356
Copihue 33, 53, 57, 89, 362, 366
Coquito 43, 44
Corbatita 278, 279
Corcolén 79, 80
Cordillera Darwin 8, 375; de la Araucanía 8; Occidental 8; Patagónica 8
Cormorán antártico 176, 177; de las rocas 176, 177; guanay 175, 177; imperial 175, 177
Cormorant Blue-eyed Shag 176, 177; Guanay 175, 177, 350, 353, 355, 356, 367, 368; Imperial 175, 177, 368, 372, 375; Neotropic 175, 177, 352, 359, 367, 369; Red-legged 175, 177, 350, 353, 355, 356; Rock 176, 177, 367, 372
Coruro 323, 325
Cotorra 233
Cowbird Shiny 288, 289
Coypu (Coipo) 324, 325, 364, 366, 368, 369, 370
Crabs 24, 25
Crowberry 60, 61, 80, 207

Crucero 43
Crustaceans (Crustáceos) 24, 25
Cuerno de cabra 37
Cuervo de pantano 180, 181; de la puna 180, 181
Culebra de cola corta 117; de cola larga 117
Culpeo (fox) 298, 299, 352–374
Cuy chico 319, 320; de dientes amarillos 319, 320; serrano 319, 320
Cypress Cordilleran 33, 47, 49, 72, 360, 362, 368; Guaitecas 33, 54, 59, 60, 73, 366, 368, 369; Patagonian (Alerce) 53, 55, 74, 366, 367, 368
Dandelion 65
Darwin's Bread 58, 59
Dedal de oro 40
Deer Fallow 307, 309; Guemal (Huemul) 306, 307, 362, 368; Pudu 307, 308, 367; Red 307, 309; Taruca 307, 308, 352
Degu 322, 325, 358, 362; Bridges' 323, 325, 362; de los matorrales 323, 325; Mountain 323, 325
Delfín austral 340; azul 342; chileno 339; común 340; cruzado 340; gris 344; liso 342; oscuro 340; pardo 342; Tonina común 342; Tonina overa 339
Desventuradas (Is.) 14
Diddle-dee 61, 80
Diuca 281, 283; de alas blancas 282
Diuca-Finch Common 16, 281, 283, 352, 356, 358, 360, 367; White-winged 282, 283, 352
Diucon Fire-eyed 259, 260, 358, 363, 367, 368, 372, 375
Diving-Petrel Common 171, 369, 374; Magellanic 171, 372, 375; Peruvian 171, 350, 353, 359
Dolphin Bottlenose 342, 343, 353; Chilean 339, 341, 368; Commerson's 339, 341; Dusky 340, 341; Hourglass 340, 341; Pantropical Spotted 341, 342; Peale's 340, 341, 367, 368; Risso's (Grampus) 343, 344; Short-beaked 340, 341, 353; Southern Right Whale 342, 343; Striped 341, 342, 353
Don Diego de la noche 37
Doradito Warbling 265, 266, 359
Dormilona cenicienta 262, 263; chica 263, 264; de ceja blanca 261, 263; de frente negra 261, 263; de la puna 261, 263; de nuca rojiza 261, 263; fraile 261, 263; gigante 262, 263; rufa 262, 263; tontita 262, 263
Dotterel Rufous-chested 199, 200, 359; Tawny-throated 199, 201, 353
Dove Eared 228, 229, 350, 354; Pacific 228, 229, 350, 353; Rock 16, 228, 229
Draba 65
Duck Andean135, 137, 352, 363, 364; Black-headed 135, 137, 359; Crested 136, 137, 352, 356, 372, 375;

INDEX OF COMMON NAMES 387

Duck (cont.) Lake 135, 137, 359; Muscovy 140; Spectacled 139, 140, 363; Torrent 134, 137, 360, 364, 366; Whistling 131
Earthcreeper Band-tailed 246, 247; Plain-breasted 245, 246, 352; Scale-throated 244, 245, 360; Straight-billed 246, 247, 352; White-throated 245, 246, 352
Easter Island flora 15, 68; map of 15; marine life 15; birds 15
Echinoderms 24, 25
Egret Cattle 178, 179, 353; Eastern Reef 178; Great 176, 179, 359, 367; Snowy 178, 179
Elaenia White-crested 264, 265, 362, 367, 368, 372
El Niño (ENSO) 21
El Yali Reserve 359
El Yeso Reservoir 359
Espinillo 39, 83, 356
Espinal 40, 41
Espino 33, 41, 42, 83, 358
Estrellita 53, 57
Euneomys Tierra del Fuego 317
Fachine 62, 63, 88
Falcon Aplomado 191, 192, 352, 363; Peregrine 191, 192, 353, 356, 360, 364
Falkland Lavender 65
Fardela atlántica 165, 167; blanca 165, 167; blanca de Cook 162, 164; blanca de Juan Fernández 162, 165; blanca de Masatierra 162, 164; capirotada 165; de alas grandes 161; de dorso gris 165, 167; de fénix 161, 164; de frente blanca 164; de Kerguelen 161, 164; de Masafuera 162, 164; de Pascua 165, 167; de Nueva Zelanda 165; gris 165, 166; heraldica 161. 164; moteada 162; negra 165, 166; negra de Juan Fernández 161, 164; negra de patas pálidas 165; negra grande 165, 166
Fern Blechnum 57, 60, 61, 66; Quilquil 57; Tree-fern 67
Field-Tyrant Short-tailed 350
Finch Black-throated 282, 283; Slender-billed 282, 283, 350; Yellow-bridlec 282, 283, 363
Fío-Fío 264, 265
Firebush (Notro) 81
Firecrown Green-backed 239, 240, 358, 362, 363, 366-369, 372, 375; Juan Fernández 17, 239, 240
Fish 12, 21, 22, 23, 24, 366, 370
Flamenco chileno 181, 182
Flamingo Andean 181, 182, 350, 352-356, 360-364, 369-374; Chilean 181, 182, 350, 352-356, 360-364, 370; James' (Puna) 181, 182, 352, 354
Flicker Andean 242, 352; Chilean 242, 358-360, 368, 370
Flor de la Cuncuna 65; del minero 37
Flowering Desert 37, 356

Flowerpiercer Black-throated 275, 277, 352
Flycatcher Vermillion 265, 267, 350
Foca cangrejera 331, 332; de Ross 331, 332; de Weddell 331, 332; Elefante marino 331, 333; Leopardo marino 331, 332
Fox Chilla 299, 354-374; Culpeo 298, 299, 352-374; Darwin's 299, 363, 367; South American Grey 299, 354-374
Fray Jorge Park 356
Frigatebird Great 16, 172, 173
Frog Banded Wood 122, 123. 363, 366, 368; Chile Four-eyed 120, 121, 355-363, 366, 368; Chiloé Ground 123; Contulmo Ground 124; Darwin's 123, 125, 363-370; Emerald Forest 123, 124, 366-367; Emilio's Ground 124; Grey Foureyed 121, 362-375; Grey Wood 122, 123, 363, 368; Marbled Water 122, 123, 352; Marbled Wood 122, 123, 363, 370; Mocha Island Ground 124 Nahuelbuta Ground 123, 363; Nibaldo's Wood 122, 123; Rosy Ground 123, 124, 363; Sapo hermoso 120, 121; Spiny-chest 123, 125, 362, 367-374; Valdivia Ground 123, 124, 367. Zapahuira Water 352
Fuchsia Magellanic 59, 60, 85, 369
Fuinque 33, 59, 60, 82
Fulmar Southern 20, 158, 159, 359, 367
Gallina ciega 235, 236
Gallinule Spot-flanked 194, 195
Gamo 309
Garra de león 37, 356
Garza azul 178, 179; boyera 178, 179; chica 178, 179; cuca 176, 179; grande 176, 179
Gastropods 27
Gato de pajonal 300; Guigna 301, 302; montés 301, 302; montés andino 300, 301; pajero 300; Puma 301, 302
Gaviota andina 221, 222; austral 219, 220; cahuil 221, 222; de Franklin 221, 222; de los Galápagos 221, 222; de Sabine 221, 222; dominicana 219, 220; garuma 219, 221; peruana 219, 221
Gaviotín antártico 224, 225; apizarrado 226, 227; ártico 224, 225; b anco 226; boreal 224, 225; chico 223, 225; de San Ambrosio 226, 227; de San Félix 224, 227; elegante 226, 225; monja 223, 225; pascuense 226, 227; piquerito 223, 225; sudamericano 223, 225
Gecko Chilean Marked 116, 356, 358; Leaf-toed 116, 350, 354; Mourning 16, 116
Gekko polinésico 116
Gentian Magellanic 64, 65

Giant-Petrel Northern (Hall's) 158, 159; Southern (Antarctic) 20, 156, 159, 350, 359, 367, 372, 374
Godwit Hudsonian 205, 207
Golondrina barranquera 270, 271; bermeja 270, 271 chilena 269, 271; de dorsa negro 259, 271; de los riscos 269, 271; grande 270, 271; peruana 270, 271
Golondrina de mar 168, 169; chica 169, 170; de collar 169, 171; de garganta blanca 169, 170; de vientre blanco 169, 170; de vientre negro 169, 170; negra 169, 171; peruana 169, 170; subantártica 169, 170
Goose Andean 132, 133, 352, 356, 360; Ashy-headed 132, 133, 363, 366, 368, 374; Kelp 133, 134, 369, 375; Ruddy-headed 132. 133; Upland 132, 133, 368, 369, 372, 374, 375
Gorrión 285
Grasses Antarctic Hairgrass 20, 70; Bunchgrass 39; Carex sedge 62; Festuca 38, 39, 50, 62, 64, 65; Juncus rush 61; Stipa 38, 39; Totora reed 68, 69; Tussock (Poa) 60, 61, 374, 375
Grassquit Blue-black 278, 279, 350
Grebe Great 141, 359, 364, 366, 367; Hooded 142; Pied-billed 141, 142, 364; Silvery 141, 142, 352, 359; White-tufted 141, 142, 352
Greenbush 64, 65
Grison Lesser 297, 298, 358, 362, 364, 366, 368
Ground-Dove Bare-faced 229, 230, 352; Black-winged 229, 230, 352, 360; Croaking 229, 230, 350; Golden-spotted 229, 230, 354; Picui 229, 230, 358; Ruddy 230
Ground-Tyrant Black-fronted 261, 263, 360; Cinereous 262, 263, 353, 360; Cinnamon-bellied 262, 263; Dark-faced 262, 263; Ochre-naped 261, 263, 360; Puna 261 263; Rufous-naped 261, 263, 352, 354, 360; Spot-billed 263, 264; White-browed 261, 263. 360, 366; White-fronted 262, 263 352
Grumbler Bibro's 114, 369, 370, 372, 374; Darwin's 114, 115, 369, 372; Leopard 114, 115; Southern 114, 115, 362, 363, 367, 368
Gruñidor del sur 114, 115
Guanaco 303, 305, 352, 356, 360, 370, 374
Guayacán 42, 356
Guaren 327
Guemal 306 (see Huemul)
Guigna 302 (see Kodkod)
Guindo Santo 48, 81, 362
Guinea Pig 318, 319; Montane 319, 320
Gull Andean 221, 222, 352, 254; Band-tailed 219, 221, 350, 353; Brown-hooded 221, 222, 354, 359,

388 INDEX OF COMMON NAMES

Gull (cont.) 367, 372; Dolphin 219, 220, 367, 368, 375; Franklin's 221, 222, 353, 354, 367, 368; Grey 219, 221, 350, 353, 354, 355; Kelp 219, 220, 350, 353, 354, 356, 367, 368, 369, 375; Sabine's 221, 222, 350, 353; Swallow-tailed 221, 222
Gunnera 57, 60, 61, 66, 82
Halcón perdiguero 191, 192; peregrino 191, 192
Hare European 327, 328
Harrier Cinereous 185, 186, 359, 364, 368
Hawk Chilean 185, 186, 358, 362, 363, 364, 366, 368; Harris's 187, 189, 358; Juan Fernández Variable 17; Puna 188; Rufous-tailed 188, 189, 363, 368; Variable 187, 189, 352, 354–356, 358, 360, 368; White-throated 188, 189, 363, 364, 366
Heron Cocoi 176, 179, 359, 367; Green-backed 178; Little Blue 178, 179, 353; Tricolored 178
Hillstar Andean 237, 352; White-sided 237, 360
Huairavillo 178, 179
Huairavo 178, 179
Huala (tree/arbol) 45, 46, 78
Huala (pájaro) 141
Hualo 33, 45–49, 78, 83, 360
Hued-Hued castaño 255, 257; del sur 255, 257
Huemul chileno 306, 307, 362, 368, 369, 370, 372; del norte 307, 308, 352
Huet-huet Black-throated 255, 257, 363, 366, 267, 268, 369; Chestnut-throated 255, 257, 363
Huilli 37, 325
Huillin 296, 297
Huingán 41, 43, 86
Huiro 31
Humboldt Current 4, 21
Humboldt Penguin Reserve 356
Hummingbird Giant 237, 238, 352, 358; Oasis 237, 238, 350
Huroncito 297
Ibis Black-faced 180, 181, 359, 367, 368, 374; Puna 180, 181, 352; White-faced 180, 181
Icefield (Hielo de campo) 8
Iquique 353, 354
Irenomys Large-footed 315, 316, 368
Isla de Pascua 13, 68
Jabalí 309
Jaeger Long-tailed 217, 220; Parasitic (Arctic) 217, 218, 350, 359; Pomarine 217, 218, 350
Jarrilla 83
Jibía 26
Jilguero 286, 287; cordillerano 286, 287; grande 286, 287; negro 286, 287; peruano 286, 287
Jote de cabeza colorada 183, 184; de cabeza negra 183, 184

Juan Bueno 66, 67, 88
Juan Fernández Archipelago 17; birds 17; flora 66; marine life 17
Kelp 30, 31, 374, 375
Kestrel American 191, 193, 355, 358, 370; Juan Fernández subsp. 14, 17
Killdeer 199, 200
Kingfisher Green 241, 242; Ringed 240, 241, 366–370, 372
Kite White-tailed 184, 185, 360, 368
Knot Red 208, 209
Kodkod 301, 302, 360, 362, 364, 366, 368, 369, 372
Krill 22
La Campana Park 358
Lady's Slipper Marsh 63
Lagartos y lagartijas 108–114
Lago Cochrane (Tamango) 370
Lago Jeinimeni Reserve 370
Lago Pañuelas Reserve 359
Laguna del Laja Park 362
Laguna de los Cisnes 372
Laguna Peral Reserve 359
Laguna San Rafael Park 369
Lakes (Lagos) 12
La Portada Nat'l Monument 354
Lapwing Andean 198, 199, 352; Southern 197, 199, 367, 368, 372
Las Vicuñas Reserve 353
Lauca National Park 350
Laucha 326, 327; Altiplano 314, 315, 352, 254; Graceful 314, 315
Lauchita andina 314, 315
Lauchón orejudo austral 315, 316; orejudo de Darwin 315, 316
Laurel 33, 47, 53, 56, 75, 360, 362
Leaf-eared Mouse Darwin's 36, 315, 316; Patagonian 315, 316, 370
Lechuza 233, 235
Leña dura 85
Lenga 33, 45, 47, 50, 52, 58, 62, 63, 78, 363–370, 372, 374
Leucheria Hahn's 65
Lichen Old Man's Beard 59; Xanthoria 71; types of 71
Liebre 327, 328
Lile 175, 177
Lilén 43, 78, 79, 358, 359
Limpets 27
Lingue 33, 41, 46, 47, 56, 76, 360
Lion's Claw 37, 356
Lirio del campo 37
Litre 33, 41, 42, 46, 86
Lizards 108–115
Llaca (Yaca) 292, 293, 356, 360
Llama 304, 305, 352
Llanos de Challe Park 356
Llareta 38, 39, 62, 86, 350
Lleuque 48, 74, 362
Lobo de dos pelos 329, 331; de Juan Fernández 329, 331; de un pelo 330, 331; marino gracil 330, 331
Loica 289, 290; peruana 289, 290
Longitudinal depression 8, 10

Los Flamencos Reserve 354
Los Huemules del Niblinto 362
Los Pinguinos Reserve 372
Luche 30, 31
Luma 33, 41, 53, 54, 56, 66, 67, 84, 85, 358, 367
Lupine 65
Magellanic Coigüe 59, 78, 364, 367, 369, 370, 372, 374
Maiden's Slipper 65
Maillico 63
Maitén 41, 46, 47, 48, 59, 60, 85, 358, 362, 369
Mañío de hojas cortas 48, 74; de hojas largas 56, 74; de hojas punzantes 56, 74; Long-leaved 56, 74; Prickly-leafed 56, 74; Short-leaved 48, 74
Manzano 66, 67
Maqui 47, 48, 66, 79
Marigold Arrow-leaved 63
Mariposas 90–102
Mariscos 24, 25; Almeja 25; Centolla 25; Choro 25; Erizo 25; Jaiba 25; Loco 25, 354; Macha 25; Ostión 25; Ostra 25; Picorocos 25; Piure 24, 354
Marsopa de anteojos 339, 341; spinosa 339, 341
Martin Peruvian 270, 271
Martín pescador 240, 241, pescador chico 241, 242
Matacaballos 233
Mata verde 62, 63, 64, 88
Matorral 40–44
Mayu 43, 84
Meadowlark Long-tailed 289, 290, 356, 359, 372; Peruvian 289, 290, 350
Medallita 53, 57
Mero 258, 259; de la puna 258, 259; de Tarapacá 258, 259; gaucho 259, 260
Metamorphosis 90, 125
Michay 51, 61, 63, 66, 77
Miner Common 243, 245, 354; Creamy-rumped 244, 245; Greyish 244, 245; Puna 244, 245, 352; Rufous-banded 244, 245, 360; Short-billed 243, 245
Minero 243, 245
Minero 244, 245; austral 243, 245; chico 244, 245; cordillerano 244, 245; de la puna 244, 245; grande 244, 245
Mink American 297
Mirlo 253, 254
Mistletoe 59
Mitique 43, 362
Mockingbird Chilean 273, 274, 356, 358–360, 363; Patagonian 273, 274; White-banded 274
Mole Mouse Valdivian Long-clawed 311, 313, 368
Molle 41, 42, 86
Mollusks (Moluscos) 24, 25
Mollymauks 152, 157
Monito del Monte 292, 293, 360, 362, 364, 366, 367, 368

INDEX OF COMMON NAMES 389

Monkey Puzzle Tree 50, 51, 72
Moorhen Common 194, 195
Moth Bella 105; Four-eyed 105; Saturniidae 104; Sphinx 105; Tebo 42, 103; Venusta 105
Mountain Berry 61, 79
Mouse Altiplano Chinchilla 315; Andean 314, 315, 352; Darwin's Leaf-eared 36, 315, 316; House 326, 327; Patagonian Leaf-eared 315; Puna 314, 315
Murciélago cola de raton 293, 294; colorado 293, 295; de Schnabel 293, 294; gris 293, 295; orejas de raton del sur 293, 294; orejón grande 293, 294; Vampiro 293, 294
Murta 53, 57, 80, 85
Muskrat Common 326, 327
Mustelids 296–298
Mutilla 80
Mutisia 38, 39
Nahuelbuta 9, 363
Nalca 82
Ñandú 64, 128
Naranjero 275, 277
Naranjillo 67
Nautilus Paper 26, 29
Negrillo 278, 279
Negrito Andean (White-winged) 266, 352, 354; Austral 265, 266, 368, 372, 375
Neotomys Red-nosed 317
Nevados de Chillán 362
Nevado Tres Cruces Park 355
Night-Heron Black-crowned 178, 179, 352, 353
Nightjar Band-winged 235, 236
Ñirre 33, 45, 50, 54, 62, 63, 78, 360, 363, 366, 370, 372
Noddy Brown 14, 16, 224, 227; Grey (Ternlet) 14, 16, 226, 227
Norte Chico 3, 12; map 357
Norte Grande 3; map 351
Notro 33, 50, 59, 60, 62, 81, 363, 369, 370, 372, 374
Nuco 234, 235
Nutria 324
Octodonts 322–324
Octopus Changos 26
Ojos del Salado 8, 355
Olivillo 46, 47, 52, 53, 54, 56, 85, 356, 364, 366, 368
Opossum Elegant Fat-tailed Mouse (Llaca) 292, 293, 356, 360
Orchid Dog 62, 63; Pico de Loro 65; Yellow 62, 63
Osprey 184, 185
Otter Marine 296, 297, 350, 353, 355, 356, 367–369, 372, 375; Southern River 296, 297, 366, 368, 369
Owl Austral Pygmy 234, 235, 358, 366, 368; Barn 233, 235, 356; Burrowing 235, 236, 350, 354; Magellanic Horned 234, 235, 354,

356; Rufous-legged 234, 235, 358, 362, 363; Short-eared 234, 235
Oystercatcher American 202, 203, 350; Blackish 202, 203, 350, 353, 356, 372, 375; Magellanic 202, 203, 369, 372
Painted-Snipe South American 214, 215
Pajarito 37
Pájaro amarillo 265, 266; plomo 279, 280
Pajonales 38
Palm Chilean 43, 44, 68, 88, 358; Chonta 66, 67, 88; Coquito 43; Juania 66, 67, 88; Kan-Kán 43, 44, 88
Paloma 223, 229; antártica 203, 205; de alas blancas 228, 229
Palomita 63
Palqui 43
Pampa del Tamarugal 10
Pan de Azúcar Park 355
Parakeet Austral 231, 232, 360, 363, 366, 368, 369, 370, 372, 374, 375; Monk 231, 233; Mountain 231, 232, 360; Slender-billed 231, 232, 363, 364, 366, 357, 368
Parina chica 181, 182; grande 181, 182
Parinacota 350, 352
Parque Pumalín 368
Parrot Burrowing 231, 360, 362
Pata de guanaco 37
Patagón 246, 247
Patagua 33, 41, 43, 79
Pato anteojillo 139, 140; capuchino 138, 139; colorado 138, 139; cortacorrientes 134, 137; criollo 140; cuchara 139, 140; gargantillo 138, 139; jergón chico 136, 139; jergón grande 136, 139; juarjual 136, 137; negro 136, 137; puna 138, 139; rana de pico ancho 135, 137; rana de pico celgado 135, 137; real 139, 140; rinconero 135, 137; silbón 131
Pearlwort Antarctic 20, 70
Pehuén 51, 73
Pelican Peruvian Brown 173, 174, 350, 353, 355, 356
Pelícano 173, 174
Pelillo 30, 31
Penguin Adelie 20, 145, 146, 147; Chinstrap 20, 145, 147; Emperor 145, 148; Gentoo 20, 145, 147; Humboldt 143, 145, 350, 353, 355, 356, 359; King 145, 148; Macaroni 145, 148; Magellanic 144, 145, 367, 368, 372, 374, 375; Rockhopper 144, 145, 146
Pepitero 276, 277
Peppertree 35, 86
Pequén 235, 236
Perdicita 214, 215; cojón 213, 215; cordillerana 213, 215; cordillerana austral 213, 215

Perdiz austral 129, 130; chilena 128, 129; copetona 129, 130; cordillerana 129, 130; cordillerana de Arica 129, 130; de la puna 129, 130
Perico cordillerano 231, 232
Pericote andino 310, 311; Bolivian 314, 315, 352, 354; Southern 310, 311, 368
Perrito 203, 204
Pescados 22, 23
Petrel Antarctic 20, 159, 160; antártico 159, 160; azulado 163, 164; Blue 163, 164; Cape (Pintado) 159, 160, 359, 367, 372, 375; Cook's 162, 164; de las nieves 159, 160; Great-winged 161, 164; Grey 165, 166; Herald 161, 164; Juan Fernández 17, 162, 165; Kerguelen 161, 164; Kermadec 14, 16, 161, 164; Masatierra 14, 162, 164, 359; moteado 159, 160; Mottled 162; Phoenix 16, 161, 164; plateado 158, 159; Snow 20, 159, 160; Stejneger's 17, 162, 164; Westland 166, 359; White-chinned 165, 166, 350, 359, 375; White-headed 163, 164
Petrel-paloma antártico 163, 164
Petrel gigante antártico 156, 159; subantártico 158, 159
Peuco 187, 189
Peumo 33, 41, 43, 46, 76, 358, 360
Peuquito 185, 186
Phalarope Red (Grey) 211, 359; Red-necked (Northern) 211, 212, 350; Wilson's 211, 212, 352, 367
Picaflor azul 238, 239; chico 239, 240; cordillerano 237, 239, de Arica, 238, 239; de Cora 238, 239; de Juan Fernández 239, 240; de la puna 237, 239; del norte 238, 239; gigante 238, 239
Pichi 295, 296, 369, 370
Picurio 141, 142
Pidén 194, 195; austral 193, 195
Pidencito 193, 195
Pigeon Chilean 228, 229, 358, 360, 362, 366, 368
Pilpilén 202, 203; austral 202, 203; negro 202, 203
Pimiento 35, 36, 37, 86, 354
Pimpollo 141, 142; tobiano 142
Pingo-pingo 38, 39, 75
Pingüino antártico 145, 147; de Adélie 145, 146; de Humboldt 143, 145; de Magallanes 144, 145; de penacho amarillo 144, 145; emperador 145, 148; macaroni 145, 146; papúa 145, 147; rey 145, 148
Pintail White-cheeked 138, 139, 359; Yellow-billed 136, 139, 352, 369, 372
Pipevine 93, 95
Pipit Correndera 273, 275, 363, 372; Yellowish 273, 275
Piquero 173, 174; blanco 173, 174; café 173, 174; de patas azules 173, 174

Pisco 12
Pitajo gris 264, 265; rojizo 264, 265
Pitío 241, 242; del norte 241, 242
Pitotoy chico 206, 207; grande 206, 207
Pitra 85
Piuquén 132, 133
Pizarrita 282, 283
Plantcutter Rufous-tailed 270, 273, 358, 359, 364, 366, 367
Platero 278, 279
Playero ártico 208, 209; blanco 208, 209; de Baird 209, 210; de las rompientes 207, 208; de lomo blanco 209, 210; enano 209, 210; grande 206, 207; manchado 208, 209; pectoral 209, 210; semipalmado 209, 210; vuelvepiedras 207, 208
Plebeyo 279, 280
Plover American Golden 198, 199; Black-bellied 198, 199; Collared 199, 201, 359; Magellanic 203, 205, 372; Puna 199, 201, 352, 354; Semipalmated 198, 199; Snowy 199, 200; Two-banded 199, 200
Pochard Rosy-billed 136, 137
Polizónte 57
Pollito de mar boreal 211, 212; rojizo 211; tricolor 211, 212
Porpoise Burmeister's 339, 341; Spectacled 339, 341, 375
Primula Magellanic 65
Prion Antarctic 163, 164
Pudu Southern 307, 308, 360–370
Puma 301, 302, 352–374
Puna 8, 38, 88, 350, 352–355
Punta Arenas 13, 372
Puyehue Park 364
Quail California 129, 130, 356, 362
Queltehue 197, 199; de la puna 198, 199
Queñoa 38, 39, 81
Quetru no volador 134, 137; volador 134, 137
Queulat Park 369
Queule 33, 48, 75
Quiaca 38, 39, 79
Quillay 33, 41, 42, 46, 81, 358, 360
Quinoa 38, 39
Quintero (city) 359
Quique 297, 298
Quirquincho 295, 296
Rabbit Old World 327, 328
Radal 33, 47, 48, 82
Radal Siete Tazas Reserve 360
Rail Austral 193, 195; Black 193, 195; Plumbeous 194, 195, 359, 364, 375
Rapa Nui (Easter Is.) 15
Rara 270, 273
Rat Norway 327; Roof (Black) 327
Rata almizclera 326, 327; andina 314, 315; arborea chilena 315, 316; cola pincel 323, 325; conejo 315, 316; negra 327; sedosa fueguina 315, 317

Ratón achallo 314, 315; andino 310, 311; chinchilla 324, 325; colilargo 313; colorado 311, 312; de los espinos 311, 313; ebrio 315, 317; hocico bayo 311, 312; negruzco 311, 312; olivaceo 310, 311; orejudo 314, 315; topo grande 311, 313; topo valdiviano 311, 313; ventriblanco 310, 311
Ratoncito de pié sedoso 314, 315; lanudo 311, 312
Raulí 33, 45, 46, 47, 49, 77, 364
Rayadito 250, 251; Masafuera 17, 250, 251; Thorn-tailed 250, 251, 358, 362, 363, 368, 372, 375
Rayador 226, 227
Repu 47, 48, 88
Rhea Darwin's 128; Lesser 128, 129 352–355, 372, 374; Suri 128
Río de los Cipreses Reserve 360
Río Simpson Reserve 369
Rivers (Ríos) 11, 12
Róbinson Crusoe (Is. Masatierra) 17
Robinsonia 67
Roble 33, 45, 46, 47, 49, 76–79, 358
Rock Rat Chilean 323, 325
Ruil 45, 46, 49, 78
Run-Run 265, 266
Rush-Tyrant Many-colored 250, 265, 267, 359
Rushbird Wren-like 250, 251, 267
Saca-tu-real 265, 267
Salamanqueja 116
Salar de Atacama 12, 354
Salar de Surire 353
Sala y Gómez (Is.) 16
Saltator Golden-billed 276, 352
Salteador chico 217, 218; chileno 216, 217; de cola largo 217, 220; pardo 217, 218; polar 216, 217; pomarino 217, 218
Sandalwood 17, 66
Sanderling 16, 208, 209
Sandpiper Baird's 209, 210, 367, 372; Least 209, 210; Pectoral 209, 210, 352; Semipalmated 209, 210; Spotted 208, 209; White-rumped 209, 210, 372
Sandpiper-Plover Diademed 199, 201, 352, 359
San Félix y San Ambrosio (Is.) 14
San Pedro de Atacama 355
Santiago 1, 2, 3, 10
Sapos 119–125 (see Frog)
Sauce chileno 79
Sauco del diablo 59, 86
Sclerophyll 40–44
Sea Cabbage 61, 203
Seal Antarctic Fur 20, 330, 331; Crabeater 20, 331, 332; Juan Fernández Fur 17, 329, 331; Leopard 20, 331, 332; Ross 20, 331, 332; South American Fur 329, 331, 372, 375; South American Sea Lion 330, 331, 350, 353–356, 367, 368, 369, 372, 375; Southern Elephant 20, 331, 333; Weddell 20, 331, 332
Seashells (Caracoles) 27
Sea urchin 25, 27
Seedeater Band-tailed 278, 279, 352; Chestnut-throated 278, 279, 350
Seedsnipe Grey-breasted 213, 215, 352, 360; Least 214, 215, 374; Rufous-bellied 213, 215, 352; White-bellied 213, 215
Semillero 278, 279
Senecio 63, 65
Shag Blue-eyed 175, 176
Sheartail Peruvian 238, 239, 350
Shearwater Buller's 165, 167, 350; Christmas 16, 165, 167; Manx 165, 167; Pink-footed 165, 167, 350, 359, 367; Sooty 165, 166, 350, 353, 359, 375
Sheathbill Snowy 20, 203, 205
Shellfish (Mariscos) 24, 25
Shoveler Red 139, 140
Shrike-Tyrant Black-billed 259, 260, 352; Great 258, 259, 360, 363; Grey-bellied 258, 259, 363; White-tailed 258, 259
Sierra-Finch Ash-breasted 279, 280, 352; Band-tailed 278, 279, 360; Black-hooded 281, 283, 352; Grey-hooded 281, 283, 358; Mourning 279, 280, 352, 360, 368; Patagonian 281, 283, 363, 369, 372; Plumbeous 279, 280, 352, 360; Red-backed 279, 280, 352, 353; White-throated 279, 281
Siete camisas 61
Siete colores 265, 267
Sisi Iris 65
Siskin Black 286, 287, 352; Black-chinned 286, 287, 356, 366; Hooded 286, 287, 352; Thick-billed 286, 287, 353; Yellow-rumped 286, 287, 360
Skimmer Black 226, 227, 353
Skink Snake-eyed 16, 114, 115
Skua Brown 217, 218; Chilean 216, 217, 350, 359, 367, 369, 372, 375; South Polar 216, 217
Skunk Humboldt's Hog-nosed 297, 298, 369, 370; Molina's Hog-nosed 297, 298, 353, 356, 358–362, 366, 368
Snail Forest 53
Snake Chilean Slender 117, 356, 362, 363, 364, 367; Elegant Racer 117, 355, 360; Long-tailed Racer 117, 355, 360, 362, 363; Yellow-bellied Sea 117
Snipe Fuegian 213, 215, 369; Puna 212, 215, 352, 353; South American 212, 215, 360
Sparrow House 16, 285, 350, 354, 367, 372; Rufous-collared 285, 350, 353, 354, 372
Squid Humboldt Flying 26
Steamer-Duck Flightless 134, 137, 367, 372; Flying 134, 137, 363, 366, 369, 375

INDEX OF COMMON NAMES

Stilt White-backed 203, 204, 359
Storm-Petrel Black-bellied 169, 170; Elliot's 169, 170, 350; Grey-backed 169, 170; Hornby's 169, 171; Markham's 169, 171, 350; Polynesian 169, 170; Wedge-rumped 169, 170; White-bellied 14, 169, 170; Wilson's 20, 168, 169, 350, 352, 359, 367
Strait of Magellan 1, 8, 13, 374
Sundew 60 61
Surfbird 207, 208, 350
Suri (Puna Rhea) 128, 353
Suspiro del mar 37
Swallow Andean 269, 271, 352; Bank 270, 271; Barn 270, 271, 354; Blue-and-white 269, 271, 350, 354, 355, 367; Chilean 269, 271, 358, 368; Cliff 270, 271
Swan Black-necked 131, 133, 356, 359, 367, 368, 369; Coscoroba 131, 133, 359, 372
Swift Andean 236, 352; Chimney 237
Tagua andina 195, 196; chica 194, 195; común 195, 196; cornuda 195, 196; de frente roja 195, 196; gigante 195, 196
Tagüita 194, 195; del norte 194, 195
Taique 59
Tamarugo 35, 36, 83
Tanager Blue-and-yellow 275, 277, 352
Tapaculo Chucao 256, 257, 363, 364, 366–370, 372; Dusky 257, 258, 358, 360; Magellanic 256, 257, 359, 363, 366; Ochre-flanked 256, 257, 363, 364, 366; White-throated 256, 257, 356
Tara 35, 36, 83
Taruca 307, 308, 352
Tattler Wandering 16
Teal Blue-winged 140; Cinnamon 139, 138; Puna 138, 139, 352; Silver 138, 139; Speckled 136, 139, 352, 363
Tenca 273, 274, patagónica 273, 274
Tepa 33, 46, 47, 49, 53, 54, 75, 356, 364, 366, 367, 369
Tepú 53, 54, 59, 85
Tern Antarctic 20, 224, 225; Arctic 224, 225, 359; Common 224, 225, 359; Elegant 224, 225, 350; Grey-backed 16, 226, 227; Inca 223, 225, 350, 353–356, 359; Peruvian 223, 225, 350, 353–356, 359; Snowy-crowned (Trudeau's) 223, 225, 367; Sooty 14, 16, 226, 227; South American 223, 225, 350, 353, 359, 360, 367, 369, 372, 375; White (Fairy) 16, 226, 227
Thick-knee Peruvian 203, 204, 350
Thrift 61
Thrush Austral 272, 273, 360, 368, 369, 370, 372, 375; Chiguanco 273, 274, 354
Tiaca 33, 53, 54, 56, 80
Tihue (Trihue) 74

Tijeral 253, 254; listado 253, 255
Tinamou Andean 129, 130; Chilean 14, 128, 129, 356, 358, 363, 366; Elegant-crested 129, 130; Ornate 129, 130, 352; Patagonian 129, 130; Puna 129, 130, 352
Tineo 33, 47, 53, 54, 55, 56, 80, 364, 366, 367. 369
Tit-Spinetail Plain-mantled 253, 254, 358, 363; Streaked 253, 255, 352
Tit-Tyrant Juan Fernández 17, 267, 268; Pied-crested 267, 268; Tufted 267, 268, 358, 363, 366, 372; Yellow-billed 267, 268, 352
Tiuque 188
Toad Atacama 119, 121, 362; Chilean 120, 121; Concepcion (Arunco) 119, 121, 362; Helmeted Water 120, 121, 358, 359, 363, 367; Patagonian 120, 121, 366. 368, 372, 375; Red-spotted 119; Sapo hermoso 120, 121, 362; Warty 119, 121, 352, 354, 356, 360, 362
Tola 38, 39 80, 88
Torcaza 228, 229
Tordo 288, 289
Toromiro 68, 69, 84
Torres del Paine Park 372
Tórtola 228, 229; cordillerana 229, 230
Tortolita boliviana 229, 230; cuyana 229, 230; de la puna 229, 230; quiguagua 229, 230
Tortuga boba 107; laúd 107; verde 106, 107
Totora 68, 69
Trabajador 250, 251
Traro 190, 191
Treerunner White-throated 250. 251, 363, 366, 368
Trevo 33, 47, 56
Tricahue 231, 360, 362
Trile 288, 289
Tropicbird Red-billed 172, 173; Red-tailed 16, 172, 173; White-tailed 16, 172, 173
Trout 12, 367 368
Tuco-tuco de Atacama 319, 321; de la puna 319, 321; del Tamarugal 36, 321; Highland 319, 321, 352; Magellanic 319, 322; Maule 319, 322; Tawny 319, 321
Tucúquere 234, 235
Tunduco 323. 325
Tupa 66, 67
Turca Moustached 255, 257, 358, 359
Turnstone Ruddy 207, 208, 350
Turtle Green 106, 107, 354, 359; Leatherback 107, 359; Loggerhead 107, 354; Olive Ridley 107, 354, 359
Tyrant Choco ate-vented 259, 260; Patagonian 264, 265, 359; Rufous-webbed 259, 260, 353; Spectacled 265, 266
Ulmo 33, 47, 53, 54, 56, 80, 362, 366

Valdivian Coastal Reserve 53
Vari 185, 186
Vencejo chico 236; de chimenea 237
Vicente Peréz Rosales Park 366
Vicugna (Vicuña) 303, 352–356
Vilches-Altos del Lircay 362
Villarica Park 364
Violeta amarilla 63
Violetear Sparkling 238, 239, 352
Viscacha Mountain 317, 319, 352, 353, 354, 358, 362, 368
Viudita 264, 265
Volcán Isluga Park 354
Vulture Black 183, 184, 356, 367; Turkey 183, 184, 353, 354, 356, 367, 368, 369, 372, 375
Weasel Patagonian 297
Whale Antarctic Minke 20, 336, 337; Beaked 346–350; Blue 337, 338; False Killer 343, 345; Fin 337, 338; Humpback 20, 334, 335; Killer (Orca) 20, 343, 344; Long-finned Pilot 343, 344, 353; Dwarf Minke 336, 337; Pygmy Sperm 346; Pygmy Right 334, 345; Southern Right 333, 335; Sei 336, 337; Sperm 345
Whimbrel 206, 207, 367, 372
Wigeon Chiloé 139, 140, 359, 372
Willet 206, 207
Willow Chilean 41, 80
Winter's Bark (Canelo) 59, 74
Wiretail Des Mur's 249, 251, 358, 366, 367
Woodpecker Magellanic 241, 242, 360, 362, 363, 364, 366, 368, 369 370 ; Striped 241, 243, 358, 359, 363, 366
Woodstar Chilean 238, 239, 350
Wren Grass (Sedge) 272 273; Southern House 272, 273, 350, 354, 368, 372
Yal 279, 280; austral 282, 283; cordillerano 282, 283
Yeco 175, 177
Yellow-Finch Bright-rumped 284, 287; Grassland 282, 287, 368, 372; Greater 284, 287. 360; Greenish 284, 287, 352, 354; Patagonian 284, 287; Puna 284, 353
Yellowlegs Greater 206, 207, 352, 367; Lesser 206, 207
Yerba blanca 39
Yunco 171; de los canales 171; de Magallanes 171
Zambullidores 141, 142
Zapatilla de la Virgen 65
Zarapito 206, 207; pico recto 205, 207
Zarcilla 77
Zarzamora 66
Zarzaparilla 51
Zorro chilote 299; rojo 298, 299
Zorzal 272, 273; negro 273, 274

QUICK INDEX TO THE COLOR ILLUSTRATIONS AND MAPS

MARINE RESOURCES 21–31
Fish 23
Shellfish (Mariscos) 25
Marine Mollusks 28, 29
Marine Algae 31

FLORA 32–89
Alerce Forest 54
Antarctic 70, 71
Araucaria Forest 51
Deciduous Forest 48, 49
Desert 35
Easter Island 69
Flowering Desert 37
High Andean Steppe 39
Juan Fernández 67
Magellanic Moorland 61
Magellanic Rainforest 59
Matorral and Sclerophyll 42, 43
Patagonian Andes 63
Patagonian Steppe 65
Siempreverde Forest 56, 57
Valdivian Rainforest 56, 57

LEPIDOPTERA 90–105
Butterflies 93, 97, 101
Moths 105
Skippers 93

REPTILES 106–117
Geckos 116
Lizards 110, 111, 115
Sea Turtles 107
Snakes 117

AMPHIBIANS 118–125
Frogs 121, 123
Toads 121

BIRDS 126–290
Avocet 203
Accipiters 185
Albatrosses 153, 157
Bitterns 179
Blackbirds 289
Boobies 173
Canasteros 253
Caracaras 191
Chilia 247
Cinclodes 247
Condors 183
Conebills 277
Coots 195
Cormorants 177
Diuca-Finches 283
Diving-Petrels 171
Dotterels 199
Doves 229
Ducks 137, 139
Earthcreepers 245, 247
Egrets 179
Falcons 191
Finches 279, 283, 287
Flamingos 181

Flowerpiercers 277
Grebes 141
Ground-Tyrants 263
Gulls 219, 221
Hawks 185,189
Herons 179
Hummingbirds 239
Ibises 181
Jaegers 217
Kingfishers 241
Kites 185
Lapwings 199
Meadowlarks 289
Miners 245
Mockingbirds 273
Nightjars 235
Ospreys 185
Owls 235
Oystercatchers 203
Painted-Snipes 215
Parrots 231
Pelicans 173
Penguins 145
Petrels 159, 164, 165
Phalaropes 211
Pigeons 229
Pipits 273
Plantcutters 273
Plovers 199, 203
Quails 129
Rails 195
Rayaditos 251
Rheas 129
Rushbirds 251
Saltators 277
Seedeaters 279
Seedsnipes 215
Shearwaters 165
Sheathbills 203
Sheldgeese 133
Shorebirds 203, 207, 209
Shrike-Tyrants 259
Sierra-Finches 279, 283
Siskins 287
Skimmers 227
Skuas 217
Snipes 215
Sparrows 285
Stilts 203
Storm-Petrels 169
Swallows 271
Swans 133
Swifts 237
Tanagers 277
Tapaculos 257
Terns 225, 227
Thick-knees 203
Thrushes 273
Tinamous 129
Tit-Spinetails 253
Tit-Tyrants 267

Treerunners 251
Tropicbirds 173
Tyrants 259, 265
Vultures 183
Wiretails 251
Woodpeckers 241
Wrens 273
Yellow-Finches 287

LAND MAMMALS 291–328
Armadillos 295
Bats 293
Camelids 305
Cats 301
Cavies 319
Coypus 325
Chinchillas 319
Cuis 319
Deer 307
Degus 325
Foxes 299
Mice 311,315, 327
Octodonts 325
Opossums 293
Otters 297
Rats 311,315, 327
Skunks 297
Tuco-tucos 319
Viscachas 319
Weasels 297

MARINE MAMMALS 329–349
Beaked Whales 347
Dolphins 341
Humpback Whales 335
Orcas 343
Pilot Whales 343
Porpoises 341
Right Whales 335
Rorqual Whales 337
Seals 331
Sperm Whales 345

REGIONAL MAPS
Aisén Region 371
Arica-Parinacota Region 353
Beagle Channel and Cape Horn 376
Central Chile 361
Chilean Antarctic Territory 18
Easter Island 15
Islas Desventuradas 14
Juan Fernández Archipelago 16
Magallanes Region 373
Norte Chico 357
Norte Grande 351
Sala y Gómez 16
South-Central Chile 365

NATIONAL PARK MAPS
Conguillo-Los Paraguas 364
La Campana 358
Torres del Paine 373
Vicente Pérez Rosales 366